Cyril of Jerusalem and Nemesius of Emesa

D1548334

General Editors

John Baillie (1886–1960) served as President of the World Council of Churches, a member of the British Council of Churches, Moderator of the General Assembly of the Church of Scotland, and Dean of the Faculty of Divinity at the University of Edinburgh.

John T. McNeill (1885–1975) was Professor of the History of European Christianity at the University of Chicago and then Auburn Professor of Church History at Union Theological Seminary in New York.

Henry P. Van Dusen (1897–1975) was an early and influential member of the World Council of Churches and served at Union Theological Seminary in New York as Roosevelt Professor of Systematic Theology and later as President.

Cyril of Jerusalem
and
Nemesius of Emesa

Edited by

WILLIAM TELFER

Westminster John Knox Press

LOUISVILLE · LONDON

Cover design by designpointinc.com

Published by Westminster John Knox Press
Louisville, Kentucky

This book is printed on acid-free paper that meets the American National Standards Institute Z39.48 standard.♾

PRINTED IN THE UNITED STATES OF AMERICA   ·

United States Library of Congress Cataloging-in-Publication Data is on file at the Library of Congress, Washington, D.C.

ISBN-13: 978-0-664-23082-1
ISBN-10: 0-664-23082-2

GENERAL EDITORS' PREFACE

The Christian Church possesses in its literature an abundant and incomparable treasure. But it is an inheritance that must be reclaimed by each generation. THE LIBRARY OF CHRISTIAN CLASSICS is designed to present in the English language, and in twenty-six volumes of convenient size, a selection of the most indispensable Christian treatises written prior to the end of the sixteenth century.

The practice of giving circulation to writings selected for superior worth or special interest was adopted at the beginning of Christian history. The canonical Scriptures were themselves a selection from a much wider literature. In the Patristic era there began to appear a class of works of compilation (often designed for ready reference in controversy) of the opinions of well-reputed predecessors, and in the Middle Ages many such works were produced. These medieval anthologies actually preserve some noteworthy materials from works otherwise lost.

In modern times, with the increasing inability even of those trained in universities and theological colleges to read Latin and Greek texts with ease and familiarity, the translation of selected portions of earlier Christian literature into modern languages has become more necessary than ever; while the wide range of distinguished books written in vernaculars such as English makes selection there also needful. The efforts that have been made to meet this need are too numerous to be noted here, but none of these collections serves the purpose of the reader who desires a library of representative treatises spanning the Christian centuries as a whole. Most of them embrace only the age of the Church Fathers, and some of them have long been out of print. A fresh translation of a work already translated may shed much new light upon its meaning. This is true even of Bible translations despite the work of many experts through the centuries. In some instances old translations have been adopted in this series, but wherever necessary or desirable, new ones have been made. Notes have been supplied where these were needed to explain the author's meaning. The introductions provided for the several treatises and extracts will, we believe, furnish welcome guidance.

JOHN BAILLIE
JOHN T. McNEILL
HENRY P. VAN DUSEN

To
MELLICE,
WHO HEARD ME MY INTRODUCTIONS

CONTENTS

CYRIL OF JERUSALEM

NEMESIUS OF EMESA

ON THE NATURE OF MAN

(The chapters, with their headings, are as in the manuscripts. The work is here, for the first time, broken up into seventy sections of approximately equal length. The section numbers in relation to the chapters are indicated below, after the chapter-headings).

Note: The figures M.35.1–38.7 at the head of Section 1 represents the page and line of the page in Matthaei's edition where the Greek text of the section begins and ends; and so for all sections.

Acknowledgment: Special thanks are due, on the part of the translator, to Dr. J. Dixon Boyd, Fellow of Clare College and Professor of Anatomy in the University of Cambridge, for counsel on points of medical history and on the medical knowledge of Nemesius.

List of Ground-plans, etc.

Conjectural Plan of the buildings on Golgotha.

Conjectural South Elevation of the buildings on the Golgotha site, with the south enclosing wall and the baptistry taken away.

The buildings on the Golgotha site as seen by the artist of the Madaba mosaic.

CYRIL

BISHOP OF JERUSALEM

General Introduction

THE AUTHOR

OUR ASSURED KNOWLEDGE ABOUT CYRIL IS THAT he was bishop of Jerusalem in the second half of the fourth Christian century, and that he died in that office on 18 March, 386. Of the circumstances of his early life we have no certain knowledge. He shows acquaintance with things which happened in Jerusalem when he must have been a boy, but that does not prove that he was then resident in Jerusalem. There is, in fact, some reason for thinking that his place of upbringing was Caesarea in Palestine. For, later in his life, he seems to have been the recipient of an appeal for help by a section of the Church at Caesarea. The relations between the sees of Caesarea and Jerusalem were not such that Caesareans would naturally turn to the bishop of Jerusalem.[1] And when, presently, it was Gelasius, Cyril's sister's son, who was consecrated by Cyril to be bishop of Caesarea, we have ground for the conjecture that Cyril was Caesarean by origin. His commemoration in the *Synaxary*[2] says that he "was born of pious parents professing the

---

[1] The see of Aelia (as Jerusalem had been called since the days of Hadrian) was suffragan to Caesarea. When, in 325, the Synod of Nicaea gave Aelia a status of honour, as the holy city of Jerusalem, it left it ecclesiastically suffragan to Caesarea. As the years brought more and more importance to the see of Jerusalem, the relationship between the two sees grew uneasy. Caesareans would not, without good reason, have taken a step which flattered the see of Jerusalem.

[2] *Synaxary* is the title of the liturgical book containing short notices of saints and subjects of other commemoration in order through the year. Many of these notices originated in antiquity and may depend upon documents now lost. The commemoration of Cyril began very early. This sentence in his *Synaxary* notice, if taken strictly, implies (what we might expect) that in 337, when Constantine died, Cyril had reached manhood.

orthodox faith, and was bred up in the same in the reign of Constantine". The statement is entirely plausible, for Cyril shows no signs of having been a convert from paganism in adult life.

In 326, the favour of Constantine towards the Holy Land, as a centre of Christian devotion and unity, began to make the fortune of Jerusalem as the Christian Holy City. To meet its new responsibilities, the Church of Aelia [3] had need of an able and cultured clergy, capable of handling a great and growing body of ascetics of both sexes, who had taken up their permanent abode in the neighbourhood, as well as caring for the holy sites and acting as hosts and chaplains to streams of pilgrims now arriving from every part of Christendom. The emperor's chief agent for the development of his Holy Land schemes was Eusebius, "the father of Church history", bishop of Caesarea. [4] That the Caesarean bishop should commend a young Caesarean, of good Christian family and personal promise, to the bishop of Jerusalem, for diaconate, has no improbability, particularly just after 326, when imperial benefactions to the church of Jerusalem made both the need and opportunity for increasing its clergy. And at this time Cyril, who must, from other considerations, have been born between 310 and 315, would have reached an age to leave home and enter a bishop's household. The matter remains one of conjecture. Cyril's family may have belonged to Aelia, and have had a married daughter living in Caesarea. [5]

For Cyril's early clerical career at Jerusalem we are beholden to a very unfriendly witness. This is Jerome, who resided within the bishopric of Jerusalem from 386 to 420. In 392, he quarrelled

---

[3] After the failure of the Jewish rising of A.D. 135, the ruins of the city of Jerusalem were forbidden to Jews, and a Gentile community, containing a proportion of Christians, occupied them. The township thus constituted received from the emperor Hadrian the name of Aelia. At first, the little Church of Aelia must have seemed one of the most insignificant in Palestine. But its importance was increasing, and the bishop of Aelia had been an important suffragan of Caesarea, for a century before the days of Cyril.

[4] Eusebius of Caesarea, who had lent support to Arius and his associates after their breach with their bishop, Alexander of Alexandria, appeared at Nicaea in the character of defendant. He received somewhat surprising protection from the emperor, which is, however, the less surprising if Constantine already saw a use for him in connection with his own schemes.

[5] The fact that Cyril appears in many respects to be a disciple of Eusebius of Caesarea does not resolve the uncertainty as to Cyril's place of birth.

violently with Cyril's successor and admirer, bishop John of Jerusalem. Jerome was therefore prepared to twist whatever he knew about Cyril to his disadvantage. So, in his *Chronicle*, against the eleventh year of the sons of Constantine,[6] he made the entry, "Maximus, who succeeded Macarius as fortieth bishop of Jerusalem, died, this year. Thereafter the succession was Arian: first, Cyril, replaced by Eutychius; then Cyril returned, and was next replaced by Irenaeus; Cyril reigned again for a third time, and was replaced by Hilary, afterwards returning for a fourth and last period. This Cyril was ordained presbyter by Maximus. After the death of Maximus, Acacius, bishop of Caesarea, with other Arian bishops, promised Cyril the bishopric if he would repudiate his ordination at the hands of Maximus. So he ministered as a deacon in the church, and for this impiety was rewarded with the see. Maximus, on his deathbed, had made Heraclius his successor, and him Cyril cajoled into reverting to the rank of presbyter from that of bishop." This notice is malicious, especially in representing Cyril's history as a squabble within Arianism, but every consideration is against its being inaccurate in its assertions of fact. It will be noted that no doubts attached to Cyril's diaconate. He was made deacon either by Macarius, or by Maximus before his episcopate became compromised in the eyes of the comprovincial bishops. We may provisionally adopt the first alternative. Macarius was bishop of Jerusalem from 311 (or 312) and died shortly before the synod of Tyre in 335. If he made Cyril deacon, it is unlikely to have been much before 330. Macarius was succeeded by a senior presbyter of Jerusalem, Maximus, who had been a confessor and suffered mutilation, with the loss of an eye, in the last persecution. He must have been well on in the fifties when he became bishop, and his long association with Macarius guarantees that his doctrinal leanings were anti-Arian. Nevertheless, one of the first acts of his episcopate was to attend the synod of Tyre, where he became implicated in passing sentence of deposition upon Athanasius. It is very likely that Cyril was in attendance upon him at this time. The new basilica built by the munificence of Constantine on Golgotha, afterwards to be known as the Martyry, was now complete, and the whole

---

6 These were Constantine II, Constans, and Constantius, who, after their father's death in 337, divided the empire between them, Constantine ruling in the west, Constans in the centre, and Constantius in the east. Constantine was killed in 340, and from then to 350 the western two-thirds of the empire were under Constans.

company of bishops came straight from deposing Athanasius at Tyre to dedicate the Martyry as the new cathedral of Jerusalem, and incidentally to enthrone Maximus therein. And in these long-to-be-remembered solemnities[7] Cyril certainly had a part. From the Martyry, the bishops dated an encyclical in which they declared that they received back into the Church the Arians.[8]

It need not be supposed that either Maximus or Cyril was involved by these events in any change of doctrinal allegiance. The trial of Athanasius at Tyre was not for heresy, but for "tyranny." The charge concerned his administration of the ecclesiastical affairs of Egypt. However much some of his judges were prejudiced on doctrinal grounds, overtly the whole matter was one of church order. Athanasius was sent into exile by Constantine, who did not allow his see to be filled. Everything stood open for his restoration by another synod when his fault was purged. But in 338 Athanasius, supported by the west, regained possession at Alexandria in contempt of the synod that had deposed him, and so, in the eyes of all easterns, probably at this time including Maximus and Cyril, he appeared to be, *ipso facto* and irretrievably, self-deposed.

The eastern episcopate met again in synod at Antioch in 341. Maximus did not attend.[9] Already, it may be, doctrinal considerations were bringing him over onto the Athanasian side.[10] Through the pilgrims, a bishop of Jerusalem was rendered sensitive to western opinion, and Pope Julius in synod had vindicated the cause of Athanasius in 340. The westerns saw all the irregularity in the synod of Tyre, and none in Athanasius, and so suspected all who condemned him of being unsound in faith. In 342 a synod was called at Sardica by the two surviving

---

[7] So Sozomen, *Church History*, ii.25, and *The Pilgrimage of Etheria* (end). And see *Journal of Ecclesiastical History*, V. (1954), pp. 78–86.

[8] Athanasius, *Apology against the Arians*, 84. Arius himself they could not readmit in person, for he had died in Constantinople in the Spring of 335. (W. Telfer, "Paul of Constantinople," *Harvard Theological Review*, 1950, pp. 52–54.)

[9] This synod, held in connection with the dedication of the new cathedral of Antioch, the "golden church" started by Constantine and finished under Constantius, was representative of the eastern episcopate, determinedly anti-Athanasian and resentful at the support lent by Pope Julius and the western bishops alike to Athanasius and others upon whom eastern synods had passed sentence.

[10] Socrates and Sozomen, church historians at Constantinople, who, about 430, each published a history designed to continue that of Eusebius, expressly give this explanation of the absence of Maximus.

emperors, Constans and Constantius, to which were bidden the bishops both of east and west. Athanasius, whom Constantine had caused to be driven from Alexandria, was now under the protection of Constans, and was sitting with the western bishops when the eastern bishops arrived. When the easterns discovered this fact, they withdrew in a body. But Maximus of Jerusalem, and fourteen other bishops of Palestine, did not withdraw, but sat in synod with the western bishops, in company with Athanasius. The breach between east and west was grave, and, from this time on, the attitude of the easterns towards Athanasius, and towards the westerns for supporting him, hardened.[11] A fortiori, the Palestinian bishops found themselves unpopular with their neighbours.

In 346, under western pressure, Constantius was fain to order the restoration of Athanasius to his see. Athanasius returned overland, and passed through Jerusalem on his way home; "where," he says, "I met with the bishops of Palestine, who, when they had called a synod at Jerusalem, received me cordially." He then gives the text of a letter which these Palestinian bishops sent to congratulate the Church of Alexandria on receiving its bishop again. Maximus of Jerusalem heads the list of sixteen signatories, from which the name of Acacius of Caesarea is conspicuously absent.[12] Of those who signed, some were perhaps less cordial than they seemed. For it was not long before Maximus appears to be alone, in Palestine, in his support of Athanasius. With this history in mind, we can return to the entry in Jerome's *Chronicle* and find it more intelligible. Maximus, dying, consecrated Heraclius to be his successor. There were, that is, no other episcopal consecrators, and the succession was utterly irregular. It is clear that, at the last, Maximus had his back to the wall, in regard to the Athanasian cause, and saw no hope but in wresting the succession from the hands of the comprovincial bishops. Socrates

[11] The cause of Athanasius created a tragic misunderstanding between the Latin-speaking ecclesiastics of the west and the Greek-speaking ecclesiastics of the east, to which the divergences of doctrinal opinion in the Arian controversy lent bitterness and obstinacy. The joint synod of Sardica in the Balkans was called in the hope that when the two bodies of bishops sat together, they would find their way to a renewed understanding. When the easterns withdrew, misunderstanding became, to all intents and purposes, schism.

[12] *Apology against the Arians*, Section 57. Athanasius excepts from the number of those who welcomed him, two or three Palestinians "of suspected character": in particular, Acacius, who succeeded Eusebius in 337, and had a more pronounced leaning than he towards Arianism.

asserts that he was actually under synodical sentence of deposition,[13] which is likely enough. In taking this desperate course, Maximus evidently had not carried Cyril with him. At the end, Cyril had come to believe that Maximus had forfeited his own bishopric in his attachment to the ruined cause of Athanasius, and that the fatal step had been taken before he laid his hands in ordination upon him, Cyril. In such a view, based solely upon considerations of canon, and church order, the fatal step would appear to be Maximus' desertion from his eastern colleagues at Sardica. We shall be right, therefore, to assume that Cyril's promotion to the presbyterate took place about 343, when he was a little over thirty. After the death of Maximus, Cyril renounced his priesthood as null and void, thereby causing Acacius of Caesarea, the metropolitan of Palestine, and the bishops of the Province, to regard him as ecclesiastically sound. That he was able, after they had given him regular consecration, not only to persuade Heraclius to abandon his claims to episcopate but actually to retain him to serve under him as presbyter, argues that he, Cyril, was the whole-hearted choice of the Church of Jerusalem. What it does not argue is that Cyril had sacrificed doctrinal loyalties to obtain the bishopric. Doctrinal loyalties were still a matter over which many, if not most, kept their own counsel. The matters on which everyone could still see how to take sides, publicly, were those of church order. In 350, Constans, the supporter of the western bishops, and so of the Athanasian cause, was slain by the usurper Magnentius. To many in the eastern Church, this must have seemed like the sentence of God against Athanasius; for the men of that age were given to interpreting the mind of providence by the course of public events. There could be no better illustration of this tendency than Cyril's letter to Constantius, announcing the "sign" seen in Jerusalem on 7 May, 351, of which the text forms part of the present selection.[14] The episcopate of Cyril thus began altogether propitiously. But his sky was soon overcast, owing to the growing jealousy of Acacius. We may suppose that, at the time of Cyril's election, the bishop of Caesarea supposed that the new bishop of Jerusalem would be very much his man,[15] particularly as having enjoyed his support against Heraclius. And Cyril owed him obedience

[13] Socrates, *Church History*, ii.38.
[14] pp. 197.
[15] If Cyril was of Caesarean origin, that would help to explain the confidence of Acacius.

under the terms of the Seventh Canon of Nicaea.[16] But tension arose, in which Acacius had the support of the other bishops of the province. Those who explain the church history of this period wholly in terms of doctrine say that Acacius and his colleagues were Arians, and that they knew that Cyril was not. But what was talked about at the time was church property. A bishop's discretion in expending the funds in the church chest was almost unlimited, but it could be a matter of complaint, and, in the end, of complaint to the bishops of the province. Now the temporalities of the Church of Jerusalem were unique. On the one hand there were great assets arising from the lavish imperial gifts, and those of the pilgrims. On the other were special liabilities, in the form of the great body of "poor saints," the resident ascetics, encouraged to reside near the holy sites, and, in time of need, looking to the bishop of Jerusalem as their only earthly father and protector. In 354 or 355, it appears that there was famine. Cyril, according to Socrates, Sozomen, and Theodoret, sold church property.[17] Sozomen, who is most favourable to Cyril, insists that he did it to feed his "poor," and that the things sold were rich curtains from the church, and other sacred ornaments, and therefore, be it noted, all imperial gifts. Socrates, at this point, draws upon a recognizable and very reliable source,[18] and says that for two years Cyril refused to answer a summons to account for his actions to the provincial synod, and that, finally, in 357, the synod deposed him from his see, in his absence. Upon this, Cyril gave notice of appeal to the emperor, and betook himself to Tarsus, where he was hospitably received by Silvanus, the bishop of Tarsus, and soon became a great favourite with the Tarsians.[19]

[16] The canon says, "As custom and ancient tradition show that the bishop of Aelia ought to be honoured, let him have precedence in honour, without prejudice to the proper dignity of the metropolitan see." Nothing seems to explain the passing of this canon so well as that it was calculated to assist the plans of the emperor, without being to the detriment of Eusebius.

[17] Socrates, ii.40. Sozomen, iv.25. Theodoret, bishop of Cyrrhus in Syria, composed a *Church History* to supplement that of Eusebius soon after 440, in which the passage is ii.25.

[18] viz. the *Collection of Synods* composed by Sabinus, the semi-Arian bishop of Heraclea, which is lost except as it can be recognized in the extracts which Socrates and Sozomen made from it. Sozomen named this source, and it has so marked a character that it can probably be detected wherever used.

[19] According to Theodoret, ii.22, Silvanus answered the protest of Acacius at his harbouring Cyril by saying that the people would not endure his being sent away.

The bishops of Palestine put Eutychius in Cyril's throne, while Cyril waited for the emperor to commit his cause to a greater synod. We have here a situation which makes the best sense if we think of Cyril as being in the position of Dean of a Royal peculiar. For his trusteeship of imperial gifts, he was answerable to the emperor alone. But it is not surprising if the Provincial synod saw, in his refusal to answer summons, a proof of the rising pride and ambition of the Jerusalem see. For an opportunity to get his cause reviewed Cyril had not very long to wait. In 359, Constantius assembled a synod for the whole eastern Church, at Seleucia "the rugged," on the coast of Isauria, no long journey from Tarsus. Thither went Cyril as appellant, but also, it would appear, as having received the imperial summons. Accordingly he took his seat in the synod. Acacius demanded his withdrawal, and a procedural struggle began. But Acacius soon felt the synod to be hostile to himself, and withdrew, and in the end, the synod pronounced his deposition. Cyril was thus freed to return to Jerusalem, as having been cleared by the synod, and Eutychius could not stand his ground against him.[20] The next year revealed the fact that the synod of Seleucia had gone contrary to the emperor's wishes, and that his favour was reserved for Acacius and his associates. Theodoret tells how Acacius took his opportunity to blacken Cyril in the emperor's eyes, and to use Cyril's discharge by the synod of Seleucia to blacken the semi-Arian cause which had predominated at Seleucia. Constantius, like Acacius, was now inclined to doctrine much nearer Arianism than the conservative "semi-Arian" position. Acacius told Constantius, Theodoret says, that among the treasures that Cyril had sold was a "holy robe" given to Macarius by Constantine, and that this garment had fallen into unsuitable hands.[21] Constantius was infuriated and ordered Cyril into exile, we are not told where.

But at this point some information given by Epiphanius, who was a Palestinian and likely to be well informed, telling of the interventions of Cyril on the side of the anti-Arians at Caesarea, suggests that Cyril made use of his return from Seleucia to

[20] The names of the three men intruded into Cyril's throne vary in different writers and even in different manuscripts of Jerome's *Chronicle*. They are here taken to be Eutychius, Irenaeus, and Hilary. Other sees may have been found for them, for we presently find a Eutychius, bishop of Scythopolis, opposing Cyril in the matter of the succession to the bishopric of Caesarea.

[21] *op. cit.*, ii.23.

consecrate a certain Philumenus to be bishop of Caesarea, in the room of Acacius, deposed by the synod.[22] Thanks to the emperor, this was a very short-lived victory. But when Constantius was succeeded in 361 by Julian the apostate, ecclesiastical fortunes swung round again. Constantius' sentences of banishment were cancelled, and Cyril returned to his see for the second time. Theodoret has an anecdote which shows that Cyril's return journey lay through Antioch,[23] which shows that the place of his exile lay in the north. The people of Jerusalem must have been devoted to Cyril, for Irenaeus, whom the Acacian party had only just made bishop in his stead, disappears without a trace.

The reign of Julian, while it enabled Cyril's return, soon led to a new crisis for him in Jerusalem, and one that sets his acumen in a very bright light. In his fifteenth Catechetical Lecture, on the Second Coming, he pictured Anti-christ as an emperor, to whom, as an enemy of the Church, the Jews would rally, and from whom they would obtain the rebuilding of the Temple at Jerusalem, in which, at the last, he would place himself as the object of their worship. This picture looked as if it might become actuality in 362. Cyril had, no doubt, a lively sense of the chagrin of the Jews in seeing Jerusalem appropriated by the Christians as exclusively *their* holy place. And it suited Julian's policy of a nominal universal tolerance, to grant the Jews aid towards rebuilding the Temple. The undertaking failed. Christian writers allege supernatural intervention, and stories of this sort obtained credence outside the Church.[24] Perhaps some credit should be given to determined resistance on the part of the Christian population of Jerusalem led by Cyril. With the death of Julian in 363, the hopes of the Jews foundered.

Cyril was left in peace through the short reign of Jovian, and the years in which Valens was engaged in consolidating his hold upon the eastern empire. In 366 Acacius died, after five years in which the Jerusalem Church had gone its own way without him. And now Cyril stepped in to give him a successor in the person of his nephew Gelasius. But in the following year, Valens adopted the ecclesiastical policy of Constantius exactly

---

[22] *Panarion*, Heresy 73. Section 37.   [23] *op. cit.*, iii.10.
[24] The pagan historian Ammianus Marcellinus (*Liber rerum gestarum*, xxiii.1) tells of thunderbolts falling on the foundations, and says, "Thus the very elements, as if by some fate, repelled the attempt, and it was abandoned." Christian writers are more explicit in their interpretation of the alleged incidents.

as he had laid it down. Cyril's banishment was reimposed and
Gelasius was driven from Caesarea. The ruling Arian party
filled the see of Caesarea with a certain Euzoius, not the most
famous of that name, but, according to Jerome, a person of
some literary distinction.[25] Hilary nominally ruled the Church
of Jerusalem, though, as it appears, the provosts of the great
churches of imperial foundation found opportunity to assert
their independence of him and of one another, to the great
detriment of the order and religion of the holy places. And this
unhappy state of things continued until the death of Valens in
378. For Cyril, these eleven years were not years of total loss.
His place of banishment enabled him to attain complete
solidarity with that body of bishops of north Syria and eastern
Asia Minor which ranged itself, as soon as opportunity was
given, behind Meletius, bishop of Antioch, to restore the Nicene
faith. Speaking of the situation in the Church at the time of
Valens' death, Sozomen says, "at this period, all the churches
of the east, with the exception of that of Jerusalem, were in the
hands of the Arians."[26] In making this exception he infers that
Hilary was dead, and possibly that the return of Cyril had been
permitted before the change in the government. When, in 379,
Meletius gathered his momentous synod in Antioch, among its
acts was the sending of Gregory of Nyssa, aided by a grant of
imperial transport from the new and orthodox government of
Theodosius, on a "mission of help" to the Arab churches of
S.E. Palestine. Nyssen undertook also to try and act as arbitra-
tor at Jerusalem. He does not say who asked him, but only that
"matters were in confusion with the heads of the holy Jerusalem
churches and needed an arbiter." But Cyril was the person to
whom the success of the mission was of most interest. Gregory
Nyssen was a sensitive soul and went home to Cappadocia with
a sense of failure and frustration that was probably out of all
proportion to the facts. He has poured out his griefs in a letter
to an unnamed ascetic in Cappadocia, commonly reckoned as
a separate opuscule entitled *On pilgrimages*, and in a letter to
three ladies living the ascetic life at Jerusalem.[27] In the first
of these letters, it is chiefly his bitter disillusionment by what he
saw of Jerusalem pilgrims. His brother Basil had passed through

---

[25] No. 113 in Jerome's *Famous Men*. Jerome makes him a benefactor to the
Church Library of Caesarea, founded by Origen and Pamphilus.
[26] *op. cit.*, vii.2. Jerome, *Famous Men*, No. 112 gives Cyril eight full years of
restoration.
[27] Gregory Nyssen, Epist. xvii.

the Holy Land in 357, the year when Cyril was deposed, and took home glowing accounts of the spectacle of religion and spirituality which he had seen.[28] Now, after thirty years, Nyssen saw conditions of pilgrimage that were anything but an aid to spirituality, while a whole race of brigands battened on the pilgrims. Moreover it would appear from the second letter that his arbitration met with hostility from some quarters, on doctrinal grounds. But despondent as he went away, his intervention, with the authority of the synod and of the emperor behind him, had probably contributed a great deal to the recovery of the unity and concord of the Church of Jerusalem under Cyril. Cyril's position was further strengthened when Theodosius called a synod of the whole eastern Church at Constantinople, in 381. If Cyril's personal association with semi-Arians at Seleucia had caused him for a while to be considered as of that group, his years of banishment had purged him, and Sozomen represents him as now taking a leading place among the neo-Nicenes. But this does not mean that he had changed his ground with the years. The doctrine of the Lectures that he delivered at the beginning of his episcopate is orthodox by the standards of the synod of 381.[29] A second session of the synod, in 382, addressed a synodal letter to the Church of Rome in which Cyril is expressly mentioned as rightful bishop of Jerusalem "the mother of all the churches," and as one who, over many years and in many places, had striven against Arianism.[30]

Cyril enjoyed four years of peace thereafter, and was succeeded in 386 by John. It may have been ten years later that there came to Jerusalem on pilgrimage a great lady from the far west by name Aetheria.[31] She wrote a journal of all that she saw, addressing it to her sisters in religion in her distant home. What she describes at Jerusalem is a magnificently organized liturgical community, in which time and place were hallowed in commemoration of the ministry, passion, and triumph of Christ. Space was hallowed in the linking together of the holy sites in one coherent programme of devotion. The "heads of the

---

[28] Basil, Epist. cxxiii. 2.
[29] Cyril's orthodoxy has been frequently vindicated; e.g., by J. Lebon, in *Revue d'histoire ecclésiastique*, xx (1924), 197 sqq., 357 sqq., or by B. Niederberger, *Logoslehre des hl. Cyril von Jerusalem* (Paderborn, 1923).
[30] Theodoret, *Church History*, v. 9.
[31] See *The Pilgrimage of Etheria*, M. L. McClure and C. L. Feltoe, in the S.P.C.K. Translations of Christian Literature, 1919, in which the journal of Aetheria is rendered into English, with Introduction and notes.

holy Jerusalem churches," at loggerheads in 378 as competitors
for the attention of pilgrims, were now colleagues in the maintenance of a co-ordinated piety towards Christ in connection
with the actual scenes of his saving work.[32] And time was
hallowed in a liturgical calendar, with a climax in Holy Week
and Good Friday leading up to Easter and its octave, and so
passing on to Ascension and Whitsunday. When Cyril first
lectured, there was the Forty-day Fast and Easter, but no Holy
Week or Good Friday. Bishop and people did not go together
from holy place to holy place, according to the subject of the
day's commemoration. But in the brilliant development of a
sacred year in the holy city to which the pages of Aetheria's
journal bear witness, we have the most impressive monument
to Cyril's genius. And through pilgrims like Aetheria, the
influence of his work spread throughout Christendom. In the
words of the late Dom Gregory Dix, Jerusalem gave to Christendom "the first outline of the public organization of the divine
office, and the first development of the proper of the seasons."[33]

CATECHESIS

The preparation of adult converts for baptism in the early
Church was long and arduous. Until they came to realize their
need of what the Church might have to give, enquirers were
handled with much discretion. But when they were ready to
submit to the conditions attaching to formal instruction, they
were enrolled as *catechumens*, and admitted to part of the
liturgical worship of the Christian congregation. The title
catechumen derives from the verb *katechein*, in ordinary use for
"instruct by word of mouth," and so means "a person who is
receiving instruction from a teacher," while the process of
giving such instruction, or the content of the instruction given,
is *catechesis*. These words had probably been taken for use in a
technical sense in Judaism before they received parallel
Christian use, for, in Romans 2:18, Paul speaks of a "*catechumen
in the Law*," meaning an instructed orthodox Jew.

The word *catechumen* first appears as a regular ecclesiastical

---

[32] At this time there were at least seven separate ecclesiastical establishments
in or near Jerusalem; the Martyry, the Eleona, or Church of the Mount
of Olives, the Imbomon, or Church of Christ's ascension higher up on
the Mount, the Church of Gethsemane, a church on the road to Bethany,
the Lazarium at Bethany itself, and the Church of the Nativity at
Bethlehem.

[33] *The Shape of the Liturgy*, p. 350.

term in the opening of the third century, in Tertullian.[34] The context shows it to mean an unbaptized person who has been accepted by the Church for instruction and training in the hope of baptism. It shows, also, that catechumens were admitted to the first part of the liturgy, and dismissed before the offerings. The way of the early Church was to hold back from the outside world any detailed knowledge of what Christians believe, and only to display the Christian way of life and moral principles.[35] Thus mere curiosity won nothing for a pagan enquirer. But if such an enquirer was moved by admiration and desire for the Christian way of life to such effect that his Christian friends bore witness of it to the clergy, these might admit him to instruction, upon his undertaking to submit himself. His first instruction was still predominantly moral, not excluding the exercise in Christian prayer and the instruction by and upon the liturgical readings which he received by his attendance at the first part of the liturgy. Instruction of a strictly credal character followed only when the catechumen had proved himself eager and ready to receive the secret of Christian living. As soon as the creed had been soundly imparted and learned by heart, the catechumen received baptism and passed into the ranks of the faithful. By the fourth century, however, a very great change had come over the scene. It was an inevitable change, resulting from the great increase in the applications for entry into the Church, and had made rapid advance already during the long period of peace in the second half of the third century. With the Peace of the Church in 313 began a process of acceleration, in this respect, so that catechumens were no longer "hand-picked" as of old, and it was quite impracticable to give the same degree of individual personal attention to catechumens as had been usual in former times. Some regimentation of catechesis now became indispensable. And as the same circumstances that made the instruction of converts more

---

34 *On prescription of heretics*, 41, *Of the crown*, 2, *Against Marcion*, v. 7. The last of these passages implies that the distinction between catechumens and faithful prevailed also among the Marcionites.

35 This reserve with regard to doctrine is notably shown by the instance of Arnobius. Arnobius was an African teacher of rhetoric, and became an enquirer in the Church at Sicca, at the end of the third century. Before he could be instructed for baptism, the bishop demanded his composition of a work in refutation of paganism and the pagan way of life. This Arnobius did, in his work, *Against the Gentiles*. The book shows excellent appreciation of the gospel way of life, but the very vaguest acquaintance with Scripture and Christian doctrine.

difficult, also made it harder to maintain the high standards of devotion required from the faithful, a double need was met by the institution of Lent, which appears to be, quite strictly, a development of the fourth century, though of the first years of the century. The Fifth Canon of Nicaea recognizes "the forty days" before Easter as an understood description of a period of the Christian year, without indicating its use or purpose.[36] But it is not long before it is made clear that the forty days are to be used for the spiritual discipline of the faithful, and for the preparation of catechumens, approved for the purpose, for baptism on Easter eve. There is evidence, earlier than the fourth century, of some disciplinary and devotional preparation for Easter, by a complete abstention from food for forty hours before the Easter liturgy. The reason for this observance was that, for those forty hours, "the Bridegroom had been taken away."[37] And a scriptural reason was, of course, equally forthcoming for the new Lent of forty days. In it the believer followed the Saviour in his days of fasting in the wilderness.

This prolonged preparation for Easter quickly spread to all parts of the Church, because it contained an idea that met the need of the Church in that hour. But the one idea clothed itself in local practice in a variety of different usages, and Lent-keeping advanced at differing paces in different parts of the Church. It is sufficient for our purpose to describe the practice of the Jerusalem Church at the time when Cyril became bishop. The Jerusalem Lent began eight weeks before Easter. This was because no Sunday or Sabbath (Saturday) could be a fast-day,[38] only excepting the Great Sabbath, or Easter Eve. The first fast-day was what we should call the Monday after Sexagesima. There were then five fast-days in each of eight weeks, of which the last was the Friday before Easter. And after that Friday's evening refection, the old and traditional total fast of forty hours began. This last fast was incumbent upon all who were capable of enduring it. But the degree of fasting on the forty Lenten fast days was left very much to individual devotion, and

---

[36] According to this Canon, the sentences of excommunication passed by a bishop are to be the subject of review by the Provincial Synod twice in the year. The first such synod of review is to be held "before the Forty Days." No doubt the purpose of this was to enable excommunication, in suitable cases, to be terminated before Easter, and the Canon shows that, at least for penitential purposes, a forty-day fast before Easter was already a recognized institution.

[37] Mark 2:20.

[38] That is, a day on which no meal was taken until evening.

was observed very differently by the ascetics and by ordinary lay people. And the observance both rekindled devotion in the faithful and brought the baptizands to approach with fit mind their baptism on Easter eve, now the general day, or rather night, of Christian initiation. Thus, on the Day of Resurrection the congregation felt its reinforcement and renewal by the accession of a body of neophytes.

It lay with each church to devise the manner in which the catechumens, who were now in the west called *competentes* and in the east *photizomenoi* (those being enlightened), should pass through this, the last, stage of their preparation, during the Lenten season. Much of their exercise was strictly devotional. Evidence drawn from different churches agrees in showing that baptizands at this stage underwent exorcism every day, as was the case at Jerusalem. And we must not, because exorcism is to us unfamiliar, underestimate the importance of the rite in this connection. The *formulae* of exorcism uttered in the most impressive manner and circumstances must have been a powerful force for decision of the will and feelings against the allurements of evil, as they had presented themselves in the past life of the convert, and for a sense of liberation into the service of God. But the most important thing about pre-baptismal exorcism was that, in those days of increased numbers, it supplied the surviving element of individual and personal ministry in the preparation of the candidates. The office of exorcist was one that called for faith and earnestness, but for little other special aptitude than might suffice for committing the *formulae* of exorcism to memory. It was therefore possible for each church to possess a corps of exorcists, who counted as a lower rank in the clerical order, of sufficient size to supply individual ministration to the now so numerous candidates for baptism. Each such candidate could therefore have an approved minister in personal charge of that part of his preparation that concerned the conversion of his will. We learn from Jerome that the place of catechesis, Constantine's basilica on Golgotha,[39] known as the Martyry, was regarded as a very special centre for exorcism, because the devils were in special terror of that sacred spot.[40] But this in turn makes it likely that the ministry of exorcism in this church was particularly well developed.

[39] The latest work on this building is *Konstantins Kirche am heiligen Grab in Jerusalem*, Erik Wistrand, Göteborg, 1952.
[40] Epist. xlvi, to Marcella.

3—C.J.

We now come to the actual instruction given to the *photi-zomenoi* at Jerusalem during the forty days of Lent. A study of the catechetical lectures of Cyril shows them to form what would be described today as a "teaching mission." They were not aimed at, or indeed open to, the outside public, and they presuppose a general understanding of the Christian faith and some familiarity with Scripture. The baptizands, who were registered after scrutiny at the beginning of the forty days, formed the expected audience at these lectures, and were given to understand that everything they would hear would be essential to them, so that they must not think them on a level with ordinary sermons. Other catechumens, not yet promoted to be *photizomenoi* were strictly excluded, and nothing said or done in the preparation of the *photizomenoi* must be divulged to them. But a large number of the baptized, some friends and witnesses of the *photizomenoi*, and some ascetics and other devout persons, were also present. Cyril delivered an introductory lecture, followed by a series of eighteen lectures forming a complete summary course of instruction in the Christian faith.

We are here faced with a numerical puzzle. It is implied that lecturing took place on every one of the forty days. And yet there is nothing about the nineteen lectures that have come down to us that suggests that they form only part of, or a selection from, a course of forty lectures. This puzzle has vexed the ingenuity of scholars without evoking any but the most tentative solutions.[41] What now follows is also tentative.

By the end of the course, Cyril found himself with more matter than time, and the eighteenth lecture is easily seen to be two lectures telescoped into one. But this is the kind of quandary that is familiar to the young lecturer. Afterwards he times more successfully, and gives the number of lectures in the way intended. We have evidence that this same course of catechetical lectures was later given with the telescoped lectures on separate days, so that there were twenty lectures in all, the introduction, and a series of nineteen instructions.[42] Now it is

---

[41] The most elaborate attempt is that of Dom F. Cabrol in chapter vii of his *Les Églises de Jérusalem*. (Paris, 1895). He supposed many lectures to be lost, put vi–xi in the sixth week (with a lecture on Saturday), xii–xvii in the seventh, and xviii on Palm Sunday. This puts xiv on Wednesday, whereas xiv. 24 shows that it was on Monday, and separates xi and xii by a Sunday. This is enough to destroy the whole construction.

[42] The evidence is in the form of a Jerusalem lectionary translated into Armenian, published as an appendix in F. C. Conybeare, *Rituale Armenorum* (Oxford, 1905), Appendix II. The manuscript, which is in

certain that a great part of the Jerusalem Christian residents spoke only *Syristē*, or Palestinian Aramaic,[43] while Cyril's lectures proclaim themselves as able and cultured extempore speaking in Greek. They could not have been followed by the less Hellenized, even if they had some colloquial Greek. It is possible, therefore, that Cyril gave a full-dress Greek lecture only on twenty of the forty days, on the remainder lecturing to the *simpliciores* appropriately in the vernacular. But, if so, the two courses were of independent construction (as would be reasonable, considering the difference between the two cultures and tongues), and were not given strictly day and day about. Sometimes we find indication of two or even three of our Greek lectures being on consecutive days. This was so with the sixth, seventh, and eighth[44] and with the tenth, eleventh and twelfth. The fourteenth was on a Monday.[45] If it were the Monday in Holy Week, the last five lectures were on consecutive

the Bibliothèque Nationale at Paris, dates from the eighth or ninth century. The remoteness of Armenia saved the Armenian church from many liturgical cross currents, and the lectionary, brought home by some important pilgrim from Jerusalem in the fourth century, was not quickly displaced and forgotten. This lectionary gives nineteen lections to be used at the instruction of those to be baptized at Easter. The first eighteen correspond with those indicated in the manuscript of Cyril's lectures. These manuscripts give only the *incipits*. The Armenian lectionary gives the *explicits* as well, so that we can now tell the whole scripture which the audience had heard before each of Cyril's lectures. The Armenian has a nineteenth lection, I Timothy 3:14-16. Now I Timothy 3:15 is cited in Section 25, early in the second part of the lecture, which breaks obviously between Sections 21 and 22. The Armenian lection is appropriate to this second part, if it were a lecture in itself. And we may conclude that it was at some time separate from the first part, as Lecture XIX. A Bodleian Armenian manuscript dated 1359 is also printed by Conybeare (p. 518), with the rubric, "For the holy quadragesima of those who are about to receive the seal (i.e., be baptized), nineteen lections." There was no lection for the introductory lecture.

43 For this dialect, see Anton Baumstark, *Nichtevangelische Syrische*. (Münster, 1921.) F. C. Burkitt shows that, on the evidence of the surviving literature in this dialect, the Church of Jerusalem was the effective metropolis of an extensive Aramaic Christianity in the fourth and fifth centuries. (*Journal of Theological Studies*, xxiv, 1923. p. 423). Eusebius tells of a lector, Procopius, of the Church of Scythopolis, a native of Jerusalem, who interpreted Greek into "Syriac" (no doubt meaning Palestinian Aramaic). (*Martyrs of Palestine*, ii. 1.) The non-Hellenic element in the Jerusalem Church was therefore not negligible. The bilingual section of the population would naturally increase with the increase of pilgrimage, but is not likely to have been very large when Cyril became bishop.

44 See VII. 1 and VIII. 1. Similarly, for the next sequence, XI. 1 and XII. 4.

45 XIV. 24.

days. In that case, how were the vernacular instructions given? This difficulty does not arise if it were the Monday in Passion week, with a fortnight of Lent still to run. We can then understand why, in Lecture xiv, Cyril is not yet painfully aware that he is running out of time, as he certainly is by Lecture xvii.[46] And if Lecture xiv was on Monday in Passion week, the lectures can be fairly evenly spaced out among the days, with four of the eight weeks having two Greek lectures, and the remainder having four, three or one.[47] The straits into which Cyril fell at the end of the course show clearly in the last four lectures. In xv, Cyril, before he closes, assures his audience that they will get the creed finished. But he had a great deal to say about the Holy Ghost. At the end of xvi he acknowledges that "the time is short." And xvii was not next day, for he begins with the phrase "In our last lecture," and not "yesterday." But xvii proved another very long lecture. And now, having dragged his audience through a positive treatise on the Spirit, he has to crowd the rest of the course into Lecture xviii. As he concludes this lecture, he shows plainly that his forty days are come to an end. His audience has next to face the forty-hour fast. So xviii was on Friday in Holy Week (not yet differentiated as the day of our Lord's passion). xvi and xvii can best be put on Monday and Wednesday in Holy Week. Now xiv and xv may be put on the Monday and either Wednesday or Thursday in Passion Week. And so we can work back through the weeks, supposing Cyril to have been determined by circumstances when to lecture in Greek and when to instruct in the vernacular. One thing can be said with certainty. Those who followed the Greek course could only retain what they heard if they also had some form of "tutorial" in which to consolidate their learning. They would have been overwhelmed by forty days of such lecturing, without intervals for assimilation.[48]

The question of the Monday on which Lecture xiv was delivered is of crucial importance, for on it depends the deter-

[46] xvii. 20. The audience flagged, and was rallied, because "Easter is at hand."
[47] Thus; 1st Week, Introduction and i, 2nd Week, ii, iii, 3rd Week, iv, v, 4th Week, vi, vii, viii, 5th Week, ix only, 6th Week, x, xi, xii, with x on Monday and xiii Friday, 7th Week, xiv, xv, Holy Week, xvi, xvii, xviii. There is the possibility that *tēi chthes hēmerai* means "in our last lecture" and not strictly "yesterday." In that case, the awkward bunching of Greek lectures disappears.
[48] Cyril's Greek is too spontaneous and fluent for him to have been rendered into Aramaic on the spot.

mination of the year in which the lectures were given. In
XIV. 24, we are told not only that yesterday was Sunday, but
that the liturgical reading referred to the ascension. If the old
lectionary in use before the development of Holy Week had
survived, the solution to our problem would be easy. But it has
not.[49] However, in XIV. 10, we learn that it was nearing the time
when Christ rose from the dead. The vernal equinox was "a few
days ago." The month Xanthicus had begun. As Xanthicus
began on 24 March, the last two pieces of information hardly
differ. With this passage we must take VI. 20, which is a
denunciation of Mani, of whom it is said that he "arose lately,
under the emperor Probus (for the error is just of seventy years'
standing)."[50] Probus reigned from July 276 to September 282.
Cyril, lecturing in the spring, thus gives us a choice of six years,
from 347 to 352. In that range of years, Easter fell respectively
on 12 April, 3 April, 23 April, 8 April, 31 March, 19 April. In
view of the information in XIV. 10, we can rule out all but 348
and 350. In 348, Monday in Holy Week was 28 March, a week
from the equinox and the 5th day of Xanthicus. In 350, the
Monday in Passion Week was five days from the equinox, and
the 3rd day of Xanthicus.

To the decision between these alternatives, we must bring in
some further considerations. Jerome's *Chronicle* places the death
of bishop Maximus of Jerusalem in the eleventh year of the
three Augusti, that is, between May 348 and May 349. So, in
Lent, 348, Maximus would be alive. His relations with Cyril at
that last stage would not prepare us to expect that he would
depute Cyril to give the catechetical lectures in his place. If he
was too ill to lecture himself, we should expect Heraclius to be
his choice. There is, moreover, nothing in our lectures to suggest
that Cyril speaks as a deputy, and not as bearing on his own
shoulders the responsibilities of the bishop's office. Thus there
are three difficulties which meet us in choosing 348, and apparently none in choosing 350. The three difficulties are, (i) in
requiring Lecture XIV to be given in Holy Week, it overloads
the lecturing of that week, (ii) in supposing that Cyril lectured
as a presbyter, and (iii) in placing so unhappy a background to

49 F. C. Burkitt, "The early Syriac lectionary system" (*Proceedings of the
British Academy*, 1923) gives us no help. As the Calendar developed,
earlier lectionaries became inappropriate and were displaced, and, with
their disappearance, the evidence we desire disappeared also.

50 For Mani and Manicheeism, see note 16 to Lecture IV. 4 (p. 101) and
note 23 to Lecture XV. 3 (p. 150). Also note 11 to Section 11 of
Nemesius (p. 259) below.

such serene lecturing. The circumstances in which Cyril succeeded Maximus would lead us to expect some delay between the death of Maximus and the consecration of Cyril. We could hardly expect that he would lecture as bishop in 349. Again, in his letter to Constantius in May, 351, he speaks of himself as newly in office, so that this was his first occasion for addressing the emperor. We should hardly expect such an expression if two years had passed since his consecration. Consequently, we must conclude that our lectures were delivered in Lent, 350, that they were among the first acts of Cyril as bishop, and that they embodied instruction for the whole forty days in the form of what was intended as twenty addresses. The tenth-century Munich codex which is our oldest manuscript source for the Lectures, follows the text of Lecture xviii with this note:

"Many and various have been the lectures delivered from year to year, whether it be the lectures before baptism, or those addressed to the newly-enlightened after their baptism. But only these lectures have been taken down in writing while they were being delivered. This was by certain religious, in the year 352 from the appearing on earth of our Lord and Saviour. In them you will find, in one place and another, instruction from holy scripture on all the necessary dogmas of the faith that profit those who come to know them, together with the answers to be made to pagans, Jews and heretics; also, by God's grace, the manifold ethical precepts of Christian living."[51]

This note cannot be much older than the manuscript that contains it, in view of the attempt to render the date of the lectures in the form of *anno Domini*.[52] If it was not the work of the amanuensis of this copy, it was of that of his exemplar. And the previous copy must have had a date note in one of the earlier systems. We have seen reason why the lectures could not have been given in 352, and we need not be troubled by what is likely to be an arithmetical failure on the part of a ninth-century scribe. But there is no reason for rejecting the account here given of the circumstances that gave us these precious pre-baptismal instructions in writing.[53]

[51] Codex cccxciv. See the footnote 20, on pp. 342–3 of Reischl and Rupp's edition of the works of Cyril. This codex was written in the Orient in the tenth century in a neat uncial hand.

[52] This method of dating was introduced by the monk Dionysius Exiguus at the beginning of the sixth century. But its general acceptance was a matter of slow development.

[53] The transcribers are described as *spoudaioi*. *Spoudaios*, literally "eager,"

We now turn to the headings of the lectures, which all declare them to have been delivered *extempore* (so that what we have is a transcript, and not the lecturer's manuscript) and to a note at the close of the introductory lecture.[54] This binds everyone who receives or makes a copy to preserve the necessary discipline of secrecy. It permits it to be put into the hands of *photizomenoi* before their baptism. The note is presumably the work of the transcribers, and it shows clearly that they had no intention of adding the post-baptismal, or mystagogic,[55] lectures, which must not, of course, be divulged to *photizomenoi*. Nevertheless, five mystagogic lectures appear in company with these Lectures in most, though not all, of our manuscript copies. Are they Cyril's? Certainly not those he gave in 350, though they might be those of a later year. But in 1942, W. J. Swaans produced an argument for attributing the five mystagogic lectures, of the manuscript tradition, not to Cyril but to his successor John.[56] It is a very cogent argument, and should be set out here in an abbreviated form, especially as these mystagogic lectures do not form part of the present selection.

The points of the argument are, (i) the Munich codex follows the note on the transcription by the text of the five mystagogic lectures, expressly attributing them to John. (ii) Other manuscripts have the prebaptismal lectures without the mystagogic lectures following, and yet others attribute the lectures to Cyril and John. (iii) Cyril, in xviii. 33 promises a mystagogic lecture for every day in Easter week and there are only five in this collection (this does not show that the five are not by Cyril, but only that they do not belong to 350). (iv) These mystagogic lectures show us the Eucharist with an

came to be used as a synonym for "distinguished" and so to be applied, in secular life, to men of standing. Thence it came to be used by Christians for those whose zeal exceeded ordinary standards, and thus came to mean ascetics. It was displaced by the word *monachos* (monk) when the isolation of the ascetics from secular life was established. Its occurrence in this passage indicates that the substance of the note has come down from the age of Cyril. The determination of these persons to take down Cyril's lectures throws a vivid light on his reputation before his episcopate.
[54] See the text, p. 76 below.
[55] So called because the rites of baptism, chrism or anointing with hallowed oil, and the Eucharist, are regarded as "Mysteries," only to be disclosed to those who undergo initiation, and in the course of their initiation. Thus the *photizomenoi* might not be told beforehand exactly what was going to happen.
[56] In *Le Muséon*, lv. 1-43.

Epiclesis,[57] and a recitation of the Lord's Prayer, assign the virtue of chrism[58] to the Third Person of the Trinity, teach a eucharistic presence of Christ by metabolism[59] of the elements, and give a eucharistic intercession for emperors (in the plural).[60] All these features would be expected in a work of the 390s. They are surprising in work of forty years earlier.

There is thus strong reason for supposing that Cyril's lectures were transcribed but the once, and only those which he gave before Easter; that by the 390s the absence of mystagogic lectures was felt to be a defect in the book in circulation, and so a copy of five short mystagogic lectures given by John was added, but without the attribution to John being always copied; so that eventually these five lectures were wrongly attributed to Cyril. It remains that these lectures give us a pattern of post-baptismal, or mystagogic lecturing. The pilgrim Aetheria witnessed the catechetical lecturing at Jerusalem, as it was conducted by John, [61] and notes these points: catechumens aspiring to baptism handed their names to a presbyter before Lent, and were called for scrutiny by the bishop on the first day of Lent (Monday after Sexagesima): for the scrutiny, the bishop sat with his clergy in the Martyry, to hear the testimony of the sponsors and question the candidates: those approved were enrolled in a register of *photizomenoi*: on every fast-day in Lent every *photizomenos* was exorcized in the early morning, and a lecture by John followed: many baptized persons heard the lectures: the bishop goes through Scripture from Genesis on, expounding first the literal and then the spiritual sense, at the same time teaching the resurrection and all things concerning the faith: in the sixth week the *photizomenoi* received the creed: the bishop lectured always in Greek, while priest-interpreters rendered what he said, the one into *Syristē*

---

[57] A prayer to the Holy Spirit to come down and sanctify the elements, so that they may become sacramentally the Body and Blood of Christ.

[58] The anointing with holy oil that took place immediately after baptism.

[59] "Metabolism," a term which is applied nowadays chiefly to the change of food, in digestion, into living tissues or blood, was applied, in the early sacramental doctrines which regarded the bread and wine as "turning into" the Body and Blood of Christ (without further attempt to say how), to the change wrought by the sacrament in the elements.

[60] In April 350, it must have been known in Jerusalem that there was only one emperor. It is questionable when, after that, intercession would be made for "the emperors," with Cyril able to give the lectures, until the days of Theodosius the Great.

[61] Aetheria does not name the bishop, but there are difficulties in fitting her descriptions to circumstances prior to A.D. 386.

for the *simpliciores*, the other into Latin for the immigrants: lectures began at six a.m. and lasted for three hours: the last lecture before baptism was on Friday in Passion Week: after it the bishop sat on his throne in the apse of the Martyry and the candidates went to him, one by one, and recited the creed: the bishop then made an allocution to the *photizomenoi*, in which he told them that their important illumination was yet to come: from then till Easter eve both *photizomenoi* and clergy were fully occupied in the Holy Week observances: lecturing was resumed on Easter Monday, not in the Martyry but in the chapel over Christ's tomb, known as the Anastasis: the bishop stood in the tomb itself, speaking as in the Person of the risen Christ: these lectures were characterized by a tone of exaltation and excited strong emotion.[62]

We shall easily see that Cyril's lectures fit, on the whole, with this picture, but that there are some marked differences.

In Cyril's introductory lecture, he seems to be pressing the candidates to face the issue for themselves, whether or not they go forward with preparation. John seems to take the matter out of their hands. Cyril treats the *photizomenoi* as all but Christians. Their postulancy is the sign of their election. The big gap is between ordinary catechumens and themselves. Their illumination is taking place all through Lent. For John, they are still catechumens till Easter eve. The real enlightenment is the sacramental experience of Easter.[63] Cyril imparted the creed in his fifth lecture, with most of Lent to go. Nowhere else do we hear of the creed being taught so long before baptism; and the disadvantages are obvious.[64] John imparted the creed at the beginning of the sixth week, and received it back from the candidates at the end of the seventh, more than a week before baptism. Cyril's practice emphasizes the intellectual aspect of

62 *Pilgrimage*, 47–49. At the mystagogic lectures "the voices of those applauding . . . are heard outside the church" for "there is no one unmoved at the things that he hears."
63 The reader of Cyril's lectures must feel sorry for the *simpliciores*. It is not surprising, therefore, that in course of time emphasis was thrown more and more upon mysterious grace experienced in the sacrament, as being the chief and general cause of the light of faith in the soul of the neophyte, and less upon the enlightening of understanding.
64 So much so as to be evidence that Cyril was a beginner. John, on the other hand, could give only ten lectures to expounding the creed. But our other evidences on catechesis suggest that the outlines of the creed were allowed to unfold in the stages of instruction leading up to the delivery of the creed itself, which only took place when baptism was drawing near, and the learning by heart had to begin.

enlightenment, as John's does not, especially as he prepares the way for the creed, in Lecture IV, by a ten-head summary of his own of essential Christian doctrine, in which he includes instruction that is not covered by the creed. Cyril spoke *extempore*. John had, presumably, a prepared script, and could pause while the interpreters rendered him to their respective groups, and resume at the same point again. Each three-hour session under John conveyed about half the matter of an average Greek lecture of Cyril.[65]

Aetheria has an observation to make on John's lectures which might well apply to Cyril's. It concerns the great part played in them by the exposition of Scripture. Thinking, perhaps, of Luke 24: 27, "Beginning at Moses and all the prophets, he expounded unto them in all the scriptures the things concerning himself," Aetheria says, of John, "Beginning from Genesis, he goes through all the Scriptures . . . explaining them first literally and then unfolding them spiritually." We shall not understand this as meaning that John gave a course on the books of the Bible, but only (what we have in Cyril) a continual proof of the things concerning Christ, first from direct prophecy in the Old Testament, and then by deduction thence of a spiritual meaning. When Aetheria says that the resurrection and all things concerning the faith are taught at the same time, we shall understand the teaching of the New Testament. Aetheria underlines the fact that both the instruction on the creed, and the doctrinal and moral instruction before the imparting of the creed, are equally based on continual exegesis of Scripture. And so, she says, these Palestinian Christians get so much more profit from the liturgical lections, all through their lives, than our western folk do, thanks to this thorough scriptural grounding at their catechesis. In this matter, it is clear that Cyril marked out the way in which John followed. John was also Cyril's faithful disciple in following his heads of doctrine. Jerome, in his book *Against John of Jerusalem*, says that John, to prove his orthodoxy, preached in the presence of Epiphanius a sermon in which he treated of "all the dogmas of the Church," just as he was wont to do in catechesis.[66] Jerome

[65] And so more nearly the length of the five mystagogic lectures. This lecturing was the bishop's special glory. Aetheria says that the audience applauds more at the catechetical lectures than they do at the ordinary sermons.

[66] Section 10. The three sections that follow confirm Aetheria's estimate of John's catechetical lecturing.

wondered that John, who "does not excel in the gifts of speech," should be thus able "to gallop through it all without stopping to take breath." The secret may have been that he had by heart Cyril's *Decalogue of Dogmas*, that is to say, his own "ten heads of faith," set out in Lecture IV before he confined himself, for the rest of his course, to the exposition of the Jerusalem creed. To sum up, the comparison of Aetheria's account of John's cate- chizing with Cyril's lectures gives us a picture of intelligible development of method and of changing emphases. But it shows clearly that Cyril, in this first course of lectures, delivered, as Jerome says, "in his youth,"[67] laid the whole foundation for a baptismal catechesis that was to be one of the chief glories of the Church of Jerusalem.

THE MARTYRY

The scene of the catechetical lectures was the basilica of Constantine known as the Martyry.[68] We have our first descrip- tion of this building in Eusebius' *Life of Constantine* (iii. 33–40). Eusebius must have known very well what he describes. And yet his description has faced scholars with a great deal of diffi- culty. This may be lessened somewhat when we consider that Eusebius was not writing as an architect but as a panegyrist extolling Constantine. He therefore chooses for mention those features of the building that were unusual or, of themselves, impressive. The ordinary basilican features of the building he passes over without description.[69] It may be guessed that Eusebius had a great share in inspiring Constantine with the plan of erecting these sacred buildings in Jerusalem. But it is his clear intention, in the *Life*, to extol the initiative of Constan- tine himself. So, in iii. 29, he declares that the emperor had

[67] *Famous men*, No. 112.
[68] *Marturion*, rendered into English as Martyry, means a proof or testimony. Cyril regards the name as inspired (see XIV. 6) since Zephaniah (3:8 in the Septuagint) says, "Therefore await me, saith the Lord, on the day of my resurrection at the Martyry". Valesius, commenting on *Life of Constantine*, iv. 45, suggests that this exegesis was produced at the dedication of the Martyry, in 335. Whereas the names Martyry and Anastasis are commonly used, as in these pages, to denominate two dis- tinct buildings, the first a basilica and the second a rotunda, both names, in Cyril's days, were alike applicable to the whole complex of buildings shown in the ground plan A. (See page 44.)
[69] He planned to append to the *Life* the text of a full description which he had sent to Constantine in 335. This appendix was never added. (See the end of iii. 40.)

CONJECTURAL PLAN OF THE BUILDINGS ON GOLGOTHA

GROUND PLAN A

conceived a plan for erecting a church near the Saviour's tomb, some time before it became practicable for him to carry it into effect. Constantine, he says, "had foreseen, as if by the aid of a superior intelligence, that which should afterwards come to pass." He means the rediscovery of the Holy Sepulchre, which he is going presently to describe.[70] This is as much as to say that Constantine had plans for the glorification of Jerusalem some time before he either became master of Palestine or was acquainted with Eusebius. The point is very important for our estimate of Constantine.[71] For it shows the kind of under-

[70] He asserts that the pagans deliberately hid the tomb beneath a mound of earth, upon which they then erected a shrine of Venus (iii. 26). Jerome attributes this, and other steps to bar Christians from the holy sites, to Hadrian, in A.D. 135 (Epist. lviii. 3). But the Christians presumably remembered. Constantine appears to say, in a letter to bishop Macarius of Jerusalem (Life, iii. 30-32), that they had applied to Licinius in vain to have the mound removed from the holy Sepulchre. Eusebius says (iii. 28) that when the mound was demolished at Constantine's command, the results "exceeded all expectation. The venerable and hallowed monument of our Saviour's resurrection was discovered." Constantine refers to the discovery of the tomb, in his letter to Macarius, as "this miracle." For Eusebius, the resurrection of the tomb is a symbol of the resurrection of Christ. In his Theophany, which survives in Syriac, he dilates on the lone rock with but one tomb as fitting the unique burial (iii. 61. p. 199 in the edition of S. Lee).
Cyril (xiv. 9) shows, what Eusebius does not, that Constantine ordered the cutting away of the face of the rock, so as to expose the chamber and its loculus to view. He also says (xiii. 39 and xiv. 22) what is confirmed by Jerome (Epist. cviii. 9), that the round stone to block the door was also found. When we remember how John 20:5-9 implies that the door to the tomb was so low, and the interior so dark, that the loculus could not be distinctly seen, the motive for the drastic step of cutting back the rock is intelligible.
[71] The greater part of the evidence that the Holy Land played an essential part in the religious policy of Constantine is to be sought in the Life of Constantine attributed to Eusebius. The authenticity of this work has latterly been called in question by H. Grégoire. But even he seems not to be prepared to deny it any Eusebian basis. Certainly the Life gives rise to problems that are not yet all solved. But recent study has tended to diminish suspicions of fiction attaching to the work, and this applies particularly to the passages in which it represents Constantine as having a lively interest in the Holy Land. If the Life is, in the main, the authentic work of Eusebius, it occupied the last days of his life, and it is probable that his autograph was still not ready for copying when he died. The autograph may have lain unnoticed in the church library of Caesarea until the days of Euzoius, whom Jerome credits with concern for its treasures. Gelasius, his Nicene successor, is, however, more likely than Euzoius to have prepared the Life for circulation, at a time when the east had, once more, in Theodosius the Great, a ruler ready to walk in the steps of Constantine.

standing of Christianity in which he excelled. The main evidence for his interest in the Holy Land is contained in the *Life*, Book iii, chapters 25–53, which give an account of the works carried out in Palestine on Constantine's orders. But other passages in the *Life* are of importance. Thus, in i. 12, Constantine is compared with Moses, as being a deliverer brought up in the palace of a tyrant, and this passage leads the way to i. 19, where the author describes Constantine as he first saw him, a magnificent young soldier in the train of Diocletian, when the emperor passed southwards through Palestine in 296 on his way to suppress the rising of Achilleus in Egypt. We know alike from Eusebius and Lactantius that at this time there were many Christians about the emperor's person. Constantine may have learned then what the topographical associations of Palestine meant for Christians, and this may have constituted one of his first impressions concerning the Christian religion. In ii. 64–72, Constantine's letter pleading with Alexander and Arius to resolve their dispute, he clearly suggests a connection between the pacification of the Church and the possibility of his coming in person to the Holy Land. The description of his death-bed baptism at Nicomedia (iv. 62) represents him as telling those present "I had thought to do this in the waters of the river Jordan." We are plainly meant to understand that church disunity was at least one reason why that hope was disappointed. There can be no doubt of Constantine's constant preoccupation with the union of Christendom. So, when we read in iii. 25 that he was inspired of Christ to make the place of his resurrection "an object of attraction and veneration to all," we may suppose him to have fostered Christian pilgrimage as something that should strengthen church unity. When we remember how the travels of an Irenaeus or Abercius created recognition of the world-wide unity of churches, and how Constantine himself may have been brought by his travels to appreciate the significance of the Church, it is reasonable to credit him with the thought that the Holy Land might be an influence for unity through the travels of pilgrims. We may judge further that he looked to the Holy Land as a place where great gestures were to be made. In 335, as the *Life* (iv. 42–6) tells us, he urged the bishops assembled at Tyre to restore unity to the Church, and followed this up with an urgent call to them to repair to Jerusalem where magnificent provision had been made for the dedication of his new church on Golgotha, the Martyry. At this dedication the bishops (as we learn from

Athanasius, *Against the Arians*, 84) asserted the emperor's assurance that "the Arians"[72] were returned to catholic obedience, and reconciled them. Constantine had, in short, a considered Holy Land policy. That he should have conceived the idea of creating a new focus of unity for the Church throughout the empire, in the Holy Land, and particularly in the holy city of Jerusalem, is a striking instance of his artistic sense of human strategy. If we will believe Eusebius, it was *his* part to be only the admiring agent for fulfilling what the genius of Constantine had initiated. But it must have been his joy to superintend the rediscovery of the tomb in the rock, which gave the point of departure for the realization of the emperor's scheme. Jerome's *Chronicle* tells us, under A.D. 326, that a Constantinopolitan presbyter Eustathius earned acknowledgment by the industry with which he built the Martyry at Jerusalem. But as Bidez, in his Berlin edition of the *Church History of Philostorgius* (p. 208), reconstructs that writer's text referring to the Martyry, Eustathius earned acknowledgment by his "apostolic life" and "supreme virtue," while he had as his colleague Zenobius the "archdeacon" (a transparent miscopy for "architect"). For practical purposes, therefore, the erection of the Martyry was an outlying part of the huge building-scheme that created Constantinople, and the emperor joined to the architect whom he sent to Jerusalem an outstanding presbyter, from among his own personal clergy, to see that everything went forward as well as he could wish.[73]

The site consisted of the garden containing the rock of the sepulchre, and the low ridge of rock, to the east of the garden, which had been identified as Golgotha. This ridge must have been clearly defined, and ran east and west, its axial line, when produced, passing close to the sepulchre itself. The garden was enclosed, on the sides away from Golgotha, within a wall, having a colonnade on the inside. In 350 the rock of the sepulchre probably still stood, in its enclosure, under the open sky. Later a rotunda was erected with the sepulchre at its

72 *Tous peri Areion*, "Arius and company," as referred to in the emperor's letter. Between the letter and its acceptance at Jerusalem Arius himself had died.

73 This again is an imaginative step on Constantine's part. It meant that the clergy and ascetics of Jerusalem had to deal with an imperial agent who had their enthusiastic confidence, and that the architect would adapt his plans both to the actual site, and to the uses to which the buildings were likely to be put.

centre.[74] This was the building known as the *Anastasis*, or chapel of the resurrection, and was entered by several doors. Its floor-space took up the western half of the garden, while the eastern half formed an open court, between it and Golgotha. The ridge of rock formed the site of the Martyry, of which the western apse towered above the garden court, while its eastern facade, with its great entrance-doors, fronted on another colon-naded courtyard, from which a gateway gave access from what Aetheria calls the *pars quintana* or market street.[75] From this street the visitor ascended a flight of steps (see elevation B) from which he could either pass through an entrance into the basilica, or along a portico, built against the flank of the church, which led, at the further end, down steps, into the garden court, and so to the Anastasis. The Martyry thus was the largest unit in a complex of building so designed as to give the authorities the greatest control over access, and that nevertheless, when it was so desired, would admit large crowds of worshippers with a minimum of delay.

Eusebius describes the basilica as a very lofty and wide nave, covered with a lead roof under which a panelled wood ceiling glowed with gold ornament. He does not say, but we can assume that it had this roof borne up upon long lines of pillars, in the way usual in such basilican halls. He continues, "along both flanking-walls upper and lower porticos were built, exactly alike on the two sides, and both running the whole length of the building. These, too, were ceiled with panels adorned with gold. The lower porticos in front of the building leaned upon enormous pillars, while the upper, lying in from these front colonnades, were borne up by masonry that, towards the out-side, was intricately ornamented."[76] The floor of the basilica was paved, he says further, with marble. And so smooth was the building of the walls, that even their external surface almost seemed like marble. We note the emphasis on the external glories of the building. To see what it all means, we may do best to think first of the preparation of the site. The rock ridge must first have been dressed to take the building, the side slopes being cut back to give a vertical wall of rock forming the back

---

[74] Wistrand, *op. cit.*, argues this probability, and places the building of the rotunda about the end of Cyril's life.

[75] *Pilgrimage*, xliii. 7.

[76] *Life*, iii. 37. Every writer on the Church of the Holy Sepulchre hitherto has assumed that Eusebius is describing pillared aisles *inside* the basilica. But it is impossible to impose such a sense upon his words.

CONJECTURAL SOUTH ELEVATION OF THE BUILDINGS ON THE GOLGOTHA SITE WITH THE SOUTH ENCLOSING WALL AND THE BAPTISTRY TAKEN AWAY

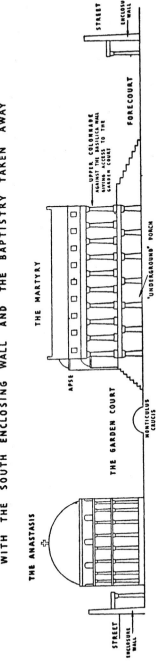

THE ANASTASIS

THE GARDEN COURT

THE MARTYRY

APSE

MONTICULUS CRUCIS

"UNDERGROUND" PORCH

UPPER COLONNADE
AGAINST THE BASILICA WALL
GIVING ACCESS TO THE
GARDEN COURT

FORECOURT

STREET

ENCLOSURE WALL

STREET

ENCLOSURE WALL

ELEVATION B

of a lower portico.[77] The roof of this portico would be of heavy masonry continuing the level of the floor of the church, and resting on a row of very stout pillars. Upon this projecting floor, upheld by the lower portico, was erected the lighter upper portico, whose more graceful and decorated columns rose to meet the eaves of the lead roof of the church. It was these upper porticos that were entered from the top of the eastern stairs of the Martyry, and so gave access, from the forecourt, outside the basilica, to the garden court and Anastasis.[78] The lower porticos were a purely external feature of the buildings, and emphasized its lavish magnificence in the eyes of the outside world. There was, according to Eusebius, one outstanding glory of the interior of the Martyry. "Over against the entrance-doors, the crowning feature of all was the hemisphere, which rose to the very summit of the church. This was ringed by twelve columns, whose capitals were embellished with silver bowls of great size." No small help to solving the riddle of this description has been given by the recent publication of a survey of the ancient basilican churches of Lepcis, Sabratha and Oea, on the Tripolitanian coast, dating from the neighbourhood of 400 A.D., and not seriously rearranged in their sixth century Byzantine restoration.[79] Before this restoration, each church had a wooden altar-table in the middle of the nave, under a baldachin supported on four columns, and surrounded by a low screen on all four sides. These churches, like the Martyry, had a western apse, and an eastern facade pierced by entry doors. There were side aisles cut off by rows of pillars and running the whole length of the basilican hall.[80] The western apse held the bishop's throne and presbyteral bench, on a platform some five feet above the floor of the nave. Conversely we may attribute these features to the Martyry, and see, in the

---

[77] We have something analogous in the siting of Durham Cathedral, and especially of its Galilee. At Golgotha, the uneven surface of the rock platform must first have been levelled, and the building and the edges of the rock adjusted each to other. The adjective which Eusebius applies to the lower porticos is "underground," which is justified according to the accompanying reconstruction, elevation B.

[78] See *Pilgrimage*, xxiv. 8, where a crowd assembles at cockcrow in the garden-court before the doors of the Martyry or Anastasis have yet been opened.

[79] See "The Christian Antiquities of Tripolitania," J .B. Ward Perkins and R. G. Goodchild, in *Archaeologia*, xcv. 1–84.

[80] At the end of each aisle was a chamber, or *secretarium*, flanking the apse on either side. In one were kept and prepared the sacred vessels, and in the other the scriptures and liturgical books.

"hemisphere" upborne by a circle of twelve columns nearly to touch the ceiling of the church, a peculiarly magnificent *baldachino*, to dignify the Holy Table. When lecturing, Cyril probably sat, facing east, before the Holy Table, with his audience between him and the entrance doors, and probably John likewise; but when John heard the candidates recite the creed, they went (Aetheria says, one by one) up the steps into the apse.[81] For exorcism, the candidates may have gone in turn along the aisles to the sacristries or *secretaria* that flanked the apse. After exorcism they would return, to sit on the marble floor east of the Holy Table until the bishop came from the Anastasis, to begin his lecture.

Neither Eusebius nor Cyril give us any hint of something that plays so great a part in the journal of Aetheria and the accounts of later pilgrims. This is the *monticulus Calvariae* outside the Martyry in the south-east corner of the garden-court.[82] It was apparently a little mound of rock with a crevice in it. On this mound, approached by steps, there was built a shrine where ostensions of the wood of the True Cross took place. Such an "invention" might have happened and become accepted during Cyril's exile. It entailed, however, far-reaching consequences, for it invested the group of sacred sites with a bi-focal character, the cave of Resurrection answering to the mound of Passion, two clearly defined objects of cult observance. This is the probable reason why a mere *paraskeuē* or eve of the eve of Easter presently turned, at Jerusalem, into Good Friday, and introduced an antithesis, previously unknown but soon to be felt throughout the Christian world, between Passiontide and Eastertide.

81 *Pilgrimage*, xlvi. 5. Aetheria's words *retro in absida post altarium* raise the question whether in her time the Holy Table had been removed from under the "hemisphere" to stand before the bishop's throne. But they certainly do not put it beyond doubt.
82 Aetheria speaks of the space between the Anastasis and the *monticulus* as *ante crucem*, "in front of the cross," and the Martyry, and everything east of the *monticulus*, as *post crucem*. This suggests that the shrine of Calvary was open to the west, facing the Anastasis. Peter the Deacon calls it a *mons* and speaks, like Aetheria, of the lamps in the shrine. By the time of Adamnus, in the late seventh century, a nave had been built out eastwards from the rotunda of the Anastasis, to contain the asserted place of the crucifixion in one building with the Holy Sepulchre, leaving the basilica of the Martyry outside the essential sanctuary. The development can be followed in P. Geyer, *Itinera Hierosolymitana* (1898), in the "Vienna corpus." Wistrand, *op. cit.*, has a suggestion as to the circumstances which led to the recognition of the *monticulus crucis*.

By singular good fortune we have an actual picture of the group of buildings on Golgotha by an artist of the sixth century. This picture forms part of a mosaic floor, in a church of that age, at Madaba in the Moabite country east of the Dead Sea.[83] The whole floor presents a map of the Holy Land, conceived, perhaps, as a New Testament Pisgah-view, for the place is near Mount Nebo. In the middle of the map is pictured contemporary Jerusalem. We see the colonnaded market street (line-drawing C) and the forecourt of the Martyry, with its flight of steps ascending to the east facade pierced by three doors. We look along the ridge of the Martyry roof to see the golden dome of the Anastasis, with, just beyond it, the city wall. Eusebius tells us that the wall of the city was carried out, so as to enclose this Christian sacred area, and to create a fresh quarter of the city, known as New Jerusalem.[84] Aetheria's reference to the ecstatic cries of the neophytes during the mystagogic lectures in the Anastasis probably means that the sound could be heard in the street outside the sacred enclosure.[85]

The Madaba picture shows us something that our literary sources do not describe, though it is the subject of a single allusion,[86] namely the baptistry. This is shown as lying to the

---

[83] See F. Cabrol and H. Leclercq, *Dictionnaire d'archaeologie et de liturgie chrétienne*, *s.v.* Madaba. The buildings so depicted were obliterated in 1009 by Caliph Hâkem, and their traces covered up by the new work of Constantine Monomachus in 1048.

[84] *Life of Constantine*, iii. 33. In 326, the Jerusalem leaders supposed the site which they identified as Golgotha and the garden of the tomb to be outside the old city wall. They could then, presumably, trace the line of that wall. Modern archaeologists have, so far, been unable to trace it, though its discovery would affect vitally the question of the authenticity of the Holy Sepulchre.

[85] There was therefore some space between the wall of the sacred enclosure and the city wall of New Jerusalem, though this, with other details, cannot be seen from the Madaba picture. In xiv. 9 Cyril speaks of the tomb as near the city wall.

[86] This is in the first of the pilgrim records edited by Geyer. The pilgrim was an unnamed man, apparently a high military officer, who made his pilgrimage from Burgundy in 333. Compared with Aetheria, he is very laconic, and does not seem to have had such good guides as were, no doubt, available later. He speaks of the *monticulus Golgotha*, not meaning the *monticulus Calvariae* of later date, but the ridge of rock forming the site of the Martyry. He speaks of the church of marvellous beauty there built by Constantine. It must have been nearing completion, at the time, but was not to be dedicated for another two years. He speaks of it as a stone's throw from the *cripta* where the Lord was buried and rose again, but says nothing of this *cripta* being surmounted by any rotunda. Eusebius says nothing of the rotunda either, but merely that Constantine enriched

THE BUILDINGS ON THE GOLGOTHA SITE AS SEEN BY THE ARTIST OF THE MADABA MOSAIC

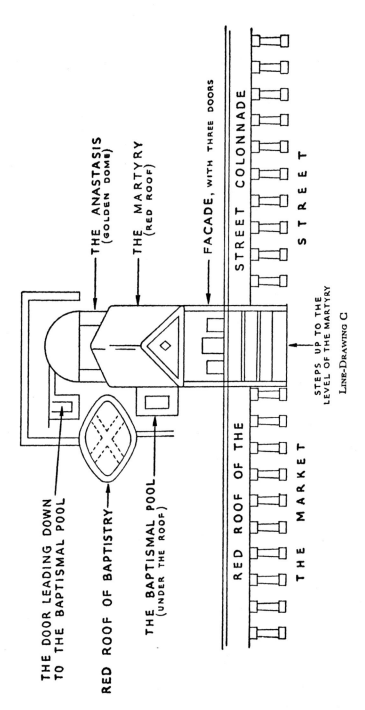

THE DOOR LEADING DOWN TO THE BAPTISMAL POOL

RED ROOF OF BAPTISTRY

THE BAPTISMAL POOL (UNDER THE ROOF)

THE ANASTASIS (GOLDEN DOME)

THE MARTYRY (RED ROOF)

FACADE, WITH THREE DOORS

STREET COLONNADE

STREET

STEPS UP TO THE LEVEL OF THE MARTYRY

RED ROOF OF THE

THE MARKET

LINE-DRAWING C

south-west of the garden-court. The mosaic-artist of Madaba imagines its roof removed, so that we see the pool. He indicates a doorway just outside the Anastasis through which, we may suppose, folk descended to the water by a flight of steps. All through the night before Easter dawned, these sacred buildings were ablaze with light. Glass candelabra and hanging lamps of burnished silver well-trimmed and filled with olive oil, turned night into day for those who passed those hours in guiding or being guided through the moving solemnities of baptism.[87] It is no wonder that it was a night never to be forgotten by even the stolidest of those whom the Church of Jerusalem received to baptism. But, then, even the daytime setting of their preparation for baptism was impressive, in having the richness and solemn grandeur that is associated for us with the word "cathedral."

JERUSALEM TRADITION

In 350, the buildings that have been described were aggressively new, and, as has been seen, the catechetical lectures delivered in that Lent seemed to some of the religious who heard them to set an excitingly new standard. But it would be a mistake to suppose this fourth-century church life at Jerusalem to be a mushroom growth. There was a Jerusalem tradition that was already venerable, though we can only form an impression of its true significance when we have considered the history of the transmission of Christianity at Jerusalem down to this time. In short, we must answer the question, What had been the history of the Church of Jerusalem? The primitive Church in Jerusalem was unique in that it was not apostolic as other churches were. According to Acts, the Church of Jerusalem inclusive of the apostles was created by a divine act of the

the sepulchre with decorations. We may conclude that the rotunda was built between the dedication of the Martyry in 335 and Cyril's death in 386. What the pilgrim of 333 saw, besides the Martyry and the *cripta*, were water-pits supplying a "bath where infants are washed," presumably a baptistry. (Geyer, *op. cit.*, p. 23.)

[87] Section 15 of Cyril's introductory lecture describes Easter eve as "that night when darkness is turned into day." Eusebius, *Church History*, vi. 9, tells how, in the early third-century days of Narcissus as bishop of Jerusalem, the lamp-oil failed for the all-night vigil of Easter. "Deep despondency seized the whole multitude." Narcissus commanded the lamps to be filled with water which was at once, by a miracle, turned into oil. Eusebius was shown a relic of this miraculous oil. Thus, in Aelia, the tradition of the Paschal illumination went back at least a century before Eusebius visited the city.

Holy Spirit. This act at the same time empowered the apostles for their mission to the world. The mother-Church of Jerusalem now took a shape of its own, the shape of a Davidic kingdom of Israel redeemed. Jesus, at once the new Moses and the Son of David, having ascended into the heavens, James, his brother after the flesh, pontificated in the City of David as a new Aaron, offering spiritual sacrifices revealed by Jesus, the high-priest after the order of Melchizedec.[88] Acts show James surrounded by a sanhedrin of Jewish presbyters who believed. And the Pauline epistles support Acts in representing James and the mother-Church of Jerusalem as receiving fullest recognition from all the apostles, and from the churches of their founding. At its source, therefore, the tradition of Jerusalem was of the richest and most significant. But in A.D. 62 James was martyred. Hegesippus, whose account is preserved in Eusebius,[89] tells us that Symeon, also a kinsman of the Saviour, was made successor to James, with the concurrence of the representatives of the apostolate and the apostolic churches. Symeon presently led forth his flock to voluntary exile at Pella.[90] But Epiphanius, who also has told us this in his *Panarion*, Heresy 29, tells us, in his *Weights and measures*, ch. 15, that after the sack of Jerusalem by the Romans in A.D. 70, Symeon and the Pella refugees returned to the ruins of the city. Presumably Epiphanius drew on Hegesippus for all this information. And there is no reason to regard the return to Jerusalem as impossible. Of our informants on this history, Josephus exaggerates the ruin of Jerusalem to flatter the Romans, and the Christian writers emphasize it to throw into brighter relief the prophetic words of Christ. But Josephus tells us[91] that Titus marvelled to find that he had captured the city with the three towers of Herod's palace, and a large piece of the adjoining western wall, undestroyed. These, then, were incorporated into a *castrum* occupying the western hill of Jerusalem, in which the tenth legion was thereafter continuously in garrison for sixty years. No such permanent *castrum* but must have its *vicus* or civilian settlement, outside its fortifications, inhabited by sutlers and a mixed population ministering to the needs of the troops. As the *castrum* at Jerusalem was finished, so civilians would find a shelter in the less ruined

[88] The position and authority of James has been discussed by Dr. Arnold Ehrhardt in the first chapter of his *Apostolic Succession* (Lutterworth Press, London, 1953).
[89] *Church History*, iii. 10.11.   [90] *Ibid*, iii. 5.3.
[91] *Jewish War*, Bk. vii, opening.

houses, to be a *vicus* to the tenth legion. In the eyes of the
legionaries, the Pella refugees would be "white" Jews. And
whereas Adolph von Schlatter has shown that rabbinic
opinion for some time held the ruins of Jerusalem to be defiling,
on account of dead men's bones,[92] the Christian leaders may
well have thought differently, although regardful of the law.
It is reasonable, therefore, to assume that the Judaeo-Christians
of Pella returned and found shelter in the south-west corner of
the city. For one thing, this may have been the least ruinous
part of the city. The Bordeaux pilgrim of 333 was shown, there,
the house of Caiaphas, and the remains of seven synagogues, of
which one only stood.[93] Epiphanius also knew about the synagogues.[94] The idea evidently lingered on that things had
survived in that quarter of the town, including the house of the
Last Supper. And fourth-century Christians called the quarter,
though furthest from the temple, "Zion";[95] something which
might have seemed appropriate if and when it was the only
part of the former city that possessed inhabitants, but hardly
otherwise. Finally, it was the most natural *vicus* for the adjoining
legionary camp. It was in the church in "Zion" that Eusebius
saw the reputed throne of James, to which marks of reverence
were accorded.[96] There is ground enough, therefore, to believe
in the return of the Pella Christians to Jerusalem, and in
Symeon's continuance there, as high-priest of redeemed Israel,
until his martyrdom, about A.D. 105. When this happened,
Hegesippus says, there was no kinsman of the Lord to succeed
him, and his flock received a bishop by election. And from this
moment, he continues, the Judaeo-Christian Church began to
be broken up into parties.[97] That group to which Hegesippus
belonged made claim to be in full accord with the apostolic
churches elsewhere, as James and Symeon had been with their
founders. And he attributes the death of Symeon to the
treachery of the "sects." Meanwhile, as Schlatter shows from

[92] *Die Tage Trajans und Hadrians* (Beiträge zur Forderung christlicher
Theologie), Gütersloh, 1897, p. 73. This monograph, in which extensive
use is made of evidence gathered from rabbinic sources, is of great importance for a true estimate of the history of Jerusalem after A.D. 70.
[93] P. Geyer, *op. cit.*, p. 25.
[94] *Weights and Measures*, c. 14.
[95] The authentic Zion, "the city of David," was certainly the eastern ridge
on which the temple stood.
[96] *Church History*, vii. 19. Until the Martyry was built, the "cathedral" or
mother church of Aelia was the so-called Upper Church of Zion, the
reputed successor to the house of the Last Supper.
[97] *Church History*, iii. 35 and iv. 22.4–6. The date is fixed by iii. 32.3.

rabbinic sources, the avoidance of Jerusalem by non-Christian Jews came to an end. The temple ruins became an object of mournful pilgrimage, and the previously deserted areas of the old city began quietly to fill again with Jews, some of Pharisee leanings and some Sadducee, but not Christian. An interesting episode is the purchase by a rabbi of the synagogue-building of that very synagogue of the Alexandrines in which Stephen once disputed, as a dwelling house.[98] Meanwhile, according to Eusebius (*Demonstration of the Gospel*, 3. 5) the Judaeo-Christian congregation was very large. At the end of Trajan's reign, Jewry was once more in conflict with the Empire, in Alexandria, Euphratensia and Crete. Palestinian Jews went to the help of their comrades at Alexandria, and brought chastisement to their own land. But Schlatter finds no sign that the Jewish population of the holy city was involved. Presumably it was reckoned as "well-affected." So we come to the reign of Hadrian and to the year 130. There was a very well-informed authority for the history of events in Palestine at this time, in the *History of the Romans* by Dio Cassius, writing only a century later than the events. This part of his work only survives as used in two works of the eleventh century, the *Chronicle* of John Zonaras, and the *Epitome* of Xiphilinus. And they say that Hadrian, in 130, gave orders to build a temple of Zeus on the Jewish temple site, as if Jerusalem was a Greek city.[99] This raises very great difficulties. Hadrian certainly gave such and more extensive orders five years later when a general Jewish revolt had been finally crushed. Schlatter argues[1] that Dio was misunderstood by the eleventh-century writers and that Hadrian ordered building at Jerusalem in 130, but of a different sort from that ordered in 135. Schlatter appeals to the *Epistle of Barnabas*, ch. 16, in confirmation of his conjecture that in 130 Hadrian ordered such rebuilding on the temple area as would enable the restoration of the temple rites of Israel. Such action on Hadrian's part is not incredible. Nor is it unlikely that he thought thereby to win the favour of the Jews, and their offering of sacrifices on his behalf. But if so, he grossly misunderstood the mentality of the Jews as represented in the rabbinic authors of the time. The Jews thanked Hadrian for nothing. It was their

[98] Schlatter, *op. cit.*, p. 81.
[99] *History of the Romans*, lxix. 12. After the replanning as a Roman colony, the temple site was known as the Quadra, and no doubt regarded as a sacred area for the erection of shrines.
[1] Schlatter, *op. cit.*, *passim*, for the outlines that follow.

God who again accepted them, whom they thanked. And so, when Hadrian withdrew from the Orient in 132, a certain Simeon, recognized by Rabbi Akiba and others as Messiah, under the title of Barcochab, "Son of a star," in reference to Numbers 24: 17 ("a star shall come out of Israel"), led the people in full insurrection. The legionaries at Jerusalem must have been taken entirely by surprise, and were driven from their *castrum*, to suffer heavy losses in the ensuing campaign. Simeon allied himself with Eleazar ben Charsom as high-priest, and the two reigned in Jerusalem for two years. What happened to the Christians of the Holy City can only be guessed. Justin (*I Apology*, 31) says that Barcochab was their bitter persecutor. Barcochab's Jerusalem can have been no place for Christians, whether circumcised or uncircumcised. But the suddenness with which the Romans were overthrown there gave the church no opportunity of orderly withdrawal, as in the days of Pella. Individuals can only have saved their lives by flight to the protection of the Roman forces, and, in the first instance to that of the legionaries to whom they were known.

Hadrian now called Julius Severus from Britain to take command of the recovery of Palestine. In the hot summer of 134, Jerusalem was beleaguered, and the failure of water caused Simeon to abandon the city, breaking through the Roman lines to reach the fortress of Bittir, seven miles to the south-west, where the insurgents made their final stand, until they were overcome in 135. There followed the severest repressive measures. Those involved in the guilt of insurrection were sold into slavery. All practice of Jewish religion was proscribed. We cannot be surprised if the Christian holy places were indiscriminately involved in this proscription. But, for the adherents of Judaism, the decrees of Hadrian, which remained unalleviated until A.D. 145, brought one of the bitterest persecutions in Jewish history. The Judaean highlands were confiscated and used in the refoundation of the "liberated" Jerusalem as a Roman colony, under the name of Aelia Capitolina. The new citizenship must have consisted, in the first place, of veterans and others to whom was accorded former Jewish land in reward for services rendered in the war. But the public buildings which the anonymous author embodied in the *Paschal Chronicle*[2] at this point records, as having been erected, on Hadrian's orders, for the colony, show that the new inhabitants were no mere handful. Moreover, the colony was to replace the tenth

[2] Dindorf's edition, I. p. 474. (*Corpus Scriptorum Historiae Byzantinae*, 1832.)

legion in securing the Roman peace, and must therefore have been planned as a concentration of loyalists. Under these circumstances it is unlikely that none of the Christian loyalists driven out by Barcochab were given a place in the new colony. No circumcised Christian could inhabit Aelia. But the Judaeo-Christianity represented by Hegesippus was in full communion with Gentile churches, and there is no ground for concluding that all the Christians of Jerusalem before 132 were circumcised. We must therefore allow for the possibility that the Christian congregation that reassembled in Aelia, in spite of its uncircumcision, was dominated by the tradition that had prevailed under bishops of the circumcision down to 132. There is no ground for supposing that the Church of Aelia in 135 was a mere chance collection of Levantine Greeks, looking up to the Church of Caesarea rather than back to the historic Church of Zion. This point is of the greatest importance in estimating the authenticity of the holy sites of Christian Jerusalem, excellently defended by J. Jeremias, in "Wo lag Golgotha und das Heilige Grab" (*Angellus* I. 141–173, Leipzig, 1925).[3] But it also has an important bearing on our estimate of the doctrinal and liturgical tradition in the Church of Aelia-Jerusalem in the days of Cyril.

Before the second century was out, pilgrimage to Jerusalem recommenced. But this time it was Gentile Christian pilgrimage. Melito of Sardis, in a passage cited in Eusebius, *Church History*, iv.26.13, says that he had "gone up to the east and come to the place where the things (of the old covenant) were proclaimed and done," and in his more recently discovered Paschal homily[4] he makes it clear that, for him, this place meant Jerusalem. It was thus to the Gentile Church of Aelia that an Asian bishop went to be assured what were the authentic scriptures of the Old Testament. And Melito died shortly before 190. Then, in Book vi of his *Church History* (chapters 8–14), Eusebius gives us a clear picture of the way in which, at the opening of the third century, the thoughts of individual Christians were turning

---

3 *Angellus* (the title was printed in Greek capitals) was a short-lived periodical founded by J. Leipoldt in 1925, with the alternative title *Archiv für Neutestamentliche Zeitgeschichte u. Kulturkunde*. Its first volume contained this important article of Jeremias.

4 Edition by Campbell Bonner, in *Studies and Documents*, xii (1940), p. 168 (text and note, p. 89). "For the Law became Word, and the old became new, going forth together from Sion and Jerusalem." The allusion is to Isa. 2:3, and the prophecy explains Melito's confidence in the Church of Aelia, which called itself Zion.

towards the Holy Land and City as the goal of pilgrimage. In
211, he tells us, Alexander, who had been bishop of an unnamed
church in Cappadocia and a confessor in the persecution under
Septimius Severus, was released from his long imprisonment.
His flock had apparently in the meantime been given another
pastor, and he had vowed that if he were set free he would visit
the scene of the sufferings of Christ. When he reached Aelia,
there seem already to have been there persons whom we should
call "religious,"[5] and some of these claimed to have had it
revealed to them that Alexander should stay and minister
among them. Narcissus, himself a "religious," to judge by the
stories that Eusebius collected about him, was now advanced
in years, and the bishops of Palestine agreed to Alexander
assisting Narcissus, with right of succession. Alexander was a
man of learning and had been a disciple of Pantaenus at
Alexandria, perhaps in company with Clement.[6] Perhaps, also,
for this reason he became friendly with Origen, and bore
responsibility for provoking Origen's breach with his bishop
Demetrius. When Origen had been ordained presbyter at
Caesarea, Alexander and he became lifelong friends, and both
fell victims in the Decian persecution.[7] During his residence at
Caesarea, Origen visited various places in the Holy Land, and
his great influence must have done much to spread the idea
of devotional pilgrimage. Through Pamphilus, this interest
passed to Eusebius, who was not only familiar with Jerusalem,
where he used the library collected by Alexander, but shows
wide acquaintance with the topography of the Old and New
Testaments.[8] At the same time Eusebius bears witness to the

[5] *Tois malista autōn spoudaiois.* The revelation was to "the outstandingly
devoted among them." By the time of Eusebius, the kind of devotedness
that entitled a person to be called *spoudaios* was coming to be recognized
as what later was called the religious life.
[6] In Eusebius, *Church History,* vi. 14.9, Alexander claims to have learned
from Pantaenus, and Clement, vi. 11.6 shows that Clement was with him
during his imprisonment. It is not certain, though quite likely, that
Alexander and Clement first met in the school of Pantaenus. At least
the Alexandrine connections explain Alexander's actions concerning
Origen.
[7] Origen died as a result of what he had suffered, some two years after the
persecution.
[8] On this subject, see Note 2, p. xv, in Prof. F. L. Cross, *St. Cyril of Jerusalem's Lectures on the Christian Sacraments,* S.P.C.K., 1951, where the debt
of Jerusalem, and the Holy Land, as a sanctuary for Christians, to Eusebius,
is well stated. For Origen's knowledge of the Holy Land, see *Against
Celsus,* i. 51 (cave of Bethlehem) or iv. 44 (wells of Ascalon), and elsewhere.

claims made by the Church of Aelia at the beginning of the fourth century to inherit a great tradition. The cycle of legend surrounding the figure of Narcissus may have been collected from word of mouth, but it shows that the Jerusalemites of the time of Eusebius believed in the past glories of their Church.[9] Associated with this hagiology was a written list of episcopal successions, containing the names of fifteen bishops of the circumcision down to Hadrian, and of fifteen Gentile bishops of Aelia.[10] C. H. Turner is no doubt right in calling this list for the most part a pious fiction.[11] But the motive for its composition was clearly to proclaim that the Church of Aelia was true successor in a line that stretched back, in the end, to the first and original Church of Jerusalem. We must not, therefore, attribute all the glories of Cyril's Jerusalem to the rise of pilgrimage, or to imperial favour. Much was a heritage from the past.

Part of this heritage was no doubt a tradition of doctrine, and in particular of norms of baptismal catechesis. For all the freshness with which Cyril handles his matter, in catechetical lecturing, we may judge that he is guided by church tradition, when we note how impervious he is to the contemporary theological disturbances. The synod of Nicaea, in 325, had declared that believers must be made safe against the errors of Arius by receiving the doctrine that the Son is consubstantial (*homoousios*) with the Father.[12] In spite of this, for a quarter of a century, a vogue for the Arian way of thinking spread among Hellenized church leaders throughout the Levant, including the metropolitan of Caesarea. Yet in his lectures Cyril teaches his *photizomenoi* as if, in their preparation, Arius and Nicaea had best be equally ignored. He warned them against Arian errors, but never utters Arius' name. Equally he never mentions the word "consubstantial." This is the behaviour of one who, in an unsettled age, relies upon a very assured doctrinal tradition.

9 Eusebius, *Church History*, v. 23.3 shows Narcissus of Jerusalem presiding, together with Theophilus of Caesarea, over a Palestinian synod as far back as the last decade of the second century.
10 Eusebius, *op. cit.*, iv. 5.
11 *Journal of Theological Studies*, I (1900), 529–553.
12 The synod took the baptismal creed of Caesarea, as divulged by Eusebius in proof of his orthodoxy, and added to it the agreed safeguards. The implication is that the safeguards were to be applied at the level of catechesis, when the baptizands received the baptismal creed of their own church: not that every church should take the Caesarean form in place of their own.

And the same explanation applies to the public behaviour of his immediate predecessors in the see of Jerusalem. Thus, when Arius wrote the letter to Eusebius of Nicomedia which forms the opening document of the Arian controversy,[13] he names Macarius of Jerusalem as one of three incurable reactionaries obstructing the advance of a more enlightened theology in the orient. He calls Macarius a man devoid of theological learning. But as he says the like of Philogonius, head of the great Church of Antioch, it is probable that he and Macarius had different criteria in matters of divine learning. Cyril's lectures make it absurd to suppose that the Church of Jerusalem was plunged in stolid ignorance. Yet three years before the sunshine of imperial favour fell upon that Church, its bishop stood out in the mind of Arius as one not to be driven in the direction he would have had him go. Maximus of Jerusalem, as we have seen, was no more to be driven in that way than was Macarius. And the whole career of Cyril testifies how little he was to be stampeded in matters of doctrine. He knew, however, what was going on in the learned world; and though his wit as an exegete is too sharpened by anti-Jewish polemic to let him lean much to allegorism, he perpetrates a few discreet Origenisms.[14] But in the lectures he is the practical ecclesiastic, first and foremost, aiming to render his Church orthodox and glorious, and his people upright and devout. There has been a time when scholars, observing that the framework of the creed of the Council of Constantinople had much in common with the arrangement of the Jerusalem baptismal creed, as that is to be gathered from Cyril's lectures, thought that it might have been in Cyril's brain that the *Constantinopolitanum* took shape. Now it appears that the probabilities are against it.[15] There is no evidence of Cyril engaging in the speculative ideas that formed the currency of the Arian controversy. His qualities, of scriptural learning and appreciation of the spiritual value of the ecclesiastic doctrine, were not foremost in many of the bishops who play leading parts in the polemics of the time. The turn in his fortunes came when, pure rationalism having entered the field in the persons of Aetius and Eunomius, bishops were shocked into a fresh

---

[13] Epiphanius, *Panarion*, Heresy 69.6, Theodoret, *History of the Church*, i. 5 and Latin sources.

[14] E.g., his doctrine of the forgiveness of angels in Lecture II. 9.

[15] Dr. J. N. D. Kelly reviews the history of this argument in treating of the Creed of Constantinople, in his *Early Christian Creeds*, London, 1950.

valuation of ecclesiastical tradition. [16] Then, from 359, he began to be trusted and admired by the eastern bishops who were beginning to feel their way back to a Nicene orthodoxy. He never lost the loyalty of Jerusalem Christians. If we may trust Jerome, three men, intruded into his throne by party politics, had in turn to yield place to him, so soon as he was able to return to the holy city. All these facts fit to one explanation, that Cyril represented and conserved a venerable teaching tradition, that of the Church of Aelia-Jerusalem, which, for all its vicissitudes, had known no absolute severance since the first days of the faith. This tradition moulded these lectures of Lent, 350, that have come down to us. And though they were delivered a quarter of a century after Nicaea, yet, by the deliberate policy of Cyril, they bring to us the voice of the ante-Nicene Church.

[16] See the history of the Synod of Ancyra, 358, and its consequences. See particularly the synodical letter of Ancyra in Epiphanius, *Panarion*, Heresy 73.6, and its rejection of "human wisdom."

Selections from the Catechetical Lectures

THE INTRODUCTORY LECTURE, OR

PROCATECHESIS[1]

1. Already the savour of bliss is upon you, who have come to be enlightened[2]; you have begun to pluck spiritual flowers with which to weave you heavenly crowns.[3] Already are you

---

[1] The transcript made for use in Jerusalem simply records Cyril's words, without preface or commentary. Fortunately Aetheria's words fit so well to Cyril's at this point that we can write our own preface, from chs. 45 and 46 of her *Pilgrimage*. The enrolling of the candidates closed by the Sunday before the eight weeks of Lent began. On the Monday morning the candidates ascended the steps of the Martyry to find the doors ajar, and door-keepers scrutinizing them as they filed in. Inside, they found that the bishop's throne had been brought from the apse, and set in the middle of the great nave. Stewards caused the candidates to sit in a semicircle facing the throne, men on one side and women the other, with the godparents standing behind them. Then there came in the bishop's procession: first the vowed virgins and widows, deacons, presbyters, and, last, the bishop. The bishop took his throne, and the presbyters their seats on either side. The rest of the procession took positions standing behind the presbytry, facing the candidates. It was at this point that the bishop began his Procatechesis.

[2] *Photizomenoi.* In the Latin west, at this stage, the title used was *competentes,* "candidates." The east regarded them as having advanced a stage, and entered on privileges which, in the catechumenate, they did not enjoy; as inceptors, rather than mere candidates. In the non-Christian Greek mystery religions, initiation involved the revealing of symbols and representations to the initiate, and this was called "enlightenment"; in fact, "enlighten" came to be a synonym for "initiate," and may be so used, in a Christian sense, in Heb. 6:4 and 10:32. So *photismos,* "enlightenment" came to mean baptism, and the title *photizomenoi* was appropriated to those in this last stage of their preparation which began with the season of Lent.

[3] These "crowns" or wreaths are not royal or triumphal, but those worn for banquets. As catechumens, they have been frequenting the first part of the liturgy, hearing the lections from Scripture, taking part in prayers, and listening to sermons. This is what Cyril likens to plucking spiritual

64

redolent of the fragrance of the Holy Spirit. You have reached the royal vestibule. O may the King himself conduct you within!

Lo, now the trees are in blossom; and grant the fruit be duly gathered!

So far, your names have been enrolled,[4] and you have been called up for service. The lamps have been kindled for the wedding procession. There is longing for the citizenship of heaven. There is good intention, with hope, to back it up. He cannot lie that saith "All things work together for good to them that love God."[5] For while God is lavish to do us good, he looks for a worthy resolve on the part of each, wherefore the Apostle continues "To them that are called according to his purpose." If your intention is worthy, that it is that sets you among these "called." For though you be present here in the body, that is no use if your heart be not here as well.

2. Once upon a time there came to the font Simon the Sorcerer.[6] He was baptized, but he was not enlightened, for while his body went under the water, his heart let not in the light of the Spirit. He plunged his body and came up, but, in his soul, he was neither buried with Christ nor did he rise again with him.[7] Now I give you sketches of failures, just so that *you* may not fail. For "these things happened unto them for ensamples: and they are written for our admonition,"[8] who follow in their footsteps, down to this very day. Let none of you be

flowers to weave themselves crowns. And now, adorned with what they have gathered on their way, they approach the banquet.

[4] The registration for "enlightenment" is now likened to enlistment in the *militia Christi*. In the next phrase it is likened to entry in the franchise-roll of the heavenly city.

[5] Rom. 8:28.   [6] Acts 8:13.

[7] It is remarkable that whereas the baptismal symbolism of Rom. 6:3-14 is the theme of the second mystagogic lecture, Cyril treats the ceremonial and ritual of baptism as already known to the *photizomenoi*. This argues that the mystagogic lectures are not Cyril's but John's. John, according to Aetheria, told the *photizomenoi* on Palm Sunday that they were still catechumens, and not yet able to hear the words which belong to the higher mystery, baptism itself. It thus appears that, in the interval between the delivery of this Procatechesis and John, a considerable change of emphasis took place. Cyril puts the stress on the conversion that has brought the candidates to register, so that, in his eyes, they begin "already" to be Christians. John puts the emphasis on the sacramental initiation, treating the class (as was the case in the west) as just candidates. It appears, therefore, that the tone of the Procatechesis in this respect, either fitted the early fourth century or is something individual to Cyril.

[8] I Cor. 10:11.

found abusing God's grace; let not any "root of bitterness springing up trouble you,"[9] as that any of you should enter here saying to himself, Come, let us see what believers[10] do. I will enter and see, and learn what is done. Are you expecting to see, and not expecting to be seen?[11] Do you suppose that you can occupy yourself with what goes on, while God will not concern himself with the state of your heart?

3. In the Gospels we are told of a man, once, who pushed his way into a wedding party[12]; how, wearing unsuitable clothes, he went in, took a place, and ate, since the bridegroom let him do so. Now when he saw that all were in their brightest clothes,[13] he ought to have changed into his. But in his appearance and by his attitude, he was an odd man out, although he was quite one of the party where the food was concerned. The bridegroom, for his part, though bountiful, was not undiscerning; and as he went round the party, giving his attention to each in turn (not, of course, with any thought what they were eating, but simply of their nice manners), he came upon this complete stranger not dressed for the occasion. So he said to him, "Friend, how camest thou in hither? I mean, in those filthy clothes? Where was your conscience? Granted that, as the host is lavish, the porter did not stop you coming in: granted that, when you entered you did not know what sort of clothes the party demanded: you came in and saw people at table in brilliant costume: ought you not to have been put right by what you saw? Should you not have taken your chance to withdraw and come back suitably dressed? Well, now, you came in unceremoniously for us to throw you out unceremon-

9 Heb. 12:15. "Let none of you be found abusing (or 'presuming upon') God's grace" is a rough paraphrase of the first half of the verse.
10 *Pistoi*, the title of Christians after baptism. Cyril gives it to his class by anticipation, to evoke their eagerness.
11 While the reference is to the all-seeing eye of God, it must be remembered that the candidates were under the continued scrutiny of the whole of the bishop's suite.
12 The reference is to Matt. 22:1-14, and specially to vv. 11-13. The parable as it stands in St Matthew is clearly the clamping together of two quite independent parables, so that no circumstance of v. 10 is applicable to the next three verses. This was obvious to Cyril, who feels himself at liberty to supply his own account of the circumstances under which the unmannerly guest arrived.
13 Or, literally, "white garments," in which sense the word is in use in classical Greek. Later the word came to be the equivalent of "dressed in one's best." But at baptism, the *photizomenoi* would be literally all in white. The man's offence is to have made no attempt to dress for the occasion.

iously." So the bridegroom orders the servants, "Bind his feet, which had the hardihood to bring him in here. Bind his hands, that could not dress him properly. And throw him out into the darkness outside, for he does not deserve wedding lights."

You, my friends, take note what happened to that man on that occasion. Make sure that what you are doing now is all as it should be.

4. For we, Christ's ministers, have received each one of you. If you think of us as, figuratively, his door-keepers, then we have left the door unfastened. There has been nothing to stop you coming here with your soul covered in the mire of sins, with purpose anything but pure. And in you have come, been passed as fit,[14] and your name inscribed on the roll. Look, I ask you, at this solemn setting of the Church. Give heed to the order and thought-out arranging of it, the Scripture lessons, the attendance of the entire ecclesiastical body,[15] the arrangements for teaching. Let the very place put you in awe, and be admonished by what you behold. Be glad to make your escape now,[16] so as to return tomorrow in a better disposition. Let us say that your soul is wrapped in avarice. When you come back, let it wear a different dress: I do not mean on top of the old one, but with the old one taken off. Strip off, I beg, fornication and uncleanness and put on that brilliant robe, self-discipline. Off with the former habit, I charge you, e'er Jesus, bridegroom

[14] Aetheria tells us that, at what would correspond to the opening of the session at which, later on, the Procatechesis was to be given, the bishop interrogated referees as to the good life and character of each person whose name had been given in. Only when thus satisfied, did the bishop inscribe the candidate's name on his official roll. Anyone with whom he was not thus satisfied would have been sent away before the Procatechesis was delivered. Cyril, on the other hand, is here, in the Procatechesis itself, pleading that any candidate should withdraw who knows himself to be in a wrong disposition for going forward. John's different procedure shows that, as the century went on, less and less reliance was, or could be, placed upon the discretion of candidates.

[15] The *canonici*, or persons on the *canon* or roll of those entitled to support from the church chest. The term includes, besides the clergy proper, the women under religious vows and perhaps some men employed by the church in lesser ministrations. The candidates are to judge how truly it is a "wedding-feast" to which they are come, by the presence of the entire staff, and it is probable that all the *canonici* were to be employed in some way in teaching the *photizomenoi*.

[16] Cyril supposes that his words have pricked the conscience of someone who came light-heartedly through such public scrutiny as then took place, so that he feels as the unmannerly guest in the parable ought to have felt. He needs to think again, but may return the next day.

of souls, comes to view your array! You have a long period of grace, forty days for repentance.[17] You have plenty of time to discard and wash thoroughly your soul's apparel, and so to clothe yourself and come back. But if you just continue in your evil disposition, I have cleared myself by telling you, but you cannot expect to receive God's grace. For though the water will receive you, the Holy Spirit will not. If any be conscious that his soul is wounded, let him receive the salve. If any have fallen, let him get up. Let there be no Simon among you, let there be no hypocrisy, let there be no idle curiosity to see what happens.

5. Perhaps you had a different reason for coming. For it is quite what might happen, that a man should be wanting to advance his suit with a Christian woman, and to that end has come here. And there is the like possibility the other way round. Or often it may be a slave that wanted to please his master, or a person that comes for the sake of his friend. I accept this as bait for the hook, and I welcome you as one who shall be saved, by a good hope, in spite of having come with an unsound intention. It may well be that you did not know where you were coming or what sort of a net it is that is taking you. And now you are inside the ecclesiastical fishnets. Let yourself be taken, do not make off, for Jesus is angling for you, not to make you die, but by his having died, to make you live. For die you must, and rise again, as you heard how the Apostle says "Dead indeed unto sin, but alive" unto righteousness.[18] Die to your sins and live unto righteousness. As from today, I say, live.

6. Look, I ask you, and see with how great a dignity Jesus favours you. You were called catechumen, which means one into whom something is dinned from without.[19] You heard of some hope, but you did not know what. You heard mysteries without understanding anything. You heard scriptures without plumbing their depth. It is not dinned in, any more, but whispered. For the indwelling Spirit is fashioning your mind into mansions for God. When you hear, in future, scriptures concerning mysteries, you will understand things you knew

---

[17] This length of Lenten fasting is not likely to have been of very long standing at Jerusalem. It was only during his first exile in 335 that Athanasius learned of the 40-day Lent observed at Rome. Before that, the Egyptian churches had only kept the fast through Holy Week.

[18] A conflation of Rom. 6:11 and I Peter 2:24.

[19] *katēchein* is to make resound. So a catechumen was literally one who was having the elements dinned into him. Cyril exaggerates a little here, to exalt the status of the *photizomenoi*.

nothing of. And do not esteem as if a trifle what you are receiving. Being but a wretched man, you are recipient of a divine title. For listen to Paul "God is faithful,"[20] or to another text in Scripture, "God is faithful and just." It was as foreseeing that a divine title would come to be applied to men that the Psalmist, speaking in the Person of God, said, "I have said, ye are gods, and are all the children of the Most High."[21] But see that when the title is faithful, the purpose is not faithless. You have entered the contest, run your course steadfastly. No other chance like this will come your way. If it was your wedding day ahead of you, would you not make light of all else, in preparing the banquet? When, then, you are going to consecrate your soul to the heavenly Bridegroom, will you not let the things of the body take their chance, so that you may take firm hold on the things of the spirit?

7. This bath is not to be taken two or three times, else you might say, if I do not succeed at the first trial, I shall go right at the second. But in this matter, if you do not succeed this once, there is no correcting it. For there is "one Lord, one faith, one baptism";[22] seeing that certain heretics repeat baptism, but only such, and of course what they did in the first instance was not baptism.[23]

8. For what God seeks from us is nothing else but a right intention. Do not ask, How are my sins wiped out? I tell you, it is by your willing it, by your believing. How can I put it more

20 *Pistos* can mean either one who puts his trust in someone, or one in whom trust can be put; believer, or faithful. *Pistos* meant a baptized Christian, taken in the sense, Believer. *Pistos*, applied to God, meant faithful. Cyril plays on the two senses of *pistos*. The texts cited are I Cor. 1:9 and I John 1:9.
21 Ps. 82:6.
22 Eph. 4:5. The possibility of post-baptismal penance is here being held in reserve.
23 Cyril is not saying that heretical baptism is no baptism, but that some heretical rites that could be called "baptisms" are devoid of that character. Any that are repeatable are devoid of that character, for it is of the nature of the sacrament instituted by Christ that it should be once for all, so that any rite conceived repeatable is *ipso facto* not baptism. The question what heretics Cyril has in mind takes us to the refutation of heresies in Lecture vi. It is probable that the Manichees are most in his mind, in the present passage, for their lustrations before prayer might make it a point of propaganda against orthodoxy that they offered a readier way of escape from sin. He may have had also the Marcionites and Valentinians in view. But his clear intention is to remove from the minds of his hearers the notion that it would be desirable that baptism were not beset with such finality as it is.

succinctly? Yet if your lips declare you willing, but your heart does not, remember that he who judges reads the heart.[24] Break off, as from today, from every evil practice. Let not your tongue run to irresponsible talk, nor your gaze lead you astray or go roving where it ought not.

9. But let your feet hasten to these times of instruction. Submit yourself to be exorcized with all eagerness. Whether it be insufflation[25] or exorcism, the concern is for your salvation. Imagine that you had crude gold, adulterated, mingled with all sorts of other substances, such as brass and tin, iron and lead. It is the gold that we want to have by itself. There is no way of getting gold purged of foreign substances except by using fire. In just the same way, the soul cannot be purged except by exorcisms. Now exorcisms have divine power, being collected out of divine Scripture. The veil thrown over your face at exorcism is so that your mind may then be receptive, and that a wandering gaze may not cause a distracted heart as well. But when the eyes are veiled, there is nothing to hinder the ears from receiving the means of salvation. For (to go back to the subject of gold) experienced goldsmiths concentrate a blast on the fire by use of fine blowpipes, and drive it onto the gold-ore hiding its gold in the crucible. So, by chafing the available flame, they find what they seek. In exactly the same way the

---

[24] *kardiognōstes*, Acts 1:24; 15:8.

[25] We might call insufflation the ceremonial act in exorcism, the ritual counterpart consisting of the fierce adjurations of the invisible evil power, with injunctions, backed up by fearful threats, to depart and leave the subject of exorcism. Gregory of Nyssa, writing but shortly after these lectures of Cyril, describes thus an exorcism performed by Gregory Thaumaturgus: "He took the linen scarf from off his shoulders, and breathed upon it with his mouth; after which he cast it over the youth" to be exorcized. If this is taken in conjunction with what Cyril says, a few lines down, of the faces of those being exorcized as covered with a veil, we may picture the exorcist as naming the Name of Jesus, invoking the Holy Spirit, breathing upon a linen kerchief, and throwing it over the face of the candidate, who was perhaps lying prone. Bending over the candidate, and stretching out his hand to sign the cross, the exorcist now pronounces the solemn and dreadful (and as Cyril presently tells us, scriptural) formulae of exorcism, cursing the fiends and consigning them to eternal punishment, in such a manner as to excite in the candidate lively fear, and a positive abhorrence of the thought of evil. Bishop John explains, in his second mystagogic lecture, that the "breathing" of Christians, with invocation of the Name of God, like fiercest flame, scorches and drives out evil spirits. Cyril sees the psychological value of the candidate not being able to see, during the exorcism, and evidently regards these exorcisms before each catechesis as an important aid to devout and receptive hearing.

exorcists,[26] by divine Spirit, excite fear, apply fire to the soul in the body for crucible. The demonic enemy is driven out, and there is left salvation: there is left the hope of eternal life. And, after that, the soul cleansed of its sins, possesses salvation. Let us, then, my brethren, endure in hope. Let us devote ourselves, side by side with our hoping, so that the God of all the universe, as he beholds our intention, may cleanse us from our sins, fill us with high hopes from what we have in hand, and grant us the change of heart that saves. God has called you, and you have your calling.

10. So persevere with the catechizings. If we prolong our discourse, never let your mind relax, seeing that what you are being provided with is your arms against the operations of your foe. You are being armed against heresies, against Jews, Samaritans[27] and pagans. Your foes are many, and you must be given many darts, for you have many to hurl them at. You need to learn to shoot down your scoffing pagan, and how to fight your heretic, Jew or Samaritan. Your weapons are all ready, and readiest of all is the sword of the Spirit. You must hold out your right hands for them, that is, have a right intention to fight the Lord's battle, to overcome the operations of your foe, and not be worsted in any heretic encounter.

11. Let this be your solemn charge; learn the things that are told you, and keep them for ever. Do not think of them as on a par with ordinary sermons. Sermons are good things, and

26 There was evidently a technique in exorcism, calling for faith, aptitude, and training; and one that met its severest test when the subject was mentally disordered, or "possessed." It is probable that the ministers of exorcism in this prebaptismal training were all persons inscribed, in some capacity, on the Canon of the Church; i.e., *canonici*, if not *clerici*.

27 The Samaritan religion may be described as an arrested development of Judaism, from which it passed into schism. The Samaritans formed a limited and dwindling community, down to present times. In the fourth Christian century they had a period of intellectual and religious awakening, under a theologian and hymnographer Marqah, Cyril's contemporary. The sect was conservative and fanatical. There were several Samaritan revolts under the Christian empire. And it can well be believed that, in Cyril's day, Samaritanism was aggressive enough in Palestine to justify a bishop "arming" his baptismal candidates against Samaritan propaganda. The promise of "arming" is fulfilled by Cyril in Lecture XVIII, cc. 11-13, where it appears that the Sadduceeism of the Samaritans was the special danger, by reason of their arguments against the resurrection of the flesh. They are coupled with the Jews in Lecture IV, c. 1, as Sabbatarians, and with the pagans in XVIII as disbelievers in the resurrection of the flesh. For fuller particulars about the Samaritans, see J. A. Montgomery, *The Samaritans* (Philadelphia, 1907).

should evoke your faith. But, suppose we neglected today's sermon; we attend to tomorrow's. In the sequence of carefully prepared instructions for baptismal regeneration, if today's lecture be neglected, when will the matter be put right? Think of this as being the season for planting young trees. If we do not now dig and set them deep in the earth, when can we find another opportunity for planting well what has been once planted badly? Or think of catechesis as like building.[28] We get no profit from toil expended, unless we dig deep to lay the foundations, unless we mortar together the successive courses of the building so as to compact our house in one, with not a crack to be found, nor the structure unsound in any way. Stone must follow stone in the appointed order, and corners be turned in each successive course. Unevennesses must be levelled off, so that the building may rise without fault. So we are proffering to you, as it were, building-stones of knowledge. You have to be told about the living God, you have to be told about the judgement, you have to be told about Christ, you have to be told about the resurrection. There are many things to be said, and in their proper order. As they are being said, they appear casual, but afterwards they present themselves as all connected together. Now if you do not do the joining of them in one, if you do not remember what went before and what came after, the builder builds his house, but the building you will have will be unsound.

12. So when the instruction is over, if any catechumen tries to get out of you what your teachers[29] told you, tell nothing, for he is outside the mystery that we have delivered to you, with its hope of the age to come. Guard the mystery for his sake from whom you look for reward. Never let anyone persuade you, saying "What harm is it that I should know as well?" So, too, sick people ask for wine, whereas, if it is given them when it should not, it makes them delirious. Thence comes a two-fold evil. The patient dies and the physician gets the blame. In like manner, if a catechumen hears something divulged by a believer, it makes the catechumen delirious; for he does not comprehend what he has heard, so that he thinks nothing of

28 The "builder" is Cyril, and the candidates are thought of as building, in their minds, copies of the course of learning which he builds up in his lectures. However sound is the course, as he builds it, their building will be unsound unless all through they take the greatest pains.
29 "Teachers" in the plural perhaps suggests that, besides the lecturing of the bishop, the other clergy took part in tutorial instruction of the candidates.

the whole matter, scoffing at what he has been told. Meanwhile, the believer is condemned as the betrayer of his trust.[30] Already you stand on the frontier of mystery. I adjure you to smuggle no word out; not because the things you are told are not worth the telling again, but because the audience is not fitted to take them in. You, too, were once a catechumen, relatively to this matter. I did not then say a word to you about the things we have now in hand. When, by what you experience, you grasp the sublimity of the things that are being taught, then you will know for yourself that catechumens are not fitted to be told them.

13. You who have been enrolled have become sons and daughters of one Mother. When you arrive before the time for exorcizing, let each of you speak only what helps to godliness. If any of the class does not arrive, go seek them. If you were asked out to dinner, would you not wait for a fellow guest? If you had a brother, would you not seek that brother's good? Whatever you do, do not start unprofitable gossip; about what has been happening in the city, or your village, or what the emperor has done, or the bishop, or your presbyter. Lift your eyes to God. It is the time for you to need him. "Be still and know that I am God."[31] If you see the believers who are assisting in the church quite at their ease, remember that they have reason to be. They know what they have received, and they are in a state of grace. You, on the other hand, are just in the balance, to decide whether you shall be received or not. Do not ape those who have reached security, but make it your aim to be in fear.

14. When your exorcism is over, until the others have come from theirs, the men are to keep together, and the women are to keep together. This is where the typology of Noah's ark comes in, for Noah and his sons were together, and his wife and daughters-in-law together.[32] For even though the interior of the

30 That is, if the *disciplina arcani* is betrayed, it is the bishop who is ultimately wronged.   31 Ps. 46:10.
32 The allusion is to Genesis 7:7-9. It is remarkable that Cyril should expect people just completing catechumenate not only to accept, as understood, the principle of typology, but also to remember that whereas the animals are said to have entered the ark two and two, male and female, it is not said that Noah and his wife entered, and his sons and their wives, but "Noah went in, and his sons, and his wife, and his sons' wives." Cyril deduces from this difference, that the men kept to one end of the ark and the women to the other. So he compares the nave of the Martyry to the interior of the ark, and draws his conclusion on the seating of the sexes in the former. It is hard to believe that the

ark was undivided and they were shut in it, yet everything was ordered with propriety. So, if the church-doors are shut and you are all inside, here too let the separation be preserved, the men together and the women together. We do not want our laying the foundation for salvation to prove the occasion of the overthrow of souls! And if this fair foundation causes you to sit near one another, then passion must be kept at a distance. In these waiting-times, let the men have some edifying book and sit down, while one reads and others listen. If there is no book available, let one man offer a prayer, and another speak to edification. Again, let the bevy of maids foregather in the same way, and sing or read so quietly that the whispered words will not be heard by anyone else. For, says the Apostle, "I suffer not a woman to speak in the church."[33] And you, matron, imitate the maids and pray, moving your lips but making no sound, that your Samuel may be granted you,[34] and that your soul, hitherto barren, may bring forth salvation from God that hears prayer.[35] For that is the interpretation of the name Samuel.

15. I shall see each man's earnestness. I shall see each woman's devotion. Burn out impiety from your mind,[36] put your soul on the anvil and your stubborn infidelity under the hammer. Let the loose scales fall from the iron and leave pure metal. Let the iron rust fall off and leave clean iron. And may God at length grant you to see that night when darkness is turned into day,[37] of which it was said "the darkness hideth not from thee, but the night shall shine as the day." Then let the gate of paradise be opened to each man and each woman among you. Then may you enjoy waters that bear Christ and have his sweet savour. Then may you receive his name of Christian, and the capacity for heavenly things. And even now,

matter was dismissed in those few words, or that the argument was not elaborated from the Bible text in tutorial instruction to follow.

[33] I Cor. 14:34.   [34] The allusion is to I Sam. 1:12–17.

[35] Cyril thus accepts a derivation of the name Samuel from Hebrew words meaning "heard of God." Modern Hebrew scholarship does not accept this derivation, but it seemed to explain Hannah's words in I Sam. 1:20. The comment suggests that Cyril had some acquaintance with Hebrew.

[36] Cyril is returning to the simile, introduced in section 9, of purifying metal by fire.

[37] When darkness fell on Easter eve, all the lights in the church and baptistry were kindled, as Aetheria tells us, from candles lit by the bishop in the Sepulchre, and the illumination was maintained throughout the night. Cyril sees Ps. 139:12, "the night shineth as the day," as a prophecy of this. See the note 21 on Lecture XVIII. 17 below.

I pray you, lift up the eyes of your mind: take thought now of angelic choirs, and God the master of the universe enthroned, with his only-begotten Son sitting on his right hand, and his Spirit with him, while thrones and dominations do him service, and likewise each man and woman of you as being in a state of salvation. Even now imagine that your ears catch those lovely strains wherewith the angels acclaim you saved. "Blessed are those whose transgressions are forgiven and whose sins are covered"[38] when, as stars of the Church, you enter paradise with glorious body and radiant soul.

16. Great is this baptism to which you are coming: it is ransom to captives and remission of sins. It is the death of sin and the soul's regeneration. It is a garment of light and a holy seal[39] that can never be dissolved. It is a chariot to heaven, the delights of paradise, the pledge of the kingdom, the gift of sonship. But a dragon is keeping watch beside the road you are walking. Take care lest he bite you with unbelief. He sees so many on the way to being saved, and seeks whom he may devour. The end of your journey is the Father of Spirits, but the way lies past that dragon. How, then, shall you get past him? By having "your feet shod with the preparation of the gospel of peace"[40] so as to take no hurt, though he do bite. Let faith dwell in your heart, have a strong hope, and be strongly shod, to get by the enemy and reach the Master's presence. Prepare your

[38] Ps. 32:1.

[39] The root-idea here connected with a seal is that it is a mark of ownership. The notion of the worshipper as the property of the god is probably of Semitic origin. The rabbis saw circumcision as Jehovah's seal on those who were his. In Romans 4:11 Paul takes up this idea. It was a token to Abraham of the covenant which had made him God's man. Soon after the close of the New Testament canon Christians had begun, at least in Rome, to apply the title "seal" (*sphragis*) to baptism, possibly as the counterpart, under the new covenant, to circumcision. But this is not explicit. Hermas, *Similitudes* 8.6, 9.16 and II Clement 7 refer to baptism as "the seal," and exhort Christians to "guard the seal." They probably reflect Roman usage, and it is the Roman Church which the epitaph of Abercius, later in the second century, calls "a people having a splendid seal." From that time forward, the use of the title "seal" for baptism becomes widespread, and attracts to itself New Testament associations. It is thus the seal attesting God's forgiveness, or that passes the believer into the Messianic Kingdom (Rev. 7:3; 9:4). The chrism of holy oil applied after baptism may have conduced to connecting the notions of seal and baptism, and it later attracted the title "seal" more particularly to itself. But as baptism left no visible mark, Cyril emphasizes the indelible character invisibly imprinted on the soul of the baptized, and calls it "a holy seal that can never be dissolved."

[40] Eph. 6:15.

heart to receive instruction, and enter into holy mysteries. Pray yet more often that God will judge you worthy of heavenly and immortal mysteries. Cease not day or night, but when sleep falls from your eyes, then let your mind free itself to pray. Should you see some unbecoming thought rising into consciousness, take the remembrance of judgement as means of safety. Devote your mind to study, and evil concerns will slip from it. If you meet someone who says "Are you getting ready to plunge in the water? Are there no city baths any more?" then know that the dragon of the sea[41] got ready these temptations for you. Mind not the lips that speak but the God that works. Guard your soul, that you be not caught, and persevering in hope may be heir of eternal salvation.

17. We are but human, who declare and teach these things. Do not you make of our building "hay, stubble," and chaff, so that we suffer loss, in our work being burnt up. But make our work "gold, silver, precious stones."[42] It is my part to tell you, yours to carry it forward, but God's to bring it to completion. Let us brace our minds, concentrate our souls, prepare our hearts. The race is run in matters of soul, and the prize consists of rewards in heaven. And God, who knows your hearts and can tell who is genuine and who but feigns, is able to keep the former steadfast and bring the latter to a state of faith. For God can turn an infidel into a believer, if he will but surrender to him his heart. May God "blot out the handwriting that is against you,"[43] wink at your transgressions heretofor, plant you in his Church, enrol you in his own host, and equip you with the arms of righteousness. May he fill you with the heavenly guerdons of the New Testament and give you the seal of the Holy Spirit, that cannot be removed for evermore, in Jesus Christ our Lord, to whom be glory, world without end. Amen.

NOTE TO THE READER[44]

You may give these catechetical lectures to *photizomenoi*, in preparation for baptism, to read, and to believers who have already received the sacrament of the font. Do not give them, under any circumstances, to catechumens or to any other

---

[41] Perhaps an allusion to Rev. 13:1.
[42] I Cor. 3:12, 15.   [43] Col. 2:14.
[44] This note after the Procatechesis corresponds to the note that follows Lecture XVIII in our oldest MS. It is therefore not the words of Cyril, but those of the persons who took down Cyril's lectures, and put them into secret and confidential circulation.

persons not actually Christian, as you shall answer to the Lord.
And, as in the sight of the Lord, you shall transcribe this note
before any copy that you make of the lectures.

LECTURE I

On the temper of mind requisite for baptism

Delivered *extempore* in Jerusalem to *photizomenoi*, by way of
introduction to those going forward to baptism. The Lesson
is from Isaiah, "Wash you, make you clean; put away the
evil of your doings from before mine eyes," and the rest.[1]

1. Disciples of the new covenant and sharers in the mysteries
of Christ (at this moment because God calls you, but in a little
while by enjoying his grace), "make you a new heart and a new
spirit"[2] that you may be the occasion of jubilation in heaven.
For if the Gospel says that "there is joy over one sinner that
repenteth,"[3] how much the more will the saving of so many
souls rejoice the heavenly hosts! The course[4] you have commenced is good and glorious: run the race of godliness with
godly fear. For the only-begotten Son of God is at hand, looking
intently to your redemption, and saying "Come unto me, all
ye that labour and are heavily laden, and I will refresh you."[5]
You who are laden with the heavy burden of your own transgressions, and are bound with the chains of your own sins,[6]
listen to the voice of prophecy crying "Wash you, make you
clean: put away the evil of your doings from before mine eyes"
that the angelic host may shout over you, proclaiming "Blessed
are they whose iniquities have been forgiven, and whose sins
are covered."[7] You who have but now kindled the torches[8] of

1 The Lection is Isa. 1:16–20, the call to conversion, with offer of pardon,
and the declaration of reward and punishment assigned to the good or
bad response.
2 Ezek. 18:31.   3 Luke 15:7.
4 Cyril now begins a changing succession of pictures based on making
one's way to a destination. It begins as just that, then it is running the
race of godliness. But just as we expect Heb. 12:2, Cyril changes the
picture to that of laborious progress by laden people, and finally again to
people in procession to a marriage feast, hastening and swinging their
torches to make them burn up.
5 Matt. 11:28.   6 Prov. 5:22.   7 Ps. 32:1.
8 Torches (*lampades*). The word is however that used in Matt. 25:1–13,
the parable of the ten virgins, where the context clearly requires lamps,
with wicks; and while that may be the image in Cyril's mind here, the
other seems to fit better his choice of words.

faith, do not let them go out in your hands, that he who once on this all-holy Golgotha opened paradise to a robber, by means of faith, may cause that you shall sing the marriage song.

2. Should anyone here be a slave of sin, let him, through his faith, be now intent on gaining that regeneration into adoption as sons that befits free men, and while he puts from him that most miserable bondage to his sins and obtains the most blessed status of the Lord's bondsman, let him become worthy to inherit the kingdom of the heavens. "Put off the old man, which is corrupt according to the deceitful lusts"[9] by making your confession,[10] so as to "put on the new man, which is renewed after the knowledge of him that created him."[11] Obtain by faith "the earnest of the Holy Spirit"[12] so that you can be received "into the everlasting habitations."[13] Proceed to the mystical sealing, so as to be readily recognizable[14] by your Master, and be counted together into the holy and spiritual flock of Christ, set apart at his right hand,[15] inheriting the life prepared for you in heaven. For those still clothed in the goat's-hair of their sins are placed on Christ's left hand, because of not going forward in the grace of God to the baptismal regeneration given through Christ, a new birth, not corporeal, but a spiritual rebirth of soul. For corporeal birth is from visible parents, but souls are reborn by means of faith; because "The Spirit bloweth where it listeth."[16] So, if you become worthy of it, you

---

9 Eph. 4:22.
10 We must not assume that secret auricular confession is here meant, after the manner in which it later came to be practised by baptized Christians in the churches of the west. The confession in this passage is a confession made by unbaptized persons of sins against the divine law committed in the ignorance of paganism. Didache iv. 14 directs "Thou shalt confess thy transgressions in church" as part of the ideal prebaptismal discipline of Gentile converts. "In church" suggests a degree of publicity. The *photizomenoi* are to be told that baptism will be plenary remission of these sins. The object of calling for confession, at this stage, must be to exercise the spiritual judgement of the *photizomenoi*. They are being exorcized, day by day, during their preparation, and this trains them to view their sinfulness as a kind of demon-possession. But there is also the fact that the evil past is something to which they are habituated, and, for this, confession also is prescribed.
11 A conflation of Eph. 4:24 and Col. 3:10.
12 II Cor. 1:22.   13 Luke 16:9.
14 Baptism is thus represented as giving an indelible character to the soul, visible to God, as that of those whom he has given to Christ out of the world. (John 10:28–29.)
15 Matt. 25:33.   16 John 3:8.

can look to hear "Well done, good and faithful servant,"[17] when
you are found with conscience void of all dissimulation.

3. Should anyone here suppose that he can presume upon
divine grace, he deceives himself, ignoring God's might. To
such I say, Keep your soul sincere, in view of him "who
searcheth the hearts and reins."[18] For just as people preparing
for a campaign look into the age and physique of the troops, so
likewise the Lord, as he reviews elect souls, searches out their
dispositions, and if he finds hidden insincerity he rejects that
person as unsuited for the warfare *par excellence*. If, however, he
approves him worthy, then he readily pours his favour upon
him. He does not "give that which is holy to dogs,"[19] but where
he sees that the disposition is good, there he grants the saving
seal,[20] the wonderful seal, at sight of which devils tremble,
which angels acknowledge; and, in consequence, the former
are driven off and put to flight, while the latter attend upon
the seal-bearer as a thing belonging to their service. Those,
then, who receive this spiritual and saving seal require also
to have the appropriate disposition. For just as a pen or a
javelin is idle unless it have a user, so likewise divine grace[21]
depends upon meeting with human faith.

[17] Matt. 25:21.   [18] A conflation of Ps. 7:9 with Rev. 2:23.
[19] Matt. 7:6.
[20] Cyril makes no attempt to reconcile the *opus operatum* conception of the
sacrament of baptism with his very wholesome insistence on the subjective side of conversion. He cannot be taken to mean that no one comes
to baptism in an unworthy state, and he does not discuss the effect of
such baptisms, beyond implying that they fail of the purpose of baptism.
But it would be a fair inference to suppose that no godly character is
stamped upon the soul that receives baptism without the right disposition.
It is not Cyril's interest to make such a definition, but rather to encourage
eagerness to receive the sacrament profitably.
[21] Literally "the grace," i.e., the supernatural gift covenanted by the
sacrament of baptism. There is no question that, in the early centuries
of the Church, the baptized commonly found themselves, after receiving
the sacrament, able to overcome the world, and live for God, in a way
they had never thought possible. A notable testimony to this experience
is Cyprian's *Letter to Donatus*, ii and iii. Here Cyprian tells how hard he
found it to credit what he heard of the power of baptism to change a
man's life, above all by affecting the strength of his habits and temptations;
but that he found himself, after baptism, "created into a new man," so
that former difficulties and confusions disappeared. But it was a natural
consequence of this insistence upon a sensible change, as the hoped-for
gift of God in baptism, that "the grace" became, in a sense, detached,
in men's minds, from the Giver, so that Cyril could compare it to a thing
which a man can use or not use. So established was this notion of a
specific effect upon spiritual life to be expected from baptism that Gregory

4. You are being armed not with perishable but with spiritual weapons. The paradise in which you are being planted is the soul's paradise,[22] wherein you will be named[23] with a name you had not heretofore. You were a catechumen till now, but now you are to be called believer. Henceforth you are transplanted among the olives of that paradise: or are being grafted on a good olive tree being taken from a wild olive[24]. You pass from sins to righteousness, from defilements to purity. You are becoming part of the Holy Vine. If, then, you abide in the Vine,[25] you grow into a fruitful branch, but if you do not so abide, you will be burnt up in the fire. Let us therefore bring forth worthy fruit. For let not that come about, that there should happen to us what happened to the barren figtree in the Gospel.[26] Let not Jesus come in these days and utter the curse upon the fruitless: but be it instead that all of you say, "I am like a green olive tree in the house of God; my trust is in the tender-mercy of God, for ever and ever";[27] not a material olive tree, but a spiritual and glorious one. It is God that plants and waters, but it is yours to bear fruit; God's to bestow the gift, and yours to receive it and keep it for ever. But do not esteem the gift lightly because it is given gratis. Rather receive it reverently and guard it with care.

5. This is the season of confession. Confess your past sins of word, and deed, sins of the night and sins by day. Confess "in a time accepted, and in the day of salvation"[28] receive the heavenly treasure. Make the time required for the exorcisms.[29]

of Nyssa, as well as Cyril, used "the grace" as a synonym for baptism. This not very happy development of Christian thought shows how salutary and indispensable to the Church was the teaching of Paul in I Cor. 12–14, on the nature of spiritual gifts.

[22] Literally "intelligible paradise." The Greeks conceived of the kinds of things in the world that we know by the senses, as having their several natures and forms because the Creator shaped them in accordance with patterns belonging to a thought-world conceived in his mind; much as a building corresponds with the blue-print, or rather with the conception in the architect's mind. So they contrasted the "intelligible world" of God's thinking, in part comprehensible to men's minds, with the "sensible world" known to us by the testimony of our senses. To Christians, the "intelligible world" is rather the age to come, or heaven.

[23] The reference is to Adam naming the things in paradise. (Gen. 2:19.)

[24] Rom. 11:17–24.   [25] John 15:1–8.

[26] Mark 11:13, 14, 20, 21.   [27] Ps. 52:8.

[28] II Cor. 6:2. The "season of confession" means Lent, when baptized sinners were doing penance, while the baptizands were parting from their unregenerate past.

[29] The exorcists were evidently in attendance early in the morning, some

Attend the instructions assiduously, and store up in memory the things that shall be said. For it is not spoken just for you to listen to, but so that the things said may be imprinted by faith upon your soul. So wipe off from it every human concern. The race is for your soul. You are leaving behind you the things of this world, and that, for good. They are but trifles that are being left behind, but the things that are being bestowed by the Lord are great. Leave present things behind and set your faith on the things that are coming. . . .[30] And may Christ himself, the great High-priest, accept your devotion of yourselves, and offer you all as an oblation, saying to his Father "Behold I, and the children whom God hath given me."[31] And may God preserve you all as well-pleasing in his sight, to whom be glory and might, world without end. Amen.

LECTURE II

On penitence and remission of sins, and concerning the Adversary

The Lection is from Ezekiel.[1]

1. A dreadful matter is sin, and disorder of life is the soul's worst sickness, which, while it severs, unobserved as it were, the sinews of the soul, puts it in danger of everlasting fire. Sin is evil of man's own choosing, springing from free will,[2] as the

time before the bishop should arrive and the period of instruction began. Unless the candidates also came early, exorcism would be hurried and perfunctory. Perhaps for this reason, exorcism, at Antioch, followed the period of instruction. This passage again testifies to the serious importance in the preparation of the candidates which Cyril assigns to the exorcisms.

30 A repetition of earlier themes of exhortation has been here omitted.
31 Heb. 2:13.
1 The Lection was Ezek. 18:20-23.
2 Literally, "from an act of deliberate choice." The technical term for free will was *autexousia*, "having it within oneself to determine." In the eyes of the Greek Fathers, the arch-heresy as touching the human will was fatalism. In reaction they tended to overlook the qualified nature of human free will, and to regard man as having absolute freedom to respond to the call to choose the right and reject the wrong. In a hortatory address to new converts, this way of representing the matter has obvious practical advantages. But the doctrine of *autexousia* was apt to wear thin under the experience of life. In this respect, the qualified doctrine of human free will that prevailed in the west, and had its great protagonist in Augustine, fared better. Nevertheless, the easterns were not without recognition of the powerlessness of unconverted man to will good, nor slow to glorify the part played by divine grace in man's salvation.

6—c.t.

prophet clearly declares that we sin of our own free will in the
passage "I planted thee a noble vine, wholly a right seed: how
then art thou turned into the degenerate plant of a strange vine
unto me?"[3] Here is a good tree that of its own deliberate purpose brings forth evil fruit,[4] and consequently he that planted
is not to blame. The vine, on the other hand, shall be burned
up, since it was planted to bear good fruit, and it has chosen
of itself to bear evil fruit. For, says the Preacher, "God hath
made man upright: but they have sought out many inven-
tions,"[5] while the Apostle declares, "We are his workmanship,
created unto good works."[6] The Creator "created unto good
works" because he is good, and then the creature turned of his
own set purpose to wickedness. As we said, then, sin is a dreadful
matter, and yet not beyond cure. It is dreadful when the sinner
clings to it, but, to the man that by penitence puts it from him,
it is easily cured. Imagine a man holding fire in his hand. As
long as he grips the live coal, without question he himself is
burning. But if he drops the coal, he rids himself at the same
time of the burning. Now if anyone thinks that sins do not burn,
Scripture tells him "Can a man take fire in his bosom, and his
clothes not be burned?"[7] For sin does burn. The sinews of the
soul are severed, and the invisible bones of the mind are
broken, and sin darkens the light that shines in the heart.

2. Someone asks, however, What is this sin you talk of? Is it
something alive, an angel or devil?[8] What is it that works sin?
It is no foe that strives against you, good sir, from without, but
an evil shoot that is growing out of you yourself, by your own
free choice. "Let thine eyes look right on,"[9] and no lust is

[3] Jer. 2:21.   [4] In allusion to Matt. 7:17, 18 and 12:33.
[5] Eccles. 7:29.   [6] Eph. 2:10.
[7] Prov. 6:27. The context indicates that sin is the fire.
[8] This question is dictated by the existence of a tradition of thought, no
doubt Semitic in origin, which makes spirits, or living creatures, out of
man's immoral tendencies, and thinks of them as fastening, like parasites,
upon the delicate and naturally good spirit which God has placed in
man. The most notable literary representation of this tradition is to be
found in the *Testaments of the Twelve Patriarchs*, and in Hermas, *Mandate*,
V. c. 1, sections 2 and 3, and c. 2, sections 6 and 7, and *Mandate*, X, c. 2,
section 6 and c. 3, sections 2 and 3, where a "liberal synagogue" source
seems to be under tribute. Cyril does not seem to regard this crude
pneumatology as important enough to need refutation. It suffices to set
it aside with picture-language of better tendency: the bad thing inside a
man is something that the man is deliberately causing to grow out of
himself, and it will wither to nothing the moment he so wills.
[9] Prov. 4:25.

stirred. Lay no hand on other people's things, and you are clear from robbery. Keep the judgement in mind, and then neither fornication, adultery, murder, nor any of the crimes will prevail over you. But as soon as you forget God, then and thenceforth you begin to ponder evil things, and fulfil lawless deeds.

3. And yet you do not stand alone as the perpetrator of the deed, but there is another as its wretched prompter, to wit, the devil. So then he prompts, but he does not master by might those whom he does not persuade. Therefore says the Preacher, "If a spirit of the powerful rise up against thee, leave not thy place."[10] If you shut to the door and keep him at his distance, he will not harm you. But if you carelessly admit consideration of lust, it will strike its roots down into you through your imaginations. So it will take your mind captive, and drag you down into a pit of evils.

But maybe you are saying "I am a believer,[11] and even though I think about it quite a lot, lust does not overcome me." Do you not know that oftentimes a root has split a rock, when suffered to remain in it? Give no lodgement to the seed of evil, seeing that it will break up your faith. Pull the evil thing up by the roots before it can bloom, lest, through not putting yourself to trouble at the start, you presently have to take axes to it and busy yourself with a fire. If you begin to have eye-trouble, see to it at once, lest, by the time you seek a doctor, you have lost your sight.

4. The devil, then, is the prime author of sin and father of all evils. It is the Lord that declared this, not I, saying "the devil sinneth from the beginning."[12] None sinned before he did. And when he sinned, it was not because he received naturally the proneness to sin, without being able to help himself, since then the ostensible cause of the sin would go back to him who made him thus. But being formed good, he turned devil of his own free choice, and got the name from the deed. For he was an archangel, and was afterwards called devil because he slandered;[13] and from being good and a minister of God, he became rightly named Satan, for the name Satan means

10 Eccles. 10:4.
11 Cyril shows here that he is aware of the dangers of laying too much stress upon the conviction of a changed life following upon the moral conversion which has brought the candidate to enrol for "enlightenment."
12 I John 3:8.
13 The word "devil," like the German *Teufel*, is merely a taking-over, orally, of the Greek word *diabolos*, "one who slanders."

adversary[14] and slanderer. These teachings are not mine but those of the inspired prophet Ezekiel. For he takes up a lamentation over him, and says, "Thou sealest up the sum, full of wisdom, and perfect in beauty: thou hast been in Eden, the garden of God,"[15] and a little further on, "Thou wast perfect in thy ways, from the day that thou wast created, till iniquity was found in thee." Quite accurately it says "was found in thee." For the iniquity was not introduced from without, but you yourself begat the evil. And, further on, Ezekiel gives the explanation, "thine heart was lifted up, because of thy beauty: I will cast thee as profane out of the mountain of God, I will cast thee to the ground." The Lord speaks to the like effect in the Gospels, again, saying "I beheld Satan as lightning fallen from heaven."[16] There you see the agreement between the Old Testament and the New.[17] Now when Satan fell he drew many into rebellion in his company. He excites lust in those who attend to him, and is the author of adultery, fornication, and every evil whatsoever. Through listening to him our forefather Adam was ejected, so as to exchange paradise which brought forth of itself marvellous fruits[18] for this thorny earth.

5. Why then, someone exclaims, we have been led astray and are lost; surely there is no being saved after that? We have

[14] Satan means adversary, but slanderer only by implication. Satan appears, by that name, four times in the Old Testament, I Chron. 21:1; Job 1:6 and 12; Ps. 109:6 and Zech. 3:1 and 2. The conception, in these passages, is of one of the courtier-spirits, in the presence of Jehovah, who has a grudge against Israel, or against righteous Israelites. He is thus primarily the adversary of Michael, the angel of the Israelite people. In Ps. 109, his accusation to Jehovah of the Psalmist's enemy is justified, in Job it is tentative, and only in Zechariah does it amount to slander. But in post-exilic Judaism the concept of a fallen archangel, who is the source and promoter of all evil, gathered into itself the exegesis of all possible passages in the Hebrew scriptures, and the Christian Church inherited this tradition.
[15] Ezek. 28:12 and 13, where the lamentation is over the "Prince of Tyre." The later verses cited by Cyril are 15 and 17. [16] Luke 10:18.
[17] As will appear later, Cyril wished to have his people particularly on their guard against Marcionism. Marcion taught that the Creator of this world and the inspirer of the Old Testament was not God the Father revealed by Christ, but an angel whose highest conception was legal justice. He found the Old and New Testaments thus in essential disharmony. Cyril, therefore, takes every opportunity to arm the *photizomenoi* with arguments for the contrary belief, namely, that there is a divinely planned accord between the Testaments.
[18] For the belief that, at the first, plants had wonderful powers that later ceased, because of the fall, see Nemesius, Section 5 (p. 239) below.

fallen, surely we cannot stand up again? We have been blinded, surely we shall never see again? We have been crippled, surely we shall never again leap and walk?[19] In a word, we are dead, surely there is no rising again? Surely, good sir, I reply, he that wakened Lazarus, dead four days and stinking,[20] will he not much more easily raise you up who are alive? He who shed for us his precious blood, he will rescue us from sin. Let us not despair of ourselves, brethren, let us not abandon ourselves to a state of hopelessness. For not putting our trust in the hope of repentance, that is the dreadful thing,[21] since he who does not at all look forward to salvation adds evil to evil recklessly. A man, on the other hand, who hopes for cure is ready enough to go on taking care of himself. For a robber who has no hope of getting off runs to excess, whereas, if he hoped for pardon, the odds are that he would repent. Or put it thus; does a snake cast its skin, and we not cast our sin? Does ground full of thistles become fertile under good tillage, and shall we think salvation beyond recovery? So, then, nature is ready for salvation, and all we have to seek for is the will to be saved.[22]

10. You who have not been for very long a catechumen, do you want proof of God's love for man? Even though the whole people sin as one man, God's loving-kindness is not overthrown. The people made a calf, but God cast not away his love for them. Men denied their God, but God did not deny his own nature. Though they cried, "these are thy gods, O Israel,"[23] as was his wont, "the God of Israel became their Saviour"[24] yet once more. Now it was not only the people that sinned, but Aaron the high-priest also sinned. For we have that from Moses when he says, "And upon Aaron came the wrath of the Lord, and I entreated for him" and (says Moses) the

---

19 Cyril uses a verb *artipodein* not found elsewhere. Its obvious meaning is to go with sound feet, in contrast with limping or going like a cripple.
20 The allusion is to John 11:39.
21 It has been said more than once in this Lecture, that sin is a dreadful thing. But equally, Cyril says, despair of good and of forgiveness is a dreadful thing. Therefore the dreadfulness of sin is no argument for despair.
22 Section 6 has been omitted, and this opening sentence of Section 7 is immediately followed by Section 10. In Section 7 Cyril is proceeding to prove the philanthropy of God from the Old Testament. He appears to think that his exposition may not be new to many in the class, and he therefore appeals to the fact that this may not be true for all of them. This seems to indicate that the length of catechumenate before being enrolled for baptism varied. Sections 8 and 9 deal with Noah and Rahab.
23 Ex. 32:4.   24 Cf. Isa. 63:8.

Lord pardoned him.[25] Well, then, if Moses importuned the Lord, begging pardon for a high-priest that had sinned, will Jesus, God's only-begotten Son, shrink from importuning God by begging pardon for you? Now God did not stay Aaron from continuing in the high-priest's office on account of his lapse, and has he stopped you from coming to salvation because you come from paganism? After that, do you, good sir, yourself repent in like manner, and grace will not be denied you. Henceforward present your way of life unblameable, for God is truly loving unto man: and all one's life would not suffice to tell out his loving-kindness as it should be told, nor if all human tongues uttered it with one consent would they, even so, be able to express more than a tiny part of that divine philanthropy. It is true that we can tell out some part of what is written in Scripture concerning God's kindness to men, but of what he has pardoned in angels we have no knowledge. For they have needed pardon, seeing that there is one only that is without sin, namely Jesus who cleanses us from sins. But I will say no more about the angels.[26]

[25] The citation is of Deut. 9:20. Deuteronomy, as part of the Pentateuch, was held by the Jews to have been written by Moses. The justification for the words following the citation is to be found in v. 19.

[26] Cyril's argument is that, whereas revelation abundantly shows forth the loving-kindness of God in his dealings with men, that loving-kindness is manifest on a vaster scale in (what has not been the literal subject of revelation, unless through an allegorical or mystical exegesis of Scripture) his dealings with the incorporeal rational creatures. If we ask how Cyril knows of such a field of knowledge, the answer is that he has taken it from Origen. But already, by Cyril's episcopate, Origen's name was breathed upon, and so, having used the notion of divine long-suffering towards angels to provide an argument *a fortiori*, Cyril refuses to pursue further the theme of angelic need of forgiveness. Origen, *On First Principles*, Bk. IV, c. iv, Section 4, teaches that the soul of Jesus is the only sinless creature, while the whole work elaborates the doctrine that the impartiality of God requires that he made all rational creatures by nature equal. The differences now manifest in the universe of visible and invisible are therefore due to varied use of creaturely free will. Origen saw the whole world-process as redemptive. Wrong choice always and everywhere entails a fall in status, while repentance always brings forgiveness and grace of recovery. How Origen represented this agelong drama of redemption is probably as much revealed as parodied in Section 19 of Jerome's *Letter to Pammachius* against Cyril's successor John in the see of Jerusalem (this letter is referred to also as *Against John*). John took Cyril as his standard of orthodoxy, and Jerome detected in John the streak of Origenism which remained in the doctrinal tradition of Jerusalem from Cyril. Jerome says that in this Origenistic scheme every soul was originally created arch-angelic, but has had a prenatal history that can be likened to the fate of

11. If you like, however, I will give you further examples relating to our condition. Come then to the blessed David, and take him for your example of repentance. Great as he was, he suffered a fall. It was in the afternoon, after his siesta that he took a turn on the housetop, and saw by chance what stirred his human passion. He fulfilled the sinful deed, but his nobility, when it came to confessing the lapse, had not perished with the doing of the deed. Nathan the prophet came, swift to convict, but a healer for his wound, saying "The Lord is wroth, and thou hast sinned."[27] So spake a simple subject to his reigning sovereign. But David, though king and robed in purple, did not take it amiss, for he had regard not to the rank of the speaker but to the majesty of him who sent him. He was not puffed up by the fact that guardsmen were drawn up all around him, for the angelic host of the Lord came to his mind, and he was in terror "as seeing him who is invisible."[28] So he answered and said to the man that came to him, or rather, in his person, to the God whose messenger he was, "I have sinned against the Lord."[29] You see this royal humility and the making of confession. Surely no one had been convicting him, nor were there many who knew what he had done. Swiftly the deed was done and straightway the prophet appeared as accuser.[30] Lo! the sinner confesses his wicked deed, and as it

a Field Marshal who suffers successive reductions in rank until he has arrived at that of simple private. This last condition represents that of a human soul, now on probation in the flesh; on probation, that is, whether it will begin thereby its recovery of rank, or desert to the traitors, i.e., the devils in deliberate rebellion against their God and Maker. Jerome rightly saw that a part of Origen's scheme could not logically be held without accepting the whole, but the Greek Fathers in general kept away from Origenism by supposing that an archangelic being could not make a partial or blundering decision, but must, in the first timeless moment of existence, have decided, immutably, either for or against God. So they assumed a pure dualism, of sinless angels, and unsaveable devils. Nevertheless, through such persons as Basil the Great, much diluted Origenism seeped into orthodoxy; as that we must not worship the good angels because they are not divinely omniscient, but are being sanctified by God, just as are the saints. While the doctrine of the sinlessness of Christ no doubt rested, for Cyril, most firmly on the literal meaning of such texts as John 8:46; 16:8–10, and Heb. 4:15, independently of any theory of the soul of Christ, it was no doubt because he was resting on Origen that Cyril could say so peremptorily that "Jesus alone is without sin." [27] II Sam. 12:7–12 in summary.
[28] Heb. 11:27. [29] II Samuel 12:13.
[30] In fact almost a year passed between the adultery and the king's repentance. But the sinful deed was not fulfilled till Uriah had been done to death, and the king's knowledge of his death might be almost simultaneous

was full and frank confession, he had the swiftest healing. For the prophet Nathan first threatened him and then said forthwith, "And the Lord hath put away thy sin." And see how quickly loving-kindness changes the face of God! except that he first declares, "Thou hast given great occasion to the enemies of the Lord to blaspheme"[31] as though he said "thou hast many that are thy foes because of thy righteousness, from whom nevertheless, thou wast kept safe by thine upright living. But as thou hast thrown away this best of armours, thou hast now, standing ready to strike, these foes that are risen up against thee."[32]

12. So then the prophet comforted David as we have seen, but that blessed man, though he received most gladly the assurance, "The Lord hath put away thy sin," did not, king as he was, draw back from penitence. Indeed he put on sackcloth in place of his purple robe, and the king sat in ashes on the bare earth instead of on his gilded throne. And in ashes he did not merely sit, but took them for eating, as he himself says, "I have eaten ashes as it were bread, and mingled my drink with weeping."[33] His lustful eye he wasted away with tears; as he says, "Every night wash I my bed and water my couch with my tears."[34] And when his courtiers exhorted him to take bread, he would not, but prolonged his fast for seven whole days. Now if a king was wont to make confession after this manner, ought not you, as a private person, to make your confession? Again, after Absalom's rebellion, when David was in flight, with many a choice of road before him, he chose to make his escape by the Mount of Olives, as good as invoking in his own mind the Deliverer who should from thence ascend into the heavens. And when Shimei cursed him bitterly he said, Let him be. For he knew that forgiveness is for those who forgive.[35] What notion have you as to Nebuchadnosor? Have you not heard from Scripture that he was bloodthirsty and savage with the disposition of a man-eating lion?[36]

with the birth of the child of guilt. Cyril is thus justified in thinking the arrival of Nathan prompt, upon the completion of the shameful episode, and in measuring, by this promptness of the messenger, the instant readiness of God to rescue the sinner from his sin.   [31] l.c., v. 14.
[32] Cyril thus reproduces the Origenistic doctrine that, in the divine order, sin always makes recovery more difficult.
[33] Ps. 102:9.   [34] Ps. 6:6.
[35] The incident is in II Samuel 15:30 ff. to 16:10.
[36] Sections 12–16 inclusive, treating of the examples of Solomon, Ahab, Jereboam, Manasses, Hezekiah and Ananias, have been omitted. This

19. Why then? When Nebuchadnosor had behaved in this kind of way and then made confession, God granted him both pardon and his kingdom. And will he not give you remission of your sins, if you repent, and the kingdom of heaven, if your conversation accords therewith? For the Lord is full of loving-kindness and swift to pardon, but slow to punish. Therefore let none of you despair of his own salvation. Peter, the highest and first of the apostles, thrice denied the Lord, all because of a serving-maid, but when he had come to repent of it, he wept bitterly. Now his weeping testifies the heartiness of his repentance. And on that account he not only received forgiveness for his denial but was actually allowed to retain his apostolic dignity.[37]

20. As, then, brethren, you have many examples of people who have sinned and then repented and been saved, do you also make confession[38] unto the Lord with all your heart, so as to receive pardon of all your sins of the time past and be accounted worthy of the heavenly gift and inherit the heavenly kingdom with all the saints in Christ Jesus, to whom be glory world without end. Amen.

LECTURE III

On baptism

The Lection is from the Epistle to the Romans.[1]

1. "Ye heavens rejoice, and let the earth be glad"[2] because

sentence is the opening of Section 17. Sections 17 and 18 develop the example of Nebuchadnosor to the same purpose, and the Lecture ends with Sections 19 and 20. There is a sameness of argument that justifies curtailment, but Cyril's treatment is never without force and freshness. The reader can find the omitted sections in Dean Church's or Dr Giffard's translation.

37 It is to be noted how Cyril harps upon the fact that his examples were not only forgiven, but allowed to keep their status which they had deserved to lose. It suggests that he was trying to break down the fear of the loss of respectability which might deter candidates from a really cleansing confession. And this would be natural where the disclosure was made before others.

38 Cyril's use of the word confession (*exomologesis*) is wider than a mere disclosure of past sins. In Section 16 for example it covers the *Song of the Three Children*, which is no personal confession of sin, but an appeal to God to vindicate Israel in spite of the shortcomings of the people. It is also a profession of trust in God. And this is no doubt part of what Cyril envisaged when he exhorted the candidates to "make confession unto the Lord."

1 The Lection was Rom. 6:3–14.   2 Ps. 96:11.

of those who are going to be "sprinkled with hyssop,"[3] and "purged with (invisible) hyssop"[4] and the power of him who during his passion drank from hyssop and a reed.[5] Yes, let the powers of heaven rejoice and let those souls get themselves ready, that are about to be wed to their spiritual Bridegroom. For lo! "the voice of one crying in the wilderness, Make ready the way of the Lord."[6] For this wedding is no light matter, nor the usual and undiscriminating union of bodies, but is the election by faith made by "the Spirit that searcheth all things."[7] For the espousals and marriage-contracts of this world are not invariably well-judged, but where there is wealth or beauty there the suitor is quick to give his hand. But in this wedding, it is not physical beauty, but the blameless conscience of the soul, that engages. Here it is not Mammon, which he condemned, but the soul's wealth of piety, that the Bridegroom desires.[8]

3. That to which you draw near is truly of great import, my brethren, and you must approach it with careful attention. Each one of you is to be presented before God in the presence of myriad hosts of angels. The Holy Spirit is going to seal your souls. You are about to be enrolled as soldiers of the great King.[9] So then get ready, be prepared, not in the sense of putting on the whitest of literal robes[10] but the devotion of a soul with conscience unburdened. Do not think of the font as filled with ordinary water, but think rather of the spiritual

---

[3] Num. 19:18; Heb. 9:19. Hyssop as sprinkler of water for purifying the unclean.

[4] Ps. 51:7. The fifty-first psalm is recognized by Cyril to be a psalm of inward and spiritual relations with God, so that literal hyssop cannot be meant.

[5] There is a combined allusion here to Mark 15:36 and John 19:29.

[6] Isa. 40:3 is rather incongruously brought into a theme based on the Song of Songs.

[7] I Cor. 2:10.

[8] The last four words must be supplied. The Mammon reference is to Luke 16:13; Matt. 6:24. Section 2 is omitted, as of less interest.

[9] It is a remarkable tribute to the success of Constantine in bringing the military profession under Christian sanctions that, by the date of these lectures, a bishop could appeal to enrolment in the imperial armies as a pleasing simile for Christian people for their own religious service under Christ. By the year of the transcribed lectures the arms of Constantius were beginning at last to be crowned with success, and the people of Palestine, long conscious of the danger from the Persians, saw in his victories a proof of the blessing of heaven.

[10] For their white baptismal robes the candidates were no doubt already making preparation, and the more this bulked in their minds, the better Cyril's opportunity to enforce the symbolism.

grace that is given with the water. For just as the sacrifices on pagan altars are, in themselves, indifferent matter and yet have become defiled by reason of the invocation made over them to the idols, so, but in the opposite sense, the ordinary water in the font acquires sanctifying power when it receives the invocation of the Holy Spirit of Christ and the Father.

4. Whereas man is a twofold being composed of soul and body, so is the means of his cleansing twofold, which is incorporeal for his incorporeal part, and corporeal for the cleansing of his body.[11] The water washes the body and the Spirit seals the soul, so that, being (by the Spirit) "sprinkled in heart, and washed in body with pure water, we may draw near to God."[12] Therefore when you are about to go down into the water, do not look upon it as mere water, but look for its saving power by the operation of the Holy Spirit,[13] for you cannot be initiated but by means of both the Spirit and the water. And this is no assertion of mine, but it is the Lord Jesus Christ, in whose power the matter lies, that says "except a man be born again" first, and presently adds "of water and of the Spirit, he cannot enter into the kingdom of God."[14] For neither does one baptized with water, but not accounted worthy of the Spirit, receive the grace whole and entire, nor shall anyone, however virtuous his conduct be, who does not receive the Spirit-seal by means of water, enter into the kingdom of heaven. That is a bold saying, but it is not mine, for Jesus uttered it. But I will make bold to prove to you its truth, out of Holy Scripture.[15] Cornelius was a just man, and held worthy to see angels in vision. By his prayers and alms he had, as it were, erected his good memorial[16] before God in heaven. Then came Peter and

---

[11] Cyril seems to think of spiritual regeneration in baptism as the work of the Spirit, coming to the baptized after the manner of the descent upon Christ at his baptism. The work mediated by the water, and affecting the body of the baptized, he apparently connects with the preparation of the resurrection body for eternal life. What is meant here surpasses therefore what appears to be said, viz. that it is a mere present cleansing by water.   [12] Heb. 10:22.

[13] As body and soul in man cannot be separated, so Cyril's picture of a twofold action of water and spirit in baptism is not a picture of two actions, independently, one by the Spirit and one by water. The water does what it does because the Spirit gives it the power, while the Spirit uses the water to prepare the bodies of the regenerate for life after death.

[14] First John 3:3 and then 3:5.   [15] Acts 10:1-8 and 34-48.

[16] Acts 10:4 makes the angel use pictorial language, in representing the good deeds of Cornelius as ascending to heaven, and there presenting an object that made God mindful of him. Cyril makes the exegesis still

the Spirit was poured forth upon those who believed, and they spoke with other tongues and prophesied. Yet the Scripture relates that after they had received the grace of the Spirit, Peter commanded them to be baptized in the Name of Jesus Christ, to the end that, whereas their souls had been regenerated through their believing, their bodies should share in this grace through the (sacramental) water.

5. Now if anyone is eager to learn why baptismal grace is given by means of water, and not by any other of the elements, he will find the answer if he takes up the Scriptures. For water is a great subject and the fairest of the four visible elements of which the world is made.[17] Heaven is the angels' home, yet heavens were made from waters. Earth is man's place, and the earth arose from waters, and before the making of all that the six days of creation brought forth, "the Spirit of God moved upon the face of the waters."[18] As water was the foundation of the world, so Jordan was the foundation of the Gospel.[19] Israel was set free from Pharaoh by means of the sea, and the world was freed from sins "with the washing of water by the (divine) word."[20]

more sharply pictorial by making the object a pillar erected in God's sight with, presumably, the name of Cornelius engraved upon it.

[17] Of the four elements, water is easily the most often mentioned in Scripture, fire coming second, but much behind, while the elements earth and air are, by comparison, little in view. The scriptural associations of water are the most poetical and pleasing. Thus Cyril's encomium on water is uniformly scriptural.

[18] Gen 1:2. The preceding sentences are commentary on Gen. 1:1–10. The first account of creation in Gen. assumes water to have been the primal matter. God's second creative word, presumably working upon water as substrate, evoked a firmament entirely surrounded by waters, within which the universe of heaven and earth took form. Below, earth rose out of the waters to form a lower firmament, while, above, a more mysterious dome enclosed heaven. In this way Cyril can assert that the dwelling places of angels and men owed their origin to water.

[19] Archē, here, would seem to mean "foundation" or "pre-requisite," rather than beginning. Cyril was no doubt aware of Greek speculation that would make water the primal element. But he keeps strictly to the terms of scripture. There was water, and the Spirit of God at work, before there was any universe of visible and invisible. This is to invest water with a mysterious and venerable character very suited to his purpose.

[20] Eph. 5:26, where it is the Church that is delivered by Christ's washing. But Cyril no doubt held the common patristic view that the world came into existence for the sake of the Church, as Jews had supposed that it was for the sake of Israel. The Jews were wrong, in that the election was out of all peoples, but Christians are right, Cyril would say, because the catholic Church is God's end in creation.

Where there is a covenant between parties, water comes into it.[21] It was after the Flood that a covenant was made with Noah. The covenant with Israel made from Mount Sinai was, you notice, implemented "with water, and scarlet wool, and hyssop."[22] Elijah was taken up to heaven, but water came into it, for he made the crossing of Jordan first, and after that the chariot took him on high.[23] The high-priest first washes and then offers the incense, for Aaron first washed with water and after that was invested as high-priest.[24] How indeed could he properly intercede for others if he had not first been cleansed with water? And the basin placed within the tabernacle was there as a symbol of baptism.[25]

6. Baptism is the ending of the old covenant and the beginning of the new. For the inauguration of the new was John, than whom there was none greater "among them that are born of women," the crown indeed of the prophets. "For all the prophets and the law prophesied until John."[26] But of the Gospel dispensation he was the firstfruits, for (we read) "the beginning of the gospel of Jesus Christ" and after some words "John did baptize in the wilderness."[27] I grant you that Elijah the Tishbite was taken up to heaven: yet he was not greater than John. Enoch was translated but was not greater than John. Moses was the greatest of lawgivers and all the prophets were admirable, but they were not greater than John. I dare not compare prophet with prophet, but it was their Master and ours that declared "among those that are born of women, there hath not risen a greater than John." Not "born of virgins" observe! but "born of women." We are comparing a head-servant with his fellow-servants, not the Son with the household, for his pre-eminence and grace are incomparable. Of this grace, do you observe what manner of man God chose to be the inaugurator? One who forsook possessions and loved solitude, but no misanthrope. He fed on locusts to make his soul grow wings. Sated with honey, the words he spoke were sweeter than honey and of more profit. Clothed in a garment of camel's hair, he exemplified in his own person the ascetic life.[28] While he was yet cradled in his mother's womb, he was

21 i.e., wherever in Scripture such a subject occurs.
22 Heb. 9:19.   23 II Kings 2:8-11.   24 Ex. 29:4.
25 Ex. 40:30-32.   26 Matt. 11:11-13.   27 Mark 1:1, 4.
28 Already Jerusalem was beginning to be populated with persons who had forsaken the world to live devoted to religion. The transcribers of these Lectures were probably such. So Cyril's lecture class knew and respected the ascetic life.

hallowed by the Holy Spirit. Jeremiah also was sanctified before he came forth out of his mother's womb,[29] but did not then prophesy. Only John "leaped in his mother's womb for joy"[30] and in the Spirit recognized his Master, when his fleshly eyes were blind. For since the grace of baptism was so great, its minister too must needs be great.

7. He, then, began to baptize in Jordan, and "all Jerusalem went out to him,"[31] taking advantage of the firstfruits of baptisms, for to Jerusalem belongs the pre-eminence in all good things. But note, citizens of Jerusalem, that those who "went out" were baptized of him, confessing their sins. First they showed their wounds, then he applied the words of healing,[32] and to those that believed he gave redemption from "unquenchable fire."[33] And if you need persuasion of this, that John's baptism redeems from the threat of fire, hear his words "O generation of vipers, who hath warned you to flee from the wrath to come?"[34] But since you have fled, leave off being a viper, and whereas you were once the offspring of a viper, slough off, said he, the skin of your former sinful life. For every snake puts off its signs of age by pushing through some narrow place, and gets rid of its old apparel by squeezing it off. Thenceforth it is young again in body. So "enter ye in at the straight and narrow gate,"[35] squeeze yourself through by fasting, break yourself away from perishing, "put off the old man with his deeds,"[36] and say, with the Song of Songs, "I have put off my coat; how shall I put it on?"[37]

But it might be that someone among you is not sincere, "a man-pleaser,"[38] feigning piety but not believing from the heart, imitating Simon Magus in hypocrisy,[39] not drawing near for the sake of participating in the grace, but with idle curiosity to see what is given. Let such a person hear the words of John, "And now also the axe is laid unto the root of the trees, there-

---

[29] Jer. 1:5, 6.   [30] Luke 1:44.   [31] Matt. 3:5.
[32] *Iatreuma* seems to be found only in figurative use, though its literal sense is simply "a remedy."   [33] Matt. 3:12.
[34] Matt. 3:7. The present tense "redeems" seems to show that Cyril thought the power of rescuing souls from damnation was inherent in John's baptism, as fore-empowered by the Gospel dispensation.
[35] A combining of Matt. 7:13 and 14.
[36] Combining Eph. 4:22 with Colossians 3:9.
[37] S. of Sol. 5:3.   [38] Eph. 6:6.
[39] Acts 8. But with the high standard of scriptural knowledge which Cyril everywhere assumes in his audience, we may suppose that vv. 21–24 (Peter's rebuke and Simon's repentance) would be, in substance, inferred from this mere general allusion.

fore every tree which bringeth not forth good fruit, is hewn down, and cast into the fire."[40] The Judge cannot be hood-winked, so put away hypocrisy.[41]

10. Unless a man receive baptism, he has not salvation, excepting only martyrs, who receive the kingdom though they have not entered the font.[42] For when the Saviour was re-deeming the universe by means of his cross and his side was pierced, "forthwith came there out blood and water,"[43] to show that in times of peace men should be baptized in water, and in times of persecution in their own blood. For the Saviour purposely spoke of martyrdom as baptism when he said "Can ye drink of the cup that I drink of, and be baptized with the baptism that I am baptized with?"[44] Moreover, martyrs make their profession of faith, "being made a spectacle to the world, and to angels, and to men."[45] In a short while, you too will make your profession of faith, but we have not yet reached the time for you to hear about that.[46]

11. Jesus, in being himself baptized, hallowed baptism. If the Son of God was baptized, who any longer can claim to be godly and yet think lightly of baptism? He was not baptized that he might receive pardon for his sins, for he knew no sin; but being without sin he was baptized to impart divine grace and dignity to those who are baptized. For just "as the children are partakers of flesh and blood, he also himself likewise took part"[47] with them, so that we, by partaking in his presence after the flesh, may also become partakers of his divine grace. Jesus was baptized for that reason further also, that besides salvation, and through our partaking with him, we may receive the dignity.[48] The dragon in the waters,[49] according to Job,

40 Matt. 3:10.   41 Sections 8 and 9 are, for brevity, omitted.
42 This belief is based on Matt. 10:32 and 39 and is testified by Tertullian, *On Baptism*, xvi and following.
43 John 19:34.   44 Mark 10:38.   45 I Cor. 4:9.
46 Cyril proposes to reach the imparting of the creed only two lectures later, interposing one lecture in which he gives an epitome of the heads of the Faith. (An epitome, it appears, of his own construction.) It was therefore simply to keep up interest and expectation that he inserted this remark at this point.   47 Heb. 2:14.
48 Or "prerogative," viz., of "treading upon serpents and scorpions." Cyril will now say that the waters were a lurking-place for powers of evil (thus reproducing a widespread and ancient theme of Semitic demonology) until Christ neutralized and reversed their dominion by his baptism. Henceforth baptism makes the recipients secure against this ambushed foe, in the might of Christ's once-for-all victory communicated by the water itself to the baptized.   49 Behemoth. Job 40:15-24.

"trusteth that he can draw up Jordan into his mouth."[50] When, then, Jesus must break "the heads of the dragons,"[51] he went down and bound the mighty one in the waters, so that we might receive the "power to tread upon serpents and scorpions."[52] The Beast was no ordinary monster, but a dread one. "No ship of fishers could bear one scale of his tail: before him ran destruction,"[53] that laid waste all it met. But life ran to meet him, to muzzle death henceforth, that all we, the saved, may cry, "O death, where is thy sting? O grave, where is thy victory?"[54] Baptism destroys the sting of death.

12. For you descend into the water laden with your sins. But the invocation of the grace causes your soul to receive the seal, and after that it does not let you be swallowed up by the dread dragon. You go down "dead indeed in sin,"[55] and you come up "alive unto" righteousness "for if thou wert planted together in the likeness of the Saviour's death, thou shalt be counted worthy of his resurrection also."[56] For as Jesus died in taking away the sins of the world, that, by doing sin to death, he might rise in righteousness, so, too, when you go down into the water and are, in a fashion, entombed in the water as he was in the rock, you may rise again to "walk in newness of life."[57]

13. Next, when you have received the grace (of baptism), there will be given you thereafter the power to wrestle against the adverse powers. For just as Jesus, after his baptism endured forty days temptation (and that not because he could not surmount it before baptism, but because he willed to accomplish all things in order and sequence), so you, who, prior to baptism, dare not engage the adversaries in strife, when you receive the grace (of baptism) and thenceforth take courage, may then fight with the arms of righteousness, and, if you will, preach the gospel.

14. Jesus Christ was Son of God, but he did not preach the gospel till he had been baptized. Now if the Master himself pursued his course in regular order, ought we his servants to venture before the proper time? From that moment when "the Holy Spirit descended in a bodily shape like a dove upon

[50] The preferable MS reading is "into his eye," due to the first half of v. 24, "He taketh it with his eyes."
[51] Ps. 74:14, but our text has "dragon" in the singular.
[52] Luke 10:19.
[53] Job 40:26 in the Septuagint, corresponding with 41:7 in the A.V.
[54] I Cor. 15:55.   [55] Rom. 6:11 in reminiscence.
[56] Rom. 6:2, 5.   [57] Rom. 6:4.

him"[58] "began Jesus to preach."[59] This was not so that Jesus should, for the first time, behold the Spirit, for he knew him before coming to earth in the body, but that John the Baptist should behold it. For said John, as I would have you note, "I knew him not; but he who sent me to baptize with water, the same said unto me, Upon whom thou shalt see the Spirit descending, and remaining upon him, the same is he."[60] And if you have a sincere devotion, the Holy Spirit will descend also upon you, and the Father's voice will sound forth from on high: not to say "This is my Son," but to say "This is now become my son." "Is my Son" was said over him only, since "In the beginning was the Word, and the Word was with God, and the Word was God."[61] To him applies the "is," since he is always Son of God, but to you applies the phrase "is now become," since you have not natural sonship, but receive the status of son by adoption. The Word is Son eternally. You receive the grace of sonship progressively. Therefore, to be made son of God, "an heir of God, and joint heir with Christ," make ready the soul's vessel.[62]

16. "Be of good courage, Jerusalem, the Lord will take away all thine iniquities. The Lord shall wash away the filth of his sons and daughters, by the spirit of judgement and by the spirit of burning: he shall sprinkle clean water upon you, and ye shall be cleansed from all your sin."[63] Angels will circle round you, crying "Who is this that cometh up in white apparel, leaning on her near of kin?"[64] For the soul that used to be but servant has now claimed the Master himself for her kinsman, and he will accept her sincere intention and cry to her, "Behold thou art fair, my love: behold thou art fair; thy teeth are as flocks of shorn sheep," because she has made her profession with a good conscience, and "each of them bearing twins" because of the twofold grace (I mean that grace completed of

[58] Luke 3:22. [59] Matt. 4:17. [60] John 1:33.
[61] John 1:1.
[62] Rom. 8:17. The sentence is the first of Section 15, the rest being omitted.
[63] Cyril here strings together Zeph. 3, parts of vv. 14 and 15, Isa. 4:4, and the first half of Ezek. 36:25, and substitutes "Jerusalem" for "daughter of Jerusalem," at the beginning. The result no doubt was that he made a mixed company of Palestinian men and women, candidates for baptism in the middle of the fourth Christian century, feel that they and not the Jews were the true heirs of the Old Testament, wherein was already set out, prophetically, the way of preparation for the newer rite.
[64] The first half of S. of Sol. 8:5 in the Septuagint.

water and the Spirit, or preached in the old covenant and the new).[65]

Now may you all persevere through this fast, remember what has been said, bear the fruit of good works, be presented blameless to the spiritual Bridegroom, and receive from God the remission of your sins in Christ Jesus our Lord, to whom be the glory, world without end. Amen.

LECTURE IV

On the (ten) dogmas[1]

The Lection is from the Epistle to the Colossians.[2]

1. Evil apes respectability, and tares do their best to look like wheat, but however close a similarity to wheat they have in appearance their taste completely undeceives the discerning. Even the devil "transformeth himself into an angel of light,"[3] not meaning to ascend again to his former place (for he possesses a heart as hard as an anvil and has no intention of repenting ever)[4], but to snare those who are living the angelic life in blinding darkness, and infest them with a condition of faithlessness. There are many wolves going about "in sheep's clothing,"[5] but though they wear the coats of sheep, they possess, none the less, both talons and teeth. They wrap themselves in the gentle creature's hide and with this disguise deceive the innocent only to inject with their teeth the deadly poison of their irreligion. We therefore need the grace of God, a sober mind, and watchful eyes, so as not to eat tares for wheat and come to harm for not knowing better; so as not to mistake the wolf for a sheep and be ravaged; and so as not to take the death-dealing devil for a good angel, and be devoured. For Scripture says, "he goeth about like a roaring lion, seeking

---

[65] S. of Sol. 4, first half each of vv. 1 and 2. Cyril's allegorical interpretation of "bearing twins" is in the style of Origen, of whom there survives the saying that it may refer to the two senses of Scripture, literal and mystical. It is probable that Cyril was a reader of Origen's Commentaries, but he is sparing in his use of Origen's favourite exegetical methods.

[1] The number of headings varies from ten to fourteen in the MSS.

[2] The Lection was Col. 2:8–end.   [3] II Cor. 11:14.

[4] The sentence in brackets may be an addition, to defend Cyril from the suspicion of Origenism, as the speculation that the devil would at last be saved was regarded as one of Origen's prime errors.

[5] Matt. 7:15.

whom he may devour."[6] That is why the Church admonishes. That is why we hold these classes. That is the reason for these readings of Scripture.

2. The way of godliness consists of these two parts, pious dogmas and good works. Neither are the dogmas acceptable to God without good works, nor does God accept works accomplished otherwise than as linked with pious dogmas. What good is it to a man shamefully committing fornication to have an excellent knowledge of theology? Again, what good is it to a man to exercise the greatest self-discipline, if he utters godless blasphemy? To have learned the dogmas is therefore a very great possession, and after that our need is sobriety of soul, since there are many that would "spoil us through philosophy and vain deceit."[7] Now the Greeks plunder you with their smooth tongues, "for honey distils from the lips of a strange woman,"[8] while the circumcision lead you astray by means of the Holy Scriptures, which they wrest vilely, if you go to them. They study Scripture from childhood to old age, only to end their days in gross ignorance.

The sectaries "by good words and fair speeches deceive the hearts of the simple"[9] coating over their poison-pills of godless doctrines with the honey of the Name of Christ. Now of all these the Lord declares "Beware lest any deceive you."[10] And that is why there is this teaching of the faith and these explanations of it.

3. But before I commit to you this faith I think it will be good now to recapitulate in brief its indispensable dogmas, lest the great number of things to be said and the intervening space of the whole forty days[11] should result in the less clever among you forgetting. But if we have now unobtrusively implanted in your minds the headings, it will mean that they

6 I Peter 5:8.   7 Col. 2:8.
8 Prov. 5:3. "The Greeks" means adherents of the Classical paganism. They had "smooth tongues" as deprecating the strictness of Christianity.
9 Rom. 16:18 reading, however, *euglottias* for *eulogias*.
10 Matt. 24:4.
11 While the oldest MSS have "the whole forty days," others read "the whole Sacred Forty Days," i.e., Lent. The later reading no doubt rightly interprets the earlier. But we need not suppose Cyril to mean that, on the day of this lecture, the whole of Lent, or practically the whole of Lent, was still to come. If that were his meaning, we should have to crowd the fourth lecture into the first week. But this consequence does not follow, if, as is most probable, he simply means that they were hearing lectures over the whole length of Lent, from the Procatechesis on, and must try to remember everything.

do not slip your memory when they are, later on, worked up into fuller form.[12] And let the more advanced of the present company bear with this arrangement, "having their senses now exercised to discern both good and evil"[13] and yet having to listen to instruction fitter for children, and to a course of spoon-feeding: just so that, at one and the same time, those that have need of the instruction will benefit, while those who know it all already may have the memory refreshed of things the knowledge of which they gained previously.[14]

4. *Of God.* Let there, then, be laid as first foundation in your souls the dogma concerning God, that God is one alone, unbegotten, without beginning, unchanging and unchangeable, neither looking to any other as the author of his being, nor to any other to succeed to his life, of which life he had no beginning in time, nor will it ever come to an end: then that he is good and just, so that if ever you hear a heretic say that there is a just God and also a good God and they are different,[15] be

[12] The suggestion which Cyril seems to make, that he is about to epitomize the remainder of the course, is not borne out by the facts. The course rather reflects the structure of the Jerusalem baptismal creed, which he communicates to the *photizomenoi* in the fifth lecture. And it is the creed, rather than the epitome of dogmas in Lecture IV, that provides the class with headings that should prevent their being befogged in the fuller treatment of the subjects, in subsequent lectures. The truth seems to be, therefore, that Cyril interposed this epitome of his own, before delivering the creed, so as not to be too closely confined by the structure of the creed. He is able, in his epitome, to treat of soul, body, and Scripture, in a way to which the structure of the creed does not lend itself. The idea of such an epitome, arranged under the major heads of dogma, had its classical expression in the work of Origen, *On First Principles,* which Cyril is likely to have known.

[13] Heb. 5:14. The preceding verse gives the simile with which the sentence concludes.

[14] This apology to the more learned *photizomenoi* implies, in them, so high a standard of knowledge and ability, that we must assume Jerusalem to have become something of a school of Christian learning, after the former pattern of the school at Alexandria.

[15] The heresy here referred to is that of Marcion, a shipmaster from Pontus, who joined the Church in Rome about A.D. 135. Brought up to the Pauline antithesis between Law and Gospel, he was influenced by a Syrian Gnostic, Cerdo, in Rome, to see the whole Old Testament as the antithesis of the Gospel, and so to distinguish between the God who created this world and gave the Law, and the Father revealed by Christ. He supposed the Catholic Church to have been deceived by the god of this world into receiving the Old Testament as scripture, and contaminating the Gospel with the principles of the Law. Marcion founded a rival Church claiming to be catholic, which had great success in the orient, and was a formidable foe in the eyes of Cyril.

straightway on your guard as you recognize the poison-pill of heresy. For some have dared, in their godless teaching to divide the one God.[16] And some have distinguished the maker and master of the soul from the creator of our bodies, a doctrine as impious as it is stupid. For how should a man that is one be servant of masters that are two? as the Lord says in the gospel, "No man can serve two masters."[17] So there is only one God, the maker of both souls and bodies. There is one creator of heaven and earth, who made the angels and archangels. He is indeed creator of plurality, but of one only was he Father[18] before all ages, that is of his only and sole-begotten Son, our Lord Jesus Christ, through whom also he made all things, both visible and invisible.

5. Now this Father of our Lord Jesus Christ is not circumscribed to some place, nor is there heaven beyond him, but "the heavens are the work of his fingers,"[19] and "the whole earth is holden in the hollow of his hand."[20] He is in everything and yet nothing contains him. Do not imagine that God is smaller than the sun, or that he is as large as the sun. For, as he made the sun, he must have been already incomparably greater than the sun, and more resplendent with light. He knows what is to come, and nothing equals him in power. He knows everything, and does as he wills. He is not subject to any law of sequence, or genesis, or fortune, or fate. He is perfect by every measure. He possesses unchangeably every kind of virtue, never less and never more, but ever in the same degree and

16 While this might apply to any of the dualistic Gnostics, it is probably meant specially to cover the Manichaean religion, founded by the Persian subject Mani, on the lines of the old Iranian irreducible dualism of light and darkness, good and evil. Mani came in contact with diffused Christian ideas, of which he adopted so much that his religion was able, after his death at the hands of the Persian king in A.D. 276, to propagate itself inside the Roman empire as if it were an esoteric Christian heresy, Manichaean salvation was based upon the escape of soul (conceived as a quantitative soulstuff) from bondage to matter.

17 Matt. 6:24. This disproof of dualism seems to be Cyril's own. For this strong Christian conviction of man's unity of soul and body, see the work of Nemesius, following.

18 The problem of the One and the Many preoccupied Greek philosophy throughout the ages. The Alexandrine Christian teachers Clement and Origen essayed to solve it by the notion of a Logos or Word of God who is one, as his Father is one, while able to enter relation with the plurality of which he is Creator. Cyril, in his present outline, is their heir.

19 Ps. 8:3.

20 Isa. 40:12.

manner. He has prepared chastisement for sinners, and crowns for the righteous.[21]

6. See, then, that many have gone astray from the one God in different ways, some deifying the sun, and so remaining atheist every night from set of sun, and others the moon, so as to have no god by day. Others have deified this or that portion of the world. Others have deified the arts, others, things to eat, others different pleasures. Men mad after women have set up on high their idol, a nude woman, calling it Venus, and by means of the visible emblem, have worshipped lust. Others fascinated by the gleam of gold have deified it and other forms of matter.[22] But if anyone first lays the foundation in his heart of the doctrine of the monarchy of God, and puts his trust therein, he cuts out at one stroke every seduction by the evils of idolatry and of heretical error. Do you, then, by means of the faith, lay in your soul as first foundation, this, the first dogma of true religion.

7. *Of Christ.* Believe also in the Son of God, who is one and sole, our Lord Jesus Christ, God begotten from God, life gotten from life, light gendered from light, like in all things to him that begat him:[23] who did not receive his being in time but was begotten of the Father before all ages in a manner eternal and incomprehensible. He is God's wisdom and power and his righteousness existing hypostatically.[24] He is enthroned at God's right hand from before all ages. For he was not, as some have supposed, crowned after his passion, as though God seated him at his right hand for his endurance of the cross,[25] but has royal dignity from that source whence he has his being, to wit, in being eternally begotten from the Father, and shares the

[21] After delighting the intellectual among the *photizomenoi* with his Platonisms, he comes back to the thought of moral decision, which concerns all.
[22] The anti-pagan polemic here epitomized is given *in extenso* in Arnobius, *Against the pagans.*
[23] This is the phrase upon which all those eastern theologians commonly called Semi-Arians attempted to base orthodoxy, rather than on the consubstantiality-formula of Nicaea. Cyril, after remaining in some degree of association with this group through middle life, ended by becoming a prominent Neo-Nicene.
[24] That is, the Son, in perfectly fulfilling the Father's will, became, in his own Person, the righteousness of God, existing not as a quality or attribute of God, but hypostatically, to be contemplated, loved, and accepted by the Father.
[25] Paul of Samosata, bishop of Antioch, was condemned in A.D. 268 as teaching that Jesus was a man uniquely indwelt by the divine Wisdom, and rewarded for obedience by exaltation.

Father's throne, being God, and, as we said, being the wisdom and power of God. He reigns together with the Father, and through the Father is creator of all things. He falls in nothing short of the majesty of Godhead and knows the Father that begat him as he himself is known of his Father. To state the matter in brief, I remind you of the gospel, "None knoweth the Son, but the Father: neither knoweth any the Father, save the Son."[26]

8. Nor must you make the Son alien from the Father[27], nor, on the other hand, put your faith in a Father-who-is-his-own-Son, by making the concepts coalesce;[28] but you must believe that there is one only-begotten Son of one God, the Word who is God before all ages. He is Word, not as though uttered[29] and diffused upon the air, nor to be likened to unsubstantial words.[30] But he is the Son-Word, maker of rational creatures, the Word that hears the Father and himself declares it.[31] If God permit, I shall speak more fully of these matters when time serves, for I do not forget my proposal, at this stage, to make introduction to the faith in the form of brief headings.

9. *Of Christ's birth of a Virgin.* You must believe that this only-begotten Son of God came down from heaven to this earth because of our sins, and took upon him manhood of like passions

---

[26] Matt. 11:27.   [27] As did Arius.

[28] As did the Modalist Monarchians or Patripassians of the second century, of whom Noetus and Sabellius are historic leaders. To safeguard faith in the full and true deity of Christ, they made him personally identical with the Father, Sabellius refining the doctrine by making the Father, for the purpose of the incarnation, "unfold" into Trinity of being.

[29] *prophorikos*, a word coined by the Stoics, to express rational thought when it externalizes itself to the parent mind in which it was conceived. Thought germinally implanted in the mind (as the Stoics said *endiathetos*) has indefinite possibilities of development. But the moment it leaves the mind as an uttered message (*logos prophorikos*), potentiality ends in actualization. The thinker's message is limited to what he has said, and even that is a wasting quantity, through failure to understand, inattention, and for-getfulness on the part of the hearers.

[30] Words are "unsubstantial" in the sense that their meaning does not arise from the sounds or syllables of which they consist, but in the existence of the thing, concrete or abstract, to which they are appropriate. Cyril is safeguarding against the associations of "Word" which would lead to its application to the Son of God in a way suggesting that the existence of the Word-Son was dependent on the world that God willed to create through him; in short Cyril was fully orthodox in his doctrine of the Son of God, but seeks to express his faith otherwise than by the formula of Nicaea.

[31] Cyril here relates the Son to the Father in the same way that the Fourth Gospel relates the Paraclete to the Father and the Son. (John 16:13).

with ours, by being born of the Holy Virgin and of Holy Spirit,[32] and this incarnation was not docetic[33] or imaginary, but true incarnation. He did not pass through the Virgin as though passing through a channel,[34] but his flesh grew truly from her flesh and he was truly fed upon her milk. He truly ate as we eat, and drank as we drink. For if the incarnation was but seeming, then did it but seem to bring salvation.[35] Christ was twofold. As to what was visible, he was man, and as to what is invisible, he was God.[36] As man, he ate genuinely as we do, for he had the same fleshly needs as we have, but as God he made five loaves feed five thousand men. As man he truly died, and as God, on the third day, he raised to life his body that was dead. As man he was really asleep in the boat, while, as God, he came walking upon the waters.[37]

10. *Of the Cross.* Christ was truly crucified for our sins. Even supposing you were disposed to contest this, your surroundings rise up before your eyes to refute you, this sacred Golgotha where we have now come together[38] because of him who was crucified here. Yes, and the wood of the cross is henceforth here and there distributed all over the world.[39] Now, he was not

[32] Cyril uses no definite article. To have done so would have been to place the Holy Spirit in the position of Father of Jesus. Without the article, the phrase is equivalent to "miraculously born of the Holy Virgin."

[33] Docetic means "seeming without genuinely being." Many of the early Gnostic heresies were docetic, in supposing that Christ was not genuinely subject to the realities and limitations of human existence.

[34] The Valentinians, in the second century, attributed to Christ a "psychic" body, which entered the world by passing through the material body of Mary "like water passing through a pipe."

[35] This argument, that a docetic Christ offered no real hope of man's salvation, meets us first in the letters of Ignatius, bishop of Antioch, martyred in A.D. 115.

[36] Here Cyril over-simplifies, and would be Apollinarian if strictly interpreted.

[37] Thus Cyril approaches Christology on the line that was to become classical in the Tome of Pope Leo, a century later.

[38] Note that Cyril, here for the first time, but repeatedly in the course of the lectures, treats these as taking place on the very site of the crucifixion. This is incompatible with the assumption that the identification of the *monticulus crucis* in the garden court between the basilica and the rotunda of the Anastasis had already taken place in 350. Equally the way in which Cyril here mentions the wood of the cross, afterwards shown in the chapel on the *monticulus*, excludes the supposition that this sacred site outside the basilica had already received recognition.

[39] From the visit of the empress mother Helena, in A.D. 326, and her "invention" (miraculous discovery) of the true cross of Christ buried *in situ*, proceeded a distribution of small portions of the cross to privileged pilgrims. The Letter of Cyril to Constantius which is printed below,

crucified for sins which he had done, but to free us from the sins that are wholly ours. And though he was, at that time, scorned of men, and as man smitten on the face, creation recognized him to be God. For when the sun saw its master being dishonoured, it shuddered and ceased to shine, not bearing to see the sight.[40]

11. *Of the Sepulchre.* Christ was truly, as man, laid in a tomb in the rock, but for dread of him the rocks were rent asunder. He went down to regions under the earth to redeem from thence the righteous.[41] For, tell me, do you want the living to enjoy the grace of God, and that when the most part of them are not deeply religious, and are you quite content that those that have been so long while imprisoned, even from Adam down, should never come to deliverance? Isaiah the prophet with clarion voice proclaimed so many things of Christ. Would you not have the King go down and redeem his herald? David and Samuel were down there, and all the prophets, including John, who sent and asked him, "Art thou he that should come, or do we look for another?"[42] And would you not have our Lord go down and rescue men like that?

designed to celebrate Constantius as no less favoured of God than Constantine, is the first document that alludes explicitly to the invention. By the time of Aetheria, as we have seen, a chapel had been erected in the garden court west of the Martyry, to house the portion of the cross retained by the Church of Jerusalem, and an annual commemoration of the invention had been established, with an ostension of the relic in the presence of the bishop. In the present passage we have our most solid historical evidence corroborating the invention. For it shows us that, despite the silence of Eusebius, fragments of what the Church of Jerusalem claimed and believed to be the true cross had been given to visitors representing churches all over the known world, in a process that must have covered a number of years.

40 Such poetical fancies connected with the crucifixion had, no doubt, their origin in a long tradition of Paschal preaching. We may compare the Sermon of Melito of Sardis (about A.D. 180), "The Master has been treated in unseemly wise, with his body naked. For this reason the lights of heaven turned away, and the day darkened, that it might hide him who was stripped upon the cross." (Edition by Campbell Bonner, *Studies and Documents*, XII, Christophers, London, 1940, p. 179.)

41 There was no clause on the descent into Hades in the Jerusalem creed, though, by this time, such a clause was present in the baptismal creeds of some churches in the Danube country. The argumentative form in which Cyril casts his section on the entombment suggests that his teaching at this point might be thought novel. That he should wish to include the subject in his epitome indicates the advanced character of theology in Jerusalem.

42 Matt. 11:3.

12. *Of Christ's resurrection*. But he that descended beneath the earth came up again from thence, and Jesus who was buried truly rose again, the third day. Now should Jews ever try to pull your faith to pieces,[43] counter them instantly by asking thus: Jonah came forth from the whale after three days, and do you then say that it is not true that Christ rose from the earth after three days? A corpse that touched the bones of Elisha came to life again, and will you argue that he who made men could not more easily than that be raised up by the power of God? So, then, Christ truly rose again, and after his resurrection was seen once more by the disciples. Twelve disciples were witnesses of his resurrection, and the measure of their witness is not their winning speech, but their striving for the truth of the resurrection unto torture and to death. Well, now, "at the mouth of two or three witnesses shall every word be established," Scripture says.[44] But those who bore witness to the resurrection of Christ were a round dozen. And after that are you going to find the resurrection incredible?[45]

13. *Of Christ received up*. When Jesus had run the course of his endurance, and redeemed men from their sins, he ascended up again into the heavens and a cloud received him from sight. Angels stood by as he ascended, while apostles gazed. If anyone does not credit these words, let him believe simply in virtue of the things he sees today. In the case of every monarch that dies, his power is extinguished in the same breath as his life. But Christ is no sooner crucified than he begins to be worshipped by the whole universe. We preach the crucified, and see, the demons tremble. Many have been the victims of crucifixion through the ages, but of which of them but of him did the invocation ever drive off the demons?

14. So let us not be ashamed of the cross of Christ, but though someone else keeps it secret, do you openly sign it upon your forehead, so that evil spirits beholding the royal cipher may fly far from you, terrified. Make this sign as you eat and drink, when you sit down, when you go to bed, when you get up again, while you are talking, while you are walking; in brief, at your every undertaking. He who was crucified then

---

[43] In Palestine and Syria, unsophisticated Christians were quite likely to be discomfited by the Jewish controversialists with whom they came in contact in the market, or on the road. The influence of Judaism was formidable enough to justify such lessons in polemic.

[44] Deut. 19:15.

[45] The imaginary Jew is the addressee throughout.

is now in heaven above. For we would have cause to be ashamed if, after he had been crucified and entombed, he had remained entombed. But now, he who was crucified on this very Golgotha ascended to heaven from the Mount of Olives there to the east. For from hence he went down into Hades and came again to us here. Again he went up from us into heaven, when the Father called him saying, "Sit thou on my right hand, until I make thine enemies thy footstool."[46]

15. *Of judgement to come.* This ascended Jesus Christ is coming again, from heaven, and not from anywhere on earth. I say "not from anywhere on earth," since there are going to be many antichrists now arising on earth. For, as you have beheld, many already began to say, I am Christ.[47] Besides, "the abomination of desolation"[48] is still to come, giving himself the usurped title of Christ. But I bid you look for the true Christ, the only-begotten Son of God coming, but from heaven, and never again from anywhere on earth; appearing to all more clearly than any lightning, or any brilliance of light, escorted by angels, to judge quick and dead and reign as king, in a heavenly and eternal kingdom that knows no end. In that point also I bid you make sure your faith; since many are saying that the kingdom of Christ has an end.[49]

16. *Of the Holy Spirit.* Also you must believe in the Holy Spirit and possess the right knowledge about him, seeing that there are many who are alien to the Holy Spirit and teach a doctrine concerning him that is no better than blasphemy.[50]

[46] Ps. 110:1.
[47] Matt. 24:5. Jerusalem folk would perhaps think of Barcochba, but see below, Lecture xv. 5.
[48] Matt. 24:15.
[49] Marcellus, bishop of Ancyra, prominent among the Consubstantialists at Nicaea, had later exposed the whole Nicene cause to the greatest suspicion, by saying that the eternal Word, consubstantial with the Father, only became the Son of God by incarnation; and was incarnate solely for the salvation of the world. When that purpose has been fully accomplished, Marcellus said, Christ's kingdom will end, and God will be all in all. Marcellus had a deacon named Photinus, who became bishop of Sirmium, and went on teaching Marcellus' doctrine unpunished till very shortly after the date of Cyril's lectures. The news of all these developments must have quickly reached Jerusalem by means of pilgrims. And, as Cyril no doubt saw, the heresies themselves might reach Jerusalem by the same means. Hence this warning.
[50] This is the earliest reference to the currency of a doctrine which reduced the Holy Spirit expressly to the status of a creature. In less than a decade from this lecture, Athanasius was beginning to refute such a doctrine as it had come to his knowledge in Egypt. While it was almost necessarily

But I bid you learn that this Holy Spirit is one and indivisible, but of manifold powers. Many are his activities, but he himself is not parcelled out among them. He knows all mysteries, and "searcheth all things, even the deep things of God."[51] He descended upon our Lord Jesus Christ in the form of a dove. He wrought in the Law and in the prophets. And it is this Holy Spirit that seals your soul now, when the time of your baptism comes. Every intelligible nature has need of sanctification from him. If any dare blaspheme against the Holy Spirit, he has no forgiveness, "either in this world, or in that which is to come."[52] In honour he is honoured with the majesty of the Father and the Son. Thrones and dominions, principalities and powers, depend on him.[53] For there is one God the Father of Christ, and one Lord Jesus Christ the only-begotten Son of God, and one Holy Spirit, who sanctifies all and makes divine,[54] who spoke in the Law and in the prophets, in the old covenant and in the new.

17. Always keep the thought of this sealing in your mind, according to what has now been told you, in a summary way just skimming the surface. But if the Lord permit, I will set it forth, according to my powers, with demonstration from the Scriptures. For when we are dealing with the divine and holy mysteries of the faith, we must not deliver anything whatsoever, without the sacred Scriptures, nor let ourselves be misled by mere probability, or by marshalling of arguments. And do

the sequel to the Arian doctrine of the Son of God, the question of the creaturehood of the Holy Spirit did not become a public issue at once. There was a reason for its early prominence in Palestine, in that Eusebius of Caesarea, in controverting Marcellus, with the works of Origen as his armoury, slipped into plain assertion that the Holy Spirit is a creature. That Cyril should so clearly dissociate himself from the Eusebian doctrine at this point, is proof of his fundamental opposition to any Arian principles. C. R. B. Shapland in Section iii, "Who were the Tropici?" of his introduction to *The Lectures of St Athanasius concerning the Holy Spirit* (London, 1951), may be consulted on the emergence of the doctrine to which Cyril here alludes.

[51] I Cor. 2:10.   [52] Matt. 12:32.
[53] This sentence seems to echo the last part of the 14th Section of Rufinus' version of Origen, *On First Principles*, Book IV, c. iii (expounding Isa. 6:2, 3) where Origen in turn acknowledges debt to his Hebrew teacher.
[54] Encouraged by II Peter 1:4, "that ye might be partakers of the divine nature," Greek Christian theologians thought of salvation in terms of being deified or made divine. Athanasius in particular adopted the watchword, "The Son of God became Man, that we might be deified." Cyril thinks of this "deification" as advancing *pari passu* with sanctification.

not simply credit me, when I tell you these things, unless you get proof from the Holy Scriptures of the things set forth by me. For this salvation of ours by faith is not by sophistical use of words, but by proof from the sacred Scriptures.

18. Next after knowledge of this venerable, glorious, and all holy faith, comes the maxim "Know thyself," who you are; that is to say that man has a twofold constitution, combining soul and body, and that, as we said just now, the same God is creator of your soul and of your body. And, you must know your soul to be endowed with free-will, and to be God's fairest work in the image of himself, its maker. It is immortal in as far as God grants it immortality. It is a rational living creature not subject to decay, because these qualities have been bestowed by God upon it. And it has the power to do what it chooses. For you do not sin because you were born that way, nor if you fornicate is it by chance. And do not take any notice of what some people say, that the conjunctions of the stars compel you to fall into unclean living.[55] Why should you avoid acknowledging that you have done wrong by blaming it onto the stars that had nothing to do with it? I beg of you, never have anything to do with astrologers, for of these men Scripture says, "Let now the astrologers stand up and save thee" and, further on, "Behold they shall be as stubble: the fire shall burn them: they shall not deliver themselves from the power of the flame.[56]

19. Learn this also, that before it came into this world, your soul had committed no sin, but that we come into the world unblemished, and, being here, sin of our own choice.[57] Do not listen, I say, to anyone who expounds "If then I do that which I would not"[58] in the wrong sense, but remember who says, "If ye be willing and obedient, ye shall eat the good of the land; but if ye refuse and rebel, ye shall be devoured with the sword,"[59] and what follows. Remember again, "As ye have yielded your members servants of uncleanness and of iniquity unto iniquity; even so now yield your members servants to righteousness unto holiness."[60] Remember also the passage

55 In Syria and Palestine there was a strong leaning to fatalism, to which astrology provided a show of reason. See Nemesius on this subject, below, p. 400.   56 Isa. 47:13, 14.
57 Cyril thus formally abjures the most offensive feature of Origenism, the doctrine, prefigured in Greek paganism by the speculations of the Orphic poets which Plato describes in his Cratylus, of a prenatal fall of the soul, in consequence of which it was united to a body and set to work out its own purgation in this present life.
58 Rom. 7:16.   59 Isa. 1:19, 20.   60 Rom. 6:19.

where it says, "And as they did not like to retain God in their knowledge,"[61] and the other, "That which may be known of God is manifest in them,"[62] and "their eyes have they closed"[63]; and again where God charges us saying, "Yet I had planted thee a noble vine, wholly a right seed; how then art thou turned into the degenerate plant of a strange vine unto me?"[64]

20. The soul is immortal, and all souls, whether of men or of women, are alike, and the sexes are distinguishable only by their bodily members.[65] There is not one order of souls that naturally sins, and another that is naturally upright,[66] but both sinning and righteous are so by their own choice, being of one form and alike in every particular essential to a soul.

Yes, I know that I am giving a long lecture, and that it is already getting late, but what ought we to think about so much as about salvation? Do you not want to take trouble to get provision for your way, against the heretics? Do you not want to know the twists of the road, so as not, through not knowing, to run over a precipice? If your teachers think it no small gain for you to learn these things, surely you who are learning them ought gladly to welcome a copious instruction!

21. The soul possesses free will. The devil has power to suggest evil, but he was not given the power to compel you against your will. Say that he prompts you to think of fornication. If you please, you have accepted the thought, but if not, then you have not. If you cannot help fornicating, for whom did God prepare a hell? If you do righteousness because you are made like that, and not because you deliberately chose to, for whom has God prepared crowns of inexpressible beauty? A sheep is meek, but no sheep was ever crowned for being it, seeing that it has its meekness by nature, and not because it exercised that choice.

22. *Of the body.* So now, beloved, you know as much as you need to know about the soul. And the next thing is to take in

---

[61] Rom. 1:28.   [62] Rom. 1:19.   [63] Matt. 13:15.   [64] Jer. 2:21.

[65] The development of psychology since Cyril's days has shown this to be an overstatement. The point from which Cyril approaches the question is that if female souls were substantially different from male souls, one must conclude that souls pre-existed and determined the sex of their bodies. Alternatively one must suppose the soul a function of body. Neither supposition would be acceptable to Cyril. Dean Church supposes that Cyril had in view Tertullian, *On the Soul*, c. 36. But it is more likely that he approached the question from review of the speculations of Origen. And his dogmatism is, no doubt, based on Gal. 3:28.

[66] Origen, *On First Principles*, Book III, c. i, Section 8 argues to this effect against Gnostics.

as much as you can about your body. Do not bear with anyone if he says that the body is alien to God. For those who believe that the body is this, and that the soul dwells in the body as in something alien to itself, are quite ready to use the body in fornication.[67] But why have they depreciated this marvellous body? Wherein does it fall short in dignity? What is there about its construction that is not a work of art? Ought not the alienators of the body from God to have taken knowledge of the most brilliant ordaining of eyes? or how the ears are placed right and left, and so receive hearing with nothing in the way? Or how the sense of smell can distinguish one vapour from another, and receives exhalations? Or how the tongue has a double ministry in maintaining the faculty of taste and the activity of speech? How the lungs, hidden away out of sight, keep up the breathing of air with never a pause? Who established the ceaseless beating of the heart? Who distributed blood into so many veins and arteries? Who was so wise as to knit bones to muscles? Who was it that assigned us part of our food for sustenance, and separated off part to form a decent secretion, while hiding away the indecent members in the more fitting positions? Who, when man was so constituted that he will die, ensured the continuance of his kind by making intercourse so ready?[68]

23. Do not tell me that the body is the cause of sin. For were the body the cause of sin, why does no corpse sin? Put a sword into the right hand of a man who has just died, and no murder takes place. Let beauty in every guise pass before a youth just dead, and he will not be moved to fornication. Wherefore so? Because the body does not sin of itself, but it is the soul that sins, using the body.[69]

[67] Cyril may here be drawing upon Irenaeus, *Against Heresies*, Book I, cc. 25, 26, where Irenaeus accuses the Carpocratians and Nicolaitans of justifying indifferent moral conduct on the strength of a dualistic doctrine of creation. The only formidable teachers of dualism that Cyril's hearers were very likely to meet would be Manichees, and the conclusion which Cyril here draws would not apply to them. It would seem rather to be a debating point which Cyril is making, his real concern being to inculcate reverence for the body.

[68] The physiological and anatomical argument for the creation of the body by God, which appears at much greater length in Nemesius, below, had clearly become a commonplace of Christian apologetic. The "decent secretion" is that of fumes through the pores, in contradistinction to the urine and faeces.

[69] In effect, this argument is a development of Rom. 6:7, "He that is dead is freed from sin." It is only valid to prove that the body is not an active

The body is the soul's tool, and also serves as a garment and robe of the soul. If then the body is given over to fornication by the soul, the body is impure, but if it cohabits with a holy soul, it is a temple of the Holy Spirit. This is not my assertion. It was Paul the Apostle that said "Know ye not that your bodies are the temple of the Holy Ghost, which is in you."[70] Take care, therefore, of the body, as the possible temple of the Holy Spirit. Do not pollute your flesh with fornication, and soil what is your fairest robe. But should you have polluted it, cleanse it now by penitence, for this is the time for washing clean.

24. Be attentive to the doctrine of chastity, and especially the order of solitaries and virgins who are successfully accomplishing an angelic life[71] in the world; and after them, let the rest of the people of the Church give heed to chastity. There is a grand crown laid up for you, brethren. Do not barter away a great dignity for a paltry pleasure. Listen to the Apostle saying, "Lest there be any fornicator, or profane person, as Esau, who for one morsel of meat sold his birthright."[72] Henceforth, on account of your purpose of chastity, your name is inscribed in the register of angels. See that you are not expunged again for commerce in fornication.

25. But, again, do not make the opposite mistake of guarding

principle of evil. Cyril is, of course, straining against the tendency to regard the body as unmanageable, to which the Manichees had provided doctrinal support.

[70] I Cor. 6:19.
[71] There grew up, in the fourth century, a fashion of alluding to the life lived by the monks and other ascetics of Egypt and Syria-Palestine, as angelic. By the fifth, as may be judged from the works of Theodoret, "angelical" had become a synonym of "ascetic" as applied to a way of life, or conversation. The primary idea was that the ascetics were giving themselves up wholly to the contemplation of God. Already we find the thought in Clement of Alexandria, who (*Stromateis*, iv, 25) describes the soul of the "True Gnostic" or perfect ascetic as "becoming as it were an angel . . . rapt in contemplation." A more obscure passage in *Stromateis*, vii, 2, sets at the summit of the visible (i.e., human) world, *angelothesia*, transference to the status of angels. Again the contemplative life is the reason. But in the present passage, while the idea of angelic life was no doubt put into Cyril's mind by the current usage, he so expresses himself as to make clear allusion to Luke 20:36, and to think of the solitaries and virgins as "equal unto the angels" because, even on this side of the grave, they "neither marry nor are given in marriage." In a place so far removed from economic independence as Jerusalem where a minimum of material goods could be spared for the unproductive, the Church gained a maximum profit from the accession of men and women devoted to her service and living single and sparingly, as ascetics.
[72] Heb. 12:16.

chastity successfully and being puffed up with disdain of those who have come down to marrying. "For marriage is honourable, and the bed undefiled"[73] in the words of the Apostle. And surely, were not you, who are keeping your purity, sprung from a marriage? Do not, I say, repudiate silver because you possess something golden. Those, on the other hand, who are in wedlock, and are using it aright, are to stand firm in hope: I mean people who see that their wedded life is lawabiding, and do not let it become wanton through immoderate licence: people who recognize times for abstaining "that they may give themselves unto prayer"[74]; people who bring clean bodies, as well as clean clothes, to join in the assemblies in church, having entered wedlock for the sake of offspring, and not for carnal pleasure.

26. Do not let the once-married set at nought those who have come together in marriage for the second time.[75] For continence is a fine thing, and admirable. But folk may be pardoned for contracting a second marriage, lest infirmity end in fornication. "It is good for them if they abide even as I," says the Apostle, "but if they cannot contain, let them marry; it is better to marry than to burn."[76] But every other kind of sex-relation must be put right away, fornication, adultery, and every form of debauchery. The body is to be kept pure for the Lord, that the Lord may look favourably upon the body.

27. *Concerning food.* Let the body have its victuals, that it may live and render its services unimpeded, but not so as to be given to daintiness. Let these be your rules regarding food, since many trip up over meats. There are those who eat things

---

[73] Heb. 13:4. [74] I Cor. 7:5.

[75] There was a very strong prejudice in the early Church against second marriage. The puritan sects, such as that led by Tertullian after he adopted Montanism, and the Novatians, declared remarriage contrary to divine law. The Fathers, giving to the Pastoral Epistles the authority of Paul, first interpreted I Cor. 7:8, 9 as a concession to infirmity, and then I Tim. 3:2, 12, as showing it to be degrading infirmity, disqualifying for office in the Church. The argument based on these texts has been that one who marries twice must be taken thereby to plead incontinence, and cannot therefore be reverenced by the people of the Church. Cyril is unusually liberal in applying the injunction "Judge not" in this connection. Perhaps it counted for something that the emperor Constantius was contemplating remarriage. In Latin Christianity the difficulty of maintaining logically the degrading character of second marriage has led to an argument based on the concept of marriage as a sacrament, which in turn has produced an infinitely complicated law of the relation of marriage to office in the Church.

[76] I Cor. 7:8, 9.

sacrificed to idols without taking any notice. There are others who practise mortification and then pass judgement on those who eat. And so the soul of this person or that is soiled in different ways, all in connection with the question of meats, through their not knowing the sensible grounds for eating or not eating. For we fast by abstaining from wine and from meat, not as though these things were abominations that we must hate, but as expecting a reward for doing so, namely that, in spurning things of sense, we may enjoy a spiritual and heavenly feast, "that sowing now in tears, we may reap in joy,"[77] in the world to come. But do not, in fasting, despise those who are taking such food, and taking it because of bodily infirmity. Do not blame those "who use a little wine, for their stomach's sake, and their often infirmities,"[78] and certainly do not adjudge them to be sinners. Do not abhor flesh-meats as if they were taboo, for the Apostle evidently knew people like that, since he says that there are "who forbid to marry, and command to abstain from meats which God hath created to be received with thanksgiving of them which believe."[79] If therefore you are abstaining from these things, let it not be as from things abominated, or your reward is lost, but as good things let them be transcended, in the quest of the fairer spiritual rewards that are set before you.

28. For the safety of your soul, never eat any food that has been offered to idols, seeing that it is not only I that am concerned about such meats, but the apostles and James the bishop of this Church were so concerned then. And the apostles and elders write a catholic epistle to all the Gentiles, bidding them abstain in the first place from things offered to idols, and after that from blood and anything strangled. For there are many savage races of men who live like dogs, lap up blood, and behave exactly like the wildest of wild beasts, also eating freely anything strangled.[80] But do you, as a servant of Christ, so eat as to eat with reverence. And I need add nothing more on food.

[77] Ps. 126:5.   [78] I Tim. 5:23.   [79] I Tim. 4:3.
[80] Canon law in the Syrian-Palestinian Church grew up at first in a succession of church orders, pseudepigraphically composed to represent the legislation of the apostles. It followed that the apostolic decree of Acts 15:29 must be made part of it, even though it was dubious what the decree meant. We see here the ingenuity of Cyril turned to the task of drawing out an edifying exegesis, by supposing that the apostles, with prophetic foresight that the most savage races would receive the faith, legislated for this in advance, leaving the more civilized to draw the moral "so eat as to eat with reverence."

29. *Of clothes.* Let your clothes be plain, and not showy; for your needful covering and not for vanity; to keep you warm in winter and cover your naked body. But take care that the excuse of covering your naked body does not carry you to the other extreme of over-dressing.

30. *Of our rising again.* Reverence, I pray you, this body of yours, knowing that you will rise from the dead and be judged together with this body. If any suggestion of disbelief should come to you as though such a thing is impossible, look at those facts about yourself that do not meet the eye. Tell me, for example, where do you suppose *you* were, a hundred or more years ago? Out of how very small and inconsiderable a primal matter have you grown up to such big stature and such dignity of form? Well then, cannot he that brought a nothing into being raise up what for a while had being and perished again? Will he who for our sakes raises up the corn that is sown and dies, year by year, find it hard to raise up us ourselves, for whose sakes he was raised up? You see how the trees have been standing now for so many months bare of fruit or leaves, but every one of them, when the winter is over lives again as if from the dead. Shall we then not live again more and more readily than they? By the counsel of God, Moses' rod was transformed into the unlike nature of a serpent, and shall not man be restored to be himself again after he has fallen into death?

31. Do not listen to those who say that this body is not raised up; for raised it is, as Isaiah witnesses, saying, "The dead shall arise, and they in the tombs shall be raised."[81] Or, as Daniel says, "Many of them that sleep in the dust of the earth shall arise; some to everlasting life, and some to everlasting shame."[82] But while rising again is the common lot of all men, the manner of rising again is not alike for all. For while we all receive everlasting bodies, those bodies are not alike for all: that is to say, the righteous receive such bodies as may enable them to join with the band of angels throughout eternity, while sinners receive bodies in which to undergo through the ages the torture of their sins.

32. *Of the font.* Because this is so, the Lord in loving kindness took the initiative and gave us baptismal repentance wherein to cast away the multitude of our sins—I might better say, the whole burden of sin—and receive from the Holy Spirit the seal, so becoming heirs of eternal life. But we have already spoken

81 Isa. 26:19 in the Septuagint.
82 Dan. 12:2.

at sufficient length about the font. So let us come to the introductory instruction that still remains to be given.

33.⌋ *Of the divine Scriptures.* These are the things that we learn[83] from the inspired Scriptures of the Old and the New Testament. For one God is the God of both covenants. In the Old Testament he foretold Christ as he appeared in the New, and was our schoolmaster leading us to Christ by way of Law and prophets. "For before faith came, we were kept under the Law" and "The law was our schoolmaster to bring us unto Christ."[84] And should you ever hear someone of the heretics[85] blaspheming the Law or the prophets, cry out against him this saving phrase and say, "Jesus came not to destroy the law, but to fulfil."[86] And be studious to learn, and that from the lips of the Church, all about the books of the Old Testament, and about those likewise of the New. But I charge you not to read any non-canonical[87] book. For while you remain ignorant of Scriptures that all confess to be inspired, why waste time on questionable reading? Read the divine Scriptures of the Old Testament, which is to say the twenty-two books interpreted by the two and seventy translators.[88]

[83] That is, all that has gone before in this Lecture. Cyril claims to base all the teaching of the Church in Scripture. It is to be noted how final an argument he seems to think it to be, with a Jerusalem audience, that a matter should be asserted in the Old Testament.
[84] Gal. 3:23, 24.   [85] Probably Marcionites.   [86] Matt. 5:17.
[87] The word used is "apocryphal," but it is used here not quite in the same sense as it is today. For Cyril seems to include under apocrypha everything that was not read liturgically in the Church of Jerusalem, while implying that the apocryphal is not all bad. Athanasius, writing some ten years after him (Paschal Letter XXXIX) similarly divides apocrypha into a few good books and an indefinite number of spurious and harmful ones. But apparently the Egyptian Church used the good apocrypha (most of what we know as the Old Testament Apocrypha, together with the Didache and Hermas) as preliminary reading for enquirers. Presumably these books were considered to be good reading, that might acclimatize enquirers to the atmosphere of the Church, but without leaving any enquirer who drew back a claim to know the sacred Scriptures of the Christians. It seems clear that this Athanasian line was not followed at Jerusalem.
[88] That is to say, the Greek version of the Old Testament known as the Septuagint. The account of the origin of the Septuagint that follows, while it seems to show knowledge of the version in Irenaeus, *Against Heresies*, Bk. III, c. xxi, Section 2, is put together with considerable learning, being the neatest summary of the legendary history to come from an ancient writer. Cyril gathers up into one account the various developments which had taken place since the spurious *Letter of Aristeas* (about 100 B.C., the work of an Alexandrine Jew) made the legend

34. For Alexander, king of the Macedonians, when he died, divided his kingdom into four dominions, the first of Babylonia, the next of Macedonia, then Asia, and last Egypt. One of the kings of Egypt was Ptolemy Philadelphus, a king very favourable to learning and a collector of books, indiscriminately. He heard from his chief librarian, Demetrius of Phalerum, of the divine Scriptures of the Law and the prophets. He judged it to be the worthier course, by far, not to get possession of the books by force, from people who gave them up unwillingly,[89] but to conciliate their possessors instead, with gifts and friendliness. He knew that what men surrender unwillingly under pressure they often spoil, whereas if it is forthcoming of the donor's free choice it is authentic throughout. So he despatched lavish presents to the temple then standing in Jerusalem, to Eleazar its high priest, and got him to send him six men out of each of the twelve tribes of Israel as translators. After that he conceived the idea of putting it to the test whether these books were divine scriptures or not. But he was suspicious lest the men sent from Jerusalem might put their heads together. So he assigned to each of the translators who had come to him his own private chamber in the quarter called Pharos in the environs of Alexandria. And there he ordered each of them to translate the whole Scriptures. The men completed their task in two and seventy days, all translating simultaneously in their separate chambers and without having any contact with one another. And when Ptolemy collected together all their translations, he found that they did not merely agree as to the meaning but were verbally identical. For what took place was not the result

popular. The historical probability regarding the Septuagint is that it is the work of a series of translators belonging to Alexandrine Jewry, made with the purpose of halting the Hellenization of their Alexandrine co-religionists, and of keeping them to the faith of their fathers. There are signs that it was at first bitterly resented by the Jewish authorities in Palestine. But as the gain to Judaism from the Greek version became evident, the opportunity arose for covering over the initial tensions by a legendary account of the Greek version that honoured the Jerusalem authorities, while implying the loyalty and missionary success of the Israelites of Alexandria. To the Church Fathers, the existence of a Greek Old Testament seemed so providential that they were ready to take up the Jewish legend as it came to them through "Aristeas," Philo, and Josephus, and to add to it freely. Cyril concludes Section 34 by deducing that the Septuagint, as it lay in the hands of the Church, is verbally inspired of God.

89 An allusion, perhaps, to the last persecution, which began by forcing Christians to surrender their Scriptures to the imperial officers. Ptolemy was more magnanimous than Diocletian.

of sophistry, or contrived by human ingenuity. But just as the Scriptures had been verbally inspired by the Holy Spirit, so the Holy Spirit guided their translation.

35. Read these twenty-two books, and do not have anything to do at all with the uncanonical writings. Give your earnest care to those books only which we read without hesitation in church. The apostles, and the bishops who were set over the churches in ancient times greatly excelled you, both in prudence and piety, and they handed down these Scriptures to us. If you are a son of the Church, you must not modify their canon. And that, as I say, means reading carefully the twenty-two books of the Old Testament, and if you are ready to learn them, I will say over their names, and do you try and commit them to memory. That is to say, in the Law the first are the five books of Moses, Genesis, Exodus, Leviticus, Numbers, Deuteronomy; next, Joshua, the son of Nun, and then the book of Judges, with Ruth,[90] numbered as seventh. Of the remaining historical books, the First and Second Books of Kings count with the Hebrews as one book, and similarly the Third and Fourth Books. In the same way they count as one book the First and Second Books of Chronicles. The First and Second Books of Esdras[91] are counted as one book, while Esther makes the twelfth; so much for the historical books. There are five poetical books, Job, the book of Psalms, Proverbs, Ecclesiastes, and the Song of Songs as seventeenth book. In addition are five prophetical books, that is one book of the Twelve Minor Prophets, one of Isaiah, one of Jeremiah with Baruch, Lamentations and the Epistle to the Captivity,[92] then Ezekiel, and Daniel as the two-and-twentieth book of the Old Testament.

[90] The Canon of Athanasius (Paschal Letter XXXIX) also counts twenty-two books of the Old Testament, but separates Ruth from Judges, and omits Esther.

[91] Not the books of Esdras in our Apocrypha, but the canonical books of Ezra and Nehemiah.

[92] In our Apocrypha, the Epistle of Jeremiah to the Captivity appears as the sixth chapter of the Book of Baruch. Baruch was regarded as canonical by Christian writers from Athenagoras (late second century) to Jerome, who saw it had no place in the Hebrew canon. The praise of Wisdom, 3:9–4:1 specially commended it to the Fathers, as praise of the divine Logos. Cyril, who treats the Wisdom of Solomon and Ecclesiasticus as apocrypha (Athanasius recognizes them as reading for enquirers) thus withdraws authority from them. Nevertheless he cites each of them three times as if they were Scripture. He also cites Susanna and Bel and the Dragon. It is likely enough that both these were incorporated in his Daniel, and not impossible, if unlikely, that Wisdom and Ecclesiasticus

36. Of the New Testament there are four Gospels only. All others are spurious and harmful. And the Manichees forged a Gospel according to Thomas[93] which is smeared with the scent of the name of Gospel to murder the souls of those who are sufficiently foolish. Receive, however, the Acts of the Twelve Apostles, and add the seven General Epistles of James, Peter, John and Jude. The seal set upon them all and the latest work of disciples is the fourteen epistles of Paul.[94] Treat all other Christian writings as in a different class. And anything that is not read in the church do not you read privately, as you have already heard me say. And that is all, on that subject.

37. But do you flee every activity of which the devil is author, and do not heed the serpent that fell away, who in substance was good but of his own deliberate choice transformed himself into what he is. He has the power, I grant you, to win over those who are willing to be won, but he cannot compel anyone to yield. Have nothing to do with astrologers.[95] Have nothing to do with augurs. Take no notice of omens, or believe in the fabulous prophecies of the Greeks. And do not suffer that you should even hear of sorcery, or charms, or the utterly forbidden practices of necromancy. Keep away from every kind of licentiousness. Be no slave to your stomach, nor to any form of pleasure. Rise above avarice of every kind, and scorn usury.

were incorporated with Proverbs. Possibly they were in a class by themselves, being read in the Church of Jerusalem without formal inclusion in the Canon.

93 The "Gospel according to Thomas" of which evidence survives was known to Origen, and cannot be the work of the Manichees. If there was not another so-called Gospel according to Thomas, either composed or revised by the Manichees for propaganda purposes, and if Cyril is mistakenly attributing this Gnostic Gospel to the Manichees, it may be taken as indicating that he regarded Manicheeism as a leading danger.

94 We note the absence of the Apocalypse from Cyril's canon. Eusebius of Caesarea (*Church History*, iii, 24, 25), while acknowledging the degree of acceptance of the Apocalypse for reading in the church, was personally inclined against it, as supporting chiliasm (belief in a thousand-year reign of Christ, coming upon earth). It is accordingly interesting that it should be left out of the Jerusalem Church canon.

95 The passage now commencing has its special interest in indicating the ways in which the Jerusalem Christian had to sever himself from the way of the world that surrounded him. It was a world permeated with superstitions from which the Christian must dissociate himself. The practical influence of Judaism was strong enough to need some determination on the Christian side, if Christians were to treat the Sabbath as a full working-day, and ignore Jewish food rules. And the fourth-century aggressiveness of Samaritanism was sufficient to put it even before Judaism, as a danger to Christian converts.

Take no part in heathen gatherings to see shows. Never, in sickness, resort to amulets. Refuse all the coarseness that goes with the frequenting of taverns. Do not be cajoled into the Samaritan sect or into Judaism, for Jesus Christ has redeemed you henceforth. Keep out of any observance of sabbaths, or recognizing any of the innocent foods as "common or unclean."[96] Have a special abhorrence for all assemblies of wicked heretics. And use every aid to keeping safe your soul, such as fasting, prayer, giving alms, reading the oracles of God: to the end that you may so live the whole remaining time of your life in the flesh in sobriety and godly doctrines, as to enjoy the once-for-all salvation of the font. Being thus enlisted in the armies of heaven by our Father and our God, may you also be accounted worthy of the heavenly crowning, in Christ Jesus our Lord, to whom be glory for ever and ever. Amen.

LECTURE V

On Faith

The Lection is from the Epistle to the Hebrews.[1]

1. How great a dignity the Lord confers on you in your transfer from the order of catechumens to that of believers, is expressed for you by the apostle Paul when he says "God is faithful,"[2] by whom ye were called to the fellowship of his Son Jesus Christ."[3] Called by a God who is faithful, you receive this epithet as well, and so are the recipient of a great dignity. For as God has the titles, good, righteous, almighty, creator of the universe, so also he has the title faithful. Think therefore to what a dignity you are promoted in now coming to share one of the divine titles!

2. That being the situation, it is to be expected henceforth that any one of you will be found sincerely a believer. For "a faithful man, who can find?"[4] It is not a case of your proving your sincerity to me, for you are not going to be "judged of

96 The allusion is to Acts 10:14.
1 The Lection was the 11th ch. of Heb. to the end of v. 31.
2 See Note 20 to the Procatechesis. Cyril chooses the moment of the communication of the creed as that in which the *photizomenoi* become believers, whereas most chose the moment of actual baptism. Cyril, in short, stresses the subjective aspect of illumination to an unusual degree.
3 I Cor. 1:9.   4 Prov 20:6.

man's judgement."⁵ It is to God that you must show the purity of your faith, and he "trieth the reins and the hearts"⁶ and "knoweth the thoughts of men."⁷ It is no slight matter that a man should be faithful, for if he is, he is richer than if he had all wealth. "For to the faithful man belongs the whole world of riches,"⁸ in the sense that he despises them and tramples them under foot. For people who are rich as far as the eye of man can see, and have great possessions, are poor so far as their souls are concerned, and in proportion as they have gathered much, they pine away with coveting what they have not got. But your man of faith, by the greatest of paradoxes, abounds in his want, as knowing that all a man needs is raiment and food: so, in having these, and being content, he has trampled riches under foot.

3. For it is not only we who bear Christ's name that set great store by faith. For all the business transacted in the world, inclusive of that of persons alien to the Church, is transacted on the basis of faith. It is on this basis that the marriage laws bring into intimate partnership persons who were strangers to one another, and because of the faith that we put in marriage compacts, a completely unknown man is made free of persons and goods that were none of his. Faith again is the basis of farming, for unless a man believes that he will gather in the fruits of the earth he will not sustain the toils of it. Faith is the basis of seafaring, wherein men put their trust in quite a small wooden structure, and leave earth, the steadiest of the elements, for the uncertain motion of the waves, because they have first committed themselves to hopes that are not certainties, and taken aboard their faith as a surer hold than any anchor. Practically all human affairs are maintained on a basis of faith, and this is not something that we alone believe, but, as we said, the non-Christian world believes it too. It may be that they do not receive the Scriptures: all the same, they have such and such doctrines of their own to propose which likewise they espouse by faith.⁹

4. Today's Lection calls you to a true faith and furthermore sets before you the way in which you must walk if you are to please God. For it says "without faith it is impossible to please

⁵ I Cor. 4:3.   ⁶ Ps. 7:9.   ⁷ Ps. 94:11.
⁸ An insertion commonly found after Prov. 17:6 in the Septuagint text.
⁹ Cyril, having used faith, in this section, with different nuances of meaning, brings it at the last to meaning assent and adhesion to dogma. All men have dogmas, and not those only who draw them (as Cyril will always do) from Scripture.

him."[10] When, I ask you, will a man be found proposing to serve God, in the absence of any faith that God rewards such service? How long will a girl guard her maidenhood, or a youth contain himself, if they do not believe in an unfading crown for chastity? Faith is the eye that enlightens every conscience and fills it with understanding. For so says the prophet, "and if ye believe not, neither shall ye understand."[11] According to Daniel faith "stops the mouths of lions"[12] in that Scripture says of him "Daniel was taken up out of the den, and no manner of hurt was found upon him, because he believed in his God."[13] Is there any foe grimmer than the devil? And yet we have no other armour against him but our faith, a spiritual shield against an invisible foe. For he goes on firing every kind of missile, and in the black night he shoots down such as are not on their watch. But against a foe who does not show himself we have, in our faith, a stout protection, according to the Apostle's words, "Above all, taking the shield of faith, wherewith ye shall be able to quench all the fiery darts of the wicked."[14] And very often it is that the devil fires the "fiery dart" of lust for some shameful pleasure. But faith conjures up the picture of judgement due, and so quenches the dart by cooling down the inflamed imagination.[15]

10. The word faith is one word in the vocabulary, but has two separate meanings. For there is one kind of faith that has to do with doctrines, and involves the assent of the mind in respect to such and such a doctrine. Such faith is a boon to the soul, as the Lord says, "He that heareth my words, and believeth in him that sent me, hath everlasting life, and shall not come into condemnation"[16] and "he that believeth on the Son is not condemned; but is passed from death unto life."[17] O how great is God's loving-kindness! For whereas righteous men of old were well-pleasing to God over many years, Jesus now freely grants to you for one hour's devotion just what they obtained for succeeding in being well-pleasing to God over many years.[18] For if you believe that Jesus Christ is Lord and that

[10] Heb. 11:6.   [11] Isa. 7:9 in the Septuagint.
[12] Heb. 11:33.   [13] Dan. 6:23.   [14] Eph. 6:16.
[15] For brevity, sections 5–9 inclusive are omitted.   [16] John 5:24.
[17] John 3:18 combined with John 5:24.
[18] The Old Testament presents us with righteous men in whom God was well pleased. Their righteousness was established under long testing. Christ's gift to us is a not-inferior righteousness, acquired in one hour. The hour which Cyril has in mind must thus be the hour of baptism. Hence the comparison which Cyril makes with the eleventh-hour faith

God raised him from the dead, you shall be saved and translated to paradise by him who led the robber into paradise. And do not doubt the possibility of this. For he who, on this holy Golgotha,[19] saved the robber for one hour of faith, will also himself effectively save you for believing.

11. But the second kind of faith is that given by Christ by a particular grace. "For to one is given by the Spirit the word of wisdom, to another the word of knowledge by the same Spirit; to another faith by the same Spirit, to another gifts of healing."[20] Now this faith that is given by the Spirit as a grace is not only doctrinal faith, but one that empowers activities surpassing human nature. For anyone who has this faith will "say to this mountain, Remove hence to yonder place, and it shall remove."[21] For when anyone by faith says this believing that it will happen, and not doubting in his heart, then indeed he is the recipient of that grace. It is of such faith that is said "If ye have faith as a grain of mustard seed."[22] For just as a grain of mustard seed is of little bulk but of explosive energy, taking a trifling space for its planting and then sending out great branches all round, so that when it is grown it can give shelter to the birds, so in like manner the faith present in a man's soul achieves the greatest things by the most summary decision. For such an one places the thought of God before his mind and, as far as enlightenment by faith permits it, espies God. His mind also ranges through the world from end to end, and with the end of this age not yet come, beholds the judgement already, and the bestowal of the promised rewards. Hold firm, therefore, to that faith in him which you possess, so that you may receive in addition, and likewise from him, that which empowers activities surpassing human nature.

12. Now the one and only faith that you are to take and preserve in the way of learning and professing it is that which is now being committed to you by the Church as confirmed throughout the Scriptures. For seeing that not everyone can read the Scriptures, some because they lack the learning and others because, for one reason or another, they find no opportunity to get to know them, we gain possession of the whole doctrine of the Christian faith in a few articles, and that to

of the penitent thief, which was, by Christ, made the means of a free grant of righteousness.

19 Cyril thinks of the holy sites as eloquent witnesses of what happened upon them.

20 I Cor. 12:8, 9.   21 Matt. 17:20.   22 *Idem.*

prevent any soul from being lost through not learning the faith. This doctrine I want you to commit to memory word for word and say it over to one another as much as you can, not writing it out on paper but using memory to engrave it on your heart. But take care lest, in giving your whole mind to this, you should, by any chance, let any catechumen overhear what you have had committed to you. I want you to retain this provision for your way as long as your life shall last, and not to receive any other faith than this henceforth: not even if I were to change my mind and say something that contradicted what you are now being taught; no, nor if a dark angel were to disguise himself as an angel of light and made to lead you astray. "For though we, or an angel from heaven, preach any other gospel unto you than that ye have received, let him be accursed."[23] And at this stage listen to the exact form of words and memorize this faith, leaving it to the appropriate season for each of the articles which it contains to be built up from Holy Scripture. For these articles of our faith were not composed out of human opinion, but are the principal points collected out of the whole of Scripture to complete a single doctrinal formulation of the faith. And in like manner as the mustard seed contains numbers of branches-to-be within its tiny grain, so also this creed[24] embraces in a few phrases all the religious knowledge contained in the Old and New Testaments together. Look now, brethren, and "hold the traditions"[25] which are now being imparted to you, and "write them on the table of your hearts."[26]

[23] Gal. 1:8, 9.
[24] Literally "faith." Cyril never uses the technical word for a creed, *symbolon*. At the same time he cannot be said to use *Pistis* (faith) as a synonym for creed. It is always the context that determines when he is using it in that sense. Perhaps he wished to avoid a specific term for something which was to be received as a secret.
[25] II Thess. 2:15.
[26] Prov. 7:3. In some manuscripts this is immediately followed by the text of the Nicene Creed. The transcribers of the lecture abstained, of course, from writing down what Cyril evidently recited, article by article, at this point, viz. the baptismal creed of the Church of Jerusalem. The work of reconstructing this creed, mainly from the language of the lectures, but with some other available evidence, has reached a degree of certainty, with the one doubtful point as to whether the Jerusalem creed contained any reference to the descent into Hades. The text as given in G. L. Hahn, *Bibliothek der Symbole und Glaubensregeln der alten Kirche* (1897, pp. 132–4) may be rendered as follows:
We believe in one God the Father Almighty, Maker of heaven and earth, and of all things visible and invisible. And in one Lord Jesus Christ, the only-begotten Son of God, true God begotten of the Father

13. Preserve them with godly fear, lest the Enemy spoil any of you through your conceit, or some heretic misrepresent any of the things you have had delivered to you. Faith, you see, is like cash paid over the counter[27] (which is what I have now done) but God requires you to account for what you have had: as the Apostle says, "I charge thee before God, who quickeneth all things, and before Jesus Christ, who before Pontius Pilate witnessed a good confession that ye keep without spot, until the appearing of our Lord Jesus Christ"[28] this faith committed to you. A treasure of life[29] has now been committed to you, and at his coming the Master looks for the deposit, "which in his times he shall show, who is the blessed and only Potentate, the King of kings and Lord of lords, who only hath immortality, dwelling in the light that no man can approach unto, whom no man hath seen or can see, to whom be honour and glory world without end." Amen.[30]

> before all worlds, by whom all things were made; who was made flesh and was incarnate, crucified and entombed, who rose again on the third day and ascended into the heavens, and sat down on the right hand of the Father; who is coming in glory to judge the quick and the dead, whose kingdom shall have no end. And in one Holy Spirit, the Paraclete, that spake in the prophets. And in one baptism of repentance for the remission of sins, and in one holy catholic Church, and in the resurrection of the flesh, and in the life of the world to come.
>
> When this creed is compared with the baptismal creed of Caesarea, as Eusebius represented it at the Council of Nicaea, its general similarity of construction is obvious. But those features of Eusebius' creed that bespeak the theological influence of Origen upon the doctrine of the Caesarean Church are largely missing from Cyril's Jerusalem creed, while, on the other hand, there are (especially in the later part of the creed) expressions which seem to represent developments that had taken place in doctrinal emphasis in the quarter-century following Nicaea. The sacredness and traditional character of baptismal formularies does not seem to have excluded the right of the bishop to add and develop, provided that there were no reversal of the tradition thereby.
>
> 27 The payment of cash by the banker only takes place when his client has handed in some bond or security for the money, such as an undertaking to repay capital and interest under such and such circumstances. Cyril implies that the *photizomenoi* are likewise under an obligation, incurred by the receiving of the creed, for which they must account at the Day of Judgement.
> 28 A joining together of I Tim. 5:21, with 6:13 and 14 of the same Epistle.
> 29 The creed here seems to be pictured as a sum of money which, if it can be produced intact at the Last Day, will purchase for its holder eternal life.
> 30 In this lecture Cyril inserts I Tim. 6:15, 16 before his usual concluding formula, making the initial "which" refer not to the Second Coming but to the "deposit" which the *photizomenoi* have just received.

LECTURE VI

Of the Monarchy[1] of God

The Lection is from the prophecy of Isaiah.[2]

1. "Blessed be the God and Father of our Lord Jesus Christ"[3]; for in the thought of God, let the thought of Father be included, so that the glory which we ascribe to the Father and the Son with the Holy Spirit may be perfectly free from difference.[4] For the Father has not one glory and the Son another, but their glory is one and the same; since the Son is the Father's sole-begotten, and when the Father is glorified the Son shares in enjoyment of his glory, and because the Son draws his glory from the honouring of the Father, and again whenever the Son is glorified the Father of so excellent a Son is greatly honoured.

2. Now the mind thinks with great rapidity, but the tongue needs expressions and a long outpouring of words before it reaches a conclusion. For, in one instant, the eye takes in a vast multitude of stars, but if anyone should want to discourse on any particular stars, as, for instance, to pick out the morning star or the evening star, or any single star, he will need to say a good deal. Again in like manner the mind comprehends earth and sea and all the bounds of the world in a flash, but it takes it many words to express what it understands in a twinkling. The example,[5] then, that I have adduced is a very strong one, and yet it is weak and inadequate for the purpose in hand.

---

[1] That is, that God is the sole original and final principle of all things. As a consequence, Newman says, the doctrine of Monarchy means "that the Second and Third Persons are ever to be referred in our thoughts to the First as the Fountain of Godhead."

[2] The Lection was Isa. 45:17–25.   [3] II Cor. 1:3.

[4] Cyril thus expresses what later took classical form in the saying of John Damascene (*Orthodox faith*, I. 15), that "the Father is the fount and cause of the Son and Holy Spirit." When we think of God as Father, straightaway the Trinity is before the mind. Arius followed the Greek ethnic approach in which God is indivisible and ultimate reality, to which concept the appelation Father applies only as a Name, and the Son, catachrestically so called, is but a created intermediary. This sentence of Cyril's therefore testifies how fundamentally alien was Arianism to his mind.

[5] The thing to be exemplified is that even the simple know, in a flash of intuition, the meaning of the word God, but to unfold that knowledge in discursive reasoning is the hopeless task of theology.

For what we say about God is not what should be said (for that is known only to him) but only what human nature takes in, and only what our infirmity can bear. For what we expound is not what God is, but (and we frankly acknowledge it) the fact that we have no sure knowledge about him; and that is to say that our chief theological knowledge is confessing that we have none. Therefore, "magnify the Lord with me, and let us exalt his name together,"[6] since one alone is unequal to the task. Rather I should say, if all of us unite for it, it will still be beyond us; and in saying that I do not mean just us who are here, but that if all the children of the Church throughout the world, both to this day and for all time to come, united to the task, we still should not be able worthily to hymn our Shepherd.[7]

3. Abraham was a great man and honourable, that is to say, by human standards, but when he looked to meet with God he declared frankly and with truth "I am earth and ashes."[8] He did not say "earth" and stop at that, lest he should name himself from the first of the elements, but he added "and ashes" to indicate how unenduring and rotten he was. It is as if he said, is there anything less substantial or lighter than ash? For (we may imagine him saying) make comparison of ash with a house, and then of a house with a city; then of a city with a province, then of a province with the Roman empire, then of the Roman empire with the whole earth as far as its furthest bounds, then the whole earth with heaven in whose bosom earth lies. Now earth has the same ratio to heaven as an axle has to the whole circumference of a wheel. Then think how that this first heaven which we see is smaller than the second, and the second than the third, seeing that that is the last named in Scripture: not that that means there are no more, but only that it is convenient that we should know so far and no more.[9] And if your mind

6 Ps. 34:3.
7 The choice of this title is dictated by the fact that the Church is the Lord's flock. If the task of theology is hopeless, so, says Cyril, is the Church's task of worship. But neither task may be for that reason abandoned. In what follows, the impossibility and necessity of either task is elaborated. 8 Gen. 18:27.
9 In early Christian writers we meet with a scheme of three heavens, and another of seven heavens. The two are not necessarily irreconcilable. The first is firmly in accord with the language of Scripture, which speaks of the upper atmosphere, the place of clouds and birds, as heaven, and of a sphere determining the motion of the heavenly bodies, as heaven, and of a heaven beyond this, inhabited by saints and angels, in which Paradise may be sited. So these three heavens might be called the aerial, the aetherial, and the third heaven. Primitive astronomy suggested that

could see in thought all the heavens, neither would those heavens be able to praise God as he deserves, though they rang with voices louder than thunder. Now if these heavens and all they contain cannot worthily sing the praises of God, how possibly can earth and ashes, the least and slightest of existing things, upraise a worthy hymn to God, "who holds in his hand the circle of the earth, and considers the inhabitants thereof as grasshoppers."[10]

4. If any would take in hand to discourse of God, let him first expound what are the bounds of the earth. The earth is your dwelling, and yet you do not know the extent of your dwellingplace, earth! How then can you have any adequate thoughts of its Creator? You see the stars, but their Maker you do not see. Then count those you see and after that tell us of him whom you do not see, "who telleth the number of the stars and calleth them all by their names."[11] Quite recently a furious downpour of rain came little short of flooding us out. Tell me how many drops fell on this city only: or I will not say the city; tell me, if you can, how many drops an hour struck your house! But you cannot, and therein see how little is your strength. And from that take knowledge of the might of God, for "by him are numbered the drops of rain"[12] not only that came down then, all over the world, but at any time in history. Or the sun is God's work, and a great work, too, though small enough compared with the sky. First have a good look at the sun, and when you have done that get busy on God! "Seek not that which is deeper than thou, and that which is stronger than thou search not out; but what is appointed thee, that consider."[13]

5. But some one will ask, If the divine Being is incomprehensible, what is the good of the things you have been saying?

the second heaven was the space between two vast spheres concentric with the earth, and this is the ground of Cyril's axle-and-wheel comparison. It was natural to go on to picture the third heaven as a still greater concentric sphere. But Gregory of Nyssa (*On the six days of Creation*, Bk. I, towards the end) expresses the reaction of philosophic Christians to this notion, by arguing, on the ground of II Cor. 12:2-4, that this third heaven is incorporeal. But no early Christian writer followed up this thought to the extent of proposing a concept of heaven divorced from all notion of spatiality. Many Christians accepted, no doubt ultimately from Jewish and oriental sources, a belief that there are seven heavens, and generally supposed them concentric with earth. Cyril seems ready to accept this idea, and the more so because it falls in with his argument of things that are greater and greater as they recede from our knowledge.

[10] Isa. 40:22.   [11] Ps. 147:4.   [12] Job 36:27.   [13] Ecclus. 3:21, 22.

Come now, am I not to take a reasonable drink because I cannot drink the river dry? Of course I cannot bear to fix my gaze upon the sun in his strength. But is that any reason for not glancing up at him if I need? Or supposing that I were to go into a huge garden such that I could not possibly eat all the fruit on the trees, would you have me leave it still hungry? I praise and glorify our Maker, seeing that "Let everything that hath breath praise the Lord"[14] is a divine command. I am now trying to glorify the Master, not to expound his nature, for I know quite well that I shall fall far short even of glorifying him as he deserves. Nevertheless I hold it to be a religious duty at least to make the attempt. For the Lord Jesus comforts me for for my insufficiency by saying "No man hath seen God at any time."[15]

6. What then, someone asks, does not Scripture say "the angels of the little ones always behold the face of my Father which is in heaven?"[16] Truly it does, but the angels do not see God as he is, but only as far as they can, being what they are. For the same Jesus says, "not that any hath seen the Father, save he which is of God: he hath seen the Father."[17] Angels see in the measure of their capacity, and archangels up to their power. Thrones and dominations have greater vision than those, but still less than the reality.[18] Only the Holy Ghost, together with the Son, has a true vision of God, "searcheth all things, and knoweth even the deep things of God,"[19] as also the only-begotten Son has essential knowledge of the Father, together with the Holy Spirit: as he says "neither knoweth anyone the Father save the Son, and he to whomsoever the Son will reveal him."[20] For he has the essential vision, and reveals God through the Spirit according to each man's capacity.[21] And this is because the only-begotten Son is, with the Holy Spirit, sharer in the Father's Godhead. He whose

14 Ps. 150:6.
15 John 1:18, where, however, the words directly form part of the testimony of John.
16 Matt. 18:10. 17 John 6:46.
18 Arius, in his *Thalia* had placed the Son of God within this series, so that the final clauses applied to him. By placing the Holy Spirit as well as the Son out of this series, Cyril not only severs himself from the Arians, but, by anticipation as we may say, from the Macedonians also.
19 I Cor. 2:10. 20 Matt. 11:27.
21 The limiting factor is not the Spirit's inability to reveal but our inability to receive.

passionless begetting was before the ages began[22] knows his
Begetter, and he who begat knows him who was begotten.
Therefore, when angels are ignorant (for the only-begotten, as
we said, reveals to each in the measure of his capacity, through
the Holy Spirit),[23] let no man be ashamed to avow his ignorance.
I am now speaking, and all of us sometimes speak. And yet we
are incapable of saying how we speak. How then can we discourse of the Giver of the faculty of speech? I have a soul and
cannot tell what is the nature of the soul. How then shall I be
able to describe the Dispenser of souls?

7. This is sufficient by itself for our religion, that we know
that we have a God, that we have one God, a God who is,[24] a
God ever existing and ever self-existent, with none from whom
he was begotten, with none mightier than himself, whom none
will follow by taking from him his kingdom, of many names, all-
powerful, and of singular substance. For the fact that he is
called good, righteous, almighty, sabaoth,[25] does not mean
anything of variance or difference in him, but that, being one
and the same, he is the source of countless divine activities. He
does not exceed in this and come behind in that, but is in all
things his own divine self. He is not less wise because of his

---

[22] Consideration of the variant readings and the awkward grammar of the
received text suggest that what Cyril said was probably "He who was
begotten knows his Begetter," and that the qualification of the begetting
of the Son as passionless and pre-temporal was introduced into the text
at a later stage, when, in the Arian controversy, the orthodox had to
defend their doctrine from the consequence drawn by their opponents
from the notion of divine generation. This was that, at a point in con-
ceptual history, something happened to God; "passionless" does not
mean, here, "without sexual passion," but "without God experiencing
change." It is unlikely that this stage of controversial argument was in
view at the time of the lecture.

[23] So Cyril withdraws from angels any direct or natural knowledge of God,
unmediated by the work of the Spirit.

[24] The reference is to God's self-revelation in Ex. 3:14. In the Septuagint
it appears as "I am that I am," which lent itself, in the mind of Greek
readers, to be regarded as a philosophic definition. The Hebrew text
was certainly not inspired by abstract thought of this kind, but saw in
this declaration the revelation of a living God who will show what he
is, and wills. Cyril is not so acutely Hellenized as to be in danger of falling
short of the Old Testament doctrine of God, although his language and
reasoning are Greek.

[25] Sabaoth is often coupled, as a title, to the name Jehovah in the Old
Testament, and means God of Hosts (primitively, of the armies of Israel).
In the Septuagint, the name and title together were rendered *Kyrios
Sabaoth*, where it appeared as if *Kyrios* (Lord) was the title and *Sabaoth*
the name. And as such Cyril regards it.

great loving-kindness, but has wisdom in the same degree as he has loving-kindness. He does not sometimes see and sometimes wink at what he might see, but is all eye, all ear, all mind.[26] He is not as we are, in one thing understanding, in another ignorant. For to think him so would be blasphemy and an outrage against the divine Being. God foreknows what will come to pass. God is holy and almighty, and exceeds all in goodness, greatness and wisdom. We shall never be able to express his shape and form. "Ye have neither heard his voice at any time, nor seen his shape",[27] says the Scripture. Wherefore Moses says to the Israelites, "Take ye therefore good heed unto yourselves: for ye saw no manner of similitude."[28] For if it is quite impossible to picture what he is like, the notion of his Being will surely be immediate.[29]

LECTURE X

On the Clause "And in one Lord Jesus Christ"

The Lection is from the First Epistle to the Corinthians.[1]

3. You are to believe "in one Lord Jesus Christ, the only-begotten Son of God."[2] We say "one" Lord Jesus Christ to show that his sonship is unique. We say "one" to stop anyone dreaming that there could be another. We say "one" lest you should hear of his work under manifold names and fall into the blasphemous notion that it is the work of a plurality of sons.[3] For he is called a door. But you must not think of a wooden

26 Dr. Gifford, in his notes to this section, calls attention to the closeness of Cyril's expressions to some passages in Irenaeus, *Against heresies*, which makes it likely enough that Cyril had read that work. The Jerusalem church library, begun by Alexander, makes it the less surprising that Cyril should have such learning.
27 John 5:37.   28 Deut. 4:15.
29 Moses treats the people as knowing God, and yet insists that they have seen nothing. Therefore, Cyril argues, they must have a means of immediate knowledge. As this knowledge would be endangered by their trying to establish knowledge otherwise, it is, as direct and mystical, a true knowledge, upon which faith should rest before all other. We thus reach the conclusion of the argument commencing in Section 2 above. The rest of Lecture VI is omitted, as also Lectures VII, VIII and IX on God as Father, Almighty, and Creator.
1 The Lection was I Cor. 8:5–9:23.
2 Two opening sections are omitted for brevity.
3 Leading gods and goddesses of Greek paganism were each known under manifold names, in accordance with their different cult-representations.

door. You must think of a spiritual door that reasons and is alive, and knows all about those that enter. He has the title way; not as if he were trodden by our feet, but as bearing us on our way to our Father in the heavens. He is called sheep, not as if he were an animal, but to express the fact that he cleanses the whole world of sins by his precious blood, that he was led "before his shearer" and knew when was the time to be "dumb." [4] This sheep is equally called shepherd, and says "I am the good shepherd." [5] By his manhood he is sheep, by his divine loving-kindness he is shepherd. Do you want to be assured that there are human sheep? The Saviour tells the apostles "Behold I send you as sheep in the midst of wolves." [6] He is called, again, lion; not of the man-eating kind, but to point out, as it were, by this name, how royal, immovable, and boldly confident is his nature. He is called lion also as opposing the lion that we are afraid of, that roars and then swallows up such as are taken in. [7] For the Saviour came to tread down our adversary and rescue those that put their trust in him, not as if he put aside the gentleness that is his by nature, but as the strong "Lion of the tribe of Judah." [8] And he is called a stone, not such an inanimate stone as is quarried by the hands of men, but such a "chief corner-stone" as that "whosoever believeth in him shall not be ashamed." [9]

4. He is called Christ, [10] not for any unction from human

What was, to the poets, the single divine identity of Zeus, or Athene was worshipped differently in the various local cult forms. But for the common people this was too subtle a thought. For them, Zeus under different names was so many different divinities. It is said that, in our own times, Italian peasants have supposed Our Lady of A to be a different being from Our Lady of B. For the simple, the local and particular is most easily grasped. To equate or identify it, on the other hand, with something elsewhere, and different in form, presents difficulty. Cyril may have had reason to fear something of this sort at Jerusalem, with regard to Christ, worshipped as the divine Babe at Bethlehem, as Sufferer on Mount Golgotha, and as King of heaven on the Mount of Olives. He accordingly follows Clement of Alexandria in teaching that the different names and offices of Christ reflect the variety of our needs, and not any division of his Person and nature.

[4] Isa. 53:7.   [5] John 10:11.   [6] Matt. 10:16.
[7] Cyril labours the point that Satan has no might, and can only be an object of fear to us by deceiving us on this point. Those only whom he deceives fall into his power.
[8] Rev. 5:5.   [9] Isa. 28:16.
[10] Christ means "anointed," and unction appears in the Old Testament as the means of dedicating to their office kings, priests, and prophets. For Cyril, it always suggests priestly unction, and so our Lord's high-priest-

hands, but from the Father's, as having been anointed for eternal high-priesthood on behalf of men. He is called the dead, not as having gone to "join the majority," like all souls in Hades, but as the one "free among the dead."[11] He is called Son of Man, not as it is said of each one of us that we sprang from earth, but in the context of his "coming in the clouds of heaven"[12] to judge both the quick and the dead.[13] He is called Lord, but not in the catachrestic sense in which the title is given to men, but as possessing Lordship by right of nature and for ever.[14] He is called Jesus because the name fits him,[15] and he has that appellation in view of the saving medicine he brings. He is called Son, not meaning that God promoted him to that dignity, but that he was naturally begotten as Son. Many indeed are the names of our Saviour. And so, lest the plurality of names should suggest to you a plurality of sons, and in view of the heretical error according to which Christ and Jesus are not one and the same,[16] with the door likewise and all the other names, the faith keeps you out of danger by saying "In one Lord Jesus Christ": for though the names are many, their bearer is one.

5. It is for the good of each individual that the Saviour comes in many characters. For to those who need cheering, he proposes himself as vine, while he stands as door before those who should be entering. He stands before those who have prayers to pray, as their mediating high priest. He is sheep,

hood. But Christ's priesthood is, for Cyril, eternal and from the beginning; it is not pictured as commencing with the incarnation. The unction is therefore an expression for something wholly spiritual and divine, whereby the Son received high-priesthood from and to the Father.

11 Rev. 1:18 and Ps. 88:5.   12 Dan. 7:13.

13 John 5:27, where the authority of the Son to judge men is based on his being Son of man, is here used to interpret Dan. 7:14 as primarily constituting him Judge of the great assize. Cyril must not, of course, be taken as saying that Jesus is not named Son of man as sharing our earthly nature by incarnation, but as saying that the name has its chief significance at a higher level. Finally Cyril fetches the exposition of this name round to support a clause of the creed.

14 W. Bousset's Kyrios Christos (1921) first brought before the modern public the difference between the catachrestic and proper use by the ancients of the epithet Kyrios (Lord). In its proper use it was a divine title. And that is what Cyril is saying in this passage.

15 Jesus is the Greek form of the Hebrew name Joshua or Jeshua meaning "Jehovah is salvation." So the angel of Matt. 1:21 says "for he shall save his people from their sins."

16 Irenaeus, Against heresies, III. xvi. 8 enumerates Cerinthians, Ebionites, Ophites and Valentinians as distinguishing between Jesus and Christ. Cyril may have the passage in view.

again, to those with sins upon them, to be slain for those sins. He "becomes all things to all men,"[17] and yet never changes from what he is in his own proper nature. For he goes on possessing the dignity of sonship that truly resists all change, and at the same time adapts himself to our infirmities as, shall we say, the very kindest of physicians or as an understanding teacher. He really is Lord, not as having step by step[18] attained to lordship, but as having by nature the dignity of being Lord. He is not called Lord by courtesy as we are, but as being Lord in sheer fact, since he bears sway over all that he has himself created, and the Father wills it so. For if we bear sway, it is over men of equal status and like passions with ourselves, and often over our seniors; and very often a young master rules over old servants. But the lordship of our Lord Jesus Christ is not like that, but he is Maker first and Lord second. First he made all things by the Father's will, and thereafter is Lord of all he made.

6. Christ is Lord, who was born in the city of David.[19] Would you be glad to know that Christ is Lord with his Father and was so before his incarnation? When I say that so it is, I do not want you simply to accept it as part of the faith, but to know how it is proved from the Old Testament Scripture. Look in the first book, Genesis. God says "Let us make man." He does not say, In my image, but, "In our image."[20] And when Adam had come into being, it says, "And the Lord created man; in the image of God created he him."[21] For it does not restrict the dignity of Godhead to the Father only, but associates the Son with him in it, to indicate that man was not only made by God, but therewith by our Lord Jesus Christ, who himself is true God. Now the Lord Jesus joins in working whatever the Father works, and he did so in the matter of Sodom, as the Scripture says, "And the Lord rained upon Sodom and upon Gomorrah brimstone and fire from the Lord out of heaven."[22] Again the Lord Jesus appeared to Moses to that

---

[17] I Cor. 9:22.

[18] *ek procopēs*, progressively. Cyril's third-century predecessor, Hymenaeus, had opposed Paul of Samosata, bishop of Antioch, for teaching that Jesus, mere man by origin, attained divine sonship in this way. Cyril was, however, probably aware of the revival by the Arians of a modified form of this doctrine, based on the combination of Phil. 2:9 with Ps. 45:7, in support of the belief that Christ was a creature. If so, he clearly severs himself from them.

[19] Luke 2:11, a text likely to be very familiar to Jerusalemites, who would need to be reminded that Christ did not begin to be, in the city of David.

[20] Gen. 1:26.   [21] Gen. 1:27 (Septuagint).   [22] Gen. 19:24.

extent to which Moses was able to behold him; for the Lord is kind and ever adapts himself to our infirmities.

7. That you may know, further, that it is the Lord Jesus that appeared to Moses,[23] listen to Paul's testimony; "they drank of that spiritual rock that followed them, and that rock was Christ."[24] And another passage; "by faith Moses forsook Egypt" followed shortly by the words "esteeming the reproach of Christ greater riches than all the treasures in Egypt."[25] It was Moses that said to him "Show me thyself." (Note that the prophets as well beheld Christ in those days, only in the degree that each was able.) "Show me thyself, that I may see thee with understanding."[26] And the Lord replied "There shall no man see my face and live."[27] This was the reason, therefore, that, inasmuch as none could behold the face of Godhead and live, the Lord took him a human face[28] that we can look upon and live. But even this, when he chose to let a small part of its glory be manifest and "his face did shine as the sun,"[29] made the disciples fall to the ground with fear. Now if his human face shone, not as he could have made it but as much as the disciples could bear, and even so they could not endure it, how could anyone look boldly upon the majesty of God?

The Lord said, It is a great thing, Moses, for which you ask, and I approve your insatiable desire. "And I will do this thing also that thou hast spoken,"[30] only so far as you can bear it. "Behold, I will put thee in a cleft of the rock,"[31] for seeing that you are small, you can lodge in a small space.

8. At this point I ask you to get a very firm hold of what will be said, with an eye to Jews. My aim is to prove that the Lord Jesus Christ was then with the Father. Accordingly the Lord says to Moses, "I will pass before thee with my glory, and will proclaim the name of the Lord before thee."[32] Since it is the

23 The theory that the Son of God, by some anticipation of incarnation, was the subject of the theophanies recorded in the Old Testament, appears first in Justin Martyr's *Dialogue with Trypho the Jew*. It was the anti-Jewish polemic that gave point to this teaching. Cyril shows, in the opening of Section 8 below, that the interest of these sections, for him, is that they arm the *photizomenoi* for argument with Jews.
24 I Cor. 10:4.   25 Heb. 11:26 with the order reversed.
26 Ex. 33:13.   27 Ex. 33:20.
28 *Prosōpon*, which could mean an actor's mask, as well as the natural face. Cyril identifies *prosōpon* with "natural face" at the Transfiguration. But in the theophany to Moses a masking of glory is related, which Cyril regards as expressing the same principle of condescension to our weakness as in the incarnation (see Note 23).
29 Matt. 17:2.   30 Ex. 33:17.   31 Ex. 33:22.   32 Ex. 33:19.

Lord speaking, to what Lord is he referring? Take note how he was teaching the religious doctrine regarding Father and Son in a veiled way. Again these exact words follow, "And the Lord descended in the cloud, and stood by him there, and proclaimed the name of the Lord; and the Lord passed before him, and proclaimed, the Lord, the Lord merciful and gracious, long-suffering, abundant in mercy and true; keeping righteousness and showing mercy unto thousands, taking away iniquities and transgressions, and sins." In the next verse Moses bows himself and worships the Lord who was proclaiming the Father, and says to him "Do thou, O Lord, go with us."[33]

9. There you have a first proof. Now take a second and obvious one. "The Lord said to my Lord, sit thou on my right hand"[34]; addressed by a Lord not to his servant but to a Lord, in fact the Lord of all things and Son of him who "put all things in subjection under him." "For when he saith, All things are put under him, it is manifest that he is excepted which did put all things under him," down to "that God may be all in all."[35] The only begotten Son is Lord of all things, but a Son obedient to his Father, who did not grasp at lordship but received it naturally from him who gave it willingly. For the Son did not grasp at the gift, nor did the Father grudge it. It is the Son who says, "All things are delivered unto me of my Father."[36] When it says "delivered unto me" it does not mean "I was previously without," but "without depriving the Giver, I guard them well."[37]

12. There is one Lord Jesus Christ, a wondrous name obliquely expressed beforehand by the prophets. For the prophet Isaiah says, "Behold the Saviour is come nigh thee, having his reward."[38] Now Jesus, for Jews, means Saviour. That is to say, the grace of prophecy foresaw that the Jews would be slayers of their Lord, and veiled his name so that they might not be all ready to conspire against him through knowing clearly about him beforehand. Now it was not by men that he was named Jesus evidently, but by an angel who came not with the authority of an angel, but in the power of divine mission. And he said to Joseph, "Fear not to take unto thee Mary thy wife; for that which is conceived in her is of the Holy Ghost. And she shall bring forth a son, and thou shalt call his name

---

[33] Ex. 34:5-9.   [34] Ps. 110:1 (Septuagint).   [35] I Cor. 15:27, 28.
[36] Matt. 11:27, a particular anti-Arian text, so expounded by Cyril.
[37] Sections 10 and 11 are omitted for brevity.
[38] Isa. 62:11 (Septuagint).

Jesus."[39] Straightway also he tells the reason for the name, saying, "for he shall save his people from their sins." I ask you, how could one not yet begotten[40] have a people unless he existed before he was begotten? And this is what the prophet says, speaking *in persona Christi* and saying, "From the bowels of my mother hath he made mention of my name,"[41] because the angel foretold how he should be called Jesus, "and in the shadow of his hand hath he hid me,"[42] referring there to Herod's conspiracy.

14. Jews admit that he is Jesus, but never that he is Christ, for which reason the Apostle says, "who is a liar, but he that denieth that Jesus is the Christ."[43] Now "Christ" means that he is high priest with priesthood that passes not away. He did not begin his priestly work in time, nor will another succeed to his high-priesthood. You heard me on Sunday on this subject when I was preaching at the liturgy[44] on the text "After the order of Melchizedek."[45] Jesus did not receive the high-priesthood in a line of descent, or by unction with prepared oil,[46] but he received it from the Father before all ages. He is a priest by oath, and is proportionately higher than all others, "for they are priests without an oath, but he with an oath by him that said, The Lord sware and will not repent."[47] It would have sufficed to establish his priesthood simply that the Father

[39] Matt. 1:20.
[40] Cyril probably uses "begotten" here, in place of conceived, because of the Nicene anathema against saying "before he was begotten he did not exist."   [41] Isa. 49:1.
[42] Isa. 49:2. For brevity, Section 13 has been omitted.
[43] I John 2:22.
[44] The Greek Christian word *synaxis*, here rendered "liturgy," is closely related to, but purposely chosen as different from the word *synagogue*. Both words represent a coming together of people. It is not until sixth-century Pseudo-Dionysius that we meet with the idea that *synaxis* is a gathering to the Lord Jesus, but it connoted the Eucharist with earlier writers. Socrates (*Ecclesiastical History*, v. 22) uses the word *synaxis* for assemblies at Church in Alexandria at which there was preaching, without the Eucharist being celebrated at the time, but this he mentions as an Egyptian peculiarity. That he should use the word, of such a gathering, suggests that he thought of it as an assembly to which the faithful were solemnly bidden. Thus the readings, and special direction for the commemoration of saints, and other festivals, was called a Synaxary. Cyril clearly does not call the gathering to which he is lecturing *synaxis*, but that would be because it was not a general assembly of the faithful summoned by the bishop, as was the liturgical gathering on Sunday, or other festal occasion.   [45] Heb. 5:10.
[46] Paraphrasing Hebrews 7:14 and 8:4, "if he were on earth he should not be a priest."   [47] Heb. 7:21.

willed it, but now it is doubly established, the will backed by
an oath, "that by two immutable things, in which it was
impossible for God to lie, we might have strong consolation"[48]
in our faith, wherein we recognize Jesus Christ to be Son
of God.

16. This is Jesus Christ, "who is come, an high-priest of
good things to come,"[49] and with the ungrudging generosity of
his Godhead he has granted to all of us to bear his name. For
whereas human sovereigns have some special title of sovereignty which they keep exclusively from use by other men,
Jesus Christ, being Son of God, has deigned to bestow on us the
title of Christians. But suppose that someone says that the
name of Christian is new-fangled and had no currency till
recently, and that people commonly object to anything new-
fangled, because they are not used to it; the prophet has already
set that doubt at rest, in saying, "But them which serve me, he
shall call by a new name, which shall be blessed upon the
earth."[50] Let us put to the Jews this question, Do you serve the
Lord or not? Well then, show us what new name you have.
For you have the names of Jews and Israelites in Moses and the
other prophets, you brought them back with you from Babylon,
and they are your names to this day. So where is your new
name? But we have our new name for serving the Lord. It is a
new name, but it is that "new name, which shall be blessed
upon the earth." It is a name that holds the world in its grip.
For Jews belong to a particular country, but Christians obtain
as far as earth extends, seeing that it is the name of the only-
begotten Son of God that they set forth.[51]

19. There are, beloved, many true testimonies to Christ. The
Father testifies of the Son from heaven. The Holy Spirit
testifies of him by descending bodily in the form of a dove. The
archangel Gabriel testifies of him in announcing the glad news
to Mary, and the Virgin Mother of God[52] bears her witness;

---

[48] Heb. 6:18. For brevity, Section 15 is omitted.
[49] Heb. 9:11.   [50] Isa. 65:15, 16 (Septuagint).
[51] This ingenious argument may be Cyril's own, and belongs to the liveliest
anti-Jewish polemic. We may judge that the Church was not allowed
to monopolize the pilgrim-interest at Jerualem without resistance from
the Jews. Sections 17 and 18 have been omitted for brevity.
[52] *Theotokos*, the word to which Nestorius took exception, and thereby
precipitated the Christological controversy connected with his name. It
is certain that it was a term already consecrated by much more use than
Nestorius imagined. On the other hand it was liable after Chalcedonian
days to be introduced by copyists into texts where it had not been. It is

so does the blessed site of the crib. Egypt testifies of him whom it received as its Master[53] when he was yet a babe in body. Symeon testifies of him, taking him into his arms and saying "Lord, now lettest thou thy servant depart in peace, according to thy word, for mine eyes have seen thy salvation, which thou hast prepared before the face of all people."[54] And Anna the prophetess testifies of him, living in most religious chastity the life of an ascetic. John the Baptist, greatest among prophets and harbinger of the new covenant, and in a sense the personal bond uniting the two Testaments, the Old and New, into one, testified of him. Of rivers, the Jordan is his witness; of seas, the sea of Tiberias. He has witnesses who were blind, were lame, were dead and came to life again. Demons bear him witness, crying "What have we to do with thee, Jesus; we know thee who thou art, the holy one of God."[55] Winds, mastered and stilled, bear witness. Five loaves multiplied for five thousand men bear witness. The sacred wood of the cross, seen to this day amongst us, and taken hence by those who have received portions with faith, to places that now cover almost the whole world, bears witness, and the palm tree in the valley[56], which provided branches to the children of those days who hailed him. Gethsemane bears witness, to the imagination all but haunted by the form of Judas, still. This Golgotha, sacred above all such places, bears witness by its very look. The most holy Sepulchre bears witness, and the stone that lies there to this day. The sun now shining bears witness, that failed, then, during the hour of his saving passion. Darkness bears witness, that lasted then from the sixth to the ninth hour, and the light that shined forth again from the ninth hour till evening. The Mount of Olive bears witness, the holy mount whence he ascended to the Father, and the rain-clouds that received from sight their Master; so also do the gates of heaven, of which the

more probable than not that Cyril used the title *Theotokos* of Mary, but there can be no certainty.
53 Legends of adoration received by the infant Jesus as he entered Egypt are present in a pseudo-Matthean Gospel a century younger than Cyril. But such legends are likely to have arisen in Christian Egypt at an early date, and Cyril's words look as if he had more in view than canonical Matt. 2:14; possibly an earlier legendary flight-story than pseudo-Matthew.
54 Luke 2:29, 30.   55 Mark 1:24.
56 It appears from the narrative of the Bordeaux pilgrim of A.D. 333 that a palm tree of great age on the road from Bethany to Jerusalem was credited with having been there at the time of the triumphal entry.

Psalmist said, "Lift up your doors, O ye princes, and be ye lift up, ye everlasting doors; and the King of glory shall come in."[57] His former foes bear witness, of whom Blessed Paul is one, for a short while his enemy, for a long while his slave. Twelve apostles bear their witness, not only by their preaching, but by their sufferings and deaths proclaiming the truth. Peter's shadow bears witness, healing the sick in Christ's name. "Handkerchiefs and aprons"[58] bear witness, which, in those days, wrought similar cures through Paul, in the name of Christ. Persians and Goths[59] and all converts from the nations bear witness who die for the sake of him whom they never saw with the eye of flesh. To this day the demons exorcised by the faithful bear witness.

20. So many are his witnesses,[60] and so varied, and there are many more besides. Can Christ so testified be still refused credit? Well then, if there is any that did not believe, after this let him believe. And if any believed, let him receive the greater increase of faith, putting his trust in our Lord Jesus Christ, and know whose name he bears. You are called Christian. Be careful of that name. Let not our Lord Jesus Christ, the Son of God, be blasphemed on your account, but rather "let your light so shine before men"[61] (by good works), that men may see it and glorify our Father in heaven in Christ Jesus our Lord, to whom be the glory both now and for ever, world without end. Amen.

LECTURE XI

On the Son of God as true God, only-begotten before all ages, by whom all things were made.

The Lection is from the Epistle to the Hebrews.[1]

6. Believe, then, in Jesus Christ, Son of the living God. He is only-begotten as the Gospel says, "For God so loved the world that he gave his only-begotten Son, that whosoever believeth

---

[57] Ps. 24:7 (Septuagint).   [58] Acts 19:12.

[59] The two great nations beyond the imperial frontiers, now partly evangelized.

[60] The point of the section is that many things the *photizomenoi* would see and hear should bring them assurance of their faith.

[61] Matt. 5:16.

[1] The Lection was Heb. 1:1–12. The first five sections of the Lecture, being largely recapitulatory, have been omitted.

in him should not perish, but have everlasting life,"[2] and "He that believeth on him is not condemned,[3] but is passed from death unto life.[4] But he that believeth not the Son, shall not see life, but the wrath of God abideth on him[5]; because he hath not believed on the only-begotten Son of God,"[6] Of him John bore witness saying, "And we beheld his glory, the glory as of the only-begotten of the Father, full of grace and truth,"[7] and him the demons trembling hailed, "Let us alone; what have we to do with thee, Jesus thou Son of the most high God?"[8]

7. So, being begotten of the Father, he is Son of God by nature, not by adoption. And "he that loveth him that begat, loveth him also that is begotten of him,"[9] while he who sets at nought him who is the begotten insults by implication him who begat. Now when you hear of God begetting, do not fall a-thinking in corporeal terms, or risk blaspheming by imagining corruptible generation. "God is a Spirit."[10] Divine generation is spiritual. Bodies are begotten from bodies, and there has to be an interval of time for it to be completed. But time does not come into the begetting of the Son from the Father. Bodies are begotten in an imperfect state, but the Son of God was begotten perfect. For what he is now, that has he been timelessly begotten from the beginning. We are begotten so as to develop from childishness to rationality. Being man, your first state is imperfect and your advance is by stages. But do not imagine anything of that sort in divine generation, or charge the Begetter with lack of power. For you might charge the Begetter with lack of power, if the Begotten was first imperfect and then reached perfection in time; that is if the Begetter did not fully grant from the beginning what was by supposition granted after the lapse of time.[11]

8. Do not think, therefore, in terms of human generation, as when Abraham begat Isaac. For Abraham truly begat Isaac, but what he begat was not the product of his will, but what another rendered to him. But when God the Father begat, it was

[2] John 3:16. [3] John 3:18. [4] John 5:24.
[5] John 3:36. [6] John 3:18. [7] John 1:14.
[8] Mark 5:7. [9] I John 5:1. [10] John 4:24.
[11] This is a new argument against the "adoption" doctrine of Paul of Samosata, against whom bishop Hymenaeus of Jerusalem had taken the field. Paul had argued that the Father is honoured by having unique Godhead, and by being believed to have divinized the Son of Mary by prokopē, or advance in grace. Cyril replies that if God is supposed to need time to produce a Son thus, the thought is dishonouring to God.

not as unknowing what should be, or only after some deliberation.[12] It would be the extreme of blasphemy to say that God
did not know whom he was begetting; nor would it be any less
blasphemous to say that the Father became Father only after
deliberating. For God was not at first childless, and then after
lapse of time became Father, but he had his Son from all
eternity, not begetting him as men beget men, but as he alone
knows who begat him true God before all ages.

9. The Father, being himself true God begat a Son like to
himself, true God.[13] Do not compare it with teachers "begetting" disciples, or as Paul says to some of his, "For in Christ
Jesus I begat you through the gospel."[14] For in such cases,
someone who was not by nature a "son," becomes such by
discipleship. But the Son of God is Son by nature, true Son.
You *photizomenoi* are now becoming sons of God, but do not
liken Christ's Sonship to that. For your sonship is one of
adoption, by grace, as it is written, "But as many as received
him, to them gave he the right to become children of God, even
to them that believe on his name; which were begotten not of
blood, nor of the will of the flesh, nor of the will of man, but of
God."[15] We indeed were begotten "of water and of the Spirit,"[16]
but it was not thus that the Son was begotten of the Father, who
at the time of his baptism addressed him, saying "This is my
Son."[17] He did not say, This man is now become my Son, but
"This is my Son," to show that he was Son prior to anything
baptism might bring about.

10. Neither did the Father beget the Son in the way in
which the human mind begets speech.[18] For mind is something
permanently present in us, but speech, spoken and dispersed in

---

[12] The Arians posed the dilemma: either God begat because he could not
help himself and without knowing the outcome, or he thought first and
begat deliberately. In the latter case, "there was when the Son was not."
Cyril parries this argument by indicating a number of ways in which the
analogy of begetting cannot be pressed, in theology, and that the Arian
dilemma is based on such an illegitimate pressing of analogy.
[13] It is impossible to find a nuance of difference between the substance of
this confession and the Nicene faith.
[14] I Cor. 4:15.   [15] John 1:12, 13.   [16] John 3:5.   [17] Matt. 3:17.
[18] This analogy for the divine generation had a great vogue with the second
century apologists, and is given in its crudest form in Theophilus of
Antioch, *To Autolycus*. It was a very effective means of commending to
the Greeks the Christian claim that one known in recent history is
nevertheless the eternal revelation of God. But by the time of Cyril it
had become clear what error could follow from pressing this analogy too
far.

the air, perishes. For we know Christ to have been begotten, not as an uttered word, but as indwelling[19] reason, and living, not spoken with lips and dispersed, but eternally and ineffably begotten of the Father, and come into being as a Person,[20] that is to say "In the beginning was the Word, and the Word was with God, and the Word was God."[21] The Word is seated at the Father's right hand, understanding his will, and creating the world at his behest, a Word descending and ascending.[22] For uttered speech neither descends nor ascends. He is Word that speaks and says, "The things which I have seen with my Father, these I speak."[23] He is authoritative Word, reigning over all, for "the Father hath committed all things unto the Son."[24]

11. So the way in which the Father begat the Son is not attainable by human analogy, but is one that he alone knows. For we do not profess to say how he begat him, but we affirm that it was not in this or that manner. And our ignorance of the way in which the Father begat the Son is shared by every created being. "Speak to the earth, if perchance it may teach thee,"[25] and then go on to question everything that is on the earth, but it will not be able to tell; for the earth cannot expound the being of its own Potter that fashions it. Earth is not alone in ignorance; the sun knows no more. For it was the fourth day when the sun was created, and it is ignorant of all that happened in the first three days; and a creature that does not know what happened in the three days before it existed will not be able to expound the Creator. Heaven will not explain it, for "the heaven also was like smoke established"[26] by Christ at

19 *Enhypostatos*, having real being within another existent.
20 *Hypostasis*, already, among the Syrians and Palestinians, beginning to be used of the Persons of the Trinity, in distinction from *ousia*, the shared reality of Godhead wherein the Three are one God.
21 John 1:1.
22 Cyril may have before his mind Isa. 55:8-11, with its notion of God's Word coming down into the world to cause his will to be done, and then "reporting back" the completion of its mission. In the later part of the section, Cyril is reserving, under safeguards, the analogy which he has begun by seeming to reject.
23 John 8:38.   24 John 5:22.
25 Cyril perhaps cites Job 12:8 as if it was said ironically. Zohar has undertaken to expound the wisdom of God, and Job replies in sarcasm that the truth about God is so obvious that earth and animals can expound it. Job means that it is impossibly difficult to understand the mind of God, and Cyril takes his cue from this to place theology above the comprehension of all creatures.
26 Isa. 51:6 (Septuagint).

the Father's behest. The heavens of heavens will not declare it; the waters that are above the heavens will not tell of it. Why then should you, good sir, be downhearted because you do not know what even the heavens do not know? It is not only the heavens that are ignorant of that begetting, but the whole order of angels as well. For suppose someone (we must imagine it possible) ascended to the first heaven and beheld the life of the angels there; suppose he then approached them with the question how God begat his own Son. They would probably answer, There are greater and higher beings than us. Ask them. Ascend to the second heaven, or the third. Make contact, if you can, with thrones and dominations, with principalities and powers. For if any man could make contact with them (a mere impossibility), they would decline him an answer, for they do not know.

12. I am ever amazed at the inquisitiveness of those rash folk who fall into blasphemy by their prosecution, as they think it, of religion.[27] For they do not know thrones and dominations, the works of Christ; they do not know principalities and powers; and yet they undertake to pry into the Creator himself. First tell me, rash man, the difference between a throne and a domination, and then go into details about Christ! Tell me what a principality is, what a power is, what a virtue is, what an angel is, and then tell me all about their Maker "by whom all things were made."[28] But you will not ask thrones or dominations; say, rather, that you cannot. What but the Holy Ghost, whose words are Sacred Scripture, "knoweth the deep things of God."[29] But the Holy Spirit himself has not spoken in the Scriptures about the Son's generation from the Father. Why then busy yourself over something that the Holy Spirit has not expressed in the Scriptures? You do not know all the Scriptures, and yet must get to know what is not in the Scriptures! The sacred Scriptures give rise to enough questions, in all conscience. We do not grasp what they contain. Why then

---

[27] Fourth-century Hellenism developed a vogue for disputation that can hardly have been equalled, still less surpassed, in any age. The theological controversy in the Christian Church of the fourth century offered material for this passion to exercise itself upon, and the most transcendent subjects became the theme, not of tried theologians but of the laity. Gregory of Nyssa, in his *Oration on the Godhead of the Son and Holy Spirit*, describes the passion for theological argument among the *petite bourgeoisie*. "Ask" the small tradesman "about pence, and he will discuss the generate and the ingenerate." Cyril seems to express a somewhat similar experience.

[28] John 1:3.   [29] I Cor. 2:10.

should we be over-curious about what is beyond them? It is enough for us that we should know that God has begotten one only Son.[30]

22. I want now to tell you something that will give an example of what I have been saying, though not a very close one, as I am aware. For how can one find a close example in visible things to represent the might of God? Nevertheless, let the feeble give the feeble this feeble analogy. Once upon a time there was an emperor who had a son also an emperor, and wanted to build a city. So he proposed the building of the city to this son who was his colleague in the purple, and he took the specification and carried the work to completion. In like manner, when the Father would have the world created the Son created it at the Father's behest, so that the initiative might safeguard the Father's sovereignty, and at the same time the Son might have all authority over his own creatures, so that the Father might have mastery over his own works and the Son rule over what was created not by anyone else but by himself. For the world was not, as I said, created by angels,[31] but by the Son who was begotten before all ages; as it is said "by whom all things were made" so that there is nothing excepted from his making. What I have now said by the grace of Christ will suffice.

23. Let us come back to the clause of the creed and bring this lecture to an end. Christ made all things, even to angels and archangels, dominations and thrones, not because the Father lacked might to create by himself what things were to be created, but because he would have his Son bear the rule over the things he had made. And he, the Father, provided to his Son the pattern of the things to be created. So the only-begotten says, in honour of his Father, "The Son can do nothing of himself, but what he seeth the Father do; for whatsoever things he doeth, these also doeth the Son likewise,"[32] and again "My Father worketh hitherto, and I work"[33] showing that there is no contrariety in their working. "For all mine are thine, and thine mine,"[34] says our Lord in the Gospels.

[30] The popular taste for theological dogma no doubt explains the length at which Cyril treats the theme of "the generate and the ingenerate" in this lecture; for which reason Sections 13 to 21 inclusive have been omitted.
[31] The creation of the world was ascribed to angels in many types of Gnostic cosmology, such as those of Menander, Satornilus, Basilides and Carpocrates. But Cyril shows no real anxiety about this form of heresy.
[32] John 5:19.   [33] John 5:17.   [34] John 17:10.

10—C.J.

This truth can be clearly known from the Old as well as the New Testament. For the speaker of "Let us make man in our image and after our likeness,"[35] was, without question, speaking to someone present. But the Psalmist expressed it most clearly of all, saying, "He spake, and they were made; he commanded, and they were created,"[36] where we see the Father commanding and speaking, while the Son is creating the world according to the Father's behest. This is mystically[37] expressed by Job, "which alone spread out the heaven, and walked upon the sea as on firm ground,"[38] whereby he indicates to the thoughtful that he who in his incarnation walked on the sea is identical with the Maker of the heavens in former time. Later God addresses Job, "Or didst thou take earth, and fashion clay into a living being, and set it with the power of speech upon the earth?",[39] and presently "Have the gates of death opened to thee with fear, and did the door-keepers of hell tremble at the sight of thee?",[40] letting us know that he who for man's sake descended into hell is identical with man's Maker from the clay in the beginning.

24. So Christ, the only-begotten Son of God, is also Maker of the world, for "he was in the world and the world was made by him," and "he came to his own"[41] as the Gospel teaches us. Christ made at the Father's behest not only the world of sense, but also the invisible order. For, according to the apostle, "in him were all things created that are in the heavens, and that are upon earth, things visible and invisible, whether thrones, or dominations, or principalities or powers: all things have been created by him and for him; and he is before all, and in him all things consist."[42] And if you mention the very ages, Jesus Christ is their maker at the Father's behest, for "in these last days God spake unto us by his Son, whom he appointed heir of all things, by whom also he made the ages,"[43] to whom be glory,

---

[35] Gen. 1:26.   [36] Ps. 148:5.
[37] That is, in such a wise that only an initiate would discern his meaning. Cyril follows Origen in supposing that the exact phrasing of the Old Testament (which meant, for him, the Septuagint text as he knew it) was often guided by the Holy Spirit to bear a meaning which would only be seen by those who knew the revelation in Christ. Job's primary and conscious meaning concerned Jehovah. Cyril finds something proved by his words which Job had not in mind, and this gives a mystic or spiritual exegesis of the text, in Cyril's eyes, because the Holy Spirit caused Job to use words referable prophetically to Christ.
[38] Job 9:8.   [39] Job 38:14.   [40] Job 38:17.
[41] John 1:10, 11.   [42] Col. 1:16, 17.   [43] Heb. 1:2.

honour, might, with the Father and the Holy Ghost, now and ever, world without end. Amen.

LECTURE XV

On the clause, "He will come in glory to judge the quick and the dead, whose kingdom shall have no end," and concerning Antichrist[1]

The Lection is from Daniel.[2]

1. What we proclaim is not one single coming of Christ, but a second as well, much fairer than the first. For the first presented a demonstration of long-suffering, but the second wears the crown of the Kingdom of God. Most things about our Lord Jesus Christ are twofold. His birth is twofold, once of God before the ages, and once of the Virgin in the end of the ages. Twice he comes down, once all unseen like dew on a fleece,[3] and a second time still future and manifest. When first he came, he was swaddled in a manger. When next he comes he will "clothe himself with light as with a garment."[4] At his first coming "he endured the cross, despising the shame"[5]; at his second, he comes surrounded with glory and escorted by hosts of angels. We do not therefore simply rest upon Christ's first coming, by itself, but let us look forward also to his second; and as we say of his former coming, "Blessed is he that cometh in the name of the Lord,"[6] so also we will say the same words again

---

1 The Lectures XII, XIII, XIV are on the historical facts of Christ's incarnate life, passion, and risen glory. Anti-Jewish polemic determines their shape. Cyril goes over the Gospel history, but finds it in every detail prefigured in the Old Testament. These lectures have been omitted for brevity. The sequel comes in Lecture XV, where, without the fulfilment before his eyes, Cyril builds up an eschatology in which, while Daniel is his leading document, many other texts are interpreted prophetically. In this lecture we see how a mid-fourth-century churchman looked round him, and looked forward.

2 The Lection was Dan. 7:13-27.

3 This is a conflation of Ps. 72:6 (in the Septuagint, "He shall come down like rain upon a fleece") with the first sign of Gideon, Judg. 6:37, the natural marvel of dew on a fleece, coming all unseen. Gideon's second sign, of the dry fleece and wet ground, departs from nature. Origen had an ingenious allegorical interpretation of the two signs of Gideon (see Homily viii. 4 on Judges), and Cyril may follow suit by taking them as prefiguring the two Advents. He has already used Ps. 72:6 in Lecture XII. 9 as prophesying the incarnation, the fleece being the flesh.

4 Ps. 104:2.   5 Heb. 12:2.

6 Matt. 21:9. (The Palm Sunday greeting.)

at his second coming, that we may meet our Master in company with angels and say "Blessed is he that cometh in the name of the Lord"[7] as we worship him. The Saviour comes again, but not to be judged again, for he will pass judgement on those who passed judgement on him, and he who aforetime kept silence as they judged him now reminds those lawless men who did their outrageous deeds to him upon the cross, and says "These things hast thou done, and I kept silence."[8] He adapted himself when he came then, and taught men by persuasion, but this time it is they who will be forced to bow to his rule, whether they will or no.

2. These are the words of the prophet Malachi concerning these two comings; "And the Lord whom ye seek shall suddenly come to his temple" (that is the first coming) "and the messenger of the covenant whom ye delight in. Behold he shall come, even the Lord almighty; but who may abide the day of his coming? and who shall stand when he appeareth? for he is like a refiner's fire, and like fuller's soap: and he shall sit as a refiner and purifier of silver."[9] And a verse or two afterwards we get the Lord himself speaking; "And I will come near you to judgement: and I will be a swift witness against the sorcerers, and against the adulterers, and against the false swearers"[10] and so forth. It is in view of this that Paul forewarns us, saying "If any man build on this foundation gold, silver, precious stones, wood, hay, stubble; everyman's work shall be made manifest; for the day shall declare it, because it shall be revealed by fire."[11] For Paul also has signified to us that there are these two comings, in his Epistle to Titus where he says, "The grace of God our Saviour hath appeared unto all men, teaching us that, denying ungodliness and worldly lusts, we should live soberly, righteously, and godly in this present world; looking for that blessed hope, and the glorious appearing of the great God and our Saviour Jesus Christ."[12] You note how he acknowledges with thanksgiving the first coming and that we look for a second. And so the phrase of the creed that I have professed, and is now committed to you[13] teaches belief in him who "ascended into

[7] Matt. 23:39. (Greeting Christ, come to judge Jerusalem.)
[8] Ps. 50:21.   [9] Mal. 3:1-3.   [10] Mal. 3:5.
[11] I Cor. 3:12.   [12] Titus 2:11.
[13] The baptismal creed of Jerusalem was committed to the *photizomenoi* at the fifth lecture. But from this passage, and a later (Lecture XVIII. 21), it would appear that, from the fifth lecture on, Cyril repeated, and made them repeat, the part of the creed that he was to expound. The clause, "whose kingdom shall have no end," was not in the Symbol of Nicaea,

the heavens and sitteth on the right hand of the Father, and will come again with glory to judge both the quick and the dead: whose kingdom shall have no end."

3. So, our Lord Jesus Christ comes from heaven, and comes with glory at the last day to bring this world to its close. For this world will accomplish its course, and the world that once came into being is hereafter to be renewed.[14] For seeing that corruption, theft, adultery and every form of sin has been poured out on the earth, and in the world fresh blood has been ever mingled with previous blood,[15] this astonishing habitation filled with iniquity is not to last. This world passes away that the fairer world may be revealed. Now would you have this proved by the express words of Scripture? Listen to these from Isaiah: "And the heavens shall be rolled together as a scroll; and all their host shall fall down, as the leaf falleth off from the vine, and as a falling fig from the fig-tree."[16] The Gospel also says, "The sun shall be darkened, and the moon shall not give her light, and the stars shall fall from heaven."[17] Do not let us grieve as if we only were to die. Stars perish also, and it may well be that they too are revived.[18] Now the Lord will "roll up the heavens,"[19] not for their destruction, but to raise them up again more fair. Listen to these prophetic words of David; "Thou, Lord, in the beginning hast laid the foundations of the earth, and the heavens are the work of thy hands; they shall perish, but thou remainest."[20] There! someone will say, he says explicitly that they "shall perish." Listen to me. This is

or in the Roman baptismal creed. As appears later in this lecture, it was valued as excluding the doctrine of Marcellus of Ancyra. It might have been added for this express purpose, but equally may be older than his heresy.

14 Cyril thus excludes belief that the material universe will be annihilated. He is not a millennarian, but presumably thinks of the regenerated universe as forming part of heaven, with which it is already, in his mind, spatially related, but it will then be in perfect and eternal union with it.
15 Paraphrased from Hos. 4:2.   16 Isa. 34:4.   17 Matt. 24:29.
18 There was an ancient and widespread Hellenic belief that the stars were living beings. Philo accepted it, and supposed them to be holy angels. Origen was influenced by Job 25:5, and by his theory of the purgation of rational beings, to think them morally imperfect beings and in fact to be like souls enclosed in fiery bodies. Jerome, in his attack on Cyril's successor John, plainly insinuates that John probably believes as Origen believed, and we may safely gather from this passage that Cyril tended to accept Origen's account of the stars (On first principles, I. vii. 2, 3).
19 Cyril seems to understand this of the first heaven, the place of the stars, which now shares in imperfection, and is to take part in final regeneration in company with the universe beneath it.   20 Ps. 102:25, 26.

how you must understand the words "shall perish," and it is clear from the context; "and they all shall wax old as doth a garment; and as a vesture shalt thou fold them up, and they shall be changed." For it is just as when one speaks of a man "perishing," as in the text "The righteous perisheth, and no man layeth it to heart."[21] Now this is said in full expectation that he will rise again. And in like manner we look for a sort of resurrection of the heavens also. "The sun shall be turned into darkness, and the moon into blood."[22] Now let those who have come to us from the Manichees be admonished and cease to think the lights of heaven divine, nor let them blasphemously suppose that this sun that "shall be turned into darkness" is Christ.[23] Again, listen to our Lord's own words, "Heaven and earth shall pass away, but my words shall not pass away."[24] So you see that the creatures are of a different level from the Master's words.

[21] Isa. 57:1.   [22] Joel 2:31.

[23] The Manichees did not identify the sun with Christ, though they seem to have made it the chief of his works for the process of salvation. Certainly, the notion that "the sun shall be turned into darkness" would have seemed to them blasphemous. But we cannot infer from this sentence that Cyril knew that he had ex-Manichees among the *photizomenoi*. His ideas on Manicheeism are mostly derived from the then recent work of Hegemonius called the *Disputation of Archelaus with Manes*, a Christian polemical writing which offers an unsparing parody of Manicheeism. In Lecture VI. 32, Cyril gives (at second hand) a single piece of information gained from persons who had frequented the Manichees. But had he been in direct contact with converts from Manicheeism, his information must have been much better than it appears to be. The profession of Manicheeism was punishable under Constantine and Constantius, with the result that there were feigned conversions from it, and people concealed the fact that they had had to do with it. We do best therefore to take this sentence as an oratorical device to influence the hearers to abhor Manicheeism. The difficulty which the church leaders had in combatting that heresy was the elusiveness of its propaganda. The part of the sun, in Manichean soteriology, was to work upon the moon, which received the light-particles coming from the souls of those who sought to be purged from the evil of the world. The sun's power effected the final purification of these particles in the moon, and the moon waned because the purified light passed thence to its final abode in the Milky Way. Jesus Christ, according to Mani, who claimed to be his final apostle, was the heavenly power who created this mechanism of salvation, and in later days appeared among men to give the knowledge of its use. The Manichee faith was so attached to the visible phenomena that it was not wholly unjust to say that their Christ was the sun. What they borrowed from Christianity did not ever include its authentic principles, which were, in fact, incompatible with those of Mani.

[24] Matt. 24:35. Cyril's deduction from this text is his best refutation of Mani.

4. So, in short, visible things will pass away and be replaced by a fairer order for which we look. But let none start investigating to find out when. For our Lord says, "It is not for you to know the times and the seasons, which the Father hath put in his own power."[25] Be neither rash enough to venture an opinion when these things will come to pass, nor careless enough to go to sleep. For the Lord says, "Watch, for in such an hour as ye think not the Son of man cometh."[26] However, we need to know the signs of the coming of the end, and we are to look for Christ, or we shall either die disappointed or be led astray by that false Antichrist. For that reason the apostles were providentially moved, by the will of God, to approach the teacher of truth and say, "Tell us, when shall these things be, and what shall be the sign of thy coming, and of the end of the world."[27] In other words, we look for thy coming again. But "Satan is transformed into an angel of light."[28] So assure us against worshipping anyone in place of thee. He, then, opened his divine and blessed mouth and said, "Take heed that no man deceive you."[29] Now you are his hearers today, and behold him, in a way, with the eyes of your mind. Then listen to him saying to *you* these same words, "Take heed that no man deceive you." That saying exhorts you all to heed what it says. We are not, you see, dealing so much with a history of past events, as with a prophecy of things to come, which are surely on the way. And that is no prophecy of mine (who am all unworthy) but of Scripture, whence I am drawing out and declaring to you the signs. Take you note what things have already happened and what things have still to come, and so be on your guard.

5. Take heed that no man deceive you "for many shall come in my name, saying, I am Christ, and shall deceive many." This has in part happened already, for Simon Magus, Menander,[30] and some others of the godless heretics made this claim. Others will also make it, either in our days, or after we are gone.

6. That is one sign: now another. "And ye shall hear of wars and rumours of wars."[31] Well, and are not the Persians fighting the Romans for Mesopotamia? Is not "nation rising

[25] Acts 1:7.   [26] Matt. 24:44.   [27] Matt. 24:3.   [28] II Cor. 11:14.
[29] Matt. 24:4. For our sakes, Cyril implies, the apostles were impelled to ask this question.
[30] Cyril is following Irenaeus in making Simon and Menander claim to be Christ.   [31] Matt. 24:6.

against nation, and kingdom against kingdom?"[32] "And there shall be famines and pestilences and earthquakes in diverse places."[33] These are things that have already come to pass. The text continues, "And fearful sights from heaven, and mighty storms."[34] So he warns "Watch therefore, for ye know not what hour your Lord doth come."[35]

7. But we seek a sign of the Lord's coming that touches us? We, as members of the Church seek a sign within the Church? Well, the Saviour says, "And then shall many be offended, and shall betray one another, and shall hate one another."[36] If you hear of bishops taking the field against bishops,[37] of clergy striving with clergy, and of lay people assaulting other lay people, even to the shedding of blood,[38] do not distress yourselves. You see, it has been foretold in Scripture. So do not be

[32] The death of Constantine had been signal for the Persian king to attempt to recover the land and cities held by the Romans beyond the Euphrates. Constantius obtained a truce in 350, which enabled him presently to defeat the western usurper Magnentius, and consolidate his hold upon the empire. But in early 350 it was still true that the Persians were fighting the Romans for Mesopotamia. By Lent 350, the news of the death of Constans at the hands of Magnentius must have been known in the east, while the truce with the Persians would not have been known. Thus, at this time, not only was "nation rising against nation" (Persians against Romans), but, within the empire, "kingdom was rising against kingdom," (Magnentius against Constans, and, by sure implication, Constantius against Magnentius), satisfying in full the prediction of Matt. 24: 7.

[33] Matt. 24:7 continued.

[34] Luke 21:11, but with "storms" instead of "signs."

[35] Matt. 24:42.   [36] Matt. 24:10.

[37] During the decade A.D. 340–350, while Constans ruled the western empire and Constantius was preoccupied in resisting the Persians, the western episcopate had used political pressure to impose its will upon the bishops of the east, especially in forcing the restoration of Athanasius, and other bishops deposed by eastern synods. As Cyril was speaking, this process was about to be reversed, and as Constantius became sole autocrat, after his overthrow of Magnentius, the leaders of the eastern episcopate moved and abetted Constantius in the humiliation of the Roman bishop and his western colleagues. Cyril may have attended Maximus to the synod of Tyre, and witnessed there the ferocity displayed in the conflict of Eusebians and Athanasians.

[38] The same decade, 340–350, had been marked, at Constantinople, by a succession of popular risings, for or against bishop Paul, in which a general was murdered and large numbers of soldiers and citizens lost their lives. Similar scenes had been witnessed in Alexandria. No doubt the attempt of the secular government to impose its will upon the freedom of religion gave excuse and cover for subversive elements of the population to overthrow public order. But there can be no doubt that religious fanaticism played a leading part in causing these melancholy disorders.

preoccupied with what is happening, but keep your mind on what Scripture says. Suppose that I, who am now teaching you, fell from grace: do not you share my ruin. On the contrary, it is quite right for a hearer to be better than his teacher, and for the last comer to be the first, seeing that the Master takes on workers at the eleventh hour. Considering that treachery found its way into the apostolate, are you surprised to discover among bishops hatred of their brethren? This sign is not concerned only with the hierarchy, however, but with the lay people as well. For the Lord says, "And because iniquity shall abound, the love of many shall wax cold."[39] I ask if anyone present can boast of his unfeigned love of his neighbour. Is it not often the case that lips kiss, face smiles, yes, and eyes light up, when the heart is devising some treason, and speaks peace while plotting evil?

8. You have also this sign, "And this gospel of the kingdom shall be preached in all the world for a witness unto all nations and then shall the end come."[40] And, as we can see, practically the whole world has been filled with the teaching about Christ.[41]

9. And when this has been completed, what happens? Our text goes on, "When ye therefore shall see the abomination of desolation, spoken of by Daniel the prophet, stand in the holy place (who so readeth, let him understand),"[42] and a little later, "Then if any man shall say unto you, Lo, here is Christ, or, there, believe it not."[43] The stage of hatred between brethren gives place to the coming of Antichrist.[44] The devil prepares

[39] Matt. 24:12.   [40] Matt. 24:14.
[41] To a Jerusalem congregation, the world-wide spread of the faith was manifest in the persons of the pilgrims who came thither. At the time of this lecture, Easter was approaching, and Christian strangers were no doubt arriving in the city daily, so as to drive home the point that Cyril is here making. The map of the distribution of churches of which we have clear evidence, drawn by Carl Pieper (Dusseldorf) under the title *Orbis Christianus saec.*, i–v, shows that in the days of Cyril churches were found from Britain, up the Rhine and along the further side of the Danube, throughout the Mediterranean lands, from the Atlantic coast of Portugal, and the Straits of Gibraltar, to Egypt and up the Nile to Abyssinia; from Georgia to the Persian Gulf, southwards, and eastwards beyond the Caspian, to Afghanistan. Of known lands, that left only India, Russia and the Baltic countries wholly unevangelized. Jerome, *Ep. xlvi ad Marcellam*, speaks of pilgrims from Armenia, Persia, India, Ethiopia, and nearer lands.
[42] Matt. 24:15.   [43] Matt. 24:23.
[44] The experience of Israel in the period between the Testaments gave rise to the expectation that final deliverance would only come to "the saints

the way by making divisions among the people so that Antichrist may have a better reception. God grant that none here nor of the servants of Christ elsewhere may desert to the enemy! The Apostle gave a clear sign, when writing on this subject, and saying, "For that day shall not come, except there come a falling away first, and that man of sin be revealed, the son of perdition, who opposeth and exalteth himself above all that is called God, or that is worshipped; so that he as God sitteth in the temple of God, shewing himself that he is God. Remember ye not that when I was yet with you, I told you these things? And now ye know what withholdeth, that he might be revealed in his time. For the mystery of iniquity doth already work, only he who now letteth will let, until he be taken out of the way. And then shall that wicked be revealed, whom the Lord shall consume with the spirit of his mouth, and shall destroy with the brightness of his coming; even him whose coming is after the working of Satan, with all power and signs and lying wonders, and with all deceivableness of unrighteousness in them that perish."[45] Such is Paul's account. And we

of the Most High" after they had endured a supreme trial from an oppressor who would embody opposition to the God of Israel. Then God would destroy the foe, and the golden age would come in. The people of the primitive Church were imbued with this idea. But Paul, in his Second Epistle to the Thessalonians, while accepting the principle of this expectation, gave the notion a fresh shape. The foe must be in every way the antithesis of Jesus Christ, a seducer, given to every form of moral iniquity, while blasphemously claiming to be divine. Under such an one, the true people of God, the Church, would experience their supreme trial, and in that trial the Lord would come again. W. Bousset, in *Antichrist* (English translation, 1893), traced the way in which Christians continually tried to set the Pauline expectation against events of their own times. He shows that in the reign of Constans a speculation arose that Constans would go to Jerusalem and offer the empire to God, and that then Antichrist would come. This fact makes it the less surprising that Cyril should show such interest in "the signs of the times." Typically, he tries here also to base his teaching wholly upon Scripture. But he has found it impossible to think of Antichrist otherwise than in relation to the Roman empire, and so produces a picture of the last days that is all his own. At a moment when Church and state are paralysed by disunity, he says, Antichrist will first restore unity to the state. Then he will attach all Jewry to his person, in that he will be accepted as Messiah. Having obtained such an ascendency as no previous emperor ever had, he will reveal himself in his true colours, and the Church will undergo its final trial till rescued by the second coming of the Saviour. The evils against which Cyril thus strove to strengthen the resistance of his hearers were accordingly those which they were likely to meet, if in less ideal intensity, under the autocracy of Constantius.

[45] II Thess. 2:3-10.

have reached the "falling away." Men, that is, have fallen away from the right faith. Some proclaim the identity of Father and Son.[46] Others dare to assert that Christ is to be held to have been in some way brought into being out of non-existence.[47] And formerly heretics were quite evident, but now the church is full of masked heretics. For men have deserted the truth and want to have their ears tickled.[48] Make a plausible case and everyone is ready to listen to you. Talk of changing one's life, and everyone makes off. The majority have fallen away from the sound doctrines, and are readier to choose what is bad than to prefer what is good. So there you have the "falling away," and the coming of the enemy is to be looked for next. Meanwhile he has begun to send out his forerunners here and there, so that the spoil may be all ready for him when he comes. Therefore, brethren, look to yourselves. Have care of your souls. The Church now testifies to you before the living God, and recounts to you the facts about Antichrist before they come to pass. Whether that will be in your time we do not know, or whether it will be after your time, we do not know. What matters is that you should know these things and be on your guard.

10. The true Christ, the only-begotten Son of God, will not come on earth again. If some visionary appears in the desert, do not go out to him. "If any man shall say unto you, Lo, here is Christ, or there; believe it not."[49] Let not your gaze henceforward be downwards and fixed upon earth, for the Master will come down from heaven, not by himself, as he did before, but in company, escorted by thousands of angels. This time he will not come all unseen, like dew upon a fleece but as visibly as vivid lightning. For he said himself "As the lightning cometh out of the east, and shineth even unto the west, so shall also the coming of the Son of man be,"[50] and later, "And they shall see the Son of man coming in the clouds with power and great glory, and he shall send his angels with a great sound of a trumpet" and so forth.[51]

11. Now when he was about to be made man, at his first coming, and there was expectation of God being born of a virgin, the devil disparaged this dispensation beforehand by

[46] Sabellians. Eastern theologians like Cyril suspected, not without reason, that the orthodoxy of the western Church covered a great deal of actual Sabellianism.

[47] Arians. Cyril must have been conscious of the revival of Arianism that was taking place among the eastern churchmen.

[48] An allusion to II Tim. 4:3.   [49] Matt. 24:23.

[50] Matt. 24:27.   [51] Matt. 24:30.

causing myths about the false gods of idolatry begetting and being begotten of women to arise, preparing the way with evil intent, supposing that if the false notion of divine birth was first on the ground, the true divine birth would be disbelieved.[52] And in exactly the same way, now that the true Christ is about to come the second time, the adversary takes the expectations of simple folk as a help, and especially those of the Jews, and introduces a certain man, a magician,[53] highly skilled in the guileful and evil art that deals in philtres and enchantments. This man will grasp in his own hands the power of the Roman empire, and falsely give himself out to be Christ. He will use the appellation Christ in such a way as to take in the Jews that are looking for their Messiah,[54] while drawing to himself pagans by his magical illusions.

12. This aforesaid Antichrist will come when the destined period of the Roman empire has run its course,[55] and the subsequent end of the world is drawing near. Ten claimants to the empire will arise simultaneously, I suppose in different parts, but all wearing the purple at the same time. Antichrist will form an eleventh after them, having seized the imperial

[52] Cyril is here using what was a commonplace of Christian apologetic, not, however, in its usual context, but for the purpose of deducing the manner in which Antichrist may be expected to display himself. He shares the common belief that Satan knows enough of the counsels of heaven to exercise his malice, but has not such perfect knowledge as to be able to thwart the purposes of God.

[53] Magic, as a seeking of supernatural aid otherwise than from God, was ever abhorred by the Church, and so formed an essential trait in the character of Antichrist. The general belief that much magic was pure deception and fraud contributed to the notion of Antichrist as the embodiment of falsehood. But magic had the associations of Satanic malignance.

[54] That is, he will not call himself Christus, but Unctus, the anointed one; using the synonym for Christus which the Jews also adopted, so as, when speaking of the expected Messiah, to avoid the word used by the Christians. Cyril's strong antipathy to Judaism comes out in this notion that, at the end of the world, Jewry will be the chosen ally of Antichrist. It arose, no doubt, from the fact that Jerusalem was not claimed as the holy city of Christendom without bitter resistance from the Jews. But Hippolytus, On Antichrist, more than a century before Cyril, had predicted that Antichrist would be patron of the Jews.

[55] The early Church accepted generally the view, which Cyril here champions, that the fourth kingdom of Dan. 7 is the Roman empire, which will last to the end of the world. While Paul has been thought to see in the Roman empire something that would stand out against the consummation of wickedness by Antichrist, Cyril's view of the empire is that, in decadence, it would form the very means for the rise of Antichrist.

power by use of magic arts. He will humble three of those who came to power before him, and cause the remaining seven to be Caesars under him.[56] At first he will feign mildness and will appear to be a learned and understanding man, with pretended prudence and kindness. Then he will take in the Jews, by making them suppose him to be their expected Messiah, by false signs and wonders produced by magical trickery. And afterwards his character will be written large in evil deeds of inhumanity and lawlessness of every kind, so as to outdo all wicked and godless men that were before him. He will display a murderous, most absolute, pitiless and unstable temper towards all men, but especially towards us Christians.[57] For three years and six months only will he have maintained his effrontery when he will be brought to nought by the second glorious coming from heaven of the only-begotten Son of God, our Lord and Saviour Jesus, the true Christ. He will destroy Antichrist "with the spirit of his mouth,"[58] and commit him to the flames of hell.

13. These doctrines are not the fruit of ingenuity but are derived from the Sacred Scriptures read in the church, particularly as gathered out of the prophecy of Daniel, in our today's lection, and according to the interpretation given by the archangel Gabriel, who spoke as follows, "the fourth beast shall be the fourth kingdom upon earth, which shall surpass all kingdoms."[59] Ecclesiastical commentators have traditionally taken this kingdom to be the Roman empire.[60] For the first remarkable empire was that of Assyria, the second was the combined empire of the Medes and Persians. After these came a third empire, that of Macedon. And now we have the fourth kingdom which is the Roman empire. Further on Gabriel continues his interpreting and says, "And the ten horns out of this kingdom are ten kings that shall arise; and another king shall rise up after them, and he shall surpass in wickedness all who were before him" (not merely the ten kings, you note, but all kings that ever were) "and he shall subdue three kings"[61]

---

[56] This appears to be Cyril's understanding of Dan. 7:24, that the skill of Antichrist will enable him to induce seven pretenders to the empire to serve under him, so as only to be driven to dispose of three rivals by force of arms.

[57] Cyril shows his liberal spirit in thinking of Antichrist not solely as the persecutor of Christians, but as the foe of humanity.

[58] II Thess. 2:8.   [59] Dan. 7:23.

[60] e.g., Irenaeus and Hippolytus.

[61] Dan. 7:24.

(clearly out of the ten that preceded him: and when he had reduced three of the ten to powerlessness it is equally clear that he will reign as eighth king)[62] "and he will speak great words against the Most High."[63] Antichrist is a blasphemer and flouter of all law. He will not succeed to the empire, but will usurp it by means of sorcery.

14. You ask who is Antichrist, and whence comes his activity. Let Paul explain to us. He says, "whose coming is after the working of Satan, with all power and signs and lying wonders."[64] What Paul implies is that Satan uses Antichrist as his tool, working through him as his proper agent. For Satan knows that there is not going to be any stay of the judgement coming upon him,[65] and so he works no longer as he has been wont, through his subordinate spirits, but from now on wages war more openly, himself,[66] but always "by signs and lying wonders." For the father of lies figures forth works of false glamour, to make the crowd suppose it is seeing a dead man raised to life, when he is not really alive, and lame men walking and blind men seeing when no real cure has taken place.

15. Paul says further, "who opposeth and exalteth himself above all that is called god or that is worshipped,"[67] that is above every divinity, so that Antichrist will be the bitter foe of the idolatrous cults. He continues, "so that he sitteth in the Temple of God." What temple is that? Paul says it is the destroyed temple of the Jews. For God forbid that it should be that Temple of God in which we are! Why should I suggest such a thing? Lest you should think me complacent about us

---

[62] Cyril's canon of Scripture did not include Revelation, and he never cites it. But it was certainly known to him, if only through Irenaeus, who has the sentence, in *Against Heresies*, Bk. V, c. 26, Section 1, in reference to Rev. 17:11, "so, clearly, since he who is to come will kill three of the ten, while the rest will be subject to him, he will be the eighth among them." Irenaeus identifies the beast of Revelation with Daniel's eleventh king, and this is the probable explanation of Cyril's statement that Antichrist is "eighth king."

[63] Dan. 7:25.

[64] II Thess. 2:9.

[65] Irenaeus and Eusebius cite a passage of Justin Martyr saying that since Christ's coming Satan is desperate, having learned the finality of his defeat.

[66] Cyril perhaps follows Hippolytus in thinking that Satan will become incarnate as Antichrist. But it is unlikely, seeing that "children and the fruit of the womb are a gift that cometh of the Lord." Rather, we may suppose, Antichrist is an abandoned man, who is possessed not by lesser demons, but by the archfiend himself. To this man Satan gives his characteristic gifts of lying marvels.

[67] II Thess. 2:4.

Christians.[68] For if Antichrist will come to the Jews as Messiah and seek worship from the Jews, he will show great zeal for the Temple so as to deceive them the more, hinting that he is that man of the house of David destined to rebuild the temple erected by Solomon.[69] Antichrist will come at such a time as there shall not be left of the temple of the Jews "one stone upon another," to quote the sentence pronounced by the Saviour.[70] For it is not until all the stones are overthrown, whether by the decay of age, or through being pulled down for building material or in consequence of this or that other happening, and I do not mean merely the stones of the outer walls, but the floor of the inner temple where the Cherubim were, that Antichrist will come "with all signs and lying wonders" treating all the idols with disdain,[71] at first adopting a show of being humane,

68 Cyril seems to imply that Antichrist will sit enthroned to be worshipped in a restored Temple, but that he would fain be so worshipped in the Church of Christ if the Christians could be deluded as well as the Jews. Cyril thinks of the Church of the Holy Sepulchre as the counterpart of the Temple, so that it would be the mark for Antichrist's most daring attempt. In Lecture XIII. 28, Cyril has claimed that Golgotha is the centre of the earth, just as Jews had claimed for the Temple. So the Jews were deceived, by many cubits distance!

69 Little more than ten years after these words were spoken, Julian the Apostate attempted to assist the Jews in restoring the Temple. Work was begun, but abandoned, according to Ammianus Marcellinus (*Liber rerum gestarum*, xxiii. 1), because thunderbolts (*globi flammarum*) rained down upon the place whenever work was recommenced. The explanation of Julian's attempt and of Cyril's prophecy is probably to be sought in the fact that the Jewish community began to agitate for a restoration of the Temple as soon as Constantine's building of churches had given the excuse.

70 Mark 13:2. The Bordeaux pilgrim in 333 saw a good deal of building standing on the Temple site, and tried to identify portions of it. He recounts that Jews came and lamented over two pierced stones on the Temple site. And this may explain Cyril's supposition (below) that one might know which was the "inner temple where the Cherubim were." The Christian inference that there was a curse upon the stones of Herod's Temple apparently resulted in the site not being despoiled for the building of churches. Chrysostom's Homily lxxv on St Matthew declares that the prophecy of Mark 13:2 was not yet fulfilled. Nor had it been, when, in the seventh century, the Saracens undertook their restoration of the Temple as a mosque.

71 Cyril thus shows no expectation of paganism proving moribund. It is not clear why he assumed that the total destruction of the Temple at Jerusalem, prophesied by Christ, was to be followed immediately by the last things. But this is clearly what he thought. And it must have had the strange result that the endurance of the Temple ruins would be, to his flock, reassurance that the end was not yet.

but later displaying his ruthlessness, especially towards the holy
people of God. For it says, "I beheld, and the same horn made
war with the saints,"[72] and in another Scripture it says, "And
there shall be a time of trouble, such as never was since there
was a nation even to that same time."[73] Antichrist is the terrible
wild beast, the great dragon unconquerable by man and ready
to swallow him up. But although I have more things to say
about him drawn from Holy Scripture, I am content to have
said so much lest I exceed the due proportion.

16. Because our Lord knew how mighty our Adversary would
be, he was tender to men of religion and said, "Then let them
which be in Judaea flee to the mountains."[74] But if anyone
knows in himself that he is tough enough to try a fall with
Satan, let him stand his ground[75] (for I am not unhopeful of
the Church's nerve). And let him say, "Who shall separate us
from the love of Christ?" and the rest of that passage.[76] But
while those of good courage should stand their ground, let the
fearful among us look for safety, "for there shall be great
tribulation, such as was not since the beginning of the world,
no, nor ever shall be."[77] But thank God for confining the height
of this affliction to a few days duration! For it says, "But for
the elect's sake those days shall be shortened."[78] The reign of
Antichrist will only be three and a half years. I go by Daniel,
and not apocryphal writings.[79] For Daniel says, "And they shall

[72] Dan. 7:21. In his applications of the details of the Daniel prophecy to
Antichrist, Cyril follows Hippolytus, *On Christ and Antichrist*, so much
that he may be assumed to have known that work.   [73] Dan. 12:1.
[74] Matt. 24:16 applied to the reign of Antichrist at Jerusalem.
[75] The Church of Jerusalem is, in Cyril's eyes, not so much the first church
as the final Church. It is at Jerusalem that Antichrist will end his reign,
and the supreme martyrs will answer their call. The conception is one that
must have paved the way for Jerusalem to claim patriarchate, since
Jerusalem would be the heart of the final battle, with great Rome on
the periphery.   [76] Rom. 8:35–end.   [77] Matt. 24:21.   [78] Matt. 24:22.
[79] The most probable reference of these words is to the Book of Revelation.
As we have seen, this book is not included in Cyril's Canon of Scripture,
as given in Lecture IV, Section 36. Hippolytus and Irenaeus, whom Cyril
followed, used Revelation, and it must be deliberate that he does not
follow them in this. Revelation was early accepted into the western
Canon, but Syria and the Orient was very late in following suit. Eusebius
(*Ecclesiastical History*, iii, 24, 25) professed doubt as to the status of Revelation, being much impressed by the criticisms of it by Dionysius of Alexandria. But he probably was loth to be assured of its canonicity because
it lent support to the chiliasts. Cyril's feelings in the matter would follow
closely upon those of Eusebius. And Revelation tended to create difficulties for the system of eschatology that he had based on the Synoptic Gospels,
Paul, and Daniel.

be given into his hand until a time and times and the dividing
of time."[80] "A time" means the single year covering his rise
to power. "Times" means the ensuing two years of his wicked
career, which, when added to the single year, make up the
three years. "The dividing of time" means the last six months.
Daniel makes the same statement in another passage, saying,
"And he sware by him that liveth for ever that it shall be for
a time, times, and a half."[81] I think that some exegetes deduced
the same meaning from later verses, "the thousand two hundred
and ninety days," and "Blessed is he that waiteth and cometh
to the thousand three hundred and five and thirty days."[82] That
is why we are to go into hiding and take to flight. For quite
likely "we shall not have gone over the cities of Israel till the
Son of man be come."[83]

17. Who, then, is the "blessed" that then bears his witness
devoutly for Christ? For I tell you that those who are martyrs
then, take precedence of all martyrs. For previous martyrs have
wrestled only with human antagonists. But the martyrs under
Antichrist do battle with Satan in his own person.[84] The perse-
cuting emperors of the past only put men to death. They did
not pretend to raise the dead. They did not show illusory signs
and wonders. But in the reign of Antichrist there will be the
evil persuasion alike of terror and deceit, "insomuch that if it
were possible they shall deceive the very elect."[85] At that time,
may it enter into the heart of none to ask, "What did Christ
more than this? For what power enables this man to do such
deeds? Unless God willed it, he would not have allowed it."
The Apostle warns you, prophesying, "And for this cause God
shall send them strong delusion."[86] Now where it says "shall
send," it is equivalent to "will suffer to be." The saying is not
meant to excuse these people, but to settle their condemnation.
And why? The Apostle replies, "they believed not the truth,"
meaning the true Christ, "but had pleasure in unrighteousness,"[87] meaning Antichrist. Now God suffers these things to
happen alike in persecutions that occur from time to time and
in those last days, not because he is powerless to prevent them,

[80] Dan. 7:25. [81] Dan. 12:7. [82] Dan. 12:11, 12. [83] Matt. 10:23.
[84] Cyril's theory is that all through history Satan has warred against God
and man, at first disdainfully, through subordinate evil spirits, but, from
the incarnation and founding of the Church, with growing desperation.
At the last, in the vain hope of replying to the incarnation he will directly
possess the evil man Antichrist, and the last martyrs will therefore meet
the full and desperate malevolence of Satan.
[85] Matt. 24:24. [86] II Thess. 2:11. [87] II Thess. 2:12.

but because it is his way to crown his own athletes for their endurance, just like his prophets and apostles. He means that after a short while of labour they shall inherit the eternal kingdom of the heavens. So Daniel says, "And at that time thy people shall be delivered, everyone that shall be found written in the book (he clearly means the Book of Life), and many of them that sleep in the dust of the earth shall awake, some to everlasting life, and some to shame and everlasting contempt; and they that be wise shall shine as the brightness of the firmament: and they that turn many to righteousness as the stars for ever and ever."[88]

18. So be warned, my friend. I have given you the signs of Antichrist. Do not merely store them in your memory. Pass them on to everyone without stint. If you have a child after the flesh, teach them to him forthwith. And if you have become a godparent forwarn your godchild, lest he should take the false Christ for the true. For "the mystery of iniquity doth already work."[89] These wars between nations frighten me. The separated Churches frighten me. Animosities among the brethren frighten me. I have said enough. God grant that these things may not come in our time, but in any case we have been warned. So much, then, for Antichrist.

19–21. But let us await eagerly and expect the coming of our Lord from heaven upon the clouds.[90] According to our day's lection, "the Son of man" shall come to the Father "with the clouds of heaven" followed by "a stream of fire" for the purging of men.[91] If any man's deeds are golden he will shine more brightly still. If anyone's manner of life is like stubble, and has nothing solid about it, the fire will burn that person up. And the Father will be seated, having "his garment white as snow, and the hair of his head like the pure wool."[92] This is spoken anthropomorphically. And its spiritual sense? that he is the King of such as are not defiled with sins. For God says, "Your sins shall be as white as snow, and shall be as wool."[93]

---

[88] Dan. 12:1–3 (Septuagint).   [89] II Thess. 2:7.

[90] The first sentence of Section 19 here given is immediately followed by the resumption of the exegesis of the Lection (Dan. 7) in the middle of Section 21, the intervening matter being omitted.

[91] Dan. 7:13 followed by v. 10. The fiery stream issuing from before the throne of the Ancient of Days, in v. 10, Cyril takes to be purgatorial, and so supposes that it follows the descent of the Son of man to earth (deduced from v. 14) to purge those capable of salvation before the final judgement. Cyril follows Origen in thinking divine punishment chiefly purgatorial.

[92] Dan. 7:9.   [93] Isa. 1:18, omitting the reference to scarlet and crimson.

Wool is the emblem of forgiveness of sins, as also of innocence.[94] Now the Lord, who ascended upon a cloud, will come from heaven on clouds. For he said, "And they shall see the Son of man coming in the clouds of heaven, with power and great glory."[95]

22. But what is the sign of his coming? Is it one that the opposing power might dare to counterfeit? Listen. "And then shall appear the sign of the Son of man in heaven."[96] Now the true and authentic sign of Christ is the cross. The sign that precedes the King is a cross of light,[97] announcing him who aforetime was crucified. So, when the Jews see it, who of old pierced him and conspired against him, let them "mourn tribe by tribe"[98] and say, "This is he who was buffeted. This is he in whose face they spat. This is he whom they bound with chains. This is he whom they set at naught upon the cross."[99] "Where shall we flee from the face of thine anger?" they will cry. But they will not be able to flee anywhere, for the angel-hosts will encompass them round. So the sign of the cross will be terror to our enemies, but joy to the friends who put their faith in him, preached him, or suffered for his name.

24. "The Son of man" it is written, "shall come in his glory, and all the angels with him."[1] Note, my friend, before how many you will come to be judged. Every race of men will be

94 White wool, in contrast with black goats' hair, is the symbol of innocence, after forgiveness as in Ps. 51:7, where the reference to washing implies wool, and in Isa. 1:18; without qualification in Mark 9:3. The part played by scarlet wool in Heb. 9:19 explains the transfer of the symbolism of forgiveness from white wool, to wool as wool, irrespective of colour.
95 Matt. 24:30.   96 Idem.
97 This assertion that the second coming of Christ will be heralded by the appearance of a cross of light in the heavens does not occur in earlier literature, unless we so interpret "First a sign of spreading out in heaven" in *Didache*, xvi. There must have been much speculation on "the sign of the Son of man" in Matt. 24:30, and Origen's exegesis of this text proposes a different explanation. As we have a cross of light in the sky recorded in Cyril's letter to Constantius written apparently more than a year after this lecture, the fully reasoned anticipation is the more remarkable. It is hardly credible that the Jerusalem parhelion of 351 could be the inspiration of Cyril's argument here, but an earlier parhelion might have suggested this understanding of "the sign of the Son of man." See the Notes to Section 4 of the Letter of Cyril to Constantius below.
98 Zech. 12:12 (Septuagint).
99 Thus the sign shatters the delusion of Antichrist, and shows the Jews that they rejected Messiah.
1 Matt. 25:31. A passage from the middle of Section 22 to the beginning of Section 24 has been omitted.

present then. Think therefore of the numbers of imperial citizens. Think what the barbarian nations amount to. Take the numbers now living and those who have died in the last hundred years. Think how many have been buried in the last thousand years. Think of all the human race from Adam till today. It is a vast multitude, and yet by comparison it is nothing much, for the angels are more numerous. They are the "ninety and nine" sheep,[2] while the human race is the lone one. For we must suppose that the multitude of inhabitants is everywhere in proportion to the space. Now the whole earth surface is like a point when compared with the heaven above it.[3] And the heaven that wraps the earth around is inhabited by a multitude proportioned to its extent. And the heavens of heavens contain a multitude beyond computation. Scripture says, "Thousand thousands ministered unto him, and ten thousand times ten thousand stood before him."[4] That does not mean that those were all there were, but that the prophet could find no expression to convey more than that. At that day of judgement there will be present God the Father of all, with Jesus Christ enthroned beside him, and the Holy Spirit present with them. The angel trumpet will summon us before

[2] Matt. 18:12. This interpretation of the parable of the lost sheep, with the notion that all space is crowded with angels, was first brought together by Cyril, and then, almost simultaneously, by Hilary of Poictiers (Commentary on Matthew, c. xviii, Section 6; Tractate on Psalm cxviii, Section 7). As Hilary spent five years' exile in Asia Minor, there is some probability that both writers were indebted to a lost Commentary, and that it was one by Origen. At the point in Origen's Commentary on Matthew where he might interpret the parable of the lost sheep, he passes it over with a reference to his Commentary on Luke, of which the passage does not survive. As Jerome refers to and rejects the interpretation which sees in the ninety and nine sheep the angels, it is the more likely that it was associated with Origen. Jerome likewise pours scorn on the notion (held by Origen) that God set angels over the propagation of irrational living creatures. (Commentary on Habakkuk 1:14). It is likely enough, therefore, that Cyril owes this exegesis to Origen.

[3] Cyril follows Origen in believing that angels are circumscribed beings, who must therefore always be somewhere and cannot be everywhere, and that they could be called bodiless in the sense of having no body that was theirs always and continuously. Cyril, accepting the idea of concentric heavenly spheres round about the earth, sees in the heaven above the earth, the first heaven. By the heaven of heavens he designates whatever superior spheres there may be. And spatially these must be vaster still. But at this point Cyril halts his speculation, before involving himself in some of the self-contradiction that befell those who followed him and were less restrained.

[4] Dan. 7:10.

them, bringing our deeds with us. Is that not good reason for us to be concerned now? Do not you think, my friend, that quite apart from any penalty, it is no small sentence to have sentence passed before such a company? And surely we would rather die many deaths than have to be sentenced by friends![5]

27. Should you ever hear someone say that the kingdom of Christ is to end, abhor it as heresy. It is a fresh head of the hydra that has recently reared itself round about Galatia. Someone[6] had the effrontery to say that Christ is King no more, after the end of the world, and dared to declare that the Word that came forth from the Father will be reabsorbed into the Father and have no more existence, blasphemies that must recoil to his own hurt. For he has not heeded the words of the Lord, "The Son abideth for ever."[7] He has not heard Gabriel declaring, "And he shall reign over the house of Jacob for ever, and of his kingdom there shall be no end."[8] Take full stock of this last passage. On the one hand you have human heretics teaching to the detriment of Christ, and on the other, there was the archangel Gabriel teaching that the Saviour abides for ever. Whom do you prefer to believe? Is not it Gabriel? Hear the witness of Daniel to what he saw, "I saw in the night visions, and one like a Son of man came with the clouds of heaven, and came to the Ancient of Days, and there was given him dominion, and glory, and a kingdom, that all people, nations, and languages should serve him; and his dominion is an everlasting dominion, which shall not pass away, and his kingdom that which shall not be destroyed."[9] This is the teaching you

---

[5] Section 24 is completed and then Sections 25 and 26 omitted for brevity.
[6] This is Marcellus, bishop of Ancyra, the metropolis of Galatia. He was an enthusiastic supporter, at Nicaea, of the doctrine that the Son is consubstantial with the Father. Ten years later, provoked by the teaching of an Arian sophist, Asterius, that the Son is the sole direct and eternal creature of the unbegotten Father, Marcellus was in trouble for writing that the Word of God had not separate being until becoming Son by incarnation, and would again cease to have separate being when the work of redemption had been accomplished. At a synod at Constantinople in 336, Eusebius of Caesarea, to the delight of the eastern bishops there assembled, convicted Marcellus of producing a new version of the Sabellian heresy. The easterns suspected that many Sabellians were sheltering under the Nicene formula. Hence one cause of Cyril's unwillingness to use that formula, although it expressed what he believed. Hence also his brisk despatch of the doctrine of Marcellus, whom he does not name, perhaps because many western pilgrims were convinced that Marcellus was orthodox. As host to such pilgrims, it is not surprising if Cyril sought peace where possible.   [7] John 8:35.   [8] Luke 1:33.
[9] Dan. 7:13, 14. Section 28 has been omitted for brevity.

should prefer. Put your trust in it and dismiss the words of heresy. For you have heard most explicitly about the kingdom of Christ that has no end.

29. Would you like to know what induces these people to be so mad as to teach the contrary? They have misread what the Apostle wrote quite clearly, that Christ must reign "till he hath put all enemies under his feet."[10] So they say that when his enemies have been put under his feet, he will be no longer King, a bad and stupid thing to say. For if he is King before he has finally defeated his enemies, must he not be all the more King when he has completely mastered them?[11]

31. Let us examine them on the meaning of "till" or "until." For I shall try to join issue with them over this word, and overturn their error. You see that they have made bold to say that the phrase "until he hath put his enemies under his feet" points to his coming to an end. So they dare set a limit to Christ's eternal kingdom, and, on the strength of that word ("until"), terminate a dominion that knows no end. Well, then, let us read similar phrases from the Apostle: "Nevertheless, death reigned from Adam till Moses."[12] So, I suppose, men died until Moses, but afterwards none died; in fact when the Law had been given there was no more death for men![13] That shows you that the expression "until" does not imply the ending of a period. Rather you see Paul's meaning to be that in spite of Moses being a righteous and admirable man, the death-sentence promulgated upon Adam reached also to him, *and* to those who came after, even though he and they did not copy the sin of Adam in disobediently eating of the tree.

32. Take, also, another like expression. "For until this day . . . when Moses is read, the veil is upon their hearts."[14] Does "until this day" mean "up to the time that Paul wrote the words and no longer"? Does it not mean until this present day and indeed to the very end? And if Paul should say, "For we are come as far as unto you also in preaching the gospel of Christ, having hope, when your faith is increased, to preach the gospel in the regions beyond you,"[15] you can see clearly that the phrase "as far as" sets no limit, but indicates what lies beyond. With what meaning, therefore, ought you to recall the

[10] I Cor. 15:25.   [11] So also Section 30 has been omitted.
[12] Rom. 5:14.
[13] A sarcastic reference to Romans 6:9, "When the commandment came . . . I died."
[14] II Cor. 3:14, 15.   [15] II Cor. 10:14, 15, 16.

words "till he hath put all enemies"? Just the same as in another saying of Paul, "But exhort each other daily, while it is called to-day,"[16] which clearly means for all time. For as we must not talk of a beginning of the days of Christ, so never suffer anyone to speak of an end of his kingdom. For Scripture says, "his kingdom is an everlasting kingdom."[17]

33. I have many other testimonies from Holy Scripture to the fact that the kingdom of Christ endures throughout all ages. But I will content myself with what I have said, because the day wears on. And do you, my hearers, worship him alone as King, and flee every misguided heresy. If God's grace permit, the remaining articles of the faith shall be explained to you in due season. And may the God of all creation keep you all in mind of the signs of the end and preserve you unsubdued to Antichrist. You have been given the signs of the coming of that deceiver. You have been given the demonstration that the authentic Christ is about to descend visibly from heaven. Flee the first, the false Christ, and look for the true. You have been taught the way to be among those on his right hand at the judgement. Retain "that which is committed to thee"[18] concerning Christ, and be adorned with good works. So you will stand with a good courage before the Judge, and thereafter inherit the kingdom of heaven. Through him and with him be glory to God, with the Holy Spirit, world without end. Amen.

LECTURE XVI

On the clause, "and in one Holy Spirit, the Paraclete, who spake by the prophets"

The Lection is from the first Epistle to the Corinthians.[1]

1. Verily I need spiritual grace if I am to discourse of the Holy Spirit: I do not mean, to enable me to speak as the subject deserves, for that is not possible, but simply to run through what is said in Holy Scripture without imperilling my soul. For what is written in the Gospels, of Christ saying unequivocally, "Whosoever speaketh a word against the Holy Ghost, it shall not be forgiven him, neither in this world, neither in the world to come,"[2] truly makes one very much afraid. And there is oftentimes reason to fear that a person may incur this condemnation for saying what he ought not about the Holy Spirit,

16 Heb. 3:13.   17 Dan. 7:27.   18 I Tim. 6:20.
1 The Lection was I Cor. 12:1–7.   2 Matt. 12:32.

either through ignorance or mistaken religion. He who proclaimed that such an one should not be forgiven is the Judge of quick and dead, Jesus Christ. After that, what hope is there for an offender?

2. Under those circumstances it must be for the grace of Jesus Christ himself to grant me to speak impeccably and you to hear with understanding. For understanding is needed by hearers as well as speakers, lest they form a wrong impression in their minds from what they are rightly told. Therefore let us say about the Holy Spirit exactly what Scripture says and nothing else, and do not let us pry where Scripture does not answer. The Scriptures were spoken by the Holy Spirit himself, and what he said about himself is exactly what he pleased, or we could comprehend. So, let what he spake be said, which is to say, let us not dare to utter anything that he did not.

3. There is one only Holy Ghost the Paraclete. And just as there is one God the Father, and no second Father exists, and just as there is one only-begotten Son and Word of that one God, having no brother, so there is but one Holy Spirit, and there is no second spirit ranking beside him.[3] So the Holy Spirit is supreme power, divine substance, and ineffable nature. For he is alive and rational, and sanctifies everything that comes from God through Christ.[4] He enlightens the souls of righteous men. He was in the prophets, and under the new covenant he was in the apostles. Such as dare to break in two the work of the Holy Spirit are to be abhorred.[5] There is one God the Father, Lord of the Old Testament and of the New. And there is one Lord

[3] When Cyril delivered this splendidly orthodox statement of the Christian doctrine of God the Holy Spirit, the Church at large had still to fight its way through a period of controversy to reach the same position. Cyril shows, in the next section, that he was aware of teaching which perhaps included the Holy Spirit under the category of creatures. In fact, from A.D. 350 Macedonius was bishop in Constantinople, teaching that the Son is of essence *like* the Father's essence, and still further subordinating the Holy Spirit. At any rate, such was the doctrinal system which came to be known as Macedonianism. In 358–9, Athanasius was face to face with a group whom he calls *Tropici*, who supposed the Spirit to be a creature. The Church began to win its way out of this controversy through the work of Basil *On the Holy Spirit*, written in 375, and the orthodox doctrine was established by the synod of Constantinople, in 381, at which Cyril was hailed as a hero of the faith.

[4] The last clause exactly expresses the debt of Cyril to Origen, in this matter.

[5] By "breaking in two the work of the Holy Spirit" Cyril means denying to the Old Testament the same degree and kind of inspiration as the New. Cyril here condemns all the Gnostics, as well as the Marcionites.

Jesus Christ, prophesied in the Old Testament and present in the New. And there is one Holy Spirit, who proclaimed the things of Christ by the prophets, and then when Christ came, came down himself to make him known.

4. Let no one therefore draw a line between the Old Testament and the New. Let no one say that the Spirit in the Old Testament is not identical with the Spirit in the New. For whosoever does so offends none other than that Holy Spirit who is honoured with one honour together with the Father and the Son; none other than that Holy Spirit whom we receive in the moment of holy baptism in the threefold Name, and by its means. For the only-begotten Son of God commanded the apostles explicitly, "Go ye, and teach all nations, baptizing them in the name of the Father, and of the Son, and of the Holy Ghost."[6] In the Father, the Son and the Holy Spirit, is our hope. We are not preaching three Gods, so let the Marcionites hold their peace;[7] but aided by the Holy Spirit through the one Son, we preach one God. The objects of faith are not on different levels, nor is our worship of different orders. We do not, like some, make different grades within the Holy Trinity, nor do we make it one by coalescence, as Sabellius does.[8] But we have godly knowledge of one Father who sent his Son to be our Saviour; likewise one Son who promised to send the Paraclete from the Father's side; and likewise the Holy Spirit, who spake in the prophets and at Pentecost descended upon the apostles in the likeness of fiery tongues. That happened here in Jerusalem in the Upper Church of the Apostles,[9] for we are

---

[6] Matt. 28:19.

[7] The life of the Marcionite sect was still strong in the Orient, and Cyril here seems to tell us that the Marcionites accused the orthodox of believing in three Gods. Perhaps they meant the Father, the Son, and the Demiurge, as there was no place in their system for a Third Person of the Spirit. But Cyril chooses to take their jibe as against the Spirit.

[8] The Arians "made grades in the Trinity" by putting Son and Spirit on separate levels of creaturehood under the uncreated Father. The Sabellians "coalesced" the Trinity by regarding the Persons of Christian theology as mere appearances assumed by one only divine Person for the sake of aiding our understanding. In the preceding sentence, Cyril gives us a condensed argument against Arianism, in saying that faith and worship cannot know a less or more. An Arian Christ cannot be believed in or worshipped.

[9] What Cyril calls the Upper Church of the Apostles was the ancient church of the City standing in the south-west corner of the walled area. Maximus removed the bishop's seat thence to the Martyry in A.D. 335. The old cathedral church was believed to be on the site of the house of the Last Supper, and the title "Upper Church" seems to point to its

privileged, here, in every matter. To this spot Christ came down from heaven, and to this spot likewise the Holy Ghost came down from heaven. And it would certainly be most appropriate that just as I talk to you of the things of Christ and Golgotha here on Golgotha, I should talk to you about the Holy Spirit in the Upper Church. Nevertheless, he who descended in that place is sharer of the glory of him who was crucified here. And so I am discoursing here of him who descended there. For religion is not to be parcelled out.[10]

22. Great indeed is the Holy Spirit, and in his gifts, omnipotent and wonderful. Think how, whatever number there is of you sitting here now, there is present that number of souls. On each one, he is at work to good purpose, and, as present in the midst, he sees how each is disposed. He sees alike the thoughts and consciences of each. He knows what we say and what we think and what we believe. What I have said might seem enough for us, but yet it falls short of the whole. For, with your minds enlightened by the Holy Spirit, I beg you to note how many Christians there are in the whole of the diocese,[11]

being the successor-building of the Upper Room. Later pilgrims speak of a very big church on this site, and there are traces of this having been the case. But it is not very probable that this new building goes back to the time of the lectures. We must therefore think of a very modest house of prayer suited to the Christian congregation of pre-Constantinian Aelia as that to which Cyril refers. In view of the destruction of the Temple, the Christians called their old church New Sion. And there, Eusebius tells us (*Ecclesiastical History*, vii. 19), the people preserved and venerated the throne of James. It was this throne, presumably, that was transferred to the Martyry. Epiphanius (*On Weights and Measures*, 14) says that Hadrian found the little church standing, and that the Christians of Aelia claimed continuity here, with the apostolic mother Church.

[10] Cyril's wisdom is shown in adopting this principle. To have done otherwise would have encouraged a popular Christian tritheism. Sections 5–21 inclusive have been omitted, for brevity, containing, as they do, a refutation of early heresies and a review of the scriptural bases for a doctrine of the Person and work of the Holy Spirit.

[11] The word is *paroikia*, which later came to mean a parish, or single cure of souls. In the fourth century, its Christian use was for that part of the universal Church that was under the rule of one bishop. And as, in the east, the charge of a bishop was still often confined to the Christians resident in a single town, it still retained its literal meaning, "the people living there." Even in the east, however, the bishop of a city ruled over an extent of country dotted with village congregations. This had in fact befallen Cyril. And all these Christians were within the Jerusalem *paroikia*. The word *dioikesis*, our "diocese," was still in civil use to mean one of the large administrative subdivisions of the empire made by Diocletian and placed under an Imperial *Vicarius*. From the fourth to the eleventh cen-

and then how many in the whole province of Palestine.[12] Next
stretch your thoughts beyond the province to take in the whole
Roman empire. Then, if you please, beyond that, into the
whole wide world, the people of the Persians,[13] the nations of
India,[14] the Goths and Sarmatians,[15] Gauls and Spaniards,

tury, the use of the word *parochia*, the Latinization of *paroikia*, for the
charge of a bishop, gradually gave way, in the west, to the use of "diocese,"
which was, fundamentally, and apart from Diocletian's use of it, a
general word for a sphere of administration. With this went the transfer
of *parochia* to designate the smaller local unit of cure of souls, of which
there were many under one bishop.

12 At this time the whole of Palestine still formed a single civil province
with its capital at Caesarea. Its subsequent division into three provinces
reduced the civil standing of Caesarea and facilitated the ecclesiastical
rise of Jerusalem to be the patriarchal Church of all the lands between
the patriarchates of Antioch and Alexandria.

13 The Persian or Parthian empire ceased to be Parthian and became Persian in A.D. 227 when the House of Sassan from Persis, the province next
to the Persian Gulf, drove out the Parthian dynasty of the Arsacids, from
the less civilized lands south of the Caspian. This revolution rejuvenated
the empire, and the Sassanid King Sapor II, who reigned from 310 to
381 (his whole lifetime) struggled without ceasing to wrest control from
the Romans of land on his western frontier. To the east, his rule extended
to the Indus and the Oxus, and even beyond the latter. To residents in
Palestine, and especially for Jerusalemites, who saw many pilgrims from
the east, the Persian empire was very real, being as another world of
people stretching away to the east, and comparable with the Roman
empire. Cyril knows that the people of the Persian empire are not one
race, but several, though forming one nation.

14 Contacts between the Mediterranean world and India go back to the
conquests of Alexander the Great, who reached N. W. India in the fourth
century B.C., and thereafter, through Bactria and Persia, information
about India reached the west, together with some luxury trade, and rare
travellers. Certainly from the second Christian century, there was a fair
volume of sea-borne trade between the Red Sea coast of Egypt and the
south and west coasts of India, where a large number of trading stations
of merchants from the Roman empire have been discovered. How much
Cyril would know about the situation in general is matter for conjecture.
It is possible that an Indian embassy designed to encourage western trade,
which, according to Eusebius (*Life of Constantine*, vi. 50) reached Constantine about A.D. 330 did much to popularize the subject of India.
This embassy claimed to represent a number of sovereigns, and it may
be for this reason that Cyril thinks of the Indians as constituting nations
(in the plural). Eusebius also told (*Ecclesiastical History*, v. 10) that
Pantaenus, in the late second century, found Christians in India who had
been evangelized by Bartholomew. It is possible, therefore, that all
Cyril's information was derived from Eusebius.

15 The Sarmatians were a Scythian race, who pushed westward across
Europe in the third century, A.D., impelled by the Goths who followed
them. Both races were represented in the fourth century along the

Moors, Libyans, Ethiopians,[16] and then all those others for
whom we have no recognized names: for not even the appellation of many nations has ever reached us. And then think how
that in each of these nations there are bishops, presbyters,
deacons, religious men and women and all the other lay people.
Finally contemplate the great Guardian and Dispenser of their
several graces, who, throughout the world, is giving to this one
chastity, and to that one lifelong virginity, making another a
generous giver, and detaching another from care for worldly
goods, while on yet another he bestows the gift of driving out
evil spirits. And just as daylight, by one act of the sun's radia-
tion, enlightens the whole earth, so too the Holy Spirit is giving
light, to all who have eyes to see. For if anyone is unreceptive
of such grace because of spiritual blindness, let him lay the
blame on his own faithlessness, and not on the Spirit.

23. You see his worldwide power, but do not restrict the
range of your thoughts to earth. Now ascend and contemplate the
heavens above. Ascend in imagination, please, as far as the
first heaven, and there behold the countless myriads of angels
who inhabit it. If you can bear it, ascend in imagination a
further stage to the next heaven. Lo the archangels! Lo the
spirits of God! Lo the virtues! Lo the principalities! Lo the
powers! Lo the thrones! Lo the dominations! Of all these the
Paraclete is the divine ruler, teacher and sanctifier. To speak
of men, Elijah has need of him, Elisha has need of him, Isaiah
has need of him; to speak of angels, then Michael and Gabriel
have need of him. Nothing that has received its being ranks
with him, so that the angelic orders, even if all their hosts were
gathered together in one, cannot pretend to equality with the
Holy Ghost. The all-gracious might of the Paraclete over-
shadows them all. While they are sent to minister, he searches
the very depths of divine Being: as the Apostle tells us, "For
the Spirit searcheth all things, yea the deep things of God.
For what man knoweth the things of a man, save the spirit of
man which is in him? even so the things of God knoweth no
man, but the Spirit of God."[17]

Danube. Constantine in A.D. 322 turned a campaign for the disciplining
of the trans-Danubian Sarmatians into the preparation for his war with
Licinius. The evangelization of the Goths was going on under Ulfilas
at the time of Cyril's lectures.

[16] Cyril, at the end of this list, seems to have forgotten that he was speaking
about nations outside the Roman empire. He here enumerates barbarian
peoples who were in fact within the imperial frontiers.
[17] I Cor. 2:10, 11.

24. He it is who through the prophets predicted the things of Christ, he again who worked mightily in the apostles.[18] To this very day it is he who in the sacrament seals the souls of those who are baptized. These [19] are all gifts of the Father to the Son, who imparts them to the Holy Ghost. That is not my saying, but Jesus himself says, "All things are delivered unto me of my Father";[20] while, of the Holy Ghost he says, "When he, the Spirit of truth shall come . . . " and so on, ending, "he shall glorify me; for he shall receive of mine, and shall show it unto you."[21] Every grace is given by the Father, through the Son, who also acts together with the Holy Spirit.[22] There are not some graces that come from the Father, and different graces from the Son, and others again from the Holy Spirit.[23] There is but one salvation, one giving of power, one faith, and yet there is one God the Father, our Lord, his only-begotten Son, and one Holy Spirit, the Paraclete. Let us be content with this knowledge and not busy ourselves with questions about the divine nature or hypostasis. I would have spoken of that had it been contained in Scripture. Let us not venture where Scripture does not lead, for it suffices for our salvation to know that there is Father, and Son, and Holy Spirit.[24]

25. In the time of Moses, this Spirit descended upon the seventy elders.[25] These seventy elders were picked out, "and the

18 Perhaps in allusion to Acts 4:33.
19 Literally "The Father gives to the Son, and the Son imparts to the Holy Ghost." The context implies that what is given and imparted is elect souls.
20 Matt. 11:27.   21 John 16:13, 14.
22 The formula is, literally, "by the Father, through the Son, with the Holy Spirit." The preposition "with" connects the Spirit with both Father and Son. All divine action is the action of the Holy Trinity. But the formula expresses an orderly relation within the Trinity in respect to divine action.
23 The characteristic of polytheism was that different favours were sought from different deities. Christian tritheism was no serious danger, with Cyril's safeguard.
24 Cyril has argued the extreme danger involved in saying anything about the Holy Spirit beyond repeating the *ipsissima verba* of Holy Scripture. And the Eusebians, with whom he had been associated, strongly deprecated any theological formulation that went outside the vocabulary of Scripture. But II Peter 1:4 declares the elect to be sharers of the divine nature, and Heb. 1:3 speaks of the hypostasis of the Father. We must suppose that these two passages are insufficient, in Cyril's eyes, to constitute a scriptural doctrine of divine nature or hypostasis.
25 At this point there has been omitted a digression which the transcribers record Cyril to have made upon seeing signs of impatience in his audience, telling them to look to the Holy Spirit for aid in listening, and for aid to the lecturer, in what he shall say. The story of the seventy elders, he assures them, has a moral for themselves.

Lord came down in a cloud, and took of the spirit that was upon
Moses, and gave it unto the seventy elders."[26] The Spirit was
not himself divided, but his grace was shared out in correspondence with the recipients and their capacity for receiving
such grace. Now sixty-eight of them were with Moses[27] and
prophesied, but Eldad and Medad were not there. This was so
that it might be shown that the grace was not from Moses but
was the action of the Spirit. For, lo! Eldad and Medad, who
had been sent for, are seen to prophesy, although they had not
arrived at the place.

26. Joshua, the son of Nun, who succeeded Moses was amazed
and came to Moses and said, "Have you heard that Eldad and
Medad are prophesying? They were summoned and did not
present themselves. My Lord Moses, forbid them."[28] But he
replied, "I cannot forbid them, for the grace is from heaven.
Indeed I am so far from forbidding them as I myself depend
on grace. However, I am not supposing you to say this from
envy. Do not 'envy for my sake'[29] because they are prophesying
while you do not yet prophesy. Wait for the due season. And,
O that all the Lord's people were prophets, whenever the Lord
shall put his Spirit upon them."[30] Now he himself prophesied
when he said "whenever the Lord shall put his Spirit upon
them." Surely he means that as yet this had not happened, and

[26] Num. 11:25.
[27] Cyril assumes that the statement in v. 26 that Eldad and Medad "were
of them that were written" means that their names were in a list of
seventy whom Moses bade to go to the tabernacle. So he supposes the
prophetic frenzy to have fallen upon the chosen men before the last two
to leave the camp had done so. For this he finds a reason, that the people
might not think the Spirit-gift lay in the power of Moses. Most exegesis,
ancient and modern, is against this reading of the passage. It will be
seen in the next section, where Cyril tries to reconstruct the scene, that
he has supplied the word "summoned," relating to Eldad and Medad,
where no such word stands in the scriptural text. Most exegetes have
supposed that, while being of the roll of elders, Eldad and Medad had
not been summoned to the tabernacle, and were additional to the seventy
who were summoned. On this view, the prophesying of Eldad and Medad
was still more significant. This view was responsible for the composition
of an apocryphal *Prophecy of Eldad and Medad*, of which traces are found
in early Christian literature. It is possible that it was antagonism to this
apocryphon that decided Cyril to regard the prophesying of Eldad and
Medad as special only in that they were not at the tabernacle with the
others when the frenzy came upon them.
[28] The last sentence is Numbers 11:28, the rest of the passage in inverted
commas being a speech of Joshua composed by Cyril.
[29] Num. 11:29.   [30] The last sentence is cited from the same verse.

so "You, Joshua, have not yet received." What, had not Abraham, had not Isaac, Jacob, Joseph, received? Had not the fathers of old received? No, but it is clear that "whenever the Lord shall put his Spirit upon them" refers to a general outpouring. It means that grace is partial, now, but will then be unstinted. Moses was hinting at what was to come to pass in our times at the Day of Pentecost. For in our times the Spirit descended. All the same, he descended before our times upon many. For it is written, "And Joshua the son of Nun was full of the Spirit of wisdom; for Moses had laid his hands upon him."[31] You note how everywhere, in Old Testament and New alike, there is this one symbolic action. In Moses' time the Spirit was given by the laying on of hands. Peter likewise gave the Spirit by the laying on of hands.[32] Now this grace is shortly to come upon you when you are baptized. I am not telling you just how, for I am not taking anything out of turn.[33]

27. The Holy Spirit came upon all the righteous men and prophets, such as Enos,[34] Enoch, Noah and so on, to Abraham, Isaac and Jacob. For, in the case of Joseph, even Pharaoh came to understand that he had the Spirit of God in him,[35] while, as for Moses, you have often heard of the wonderful works which he did, that came from the Spirit. A most doughty man of the Spirit was Job, and likewise all the saints whose names I will not pass in review. It was the Holy Spirit who was sent to fill with wisdom the cunning men who worked with Bezalel upon the construction of the tabernacle.[36]

28. As we read in the book of Judges, Othniel judged in the might of this Spirit,[37] who empowered Gideon,[38] gave Jephthah victory,[39] enabled a woman, Deborah, to wage war, and caused Samson,[40] so long as he behaved righteously and did not grieve him to do deeds beyond the might of man. Likewise in the books of Kings we read about Samuel and David, how

31 Deut. 34:9.   32 Acts 8:14–18.
33 Cyril implies that, in a later lecture, he will tell them how a laying on of hands will bring to them at baptism the gift of the Spirit. The implied promise is unfulfilled. The existing third mystagogical lecture, on Chrism, makes no reference to the laying on of hands, and the only reference to Moses in it is to his anointing Aaron. This is the less surprising if the mystagogical lectures are not those that Cyril went on to give.
34 Of Enos, son of Seth, Cyril read in Gen. 4:26, according to the Septuagint, that "he began to call upon the name of the Lord." This, coming after the sacrifices of Cain and Abel, called for interpretation. Cyril apparently decided that it meant "began to prophesy."
35 Gen. 41:38.   36 Ex. 31:1, 2; 36:1, 2.   37 Judg. 3:10.
38 Judg. 6:34.   39 Judg. 11:29.   40 Judg. 14:6.

they prophesied in the Holy Spirit and were chiefs among the prophets. And while Samuel was called the Seer,[41] David says clearly, "The Spirit of the Lord spake by me,"[42] and in the Psalms he says, "And take not thy Holy Spirit from me,"[43] and, in another place in the Psalms, "Let thy good Spirit lead me into the land of uprightness."[44]

Likewise we read in the books of Chronicles how "the Spirit of God came upon Azariah"[45] in the days of King Asa, "then upon Jahaziel"[46] in those of King Jehoshaphat, and then on Azariah who was stoned.[47] And Ezra says, "Thou gavest also thy good Spirit to instruct them."[48] And how it was with Elijah who was translated and with Elisha, those Spirit-borne and wonder-working men, everyone knows without my saying, that they were full of the Holy Ghost.

29. If, further, one works through the books of the twelve minor prophets, many testimonies to the Holy Spirit are to be found. Thus Micah speaks as God's mouthpiece and says, "Truly I am full of power by the Spirit of the Lord."[49] Joel cries "And it shall come to pass afterwards, saith God, that I will pour out my Spirit upon all flesh" and what follows.[50] Haggai said "for I am with you, saith the Lord of hosts . . . my Spirit remaineth among you."[51] And in like manner Zechariah says "Unless ye receive my words and my statutes which I commanded my servants the prophets."[52]

30. Other testimony is borne by Isaiah, chief of prophetic voices, saying "And the spirit of the Lord shall rest upon him, the spirit of wisdom and understanding, the spirit of counsel and might, the spirit of knowledge and godliness; and the fear of the Lord shall fill him"[53] (making it plain that the Spirit is one and undivided although his activities are manifold) and in another place "Jacob my servant . . . I have put my spirit upon him,"[54] in another "I will pour my spirit upon thy seed,"[55] in another, "And now the Lord God, and his spirit

[41] I Sam. 9:11.   [42] II Sam. 23:2.   [43] Ps. 51:11.
[44] Ps. 143:10.   [45] II Chron. 15:1.   [46] II Chron. 20:14.
[47] The reference is to Zechariah, and the passage is II Chron. 24:20, 21. The name is given as Azariah in some texts of the Septuagint. In II Chron. 26:5 and 20, the names Zechariah and Azariah seem to be interchangeable. The confusion did not originate with Cyril.
[48] Cyril calls what we call the book of Nehemiah a part of the book of Esdras (Ezra). The reference here is to Neh. 9:20.
[49] Micah 3:8.   [50] Joel 2:28.   [51] Hag. 2:4, 5.
[52] Zech. 1:6 (Septuagint).   [53] Isa. 11:2 (Septuagint).
[54] Isa. 42:1 (Septuagint).   [55] Isa. 44:3.

hath sent me,"[56] in another, "This is my covenant with them, saith the Lord; my spirit that is upon thee,"[57] in another, "The spirit of the Lord God is upon me; because the Lord hath anointed me . . ."[58] and in yet another (where he is accusing the Jews), "But they rebelled and vexed his holy spirit" ending "where is he that put his holy spirit within him?"[59]

In Ezekiel, also, (if you can still bear to hear more) the passage I cited "And the spirit of the Lord fell upon me, and said unto me, Speak: Thus saith the Lord."[60] We must give a good signification to the words "fell upon me." They mean "affectionately," as when Jacob having recovered Joseph "fell upon his neck,"[61] or like the affectionate father in the Gospel parable who saw his son returning from his absence abroad, and "had compassion, and ran and fell on his neck, and kissed him."[62] There is another place in Ezekiel, "And he brought me in a vision by the spirit of God into Chaldea, to them of the captivity."[63] In the lecture on Baptism you heard other Ezekiel texts, "Then will I sprinkle clean water upon you . . . a new heart also will I give you, and a new spirit will I put within you . . . I will put my spirit within you,"[64] and later "The hand of the Lord was upon me, and carried me out in the spirit of the Lord."[65]

31. It was the Holy Spirit that filled the soul of Daniel with wisdom so as, youth as he was, he sat in judgement on elders.[66] Susanna, though chaste, had been pronounced a wanton, and there was no one to defend her. For who was going to take her out of the hands of the magistrates? She was summarily condemned to death; already she was handed to the executioners. But rescue was at hand in the form of an advocate,[67] to wit the Spirit that hallows all intelligence. "Come to me" he said to Daniel. So a youth convicted elders of thinking the sinful thoughts of youth. For it is written, "God raised up the holy spirit upon a young stripling."[68] And to round it off in one phrase, the chaste lady was saved by the decision of Daniel. I adduce this as an example to show the point, for there is no time now for commentary.[69]

---

56 Isa. 48:16.　　57 Isa. 59:21.　　58 Isa. 61:1.　　59 Isa. 63:10, 11.
60 Ezek. 11:5 cited in Section 14.　　61 Gen. 46:29.　　62 Luke 15:20.
63 Ezek. 11:24.　　64 Ezek. 36:25–27 (Lecture III. 16).
65 Ezek. 37:1.　　66 "Daniel" (Susanna) 13:22.
67 "Paraclete." Daniel was her visible advocate, but her true "Paraclete" was the Holy Ghost who inspired Daniel.
68 "Daniel" (Susanna) 13:45.　　69 A short final passage is omitted.

12—C.J.

LECTURE XVIII

On the resurrection of the flesh, the Catholic Church, and eternal life[1]
The Lection is from Ezekiel.[2]

1. The hope of resurrection is a root of every kind of good work, for the expectation of reward braces the soul to productive toil. And whereas every worker is ready to sustain his toil if he can look forward to being repaid for his labours, where toil has no recompense the soul is soon discouraged and

[1] Lecture XVII, which contines the theme of belief in the Holy Spirit from Lecture XVI, has been omitted. For the modern reader, it does not add anything very material from its review of New Testament passages. Cyril likens the relation of the Pentecostal gift to the man who receives it to the fire of incandescence in red-hot metal, and describes this fire as discriminating, in that it consumes sins while it causes the soul to glow.

In Section 20, Cyril acknowledges that his Lectures XVI and XVII are very long, and that he has come so close to Easter that there is no possibility of making a third opportunity for treating of the Holy Spirit. In Section 30 he hints that he and his auditory are tired out, and in 34, again, that time is running out. The first sign of doubt on his part whether he will be able to cover the remaining heads of the creed before Easter may perhaps be read into the final section of Lecture XV, where the promise to complete the course is qualified by the phrase "if the grace of God permit." But Cyril had made an original study of the Scripture doctrine of the Holy Spirit, and had much more matter than the time would allow. So, when he came to treat of the three clauses following that concerning the Holy Spirit, he changed the order, so as to get adequate. time for dealing with the resurrection of the flesh. What we have in the transcript as the close of Lecture XVIII, on the Church and eternal life, is so compressed that we can safely conclude that Cyril had planned to give a nineteenth lecture. It is probable that in later years he succeeded, for the Armenian calendar to which reference has been made supplies a nineteenth Lection, I Tim. 3:14–16, of which the middle verse, ideal as text for a lecture on the Catholic Church, is quoted in Section 25. In this case, the reversal of order, by which the resurrection of the flesh was taken before the Catholic Church, and eternal life treated as a pendent on the doctrine of the Church, was perpetuated in later lecturing. It thus appears that Cyril planned to give in all twenty lectures in forty days, but that, for whatever reasons, in 350, progress was too slow in the earlier part of the course. It is at least possible that difficulties arising from the instruction in Aramaic were a chief cause, and it is hard to see how that instruction was covered at all in the last days of Holy Week. But at least there is some probability that, in this year of transcript, Cyril was intending to give alternate days to the instruction in Greek and Aramaic.
[2] The Armenian Calendar gives the whole passage Ezek. 37:1–14 as Lection.

the body flags with it. A soldier who expects his share of the spoils is ready for war. But no one is prepared to die serving a king so undiscerning that he does not provide rewards for labours. In the same way, any soul that believes in resurrection takes care for itself as is meet, but any soul that disbelieves the resurrection abandons itself to destruction. A man who believes that the body survives to rise again is careful of this his garment and does not soil it by fornicating. But a man who does not believe in the resurrection gives himself up to fornication, abusing his own body as if it were nothing to him.

A mighty message and teaching of the holy Catholic Church is belief about the resurrection of the dead; mighty and most indispensable. While many gainsay it, the truth claims credence for it. Greeks gainsay it, Samaritans disbelieve, while heretics tear away the half.[3] Truth never appears but in one shape, while contradiction assumes a hundred.

2. Now this is what the Greeks join the Samaritans in saying against us; "your dead man falls down, decays, and is wholly dissolved into worms, and then the worms die. There is the kind of decay and ruin that is the body's lot! How, after that, does it rise again? Those that are drowned at sea the fish will have devoured, only to be devoured in their turn. Those that perish fighting with wild beasts, bears or lions consume, crunching up their very bones. Vultures and crows eat the flesh from corpses lying on the ground and then fly off to every point of the compass. Can such a body be reassembled? For it is on the cards that, of the birds that devoured it, one dies in India, another in Persia, and another in the land of the Goths. Other men are burnt to cinders in a fire, and then rain or wind disperses the very ashes. Can their bodies be reassembled?"

3. And this is my reply: "To small and feeble man, like you, it is a long way from India to the land of the Goths, from Spain to Persia. But it is no way to God, who holds the whole earth "in the hollow of his hand."[4] Therefore, do not attribute to God an inability that may match your own feebleness, but rather heed his might. Does the sun, then, warm the whole world by one instantaneous pouring forth of rays? Yet the sun

---

[3] As Cyril goes on to show, in Sections 11-13, the Samaritans received the Pentateuch but not the prophets, so that the Ezekiel passage carried no weight with them. They acknowledged a survival of holy souls but as disembodied only. Heretics believed in survival after death, but "tore away" the resurrection of the flesh from such survival.

[4] Isa. 4ɔ 12.

is but a small part of God's works. Does God's creature, air, enwrap everything in the world? Then the divine Maker of sun and air is surely far above the world."

Imagine, please, that you have a mixture of flower-seeds (it is only fair that if you are feeble where faith is concerned, I should give you feeble examples) and that you have all these mixed seeds in the palm of your hand. Tell me, is it hard or easy for you, a man, to sort your handful, collecting each of the kinds together again by itself? So *you* can sort out what lies in the hollow of your hand. And will you tell me that God cannot see and put back things that lie within the hollow of his hands? [5] Mark my words, and see if it be not impiety to deny them.

4. Please consider now the mere notion of justice and apply it to your own case. You have your different servants, some of them good and some of them bad. Well then, you honour the good ones and beat the bad ones. And if you are a magistrate you praise good men and punish criminals. If, then, justice is maintained by you, a mortal man, will not justice be meted out by God, the perpetual King of the universe? It were impiety to deny it. But now mark what I say. Many a murderer has died unpunished in his bed. Where was God's justice there? And it often happens that a man with fifty murders on his head loses it but once. Where, then, will he pay the penalty for forty-nine of them? You must charge God with lack of justice, if there be not judgement and recompense after this world. Do not be surprised, however, if judgement be delayed. It is only after the contest is over that any competitor in the games is crowned, or disgraced, as the case may be; while the presiding umpire never awards anyone a crown before the contest ends. On the contrary, he waits till he has seen how every competitor finishes, and after that he knows how to award the prizes and the wearing of the crown. In like manner God, so long as our battle in this world is still going on, accords the righteous only a measure of his aid. But hereafter he distributes to everyone their recompense in full.

16. And there are many Scriptures that bear witness to the resurrection of the dead. For there are more things said on that

---

[5] That is, God can cause the particles of matter that constituted a dispersed body to come together again. This is only an *ad hominem* argument, to counter an objection, and is not meant to be the basis of a constructive Christian doctrine. The second-century Christian apologists had, in fact, advanced most of Cyril's arguments.

subject besides.⁶ I mention the resurrection of Lazarus after four days⁷ without, at this point, stopping to do more than call it to mind. Because of lack of time, I must pass by the raising of the widow's son.⁸ Next let me just recall to you the daughter of the ruler of the synagogue,⁹ and mention the rocks being rent, and how "many bodies of the saints which slept arose"¹⁰ when their graves were opened. But principally let it be remembered how that "Christ has been raised from the dead."¹¹

I passed over Elijah, and the widow's son whom he revived,¹² and Elisha who raised a dead man to life on two occasions, one in his lifetime¹³ and the other after he was dead.¹⁴ For when Elisha was alive it was through the energy of his own soul that he caused a resurrection.¹⁵ But the corpse that was thrown into Elisha's tomb and was restored to life again when it touched the dead body of the prophet was revived so that not the souls only of just men should receive honour, but that credit should be given to the bodies of such persons for possessing inward virtue. The prophet's dead body accomplished a soul's work and what lay defunct gave a dead man life, only to remain itself among the dead after thus imparting life. And why? So that, if Elisha should revive,¹⁶ the fact would not be attributed to the mere vitality of his soul;¹⁷ but to show that a certain

6 Sections 5–15 inclusive, dealing with the arguments of unbelievers, have been omitted for brevity. But in dealing with the Samaritans, Cyril has adduced from the Pentateuch proofs of the resurrection of the flesh, and gone on to find further proofs in some prophetic passages. Now, in Section 16, he is about to deal with New Testament doctrine on the same subject.

7 John 11.   8 Luke 7:11–15.   9 Mark 5:22–end.
10 Matt. 27:51–53.   11 I Cor. 15:20.   12 I Kings 17:17–24.
13 II Kings 4:34.   14 II Kings 13:21, 22.
15 Cyril has inferred that the vitality of the prophet's soul played some part in resuscitating the Shunamite's son. If Elisha had risen from death, might it be the same quality of his soul reasserting itself in his dead body? No, Cyril argues, if Elisha rose again it would be purely because God raised him up. And this is shown by the fact that he did not resuscitate his own corpse, when his corpse resuscitated another. The conclusion might seem academic if the whole argument were not transferable to Jesus. That Cyril should drop the argument at that point is evidence how much his prepared matter exceeded the time that he now found at his disposal.
16 For the sake of argument, before the general resurrection.
17 Cyril here provided a classic argument in favour of the veneration of relics. The interesting point is the relation of his teaching to the development of the practice which he thus signally assisted. It may have been in the year of the lectures that Gallus Caesar caused the body of Babylas, martyred bishop of Antioch, to be translated to the adjoining suburb of

virtue resides in the body of saints when the soul has departed, by reason of the righteous soul having inhabited it for so many years, to which it served as instrument. Let us not be so childish as to disbelieve, as if this thing had not happened. For if "handkerchiefs and aprons," things external to the saint's body, so touched the sick that they were raised up,[18] how much more might the prophet's actual body revive the dead?

17. There would be a great deal to say about the incidents I have mentioned, if I explained the wonder of the things that happened, one by one. But because of the strain that you are to meet[19] from the prolongation of Good Friday's fast[20] and the subsequent all-night vigil,[21] let them for the time being be taken

Daphne, to counteract the baleful influence of the shrine of Apollo there (Sozomen, v. 19). Some five years later, Constantius brought the reputed bodies of Andrew and Luke from Achaia, and of Timothy from Ephesus, to enrich the restored Church of the Apostles at Constantinople, where the body of Constantine lay (Philostorgius, iii. 2). This (apart from relics of the Holy Cross taken to Constantinople by Helena) seems to begin the long process of making the new Rome equal the old in the prestige and degree of protection held to go with the possession and veneration of relics. Palestine does not seem to have had at all a lead in this development, and that Cyril should thus have interested himself in it may perhaps be regarded as due to the pilgrim impact on Jerusalem Christianity.

18 Acts 19:12.

19 In this passage, the translator is offered three alternatives. He can take *kamaton* as "weariness" or as the toil or strain that causes it; *progignomai* as "I precede" or as "I come forward"; the aorist participle *progenomenon* as referred to past fact or present fact. Former translators have taken the three first alternatives, and so made Cyril say that his hearers are wearied because they have already endured a continuous fast and all-night vigil. These things extended from Friday evening to Easter morning, and therefore cannot have happened when Cyril delivered this lecture. If we take the second set of alternatives, the *photizomenoi* are just about to meet this strain; and the time of the lecture is the Friday morning before Easter, not yet observed as "Good Friday."

20 For Cyril in 350 the Friday before Easter was the last of his forty lecturing days. The *photizomenoi* would fast till evening and then break their fast in the way normal for fast days. That meal, however, would be their last until they began the feast at Easter. Cyril recognizes that they must not be over-tired before the strain of the forty-hours abstinence from food.

21 Dr J. Jeremias, *s.v.* Pascha, in Kittel's *Wörterbuch zum N-T.*, says that the primitive Church kept Passover with the Jews, only with Christ as Paschal Lamb, and Christian salvation as the deliverance from Egypt. But anti-Jewish polemic in the second century led to the attempt to be "out of step" with the Jews where possible. So now the Christians fasted while the Jews kept Passover, and kept their Easter Eucharist with the dawning of 15 Nisan. They gathered to hear the Scripture, and such preaching as we now know in the Paschal homily of Melito, and, while the Jews feasted, were "like unto men that wait for their Lord, when he

as said in passing, a thin sowing of the seed, which seed when you, being soil of the richest have received, you will bear an increased yield. Now let it be recalled that the apostles also raised the dead. Peter raised up Tabitha at Joppa,[22] Paul raised up Eutychus at Troas,[23] and all the other apostles worked wonders, each in his own way, though they are not all recorded in Scripture.

You remember all that Paul says in his first epistle to the Corinthians in reply to folk who say "How are the dead raised up? and with what body do they come?" namely that "if the dead rise not, then is not Christ raised."[24] You remember that he apostrophizes unbelievers as "fools," and you recall his whole teaching in that passage concerning the resurrection of the dead. You remember how he wrote to the Thessalonians "But I would not have you to be ignorant, brethren, concerning them which are asleep, that you sorrow not, even as others which have no hope" and that whole passage, but particularly the words "and the dead in Christ shall rise first."[25]

18. Now take special note of this, how Paul says, as though he were pointing us where to look, "For this corruptible must put on incorruption, and this mortal must put on immortality."[26] For this very body will be raised up, but it will not continue to be weak, as it is now. Yet while the identical body is raised up, it will be transformed by the putting on of incorruption, as iron exposed to fire is made incandescent, or, rather, in a manner known to the Lord who raises up the dead.[27]

So, this body will be raised up. It will not continue just as it

will return." At the hour of his resurrection they broke the Eucharistic bread. Presently a new way of "breaking step" was found, by ignoring 14 Nisan and carrying the forty-hour fast over to the end of the week in which it fell, so as to have the Easter Eucharist on the first day of the week; in short, making Easter always a Sunday. For a long while, many Christians refused to follow this development, and remained "Quartodecimans," people who tied their observance to the 14th Nisan.

The starting-point for the Easter-eve illumination was the lamplit room of Passover. When fast took the place of supper the illumination was made more brilliant, on the rule "when thou fastest, anoint thine head." Thus in the fragment of a paschal sermon commonly printed as chs. 11 and 12 of the *Epistle to Diognetus*, we read that, the Pasch being now come, "the wax candles are brought and handsomely bestowed." This is probably earlier than the days of Narcissus. (See Introduction, Note 87.)

22 Acts 9:36–42.   23 Acts 20:7–12.   24 I Cor. 15:35, 13.
25 I Thess. 4:13–16.   26 I Cor. 15:53.
27 Note how Cyril leaves the genesis of the spiritual body as unrevealed. The redhot iron simile is not pressed.

is now, but will be everlasting. No longer will it need such food to sustain its life as it needs now. It will not need stairs to ascend by, for it will be spiritual, and that is something wonderful beyond anything that I am equal to describing. It is said "Then shall the righteous shine forth as the sun,"[28] as the moon "and as the brightness of the firmament."[29] And God, who foreknew that men would not believe, has given tiny little worms the power, in hot weather, to give off gleams of light from their bodies, just so that what is to come might gain credence on account of present phenomena. For he who can provide a part can also provide the whole. And the God who makes a worm[30] radiate light is so much the more able to make luminous a righteous man.

19. In the resurrection, therefore, we shall all have bodies that are everlasting, but not all in the same manner. If any man is righteous, he will receive a celestial body, to be able fittingly to converse with angels. If any man be a sinner, he will receive an everlasting body in which to undergo the penalty of sins, a body that will be eternally burned in the fire and yet never be consumed.[31] And this is a just disposition of God in respect of both orders, for nothing that we do is done without the body. We use our mouth to blaspheme, and we use our mouth to pray. It is by means of the body that we commit fornication, and by means of the body that we are chaste. With the hand we snatch and with the hand we give alms. And it is the same with every member. Therefore, since it is the body that has served to every work, the body will have its share in what comes to pass in the hereafter.[32]

20. So brethren, let us take good care of our bodies and not misuse them as if they were no part of ourselves. Do not let us say what the heretics say, that the body is a garment,[33] and

---

[28] Matt. 13:43.   [29] Dan. 12:3.

[30] Ancient writers pillaged the *Natural History* of Aristotle for didactic marvels in nature.

[31] This section epitomizes a Christian apologetic tradition going back to the third century or earlier.

[32] Adopting the reading *ginomenōn* in preference to the more common reading *genomenōn*. Gifford takes the other alternative, which makes the body share, in the hereafter, the reward of past deeds.

[33] The allegorical interpretation of Gen. 3:21 by Origen, saw, in the clothing of Adam and Eve in Eden after their fall, the putting into bodies of souls that had suffered a premundane fall, so that, in bodies, they might be purged through the world-process. In 350, however, Origen was not yet branded as a heretic. The heretics whom Cyril usually has in view both rejected the Old Testament and regarded the body as much worse than

not part of us, but let us take care of it as being our own. For we shall have to give account to the Lord for everything that we have done with the body as instrument. Do not say, No one sees me. Do not imagine that you do anything unwitnessed. Often, it is true, there is no human witness. But our unerring Maker remains "a faithful witness in heaven"[34] and beholds what is done. Moreover the stains made by sinning remain in the body. For just as a scar remains, notwithstanding the healing up, however complete, of a wound that has gone its course in the body, so likewise sin wounds both soul and body, and the marks of the scars remain every time, and are effaced only in those who receive baptism. The former wounds, then, of soul and body, God cures by baptism, but let us one and all hereafter guard ourselves from future sins, to keep clean this garment, the body, and not lose heaven's salvation through commission of some few acts of fornication, self-indulgence or any other sin. Let us, on the contrary, be heirs of God's eternal kingdom. And may God grant you all, by the help of his grace, to be worthy of it.

21. So much by way of development of the clause on the resurrection of the dead. As for the profession of faith, as I repeat it to you again, I want you to use every endeavour to say it over with me and to memorize it.

[At this point it would appear that Cyril stopped lecturing and received the repetition by heart of the baptismal creed from the *photizomenoi*, one by one; and, this completed, what was in effect a second lecture was begun.]

The faith we profess comes in due course to the words "and in one baptism of repentance for the remission of sins, and in one holy Catholic Church, and in the resurrection of the flesh, and in eternal life." I dealt with baptism in relation to repentance in my opening lectures.[35] And what I was saying just now on the resurrection of the dead covers the resurrection of the flesh. The rest of my lecture is to discourse for a while on "and in one holy Catholic Church." It is a subject about which there is a great deal to say, but I shall speak of it quite briefly.

a garment, as indeed a tomb or prison of the soul. Cyril's emphasis is on the negation, "not part of us." The orthodox continued to accept the simile of the body as a garment, which Origen's exegesis had made popular, after his doctrine of the prenatal fall of souls had been condemned.

34 Ps. 89:37.
35 In Lectures II and III.

23. The Church, then, is called Catholic[36] because it is spread through the whole world, from one end of the earth to the other, and because it never stops teaching in all its fulness every doctrine that men ought to be brought to know: and that regarding things visible and invisible, in heaven and on earth. It is called Catholic also because it brings into religious obedience every sort of men, rulers and ruled, learned and simple, and because it is a universal treatment and cure for every kind of sin whether perpetrated by soul or body, and possesses within it every form of virtue that is named, whether it expresses itself in deeds or words or in spiritual graces of every description.

24. The Church is well named *Ecclesia* because it calls everyone out[37] and assembles them together, according as, in the book Leviticus, the Lord says, "And assemble thou (*ecclesiason*) all the congregation to the doors of the tabernacle of witness."[38] We should note that this is the first time that this word for "assemble" (*ecclesiason*) occurs in Scripture, and does so at the point where the Lord places Aaron in the office of high priest. In Deuteronomy, also, God says to Moses, "Assemble to me the people, and I will make them hear my words, that they shall learn to fear me."[39] The name Church is recalled again in the passage about the tables of the Law, "And on them was written according to all the words which the Lord spake with you in the mount out of the midst of the fire on the day of the assembly (*ecclesia*)"[40]; which is the same thing as saying, in plainer words, "on the day when God called you out and gathered you together." And the Psalmist says, "I will give

---

[36] *catholicos* means "general," in distinction from "particular"; "universal" in contrast with "limited." Cyril proceeds to find all the ways in which the Church is thus "Catholic." There is no saving doctrine that it fails to teach, no class of person that it does not contain, no evil for which it has no remedy, no virtue that it does not inculcate.

[37] *Ecclesia* is derived from the verb *ekkalein*, to call out, and was used by the Greeks to denote the public gathering of citizens at the summons of the magistrates, when the magistrates wanted to find, or influence, the mind of the people, on some issue. The idea of the word is that the people are called out of their houses to go to the public assembly. As Cyril goes on to say, the Israelites in their camp in the wilderness were summoned from their tents to the space in front of the tabernacle, in exactly the same way, only that now the assembly has, from the first, sacred associations. Hence the name *Ecclesia* passes, *via* Israel, to the Christian Church, which is an assembly of those whom God has called out from among men to have faith in Christ.

[38] Lev. 8:3.   [39] Deut. 4:10.

[40] Deut. 9:10.

thee thanks in the great assembly: I will praise thee among much people."[41]

25. So, then, in the old dispensation, the Psalmist sang, "Bless ye God in the churches, even the Lord, from the fountain of Israel."[42] But since then the Jews have fallen out of favour because of their conspiring against the Lord, and the Saviour has built up a second holy Church, our Christian Church, from out of the Gentiles, and spoke of it to Peter, saying, "And upon this rock I will build my Church, and the gates of hell shall not prevail against it,"[43] David prophesied clearly concerning the two Churches, of the first, that it is cast off, "I have hated the church of the evil doers"[44]; and in the same psalm of the second church that is abuilding, "Lord, I have loved the beauty of thine house"[45]; and straightway after, "In the churches, will I bless thee, O Lord."[46] For since the single church that was in Judaea was cast off, henceforth the churches of Christ abound in all the world. These are they of which it is said in the Psalms, "Sing unto the Lord a new song, and his praise in the church of the saints."[47] In agreement with these passages is that where the prophet said to the Jews, "I have no pleasure in you, saith the Lord of hosts," and immediately afterwards, "For from the rising of the sun even unto the going down of the same, my name shall be great among the Gentiles."[48] Paul writes to Timothy about this holy Catholic Church and says "That thou mayest know how thou oughtest to behave thyself in the house of God, which is the church of the living God, the pillar and ground of the truth."[49]

26. But since the word "assembly" (ecclesia) has different applications, as when it is used in Scripture of the crowd that filled the theatre at Ephesus, saying, "And when he had thus spoken, he dismissed the assembly,"[50] or when one applies it, quite properly and correctly, to heretical gatherings, since there is a "church of the evil doers,"[51] I mean the conventicles of the Marcionites, Manichees and others; because of this variety of use, there has been given to you the article of faith "and in one holy Catholic Church," so that you should flee their wretched gatherings, and ever keep within the holy Catholic Church in which you are regenerate. Should you ever be staying in some strange town, do not just ask, Where is the

41 Ps. 35:18.   42 Ps. 68:26 (Septuagint).   43 Matt. 16:18.
44 Ps. 26:5.   45 Ps. 26:8 (Septuagint).   46 Ps. 26:12.
47 Ps. 149:1.   48 Mal. 1:10, 11.   49 I Tim. 3:15.
50 Acts 19:41.   51 Ps. 26:5 (Septuagint).

church (*kyriakon*,[52] "kirk")? seeing that all those sects of the ungodly would have their dens called churches. And do not be content to ask, Where is the assembly (*ecclesia*)? but say "Where is the Catholic congregation?" For that is the unequivocal name of this holy Church and mother of us all. She is the bride of our Lord Jesus Christ, the only-begotten Son of God, as it is written, "As Christ also loved the church, and gave himself for it . . ." (Read the whole passage.)[53] She also presents the form and image of "Jerusalem which is above" which "is free and the mother of us all," that once was barren, but now hath many children.[54]

27. For after the first church was cast off, as Paul says, in the second and Catholic Church, "God hath set first apostles, secondarily prophets, thirdly teachers, after that miracles, then gifts of healings, helps, governments, diversities of tongues"[55]; yes, and every sort of virtue, such as wisdom and understanding, moderation and uprightness, generosity and kindness, and patience that will not break down under persecution. "By the armour of righteousness on the right hand and on the left, by honour and dishonour,"[56] this Church in days of old, when persecutions and afflictions abounded, wove chaplets for the holy martyrs of the many tints and flowers of patience. And now, when God has favoured us with times of peace, this Church receives from emperors and men of high estate, as from every condition and race of men, the honour that is her due. And while the sovereigns of the nations in this or that part of the earth have borders set to their dominion, the holy Catholic Church alone bears sway in all the world, and knows no bounds: as it is written "for God hath made her border peace."[57] I should need to lecture for many more hours if I were to say everything about the Church that I would like to say.

28. Now if, in this holy Catholic Church, we receive her teaching and conduct ourselves aright, we shall possess the kingdom of heaven and inherit eternal life. That is something for which we endure all labours, so that we may enjoy it at the Lord's hands. For what we aim at is nothing trivial. We are striving after eternal life. In the profession of the faith, therefore, after "and in the resurrection of the flesh (or dead)" on which

---

[52] The church building was not called *ekklesia* but *kyriakon*, "the Lord's house."
[53] Eph. 5:25.   [54] Gal. 4:26.   [55] I Cor. 12:28.   [56] II Cor. 6:7, 8.
[57] Ps. 147:14 (A.V. He maketh peace in thy borders).

I have spoken, we learn belief "and in eternal life," for which as Christians we are striving.

29. Now the life that is really and truly life is God the Father, the fount of life,[58] who pours out his heavenly gifts upon all his creatures through the Son and in the Holy Spirit, and the blessings of eternal life are faithfully promised even to us men, through his love for us. There must be no incredulity about the possibility of that. For we ought to believe, because our mind should be set on his power, not on our feebleness. For anything is possible with God, and that our eternal life is both possible and to be looked forward to by us, is shown when Daniel says, "the understanding . . . from among the many righteous shall shine as the stars for ever and ever."[59] And Paul says, "And so shall we be ever with the Lord."[60] For "being ever with the Lord" means the same thing as eternal life. But clearest of all, our Saviour himself says, in the Gospels, "And these shall go away into everlasting punishment, but the righteous into life eternal."[61]

30. Moreover there are many demonstrations of the manner[62] of eternal life. And if we are eager to obtain this eternal life, the Holy Scriptures suggest to us the ways of doing so. But in view of the length of this lecture, I shall, for now, set before you a few of the testimonies, and leave the diligent among you to search out the rest. In some passages it appears that faith is the means to eternal life, for it is written "He that believeth on the Son hath everlasting life"[63] and the rest of that passage. Again Christ says, "Verily, verily, I say unto you, he that heareth my words, and believeth on him that sent me, hath everlasting life . . ."[64] In other passages it is the evangelic preaching. For Christ says, "he that reapeth receiveth wages, and gathereth fruit unto life eternal."[65] In other passages it is by being a martyr or confessor in Christ, for he says, "And he that hateth his life in this world, shall keep it unto life eternal."[66]

---

58 Within the next thirty years, as the formulation of the doctrine of the Trinity reached stability, God the Father came to be called "fount of Godhead," and the Holy Spirit came to be confessed as "Life-giver." Cyril, however, who calls the Father "fount of life," recognizes fully that "eternal life" is no natural attribute of man, but can only come to man by his union with God.

59 Dan. 12:3 (Septuagint).   60 I Thess. 4:17.   61 Matt. 25:46.

62 Cyril regards the last three texts as assurance of the fact that eternal life is possible, as a gift of God, for man. He now collects passages to show how it is mediated.

63 John 3:36.   64 John 5:24.   65 John 4:36.   66 John 12:25.

In others it is by preferring Christ before possessions or kins-
folk; "And everyone that hath forsaken brethren or sisters . . .
shall inherit everlasting life."[67] In others it is by keeping the
commandments, "Thou shalt not commit adultery, thou shalt
not kill" and the rest of that passage, as in Christ's reply to
the man who came to him and said, "Good Master, what shall
I do that I may have eternal life?"[68] And in others again it is
by forsaking evil ways and thenceforth serving God, for Paul
says, "But now, being made free from sin, and become servants
to God, ye have your fruit unto holiness, and the end everlasting life."[69]

31. Yes, the discovering of eternal life takes place in many
ways that I have passed over because they are so many. For
the Lord is so loving towards us that he has not opened one
door, or just two, but many doors of entry into eternal life,
so that all might enjoy that life without hindrance, so far as
lies with him. And for the present I will not exceed what I
have said about eternal life, which is the last of the doctrines
in the profession of our faith, and its conclusion. Grant that all
of us, by God's grace, both I your teacher and you my hearers,
may attain to eternal life!

32. Finally, dear brethren, this course of instruction moves
you all to prepare your souls to receive the heavenly gifts. As
concerns the holy and apostolic faith that was committed to
you to profess, I have, in the course of these forty days past,
by the grace of the Lord, given as many lectures as was
possible.[70] Not that these have said all that I should have said,
for many points have been omitted, and things perhaps that

---

[67] Matt. 19:29.   [68] Mark 10:17-19.   [69] Rom. 6:22.

[70] It thus appears that, for some reason, a second morning was required in
connection with every lecture. The *photizomenoi*, as has been said, included many who understood only Palestinian Aramaic, and so everything
said in Greek must have been said also in Aramaic. If an interpreter had
rendered Cyril's phrases, sentence by sentence, as he went along, his
Greek lectures could hardly have had the freshness and spontaneity
which they have. Also they would have consumed an intolerable length
of time. The greater probability seems to be that Cyril was himself
bilingual, and repeated in Aramaic the substance of each lecture delivered in Greek, on a later day; or anticipated the Greek lecture, in
Aramaic, on the previous day. A regular alternation does not seem
possible, when one Greek lecture refers to the previous one as having
been given "yesterday." Also there seems no possibility that this final
"double-lecture" could have been given again, afterwards, in Aramaic.
How the language-group that was not being lectured to employed itself
cannot be determined.

have been the subject of sublimer thought by better teachers. For the rest, the holy Paschal day is at hand,[71] and the enlightenment of your dear selves through "the laver of regeneration"[72] in Christ. So you will be instructed once again,[73] God willing, in the appropriate things, with what devotion and good order you are to enter as you are called, and for what purpose each of the holy mysteries of baptism is accomplished; and again with what reverence and good order you are to go forward from your baptism to the holy altar of God and enjoy the spiritual and heavenly mysteries that belong to it. And this is to the end that your souls may be enlightened beforehand by the course of instruction to appreciate the greatness of each of those graces that God vouchsafes to you.

33. After the holy and salvation-bringing feast of Easter, beginning on the Monday, you shall, God willing, hear further lectures, if you will come into the holy place of the resurrection each day of Easter week after the liturgy.[74] In these you will be instructed again in the reasons for each of the things that took place. You will be given proofs from the Old and New Testaments, first, of course, for the things that were done immediately before your baptism, and next how you have been made clean from your sins by the Lord "with the washing of water by the word,"[75] then how you have entered into the right to be called "Christ" in virtue of your "priesthood,"[76] then how you

[71] They have only one night's sleep between then and Easter.
[72] Titus 3:5.
[73] This appears to refer, not to another lecture, but to preparation carried out by the inferior clergy, the baptizands being taught individually.
[74] Cyril appears thus to propose six "mystagogic" lectures. In the MSS we have only five. It is not very likely that the mystagogic lectures were transcribed in the same year that the prebaptismal lectures were first transcribed. There is thus a strong probability that the lectures which Cyril is here announcing were not transcribed. The neophytes, for these post-paschal lectures, went into the courtyard west of the Martyry, where they stood around the sepulchre, and the bishop spoke to them from the very place where Christ rose from the dead. It is to be supposed, therefore, that these post-paschal lectures were much shorter and simpler than the Lent lectures; and the five mystagogic lectures in the manuscripts have this character. They do not, however, fulfil accurately the forecast which Cyril is here giving.
[75] Eph. 5:26.
[76] *Hieratikōs.* The idea is that the chrism or anointing with oil, is the unction of priesthood, such as Aaron received, so that every Christian initiate is the Lord's anointed (and since "Christ" means anointed, is a Christ). The third mystagogic lecture in the manuscripts seems to avoid any such emphasis upon the priesthood of the baptized laity as Cyril here lays.

have been given the "sealing" of fellowship with the Holy
Spirit, then about the mysteries of the altar of the new covenant
which had their origin here,[77] what Holy Scripture tells us
about them, with what virtue they are filled, then how these
mysteries are to be approached and when and how received,
and so, finally, how for the rest of your life you must walk
worthily of the grace you have received both by deed and word,
so as all to attain to the enjoyment of eternal life. If God will,
then, these lectures will be given.

34. "Finally, my brethren, rejoice in the Lord[78] alway; and
again I say, Rejoice[79]: for your redemption" hath drawn
"nigh."[80] The celestial army of the angels looks for your
salvation. And now is "the voice of one crying in the wilderness, Prepare ye the way of the Lord." The prophet also
cries "Ho, everyone that thirsteth, come ye to the waters,"
and forthwith "Hearken diligently unto me, and eat ye that
which is good, and let your soul delight itself in fatness."[81]
It will not be long before you are listening to the reading of
that lovely passage, "Be light, be light, O thou new Jerusalem;
for thy light is come."[82] And that is the Jerusalem of which the
prophet said, "And afterwards thou shalt be called the city of
righteousness, the faithful city Zion; for out of Zion shall go
forth the law, and out of Jerusalem the word of the Lord."[83]
That word, in going forth from thence has been a gracious
rain upon the whole earth. And the prophet speaks to that new
Jerusalem concerning you, and says, "Lift up thine eyes round
about, and behold thy children gathered together,"[84] while
she replies "Who are these that fly as a cloud, and as doves
with their young ones to me?"[85] ("cloud" because you are
spiritual, and "doves" because you are innocent). She proceeds,
"who hath heard such a thing? who hath seen such things?
shall the earth be made to bring forth in one day? or shall a
nation be born at once? for as soon as Zion travailed, she
brought forth her children."[86] The world shall be full of joy
unspeakable, since the Lord hath said, "Behold I create
Jerusalem a rejoicing, and her people a joy."[87]

[77] In Jerusalem. [78] Phil. 3:1. [79] Phil. 4:4.
[80] Luke 21:28. [81] Isa. 55:1, 2. [82] Isa. 60:1 (Septuagint).
[83] Isa. 1:26; 2:3. [84] Isa. 49:18 (Septuagint).
[85] Isa. 60:8 (Septuagint). [86] Isa. 66:8.
[87] Isa. 65:18. The last Section (35) of this lecture has been omitted for
brevity.

A Letter of Cyril to Constantius

A letter of Saint Cyril, archbishop of Jerusalem, written on the seventh of May to the most religious sovereign, Constantius, concerning the portent of a cross of light that appeared in the sky and was seen from Jerusalem[1]

To the emperor most beloved of God, the most religious Constantius Augustus, from Cyril, the bishop in Jerusalem, greeting.

1. This first letter from Jerusalem I send to you, emperor beloved of God; by way of first fruits,[2] and one both fitting for your reception and for me to send. I have filled it, not with words of flattery but with divine portents full of heavenly meaning, not with the winning persuasiveness of rhetorical composition but with witness borne to you, by the course of events, of the truth of the things predicted in the holy Gospels.

2. For while other men have wherewith to weave many a crown for your beloved head, and offer circlets of gold set with many-coloured and glittering stones, I offer you no earthly crown at all (since earthly gifts return to earth at last) but that which divine working has brought to pass in the heavens, accomplished in these times of your godly reign, which

---

[1] The heading goes back to eleventh-century MSS. In the Munich MS made by the sixteenth-century copyist Andrew Damarius it is simpler, and omits the date. This copy may well have been made from an examplar older than the eleventh century. The day and month are in the text of Section 4. The year is certainly A.D. 351, since fourth-century witnesses place it between Gallus being made Caesar (15 March, 351) and the battle of Mursa (28 September, 351). Magnentius, a commander in Gaul, conspired against the emperor Constans in the early days of 350. Constantius, soon afterwards, experienced relief from the pressure of the Persians, after their failure in the siege of Nisibis (end of 349), and declined negotiations with Magnentius, whom he defeated first at Mursa, and destroyed somewhat over a year later. Thus in May 351 Constantius was gathering his force against the western usurper.

[2] The implication is that Cyril had not been bishop very long. On the other hand, some delay in presenting first-fruits to the emperor is excused by the choice character of the gift now for this purpose placed from heaven in Cyril's hands. Cyril speaks as if, from him, first-fruits might be considered due; because, presumably, of the imperial foundations in his see, giving him a position analogous to that of a Dean of the Chapels Royal. Canon 7 of Nicaea had left Jerusalem suffragan to Caesarea *in spiritualibus*, but Cyril might feel himself directly a client of the emperor in administering his temporalities.

I hasten to bring to the knowledge of your piety. I do not, of course, mean that you are coming now for the first time from ignorance to knowledge of God (for you have been forward to teach others by your religious conversation), but I write to add confirmation to what you know, so that as you have received imperial sovereignty by paternal inheritance[3] you should learn to be honoured by God with greater heavenly crowns, or rather that you should now both return fitting thanks to God the King of all, and also be filled with greater courage in the face of your enemies,[4] as you understand, from the marvellous work of God on your behalf, to what effect your sovereignty is made the object of his love.

3. For, in the days of Constantine your father, most dear to God and of blessed memory, there was discovered the wood of the cross fraught with salvation,[5] because the divine grace that gave piety to the pious seeker vouchsafed the finding of

[3] There was nothing of heredity in the notion of the office of emperor (*imperator*). But Constantine (himself the natural son of Constantius Chlorus) being, like his father, very much a leader of Gaulish and Germanic soldiery, was familiar with the hereditary kingship that prevailed among nations outside the empire, and succeeded in getting the armies to accept his sons as co-emperors. With the usurpation of Magnentius, the dynastic conception was again in jeopardy. But it was one that commended itself to the people of the east.

[4] As a centre for pilgrims, Jerusalem received the world's news. Cyril shows a fine appreciation of the moment of crisis in the emperor's life at which (as he held) God had declared that the cause of Constantius was beloved to him. Cyril's letter, no doubt, was of no small effect upon the spirit of Constantius, and so upon the course of events.

[5] Cyril refers to the wood of the cross having been discovered, and widely distributed, in Lectures IV (10), X (19) and XIII (4). But he tells nothing of the circumstances. The story of Helena, the mother of Constantine, discovering three crosses, and distinguishing the cross of Christ by a miracle, is due to Rufinus (*Church History*, x. 7, 8), in whose Latin version and continuation of the *Church History* of Eusebius it appears for the first time. This work dates from 403, six years after the author had returned from Palestine to Italy. The story was probably that current in Jerusalem in the 390s. It makes Helena discover the crosses on Golgotha under a mound surmounted by a shrine of Venus. This is so similar to the story in Eusebius, *Life of Constantine*, (iii. 26–28) of the discovery of the holy sepulchre under a mound surmounted by a shrine of Venus, that Theodoret makes the two stories into one. As Rufinus speaks of silver caskets containing pieces of the wood of the cross found by Helena as being still shown for veneration in Jerusalem, we may reasonably connect the discovery of the cross with the empress' visit; but conclude that popular fancy had early confused the circumstances with those of the uncovering of the sepulchre, as well as adorning with legend the historical facts of the "invention" of the cross.

the buried holy places.[6] But in your time, your Majesty, most religious of emperors, victorious through a piety towards God greater even than that which you inherited, are seen wonderful works, not from the earth any more, but from the heavens. The trophy of the victory over death of our Lord and Saviour Jesus Christ, the only-begotten Son of God, I mean the blessed cross, has been seen at Jerusalem blazing with refulgent light!

4. For in these very days of the holy feast of Pentecost,[7] on the Nones[8] of May, about the third hour[9] a gigantic cross formed of light appeared in the sky above holy Golgotha[10] stretching out as far as the holy Mount of Olives. It was not seen by just one or two, but was most clearly displayed before

6 The discovery of holy sites in Jerusalem seems to have begun with the unearthing of the sepulchre. In the *Life of Constantine*, iii. 26, Eusebius implies that the position of the sepulchre was known to the Christians, while Constantine's letter (iii. 30) would seem to show that they had sought excavation under Licinius and been refused. See also Eusebius, *Theophany*, iii. 61 describing the isolated rock with one single tomb, fit for an unique burial. Eusebius says that Constantine ordered the building of a "house of prayer" "near the Saviour's tomb," and goes on to describe the Martyry. To this we must join the references to be found in Cyril's lectures, where (in IV. 10, 14, X. 19, XIII. 4, 39) the Martyry is said to be on Golgotha. Golgotha may have been determined as being between the sepulchre and the road to the north, though Cyril (XIII. 39) says the rock there was riven, which may have determined, or partly determined, the identification of the site. Cyril, in the Epistle, may mention the finding of the cross before the finding of the holy places because of the theme of this letter being the cross. The silence of Eusebius regarding the cross would suggest that the discovery of the sepulchre came first. But Cyril's reference, in the letter, to "buried holy places" (in the plural) may mean that the wood identified as the cross was dug up on Golgotha. While he chiefly associates the Martyry with the crucifixion, he calls it (XIV. 14) "this holy Church of the Resurrection of God our Saviour," since the sepulchre, garden court, and Martyry, together, formed one complex of buildings to testify to the acts which accomplished our salvation.

7 May 7 always falls in the "fifty days" between Easter and Whitsun.

8 The name Nones was given to the ninth day before the Ides (or "half-month-day") in each month. In March, May, July and October the Ides was the 15th day, and in the other months the 13th. So, in May, the Nones fell on the 7th, the Ides being included in the nine days.

9 Nine, a.m.

10 The phenomenon may be reasonably supposed to have been a parhelion, arising from some atmospheric condition of the time. It was witnessed from Golgotha, and so would appear in the sky to the south-east of the city. It would only be "above holy Golgotha" in Cyril's mind, but the northern arm might seem to him to be above the Mount of Olives to his east.

the whole population of the city.[11] Nor did it, as one might have supposed, pass away quickly like something imagined, but was visible to sight above the earth for some hours, while it sparkled with a light above the sun's rays. Of a surety, it would have been overcome and hidden by them had it not exhibited to those who saw it a brilliance more powerful than the sun,[12] so that the whole population of the city made a sudden concerted rush into the Martyry, seized by a fear that mingled with joy at the heavenly vision. They poured in, young and old, men and women of every age, even to maidens hitherto kept in the seclusion of their homes,[13] local folk and strangers together, not only Christians but pagans from elsewhere sojourning in Jerusalem;[14] all of them as with one mouth raised a hymn of praise to Christ Jesus our Lord, the only-begotten Son of God, the worker of wonders. For they recognized in fact and by experience that the most religious creed of Christians is "not with enticing words of wisdom, but in demonstration of the Spirit and of power,"[15] not something merely preached by men, but having witness borne to it by God from the heavens.

5. Therefore, seeing that we, the dwellers in Jerusalem, have

---

[11] The cross of light seen by Constantine in the afternoon sky during one of his Gaulish campaigns before A.D. 313, of which he told Eusebius, who recorded the story, with all appearance of careful accuracy (*Life of Constantine*, i. 28), was witnessed by the whole army on the march. It, also, may have been a parhelion, and as important in its effect upon the mind of the emperor concerned as the subject of Cyril's letter. It is one of the curiosities of history that, in 351, the manuscript of the *Life of Constantine* was lying at Caesarea uncopied, and perhaps unread. It is quite likely that we owe its publication to Cyril's nephew Gelasius, in the later days of his episcopate at Caesarea. Gelasius wrote a continuation of the *Church History* of Eusebius which furnished Rufinus with a good deal of his supplement to his translation of Eusebius, and survives only by that means.

[12] Had the direct view of the sun not been greatly tempered by the atmospheric condition that caused the cross-shaped parhelion, the cross, on Cyril's showing, would have been too fiercely bright to look at. Clearly this was not so, and the explanation in terms of a parhelion is accordingly strengthened.

[13] Such girls went out, as need might be, escorted and closely veiled. On this occasion their coming out was so hasty that the proprieties were sacrificed.

[14] It thus appears that residence in Jerusalem was almost as much controlled as in the days of Nehemiah, but now as a Christian sacred city. Sozomen, *Church History*, iv. 5, says that pilgrims carried the news of the Cross in the sky at Jerusalem all over the world.

[15] I Cor. 2:4.

seen with our own eyes this marvellous occurrence and have
rendered to God the universal King and to the only-begotten
Son of God the thankful adoration that is due, and will so
tender: and have moreover made, as we will yet make, in the
Holy Places, continued prayer for your reign as emperor dear
to God,[16] we must not consign these God-given sights in the
heavens to silence, but tell your sacred piety the joyful news.
Without delay, I have hastened to dispatch this letter, so that,
upon the good foundation of the faith you already possess, you
might build up the knowledge of the recent divine manifestation, and so receive yet stronger confidence in our Lord Jesus
Christ. At the same time you will be filled with your usual
courage as having God himself upon your side, and will the
more readily advance under the trophy of the cross,[17] using
the sign that appeared in heaven as a crowning glory, in which
heaven itself has gloried the more in showing forth its shape to
men.

6. Now this portent, God-beloved emperor, has been now
accomplished in accordance with the testimonies of the prophets[18] and with the sacred words of Christ contained in the
Gospels, but in days to come it will be accomplished more
fully.[19] For in the Gospel according to Matthew the Saviour
gives a knowledge of things to come to his blessed apostles,
and, through them, spoke to those who came after them, saying
in the most lucid way, "And then shall appear the sign of the
Son of man in heaven."[20] And if you will take into your hands
this sacred book of the Gospels, as you are wont to do, you
will find therein written down the prophetic testimony to this

[16] The Christians of Jerusalem feel themselves, more than other citizens,
bound to this duty as clients of the emperor.

[17] Constantius' troops marched under the Christian form of standard with
which Constantine had largely replaced the legionary eagles. The prestige
of this form of standard would be renewed, Cyril implies, by the sign
which had just been given from heaven. What he is writing to the emperor, it is his hope will be used to reinvigorate the morale of his soldiery.

[18] In Lecture XIII. 41, Cyril supposes Zech. 12:10–12 to foretell the second
coming of Christ accompanied by the sign of the cross. The same lecture
has many asserted prophecies of Christ's crucifixion.

[19] In Lecture XV. 22, Cyril interprets Matt. 24:30 as meaning that when
Christ comes in judgement, his presence will be heralded by a sign of a
luminous cross. As Antichrist could not use this sign, it secures the faithful
against deception. That the Christians of Jerusalem had received such
teaching, fully explains their behaviour on 7 May, 351. The morrow's
retrospect brings Cyril to the conclusion that what has just happened
is the more significant because it bears the seal of Christ, in an anticipation
of his final sign.   [20] Matt. 24:30.

fact. And I beseech your majesty in particular to make these things the subject of your more frequent meditation, because of the other things that are written out in order in the same place.[21] These matters that were foretold by our Saviour call for diligence mingled with great reverence, if we are to take no harm from the power that works against us.

7. To you, emperor most dear to God, I offer these words as first fruits. I send forth from Jerusalem this first call,[22] to you who are the noblest and most religious fellow-worshipper with us of Christ the only-begotten Son of God and our Saviour, who accomplished the world's salvation by dying according to the Scriptures at Jerusalem, where he trod death underfoot,[23] washed out the sins of men with his own precious blood, and obtained for all those that believe in him life, and incorruption, and spiritual grace from heaven. May his power and grace cheer and protect you with the adornment of brighter and greater religious deeds, and may almighty God, the giver of all goodness make you proud with royal shoots of noble sons,[24]

---

[21] Cyril means the signs of the coming of Antichrist, to be sought in the political sphere, taken to be implied in the warning of Matt. 24:36-end; so that in minding this warning we shall not be caught when Antichrist reveals himself.

[22] The imperial benefactions make Constantius a sharer in the privileges of the Jerusalem Church, which thus has a special responsibility to him.

[23] Appreciation of the empty tomb as evidence of Christ's victory was evidently much revived by the recovery of the sepulchre.

[24] In the summer of 350, Magnentius proposed alliance to Constantius, based on the marriage of Magnentius to Constantius' sister, and of Constantius to Magnentius' daughter. The proposal argues that the first wife of Constantius, married in 336, was now dead, leaving him a childless widower. Constantius had only Gallus and Julian as kinsmen and so possible colleagues and successors, now that Constans and Nepotian were dead. Constantius' need of a son was urgent, all the more in his rejection of alliance with the murderer of Constans. Cyril evidently knew, in May 351, that the two things which Constantius sought from heaven were success in the field and success in marriage. The first came to him at Mursa in September. Julian, in his panegyric upon the empress Eusebia, a noblewoman of Thessalonica and of great personal gifts, says that Constantius, when he had repossessed himself of his inherited empire by the defeat of the usurper, sought marriage for the sake of sons who should inherit his honours and authority. Only after long deliberation and careful enquiries did he decide that Eusebia was the person worthy to be empress of the whole world. If this last point is not purely rhetorical, the emperor's intention to marry again must have been known for some time before it was accomplished. It is likely to have been made public before Gallus was made Caesar in March 351, to set that political step in its right perspective. Eusebia did not in fact bear a son, so that Julian became Constantius' heir.

and keep you and all your house, for many cycles of peaceful years, the boast of Christians and the pride of the whole world. 8. May the God of all grant to us and all people that you, Augustus and emperor beloved of God, may be strong, adorned with every virtue, displaying your wonted solicitude for the holy churches and the sovereignty of Rome, and shining with yet greater rewards of piety through many cycles of peaceful years, ever to glorify the holy and consubstantial[25] Trinity, our true God, to whom, as is due, be all glory, world without end. Amen.

[25] The appearance of this word (*homoousios*) in the conclusion of the letter has caused doubts of its authenticity to be entertained. But the whole phrase beginning "ever to glorify" is missing from the manuscript of Damarius, who habitually copied ancient MSS, to sell the copies in the west. There is probability that this omission in his sixteenth-century Munich transcript reflects the fact that a copy of Cyril's letter to Constantius considerably older than the surviving copies, had not the conclusion containing the suspect phrase. The addition of such an ending is entirely comprehensible on the part of an ecclesiastical scribe, particularly in vindication of Cyril's reputation for orthodoxy. On the side of the authenticity of the letter there is the improbability of a forger seizing so accurately the situation of early 351, or getting Cyril's style and vocabulary so well. This last point is debated in the Abbé Touttée's preface (reproduced by Reischl and Rupp, p. 430). The striking expression for "a crowning glory" (*kaukēma kaukēmatōn*) used at the end of Section 5 appears also in Lecture I. 13. And there are a number of other, if less striking, correspondences with the language of the lectures. The text of the letter may therefore be trusted, if suspicion is confined to the conventional concluding phrase, which we may regard as being a scribal addition.

NEMESIUS

BISHOP OF EMESA

General Introduction

THE AUTHOR

A NUMBER OF MANUSCRIPTS OF THE WORK *On the nature of man* are headed with the name of Nemesius, bishop of Emesa. The first mention of any such person by other writers is not till the seventh century, when Maximus the Confessor[1] (580–662) and Anastasius Sinaita[2] (630–700) cite passages from the work in question and name the author as Nemesius, bishop of Emesa. But they show no signs of knowing anything about him, and we must suppose them to have been, just as we are, dependent on the manuscript heading for their ability to name the author of the work. The tendency is for works of obscure authors to be fathered upon someone better known.[3] Where, as here, the name of an otherwise unknown person comes down in manuscript tradition, it can safely be accepted as that of the true author.

Of the author's see, at least, something is known. Emesa is

[1] Maximus, *Opuscula theologica et polemica*, Migne, *Patrologia Graeca*, xci. 277.
[2] Anastasius, *Quaestiones* (xviii), Migne, *Patrologia Graeca*, xcix. 505.
The Syriac writer Moses bar Cephas (tenth century) cites our author under the title "Numysius the Christian philosopher," but this is likewise pure inference from the work itself. (*De Paradiso*, Pt. I. c. 20, Migne, *Patrologia Graeca*, cxi. 508.)
[3] This happened to all or parts of our work. Chs. II and III are often found, under the title *On the soul*, attributed to Gregory of Nyssa. The whole work is attributed to Gregory in an eleventh-century Augsburg manuscript among others. One eighteenth-century Augsburg manuscript attributes it to "Adamantion," while a twelfth-century Florentine copy, and one at the Bodleian at Oxford, calls the author "Adamantion, who is also Nemesius, bishop of Emesa." So much confusion arose that there are copies that attribute the work to "Gregory of Emesa," or "Nemesius of Nyssa." The attribution to Gregory Nyssen probably helped to get the work more widely known than it would have been under its rightful name.

a city on the upper reaches of the Orontes, where the river, emerging from the valley between Libanus and Antilibanus, flows through a fertile plain. It stood on the trade-route that ran southwards through Damascus, and at the point of shortest transit across the desert to Palmyra.[4] It throve upon nomad industries, as well as on those of rural Syria. It was, in short, though not one of Syria's greatest cities, at least a prosperous and important city of the second rank. From pre-Christian antiquity its celebrity arose from a famous temple of the sun-god, whose cult was served by a dynasty of Syrian priest-princes,[5] who ruled over a sacred territory in the Orontes plain. The fortune of Emesa began to be made, towards the end of the second Christian century, when a daughter of this priestly house, Julia Domna, married the African, Septimius Severus, who was emperor, 193–211. Her son, the emperor Caracalla, raised Emesa to the status of a Roman colony. In 218 the legions in Syria called to the purple the young prince-priest of Emesa, Elagabalus. He was succeeded as emperor by his cousin Alexander Severus, and under these Syrian emperors Emesa received the *jus italicum* and the title of metropolis.[6] In 272 Aurelian beautified the famous temple at Emesa, and not far from the city inflicted upon his eastern rival, the empress Zenobia of Palmyra, a final defeat.[7] Emesa received its last

---

[4] The oasis city of Palmyra enabled travellers to cross the desert between the Euphrates valley and Syria-Palestine in two stages, and, at troubled times, with greater safety than by the roads of north Syria. Palladius, in his *Dialogue* (c.71) on the history of John Chrysostom speaks of Palmyra, at the beginning of the fifth century, as a barbarous outpost of empire over against the Persians, to which the Joannite Cyriacus, bishop of Synnada in Phrygia, was exiled. He describes Palmyra as "80 miles further inland than Emesa." Le Quien, in his *Oriens Christianus* (ii. 837), mis-read this to say that Cyriacus was bishop of Emesa, and so gives Nemesius a successor who never existed. The blunder is perpetuated by P. B. Gams, *Series Episcoporum* (Ratisbon 1873).

[5] The dynasty was of Arab race and unknown antiquity. Cicero names Sampsigeramus as prince of Emesa, and the names of two other princes, before Elagabalus, are recorded. The dynasty assisted Rome in the Jewish war of A.D. 68–70 (Josephus, *Jewish Antiquities*, xix. 8). Aristobulus married the daughter of Sampsigeramus (Josephus, *Jewish Antiquities*, xviii. 4). Drusilla, wife of Felix, of Acts 24:24, had been proposed as wife to Azizus, prince of Emesa, who was succeeded by Zoemus (Josephus, *op. cit.* xx. 7–8), ally of the Romans (Josephus, *Jewish War*, vii. 7). The Emesenes were thus strongly Romanophile.

[6] The evidence is numismatic.

[7] After the defeat and capture of Valerian by the Persians in 258, Odenae, prince of Palmyra, thus obtained control of the eastern empire and was succeeded by his widow Zenobia. The Hellenized cities of Syria grew

secular advancement at the end of the fourth century, when Arcadius created a new province of Lebanese Phoenicia and made Emesa its capital.

How Christianity came to Emesa is not known, but it was probably before the third century. The *Augustan History* credits Elagabalus with intending to build at Rome a temple of all the cults, including the *christiana devotio*, and Alexander Severus with similar syncretism, embracing a recognition of Christ.[8] Emesa claimed to have had martyrs in the last persecution, though whether belonging to the church of the city is uncertain. Eusebius tells of martyrdoms at Emesa, including that of Silvanus "bishop of the churches about Emesa," a phrase which is probably equivalent to "bishop of Emesa," but might mean that within Emesa the church was not established in strength.[9] The church of Emesa comes clearly into the light of history when, in 341, the Edessan Eusebius, whom Jerome calls "the standard-bearer of the Arian party" became its bishop and so continued till 359.[10] Emesa had another famous bishop in the fifth century, in the person of Paul who secured from Cyril of Alexandria in 433 the acceptance of the Formula of Union, drawn up by the Syrian bishops who had broken with him in 432 after the Council of Ephesus.

Sozomen, writing at about that date, says that "the church of Emesa is one most worthy to see, and famous for its beauty."[11] The great mosque of Homs (as Emesa is now called) appears to embody remains both of a Christian church and of an older pagan temple. So the "fair church" of 430 may have replaced, and in part used, a former temple; though not the famous temple of the sun, since that was on a hill outside the city. From 453 the Church of Emesa claimed to possess the head of St. John Baptist, brought there secretly, it was said, from

restive under this Arab rule and appealed to the western emperor Aurelian for deliverance.

8 The *Augustan History* recounts that Alexander had a statue of Christ in his domestic chapel.

9 *Church History*, viii. 13 and ix. 6. These martyrdoms are recorded as taking place under Maximin Daia, Augustus in the east after the death of Galerius. They are therefore to be dated 312. The martyrs may have been brought into Emesa, for trial and execution, from the surrounding country.

10 Jerome mentions Eusebius in these terms in his *Chronicle* under the tenth year of Constantius, and in his work *On famous men* speaks of him as a writer. He enjoyed popularity as an exegete. George of Laodicea delivered a panegyric on him, which Socrates summarizes in his *Church History*, ii. 9.

11 *Chnrch History*, iii. 17.

Jerusalem.[12] Through that relic it is probable that Emesa gave to the Church universal the observance of 29 August as the Feast of the Decollation of St. John Baptist. Pagan Emesa claimed among its sons the sophist Fronto in the third Christian century, and Ulpian and Sallustius in the fourth. From these particulars concerning the church and city we may conclude that the author of our treatise was a person of some importance in his times. We have now to see what the treatise itself reveals about him.

First, Nemesius knows that the name of Origen is breathed upon, but not that his memory has been subject to formal condemnation.[13] He can hardly, therefore, have written later than the year 400 at latest. He treats the heresies of Apollinarius and Eunomius as affairs of his own time, and seems to know about the Antiochene Theodore who became bishop of Mopsuestia in 392. All these facts point to the last decade of the fourth century as the time when Nemesius was writing his book. As to his own personality Nemesius had no intention of revealing anything. He writes in the impersonal style that was in the best literary tradition of his times, weaves together accepted views and ideas, and eschews all appearance of originality. Nevertheless, we cannot miss the fact that he is a man of liberal Greek education, widely read in philosophy, and having an independent and considered attitude towards the Neo-Platonic revival of philosophy that had been in progress for some two centuries. But the most striking fact about his learning is the extent of his medical knowledge. No less than fifteen treatises of Galen, the "father of Greek medicine,"

---

[12] The story as told in the *Chronicle* of Marcellinus Comes is that two Syrian monks went, in the days of Constantine, as pilgrims to Jerusalem. The Baptist revealed to them in a dream the spot (in the ruins of Herod's palace at Jerusalem, not at Machaerus) where his head lay. On their journey home they were robbed of the wallet containing the sacred relic by an Emesene potter who supposed it to be full of treasure. The Baptist now warned the thief of the nature of his booty, and he hid the relic in a cave near Emesa where, in the fifth century, it was rediscovered by monks. The *Paschal Chronicle* says that the Baptist's head was discovered in the city of Emesa in Holy Week of the year of empress Pulcheria's death (452). (*Corp. Script. Hist. Byzant,* Pasch. Chron. II. pp. 418–9.)

[13] In the late fourth century, Origen became the object of hatred by the native Egyptian monks, to please whom Theophilus, patriarch of Alexandria, proclaimed the condemnation of his memory in 399. This condemnation was repeated at Rome in 400. Epiphanius and Jerome led an attempt to purge the east of the theological influence of Origen which was violent in the early years of the fifth century.

have left their mark upon his pages, and he shows a power of
going beyond Galen and even of correcting him. The inference
that would seem obvious today, that he had been in practice
as a physician before he became a bishop, cannot safely be
drawn, because of the conditions of medical knowledge and
practice in the ancient world. Medical knowledge developed
among the Greeks as a branch of philosophy and a part of
general education. The treatment of sicknesses and wounds,
on the other hand, was recognized to be an art, which required
apprenticeship and placed its possessor on very special terms
with society in view of the intimacy of his relations with his
patients and their households. To the lasting profit of mankind,
Greek medical practitioners recognized that their office
required of them a high standard of professional honour. So
they bound their apprentices with a religious oath, the Hippocratic oath,[14] to a code of professional etiquette which protected
the interests of the profession and of its patients at one and the
same time.

We must note that medical science and the physicians' art
were, even more than they are today, distinguishable quantities.
The professional physician was ideally[15] a man of science, as
well as trained in his art. But it was possible to have medical
science and not practise. Men of science were, in fact, to be
found in great number among those whom high social position
freed from the necessity of earning a livelihood, while the
apprenticed physician looked to live on his fees. We must
consider the possibility that Nemesius was not a practitioner
but a gentleman amateur. On the one hand, no single passage
in his book betrays the practitioner. On the other, he describes
the false goods with which men delude themselves as follows:
"to be rolling in wealth; to plume oneself on public honours;
and to find complacency in the possession of other blessings of
this present life." The phrasing might fit a person who had
known these things. We are fortunate in having an example of
a gentleman-amateur of medicine in Caesarius,[16] the brother
of Gregory Nazianzen, of Nemesius' own generation. Son of a

14 See W. H. S. Jones, *The Doctor's Oath*, Cambridge, 1924, or Vol. I of the
Loeb edition of Hippocrates, pp. 291–301.
15 There was no public control of medical practice to ensure qualification
or to prevent the public being victimized by charlatans. Accordingly the
medical knowledge possessed by amateurs in medicine who were men
of respectability was at a premium.
16 The story is told by Gregory in the funeral oration which he made over
his brother.

Christian landed family in Cappadocia, Caesarius was born about 330, and went, some twenty years later, to seek a general education at Alexandria. His principal studies were mathematics and "medicine in so far as it treats of physiology and temperament and the causes of disease, in order to remove its roots." There is no word here of surgery or the physician's art. It is medical science, and the assisting of nature to maintain health. At these studies Gregory declares his brother to have been brilliant. Caesarius now betook himself to Constantinople to seek a career at court. It was his medical knowledge, Gregory says, that gained him notice and so won him a place in the Imperial household. But this post was financial, and in due course it was to high financial office in the province of Bithynia that it led him. Meanwhile, Gregory says, many called Caesarius in as a physician, although he had not taken the Hippocratic oath, and he gave his services without fee. This example invites three observations. First, good family and some reputation for learning or letters (and sometimes the latter without the former) opened the way to high public office without any apprenticeship in lower offices.[17] Next, medical knowledge was suited to an aristocrat because he owned slaves whose health was his wealth. Finally, as Christians could not take the Hippocratic oath, and the Christian part of society was increasing daily, emphasis at this time was on medical science without apprenticeship. Eunapius[18] tells us of Magnus of Nisibis, indentured pupil of the physician Zeno of Cyprus, nevertheless going to Alexandria and opening a "public" school of medicine.

It was, no doubt, in consideration of such facts that the seventeenth century prince of church historians, Le Nain de Tillemont, so far from thinking that our author had been a practitioner, suggested his possible identity with the Nemesius who was provincial governor of Cappadocia for a short while

[17] Thus Aurelius Victor, a man of humble origin, but a man of letters and historian, was given governorship in Pannonia by Julian and continued a public career under his successors. The poet Cyrus gained the favour of the Empress Eudocia and was made exarch of Constantinople. Examples of men of social as well as literary distinction thus advanced to public office could be multiplied indefinitely.

[18] Eunapius, born in 347 and living into the fifth century, was a historian of his times, with a strong anti-Christian bias. He wrote *Lives of the sophists* to record the pagan men of learning of the cultural age that was in rapid decay after the death of Julian. In this work he records the physician Zeno of Cyprus, and his pupils Magnus, Oribasius and Ionicus, as *iatrosophists*, practitioners who were also men of science.

between 383 and 389,[19] and known to us through Gregory Nazianzen,[20] who spent those last six years of his life in retirement in Cappadocia. The governor was not a Christian, but admired Gregory as a man of letters and sought his friendship. Gregory tells us that while Nemesius made philosophy of governing, he longed for release from public office that he might devote himself to pure philosophy. Gregory claims that Nemesius undertook, when freed from office, to discuss with him the dogmas of the faith. He urges that the best monument of his governorship that Nemesius can leave is that he should leave it to become a Christian, and that the best spoils he can have from his tenure of office is to have found "the pearl of great price." As Gregory describes himself as aged and ill, and as we can assume a short tenure of office on Nemesius' part, the whole episode may be included in the span 385–8.

Assuming that Nemesius was baptized by 390, he would be marked out as a recruit to the clerical order, so soon as he ceased to be a neophyte. Having passed a governorship, no obstacles to ordination under the Theodosian law of 390[21] against ordaining curials could apply to him. We might almost expect him to be a bishop before the century ended. And if he was not the bishop of Emesa, we might wonder how history lost sight of him.

One difficulty must be noticed. Gregory calls Nemesius a jurist trained in the Roman law. The work *On the nature of man* shows no interest in questions of law. Its ideal of society is the free Greek city, not the empire. And yet these traits are not incompatible with an ex-governor who had put the unloved circumstances of his secular career behind him when he entered the font. Tillemont's suggested identification cannot therefore be called unreasonable. It was generally accepted till the beginning of the nineteenth century, when J. A. Fabricius urged that many men named Nemesius may have been prominent at the time. He thus started a wave of scepticism, which encouraged Canon Venables, in the *Dictionary of Christian Biography*, to say "we may safely reject the suggestion favoured by Tillemont." And six years later, Dietrich Bender set out to prove that our author could not be Gregory's friend, but with signal

19 *Mémoires*, ix. 541, 601.
20 Epistles 79, 183, 184, 185 and a poem, No. 61, of 334 lines addressed to Nemesius.
21 Theodosian Code, xii. 1. 121, dated 17 June.

14—C.J.

unsuccess.[22] We shall do best to return a verdict of *non liquet.*
But the careers of Gregory's friend and Gregory's brother bring
before the imagination the kind of history our author is likely
to have had. When we consider the theme of our treatise, it
ceases to be surprising that the author gave such pride of place
to medical science. His fundamental interest is in ethics and
the pursuit of true virtue. His originality is to have seen that
however separable body and soul may be, notionally, at least
in waking life their union is absolute. Before we can discuss
what soul should do, we must be fully informed what body does.
The seeker after a true ethic must therefore go to school with
the physicians, and learn the facts of the body. The classical
teachers of ethics had made ethics comparable with equitation,
with soul as horseman and body as mount.[23] Nemesius sees that
what we have to do with is more like a centaur than man and
mount. The fact that Galen is his favourite author therefore
needs no further explanation. It is evident that Nemesius had
thought deeply about ethical problems in independence of the
Bible and Christian dogma. This suggests that conversion came
to him late in life. His mind is in some ways very "unecclesiastical." Thus, while he criticizes the heretics Apollinarius and
Eunomius with acuteness (for he has a very fine sense of
orthodoxy)[24] there is no trace of *odium theologicum.* He applies

---

[22] In *Untersuchungen zu Nemesius von Emesa,* Leipzig, 1898.

[23] The simile of the centaur, not actually used by Nemesius, is used by
Basil, bishop of Ancyra, 336–360, in a work *On virginity* marked by a very
realistic view of the relation of soul and body. Jerome, in his notice of
Basil in his work *On famous men* mentions this work and says that Basil
was learned in medicine. Suidas, in the tenth century, says that Basil
was a physician by profession, but this may be no more than a misunderstanding of Jerome. Basil's career would suggest the probability that he
was another gentleman-amateur in medical science.

[24] Nemesius belongs recognizably to the Antiochene school of Christian
doctrine which was reaching the height of its achievements at the time
of his episcopate. Its leading exponents were Diodore, bishop of Tarsus,
Theodore, bishop of Mopsuestia, and, later, Theodoret, bishop of
Cyrrhus, all natives of Antioch. John Chrysostom, greatest of preachers
and exegetes, and Nestorius, condemned for heresy, were also Antiochenes, who both held and were deposed from the patriarchate of
Constantinople. The Antiochene school was strongly interested in the
historical character of the Gospel and the true manhood of Christ.
Antiochene exegetes avoided allegorism and sought the literal sense of
Scripture. Antiochenes generally found it difficult to show adequately
the unity of Christ's theandric person, and it is one of the distinctions
of Nemesius that, as far as can be judged from a work that does not
explicitly expound a Christology, he would have been clear from the

Wisdom 4:10,11 to Socrates equally with the Christian martyrs. This, naively done, is like a man who has not had time to be shaped to ecclesiastical rigidity. His book, moreover, is unfinished, and bears the signs of lack of revision, so that we may conjecture that death overtook him.[25] We may conclude that when he became a bishop, he had not been many years a Christian, and that his episcopate was short. Nevertheless, it would appear to have made him change the character of a book projected in lay, if not in pre-Christian, days. He set out to write an anthropology. He ended with a polemic against fatalism, and a defence of the Christian doctrine of divine providence. In this we may see the effect of pastoral experience in a Syrian city, where fatalism was the perennial foe.

Our author's medical knowledge is not limited to the written word of Galen, whom, on occasion, he both supplements and corrects. The probability therefore is that, like Caesarius, he was first schooled in medical science in youth, before he pursued it for philosophic reasons. We may sum up by saying that, in these ways, though without his knowing it, the book discloses the man, in no slight degree.[26]

charge of "Nestorianism," or seeing in Christ the moral union between a divine and a human person.

    The Cappadocian school, led by Basil the Great, Gregory Nazianzen, Gregory Nyssen, and Amphilochius of Iconium shared many of the Antiochene interests, but were influenced by Origen as the Antiochenes were not. Nemesius' attitude to Origen would be explained if we could surely identify him with the governor of Cappadocia. While both schools combined Platonic and Aristotelian ideas in the philosophic background to their doctrinal thinking, the Cappadocians inclined towards Platonism while the Antiochenes leaned rather towards Aristotle. Nemesius passes judgement on the Christological principles of the Antiochene Theodore, with acuteness.

25 Thus the third paragraph of Section 61 promises to discuss creation and the difference between creation and providence. No such discussion is reached. There are similar unfulfilled forecasts earlier in the book, as when the end of Section 4 promises a discussion of the difference between the pursuit of godliness and the pursuit of virtues. Signs of unrevised drafting are frequent, and attention is called to them in the notes.

26 W. W. Jaeger, *Nemesios von Emesa*, Berlin. 1914, deduces, from Nemesius' teaching that contemplation is man's highest activity and from the double standard in c. xviii of front-rank men and rear-rank men in virtue's army, that Nemesius was a monk. This seems to go too far. Nemesius is so tolerant of the world in which men enjoy the cheer of society and the comforts of home that it is more likely that, however he venerated those who went into the desert for the sake of contemplation, he had not taken that step himself before his ordination.

THE WORK

Hippocrates,[27] who lived in the fifth century before Christ
and may be called first father of scientific medicine, wrote a
tract *On the nature of man*[28] in which he argued that pleasure and
pain would be inconceivable but for the differences between the
material elements of which the body is composed, and that
the physician's work would fall to the ground if it did not lie
in righting the maladjustment of elements in the human
constitution. Equally, where there is suffering it must have a
subject. This theme is the clue to Nemesius' argument for the
continual interaction of soul and body. Nemesius may, in fact,
be taken to acknowledge his debt, in adopting the title first
used by Hippocrates. But the interest of Nemesius is not purely
medical, or even ethical. It is religious and spiritual. His book
On the nature of man is, in short, essentially a piece of Christian
apologetic. Starting from the axiom that man consists of soul
and body, Nemesius spends his first three chapters in establishing, against all rival theories, that the soul is an incorporeal
substance, self-moving, and having the body as its instrument.
Into this argument he weaves a theme for which he was
(indirectly) indebted to Posidonius[29]; that of the universe as a
continuous ascending scale of being, in which the lower and
simpler subserves the needs of the higher and more complex,
until the crown of all is reached in man, whose possession of

[27] See note to Section 15. There is an edition of the Hippocratic writings
in the Loeb Library, with a useful introduction by the editor, Dr. W. H. S.
Jones.
[28] The relation of the existing text to Hippocrates is much debated. What
matters for our purpose is that Nemesius knew a tract *On the nature of man*
attributed to the great physician of antiquity.
[29] Posidonius, pupil of the Stoic Panaetius, flourished a century before
Christ, and travelled much in the west, where he counted Cicero as
among his disciples. His philosophic achievement was to combine the
dialectic of ideas, and the doctrine of *daemones* (spiritual powers at work
in the universe) from the Platonic tradition with the doctrines of natural
law and of destiny from Stoicism. He thus constructed a grandiose picture
of one universe of visible and invisible in which the two distinct orders
unite to form one totality of being. The actual writings of Posidonius have
almost entirely perished, but his influence is to be traced all down the
five centuries that separate him from Nemesius. During those centuries,
the loss of the works of Posidonius had been progressing, and it is very
uncertain if Nemesius had read any of Posidonius at first hand. The
nature of his debt to Posidonius is discussed *passim* in the notes. Scholars
have lately tended to overwork the responsibility of Posidonius for ideas
found first in later writers, but the fault is excusable.

reason causes him to project beyond the sensible or phenomenal universe altogether, so as to have entry into the world
of intelligibles, and to converse with the unseen and eternal
order. Having thus re-echoed the Posidonian panegyric on man,
Nemesius crowns it with the proof provided by the incarnation
of the Word of God.

Next he descends abruptly, to the bottom rung of the ladder
of being, and treats of matter, the four elements, and their
intricate combination, by way of the four humours, in the
constitution of the human body. At this point, he is ready to
take up the theme of Hippocrates, the connection of man's
psychological experiences and reactions with his physical being.
If the body is the soul's instrument, how are the soul's faculties
related to bodily structure? Here Nemesius appropriates
Galen's observations upon the localization, in the structure of
the brain, of the cerebral sources of the faculty-activities. The
movements of impulse, intellect, and memory have their
actualization in corresponding physical processes. But in
assigning to what is psychological its physical counterpart,
Nemesius discovers that the soul's life is, like the universe,
disposed in a series of ascending grades with, at the bottom,
an unconscious and uncontrollable irrational life-urge, and
at the top, the detached and rational activity of the human
spirit contemplating God and the world of intelligibles. Next
Nemesius observes that while pain enters life as altogether
belonging to the world of sense, pleasure proves to point upward to the life of heaven, in that it changes its character as we
choose the better and reject the worse. So Nemesius reaches
the problem of man's free will, and finds that it plays but a
limited part in human life, though one that is morally all-
important. Here we might seem to be coming to the natural
conclusion of the book, namely, that this embodied life,
illumined by the Gospel, prepares man for a redeemed and
heavenly life to come. And this should have involved a discussion of the resurrection-body, rounding off the theme of the
nature of man. Instead, when the investigation of man's
freedom has revealed it to be confined to moral issues, the
theme is abruptly changed. A second part of the book begins,
with ch. xxxv, and concerns itself with vindicating Christian
faith in the beneficent providence of God, over particulars, as
well as over universals. Nemesius joins battle not only with the
crude fatalism of the astrologers, but with every ethnic system,
showing each in turn to be but fatalism in disguise. In these

last chapters, the bishop of Emesa is seen to be feeling his way forward. Already he sees that he must treat of the divine purpose in creation, to which the work of providence is ancillary. Perhaps he saw, here, the appropriate end of his undertaking with regard to the nature of man. But while he was still engaged in relating particular providence to human sin, the pen fell from his hand. As early as the second chapter,[30] a reference to Plato's doctrine of the world-soul ended in a promise to return to the question, "in the chapter on Destiny." But when that subject was reached, it had expanded to fill four chapters, in the last of which the promise was but briefly redeemed. Clearly, therefore, the plan of the book developed as it went along. And the most obvious explanation is that his experience as a pastor revealed to Nemesius new directions in which the work of Christian apologetic was required.

Classical scholars have been apt to speak of Nemesius as a plagiarist and as having no great weight as a thinker. Their interest in him is due to the fact that something can be learned from him about the succession of Greek thinkers of the post-classical era. It is, however, quite out of reason to look for an acknowledged effort to break new ground in a fourth century writer. In that age, the unforgivable sin was to innovate (*neoterizein*). The man of wisdom and learning looked to serve his day and generation by giving topical rearrangement to the accepted wisdom of antiquity. But while this was the approved course for every kind of writer, it had a double advantage when used by a Christian apologist like Nemesius. And we must give Nemesius credit for showing no small skill in so selecting passages from his library of past Greek thinkers as to make the mosaic which he constructs convey the message which he wants conveyed. His pagan readers can never turn on him to say "I do not agree with you" without finding themselves in conflict with some reputable authority outside the Church. The originality of Nemesius lies first in the ethical aim which he set himself, in doing justice at once to the reality of soul and the intimacy of the union of soul with body. It was perhaps this that prepared him to see in the Christian doctrine of the divine incarnation a profounder variant of the same theme. His second originality was to take the leap that carried him from the thought-world in which he had been confined into the new thought-world of learned Christianity. After the leap of conversion, the centre of the convert's consistency lies in his

[30] See Section 18, just before the last paragraph.

new faith. He no longer strives to maintain the consistency of the thought-world he has left behind, for he sees it no longer as a building, but as ruins. But that does not mean the abandonment of all his past studies. They become material, in as far as he finds them still sound and tenable, fit to contribute to a structure whose inspiration is new. Pisa cathedral is a parable. It is a Christian fane, expressive of nothing but the faith and cultus to which it is now dedicated. And yet there is in it no single piece of marble that was not first quarried and squared for the building of temples or palaces of the old pre-Christian days. So Nemesius made his treatise; in which the harshness of mosaic is somewhat mitigated, and a reasonable smoothness of style maintained, through Nemesius more often giving the gist of a passage than citing it word for word. And if we will stand back and take a view of his essential outlines, we find them faithfully representing the Christian outlook characteristic of the heyday of the Antiochene school. From the Christian side, Nemesius has incurred a suspicion of Pelagianism. *Sapit Pelagianismum*, says Bellarmine (*De scriptoribus ecclesiasticis*, ad ann. 380). The ground is that, without referring to supernatural grace, Nemesius asserts that it is in a man's power to be good or bad as he chooses. This charge, like that of his lack of originality, arises from failure to take account of the apologetic nature of the work of Nemesius. Using, as he does, traditional Greek aretology to suggest to his readers that Christianity and virtue go together, it is an unavoidable consequence that Christian disbelief in the sufficiency of aretological ethics is obscured. On the other hand, the spirit of Nemesius is not that of Pelagius. Neither is there any expression relating to human freewill in his work that cannot be paralleled in reputable Greek Christian Fathers. None of these, even John of Damascus, the standard-bearer of Greek orthodoxy, who resumes so much of Nemesius' teaching, reaches such a conception of mysterious grace as was taught by Augustine. Nevertheless Nemesius, in his last chapter, so relates our free-will to God's providence, as to exhibit a faith in God's mercy, and such humility regarding the powers of man for good, that he must be absolved from any real Pelagianism of mind. When he argues of free-will, his view is limited to the realm of nature. Against the determinists, he demonstrates that man can by nature attain what the natural man calls virtue. He says no word of man being able to merit eternal life. To say so much would be cold defence, if we supposed Nemesius to be on trial for his doctrine as a Christian theologian. But as he writes as an apologist, his true defence is that *sapere Pelagianismum* is something which no Christian apologist can avoid, when he speaks of morality to non-Christians.

SUBSEQUENT HISTORY OF THE WORK

Since the book *On the nature of man* left the hands of its author, its fate has been to suffer alternations of oblivion and rediscovery. The decline of the fortunes of the Antiochene school of doctrine after the secession of the Nestorians brought a period of oblivion, from which the work was rescued, in the first half of the eighth century by a priest of Jerusalem known to history as John Damascene,[31] whose *Exact exposition of the Orthodox Faith* became a classic of Greek Orthodoxy, commonly regarded as closing the patristic age. John does not name Nemesius; but his anthropological chapters (Book II. cc. 12–29) are full of citations from Nemesius. There are citations from chs. 1, 6–13, 18–23, 29–33, 37, 39–44, and they prove that John was very much indebted to Nemesius for the shape and character of his anthropology. As might be expected, the citations do not reproduce what is most individual in Nemesius, but they are verbally close enough for the passages to be identified. Perhaps the work *On the nature of man* came to John without any author's name. But it may have come to him under the name of Gregory of Nyssa, who is one of John's favourite authors. For, about a century later, we have some evidence, which Dräseke[32] explains as showing how the attribution of the work to Nyssen came about. The Nestorian *catholicos* Timothy I, who, under Harun al Raschid, and in response to Muslim interest in the learning of the Greeks, became a notable promoter of translations from Greek into Syriac, writes to a certain Rabban Pethion to ask him to seek for a copy of a book by "the philosopher Nemesius" on the constitution of man. Timothy gives in Syriac an *incipit* and *explicit* that define ch. 1 of the work of Nemesius. In his *explicit* occur the words in which Nemesius speaks of being about

---

[31] i.e., of Damascus. John, who died in old age in A.D. 749, came of an important Christian family in Damascus, where he himself held secular office under the Caliph. In 725 he appears, but now as a Christian priest under John IV of Jerusalem, and a protagonist against iconoclasm. He was a great polemical theologian, and a number of his works survive besides the *Exact exposition*.

[32] For this citation of Timothy, and the argument based upon it, see J. Dräseke, in *Zeitschrift für wissenschaftlich Theologie*, Bd. 46, Leipzig, 1903, pp. 505–512, "Ein *Testimonium Ignatianum*."

to treat of the soul. Timothy, who evidently possessed a Greek copy of ch. I, which he regarded as a work in itself, tells Pethion that he has no copy of this further work, and wants him to look for a copy. Dräseke suggests that this decapitation of the work was due to chs. II and III having been identified with a work attributed to Nyssen, *On the soul*. This led, he thinks, to the title "Nemesius, bishop of Emesa, *On the nature of man*" being supposed to apply only to the contents of ch. I, while those of the next two chapters were placed under the heading "Gregory of Nyssa, *On the soul*." Those who made this attribution failed to notice, what Timothy does notice, that ch. I makes claim, for its author, to what follows. Nevertheless, we have here a very probable explanation of the eventual heading of entire copies of *On the nature of man* with the name of Gregory of Nyssa. The attribution may have taken place by the time of John Damascene. About a century passed from the days of Timothy till the next rediscovery of Nemesius. This was due to a monk and physician of the monastery of the Holy Trinity in the neighbourhood of Tiberiopolis in N. Phrygia called Meletius.[33] This man, disclaiming scientific originality, compiled a *Synopsis of the views of Church Fathers and distinguished philosophers on the constitution of man*, to which we owe citations from Soranus, the Alexandrine surgeon and gynaecologist who practised in Rome under Hadrian. Whether Meletius thought our author to be a Father or a philosopher, does not appear. He does not name him, but cites him *verbatim* to such an extent that the numerous MSS of the *Synopsis* form part of the *apparatus* for an edition of Nemesius. We see here a particular interest leading to a rediscovery of Nemesius, that of the Byzantine medical practitioner, who regarded medicine as almost a branch of orthodox theology. This observation helps to explain the next rediscovery, about a century later. At this time a school of medicine had arisen, it is not quite clear how, at Salerno, in southern Italy. In the mid-eleventh century, Nicholaus Alfanus,[34] classicist, hymnographer, and learned in Greek, came to Salerno from Monte

[33] No proper edition of the *Synopsis* of Meletius exists. There are a number of MSS of which some of the best are at Oxford. In 1552, Nicolas Petraeus of Corcyra printed a Latin version of the *Synopsis* at Venice. In 1836, J. A. Cramer printed a text from three MSS at the Bodleian, in volume III of his *Anecdota Graeca*, under the title *On the constitution of man*. In the same year Friederich Ritschl produced a good text of about the first quarter of the work at Wratislaw. This may be the same Meletius as the author of *Aphorisms of Hippocrates*.

[34] Hymns of Alfanus are printed in Migne, *Patrologia Latina*, 147, 1219-1282.

Cassino to be abbot of the San Benito monastery and afterwards (1058–1085) to be archbishop there. Alfanus contributed to medical studies a tract *On the four humours.* He also made an excellent Latin rendering of Nemesius under the title *Premnon physicon* ("Key to nature"). As he does not mention Nemesius' title, or his name, he perhaps worked from a copy of the Greek text with no heading at all. The work appealed to him, as his preface shows, as a condensed doxography of medicine and theology, such as might benefit the Latin world.

Less than a century elapsed before another Italian learned in Greek produced a Latin version of Nemesius. This was Richard Burgundio, Professor of Law in the University of Pisa. By some means Burgundio came to be in Constantinople in 1137, and was sent thither again in 1172 as an envoy of the city of Pisa. It is not clear if he brought to Pisa, in 1137, a copy of the *Pandects* of Justinian (the digest of decisions in Roman law collected from the leading jurists by order of Justinian in the sixth century). What is clear is that a copy of the *Pandects* was treasured at Pisa, and that Burgundio supplied Latin versions of the passages of Greek embedded in the Latin text of the *Pandects.* In 1160, Burgundio made suit to the emperor Frederic Barbarossa, who was now the stronger for the papal schism, to patronize a grandiose scheme of translations of the learned books of the Greeks, to bring the benefits of science to the emperor's subjects. The emperor smiled on the project, and Burgundio began the series with a closely literal translation of Nemesius, more useful as a witness to Greek readings than the more literary Latin of Alfanus. The book was dedicated to Barbarossa and made from a Greek MS that named Nyssen as the author. It was followed by several works of Galen. At that point the emperor's support had so failed to fulfil his promise that the translation scheme foundered. In 1190 the emperor was drowned, while on crusade, and Burgundio died in 1193. His version of Nemesius was known to Peter Lombard and Aquinas, while that of Alfanus was known to Albert the Great. In this way, much that is characteristic of the anthropology of Nemesius passed into the structure of scholastic theology.

The renascence brought forth two new Latin versions. The first of these was the work of an Italian encyclopaedist, Georgio Valla,[35] a native of Placentia, who became professor of the sciences at Venice and died there in 1499, as was remembered,

[35] Valla was chiefly a writer on medical subjects, and translated two other small works of medical interest from the Greek.

while lecturing on the immortality of the soul. His posthumous *Encyclopaedia* bears witness to the importance which he placed upon the work of Nemesius. He was no great Greek scholar, and the Latin version of Nemesius which he left was, no doubt, made for his own use. But by some means it came into the hands of Sebastian Gryphius, publisher, at Leyden, who printed it in 1533.[36] The second of the two versions was made by John Cono,[37] or Konow, of Nuremberg, at the invitation of the noted humanist Beatus Rhenanus of Basle, whither Cono, as a friar, had come to the Dominican convent. In the convent library there was an imperfect manuscript of Nemesius, in which the work was ascribed to Gregory of Nyssa. Burgundio's version was likewise made from a Greek text that ascribed the work to Nyssen, and Cono used Burgundio's Latin to fill in the gaps which comparison discovered in the defective text of the Basle manuscript. Cono's version was published at Strassburg in 1512, and reprinted in the Basle edition of Gregory of Nyssa in 1562. Between Valla and Cono, an Italian named Domenico Pizzimenti[38] came upon a manuscript of the work of Nemesius and translated it into the vernacular, under the title of *Operetta d'un incerto, della natura degli animati.* It would seem that his Greek text, like that used by Alfanus, was without heading.

The first edition of Nemesius issued from the Plantin press at Antwerp in 1565. The editor was Nicasius Ellebodius, of Cassel, and he used but two very inferior manuscripts. He knew Valla's version,[39] but thought so ill of it that he made one of his own, which has held its place, as companion of the Greek text, in subsequent editions and reprints. An independent text of chs. 2 and 3 of the work *On the nature of man* was printed by Giles Morelle in his Paris edition of Nyssen, 1638, seemingly from a

---

[36] The Netherland presses had wide contacts, and were able to obtain works of the new learning for publication from far beyond the Low Countries.

[37] Konow was born in 1463, and, as a young man impelled by love of learning, went to Italy and acquired a knowledge of Greek. There, in 1507, he became a Dominican friar, and was presently sent to the convent in Basle, where he became acquainted with many of the humanist scholars of the circle of Rhenanus; and with their publishers. A number of his versions of Greek patristic writings were printed. He died in 1513.

[38] Pizzimenti or Pizimenius translated a number of Greek classics, one being published in Cologne in 1574.

[39] Gryphius' publication of Valla may, indeed, have paved the way. Ellebodius learned his Greek at the University of Padua whither he had gone to study medicine. For his literary work he obtained high ecclesiastical patronage, including that of the great Cardinal Granvella, to whom he dedicated his edition of Nemesius. He died in 1577.

manuscript in the library of Cardinal Federico Borromeo. It appears as an opuscule of Nyssen, entitled *On the soul*.

It was next the turn of England to discover Nemesius. The discoverer was the eccentric London poet and pamphleteer, George Wither, 1588–1667, best known to-day as author of "Shall I, wasting in despair?". After a stormy literary career, between 1611 and a journey to Holland and the Continent in 1632–3, Wither shortly withdrew from London to a "rustic habitation" under Beacon Hill, Farnham, in Surrey. Hither he apparently took two of his purchases in the Low Countries, to wit, Valla's translation of Nemesius printed in Leyden, and the Antwerp edition, by Ellebodius. The first work of his retirement was to turn Valla's Latin into English. It seems unlikely that he gained much from his copy of Ellebodius, for if he had been able to decipher Ellebodius's Greek preface, he might have laid Valla aside. He could, however, read Christopher Plantin's *Address to the Reader*, which was in Latin, and so learned to identify the author of *On the nature of man* with the friend of Gregory Nazianzen. The result of his labours was a stilted English version that would drive most modern readers to ask for the Latin instead. This he dedicated to John Selden, and had printed by Henry Tainton, in St. Dunstan's Churchyard, in a little *duodecimo* volume of 665 pages, meant, no doubt, as a gentleman's *Vade mecum* for the profitable employment of odd moments. It bore the date 1636, and the *Imprimatur* of Thomas Weekes, chaplain to the Bishop of London.

The Farnham interlude was short. Indeed, quiet was soon at an end, for Wither and England alike. In 1642, Wither sold everything he possessed, to raise a troop of horse for Parliament, and went to garrison Farnham castle, and the rest of his quaint career is not relevant to our theme. What is relevant is that he apparently sold the remaining stock of his Nemesius. For, in 1657, one Robert Crofts, bookseller at the Crown in Chancery Lane "under Sergeants Inne," put out a little volume called *The Character of Man, or His Nature exactly displayed, in a Philosophical Discourse by the Learned Nemesius, now made English*. It is, in fact, nothing but the remainder stock of Tainton's *duodecimo*, stripped of the first two leaves (containing the Dedication, *Imprimatur*, and Wither's name), since, at this juncture, Wither's was a dubious name with which to sell a book. Croft therefore had printed a title-page and a jejune preface "To the Reader," and bound these into each several copy. What all this did for the knowledge of Nemesius remains obscure. But the fact is clear that Dr. John Fell, the Restoration dean of Christchurch, who, from 1675 to his death in 1686 was also bishop of Oxford, among his many works of editing, in 1671 produced, from the Sheldonian, an edition of Nemesius, with notes. The notes show that Nemesius had been something of a discovery for Fell, and had exercised his learning. He had discovered, also, that the Bodleian possessed two manuscript copies of Nemesius, one of which was under the name of Adamantion. But it was clearly not the finding of these manuscripts that had incited him to the work, for his edition is, in fact, nothing but a hasty revision of Ellebodius, with very little added, in apparatus, from his Oxford texts. Gallandi reprinted Fell, in his *Library of the Fathers*, at Venice, in 1770.

More than a century passed before interest in Nemesius stirred again. This time the stirring took place in Germany. Christian Friedrich Matthaei, professor at Wittemberg, having become acquainted with manuscripts of Nemesius at Dresden and Augsburg, projected a new edition. He made use of Ellebodius, Fell, and the versions of Alfanus and Burgundio, together with some five good manuscripts to which he had access. The result was his Magdeburg edition of 1802, which remains unsuperseded to this day. In 1819, by using this edition, Dr. Osterhammer, a Bavarian physician, made a German translation of the first eleven chapters, which he published at Salzburg. In 1844,[40] also as a consequence of Matthaei's work, the house of Hachette of Paris published *Némésius, De la Nature de l'Homme, traduit pour la première fois du grec en français par M. J. B. Thibault*. This is a good complete version, with some notes. In 1925, Dr. Emil Orth, of Saarbrücken, published locally an excellent German translation of the whole work, and of the Latin prefaces of Alfanus and Burgundio. But in the 1880's, interest of a new kind was beginning to be taken in Nemesius. In 1887, C. Holzinger published a text of Alfanus from a manuscript unspecified. In 1888, Karl I. Burkhard, of Vienna, began a series of articles in *Wiener Studien*[41] extending over twelve years,

---

[40] In this year the editors of the Oxford *Library of the Fathers* advertised a volume in preparation by the Rev. E. Marshall, Fellow of Corpus Christi College, Cambridge, and W. A. Greenhill, M.D., to contain Nemesius, *On the nature of man*, and the *Synopsis* of Meletius, the latter, no doubt, from Cramer's text. The volume failed to appear.

[41] Volumes x (1888), 93-135, xi (1889) 143-152, 243-267 review the manuscript tradition. See also Volumes xv, xxvi, xxx, and finally xxxii (1910) 35-9. The Burgundio edition begins in the eighteenth *Jahresbericht* of the Karl-Ludwig Gymnasium at Meidling.

preparing the way for a new critical edition of Nemesius. The first articles reviewed the considerable field of manuscripts known to exist. Other scholars now began to take notice, and after the publication by the Mechitarist Father J. Tasean, in 1889, from the San Lazzaro press at Venice, of an Armenian version of Nemesius, apparently the work of an eighth-century Armenian ecclesiastic at Constantinople, and slavishly literal in its rendering of the Greek, Emilio Teza and Almo Zanolli demonstrated its great value as a witness to the ancient Greek manuscript from which the version was made.[42] Meanwhile Burkhard had been busy upon the Latin versions. Starting in 1891, and continuing for ten years, he used the annual *Programm* of the Gymnasium at Meidling to print, in instalments, an edition of Burgundio. He had carried an edition of Alfanus practically to completion, when he died in 1914. Dr. Friedrich Lammert saw the edition through the press, and it appeared in the Teubner series at Leipzig in 1917. He had it in mind, also, to take up Burkhard's longer task, and bring out the new edition of the Greek.[43] But not only was not the tenth-century codex on Patmos, the oldest known text, yet collated,[44] but the whole subject had been complicated by the results of a study of the sources of Nemesius, now going forward. It began as far back as 1882, at Berlin, where a Greek student, Margarites Evangelides, afterwards to be professor of Ancient History at Athens, presented for his doctorate in philosophy a thesis entitled "Two chapters

---

[42] In the Proceedings of the Royal Venetian Institute of Science, Letters and Arts, for 1892, Teza drew attention to the fact that both Tašean's Armenian and Pizzimenti's Italian must be taken into account by the next editor of Nemesius. (*Atti del R. Istituto veneto*, series iii, vol. 7, pp. 1239–1279.) In the next year, he followed this up with some studies of passages in the Armenian version, in the Proceedings of the Academy dei Lincei. (*Rendiconti della R. Accademia dei Lincei*, series v, vol. 2, pp. 1–16).

In 1907, Zanolli gave further studies on the light thrown by the Armenian upon the Greek text, in the Journal of the Italian Asiatic Society, and again in 1909. (*Giornale della Società Asiatica Italiana*, Vol. xix, Pt. ii, pp. 1–39. Vol. xxi, pp. 84–99, 155–178.)

[43] This, like the Alfanus, was to form a volume in the Teubner series. But in 1931, Dr Lammert gave notice in *Bursians Jahresbericht* (265–6) that the publication must be some while delayed.

[44] For this, see J. Sakkelion, *Patmiakē Bibliothēkē* (catalogue of the library of the monastery on Patmos, in Greek), Athens, 1880. Apart from this important Codex, the Greek libraries seem to have little to offer. Some fifteenth-century manuscripts contain single chapters, or extracts from Nemesius, showing that he was never wholly forgotten in the east.

from a monograph on Nemesius and his sources."[45]? So began a study of Nemesius, as himself a source of knowledge of Hellenistic thought during the early Christian centuries. A succession of scholars have engaged in this quest, D. Bender, B. Domanski, W. W. Jaeger, H. A. Koch, H. Krause, A. Ferro, and, most recently, Professor E. Skard of Oslo.[46] In 1941, Dr. Lammert himself took part; in a valuable little study of the medical learning of Nemesius, in *Philologus*.[47]

There is no patristic text more overdue for re-edition than Nemesius. A better text would probably lay bare fresh points of interest. The work itself is an expression of the Christian spirit unique among patristic writings, as well as a source of knowledge of non-Christian thought, and of some Christian thought, otherwise lost to us.[48] It is a handicap that it lies outside the leading interests of ecclesiastical historians. And the task of producing a worthy edition is undoubtedly onerous and costly. The greatest hope of it being carried through is that a wider public shall be interested in it, and here an English version, now for the first time made from the Greek, may be of some assistance towards creating the necessary conditions of demand.[49]

In any case, the work has qualities which may commend it to many modern readers who would find other patristic authors less congenial. It is liberal in spirit, and ready to follow scientific enquiry to its proper goal, to a degree that renders it surprisingly modern. It contains the fruits of a vast deal of human thinking in a very small space. In fine, to borrow the words with which Dr. Orth concludes his preface, "both the work itself, and the teaching of Nemesius contained in it, repay continued study."

[45] *Zwei Kapitel aus einer Monographie über Nemesius und seine Quellen*, Inaugural Dissertation in the Faculty of Philosophy at the Kaiser Friedrich-Wilhelm University (Berlin 1882). Professor Evangelides retired in 1924 without having ever resumed this "monograph."

[46] For these studies, see the notes to the text, *passim*.

[47] *Philologus* (Leipzig) xciv (1941) 125–141. "Hellenistic medicine in Ptolemaeus and Nemesius; a study in the history of Christian anthropology."

[48] E.g. of some Apollinarian and Eunomian ideas. It throws a good deal of light on the lost Commentary on Genesis of Origen.

[49] A letter from Dr. Lammert at the beginning of 1954 brought the welcome news that the new edition was substantially ready for printing, and some of it in galley-proof. All that lies between it and publication is some final checking and correction, for which the gallant editor has to find time from the leisure left to him as the head of a big city Grammar School. Meanwhile he hopes to publish, in *Hermes*, in a special number in celebration of the eightieth birthday of Professor M. Pohlenz, an exposition of ch. v of Nemesius' work.

A Treatise on the Nature of Man

[M.35. 1–38. 7]

I. *Of the nature of man*

1. Not a few persons of standing have asserted that man is admirably composed of an understanding soul and a body, and, indeed, that he could hardly exist, or be composed, otherwise. But the phrase, "understanding soul" is ambiguous. Did one thing, understanding, come to another thing, the soul, and beget understanding in it? Or did the soul, by its own nature, include understanding, as its most excellent member, so that understanding is to the soul what the eye is to the body?

Some, and these include Plotinus,[1] hold that soul and mind are different entities, and make man consist of three distinct components, soul, body, and mind. Apollinarius, when bishop of Laodicea,[2] followed this school, and made their notion the basis of his own opinion, building up the rest of his system upon it.[3] Others, instead of thus making soul and mind different

---

[1] The greatest of the Neo-Platonists, born at Lycopolis in A.D. 205. At Rome, 244–263, he died in Campania in 270, leaving works which his pupil Porphyry edited, arranging the matter of each section under nine headings, from which circumstance the work of Plotinus, thus edited, is known as the *Enneads*.

[2] Apollinarius, born in Egypt, A.D. 315, migrated in youth, with his father, also named Apollinarius, to Syria, where they settled at Laodicea. He was bishop from 363 of what would claim to be the orthodox congregation at Laodicea, to his death in 392, though we hear of a rival in Laodicea named Pelagius. Apollinarius was certainly the outstanding figure, as exegete and man of letters. His doctrine was condemned at Rome, without mention of his name, in 376. As Apollinarianism, it was proscribed by the first canon of the Council of Constantinople in 381. Writing in Syria about 400, Nemesius counts that his readers will know that Apollinarius, now dead, had been a (heretical) bishop in Syrian Laodicea.

[3] The importance, for the history of doctrine, of Nemesius' three references to Apollinarius was noticed by J. Dräseke in *Zeitschrift für wissenschaftliche*

entities, suppose understanding to be the guiding principle inherent in the soul's being. Aristotle,[4] in fact, holds the opinion that a potentiality of understanding is coeval with man's constitution, but that we acquire actual understanding from without, and that, when acquired, it does not contribute anything fresh to man's being and nature. What it does is to increase knowledge of physical things and to advance speculation about them. And that is why Aristotle credits few men, and those only such as have given themselves to philosophy, with the possession of actual understanding.[5]

Plato[6] seems not to regard man as a twofold being of soul and body, but as a soul that makes use of such and such a body; this he does to set human nature in a more dignified light. From the start he concentrates all our attention upon the divinity and preciousness of the soul, so that, once we are persuaded to identify ourselves with the soul, we shall give ourselves up

Theologie (Leipzig, 1886), Vol. 29, pp. 26–36. Nemesius, no doubt, had in view the *Demonstration of the divine Incarnation* of Apollinarius, just as Gregory of Nyssa had, where Apollinarius used the words "If then man is threefold, and the Lord is man, then is the Lord by all means threefold, of spirit, soul, and body." It is only Nemesius who sees here a following of Plotinus. And it is typical of the unecclesiastical approach of Nemesius that he points out this relationship without making polemical use of it.

4 Aristotle, son of a physician named Nicomachus, of Stagira, lived from 384 to 322 B.C. He was a pupil of Plato, and was later (345) appointed tutor to Prince Alexander of Macedon, afterwards Alexander the Great, in which employment he spent ten years. He then returned to Athens, to spend the rest of his life in founding what came to be known as the Peripatetic school of philosophy, because Aristotle was said to be addicted, in discussion, to pacing to and fro.

5 This passage is meant to refute, out of the mouth of Aristotle, the trichotomy of man taught by the Neo-Platonists. If mind were a complete and independent entity, distinct from soul, and every man is endowed with mind, there is no assignable reason why actual understanding should be so partial and variable from man to man. But if understanding is a potentiality in the soul, which becomes actual through exercise of discursive reason, mind and soul are not separable as the Neo-Platonists assert.

6 Plato, who lived from 427–347 B.C., was an Athenian aristocrat who became a disciple of Socrates, continuing with him until his execution in 399. Socrates held his disputations in the market place. But when his philosophy had been adjudged subversive, his disciples found it necessary to withdraw from Athens. After a while, however, Plato returned, and gathered a school of philosophy in the privacy of a garden which he possessed, called Academeia, from a shrine of Academus which it contained. The garden gave its name to the philosophic school which, after the formation of the Peripatetic school by Aristotle, maintained more exactly the Platonic tradition, and was known as the school of the Academics.

wholly to the quest of virtue, godliness, and whatever else is for
the soul's good. Likewise, we shall not love carnal desires, since
they are not characteristic of man as such, being primarily
characteristic of him insofar as he is animal, and only secondarily characteristic of him as man, inasmuch as man is, but
incidentally, animal.

There is, in fact, general consent that the soul deserves more
regard than the body, and that, indeed, the body is only an
instrument employed by the soul. The truth of this is proved by
death. For, when death severs soul from body, the body lies
completely still and passive, just like a workman's tools after he
has gone away and left them lying.

COMMENTARY

1. *Man consists of soul and body.* Nemesius starts his argument
from the received opinion (*doxa*) that the nature of man is composite of soul and body. Stated in this general form, he does not
expect the opinion to be controverted. But he proceeds to review the three ways in which this opinion finds particular expression in Plotinus, Aristotle and Plato. It was characteristic
of the Greek approach to knowledge, in the early Christian
centuries, to start from the opinions of famous thinkers on a
subject under discussion, and reach a conclusion by analysis
and criticism of the rival opinions. Thus there arose a particular
type of literary composition known as a doxography, an arranged compilation of such opinions, to serve as the basis for
further discussion. Such works were plentiful, and it need have
cost Nemesius little labour to make his summary statement of
the opinions of the three philosophers on the constitution of
man. But at once it transpires that the interest of Nemesius in
the discussion is connected with a controversy in Christian
doctrine. As a representative of the school of Antioch, Nemesius
holds that, in the incarnation, the Son of God took man's nature
perfect and complete, and that, had there been any component
of that nature which he did not take, that component would remain, in man, unredeemed. Antiochenes were therefore very
critical of Apollinarius, and his trichotomy of man, as body,
soul, and mind, upon which he based a Christology according
to which the divine Word took human flesh and soul, but was,
in his divine being, in place of mind, relatively to them. For, on
the Antiochene canon, man's mind would, on such a supposition, remain unredeemed. Nemesius claims that Apollinarius

took his trichotomy from the Neo-Platonist school of philosophy, of which Ammonius Saccas, in the early third century of our era, is generally accounted the founder, although the principles of the school were developing in the philosophic syncretism of the preceding three centuries. W. W. Jaeger, *Nemesios von Emesa* (Berlin, 1914) p. 5, Note 2, notes passages in the *Enneads* of the Neo-Platonist Plotinus as justifying Nemesius' association of Apollinarius with the Neo-Platonists. Therefore Nemesius rejects the opinion of Plotinus on the subject under discussion, since the philosophy upon which a Christian heresy can entrench itself must be false. But he accepts the opinions of both Aristotle and Plato. Aristotle made the study of the actual the road to a knowledge of universal principles, and so developed a scientific method for the extension of knowledge. The predominant interest of Plato was in the soul as conversant with the world of ideas. Regarding the actual as in some way derived from the ideal, Plato tended to give it too fleeting attention, so that Aristotle was driven to redress the balance by an opposite emphasis. The Neo-Platonists exaggerated the tendency of Platonism, until they made the actual almost irrelevant to true knowledge. It was characteristic of the Greek culture of Syria at the end of the fourth century to be divided between admiration of the idealism of Plato and attachment to Aristotelian method. In this Nemesius was typical of his time and country, as he is in the coolness with which he treats Neo-Platonism. As Platonist, he believes man to be more than the physical organism that appears, and, as Aristotelian he asserts that that organism is truly constitutive of his nature. How both things can be true, and what their simultaneous truth means for morality, and the Christian hope, is the theme and problem of the whole work.

It is significant of the nature and purpose of the work of Nemesius *On the nature of man* that while Apollinarius is introduced as a modern Christian thinker associated with the Neo-Platonists, the question of Christology is kept in the background. This would be absurd in a book of doctrine meant to be read only by Christians. The work must be intended as Christian apologetic, addressed to the moderately cultured public, outside the Church, that had, nevertheless, some knowledge of the character of Christianity, and of the contents of Scripture. It must be addressed, in short, to just such persons as Nemesius had been himself, a few years earlier.

TEXT

[M.38. 7–40. 10]

2. It is well known that man has some things in common with the inanimate creatures, and shares life with the plant and animal creation, while partaking intelligence in common with all beings endowed with reason. With inanimate things he shares a material body mingled of the four elements.[1] With plants he shares not only this but also the faculties of self-nutriment and generation. With irrational animals he shares all these things, and, in addition, a range of voluntary movements, together with the faculties of appetite, anger, feeling and respiration.[2] All these things man and the irrational animals have in common, if not everywhere on equal terms. Finally, by being rational, man shares with the incorporeal rational intelligences[3] the prerogative of applying, to whatever he will,

[1] The four elements of the material universe, as the ancients enumerated them, were earth, water, air, and fire. By earth they understood the basic solid, of which actual earth is typical. They recognized that this element is never encountered in nature as pure solid and nothing but pure solid. Always it is either porous, or moist, or warm, or otherwise mingled with a portion of one or more of the other elements. In fact, they acknowledged, no element occurs in a pure state. The element fire was considered to have heat as its first attribute, and incandescence only as a secondary attribute. Thus it was thought to be even more mobile and pervasive than air. Every object filling space must, it was believed, be composed of the four elements mingled together in some particular proportion. So man's body must be mingled of the four elements, and suffer destruction from the deficiency of any. The immediate arbiter of health, however, was held to be the proportion in which four fluids or juices were mingled in the body, namely blood, phlegm, yellow bile, and black bile. The last two were also known respectively as spleen (or choler), and bile, while the four together were called the four humours. The humours, like the rest of the body, were believed to contain the four elements. And the exact proportions in which the humours occurred were thought to have an important bearing on health and disposition, and in any individual were said to constitute his "temperament." Thus temperament, in the first instance meaning the adjustment of the humours in any person's system, came to have its chief present meaning, the physical and natural character or disposition peculiar to the particular person. Thus the elements, things which man shares with the inanimate creation, prove to affect the highest ranges of his being, in the argument of Nemesius.

[2] The justification for classing these activities as voluntary appears later in the book.

[3] The ancients assumed, as needing no proof, the existence of many kinds of incorporeal beings endowed with reason and free-will. Jews and Christians thought principally of good angels and evil demons. But the Greeks thought of many kinds of principalities and powers, semi-divine creatures,

reason, understanding, and judgement. So he pursues virtues, and follows after godliness, in which the quest of every several virtue finds its goal.[4]

It follows from these considerations that man's being is on the boundary between the intelligible order and the phenomenal order. As touching his body and its faculties, he is on a par with the irrational animate, and with the inanimate, creatures. As touching his rational faculties he claims kinship, as we said, with incorporeal beings.[5] It would seem that the Creator linked up each several order of creation with the next, so as to make the whole universe one and akin.

We may see herein the best proof that the whole universe is the creation of one God.[6] For not only has he united all particular things in making them members of one order of reality, but he has made them fit together, each to each. Consider, for example, how, in every animate creature the Creator joined insensible parts, such as bone, fat, or hair, with sentient tissues, like the masses of flesh, and fleshy organs, to make, out of the

to whom departments of nature were assigned for government. No particular moral character is implicit in this conception. But, as it came to be accepted into Christian thought, and owing to the doctrine of the Fall, the "world-rulers" were assimilated to the demons. Without being implicated in the material universe by having bodies of their own, all these beings were believed able to affect the material order. By their own nature they were held to belong to an invisible universe, called the intelligible world, because the mind can conceive and know it, though it is unknown to the senses.

4 The intelligible world was held to be more immediate to God than the material (or phenomenal or physical) world. Therefore Nemesius sees, in man's capacity for the pursuit of godliness, the proof that man, though visibly a denizen of this world, is already beginning to be enfranchised in the world of spirits.

5 It was a fundamental conviction with the Greeks that *logos*, the faculty of ordered reason which finds its proper instrument in articulate speech, is the thing that distinguishes man from the animals. They were aware of what can be called intelligence in animals. But they explained it away, as instinct, and attributed to man, alone of embodied creatures, true intelligence, a quality supposed characteristic of spiritual beings.

6 Nemesius has here taken the Stoic argument that the binding of the world together in unity proves the existence of a single world soul, and has used it for the overthrow of polytheism. By the time of Nemesius, this was good apologetic. There was widespread readiness in non-Christian society, now, to postulate one divine principle over the whole universe, to which principle the gods of polytheism were in some way subordinate. This opened the apologist's way for the doctrine of the creation of the world by one Creator, which Nemesius now drives home with his rehandling of the Stoic argument. Compare Origen's argument for "the one Author of one effect," in *Against Celsus*, i. 23.

insensible and sensitive parts, one composite living thing.[7] See how he has demonstrated such a creature to be not merely a composite whole but an individual unity![8] Or consider, again, how he made all the different kinds of things in the rest of creation to fit each to the next, by the introduction of some small difference into a general agreement.

COMMENTARY

2. *In man's nature two worlds meet.* Nemesius has rejected the Neo-Platonic trichotomy because it makes a discontinuity between man's higher faculties of mind, and his lower powers of soul and body. He now turns to the physical universe to find the principle of continuity binding higher to lower in a series of ascending grades of being, from the inanimate up through plants to animals and so to man, and to that which is above and beyond man, the intelligible universe. At each step the higher has roots in the lower, which in turn is united to that below it in like fashion. So, as man's nature is rooted in the orders of the physical universe beneath him, the intelligible orders of being are rooted in the physical order by means of man's highest faculties of mind and soul. Thus, in as far as the phenomenal and intelligible worlds are distinct, man marks the boundary, and constitutes a link, between them.

We have here two independent ideas expressly connected. The first is concerned with the physical universe and its unity arising from the fact that, in its ascending orders of being, the higher always shares in the attributes of the lower. The second is concerned with the nature of man, which is composite because he is a link between two worlds. It is certain that neither idea is original with Nemesius. And it has been conjectured that whatever the immediate source from which he drew the sub-

---

[7] See Jaeger, *op. cit.*, p. 103, for the Posidonian character of this observation.

[8] Nemesius again goes to the Stoics for an apologetic argument. The Stoic principle of the correspondence of man with nature, pursued with a moral aim, led to the observation of such parallels between man and the universe as that man's body, in the manner in which it is knit into unity, reflects the unity prevailing in the physical world. As Reinhardt points out, Nemesius, in his Christian-Platonic rehandling of Stoic themes, takes liberties that would have been intolerable to an orthodox Stoic, such as describing human flesh as, in itself, inanimate. Such behaviour is explained by the fact that long-continued syncretism had confused the boundaries of the classical systems of philosophy in the minds of the reading public. The Christian apologist had the less need to be guarded in his arguments.

stance of this section, his ultimate debt is to a philosopher who flourished about a century B.C., the Syrian Posidonius of Apamea. Though the works of Posidonius have not survived, he exerted an immense influence. He was trained under Panaetius in the Stoic school of philosophy, and, travelling widely, spread interest in Stoicism in the Roman world. He was a teacher of Cicero, who is a principal source of our knowledge of his particular version of the Stoic doctrine of the linked unity of all orders in the material universe, a version which owed much to the *Timaeus* of Plato. Posidonius explained the world-process as carried on by a system of energies or faculties (*dynameis*) each with its appropriate function, thus finding a parallel between the universe and the human body. The relation of Nemesius to Posidonius, in this respect, is discussed by Dr. K. Reinhardt, in Pauly-Wissowa, xxii. 1, in Section 9 of the article, *Poseidonios von Apamea.* Here the point is made that the two ideas, of the ascending orders in the universe, and man as the link between two worlds, are nowhere found united elsewhere, as they are in this section of Nemesius. They are found separately in a number of writers, and in Nyssen, *On the making of man*, ch. 8, they occur in the same writer, but unconnected. Yet, Reinhardt argues, as seen in Nemesius they fit together to such good purpose that it is unlikely that they had never been united previously. In brief, he thinks that Posidonius crowned his doctrine of man as crown of the universe, by making him join the universe with the gods. But if it is thus the doctrine of Posidonius that Nemesius reproduces, he reproduces it Platonized and Christianized. The Stoic monism of Posidonius included heaven and the gods in the categories of space and matter, but Nemesius conceives of two worlds, to one of which these categories are inapplicable, in accordance with Platonic dualism. It is unlikely that Nemesius worked directly upon Posidonius, or that his hands thus transformed the Posidonian theme. Origen is the man, and his lost *Commentary on Genesis* is the work, that probably brought to Nemesius the Posidonian theme in the Platonized and Christianized form in which he reproduces it. There are, as we shall see, other traces in Nemesius of the influence of this commentary; while it is in connection with Genesis that a Christian writer might find Posidonius specially interesting. That Nemesius does not acknowledge use of the commentary is the less surprising since the name of Origen had begun to be under a cloud. There are, however, passages in Nemesius of an evident Posidonian derivation that have undergone no Platonization, so that Origen's commentary cannot have been the only intermediary through which Nemesius acquired the thoughts of Posidonius. It is Posidonius who, by whatever intermediaries, has provided Nemesius with the means of setting, in this second section, the nature of man against the widest and most stimulating background. If two worlds are found conjoined in man, no wonder if body and soul form a unity in him. (See E. Skard, *Nemesios-studien*, i, in *Symbolae Osloenses*, Fasc. xv. pp. 23–43. (Oslo, 1936), and W. W. Jaeger, *op. cit.* Pt. II, ch. 2 "Syndesmos".)

TEXT

[M.40. 10–44. 1.]

3. There is no so marked difference between inanimate things and plants, but for the self-nutrient faculty of the latter. Likewise plants are not so different from irrational, but sentient, animals, nor are these, in turn, in total contrast with the rational creatures. One order is not unrelated to another, nor do they lack palpable and natural bonds of union. For example, while some inherent power[1] makes one kind of stone differ from another, the lodestone[2] seems to stand out, in comparison with other stones, by its celebrated power of first attracting, and then holding, iron to itself, as if it would feed upon it. More extraordinary still, when it has gripped one piece of iron, and by imparting to every such piece held by it, its own power of attraction, it uses that piece to get hold of another. In fact, iron, after it has been in contact with lodestone, attracts iron.

Again, when the Creator passed in turn from the creation of

---

[1] The four-element theory left the differences between minerals unexplained. What makes one mineral harder, heavier, or brighter than another? Posidonius sought to answer this question by postulating particular powers or virtues (*dynameis*) in things which account both for their actual qualities and for the change or permanence of their relations with other things. The aim of Posidonius was to describe and explain the universe as a living and moving, not as a static, structure.

[2] Nemesius means that the "powers" of the lodestone resemble, and in that sense "predict," the self-nutrient faculty of plants as it becomes manifest in the next, or vegetable, stage of creation. The ancients were fascinated by the qualities of the magnet, so called because the oxide of iron still known as magnetite was known to them as a product of Magnesia in Thrace. Magnetite was often found in polarized pieces which produced the phenomena that Nemesius describes. Such stones were called by the Greeks Magnesian stones, and from the Greek word is derived our word magnet. On the other hand, the English word lodestone is simply "the stone that leads or draws."

plants to that of animals, we may suppose that he did not, so to say, leap from the one order to the next, and suddenly make creatures endowed with the powers of locomotion and sensation. Rather, he advanced towards this end by slow degrees and seemly moderation.[3] He framed the marine animals called *pinna* and sea-nettle[4] to have all the appearance of sensitive plants. Like plants he fixed them to the bed of the sea as if with roots. He surrounded them with shells as trees grow bark, rendering them stationary like plants. Nevertheless, he implanted in them the sense common to the whole animal creation, the sense of touch. They are thus like plants in being rooted and stationary, and like animals in their possession of feeling or perception. Aristotle observed that sponges, in like manner, though they grow on the rocks, close and open, or, rather, spread themselves out, as in self-defence, when they perceive anything approaching. For this reason the scientists of ancient days used to call them, and all such creatures, Zoophytes.[5] After the *pinna* and such like creatures, God made next the animals with but a very limited range of movement, yet

[3] Nemesius sees two virtues in the gradualness of evolution. The first is that which Posidonius also saw in it, that it establishes a continuity in the phenomenal universe which, in turn, makes it a unity. The second he owes to the biblical doctrine of creation. It invests creation with an unhasting deliberation that beseems God.

[4] At this point Nemesius is drawing upon Aristotle's *Historia animalium* or *Story of the animal Kingdom*. The Mediterranean *pinna* is a bivalve mollusc in a horn-shaped shell which anchors itself to the sea-bed by a byssus of silky strands. Sea-nettles are usually floating jelly-fish. But Aristotle seems to include sea-anemones under *Acalephae* (sea-nettles). Even sea-anemones, though rooted to the sea-bed, have no "bark," however. Dr. H. B. Cott suggests the possibility that Nemesius (or rather his source) recognized the coral polyp as among *Acalephae*. The coral polyp only differs from a tiny sea-anemone by the fact that it develops a limy skeleton about it, secreted through its skin. The ancients prized red coral very highly, and they are likely to have observed the polyp, small though it is.

[5] Zoophyte means part-animal, part-plant. The question is, what Nemesius means by "the scientists of ancient days." The classical writers do not use the term zoophyte; which does not, in fact, appear before the second century, A.D. Apart from the statement about the ancients, this passage about the zoophytes is word for word identical with one in Galen, *The agreement between Hippocrates and Plato* (hereafter cited as the *Agreement*), where he is citing a work of Posidonius, *On the passions*. (See W. W. Jaeger, *op. cit.*, p. 104, Note 2, and p. 116.) It is possible that Nemesius copied the passage from some collection of passages which misled him into thinking that the word zoophyte had been coined by the classical naturalists.

able to move themselves from one place to another. Such are most of the shell-fish, and earthworms. Next he endowed particular species with more of this or that faculty, such as sentience or locomotion, until he reached the highest types of animal. By that, I mean those animals which possess all the senses, and are capable of unrestricted movement. And when God passed from the irrational animals to create a rational living creature, man, he did not introduce this rational creature abruptly, but led up to it, by the development, in certain animals, of instinctive intelligence, of devices and clever tricks for self-preservation, which make them appear almost rational. Only after them did God bring forth man, the truly rational living creature. You may observe the same progression if you investigate the particular vocal sounds that living things emit. Beginning with the simple and monotonous noises made, for example, by horses and cows, the Creator advanced gradually to the varied and remarkably inflected utterance of daws or talking-birds,[6] and only left off when he reached man's articulate and perfect speech.

Again, he attached articulate speech to thought and reasoning, so that it should communicate what was going on in the mind. Thus God, everywhere fitting one thing to another harmoniously,[7] bound them all together, uniting in one bond things intelligible and things phenomenal, by means of his creation of man.

COMMENTARY

3. *The visible creation was made a unity by gradual evolution.* Nemesius now retraces in more detail the ground traversed in Section 2. He shows how, rising through the mineral, vegetable, and animal kingdoms in succession, the principle of gradual differentiation both divides those kingdoms into distinguishable kinds, and, at the boundary between two kingdoms, is manifest in creatures which possess characteristics of either kingdom. Nemesius treats his theme teleologically. The facts which he described are, in his eyes, a demonstration of the Creator's will and indication of his nature. But the scientific material which he uses for this purpose was not collected by him, nor with a

6 Presumably "talking-birds" means parrots.
7 Nemesius is here comparing the order observable in nature with musical harmony. Certain notes, high and low, have the quality that enables them to be combined in a harmonious chord. So, if we compare the evolutionary scale to a musical scale we can liken the unity perceived in nature to a harmonious musical chord.

view to the use which he makes of it. The interest which inspired its collection was philosophic, and concerned with the
unity of the natural order. This interest was Stoic, and not
Platonic. It follows that it was not through Origen's *Commentary
on Genesis* that the matter of this section came to Nemesius. It
came, as Professor E. Skard has demonstrated, (*Symbolae
Osloenses*. Fasc. xvii, pp. 18–23, Oslo, 1937) through the medium
of the physician Galen. The original source was Posidonius,
less altered in Galen than in Origen. In fact, if this section were
purged of its references to creation, and if the word "Nature"
were put wherever God is named, it might have come from
Posidonius' hand.

TEXT

[M.44. 1–45. 17.]
4. The foregoing considerations justify the Mosaic story of
creation when it makes man the last to be created.[1] For, not
only was it logical that, if all other creatures were made for his
sake, they should be provided in advance for him to use, and
that, then, he, the intended user, should be created only when
all was ready, but there was another reason besides. God
created both an intelligible and a phenomenal order, and required some one creature to link these two together, in such
wise that the entire universe should form one agreeable unity,
unbroken by internal incoherences.[2] For this reason, then, man
was made a living creature such as should combine together the

1 Philo, the Jewish exegete and philosopher who flourished at Alexandria
about the time of Christ's birth, commenting upon Genesis 1:26, in his
work *On the creation of the world*, posed the question why man was the last
to be created. There are several passages in Nemesius that recall parts of
this work. The reason, no doubt, is that Origen's *Commentary on Genesis*,
which Nemesius acknowledges to be known to him, served as intermediary
between Nemesius and the thoughts of Philo. It has been observed that
the signs of the influence of Philo upon Origen appear most when his
subject is cosmology and the associated themes that would most naturally
enter into a Commentary on Genesis, and so reach Nemesius. The middle
part of the present section of Nemesius rings of Origen, while we may
compare the later part with this passage in Origen's *Third Homily on
Jeremiah*: "But the righteous man is not earth. For though he is on earth,
he has his citizenship in heaven: wherefore he will not hear, Earth thou
art, and the rest; but it may be very likely this, Heaven thou art, and
into heaven shalt thou go, for thou bearest the image of the heavenly."
In short, it is to Origen that Nemesius owes his elaboration of the destiny
of man in this Section.
2 The Posidonian thought that man, by his existence, turned the duality
of the intelligible and phenomenal worlds into an organic unity is
Christianized by Nemesius, and the school of Antioch, in the form that

intelligible and phenomenal natures. So then, to put great matter in few words, we see how wonderful is the wisdom of our Creator.

In being so constituted, man finds himself on the border that separates rational from irrational. If he leans towards the things of the body,[3] and finds his satisfaction in carnal pleasures, he thereby makes his choice to live like the irrational animals. So he should be accounted one of them, and be called, in Paul's words, "a man of earth," to whom is said, "Dust thou art, and unto dust thou shalt return,"[4] and "He shall be compared unto the beasts that have no understanding, and is likened unto them."[5] If, on the other hand, man advances in the direction of reason, despises all carnal pleasures, and pursues the divinely favoured life that is specifically man's, he will then deserve to be called a "heavenly man," in accordance with the Apostle's words, "Such as is the earthy, such also are they that are earthy, and such as is the heavenly, such also are they that are heavenly."[6]

The chief characteristic of the nature that is ruled by reason is to avoid and avert evils, and to search out and choose the good. One sort of good applies alike to soul and body, such as virtues, which have their reference indeed to the soul, but to the soul in so far as it makes use of body. Another sort of good concerns the soul only, in its own proper functions, without involving the body, such as godliness or philosophic contemplation.[7] Wherefore, those who choose to live as men indeed, and

Christ, by his existence and work, achieves this. The thought lived on in the more philosophic of western Christian thinkers, and English churchmen encounter it in J. M. Neal's version of the Eastertide hymn of Fulbert of Chartres, where Christ "joining heaven and earth again, links in one common-weal the twain."

[3] This does not mean the same thing as yielding to motions that originate in the body. Gen. 6:2 and "the sons of God" who "saw the daughters of men that they were fair," formed a foundation for the belief that incorporeal rational beings could, mentally, "lean towards the things of the body." It transpires that Nemesius credits man with a power of choice that consists exactly in contemplating and finding satisfaction in whichever of the two worlds he will, the phenomenal world in which he inheres primarily through his body, and the intelligible world to which he has entry as a rational soul. Origen uses this phrase "leaning towards the things of the body" in his surviving *First Homily on Genesis*.

[4] Gen. 3:19.   [5] Ps. 49:20 (Septuagint).   [6] I Cor. 15:48.

[7] The ascetic movement enjoyed a prestige which extended beyond the membership of the Church, and brought it about that what Nemesius here said would be readily understood, viz. that there may be spiritual gains that can only be obtained at the expense of the body.

not just to live that life which is at animal level, pursue virtue and godliness.

What the difference is, between the pursuit of godliness and the pursuit of virtues, shall be discussed. But we must first give an account of the relationship between the soul and the body. For, until we have discovered what, in its essence, the soul is, we are not in a position to go on and treat of its activities.

COMMENTARY

4. *Man was created to be the link between two worlds.* Nemesius has, so far, been interpreting Posidonian evolution in a teleological sense. So interpreted, evolution seeks its aim or end, and its final product must be that for which it was put in motion. Nemesius now claims, on the authority of Genesis, that man is the final creature. The whole gradual process by which the phenomenal world has been evolved was directed towards the production of man, in whom the phenomenal world is joined to the intelligible. Man is thus in a position of cosmic responsibility, only to be fulfilled by his retaining unimpaired his hold upon the intelligible. The section ends with an examination of the means to this end.

There is nothing, however, in the section more significant than what the author abstains from saying. For Nemesius certainly believed that, however it might be that God had created mankind to bind visible and invisible together, mankind was fallen in Adam. It had sunk to the level of the beasts that perish. It had no longer such hold upon the intelligible world as to be the link that God destined it for. The argument of Nemesius thus requires, for its completion, the gospel that there is, nevertheless, a link that holds, in the incarnate Son of God, the sinless and perfect Man. The completion of the argument is amply present in the works of the greatest theologian of the School of Antioch, Theodore of Mopsuestia. Writing a quarter of a century after Nemesius, Theodore teaches that man is a "pledge of friendship" between the members of a divided universe. The word "pledge" indicates that the fulfilment of the reconciliation is yet to come. But the pledge would have no substance if the link were not made secure in Christ. Christ's death and resurrection were, for Theodore, specific acts that relinked the phenomenal world with the intelligible. At the same time he saw them as redemptive of the race created for the purpose which he alone had yet fulfilled. For by them there comes,

38

NEMESIUS OF EMESA

for believers in them, reconciliation with reason and with God. Nevertheless, man is not restored, here and now, to the office for which God destined him. That will only be fulfilled, as Theodore says, "in the next world, after the resurrection . . . after we have become truly immutable and worthy to be always with Christ." For the present, he had said earlier, "it is necessary that this decrepit and mortal world should go on existing for some time further, in order that mankind might believe in Christ." (Theodore of Mopsuestia, *On the Nicene creed*, edited and translated from the Syriac by A. Mingana, 1932, Woodbrooke Studies, v., p. 115 and p. 70). Such was equally the private mind also of Nemesius, upon man as the link between two worlds. And his reticence proves that he is writing for those who have not yet entered into the Gospel.

TEXT

[M.45. 17–48. 4.]

5. The Jews[1] say that man was created at first neither avowedly mortal nor yet immortal, but rather in a state poised between the two, in the sense that, if he gave himself up to his bodily passions, he should be subject to all the changes of the body, but that if he put the good of his soul foremost, he should be deemed worthy of immortality. For if God had made man mortal from the first, he would not have appointed dying as the penalty of his offence, seeing that no one would condemn to mortality someone who was already mortal. If, to take the other case, God had made man immortal, he would not have subjected him to the need of nourishment. No immortal being

---

[1] This is the formula with which Origen commonly introduces his borrowings from Philo, and Nemesius has taken it straight from the text before him. The passage in Philo which Origen had in mind may be that towards the close of his work *On the creation of the world* where he says, "One might properly say that man is the boundary-mark between a mortal and an immortal nature, and shares in each just so much as he must." As Professor Skard points out (*Nemesiosstudien* i, p. 30) Philo is here commenting on Gen. 2:7, and the passage of Origen's commentary before the eyes of Nemesius was, no doubt, his exposition of the same verse. The text of Philo continues that man is mortal as touching his body and immortal as touching his mind. But if Origen reproduced this piece of extreme Platonism, Nemesius has not followed suit. It is interesting that the line he follows instead is that taken by Theophilus, bishop of Antioch at the end of the second century (*To Autolycus*, i. 27). We may assume, therefore, that Theophilus represents the doctrinal tradition of the Syrian Church, in handling this question.

is dependent upon bodily food.[2] We cannot suppose, either, that God created man immortal and then so lightly changed his mind and made him mortal. He did not, evidently, do any such thing to the angels that sinned. They remained immortal, according to their original nature. They look for judgement upon their offences, but in a form other than death. We had better, therefore, accept this account of the matter,[3] or else suppose man to have been created mortal, but capable of becoming immortal when brought to perfection by moral progress;[4] which is the same thing as being potentially immortal.

Until man had attained his perfection, however, it was not at all suitable for him to know how he was constituted. God, for that reason, forbad him to taste the fruit of the Tree of Knowledge. In those days plants possessed singular powers. Rather, we might say, they do so still. Then, however, in the beginning of creation, virtues of plants had suffered no deterioration, and so were correspondingly powerful.[5] Thus the mere eating of a certain fruit was then capable of imparting an understanding of one's own nature. But God would not have man attain such knowledge prematurely. For, if man knew the whole extent of his physical indigence, it would draw all his concern towards the care of his body, and leave him none to spare for his soul. And that is why God forbad man to eat the fruit that gives such knowledge.

Man disobeyed and learned the truth about himself. But, in so doing, he sacrificed his own advance towards perfection, and became the slave of bodily needs. Straightway, he set out on the search for something wherewith to clothe himself. Moses says that the man was naked, and now knew it, whereas, until that

[2] That angels have no wants is a theme of Origen.

[3] The phrase appears to refer to the whole preceding argument, and not just to the Jewish theory with which it opens, thus indicating that Nemesius has a commentary before him, and finds the conclusions which it reaches acceptable.

[4] That perfection may be reached by moral progress is a characteristic theme of Origen.

[5] See Cyril, Lecture II. 4 above. It was a Posidonian doctrine that nature was once fresher and more dynamic than now. Origen may have combined this conception with Gen. 3:17 (the curse upon the earth that was uttered as part of man's punishment), and so explained the presumed decline in quality. Thus the truth of Scripture might seem to be confirmed and enhanced by the teaching of Posidonius. Jewish and Christian writers explained the power of pagan thinkers to enhance revelation either as due to partial inspirations, or to unacknowledged deductions from the revelation in Scripture.

moment, God had caused him to be entranced with existence and happily unconscious of himself. When man lapsed from the way of perfection, he likewise lost the immortality which, by favour of his Creator, he is to recover at the last.

After his fall, God gave him permission to feed on flesh, whereas, before his fall, God had assigned to him a sufficient diet wholly provided by things that grew from the soil. This, of course, was in paradise. But now that he despaired of perfection, man was, thereafter and in condescension, allowed to feed himself as he chose.[6]

COMMENTARY

5. *Man is incapacitated, by Adam's fall, for being the link.* Nemesius has spoken, in Section 4, as if man was capable of fulfilling his office of link between the phenomenal and intelligible worlds. He now proceeds to show, with the help of Genesis, how man came to be incapacitated for his office. Once more he is evidently drawing upon Origen's *Commentary on Genesis.* For this section, see E. Skard, *Nemesiosstudien* I. pp. 27–31.

TEXT

[M.48. 4–52. 12.]

6. As man is corporeal and the body is composed of the four elements, it follows that he is liable to all contingencies to which those elements are liable, namely scission, mutation, and flux, three things affecting the body only. By mutation we mean change of qualities,[1] and by flux the evacuation of constituents. For, a living creature keeps passing off matter, through the visible orifices, and through others that are concealed, as well. These we shall consider later. Whatever is evacuated must, of course, be fully replaced, or the living organism would perish from the deficiency of replacements. Dry matter evacuated by a living creature must, of necessity, be replaced by dry food,

---

[6] Nemesius is almost certainly parting company with Origen at this point. Origen supposed men to have begun to sacrifice and eat flesh after the Flood. The theory which Nemesius substitutes, that meat-eating came of man's desperation after his fall, may be associated with the belief, prevalent in Christian Syria, that a man of God abstains from flesh. A somewhat similar idea about the origin of meat-eating appears in the *Clementine Homilies,* of third-century Syrian provenance. The *Didache,* which is probably a Syrian composition of the second century, teaches abstinence from flesh-meat as a counsel of Christian perfection (ch. 6).

[1] Mutation means change of quality, flux changes bulk, and scission alters shape.

moisture by wet food, and exhalations by corresponding inhalations. Our food and drink are made up of just those elements[2] of which our bodies are composed. So, each living
creature is nourished by taking in what accords with, and resembles, its constitution, and is cured by taking in their opposites.[3] Some elements we take into the body just as they are, and
others by the means of some vehicle. Thus, to gain moisture,
either we drink plain water, or we imbibe it contained in wine,
oil, or any of the kinds of fruit that we denominate moist. Wine
is nothing other than water produced in the vine.

In like manner, we take in the element fire, it may be directly,
by warming ourselves at it, or it may be by means of hot meats
or beverages. In fact, there is a modicum of fire diffused through
all comestibles, in greater or less degree. In like manner, again,
we either breathe in air, directly, from the surrounding atmosphere, or we extract it from the various other things that we
consume in eating or drinking. Earth, on the other hand, we
never consume just as it is, but only as a constituent in this or
that food. Thus, earth becomes wheat, and we eat the wheat.
Larks, pigeons frequently, and partridges feed on earth,[4] but

2 The four elements are present in the body in a particular proportion
and quantity, which, through the balance of the humours, determines
life and health. The same four elements are present, in particular proportions, in different kinds of food. So food sustains life and health by
replacing wastage of elements in the body.

3 In the end of a sentence, Nemesius introduces the new subject of physic,
or cure. The theory of health which Nemesius takes from Galen, and the
Greek medical tradition, makes health consist in maintaining an ideal
balance of qualities which constitutes the "temperament" of the subject.
Feeding is simple, by comparison, for it only aims to make wastage good.
But health is most often overthrown not by a deficiency but by an excess.
As there is no means of getting rid of an excess of some constituent of
the body, the physician's art is to produce in the body the quality the
exact opposite of that of the thing that is in excess, and to produce it
in exactly the right amount. Thus the balance of temperament will be
restored. Nemesius illustrates the point by the case of a fever-patient.
A fiery quality is in excess, with such a patient. It is no cure, however,
to place the patient in the cold. Cure comes by the administration of the
right food and medicine, which will introduce the required solid and cool
qualities into the body itself, and so restore the balance of temperament.
Thus the art of the physician is to discover the diet and medicine that will
restore the temperament of the patient.

4 The ancients supposed birds to be feeding on earth when they were
actually devouring ants or grubs hidden in the soil. That this is the
explanation, and not that birds pick up grits for their crops, is clear from
the fact that named species of birds are here credited with eating earth,
such as partridges, which are inveterate eaters of ants, or larks which

man consumes earth only as a constituent of seeds, fruits, or flesh.

Alike for dignity,[5] and for the greater delicacy of his sense of touch (wherein man excels all other animals) God wrapped us neither in thick hide, like oxen and other leathery-coated beasts, nor in a long hairy covering, like goats, sheep, or hares, nor in scales, like snakes or fishes, nor in hard shells, like tortoises or oysters, nor in soft shell, like lobsters, nor in feathers, like birds. Perforce, therefore, we need clothes, to take the place, for us, of the covering with which Nature endowed the other animals.

These, then, are the reasons why we stand in need of food and clothes. And for the very same reasons, we need houses, not the least function of which is to afford us a refuge from the wild beasts. Further, because of disordered mingling of qualities, and of broken continuity, in the body, we require physicians and their art. When change takes place in some quality, we need to restore the balance by introducing the opposite quality, so as to bring the constitution of the body back to normal. The physician's art is not, as some think, just to cool a fevered body, but to restore it to an equable temperament. For were one merely to cool a man in a fever, his condition would turn into the exactly opposite ailment.

So, therefore, man has need of food and drink, because of evacuation and perspiration; of clothes, because Nature provided him with no stout envelope; of a house to keep out the harsh weather and wild beasts; of healing, in view of changes in the qualities and internal feeling of the body. For if we had no such feeling, we should not suffer; and not suffering, should not feel the need of healing; and so, by not curing our ill, we should perish through not knowing that we had any.[6]

feed on small grubs and seeds. Skard, *Nemosiosstudien* II, p. 13, notes that Nemesius is so absorbed in his secular sources as not to remember the serpent (on the strength of Gen. 3:14) among the eaters of earth.

[5] This sentence might be taken to mean that it is man's glory to be covered by art and not by nature. The opposite sense is more probable. Man in paradise was naked because, for beauty and dignity, there is no equal to the "human form divine." Many of the Fathers supposed that the sin of our first parents was that they anticipated the time of their destined wedlock, and so turned nakedness, which should have been their dignity, into shame. Thus clothes are a consequence of the fall and the badge of our disgrace.

[6] Jaeger (*Nemesius*, p. 126, Note 1 and p. 127) shows reason for tracing back to Posidonius the foregoing series of observations taken from the fields of chemistry, zoology, and medicine.

Because of the arts and sciences and the useful things to which they lead, we have mutual need of one another. And because we need one another, we come together into one place in large numbers, and share with each other the necessities of our life, in common intercourse. To this human assemblage and cohabitation we have given the name of city. And therein we have profit one from other, by propinquity, and by not needing to travel.

For man is a naturally sociable animal, and made for citizenship. No single person is in all ways self-sufficient. And so it is clear, how that cities exist for the sake of intercourse, and for the sake of learning from each other.[7]

COMMENTARY

6. *Man's precarious constitution leads to his being a social creature.* Nemesius now leaves Origen, as Skard demonstrates (*op. cit.* Fasc. xvii. pp. 9-18), to resume the Posidonian doctrine of man as mediated through Galen, with facts and phrases from Galen thickly scattered through the section. The facts of nutrition and

---

[7] There were, in later Greek thought, two rival views on the subject of the city. On the one hand, there was the "high," or Platonic, view, which regarded the city with veneration. In Platonism, all culture derived from the idea of the city. And Greek cities claimed to owe not only their existence but their laws and constitutions to their divine or heroic founders. With such a view of the city, politics ranked but little below religion. On the other hand there was the Epicurean reaction, which flouted the doctrine of the golden age, the source of all good institutions, including the city. Epicurus characteristically derived civilization from man's striving to escape from the anguish of his needs. Posidonius may be credited with mediating between these opposed views, with the doctrine that civilization is the child of need and reason. Origen reproduces such a doctrine in *Against Celsus*, iv. 76, and it is likely that he did so in the *Commentary on Genesis* in connection with the biblical history. Even Christian Platonists shrank from the "high" view of the city, as likely to attach men's hearts and minds to this world (cf. Heb. 13:14). Also Scripture gave an unfavourable account of the origin of cities. (Gen. 4:17, "Cain builded a city," and Babel, Gen. 11). Christian opinion must have been known to be unfavourable to glorification of the city, for Celsus and Julian the Apostate alike gird at Christianity as unfitting men for political life. Origen was sensitive to this charge, and ready, on this question, to follow Posidonius rather than Plato. And here we may have the explanation of the solution adopted by Nemesius, to the question of the city, to wit that the city is the remedy permitted by providence for the clamorous needs which man incurred through the Fall. As Nemesius states this solution, at the end of the section, he provides a mediating view on a controversial subject, such as might prove to be good apologetic.

wastage, of sickness and vulnerability, combine to enforce the
moral of man's neediness. But necessity is the mother of invention. And man's supreme invention is the city, which brings to
him his chiefest blessing, which is to be social. Where Posidonius
extolled the cleverness of man in making assets of his infirmities,
Nemesius connects man's neediness with his fall, and so suggests
that the happy outcome is a mercy of Providence.

TEXT

[M.52. 12–56. 6.]

7. Man has two choice prerogatives, which are as follows,
and are shared by no other creature. Man, only, on repenting
can gain forgiveness. And only man's body, though mortal, is
immortalized. This privilege of the body is for the soul's sake.
So, likewise, the soul's privilege is on account of the body. For
it is only man, among the rational beings, that has this unique
privilege, of claiming forgiveness by repenting. Neither demons
nor angels repent and are forgiven. In this fact, most particularly, God shows himself both just and merciful, and is so acknowledged. As for angels, seeing that there is no compulsion
drawing them to sin, and that they are by nature exempt from
bodily passions, needs, and pleasures, there is plain reason why
they cannot claim pardon by repenting. Man, on the other
hand, is not only rational but a living organism. The wants and
passions of a living creature often distract his consideration.
Afterwards, when he comes to his senses again, and, fleeing
lust, returns to the way of the virtues, he obtains both justice
and mercy in pardon. Now, just as laughter is a peculiar mark
of man's being, because it is something that pertains to him
only, to every single man, and to all men at all times, so, in like
fashion, it is peculiar to man that he, in distinction from all
other creatures endowed with reason, should, by God's grace,
be released, upon repentance, from the guilt of former transgressions. This, too, pertains to man only, to every single man,
and to all men at all times, while still living in this world,
though not after death.[1]

---

[1] The only thing that Nemesius here reveals of the Christian doctrine of
the forgiveness of sins is that man has his privilege of pardon only on this
side of the grave. He says nothing of the terms of such pardon. It had
been thought, in the primitive church, that there was only one pardon,
granted in baptism. Early in the second century, this belief began to be
controverted. A principal document of the controversy is the sermon

Some will have it that, in like manner, the angels have no
more any place of repentance unto pardon since the Fall, seeing
that the Fall took the place of death for them. Before the Fall, in
what, for them, corresponded with man's lifetime, angels also
had a claim on pardon. But since they did not make good their
claim, it remains that they receive the fitting sentence of punishment, without pardon and without end.[2] These considerations

known by the misleading title of *Second Epistle of Clement*, in which (ch. 8)
it is argued that, while we live on earth, we can be compared with clay
in the hands of a potter. Till the pot is fired it can be remoulded. The firing
of the pot represents a man's death. Thereafter repentance and pardon
are possible no more. But while we live in the body pardon is still possible.
This teaching played an important part in opening the way to a recognition, in the Church, of post-baptismal penance. But it is teaching that
rests on reason, and not on revelation. And so Nemesius might rightly
feel that he could use it, as here, for an apologetic purpose.

[2] The doctrine here enunciated of the probation and pardon of angels is
not likely to be original with Nemesius; but it has only come down to us
in this passage, reproduced by John of Damascus in the eighth century
without any sign of knowledge other than that of the passage itself.
Origen allotted indefinite repentance to all spiritual beings, with the corol-
lary that all spiritual beings might at last be saved, not excepting the
devil. The vast theory of creation and redemption of which this universal-
ism is the end was generally disowned by Christian theologians. In reaction
from it, the view was adopted by many that incorporeal spirits must, in
a flash, have made their irreversible decision, for or against fidelity to
their Creator. This view, however, lacked the support of Christian antiquity, which inclined to belief in some kind of probation of the angels.
Thus Ignatius, bishop of Antioch, writing about A.D. 115 to the Church
of Smyrna says, "the angels who do not believe in the blood of Christ
are judged." (ch. 6.) And Irenaeus (late second century), as quoted by
Eusebius in his *Church History*, iv. 18, cites in turn Justin Martyr (mid-
second century) as saying that "before our Lord's coming, Satan never
dared to blaspheme God, since he did not know, till that time, that he
himself had been condemned." This should apparently mean that Satan's
condemnation did not become final, nor Satan desperate, until he had
slain Christ. The idea is repeated later in Epiphanius (*Panarion*, Heresy
39), and by Isidore of Pelusium. We may supply what is lacking in the
reference of Nemesius to the probation of angels, with the help of fourth
century writers who were not in sharp reaction from Origen. Thus, Basil
the Great, in his first *Homily on the six days of Creation*, ch. 5, says that the
spiritual and incorporeal orders of being were created before the material
universe, which, when it had been created, was put under the government
of angels, whose fidelity was thus under probation. Gregory of Nyssa
accordingly supposes (*Catechetical Oration*, ch. 6) that Satan was the archangel set in charge of the sublunary world, and that his envy of the final
creature, man, led to his fall and that of the world he ruled. Gregory
Nazianzen (Sermon xxxviii) supposes that the nature of angels is such
as to be moved from godliness only with great difficulty, but that when
this has happened, the fallen angels become creators of evil. As we have

make it clear that any who will not repent, renounce a gift unique and peculiar to man.

Peculiar also to man, and unique, so that man alone of living creatures enjoys it, is for his body to rise again after death and enter upon immortality. It has this privilege on account of the soul's immortality, just as the soul has the other privilege for the body's sake, which is infirm and troubled by many passions.

Further, it is peculiar to man to learn arts and sciences, and to practise the arts; so that man has been defined as a rational living creature, mortal, and capable of intelligence and knowledge.[3] He is said to be a living creature because man is essentially ensouled and sentient, whereby he fulfils the definition of a living creature. He is said to be rational, in contradistinction to the irrational beasts, and to be mortal, by contrast with the immortal rational beings. And the phrase, "capable of intelligence and knowledge," points to our being able to learn arts

seen above, Cyril of Jerusalem (*Catechetical Lecture*, II. 10) says, "We know not how much God forgave to angels, for them also did he forgive, since one only is sinless." In the light of these passages, we can make the following hypothetical reconstruction of the doctrine to which Nemesius makes what is, in fact, no more than a suggestive allusion. God first created angels, to whom his being and will were, for the most part, mysterious. Their fidelity was, like their knowledge, imperfect. But while they presumed, and needed forgiveness, they were being progressively sanctified by the Holy Ghost. At last God disclosed his will to create a material world for the sake of a new and embodied spiritual being, man. This was the most difficult mystery for angels to receive. Lucifer, set in charge of the sublunary world at its creation, envied his charges, Adam and Eve, and lured them into sin, thus precipitating the final mystery, that of redemption. Thus it was the doom pronounced upon the serpent, ending with the prophecy concerning the seed of the woman, that might appear to mark the decisive moment for the fall or salvation of the angelic host. The angels either then vowed themselves to adore the mystery of redemption, and were pardoned and saved (and these are Michael and his angels, who are the ministers of providence, until the final restoration) or rebelled against it, so as to have no more hope or desire for pardon. So Satan fell "like lightning from heaven," to seek furiously, with his associates, to establish their rebellion, in the subversion of providence in its task of redemption.

[3] Professor Skard (*loc. cit.*, p. 43) points out that this definition of man is cited also by Basil the Great and Apollinarius. Presumably it was coined by a philosopher. And Nemesius clearly cites it from a commentary on this philosopher, in which the definition is examined and justified by the observation, so strangely transcribed by the Christian author, that the last part of the definition is needed to distinguish man from "nymphs and other minor deities." Ammonius, or one of the early Neo-Platonists, may be conjectured, as the author of the definition.

and sciences, since we have, indeed, a capacity both for intelligence and for arts, but only attain the practice of them by learning them. Some say that this phrase is an addition to the definition, which, as a definition, is sufficient without it. It is used because certain others have brought into the argument nymphs[4] and suchlike minor deities that are credited with vast longevity, though not with immortality. So, to differentiate from man such beings, there has been added to the definition the words "capable of intelligence and knowledge," since those beings are not supposed to learn, but to know whatever they know by gift of nature.

[4] The belief in nymphs, in classical religion, is a survival from animism, the stage of culture at which every individuated aspect or part of Nature is supposed to be indwelt by its own particular spirit. Nymphs were poetically pictured as beautiful maidens, and thus corporeal. But the proverb that a man who saw a nymph would be doomed to hopeless passion suggests that nymphs were thought of, alternatively, as invisible spirits. Their part was to personify a place, tree, or stream. As such they came to be thought of as minor deities, and Homer, in the *Iliad*, makes Zeus summon them to a meeting of the immortals. But Bishop Fell, in a note on this passage in his Oxford edition of Nemesius, cites passages in Pliny's *Natural History* showing that nymphs were not themselves immortal. Naturally, a dryad, or tree-nymph, might be supposed to be involved in the mortality of the tree. Accordingly Pliny attributes to nymphs not immortality but fabulous longevity. Our surprise that Nemesius should include such pagan matter in his work may be lessened by consideration of the way in which the sibyls, who might be classed with "nymphs and other minor deities," were generally accepted into Christian lore. The name "Sibyl" means "will of God." The sibyls of Greek mythology were women of incredible age, possessing a knowledge of the will of heaven which they declared in oracular sentences. Jewish apologists, shortly before the Christian era, saw in the sibyls some parallel to the Hebrew prophets, and conceived the plan of commending biblical notions of providence and of morality to Greek pagan readers by couching them in fictitious "sibylline oracles." These sibylline books were accepted at their face value in the Church, and were even improved upon by Christian pseudepigraphers. Thus, while the gods of pagan worship were identified by Christians with the fallen angels, sibyls, nymphs and fairies were allowed a character of innocence, so as even to be accounted minor ministers of providence.

If a sibyl was supposed to possess her knowledge by gift of nature, and not by process of learning, so, *a fortiori*, must it be with incorporeal beings. In this way the allusion to the nymphs which Nemesius found in his Neo-Platonist commentary helped him to complete his account of the relations of the mortal corporeal rational creature man with the intelligible world, in that, whereas the incorporeal beings possess knowledge by gift of nature, man attains it by understanding and learning.

COMMENTARY

7. *Man's remaining prerogatives: in life, pardon and progress, and after death the hope to rise again.* So far, the Posidonian doctrine of man, mediated either by Origen or Galen, has provided most of the matter for Nemesius, and is to be resumed again after this section. But now there is a break of continuity. The vocabulary of this section is sharply un-Origenistic (see E. Skard, *Nemesiosstudien* I, Anhang). Section 7 is made up of the combination of two articles of the creed (the forgiveness of sins, and the resurrection of the body) with two secular maxims (man is a laughing animal who learns). The total effect of this bizarre combination is to set man in contrast with all incorporeal beings and in a unique position relatively to corporeal beings. It is as if Nemesius would answer the question, what prerogatives or liabilities of man's nature have gone as yet unnamed? Then, having briefly named them, he returns to them no more. That fact, however, is hardly so strange as that a Christian author should have at all introduced credal themes into a work of apologetic; though nothing of a specifically Christian character is revealed, on either subject. Perhaps Nemesius felt that man's relationship with the phenomenal universe was so well elaborated in his sources that he must try to dress the balance by supplying all he could, bearing upon man's relations with the other universe, the world of incorporeal creatures. What Christian source Nemesius used in this section is uncertain.

TEXT

[M.56. 6–60. 7.]

8. It is a doctrine of the Jews that the whole world was made for the sake of man; some things directly for his sake, such as beasts of burden and oxen for farm work, while grass was made for provender for these creatures. Some things were made for their own sakes, and some for the sake of other things. All rational beings were created for their own sakes, while the irrational and inanimate creatures exist for the sake of others than themselves. Now if they exist for the sake of others, we must ask, What others? For the angels, perhaps? No man of sense could argue that! For things that exist for the sake of other things serve for the constitution, the continuance, or the restoration of those things; which is to say, either for the propagation of the species, or its nourishment, covering, cure, welfare, or

recreation. An angel needs none of these things. For angels have no progeny, want no bodily food or clothing or any such requirement. Now if that is so for an angel, it is clear that it must be true of any super-angelic being. The higher the order, so much the less its needs.

So we have to seek out some being whose nature is rational, which nevertheless requires to propagate its kind, and so on. If we leave man on one side, what other such nature can we find? It is to be inferred, therefore, that it is man for whose sake irrational living creatures and inanimate things were made. If, then, they were made, as has been shown, for man's sake, that is why he was constituted lord over those creatures. A lord's business it is to make a temperate use of whatever is under his authority, not to wax wanton and sate appetite with pleasure, nor to treat his subjects tyrannously or harshly. Such as ill-use the irrational beasts, sin, therefore, for they do not play the part either of lord or righteous man; as it is written, "The righteous man hath compassion on the life of his beast."[1]

But, like as not, someone will assert that there is nothing but was made for its own sake, and not for the sake of something else. Let us, then, separate inanimate from living things, in the first instance, and look whether inanimate things are likely to have been made for their own sakes. If they were so made, how or on what should living things be fed? For we behold Nature producing the nourishment of all animals (at least, if we except the carnivores), in the form of fruits and herbs, from the earth. And even the carnivores live on those animals that graze on the earth, as when wolves and lions devour lambs, goats, pigs or deer, or eagles raven on partridges, wood pigeons, hares, and suchlike creatures that feed on the fruits of the earth. It is of the nature of fishes to live on one another. And yet flesh-feeding does not extend to all of them, but we come in the end to fishes that feed on seaweed and certain other things that grow in the water. Had all types of fish preyed on others, and had none turned from a carnivorous diet, fishes would not long have endured, but would have died out, some destroyed by others, and some of mere starvation. So that that might not happen some fishes were so made as to abstain from flesh, and graze, so to speak, on sea-pasture while the others are kept alive by feeding on them. Seaweed is fodder for the one kind, which in turn forms the diet of the other kinds, and these of yet others. Thus, through the feeding of the basic orders of fish, provided to them

[1] Prov. 12:10 (A. V. "regardeth the life").

without stint by the earthy flooring of the sea, the other types of fishes are kept going. Our argument has proved, therefore, that the creation of plants cannot have been for the sake of plants, but must have been for the nourishment and subsistence of men and other living creatures. And if they were thus made for the sake of men and other living creatures, it is evident that the means of growth and propagation of the latter is provided by the former.[2]

Then, next, the motions of the heavenly bodies, the firmament, the seasons of the year, the rains, and all such natural processes, were therefore ordained so that the nature of the fruit-eating creatures might continue, and so the whole cycle of nourishment be provided without a break. We thus find that the celestial cycle is for the sake of the fruits of the earth, and these fruits are for the sake of living creatures, and, in the end, of man.[3]

COMMENTARY

8. *The world was made for man.* In this section we return to the Posidonian doctrine of the nature of man, mediated by Philo, *On the creation of the world*, through Origen's *Commentary on Genesis*. Therefore it is introduced with a reference to "the Jewish doctrine" that the world was made for man; a doctrine actually stated in these terms, "that the Lord resolved the age for the sake of man," in the Sclavonic *Secrets of Enoch*, LXV. 3 (R. H. Charles, *Apocrypha and Pseudepigrapha of the Old Testament*, II. 467). The idea itself, however, had been in course of development from some while before the Christian era. In

[2] E. Skard, *Nemesiosstudien* II, pp. 23–25, argues that Galen is the immediate source for this argument from zoology.

[3] The argument that lower creatures do not exist for their own sakes, but for the use and sustenance of higher orders, is contained in Origen, *Against Celsus*, iv. 74–78. As a similar argument appears in Basil the Great, *On the Six days of Creation*, ix. 2, and in Gregory of Nyssa's *On the constitution of man* (ch. 8), it is highly probable that it was rehandled by Origen in his *Commentary on Genesis*, which was used by both these writers. Moreover, that the argument derives from Posidonius is made probable by the fact that Origen admits it to be an argument "of the Stoics"; also because it is reproduced by Cicero, in *On the nature of the gods*, ii. 133 and following, and in Seneca, Letters 92 and 94, both these writers being strongly influenced by Posidonius. Again, Origen's views on the heavenly bodies expressed in his *First Principles* would not lead us to expect the doctrine which he teaches in *Against Celsus*, iv. 77, that the heavenly bodies subserve the needs of man. A reasonable explanation is that the latter passage reflects the influence upon Origen of the Posidonian doctrine of the nature of man.

Wisdom 7:1-14, man is the nursling of divine Wisdom, while in 10:1-2, the thought is applied to Adam. It has been conjectured that the doom pronounced upon the Prince of Tyre in Ezek. 28:13-15 originated in a "Doom of Adam," in which was expressed the doctrine that man is the crown of God's purpose in creation. For the Jews, however, the crown of mankind is the chosen people, and the Son of man in Dan. 7:13 is no doubt their personification. The passage expresses the belief that God made the world for the sake of Israel. By the second century this idea was transferred by Christians to apply to the new Israel, the Church. The *Shepherd of Hermas* and the *Second Epistle of Clement* are at one in teaching that the end of creation, which God set before him from before all ages, was an ideal and everlasting Church. It thus appears that the doctrine that the world was made for man is of religious and scriptural inspiration, rather than philosophic. Nevertheless, the syllogistic argument of this section came from Posidonius, an argument proving deductively that man is the crown of the natural order, because the lower grades of being, directly, and the celestial bodies, indirectly, serve his needs. The *Commentary on Genesis* is the probable intermediary through which the substance of the Posidonian argument came to Nemesius, but the debating style into which it is worked up in this section may be credited to our author himself.

TEXT

[M.60. 7-63. 14.]

9. For the rest, we have to consider whether the category of irrational creatures was made for its own sake or for that of man. There is obvious absurdity in the suggestion that things incapable of purposeful cogitation, living solely by natural impulse, whose attitude bent down to earth indicates that they are slaves,[1] should have been introduced for their own sakes. Much could fitly be said on this point; so much, in fact, as to call for almost a whole book to itself. But lest the volume of my argument get out of hand, I had best turn to a summary statement that nevertheless includes the chief points.

If, then, we look into the things of the external universe re-

[1] This common-place, drawing a lesson from the singularity of man's erect stance, while found in a wide range of settings, from the opening of Sallust's *Cataline* to Basil's, *Six days of creation*, appears here, according to Jaeger (*Nemesios*, pp. 129-31) in its original setting, as it stood in the argument of Posidonius.

flected in man as in a mirror, we shall be basing our demonstration upon the reality of the subjects of our enquiry.[2] For we see that in the human soul there is an irrational element with its own characteristic functions; such, I mean, as appetite or anger. When a man is keeping the laws of nature, these irrational functions are given to him to be subservient to the rational, which is the ruler while they are the governed, which gives commands while they receive them and minister to whatever purposes reason dictates. Now if the rational in us bears rule over the irrational in us, why should we not conclude that reason also rules the irrational creatures in the universe outside us, and that they have been provided to serve its ends? For the irrational is naturally subject to the rational, as has been proved by introspection.

This, and the creation of many kinds of animals adapted to provide service to man, such as oxen and all beasts of burden for farming and transport, the multitude of things that fly in the air or swim the seas or swarm upon dry land which prove to man's advantage, and talking birds[3] that serve for his delight and

[2] Nemesius is here making his appeal to the current doctrine that man is a tiny reflection of the universe. From the third century B.C. the Stoic school of philosophers worked upon the assumption that the universe is a living creature with its own rationality and order. Man being also a living creature, comparison between man and the universe followed. Difference was observed between human ways and the ways of Nature, between man-made laws and customs and the laws governing the universe. It was acknowledged that the impulses given by nature were directed to the right ends, with the consequence that human happiness must be sought in understanding and accepting the world-order. So the Stoic ethic was an ethic of correspondence with Nature, and concentrated attention upon the correspondences between elements of man's nature and the characteristics of the universe. By the time of Nemesius, these correspondences had come to be regarded as complete. Thus Gregory of Nyssa had written, a few years before Nemesius, "Man is said by the philosophers to be a little world, containing in himself all those elements of which the universe is made up." Nemesius accepts this as dogma, and expects a constant analogy between man and the universe. Accordingly he argues, here, that truths about the universe can be deduced from observation of man, and *vice versa*. This dogma was revived by the alchemists of the fifteenth-sixteenth centuries. The half-chemist, half-charlatan, Paracelsus invented the term "microcosm" applied to man. This final stage of its history shows up the element of superstition latent in the notion of man as a microcosm, which may be described as anthropomorphism applied, not to God, but to the knowable universe.

[3] Literally, "imitating-creatures." Nemesius is possibly thinking of monkeys. His explanation here is that God made these creatures for the amusement of man. In Section 3 above we found him suggesting that God made them as a prelude to making articulate man.

recreation, combine to put the conclusion beyond all doubt. If all creatures do not, on the other hand, have such pleasant uses, but there are some, even, that do man harm, we must know that when the animals intended to be useful to man were created, all other possible animals were also prepared, lest creation should lack anything possible. Neither do these creatures wholly avoid conferring profit on man, for reason turns the evidently venomous creatures to its own advantage. It makes use of them, for example, in curing the harm which they themselves have done, as well as to provide medicaments for other ailments, such as certain preparations called theriacs,[4] which reason has discovered, wherewith to overcome these harmful creatures by their own products, so as to take spoils, as it were, from conquered foes. Man has, by grace of his Creator, myriad powerful antidotes to these kinds of harm, and such as can hinder, ward off, or correct, their assaults.

Other animals are adapted to other needs. All kinds are at one in contributing naturally to the healing of man, even those that seem to serve no other human purpose.

Let so much be said as applicable to the present state of our life, seeing that, in the far-off beginning, no other living creature dared to do man harm. They were all slaves and subjects of his, and obedient, so long as he controlled his own passions and the irrational element within him. But when he did not control his own passions but was conquered by them, he was also easily overcome by wild things outside him. For together with sin there entered in also harm from these creatures.[5]

The truth of this is confirmed by the instances of those who have lived the best of lives. For these were seen to be, beyond all gainsaying, superior to the evil assaults of wild beasts;

4 A theriac is an antidote for the bite or sting of a wild beast or poisonous reptile. As the flesh of an adder was supposed to be the essential antidote for an adder-bite, the physicians, when making up a theriac for adder-bites, would inevitably include dried and pounded flesh of adder, as an ingredient. They may well have chanced upon other ingredients of practical value. Nemesius accepts the notion that the essential of a theriac is a derivative of the harmful creature, and is seen again to be in superstition. But his argument would appear convincing and scientific to men of his age.

5 The belief in a golden age at the beginning of the world was widespread. Christians, with the prophecy in Isa. 11 of a golden age to come, to suggest it, concluded that the animals had all been harmless in Eden, and that their deterioration, and that of the earth and plants and other creatures, was the fruit of man's sin.

Daniel was superior, for example, to attack by lions, and Paul to the bite of an adder.[6]

COMMENTARY

9. *Lower creatures exist for man's sake.* This section retraces the argument of the last, with the particular application to supposed evidence that the lower animals were created for the sake of man. We here see the scientific apologetic of Nemesius at its weakest, not because he is Christian, but because he represents the somewhat shallow optimism of a current philosophy for which "no phenomenon is without a name, and no problem without a solution." It was impatience, and certainly not the lack of ingenuity, that was the besetting sin of fourth to fifth century science. An explanation must be found for everything, and often more than one explanation. And these hastily invented explanations blocked the way to further fruitful study of the facts. The Christian apologist cannot transcend the science of his age, and is therefore apt to be involved in its errors, like Nemesius in this section, which is still (apart from the biblical conclusion) in the Posidonian tradition. Jaeger, *op. cit.* pp. 132–3, notes the parallels in our section with Cicero, *On the nature of the gods*, ii. 148–159, also Posidonian. That Origen is again the medium through whom this, or much of it, has reached Nemesius may be gathered from Skard, *Nemesiosstudien* I. pp. 33–35.

TEXT

[M.63. 14–67. 1.]

10. When we consider these facts about man, how can we exaggerate the dignity of his place in creation? In his own person, man joins mortal creatures with the immortals, and brings the rational beings into contact with the irrational. He bears about in his proper nature a reflex of the whole creation, and is therefore rightly called "the world in little."[1] He is the creature whom God thought worthy of such special providence that, for his sake, all creatures have their being, both those that

---

6 The incidents of Dan. 6 and Acts 28 are thus interpreted as anticipations of the coming age. Jaeger, *op. cit.*, p. 133, thinks that this thought is not original with Nemesius, but comes from a Christian source known also to Basil. Skard, *l.c.*, points to the parallel in Theodoret, *On Providence*, v, and hints that this source may be some work of Origen.

1 The title *mikros kosmos* which man here receives is the nearest that antiquity approached to the term microcosm, coined in more modern times.

now are, and those that are yet to be.[2] He is the creature for whose sake God became man, so that this creature might attain incorruption and escape corruption, might reign on high, being made after the image and likeness of God, dwelling with Christ as a child of God, and might be throned above all rule and all authority.[3] Who, then, can fully express the pre-eminence of so singular a creature? Man crosses the mighty deep, contemplates the range of the heavens, notes the motion, position, and size of the stars, and reaps a harvest both from land and sea, scorning the rage of wild beasts and the might of whales. He learns all kinds of knowledge, gains skill in arts, and pursues scientific enquiry. By writing, he addresses himself to whom he will, however far away, unhindered by bodily location.[4] He foretells the future, rules everything, subdues everything, enjoys everything. He converses with angels and with God himself. He gives orders to creation. Devils are subject to him. He explores the nature of every kind of being. He busies himself with the knowing of God, and is God's house and temple. And all these privileges he is able to purchase at the cost of virtue and godliness.

But we must not let ourselves appear to any to be making, out of place, a panegyric on man, instead of a straightforward

2 Nemesius cannot mean that God will create, for example, new kinds of animal, in the future, since he has asserted, in the last section, that every possible form of animal was created when the animal world received its being on the sixth day of creation. The things here referred to, as yet to be created for man's sake, are those which will replace present creatures, at the final restoration of all things.

3 Skard (*Nemesiosstudien* I, p. 36) claims that Christian phrases are here grafted on to matter to which they are quite foreign. To say this is to suppose Nemesius unable, through ignorance of the meaning of pagan thought, to recognize the incongruity. But he had lived in the pagan setting, and had passed from it, by conviction, into Christian belief. We must say, rather, that, as a convert, he believed that pagan thought about the dignity of man might be a bridge to Christianity.

4 The translation here offered requires the stop to be placed after *empodizomenos*, whereas Matthaei (p. 65, line 4) puts it after the phrase next following. His argument for doing so is that it gives the sense, "Man . . . prophesies things to come, unhindered by the body," and that this is an anticipation of what is said in Section 21 about prophetic dreams. However, the opening of Section 32 shows that Nemesius did not confine prophetic foreknowledge to that derived from dreams. There is the less reason, therefore, for expecting him to account prophecy by dreams worthy to be singled out as one of the special glories of man; as we must suppose is the case if we punctuate and translate with Matthaei. On the other hand, the reference to bodily location is quite appropriate, in connection with communication by writing.

description of his nature, as we proposed to do. Let us, therefore, intermit, at this point, our discourse on man; albeit we are
discoursing of his nature while we are recounting his prerogatives.

Knowing, then, the nobility of which we are partakers, and
how we are "a planting from heaven,"⁵ let us do nothing that
would put our nature to shame, or publish us as unfit to be the
recipients of so great a bounty. Let us not cheat ourselves of all
this power, glory, and blessedness by bartering the enjoyment of
all eternal things for a brief season of pleasure that cannot last.
Let us, rather, safeguard our high standing by doing good and
eschewing evil, and by keeping before us a good aim, whereby
divine grace is specially wont to be invoked; and, of course, by
prayer.

So much concerning man's high estate. But the common saying has it that man consists of soul and body. Therefore let us
treat first and definitively of man's soul, avoiding over-subtle
and dry investigations and all problems too hard for the man in
the street to understand.⁶

<h3 align="center">COMMENTARY</h3>

10. *A panegyric on man.* The panegyric on man with which
Nemesius ends his first chapter owes much to the Posidonian
doctrine that man is the crown of the natural order, but is
much more general in scope than the theme elaborated in the
earlier part of the chapter. Navigation, astronomy, agriculture
and fisheries, science and letters, versatility, contemplation,
and exorcism are all subjects now laid under tribute, for the
glorification of man, that have not appeared earlier. The terms
in which the panegyric is here presented are those of a popular
theme to which Stoic, Neo-Platonist and Christian have each
contributed their characteristic thoughts. Jaeger (*Nemesios.*
p. 134) illustrates the similarities between this section and the
panegyric on man in Cicero, *On the nature of the gods*, II. 153; for
the fact is that they are both in a succession of rhetorical commonplace. While Nemesius is a writer whose sources become

⁵ Cf. Isa. 61:3.
⁶ We thus have an indication of Nemesius' own idea of the scope and purpose
of his book. It is a persuasive addressed to the ordinary reading public
of his land and generation, poised between the new faith and traditional
Hellenic culture, and to the yet humbler folk to be reached through such
readers. If it may seem to us that his argument is pitched rather high for
"the man in the street," we must allow something for the high level of
Syrian Greek culture at the end of the fourth Christian century.

obvious with study, he is more spontaneous than some of the source-critics give him credit for being. In this section he is freely rehandling a well-worn theme. The result is a wonderful patchwork, because, presumably, he wants every reader to find some watchwords of his own. But it is good apologetic; above all by the way in which it insinuates that Christianity has means to enhance the theme of man's glory, beyond anything that pagan rhetoricians can make of it. It is, moreover, something of a *tour de force* to have taken thought so pagan and secular as is the greater part of the content of this panegyric, and imposed upon it a Christian interpretation.

II. *Of the soul.*

TEXT

[M.67. 1–69. 12.]

11. The subject of the soul is differently handled by almost every ancient author. Democritus, Epicurus, and the entire school of Stoics, affirm categorically that the soul is corporeal.[1] But these very people, when they have agreed that the soul is corporeal, cannot agree about its essence. The Stoics assert it to be a hot and burning breath. But Critias identifies it with blood,[2] the philosopher Hippon with water,[3] and Democritus with fire, to the extent that the spherical shape of the atoms of fire and air causes them to separate out from other matter and

1 The Stoic school of philosophy was founded at Athens in the middle third century, B.C., by Zeno, who taught in the Stoa, or portico. The Stoics were monistic, holding that every real existent must be actualized in some kind of body. They supposed any living creature to be animated by a soul consisting of a subtle and tenuous substance, capable of permeating the grosser material organism. This belief, which Nemesius rejects, was accepted by many Christians, of whom the most famous was Tertullian, about two centuries before Nemesius.

2 It does not seem possible to identify this Critias. The idea that the blood is the seat of the life or soul is primitive and widespread. (See Lev. 17:11, 14, and Aristotle, *On the soul*, i. 2). The Stoic view had the advantage of explaining why living bodies are warm, but met with a difficulty in the fact of cold-blooded animals.

3 The *Physicum* or *Book of Nature* of Hippon is much quoted, and it seems likely that its author was of the Ionian school of materialistic philosophers which flourished in the sixth century B.C. He held heat and water to be the two basic existents. Observing semen to be liquid, he supposed soul to be something conveyed in semen, and hence defined it as "generative water."

unite to constitute soul.⁴ Heraclitus, on the other hand, supposes that the soul of the universe is an exhalation of vapour from all moist things, while the souls of living creatures are made of a combination of the general exhalation from without and the exhalation from within their own bodies, so as to give them the particular nature appropriate to their kind.⁵

Amongst those who do not suppose soul to be corporeal the differences of opinion are almost without number. Some say that the soul is a self-subsisting thing, and immortal. Some, while denying the soul corporeity, grant it neither self-subsistence nor immortality. Thales was the first to say that the soul is a perpetual self-movent.⁶ Pythagoras called it a self-moved number.⁷ Plato held it a self-subsisting thing, intellig-

---

⁴ Democritus was born at Abdera in Thrace early in the fifth century, B.C., and is accounted the greatest of the Greek physical philosophers. Having studied mathematics in Egypt, he conceived a mechanistic universe, consisting of an infinite number of tiny atoms moving in space. He supposed the atoms of solid substances, say iron, to be rough and jagged, so that, when brought together, they interlock and become immovable. Atoms of water he supposed smooth and spherical, whence water runs. Atoms of air and fire he supposed to be small enough to slip in among the atoms of solids and liquids. Thus he conceived the idea that the soul of a living organism was due to a marriage of these tiniest atoms. Such a soul would be corporeal, and the dissolution of soul and body would take place together. A century later, Epicurus developed an ethical philosophy on the basis of the physics of Democritus, but one giving soul a particular substance of its own, apart from air and fire. Nemesius thus groups the atomists with the Stoics, as advocates of a corporeal nature of the soul.

⁵ Heraclitus of Ephesus, 540–475 B.C., in criticism of the materialist physical theories, insisted on the unreliability of the senses. Sure knowledge comes only from reason and mind. The philosophy of Heraclitus was metaphysical. The order in the universe is intelligible, while the physical being of the universe is not. The soul of a living creature may be more surely known than anything else about it. The theory of soul, in this passage, seeks to explain the individuality of species in relation to the universal order.

⁶ Thales of Miletus, seventh century B.C., is regarded as the father of Greek philosophy, properly so called. Nemesius is here found in accord with Stobaeus (fifth century A.D.) against the testimony of Aristotle, in crediting Thales with being the first to recognize "soul" as a principle, setting matter in motion.

⁷ Pythagoras, in the sixth century B.C., taught a mystical creed in which number had prime significance. With his dictum "All things are numbers" we may compare "God is three and God is one" in "St Patrick's breastplate." In modern terms, the character and identity of each living individual persist, through changes, because "each has its own formula." Pseudo-Plutarch (*op. cit.*, iv. 2) criticizes Pythagoras for saying that the soul *is* a number, but would agree to saying that the soul was ruled by a number, differentiating the soul, as an existent, from the "number,"

ible, self-moved, and harmonious according to number.[8] Aristotle, on the other hand, held the soul to be the fundamental energy possessed by a physical organic body, giving it the power to live.[9] Dicaearchus defined soul as the harmonious combination of the four elements. He means by this an agreeable mingling of the elements, for it is a harmony not composed of sounds, but is the harmonious blending and concord of hot and cold, of moist and dry, in the body.[10] So we see that Aristotle and Dicaearchus hold the soul not to be a self-subsisting thing, while all the others whom we have mentioned assert that the soul is a self-subsisting thing.

There have been others, again, who believed that one and the same universal soul is parcelled out to the several animate beings, and will return to exist by itself again; as think the Manichees[11] and some others. Some there are that suppose

or formula governing its life. But pseudo-Plutarch, on whom Nemesius here depends, whether directly or indirectly, is wrong in attributing to Pythagoras the definition of the soul as "self-movent number." The Neo-Platonists derived this definition from Xenocrates (on whom, see Section 12, note 6).

[8] Plato was the first to assert, against the Pythagoreans, the substantive being of the soul. He followed them, however, in saying that though the soul is not number, reason, or harmony, it possesses number, reason, and harmony as its attributes.

[9] Aristotle's doctrine of the "entelechy" (here translated "fundamental energy") of individual existents draws back somewhat, as Nemesius claims, from the Platonic doctrine of the soul as a substantive existent, so as to represent the soul as an abstraction, while recognizing that the power by which the thing maintains itself derives from the soul. The phrase "the soul is the first entelechy of the body" comes from Aristotle, On the Soul, ii. 1, but here, perhaps, through pseudo-Plutarch.

[10] The text of Nemesius, at this and two other places, gives the name Dinarchus. But it would appear that this is either an uncorrected slip on the part of Nemesius (and so possible evidence for lack of revision) or an error introduced by a copyist very early in the MS tradition. The name Dicaearchus has been substituted by Matthaei for that of Dinarchus, because the opinions attributed by the MSS to Dinarchus are those attributed by pseudo-Plutarch (op. cit., iv. 2) and by Diogenes Laertius, in his Lives of the philosophers, to Dicaearchus. Dicaearchus of Messina (floruit) 320 B.C., was a disciple of Aristotle, who followed him in representing the soul rather in the light of an abstraction that explains the behaviour of the body. Nevertheless, for Dicaearchus, although he represents the reaction from Plato's metaphysic, the soul was so far an actualized existent that he claimed to prove it mortal.

[11] The Manichaean religion developed out of the Mandaean religion of Persia through contact with Christianity within the Roman empire. It was founded by a "prophet" called Mani whom the Persian king caused to be put to death in A.D. 277. But the religion rapidly spread both east and west, becoming a competitor of Christianity in all parts of the empire,

there to be innumerable different kinds of soul, while some believe in one only soul-substance which is shared by many actual souls.

There is therefore every reason why we must face a long discussion, since we have such a host of opinions to refute.

COMMENTARY

11. *The difficult subject of the nature of the soul has given rise to diverse opinions.* In this chapter Nemesius attacks his most difficult argument, concerning the nature of the soul. It was not difficult for him to marshal an array of diverse opinions of philosophers, because a class of book was available, called a Doxography, which tabulated the notions of famous thinkers upon various subjects. From Thales to Aristotle, in this section, is practically identical with a passage of pseudo-Plutarch, *On the opinions of the Philosophers*, Bk. IV, ch. 2, while ch. 3 provides, almost word for word, what Nemesius says of Heraclitus.

But Nemesius could hardly head this chapter with the words *On the Soul* without remembering that Aristotle had written a tract in two books under that title. And in fact it meets the eye that sections 11–14 stand related in some way to the work of Aristotle. Now the great philosopher begins his work *On the Soul* by explaining his own approach to the subject, and then goes on, as in Nemesius' section 11, with a doxography, or survey of the opinions of philosophers of the past, on the subject. At two points, namely in mentioning Democritus and Critias, Nemesius practically reproduces the very words of the corresponding mentions of these philosophers in Aristotle, while, with the exception of the mention of the Manichaeans, all of the rest of the section seems to be taken, if not quite exactly, from pseudo-Plutarch. Plutarch was a popular writer and en-

and this competition was reaching its zenith in the lifetime of Nemesius, who must have had first-hand knowledge of it. The Manichaeans supposed the world to have resulted from an assault upon heaven made by the demon of darkness, in the course of which particles of the heavenly soul-substance became mingled with the gross material created by the power of darkness. The souls of elect men were believed to be such heavenly particles of light, desirous of their redemption from imprisonment in matter by means of knowledge, of heavenly aid, and of ascetic practices. Their salvation after death would be by their return and reabsorption into the heavenly world of light. Nemesius regards this doctrine as parallel to Greek notions of a single soul-substance parcelled out as a plurality of individual souls. See also note 50 to the Introduction to Cyril (p. 37) above.

OF THE NATURE OF MAN 261

cyclopaedist of the first century of our era, who still enjoyed a very great vogue in the fourth to fifth centuries. Our problem does not lie in the use Nemesius makes of pseudo-Plutarch, but in his use of Aristotle. Whatever might be the case with a man of learning, like Nemesius, the public for whom he wrote would no more have had first-hand knowledge of such an author as Aristotle, except through commentaries, than modern visitors to Canterbury would go to Chaucer's *Canterbury Pilgrims* except as mediated by modern writers. In like manner it is probable that the relation of our sections to the text of Aristotle, *On the Soul,* was mediated by some more recent Commentary on that work.

B. Domanski, *Die Psychologie des Nemesius,* pp. 1–3 (in Bäumker and Hertling's *Beiträge zur Geschichte der Philosophie des Mittelalters*) observes that Nemesius is unjust to Aristotle when he says that Aristotle held the soul "not to be a self-subsisting thing." In fact, Nemesius' own doctrine of the soul might fairly be characterized as Aristotelian. In any case, it would be unlike Nemesius, with his apologetic aim, to air a novel and unfavourable interpretation of the great philosopher, likely to rouse the opposition of his readers. We may assume that the view which he expresses was current in the Syria of his day, and we may go on to father it upon the Neo-Platonic school. Putting these facts together, we may conclude that Nemesius, as he commenced this chapter, had before his mind some recent Neo-Platonic commentary on the work of Aristotle *On the Soul.* It might be this commentary that drew upon pseudo-Plutarch.

There has survived a Neo-Platonic commentary on this work of Aristotle written a little before Nemesius. This is the work of the Constantinopolitan Neo-Platonist Themistius. It contains passages that come fairly near to Nemesius, but it does not express his critical view of Aristotle, and in other ways it is clear that it was not the document that stood between Nemesius and the text of Aristotle. But the knowledge by Nemesius of a work in general character resembling Themistius, and asserting the substantiality of the soul in a more polemical manner than Themistius, would explain what we have before us. In the next section, further reasons will be found for holding to such a hypothesis.

TEXT

[M.69. 12–76. 11.]

12. Now, as regards those who assign corporeity to the soul, it suffices to recall the argument of Ammonius, the master of

Plotinus, and of Numenius the Pythagoraean.[1] It runs thus: bodies, by their absolute nature, are mutable, dissoluble, and, throughout their extent, divisible indefinitely, without there remaining anything of body that is not thus liable to change. Therefore a body requires some principle keeping it together, assembling its constituents, and (so to express it) binding and holding them in union. And this principle we call soul.

But if the soul is, in any kind of way, corporeal, even though its body were of the most rarefied stuff, the question is, What is the principle that holds *it* together? For it has been demonstrated that everything corporeal needs a principle of cohesion. And so the argument is carried back indefinitely, until we arrive at an incorporeal soul.[2] Now, if anyone, one of the Stoics for

[1] Ammonius Saccas was, according to Prof. E. Benz, probably an Indian (Ammonius the Sakka) who came to Alexandria about A.D. 225, and, without leaving any literary remains, started the eclectic, but thoroughly Hellenic, revival of philosophy known as Neo-Platonism, of which his pupil Plotinus (A.D. 205–270) was leading figure. The Neo-Platonists owed much to the Neo-Pythagoraean Numenius, who flourished at Apamea in Syria in the later second century A.D. The argument here retailed by Nemesius was presumably developed by Numenius in criticism of the Stoics, and adopted from him by the Neo-Platonists.

[2] The notion that living body must have an integrating principle leads to an absurdity if that principle is supposed to be itself corporeal. For a corporeal soul needs its own (corporeal) soul, and so on, *ad infinitum*, unless the series is broken by bringing in some incorporeal integrating principle. If that is ever to be done, why, Nemesius asks, should it not be at the first stage, so that man's soul is held incorporeal? Nemesius, as we see, attributes the argument to two people, the first of whom, Ammonius, left no writings, while the second, Numenius, is to be regarded as the next precursor of the Neo-Platonic movement which claimed Ammonius as its founder. The argument appears in the following form in a commentary to Aristotle, On the Soul by John Philoponus, Alexandrine churchman and philosopher in the late sixth century: "Every body is, by its absolute nature, dissoluble and indefinitely divisible. Therefore it is in need of some principle holding it together. This thing keeping it together is either its soul or some other power, and is either corporeal or incorporeal. If, then, it is corporeal, it will, in its turn, need something to hold it together. So we shall ask, once more, whether this is corporeal or incorporeal, and so on indefinitely. It must surely be that the power that holds bodies together is incorporeal. Now the thing that holds together ensouled bodies is the soul." (Philoponus, edited by Michael Hayduck, Vol. xv of *Greek Commentaries on Aristotle*, p. 12, lines 28–32). This is not the only reminiscence of Nemesius in the work of Philoponus. Some have thought this was because Philoponus knew the work of Nemesius. But what Nemesius says shows that the argument was current in Neo-Platonic circles (and probably current in writings) long before the days of Philoponus. It was therefore likely to have had a place in commentaries to Aristotle, *On the soul*. We have, therefore, further reason

example, retorts that there is something in bodies that moves them and sets up a tension, that it is a movement inwards and a movement outwards, the movement outwards effecting size and quality and the movement inward giving the body its unity and identity,[3] we must then ask them what is this force (since force there must be, where any movement is caused) and in what has it its substance? And if they will even have it that this force is material, we retrace our previous arguments. If, on the other hand, it is said not to be matter, but only to be connected with matter, then a distinction is drawn between what is connected with matter and matter itself. For, what plays any part in relation to matter may be said to be connected with matter. Which, then, is this something connected with matter? Is it material or immaterial? If they answer, Material, how can it be something connected with matter but not actually matter? If they say that it is not matter, then, surely, it is immaterial; and if immaterial, then incorporeal, since any kind of body is material. But suppose they say that bodies are three-dimensional, and that soul, since it pervades the whole body, must be three-dimensional, also, and therefore must clearly be corporeal: we then reply that all bodies are, indeed, three-dimensional, but that everything extending in three dimensions is not therefore body. For position and quality[4] are, in themselves, incorporeal, and yet may be accounted the accidents of a solid body. It is just the same, then, with the soul, which in its own nature belongs to things that have not dimension, yet appears itself to be three-dimensional, in being seen as an accident of the three-dimensional body in which it is. Further, every body is moved either from without or from within, and if only from without, that body is inanimate. If, however, the body is moved from within, it is an animate body.[5] But if the soul is corporeal, and is moved from without, it is inanimate, and if from within, it is animate. To call the soul either inanimate or animate is ridiculous. Surely, therefore, the soul is incorporeal.

for thinking that Nemesius had before him a Neo-Platonic Commentary to Aristotle, *On the Soul.*

3 The size and quality of a body are here thought of as obtruding themselves upon the observer. This the Stoics attribute to a kind of outward thrust of the body towards the observer. And they attribute the fact that the body does not disintegrate, but remains itself, to a kind of inward strain taking place in it.

4 An example of quality is colour. A solid white body is white in three dimensions. But whiteness is itself without dimension.

5 A maxim from Plato's *Phaedrus.*

Again, if the soul is nourished, its nourishment is incorporeal; for, the soul's nourishment is learning. No body is nourished by incorporeal nourishment; so, surely, once more, the soul is incorporeal. This form of the argument is given by Xenocrates;[6] if the soul is not nourished, but the body of every living creature is nourished, the soul must be incorporeal. And this argument refutes the whole range of arguments in favour of the soul being corporeal. But a separate argument is called for to deal with those who suppose that the soul is either blood or breath, because a living creature dies when it loses its blood or breath. Yet this is what certain folk have written, who thought themselves to be someone, but they had better been silent.[7] On their showing, when some blood has been shed, some soul is lost, which is but idle talk. For what remains is everywise the same as the homogenous matter that is gone. Water, for instance, is water, whether in bulk or a drop; and likewise with gold or silver or anything else of which the parts do not differ in substance. So, then, if soul is blood, the blood that remains, whatever the amount, is soul. Rather than say that soul is blood, we ought to say that anything is soul the loss of which brings about a living creature's death. So phlegm is soul, and bile and gall are soul, since the loss of a sufficient quantity of either brings life to an end. On the same lines, the liver, the brain, the heart, kidneys, stomach and intestines might equally be taken to be soul; for of which of these can a living creature be deprived and not die? Or another argument is this: a lot of things without blood are animate, such as cartilaginous and jelly fish; for example, squids, cuttlefish, stinking polypus, and all the *testacea* and *crustacea*, including lobsters, crabs, and oysters. So, if there are animate things devoid of blood, it is clear that the soul is not blood.

Again, to those who say that the soul is water, because water seems to promote all life, and it is impossible to propagate life without water, there are many objections to be urged. For nothing can live without food, and so, according to these folk, every single kind of food in turn should be identified with soul.

[6] Xenocrates of Chalcedon, born 396 B.C., may be called the literary executor of Plato. Zeno and Epicurus are said to have heard him at Athens, but, so far from their learning from him the notion of a corporeal soul, he revived the Pythagoraean doctrine of the soul as number.

[7] These persons can hardly have been Greeks. The sarcasm of Nemesius suggests that they made some special claim for themselves. His attack may be here directed against some oriental prophets or magicians whose opinions were known in Syria.

OF THE NATURE OF MAN

And then there are many living creatures that do not drink, as is recorded of some of the eagles. Partridges also can live without drinking. And why should water be soul, rather than air? For we can go without water for quite a while, but cannot abstain from breathing except for the shortest of periods. But neither is the soul air; for there are many living creatures which do not breathe air, for instance all insects, such as bees, wasps, and ants, bloodless creatures and the myriad denizens of the sea, together with every creature that has no lungs. For nothing that has no lungs breathes air, and, conversely, no creature that breathes no air has lungs.[8]

COMMENTARY

12. *The soul is not corporeal; general arguments.* In this section are reviewed two typical ancient approaches to the question of the soul. The first and more sophisticated rests upon observing the disintegration of corpses. There must be, it was inferred, some vital force or principle that integrates and imparts motion to a living body. The soul was then identified with this force or principle, and its nature deduced. The cruder and more primitive approach identifies the soul with whatever is most fundamental to life, such as blood or breath. Equally, Nemesius combats the view that the soul is an aetherial shape invisibly pervading the visible organism.

TEXT

[M.76. 11–82. 14.]

13. As certain arguments of Cleanthes, the Stoic, and of Chrysippus,[1] are recorded, even though they are not well reasoned, we ought to set out the answers which the Platonists returned to them. Cleanthes made up this syllogism: "Not only do we resemble our parents in feature," he said, "but also in soul, by our passions, manners, and dispositions. Now 'like' and 'unlike' are applicable to bodies, but do not apply to the incorporeal. The soul therefore is corporeal."

---

[8] The obvious conclusion, which Nemesius does not explicitly draw, is that the soul is not breath.

[1] Cleanthes, 301–252 B.C., followed Zeno as leader of the philosophic school in the Stoa at Athens. Chrysippus, 280–206 B.C., famous for his dialectic skill, was pupil and successor to Cleanthes.

We must observe, first, however, that universals do not follow the same pattern as particulars.[2] We must, further, object that the assertion "resemblance is inapplicable to the incorporeal" is not true. For we call such numbers similar of which the factors are in the same proportion; for example, 6 and 24, since the factors of 6 are 2 and 3, and the factors of 24 are 4 and 6. Two has the same ratio to 4 as 3 has to 6, since each of the former is seen to be doubled in the latter, 4 being double 2, and 6 double 3. Yet numbers are incorporeal. Shapes also are like other shapes, when their angles are the same, and the sides enclosing these angles are in the same proportion. And the Stoics themselves admit that shapes are not corporeal.

Once more, it belongs to quantity to be equal or unequal, and, likewise it belongs to quality to be like or unlike. Quality is not corporeal. So it appears that one incorporeal thing can resemble another incorporeal thing.

Cleanthes' next argument runs thus: "an incorporeal thing cannot be affected by what happens to a body, or *vice versa*, but one body is affected by what happens to another body. It is evident, however, that when the body is sick or hurt, the soul suffers with it; and, conversely, the body with the soul. For, when the soul feels shame, the body blushes, and when the soul feels fear, the body blenches. Therefore, the soul is corporeal." One of his assumptions is false, to wit, that an incorporeal thing cannot be affected by what happens to a body. What if the soul is the exception to this rule?

It is as if someone said, "No animal moves its upper jaw. A crocodile moves its upper jaw. *Ergo*, a crocodile is not an animal." The proposition is false, and thence comes the false assumption that no animal moves its upper jaw. For, see! The crocodile both is an animal, and moves its upper jaw.[3]

Similarly, when Cleanthes argues that no incorporeal thing is affected by what happens to a body, he assumes the conclu-

[2] The first objection of Nemesius is that Cleanthes is basing upon the facts of heredity a generalization which they are insufficient to support. This child is like its father in such and such particulars. That child resembles its parent in such and such other respects. The most that that proves is that some children resemble their parents in some respects. To leap from the observation "he has a disposition like his father's" to the conclusion "the soul of a child is like the soul of his father" is to make universals follow the pattern of particulars, and is unjustified. Thus both members of the syllogism that Cleanthes constructed on the basis of human heredity are at fault, and its conclusion falls to the ground.

[3] The logicians presumably derived the instance of the crocodile from Aristotle's *Natural History*, I. 11.

sion in his premiss. But if anyone were to accept as true the proposition that no incorporeal thing is affected by what happens to a body, he ought not, at the same time, to accept the second proposition of Cleanthes, that if the body is sick or hurt, the soul suffers with it. The question is whether the body is the sole sufferer, deriving perception from the soul while the soul remains itself impassible, or whether the soul suffers together with the body. Most learned authors[4] take the first alternative. Cleanthes ought to base his argument, not on what is in dispute, but only on what is agreed. It is abundantly clear that some incorporeals do suffer with bodies, for the qualities of the body (which are incorporeal) are necessarily affected by changes in the body; for they change concurrently as the body corrupts, as they did when it was being conceived.

Chrysippus takes as his premiss that death is the severing of soul from body. Now no incorporeal thing, he says, can be separated from a body. For an incorporeal thing cannot be connected with a body. But the soul is both connected with a body and separated from it. *Ergo*, the soul must be corporeal.

Now his major premiss, that death is the severing of soul from body, is correct. But the generalization that an incorporeal thing cannot be connected with a body is incorrect, even though it were true in its particular application to the soul. Its falsity as a generalization is shown by considering a geometrical line, which is incorporeal, and yet can be in connection with and in separation from a body.[5] The same would be true, say, of whiteness. Nevertheless, it is true that soul is not thus related to body, for soul is not connected with body. If soul were connected with body, it must plainly extend throughout the same space. If soul is corporeal, it cannot extend throughout the same space, else there would be two bodies exactly occupying the same space, which is impossible; and so the body is not

4 B. Domanski, *op. cit.*, p. 25, shows reasons for thinking that the indefinite plural "most learned authors" really covers an allusion to Plotinus. Nemesius' point is that the argument of Cleanthes requires that suffering is something in which soul and body participate on equal terms: so that, if that article is not conceded (and Plotinus does not concede it), neither is the consequent conclusion.

5 A body has its particular geometrical configuration. Our geometrical line might either enter into this configuration or be entirely external to it. In the former alternative, it is "an incorporeal in connection with a body." "Whiteness," which Nemesius next mentions, in being a quality is incorporeal, like the geometric line, and may be connected with a body, e.g., that of a snowman. Nemesius does not elaborate the argument in this connection, but it is necessary for the understanding of what follows.

ensouled throughout. So we have the alternatives: either the soul is connected with the body and is corporeal, but the living creature is not ensouled throughout; or the living creature is ensouled throughout, and then the soul is not connected with the body, nor is it corporeal. Now a living creature is ensouled throughout. Surely, then, soul is neither connected with the body, nor corporeal, but is separated from the body, although incorporeal.[6] So, from what we have said, it is established that the soul is not corporeal.

COMMENTARY

13. *Stoic arguments for a corporeal soul refuted.* It is evident throughout this work that Christian faith and the belief that the soul is a real but incorporeal entity are, for Nemesius, very intimately connected. Hence it was of the greatest consequence to him to reach a decisive refutation of all Stoic arguments favourable to the corporeity of the soul. He was, however, far from being the first to take in hand such a task. H. Krause (*Studia Neo-Platonica*, Leipzig, 1904) suggests, very plausibly, that the work of Porphyry *On miscellaneous questions*, which is known to have been a work of review and criticism of earlier philosophies, supplied the model for the argument in this and the next two sections. In favour of this suggestion is the fact that Nemesius explicitly makes a citation from this work in Section 22, naming the second of its seven books as the place from which it was taken. Also such a work would fit admirably the opening of this section, in which its contents are described as setting forth "the answers which the Platonists returned" to the Stoic arguments. At any rate, we shall not credit Nemesius with

---

[6] The final argument is best illustrated by the example of whiteness. The Stoics thought of the connection of the soul with the body of a living creature as exactly like that of whiteness with the body of a snowman. Nemesius will allow the connection of whiteness with the body of a snowman, but not that of the soul with the body of a living creature. If it were allowed, he argues, then soul is spatial, and if spatial, then corporeal. So, since the soul in being connected with the body is connected with all the body, the soul must be coextensive with the body. We thus have to choose between alternative absurdities. Either, the soul being corporeal, we have two bodies coinciding or filling entirely the same space, or, soul and body are mutually exclusive within the same boundaries (as if the fine atoms of soul pervaded the interstices between the coarse atoms of body), in which case the body is not ensouled throughout, nor indeed at all. Q.E.A. The heart of the controversy is that Nemesius believes the soul to be bound to the body not by spatial confinement but only by imposed habit, as will appear later.

having excogitated this reply, but, at the most, with having collected it in the course of his philosophic reading.

TEXT

[M.82. 14–86. 11.]

14. We have now to show that the soul is a real entity.[1] For Dicaearchus defines the soul as a state of harmony. Simmias also said that the soul was harmony, when arguing with Socrates, and added that, while the soul may be likened to harmony, the body may be likened to the lyre. The answers to this assertion are to be set forth as they are given in Plato's dialogue entitled *Phaedo*. The first, then, is dependent on something that Plato had previously demonstrated, for previously he had shown that things we suppose we learn, we really recollect. Taking this, then, to be agreed, Plato constructs the argument as follows: if what we learn, we really recollect, our soul pre-existed, before it took a human form. If soul is harmony, it had no prior existence, but came into being subsequently, when the body was compacted. For no synthesis is otherwise than according to the elements of which it is composed. And if the synthesis is harmony, there is a certain communion between the component elements. But that is no argument against the synthesis being subsequent, and not prior to, the elements combined. Therefore, that "the soul is harmony" and that "learning is recollecting" are mutually exclusive doctrines. Now, it is true about the recollections. So, surely, it is false that the soul is harmony. Again, the soul stands in contrast with the body, and takes upon it the rights of a governor, as ruling the body. But harmony neither governs, nor is in contrast. So, surely, soul is not harmony. And again, one harmony is more harmonious, or less so, because of the slackening or tightening of strings, and not because harmony is a comparative term. The notion of harmony can know no more and less. That is all in the combining of notes. For, if a high note and a deep note mingle, and then go flat, the notes preserve the same relation as volumes of sound, but the harmony is modified, being more intense, or less so, according to the notes that combine to form it.

1 Literally "is not unsubstantial." Nemesius, in accusing Aristotle, Dicaearchus, Galen, and Pythagoras, in Sections 11–17, of teaching that the soul is "unsubstantial," is more severe than Christian orthodoxy would require. Once more it is a Neo-Platonic source that is most likely to have set the standard.

But one soul is not more a soul than another, nor less. Surely, then, the soul is not harmony.

Once more, the soul is receptive of virtue or vice. But harmony is not receptive of harmony or discord. So, surely, the soul is not harmony. And, finally, the soul, in being receptive of a measure of things that are mutually contradictory, must be a subject or entity. But harmony is a quality, and needs a subject. Substance and quality are different things, and the soul and harmony are different things. However, there is nothing absurd in saying that the soul partakes harmony, and yet, for all that, is not harmony. For neither is the soul virtue, because it partakes of virtue.

COMMENTARY

14. *The soul is not "harmony," but has substance.* In this section, Nemesius reproduces, loosely, the discussion between Socrates and Simmias, in chs. 36–41 of Plato's dialogue, *Phaedo.* Socrates, born about 470 B.C., was, in 399 B.C., accused, before the Athenian assembly, of dishonouring the deities recognized by the State, and of corrupting the youth. The assembly condemned him to death by a majority vote. The *Phaedo* depicts him, while awaiting death in prison, in converse with disciples. A slight readiness to compromise would save his life. So Simmias urges upon him the thought that the soul, with all its interest and knowledge, will disappear, at death, just as a tune ends, when the instrument is put down.

In the ensuing discussion, the dialogue represents the group of companions as all agreed to Plato's root principle, that we are able to master knowledge at all because we are born with an endowment of knowledge, which discursive learning only develops, or, rather, revives. If so, the soul must be pre-existent before birth, and so may survive death. While Nemesius does not fully endorse the Platonic creed, he finds sufficient in this dialogue to establish the point he requires, that the soul is not evanescent.

Simmias of Thebes was a historic personage, and himself the author of dialogues. In Plato's *Crito* he is represented as bringing money with which to buy the release of Socrates.

TEXT

[M.86. 11–92. 11.]

15. Galen[1] says nothing about the soul, and further in his *Demonstration*[2] declares that he has said nothing about it. Yet it may be presumed, from what he does say, that he inclines to identify the soul with temperament.[3] For he says that differences

[1] Claudius Galen (his name was Galenos, "the peaceful") was born at Pergamos in A.D. 131. After an eclectic training in philosophy, he studied medicine, and brought together all the best in the work of the Greek physicians, while advancing knowledge very much by his own observation and dissections. His medical works, some fifty in number, became the staple library for physicians for more than a thousand years. He practised in Rome, and was appointed by Marcus Aurelius to be in medical charge of his son Commodus. Galen died about A.D. 200.

[2] Literally, "demonstrative reasons." Galen wrote a work entitled *On demonstration*, in five books, and it partly survives in Arabic fragments. From these, and from Galen's own frequent reference to this work, it was evidently a treatise on the logical principles of proof. In Section 40, Nemesius refers to "the third book of the Demonstration." The context shows, however, that this must be a slip, and that Nemesius really meant the third book of the commentary by Galen on the *Prognostic* of Hippocrates, as see C. G. Kühn's edition of Galen, vol. xviiiB, p. 286. (Leipzig, 1821–33.) It is indeed altogether unlikely that the work *On demonstration* should be quoted in this work of Nemesius. But Domanski (*op. cit.*, p. 9, Note 1) observes that what Nemesius says in the first part of this section agrees admirably with the theme of the tract of Galen entitled "that the faculties of the soul are affected by the temperament of the body." (Kühn, IV. 767–822.) To this title there might well be prefixed the words "demonstrative reasons," so that the short citation became what might be rendered into English by *Demonstration*. This tract argues first for the mortality of that portion of the soul which is the seat of courage and desire. From this it goes on to make the irrational part of the soul mortal. It then reviews what Plato, Aristotle, and Hippocrates have to say about the influence of temperament, blood, climate and age upon the functions of the soul; then the assertion of Andronicus the Peripatetic (Rome, first century, B.C.) that temperament and life-energy are the substance of the soul. At this point Galen dissociates himself from the view that the life-energy of the soul is mortal, stressing the difference between the rational and irrational functions of the soul. So he rallies to the Platonic view, but says that he cannot prove Plato right, because he does not know of what sort the substance of the soul should be. Nemesius' summary is not unfair, and he only dissociates himself from Galen for his unwillingness to go further towards Plato. In this, of course, he would please a public that respected Neo-Platonism.

[3] Temperament means, literally, "mixing." The mixing here meant is that of the constituents of the body. It could be, as Nemesius here uses it, the mingling of the four elements in the body, that is, of earth, air, fire and water. But the physicians, when they spoke of temperament, had in mind "the four humours," blood, phlegm, choler, and black bile. A

of behaviour are consequent upon temperament, constructing
his argument with the help of Hippocrates.[4] But if he thinks
that the soul is temperament, it is clear that he also thinks it to
be mortal. That statement does not apply, however, to the
whole soul, but only to the irrational soul, of man. About the
rational soul he is in doubt, and says . . .[5]

Now, that the temperament of the body cannot be the soul is
clear from what follows.[6] All bodies, animate or inanimate, consist of the four elements tempered together, for it is the tempering of the elements that constitutes such bodies. So, if the
temperament of a body is its soul, there is no such thing as an
inanimate object. The argument runs thus: If the temperament
of a body is soul, and every body has temperament, every body
has soul. If every body has soul, there is no inanimate body, not
even a stone, a bit of wood, or iron, or anything else inanimate.
Supposing, however, that he does not mean that every tempering of a body is soul, but only some particular kind of temperament, we must ask, What sort of temperament is it which constitutes a living creature, and introduces the further principle of

temperament was the proportion in which these were mingled in the
individual concerned. They observed that a preponderance of one of the
four humours went with a characteristic temperament in the psychological
sense. When blood was in excess, it went with a sanguine temperament,
when phlegm predominated there was a phlegmatic temperament, when
yellow bile, a choleric, and when black bile, a melancholy temperament.

[4] Hippocrates, "the father of medicine," born about 460 B.C., was a temple
attendant at a shrine of Asclepios, the god of health. He studied philosophy, and conceived the notion that Nature is the principle of health.
He taught that those who would practise medicine must "support
enfeebled and coerce outrageous Nature," especially by diet and regimen.
Galen venerated the memory of Hippocrates, from whom he accepted the
notion of the four humours, of their *eucrasia* (ideal balance), and of their
dyscrasia (troublesome disproportion).

[5] In all our MSS, at this point, what Galen said is missing. But if we accept
Domanski's identification of the *Demonstration*, we can fill in what is
needed. It is "I have no proof of Plato's teaching to contribute, since
I do not know the substance of the soul, of what sort it is." It is very rare
that Nemesius transcribes a passage from a surviving work of Galen.
He seems generally, when drawing upon Galen, to reproduce from memory
the gist of what he has read. But here it would appear that he wished to
give Galen's exact words, and left a blank until he could look up the
passage. This he apparently never did. So we have a further reason for
thinking that he died with his draft unrevised.

[6] Nemesius has admitted that Galen did not even identify animal soul
with temperament, still less the human soul in its completeness. The
argument that follows, in which Galen is refuted out of Galen, would
seem, therefore, to be aimed at the materialistic physician who thinks
of physical health as the sum of human hope.

soul? Whatever kind of temperament he says, we shall find also exemplified in inanimate objects. For there are nine temperaments, as he shows in his book *On temperament*.[7] Eight are bad, and only one is wholesome. He says that man is constituted according to the good temperament (not every man, that is, but men of normal temperament), and that according to the other bad temperaments, with varying degrees of ease or tension in the tempering, are constituted the other kinds of living creatures. But, as Galen himself shows in his work *On simples*,[8] the nine temperaments are also found in inanimate things.

Again, if the soul is temperament, and temperaments fluctuate with age, season, and diet, the soul fluctuates, too. And if the soul fluctuates, we have not always the same soul, but now the soul of a lion, and now of a sheep or of some other creature, according to our state of temperament; and that is absurd. Again, temperament is not antagonistic to the bodily lusts, but rather furthers them, for it is temperament itself that produces them. But the soul opposes them. Surely, therefore, temperament is not soul. Or again, if temperament is soul and temperament is a quality, and if a quality can be present or absent without destruction of the subject, then surely the soul can be severed from the subject without it dying; and that is not the case. Surely, then, the soul is not temperament, nor any quality. For people never say that either of two opposites is part of the nature of a living creature, in the way that heat is part of the nature of fire, seeing that that is unalterable. But temperament is seen to alter, and it is just these people that practise the physician's art who most cause change of temperament.[9]

Once more, the qualities of any body are perceptible. The soul is not perceptible, but is intelligible. Surely, then, the soul is not a quality of body. And once again, the good tempering of blood and breath with the neighbouring flesh, sinews, and other things, is strength. And the good tempering of hot and cold, of dry and moist, is health. The symmetry of members, with good

[7] I. 8 (Kühn, I. 559). Man the standard, I. 9 (Kühn, I. 564).
[8] The full title is "On the mixing and powers of simple medicines." We may gather this point from Book IV, chs. 16, 17 (Kühn, XI. 675-9).
[9] The argument here is obscured by condensation. It may be paraphrased thus: Temperament might be claimed to be something more profound than a quality, since there could no more be a body without temperament than fire without heat. But (as doctors ought to be the first to know) temperament *can* be changed. Therefore, temperament is no more than a quality, and therefore cannot be the soul.

18—C.J.

complexion, makes physical beauty. If, therefore, the harmonious concurrence of health, strength, and beauty, is soul, it were impossible for a living man to be sick, weak, or deformed. But it often happens that not one only but all three of these good temperaments is lost, and yet the man lives. For it happens that the same man is deformed, weak, and sick, all together. Surely, therefore, the soul is not the good tempering of the body.

How is it, then, that certain vices and virtues come naturally to men? It is true that it proceeds from their bodily temperament. For just as men are naturally healthy or sickly by temperament, so some are naturally choleric, some proud, some craven, some lecherous. Nevertheless, some such persons master these tendencies, and prevail. Now, it is clear that they master temperament. And what masters and what is mastered are different things. So temperament is one thing and soul another. For the body is the soul's instrument.[10] If it is well constituted, it helps the soul, and is, itself, in good shape. But, if the body is not well constituted, it impedes the soul, and then the soul needs to bestir itself to make head against the defects of its instrument. Moreover, unless the soul is watchful, it, too, is perverted, together with its instrument, just as a musician is thrown out of tune through his lyre being out of tune, if he does not tune it well before his performance. Therefore the soul needs to take care of the body, and render it a fit instrument for its own use. And this it accomplishes by means of reason and manners, here easing and there tightening, as in harmony, to prepare its instrument well fitted to itself. And it will employ an instrument so fitted, lest it, too, be perverted in company with its instrument; as we often see happen.

COMMENTARY

15. *The relation of soul to temperament.* Nemesius now introduces the author whose influence upon his anthropology exceeds all others. This is Galen, "the father of Greek medicine." Medicine was neither so specialized nor so technical as it is today. It was viewed as a department of philosophy, and therefore as a subject which concerned all men of culture. The voluminous works

---

10 In this conclusion, Nemesius gets things into their right order and proportion. Body is for the sake of soul. Temperament is for the sake of body. Therefore, the proper care of temperament (that is, the intelligent maintenance of health, and the understanding of oneself) is a prime spiritual duty.

of Galen can be divided roughly into two groups. On the one hand are the treatises dealing with the art and science of the physician. Of these the greater part have survived. But there was also a number of works of ethical and logical philosophy, which have not fared so well in MS tradition. We should be wrong to suppose that because Nemesius had read extensively in both categories of Galen's writings he must have been a practitioner: though it would be a legitimate conjecture that his interests (or alternatively, his family connections) had made him unusually well-informed on medical subjects. In his reproduction of the medical learning of Galen, his interest is always that of the non-technical thinker, who thinks of practitioners as a group to which he does not belong. He never records a personal observation, or falls into a reminiscence betraying the practitioner. Chrysostom's works contain passages showing knowledge of and interest in human anatomy and physiology. And he certainly was not a practitioner. We do best to conclude that, in the atmosphere of Syrian humanism in the days of Nemesius, Galen was widely read.

The nature and degree of Nemesius' use of Galen is discussed by Professor E. Skard in his *Nemesiosstudien* II, III, IV and V (*Symbolae Osloenses*, Fasc. XVII, pp. 9–25; XVIII, pp. 31–41; XX, pp. 46–56 and XXII, pp. 40–48). He finds signs that, even in ch. I, Nemesius has derived some of his matter from passages in works of Galen. The wide reading of Nemesius in this author is not to be severed from the conviction (which runs through the whole of his work), so unique among early ecclesiastical writers, that the spiritual life of man is essentially conditioned by the body, with its functions and its limitations.

TEXT

[M.92. 11–102. 3.]

16. In saying that the soul is entelechy,[1] Aristotle agrees, no less than does Galen, with those that make the soul a quality.

[1] The word "entelechy" was invented by Aristotle, who formed it from three words meaning "to have in the end." It can perhaps be rendered "self-fulfilment" or "completion."

Aristotle started from investigable Nature, and found living creatures each to be in the course of development through the working of powers resident in themselves. He saw this development as continuous alteration approximating towards some conjectural goal. All of a living creature that can be actually known is its form, that is, the internal constitution which makes it the creature it is. Shape is one, but only one of many,

So let us begin by making clear what Aristotle means by entelechy.

He uses the word "essence" in three senses: first for the basic matter of which a thing is composed, which indeed has no existence proper to itself, but contains the potentiality of what the thing may become;[2] next for the fashion and form in which the matter of the thing is disposed; and thirdly for these two things combined and combining what belongs to matter with what belongs to form. So, then, it is the essence of the thing in this third sense that is ensouled.[3] The potentiality resides, therefore, in the matter, and the entelechy in the form.[4] But form has two meanings: first it is the subject of knowledge, and then it is the contemplation on our part whereby such knowledge is gained; the first meaning, that is, pertains to it as being

among the constituents of form. While we can think of form as immanent in the thing, it is primarily something thought by us, however much we may be caused to think it by the object itself. But recognizing form leaves us ignorant of trend. So entelechy is needed, to explain the history of the form of a living creature throughout its life. In as far as we can conceive its entelechy we obtain our most significant understanding of the living creature. So, according to Aristotle, what we recognize in a living creature is its form, and what we divine is its entelechy. The following illustration has been given of the relation between entelechy and form:
The form of a block of marble in a sculptor's work-room is what distinguishes it from, say, a block of ice. The statue carved out of it is its first entelechy. The sculptor's vision, and the art which actualizes it in marble, is the second entelechy. The concept of second entelechy lies nearer to that of soul than does that of first entelechy. To do Aristotle justice we must recognize that he does not say that soul is nothing but entelechy. He only says that the concept of entelechy covers much of what can be scientifically apprehended about the soul of a living creature.
² Aristotle saw the objective world through the data of sense-perception. These revealed a process of incessant change. Material objects are ever becoming what they were not. Even the four elements seemed to be transformable one into other. Aristotle was thus driven to think of a hypothetical something, which he called "matter," that now condensed itself and was earth, and now rarefied itself and was air. This "matter" he supposed to form a basis underlying every material being. Aristotle thought of "matter" as an inveterate "becomer," and source of the incessant change going on in the material universe. It had no character of its own, but contained indefinite potentiality, upon which depended entelechy, while entelechy expressed itself in terms of form.
³ Aristotle, therefore, did not think of soul as latent in matter, though Nemesius tries to drive him into that position. His concept of soul as entelechy starts from that of the living creature as constituted of form and matter.
⁴ Form, in a living creature, changes with its development. Entelechy may be called a function of this variable.

a particular disposition of matter, and the second as being an activity.[5] We say, then, that form is a subject of knowledge because, where there is soul, there are two states, sleep and waking.[6] Now what answers to waking is the activity of contemplation, while what answers to sleep is the mere storing of knowledge without its active development. Of the two, knowledge in active development takes precedence. And for that reason Aristotle calls form the first entelechy, and the corresponding activity of mind the second entelechy.

To take an example, an eye consists of a basis and a form. The basis is the physical eye itself, and the form, to speak correctly, is the capacity for sight, which is what makes an eye. Derivatively, sight is called eye as well. Now the first entelechy of eye is its form, which is nothing else but sight providing the eye with its capacity for seeing, while the eye's activity of looking is its second entelechy. Whereas, then, a new-born puppy lacks either entelechy, it has the potentiality of attaining it. Now this is how, says Aristotle, we should think of the soul. For as sight, when it is begotten in the eye, completes the eye, so, in the other case, when soul is ingendered in a body, it completes the living creature; in such wise that there never was a time when the soul existed without the body, nor when the body existed to the exclusion of soul. For the soul is not body, but is from body, for which reason it subsists embodied and in its own particular body. Soul does not exist by itself, Aristotle says. And he gives the name of soul first to the vital principle in the soul, leaving its faculty of reason out of account. But one must take the human soul whole and entire, and not make a part stand for the whole; least of all the feeblest part.[7]

To continue, however, Aristotle says that the body possesses the potentiality of living, and does so before there is soul. For he declares that the potentiality of living resides in the body itself. But if the body contains within itself the capacity for living, it must, before it receives life, be constituted a body; and it cannot be constituted a body until it has been given form. For matter is

---

[5] Form gains significance in the thinking mind as it is there, by the mind's activity, set in relation with the universe of knowledge.

[6] Mind does not create form, which exists whether mind is active upon it or not.

[7] Aristotle's biological approach to the concept of soul begins from what Nemesius calls the irrational part of the soul and looks upon as soul in its lowest terms. Nemesius will not, however, follow the Neo-Platonists and sever mind from animal soul. He asserts the superiority of the rational, but insists on the soul's inclusive unity.

a mere indefinite and does not constitute body. Now it is a manifest impossibility that nonentity should be able to constitute itself something out of nothing. But even suppose matter to be potentially body, how can merely potential body have inherent in it the capacity for life?

Or to take another point of view, one can, in general, possess some capacity and yet make no use of it; for example, have sight and not use it. But the like does not apply in the case of soul. For the soul even of one sleeping is not inactive, seeing that he is digesting and growing, dreaming and breathing, of which the last is prime evidence that the person is alive. From these facts it is plain that one cannot have merely the capacity for living and not be actively alive. For first and foremost it is life and nothing else that constitutes the soul's form; since life pertains to the nature of soul, while it belongs to body only by participation. Therefore if anyone says that a person's health is in proportion to his life, he is not referring to life as it is in the soul, but to bodily vitality, and is quibbling. For it is in the nature of body to admit, in some ratio, conflicting qualities.[8] But it is quite otherwise with form. For if the distinctive form of a living creature were altered, it would not be the same living creature any more; so that nothing can admit conflicting qualities as touching its form, but only as touching its basic substance or corporeal being. This plainly proves that the soul cannot in any way be the entelechy of the body. It must be something that seeks a perfection of its own, apart from body. For the soul admits degrees of conflicting attributes, such as vice and virtue; and that is what form could not admit.[9]

But to proceed with Aristotle; he says that as the soul is entelechy it is, in its proper nature, an unmoved, and yet that, contingently, it is moved.[10] Now there is nothing paradoxical in the soul moving us while being itself unmoved. For beauty is an

---

[8] The body has a degree of health and a degree of ailment, and its vitality is in proportion to its health. No such variation applies to life in the soul.

[9] Since entelechy resides in form, and form cannot admit conflicting qualities, neither can entelechy. But soul can. Therefore soul cannot be entelechy.

[10] An "unmoved" means an abstraction. When Aristotle is admitted to say that the soul is moved contingently, it is plain that he did not really equate entelechy with the soul. The soul being moved contingently means that it reacts to experience. From this point Nemesius sets out to show that the soul, and not anything belonging to the world of matter, is the prime source of motion. The activity of man's soul works from thoughts to incitements of the body. The transmission would be in the reverse direction if motion originated in matter.

unmoved that yet moves us. But if something that is unmoved imparts motion, of course a concrete thing of mobile nature imparts motion. Suppose, then, that a living creature's body had its own motion, still there would be no anomaly in its being moved by an unmoved. What *is* impossible is that an unmoved should be moved by an unmoved.[11] Whence, then, comes a body's motion if not from its soul? For the body does not in fact move of itself. So Aristotle, in trying to point to the primary cause of motion, has really indicated the secondary cause and not the primary. It is a primary cause of motion when an unmoved imparts motion; but if something that has been set in motion, whether of itself or otherwise, imparts motion, we have merely exposed a secondary source of motion.[12] Whence, then, has the body its primary source of motion? The assertion that the elements set themselves in motion by being some of them naturally light and others heavy is false. For if lightness and heaviness create motion, the light and heavy things would never cease moving; whereas they come to rest on reaching each its proper place. Surely, then, heaviness and lightness are no primary cause of motion, but mere qualities of the elements. But even if the origination of motion were conceded to them, how can lightness and heaviness give birth to deliberation, the forming of opinions, and the passing of judgements? And if those are not the work of lightness and heaviness, neither are they due to the elements; and if not to the elements, then not to bodies.

Once more, if the soul is only contingently moved, while for the body to be moved is in its nature, it follows that when there is no soul the body will be self-moving. And if so, we have a living creature without a soul, which is absurd. But the absurdity is latent, surely, in the first assumption.[13] Nor is it truly said that everything by nature mobile is likewise being moved by some application of force, or that anything in motion under applied force is naturally endowed with motion. For the universe is in motion naturally, and not because of the application to it of any

[11] But beauty moves the soul. Therefore, since beauty is an unmoved, the soul is not.

[12] Aristotle, observing the material order to be in motion, sought the cause of motion in that order. Observing in particular the tendency of heavy things to move down and light things up, he gave the explanation that "the motion of a body to its own place is motion to its own form." So he found the source of motion in the things themselves. The argument of Nemesius that now follows is intended to refute this.

[13] That the soul is an "unmoved" or abstraction.

force.[14] Nor, again, is it true that if any thing is naturally in motion it must be its nature also to come to rest. For it is the nature of the universe and the sun and moon to be in motion, and equally it is their nature to be incapable of rest. Likewise also the soul is by nature in perpetual motion, and its nature is incapable of rest, seeing that rest is destruction to the soul, as to any perpetual mover.

In addition to all these arguments we must note that Aristotle leaves unsolved the problem that faced us from the start, namely, what it is that holds the body together, despite its natural liability to disintegration. Nevertheless, the above arguments, taken from a wider field, suffice to show that the soul is neither entelechy, nor an unmoved, nor any by-product of body.

COMMENTARY

16. *The Aristotelian doctrine of the soul.* Nemesius now returns to Aristotle, *On the soul,* to take his argument up at the beginning of Book ii. It helps us to follow Nemesius if we keep in mind his own doctrine of the soul, that it is a self-subsisting rational living creature, ceaselessly in motion, the indispensable integrator of a living body, implicated in the material universe, and yet no part or product thereof. Nemesius criticizes not so much the real Aristotle as a popular secularism which defended its disregard for the things of the soul by claiming the assent of a great teacher of antiquity. Almost all that Nemesius says is as much to the profit of Neo-Platonism as of Christianity, and he is likely to owe much of the structure of his argument to Neo-Platonist writers.

TEXT

[M.102. 3–110. 5.]

17. Pythagoras was accustomed always to represent God and all things by numerical symbols, and defined the soul as a self-moving number. Xenocrates took over this definition from him.[1] It does not mean that the soul is literally a number, but that it is one of the things susceptible to numerical symbolism, and a thing that involves the idea of increment. It means that it is the

---

[14] Nemesius, seeing that the Aristotelian doctrine that the "heavenly sphere" rotates perpetually by reason of the "Intelligences" played into his hands, uses it to give the *coup de grace* to the theory that the source of motion is contained in matter.

[1] See Section 11, note 7.

soul which makes distinctions between things, by assigning each
to its proper kind and character. For it is the soul that distinguishes form from form, and pronounces them different by
means of the contrast of one form with another, and the ratio of
the corresponding numbers, representing everything mathe-
matically.[2] Wherefore the soul itself is not altogether to be
severed from the notion of number. Pythagoras further testified
that the soul is self-moving.

Now, that the soul is not number is clear from the following
considerations: number is quantitative, and the soul, being substance, is not; and the soul is surely not number, especially if
they want to give number a place among the intelligibles, as we
shall relate presently. Again, the soul has continuous existence,
while number goes by jumps; so the soul cannot be number.
Further, a number is either even or odd, but the soul is neither;[3]
so surely again the soul is not number. Again, a number is increased when another is added to it, but one cannot add something to the soul to increase it. Again, the soul is self-moving,
but a number is a finite unmoved. Again, while it is in the nature
of a number to remain one and the same, and it cannot undergo
change as touching any of the qualities appropriate to number,
the soul, as touching its substance, remains one and the same,
but, as touching its qualities, undergoes change, passing from
ignorance to knowledge, and from vice to virtue. So, then,
surely the soul is not number.

We have now reviewed the doctrines of the ancients concerning the soul. Eunomius[4] defined the soul as an incorporeal being

2 Pythagoras seems to have had an intuition of the importance of mathematics to physics, of number to the universe. He saw the life of the human
body as explicable in terms of the proportion in which its several ingredients are tempered, and supposed this to be in a measure imposed upon
body by soul. When this proportion is harmonious, there is health and
growth for both body and soul, and when otherwise, loss and evil. The
doctrine of transmigration of souls may have had its attraction for
Pythagoras because, as a soul changed numerically, it became unfitted
for its body and fitted for a different body. To things outside the body,
the soul is like number in "sizing them up," and self-moving in imposing
proportion within its body.
3 Since the Neo-Pythagoreans called masculine even and feminine odd,
this is a denial that soul has sex.
4 Eunomius was born early in the fourth century of our era, near the
borders of Cappadocia and Galatia. In A.D. 356 he became the disciple
of Aetius, who was, at Antioch, launching a new version of Arianism,
based on pure dialectic, and contemptuous of church tradition, and they
worked together there till 360. Later, Eunomius was for a while bishop
of Cyzicus near Constantinople. In 382, he refused to conform, at the

created in body, an opinion that agrees at once with Plato and with Aristotle. For Eunomius took "incorporeal being" from Plato and "created in body" from Aristotle, not seeing, for all his sharpness,[5] that he is attempting to bring into agreement things that are incompatible.[6] For everything of which the genesis is in body and time is corruptible and mortal. The words of Moses agree to these things. For, when describing the creation of the sensible universe, he did not expressly say that the nature of the intelligibles was also established by that creation. Admittedly there are those who think so, but not everyone agrees with them. It would be a perversion of the truth, however, if one were to suppose that, because the soul was put into the body after the body had been framed, therefore the soul was created after the body. Moses does not say that the soul was created at that moment at which it was put into the body, nor would it be reasonable to suppose it.[7] Therefore, either let Eunomius say the same as Aristotle, who declared the soul to be begotten with the body, and as the Stoics, or, if he will have it that the soul is incorporeal being, let him refuse to say that it is created in body, lest he present us with a notion of the soul as mortal and wholly irrational.[8]

order of Theodosius the Great, with orthodoxy as defined by the Council of Constantinople, and was relegated to Cappadocia, where he spent his last years in literary controversy with Basil the Great and Gregory of Nyssa.

[5] A hit at the claim of Eunomius to prevail by dialectic.

[6] The orthodox opponents of Eunomius found him difficult to understand, and Nemesius is evidently uncertain where he stands. The difficulty seems to arise from the fact that Eunomius regarded creation as not instantaneous but a process. Similarly he thought of the generation of the Word as something which only came to completion when the Word became Son (as he held) by incarnation, and so gave, for the first time the name of Father to the eternal ingenerate God. Eunomius taught that the Word began to create souls at the creation of the world. In that sense they pre-existed. But their creation only came to completion, in the view of Eunomius, as the body destined for each came to be conceived. When all the elect souls created at the beginning have found their actuality in this way, the purpose of the material world would have been served, and the world would come to an end.

[7] The opinion of Nemesius is that the intelligibles, including the soul of Adam, were created before the material universe.

[8] There were three main views, in the early Church, about the origin of the soul. The first is traducianism, the belief that soul is born of the soul as body is of body, ex traduce, by a handing on of substance. The next is creationism, which supposes that God, when a human body, under his providence, begins to be conceived, creates the soul that is to ensoul that body. The third theory was that of pre-existence, according to which God

Or we may put the argument in another form. According to Eunomius, the world is not yet full, but, to this day, is only half-full, while our race continues to be in need of additions. For at least fifty thousand rational beings are added to it daily. But the hardest thing to accept is that, according to Eunomius, when this process has come to its destined conclusion, the universe will be dissolved in that very moment when the tale of human souls is fulfilled with perfect men who are to rise again. What could be more senseless than to say that the world will be destroyed in the moment of its completion? It is exactly the way of tiny children who knock their sand-castles to pieces the moment they have completed them![9]

Another thing that might be said is that souls are not being created now, but have been created beforehand for this moment, so that no new being is added, nor anything besides what already existed, but simply that something already in existence under providence receives actualization. But no one could say it if they knew how to distinguish creation from providence. For it is a work of providence to preserve the succession of corruptible living creatures by means of procreation (I am excluding, of course, those creatures that are bred of decay, since there is again another providential way of securing their succession, which is decay itself). But the peculiar character of creation is that it is production out of nothing. If, then, souls are procreated, that is a work of providence, and they are corruptible, just like everything else that exists by racial succession.[10] But if

created all souls at the beginning of the world, each to join its predestined body at the appointed time. The third view remained suspect from the time that the Church condemned the form of pre-existence-doctrine taught by Origen. The crux of creationism, as Nemesius sees it, was that the separate creation of each several soul at its own moment in time seemed to put God at the beck and call of human lust. To remove the origin of the soul from the time of begetting to the beginning of the world softened, if it did not really overcome, this difficulty. That in a sense, is what Eunomius did. Nemesius did it more definitely, adopting the doctrine of Origen except for the prenatal fall of souls which Origen held.

9 The simile of play-sand is used against Eunomius also by Gregory of Nyssa. Gregory says that Eunomius heaps up words and calls it an argument, just as children say, this is my house, or anything else that they fancy, when they have just made a heap of sand. But Nemesius means that God, according to Eunomius, builds a sand-castle whose grains are human beings, and when the last man has entered the world, he will destroy the race, and the world in which it is a race.

10 Nemesius is guilty of the false argument, "Providence preserves the species. If, therefore, providence exists, there must be a species that needs preserving."

souls arrive out of non-existence, then creation is still going on in defiance of the word of Moses, that "God rested from all his works."[11] Both alternatives are unacceptable, and souls are not coming into existence at this moment. For the saying, "My Father worketh"[12] does not refer to creation but to providence. And that, indeed, is how Eunomius understands it.

The opinion of Apollinarius,[13] on the other hand, was that souls are born of souls, just as bodies are born of bodies, because the soul of the first man comes down, with the bodily succession, to all his offspring. For Apollinarius denies either that souls pre-existed or that they are being created now. For, he argues, those who say that souls are being created now make God a "partaker with the adulterers,"[14] seeing that from adulterous unions children are born. He adds that the saying, "God rested

---

[11] Nemesius takes Gen. 2:2 to mean that, at the end of the seven days of creation, all that ever was to be created was created. Eunomius took it to prove that creation is a process, seeing that the sabbath, which commemorates creation, is not kept on the first day of the week (when creation began) but on the last (when it was completed). Similarly, what received its creation in the seven days would not have its completion till the end of the world.

[12] John 5:17. This presented a problem to Eunomius, who resolved it by saying that it meant the Holy Spirit, whom the Ingenerate put forth through the Word before the incarnation, to be the Word's fellow-worker. When the Word was incarnate as Jesus Christ, he honoured the Ingenerate by attributing to him the work of the Spirit.

[13] Apollinarius taught uncompromisingly that the Word took flesh, with its animal faculties, but did *not* take a human soul. He said this in the interests of a Nicene theology, holding it possible for a co-equal Son of God to take flesh, but not conceivable that he should unite to himself a human soul. Nemesius sees that this refusal was due to a low view of the soul and supposes this to be inevitable, where traducianism is held. But Gregory of Nyssa was traducianist, too; and therefore had no quarrel with Apollinarius on that score. It may be from the *Demonstration of the divine Incarnation*, once more, that Nemesius gained his information on the doctrine of Apollinarius, though other possibilities are obvious.

[14] The Greek words used by Nemesius do not imply any allusion to Ps. 50:18 (LXX. 49:18). He is simply accepting the argument of Apollinarius against pure creationism, the point of which is that, if a child is born of an adulterous union, God, on a creationist view, condones the crime by giving the criminals the reward for which they committed it. There is, however, nothing that really would remove this difficulty except that adulterous unions should never be fruitful. Nemesius ignores the scriptural answer given by II Sam. 12:15-25, and wrongly treats Solomon as the child of adultery. He seems to think that if providence allows a pre-existing soul to take advantage of an adulterous conception to enter the world, the moral holiness of God is not affected, as it would be on the creationist supposition.

from all his works that he began to make" is false, if he is still creating souls.

We reply to him that all things which depend upon successive procreation for their existence are thereby shown to be mortal. For that is the reason that they beget and are begotten, namely that a race of corruptible creatures may be preserved. So it must be either the one thing or the other, that the soul is mortal and *ex traduce*, or that souls are not being begotten, soul from soul, in succession. Let us leave the case of children begotten in adultery to be justified by providence, whose ways we do not know. And if one must even make a guess about providence, it is that a child born of adultery is one that God surely knows will serve either his generation or God himself, and he therefore allows the ensouling to take place. Of this we may take Solomon, the son begotten by David of Uriah's wife, as sufficient assurance.

COMMENTARY

17. *Further refutation of heterodox ideas on the soul.* Nemesius begins the section with a favourable account of the doctrine of Pythagoras on the soul, followed by a group of arguments against it, the force of which is largely nullified by what goes before. In the course of these arguments he promises to deal with the Pythagorean assertion that number is an intelligible. He does not fulfil this promise, and there is no obvious reason why he should. We may suspect that the promise belongs to the author of the set of arguments, whom we must suppose other than the author of the favourable review of Pythagoreanism which precedes it. In short, Nemesius seems to have made up this part of the section by drawing on two works. The first might be Neo-Platonist. The Neo-Platonists were, in many ways, successors to the Neo-Pythagoreans of the first and second Christian centuries, with Numenius in the third as last representative. The set of contrary arguments, on the other hand, seem directed against a superstitious and popular development of Neo-Pythagoreanism. When Nemesius passes from Pythagoras to two Christian heretics who were his elder contemporaries, and cut a figure in the life of Syria that made them known far beyond the pale of the Church, his own personal interest can be clearly discerned. He had seen the Nicene cause triumph in Syria against Arianism, the heresy that there is only one eternal divine Person, who, when he chose, brought into being Son and Spirit. While Eunomius gave

new life to Arianism, Apollinarius opposed it. Both Arianism
and Apollinarianism equally outraged the dearest conviction
of the Syrians, that the incarnate Son was complete in human
soul. This passage of Nemesius is of value in showing that
Eunomius broke away from other Arians, in adopting a view of
the soul which would leave open the question of a human soul in
Christ. A side aim of Nemesius, in writing his book, was, no
doubt, to support the orthodox Syrian view against the heresies.
The paragraphs on Pythagoras, on the other hand, would seem
to be aimed at little more than giving his work a comprehensive
appearance.

TEXT

[M.110. 5–118. 7.]

18. Next let us go on to review the opinion concerning the
soul held by the Manichaeans.[1] For they indeed say that the
soul is immortal and incorporeal, adding that there is but one
single soul for the whole world, which is subdivided and
parcelled out to particular bodies, whether those bodies be inanimate or ensouled. Some, to wit ensouled beings, receive
more, and some, inanimates, receive less, while much the most
part of all resides in heaven. In this wise the portions of the
universal soul constitute particular souls. Now if the Manichaeans simply said that the soul of the world was indivisibly
participated, as sound is among hearers, their error would not
be gross. But in fact they assert that the soul-substance is divided
up. And the worst thing of all is that they would have us believe
the soul-substance to be literally mingled with the elements,
and that, when bodies are generated, the portion of soul for
them is separated off, together with those elements; finally, that
when in course of time the bodies disintegrate, their portion of
soul rejoins the soul mingled in the elements, just as a separate
cupful of water eventually returns to be mingled with all the
rest. They say that pure souls depart to the light, as being themselves luminous, but that the souls that have defiled themselves
with matter go back into the elements, whence, once more, they
are separated off to go into plants and animals. Thus they make

[1] Nemesius must certainly have had a first-hand interest in the doctrine
of the Manichaeans, which was a strong competitor of Catholicism in
his day. It was also a hated rival in the eyes of the Neo-Platonists. The
summary of the doctrine, and the retailing and refutation of one of the
arguments of the Manichaeans which Nemesius here gives is unique.
There is also a strong probability that it was attained by the use of
Neo-Platonic sources.

the soul immortal at the expense of parcelling out its substance, representing it as corporeal, and subjecting it to passions. And in doing so, they fall into various contradictions. For first they assert that defiled souls go back into the elements and there mingle with other souls, and then they turn round and say that defiled souls are punished in proportion to their offences by transmigrations, thus, in effect, collecting them back out of dispersion and restoring to them their several individualities. For (say they) when it is light, shadows are given each its separate individuality, but when the sky darkens the shadows mingle into one; quite an improper simile to apply to things belonging to the intelligible order. For if it be granted that shadows can be separated and then mingled together in one, it remains that shadows are things cast by sensible objects.

Plato also asserts that there is one soul and many souls, the one soul being the soul of the universe[2] and the others being the souls of particular things; so that the universe is ensouled in its own way, and particular things are severally animated by souls of their own. And Plato says that the world-soul stretches all the way from the centre of the earth to the furthest confines of the heavens, though he does not use the word "stretch" in a spatial but in a notional sense. It is this soul, he says, that causes the universe to be spherical in form, and holds together and compacts (as one might say) the world's body. For it was shown in what has gone before that bodies need something to hold them together, and that the soul does this by imparting form to them. For each thing that exists enjoys its own life, and suffers its appropriate form of dissolution. For so long as the body is held and bound together, we call it a body, but when it disintegrates, the body is said to be destroyed. Everything lives, indeed, but not everything is a living creature. For the Platonists distinguish plants from inanimates by their growing and being nourished, that is, by their possession of the nutritive and vegetative faculties. They distinguish irrational beasts from plants by their having perception, and rational beings from irrational beasts by their possession of reason. So when Platonists say that everything lives, they must go on to distinguish degrees of living. The life they must allot to inanimate things is simply continued identity, wherein they are held together by the world-soul, so that they subsist and do not dissolve. For they say that it is the world-soul that guides the universe on its way, and assigns

2 The Platonic doctrine of the world-soul here in view is that of the *Timaeus*, ch. vIII.

particular souls already formed by the Creator to their bodies; which is to say that the Creator himself gave the world-soul laws in accordance with which the universe must be carried on (which laws Plato also calls "destiny") and supplies sufficient power for the world-soul to carry us along. These matters will be treated further in the chapter on Destiny.

All Greeks, then, who represent the soul as immortal agree in believing in transmigration.[3] Where they differ is as to the forms of souls. For some say that there is but one form, rationality,[4] and that this form passes into vegetable and animal embodiment. Of these thinkers there are some who hold that this happens at stated periods of time, and others who hold that it happens fortuitously. There are others who do not allow that all souls have one form, but divide souls under the two forms of rational and irrational. Others again say that there are many soul-forms; in fact, as many as there are forms of living creatures. The Platonists were particularly divided on this point. For Plato said that wrathful, proud, and grasping souls exchange bodies with wolves and lions, and that those who have run to excesses will receive the bodies of donkeys and other animals of that sort. Some took him to mean literal wolves, lions, and donkeys, and others thought that they discerned that he spoke in parables, and by naming animals alluded to manners of behaving. For Cronius,[5] for example, in his work *On regeneration* (for that is the term that he uses instead of transmigration) will have it that souls always remain rational. The

---

[3] The doctrine of transmigration is that when a soul leaves a body it becomes reincarnate in another body newly conceived, whether of the same kind or of a different kind.

[4] Form here means not shape or description but basic principle. So the thinkers in question suppose that wherever there is soul, there rationality is in some way coming to expression. Thus, if a sunflower turns its face to the sun, rationality is exemplified in a vegetable context, and we have a manifestation of soul in plant embodiment.

[5] Cronius was a Pythagorean who lived in the second century of our era, and was commented by Plotinus. Theodore the Platonist probably belongs to the same philosophical movement as Cronius and Numenius, but nothing certain is known of him. Porphyry of Tyre, A.D. 233–304, became the pupil of Plotinus in Rome in A.D. 262. He edited his master's writings under the title of *Enneads*. Porphyry was a bitter opponent of Christianity. There is, however, no proof of the assertion, repeatedly made, that he had once been a Christian. And Eusebius, in his *Preparation for the Gospel*, calls him "a genuine philosopher, an admirable theologian, and a prophet of things ineffable." Iamblichus, a Syrian, and the principal pupil of Porphyry, was the author of a collection of writings under the title *Summary of Pythagorean Doctrine*. He died about A.D. 330.

same view is taken by Theodore the Platonist, in *The soul is omniform*. Porphyry follows suit. But Iamblichus goes clean the other way, and declares that there is a form of soul appropriate to each form of living creature, and that these forms differ from one-another. He accordingly wrote a monograph in which he argued that there is no transmigration of souls from men into irrational beasts, nor from beasts into men, but only from one beast into another, and from one human being into another. And it seems to me that, for this reason, Iamblichus, more than all the others, both hit upon Plato's meaning and lighted on the truth itself.[6] This stands to be established by many and different proofs, but particularly by those now to follow.

COMMENTARY

18. *The world-soul and transmigration of souls.* The order in which Section 11 deals with opinions on the soul has been followed in the next sections, which treat the same subjects *in extenso*. And, with Section 18, we come to the last subject of Section 11, namely the opinion that, over against individual souls, there exists some universal soul or soul-substance. This subject is treated first as it appears in the doctrine of the Manichaeans, according to which one soul-substance, while essentially belonging to heaven, has been drawn down into the world of matter, and is now in process of redemption from the evil that is in matter, by means of the temporary existences of individual souls. In the second place this section reviews the Platonic doctrine of the world-soul, its relation to individual souls, and the Platonic and Neo-Platonic doctrines of the transmigration of souls.

TEXT

[M.118. 7–125. 7.]

19. We do not see any of the rational activities in the behaviour of the irrational animals. For neither arts, learning, counsel, virtues, or any other intellectual pursuits are to be seen in them. And from this it is plain that they are not endowed

---

6 This appraisal of Iamblichus is more likely to be the opinion of some Neo-Platonist upon whom Nemesius is drawing than that of the Christian apologist himself. Nemesius might express agreement with Iamblichus, but the Neo-Platonist interest betrays itself in vindicating his right to be the interpreter of Plato. In this setting of Plato and truth side by side, Skard sees an allusion to the proverb known to us in the form, *Amicus Plato, magis amica veritas*. (*Symbolae Osloenses*, Fasc. xxii. p. 40.)

with a rational soul. Indeed it is absurd to speak of reason in connection with the irrational animals. For although it is true that only the animal propensities are present in new-born babies, we nevertheless credit them with the possession of a rational soul, forasmuch as in fact they exhibit rational activities as they grow up. But your irrational animal does not manifest rationality at any age. It would be superfluous for it to have a rational soul, seeing that its rational powers are bound to be for ever useless. Now it is generally agreed that God has made no superfluous creature. Admit that, and then observe how superfluous a work it would be to put a rational soul in cattle or wild beasts, seeing that it would never have opportunity to exercise its proper function. It would, moreover, be blameworthy in a Creator to give to a body a soul unsuited to it; for to do such a thing would not be workmanlike or show any sense of order or harmony.

Suppose, however, that someone urges that animals in their inward disposition have rational impulses, but that their physical shape does not lend itself to the practice of the arts, the argument being based on the fact that men have but to lose the fingers of their hands and they are no more use for most of the arts. That, however, does not settle the question. For there still remains the absurdity with which we began, of God implanting in a body a soul that is no help to it, a soul superfluous, foolish, ineffectual, a soul that hinders the proper activity of the body at any stage of its life. And to this we must add that the assertion that animals have rational impulses rests on dubious grounds, upon which there is no general agreement. For whence is it proved that animals in their inward disposition have rational impulses? It is better, therefore, to assume that in each kind of body there is implanted a soul serviceable to it, and that, as regards their inward disposition, animals have nothing more than the natural simplicity that is manifest in their actions. For each kind of irrational creature is moved by its own characteristic impulse towards that advantage or that activity which was appropriate to it from the beginning. And for these things the creature had also a suitably shaped structure. Certainly the Creator did not leave the animals without succour, but provided each kind with its instinctive (not rational) intelligence. In some, indeed, he implanted a degree of cunning that mimics art and counterfeits reason. And this he did for two ends. The first was to make them avoid immediate snares, and to guard them from those with which they may meet in the future. And the second was to bind together the whole creation in the way we have already described.[1]

That the explanation of animal cunning is not their possession of reason is evident from the fact that each animal of a particular kind does the same things in the same way, that animal behaviour does not vary in the whole range of individuals (except that in some it may be more marked, and in others less) and that the whole of a kind of animal is moved by a single impulse. Every hare has the same way of doubling, every fox the same kind of craftiness, every monkey the same sort of mimicry. And that is not how man behaves. There are a thousand ways in which men may act. For reason being unconstrained and self-determining, it follows that there is not one and the same thing that all men do, in the way that there is for each particular kind of irrational animal. Animals are moved in accordance with natural instinct only, and what nature dictates is the same for every individual of a kind. But rational behaviour differs from individual to individual, and is not inevitably the same for all. To say that human souls are sent down into the bodies of this or that kind of animal in punishment for the sins of a previous human life is proving the argument from the conclusion. How came rational souls to be sent into the bodies of the first created animals? It could not be because of having sinned in human bodies before there were any human bodies to sin in![2]

Probably Galen, that most admirable of physicians, took our view, and held that every different kind of animal has a form of soul appropriate to it. For at the very beginning of the first book of his tractate *On the use of the parts (of the human body)* he says, "If this be true, then animals have many parts, some of them being main members, some lesser members, and some so small as to be irreducible to smaller components. And that which makes use of every part is the soul. For the body is the instrument of the soul, and the reason that the parts of different animals were made so very different is that their souls are different."[3] A little

---

1 See Section 3. The mock-rationality of the higher animals is a step in the rising order of intelligence, and a link in the ascending *continuum* of sensible creation.

2 Nemesius tacitly assumes the Genesis account of creation, where all animals were created before man.

3 The end of ch. 1 and the beginning of ch. 2, Bk. 1 (Teubner edn., by G. Helmreich, vol. 1, p. 1, Leipsig, 1907). The citation follows the opening definition of a member of an integral body. In Matthaei's text of Nemesius the second set of inverted commas are out of place.

later in the same book, again, Galen speaks addressing the ape and says, "Now, you clever little tease, Nature might retort to you that a ridiculous soul must needs be given to furnish the body of a ridiculous animal."[4]

If we have now proved that the soul is not body, nor harmony, nor temperament, nor any other quality, we are clearly left with a single possibility, namely, that it is incorporeal being. For everyone agrees on the soul's existence. And if it is not body, nor accident, clearly it must be not any of those things that depend for their existence on something else, but an incorporeal being. For those other things can come and go without affecting the thing which they need for their existence. But when the soul departs from the body, the body breaks up completely.

We can borrow the same arguments to prove the soul immortal. For if it is not a body (which has been shown to be liable by its nature to disintegrate and become corrupt) nor quality, quantity, or any other of the things that can be annulled, it plainly is immortal.

There are numerous proofs of the soul's immortality offered by Plato and others, but they are difficult and full of obscurities, and can scarcely be understood by those who have been brought up to such studies. But for us the sufficient demonstration of the soul's immortality is the teaching of Holy Scripture, which is self-authenticating because inspired of God.[5]

To those who, on the other hand, do not accept the Christian Scriptures, it is enough to point out that the soul is not any of the things that are subject to destruction. And if it is not one of these it is indestructible. Enough has been said, and we should now pass on.

COMMENTARY

19. *Not all souls are rational, but all are incorporeal and immortal.* By bringing the course of Section 18 back to the Platonic doctrine of the soul, Nemesius has prepared for the conclusion to his chapter on the soul. He answers the question whether the soul has one form or many by arguing that the form of the souls of animals does not involve rationality. The argument has been

---

[4] Bk. i, ch. 22. (Edn. cited, p. 59.) The importance of fingers has led up to the fingers of monkeys, and their laughable resemblance to man, in all respects. "Tease," literally "accuser," in the sense of one who shows you what you have done, a mimic or "take-off."

[5] It would be interesting to know how Nemesius deduced from Scripture the doctrine of unconditional immortality in which he believes. He is a precursor of the schoolmen in thinking thus.

the subject of two studies, the first by M. Pohlenz (*Hermes*, LXXVI, 1–13, Berlin, 1941) entitled "Tierische und menschliche Intelligenz bei Poseidonios," and the second by E. Skard (*Symbolae Osloenses*, Fasc. XXII, 40–48, Oslo, 1942) in the fifth of his *Nemesiosstudien*, "Galens Lehre von tierischer und menschlicher Intelligenz." Pohlenz thinks that the opening of the section takes up the argument of Iamblichus, and that the theme is Posidonian. Skard shows that the structure of the section reflects Galen most closely all through, and not only after the acknowledgement by Nemesius of his debt to his favourite author. The subject of animal intelligence was much canvassed (e.g., by Plutarch and Aelian), and might reach Nemesius by many routes; including the doctrine of Posidonius that animal intelligence is instinctive and not rational. Nemesius might start with the argument of Iamblichus, as given by his Neo-Platonic source, and develop it under the guidance of his great knowledge of the works of Galen.

Nemesius concludes that soul, in all its forms, is incorporeal and therefore "indestructible" being. His interest, however, is only in the rational human soul. But his argument has established the principle that a human body must be the fit habitation for a human soul, so that the study of the nature of man is the study of soul in union with body.

III. *Of the union of soul with body*

TEXT

20. Our next subject of enquiry concerns the manner of union between soul, on the one hand, and body as it is apart from soul, on the other. It is a subject enveloped in uncertainties. And if, as some will have it, man consists not only of soul and body but also of mind, the subject is more puzzling still. And when some would even add to man a fourth constituent, they make the problem frankly insoluble.[1] For all that comes to-

[1] The reference is probably to some of the Apollinarians. Apollinarius himself was trichotomist. That is, he distinguished three elements in man, distinguishing soul, conceived as the seat of the passions and the recipient of sense impressions, from the mind. In this, Nemesius (Section 1) charges Apollinarius with being a follower of the Neo-Platonists. Nemesius is, of course, a stout upholder of the unity of the soul, and he probably does less than justice to either Apollinarius or Plotinus when he accuses them of destroying that unity. Certainly, both laid emphasis upon the difference between the soul in its higher activity of thinking, reasoning and contemplation, and the soul in its lower activity of sense-perception

gether to make one single being is made in all ways one, but in being thus united the constituents all undergo change, and no longer remain what each was in isolation, as will be shown in our chapter on the four elements.[2] For things that have undergone union with other things become different. How is it possible, then, on the one hand, for body to be united to soul without losing corporeity, or, on the other hand, how is it possible for soul, being incorporeal and self-subsistent, to be joined to body, and become part of a living creature, still keeping distinct and uncorrupted its own entity? We have but two alternatives. Either, when soul and body are united, they are changed both together, and die away into each other, as the elements do, or (since such suppositions are absurd), soul and body are, in fact, not really united, but merely in juxtaposition; as it were, like partners in a dance, or one counter added to another; or they are mixed, like wine and water. But we saw, in the last chapter,[3] that soul is not in juxtaposition with its body, for, otherwise, only that part of the body would be alive that was in proximity to the soul, and that part that was out of contact with the soul would be lifeless. Furthermore, it cannot be said that things which are in contact are therefore in union; to take an example, bits of wood placed in contact are not thereby united, nor bits of iron, or anything of that sort. The mixing of wine and water destroys the nature of both together. The mixture is neither clean water, nor is it wine. Though such mixture is by juxtaposition, the senses cannot perceive it, because the particles of the mingled liquids are too tiny. But that these particles are in juxtaposition is plain, because, for sure, the two liquids can be separated again, by employing an oiled sponge or a piece of paper to draw the water up clean. Things truly united could not possibly be separated, thus perceptibly.[4]

and the maintenance of animal life. Apollinarius and his first followers accepted a trichotomy of body, animal soul, and mind, equating mind with spirit, as spirit is used in the vocabulary of Paul. There was a difficulty, however, in maintaining this equation, occasioned by I Cor. 14:15, where mind is contrasted with spirit. This seems to have driven some later Apollinarians to adopt the fourfold division of man into body, soul, mind, and spirit. These will be the people who, according to Nemesius, render the problem of man's unity insoluble. The other Apollinarians are stigmatized as making the problem unnecessarily difficult.

[2] Ch. v, below.   [3] Section 13.

[4] By the wine-and-water experiment, Nemesius has, in addition to confused union and mere juxtaposition, ruled out union by mixture. Bishop Fell points out that the experiment is not as successful as Nemesius suggests. The capillary attraction in the sponge or paper raises pure

If, therefore, we must rule out union, juxtaposition, or mixture, in what manner can we say that a living creature is a unity? This was the perplexing question that made Plato unwilling to say that a living creature consists of soul and body, and define it as a soul using a body, or figuratively putting on a body.[5] But this definition raises its own difficulties. For how can the soul be one with the body it has put on? When a coat is put on, coat and wearer do not thereby become united. However, Ammonius, the master of Plotinus, solved the problem thus.[6] He said that it is in the nature of intelligibles both to be capable of union with things adapted to receive them, just as much as if they were things that would perish with them, and to remain, nevertheless, unconfused with them while in union, and imperishable, just as though they were merely juxtaposed. For, the union of bodies always involves some alteration in them as they enter into union, even, possibly, a being transformed into other bodies, as in the case of elements entering into compounds, food turning into blood, or blood turning into flesh or into other parts of the body. In the case of intelligibles, on the other hand, union takes place, and yet no change in them results. For an intelligible being is essentially such as not to suffer alteration. The alternatives are for it to withdraw from the union, or to suffer annihilation. An intelligible will not suffer transformation. Now, an intelligible cannot be annihilated, for if it could, it would not be immortal. And, as the soul is life, if it were altered through mingling with the body, it would become something different, and would not be life any more. What then would it contribute to the body, if it did not endow it with life?

Surely, then, the soul suffers no change, as the result of union with body. And if we may assume it proved that intelligibles cannot suffer any change of being, it follows of necessity that

water, ahead of wine, and thus makes a beginning of separation, very soon arrested. Fell says, however, that, with the help of a retort, the separation can be completed, and that is enough to justify the argument which Nemesius bases on the experiment. Needless to say, Nemesius did not invent the experiment. Domanski points out that Stobaeus appears to attribute it to Chrysippus.

5 These phrases, which Nemesius attributes to Plato, appear to belong to Plotinus and Porphyry respectively.

6 This is the second mention by Nemesius of an opinion of Ammonius. We must suppose that he was drawing upon some work lost to us. And as, in Section 12, Ammonius is bracketed with Numenius in regard to his opinion, it is possible that the work in question was a Neo-Platonist doxography.

when intelligibles are in union with bodies, they do not perish in company with those bodies.

COMMENTARY

20. *Soul remains soul, though in union with body.* In this third chapter, Nemesius attacks the problem of the union of soul and body. He is at a great advantage, in this, through having established, in the previous chapter, his Neo-Platonized Aristotelian psychology, in which was vindicated the claim of the human mind to be a denizen of two worlds at once. Plato, by his recollection-theory, made man's mind an exile from the intelligible world in the world of sense. But the theory of Aristotle was that man's mind, by a faculty or power inherent in it, discovers intelligibility in sense-perceived objects, so as to be able to relate them to universal reality. Not that mind invests an object with intelligibility, which, indeed, it possesses in its own right, but that it finds in it so much that is intelligible as is commensurate with its own powers of understanding. This is to make mind equipped for life in this world. But the Neo-Platonist revision of the doctrine of Aristotle restores the balance in favour of the intelligible world, as that which is the true home of mind. And this confers upon the concept of the soul an otherness in relation to body which is greatly enhanced by the reference to Ammonius at the end of this section. For Ammonius seems to have compared the union of soul and body with the immanence of the idea in a particular representation of it in the phenomenal world. Nemesius accepts this very Platonic estimate of the nature of the soul with such good will, that he is in no danger of falling, in this third chapter, into any form of union by confusion. Domanski (*op. cit.* p. 59, Note 1) suggests that the source of the argument, in this section, is Porphyry's *Miscellaneous questions*; which is likely enough; except for the final passage about the opinion of Ammonius, which differs both in style and thought from the rest of the section. But this, if not Porphyry, is clearly from some other Neo-Platonist source.

TEXT

[M.131. 3–137. 4.]

21. So the soul is united to the body, and, further, this union is without confusion. For union there is, as the sympathy shows, to wit, the community of feeling which is throughout the living

creature, because it is one subject.[1] And that it involves no confusion is clear from the way the soul has of separating itself from
the body in sleep, leaving the body lying as if dead, only that it
keeps the life just breathing in it, lest it should actually perish.
Meanwhile the soul carries on an activity of its own in dreams,
divining things to come and consorting with intelligibles. The
same thing happens, also, when the soul meditates on some intelligible. For at such times, the soul seems to sever itself from
body and claim its independence, that thus it may devote itself
to realities.[2]

The soul is incorporeal, and yet it has established its presence
in every part of the body, just as much as if it were a partner to
union involving the sacrifice of its proper nature.[3] Nevertheless,

[1] This resumes the unresolved question in Section 13 whether an incorporeal
entity can be conjoined with body in the experience of feeling. "The
most learned authors," said Nemesius, meaning particularly Plotinus,
think the soul to be, in its proper nature, impassible. Nevertheless, the
vital power which is pre-requisite to feeling is acknowledged to be derived
by the body from the soul. It is therefore legitimate to speak of the soul's
"sympathy" with its body, thus recognizing that while soul and body are
not partners on equal terms, in this respect, they are partners.

[2] Two experiences were supposed by the ancients to show that the soul
could escape for a while from the bond of natural predilection for its
body. The one was dreaming, and the other ecstasy. Because there was no
clear concept of consciousness as a state of the soul, the difference between
dream-consciousness and waking-consciousness was too little considered.
Dreams take place in sleep, and the things which the soul encounters in
dreams are not encountered in the body, like its waking experiences.
Thus it was supposed that the soul left the body in sleep, and had its
dream experiences away from the body. The Neo-Platonists, on the other
hand, set great store by the contemplative ecstasy, in which again the
suspension of sense-consciousness seemed to argue the absence of the
soul from the body; this time, as Nemesius says, for the purpose of
"consorting with the intelligibles." When he speaks of the soul in absence
from the body "divining things to come," it is not ecstasy, but dreaming,
that is in view. Nemesius shared with all Christians of his age the belief,
resting on scriptural testimony, that the future may be revealed in dreams.
And he finds an explanation in the thought that the soul when freed from
the body may voyage into the future. But these excursions of the soul are
limited. Presently the soul must return and awaken its body, and resume
the normal tenor of life. But, as the Neo-Platonists believed, the soul
came back from such sleep, or ecstasy, enriched. (See Note 2 to Section 32
below.) It is very likely that Porphyry is the authority on whom Nemesius
rests, at this point.

[3] Nemesius is thinking of the union of elements in a compound, where
each undergoes some sacrifice of its proper nature. Such a union extends
throughout the compound, just as the soul establishes its presence in
every part of the body. But in the compound, wherever there is the
union of elements, there is a sacrifice of *propria* of the elements thus in

it remains uncorrupted by body, just as if it were something quite distinct from it. Thus, on the one hand, the soul preserves its own independent unity of being, and on the other, it modifies whatever it indwells, in accordance with its own life, while itself suffering no reciprocal change. For, as the presence of the sun transforms the air into light, making the air luminous by uniting light with air, at once maintaining them distinct and yet melting them together, so likewise the soul is united to the body and yet remains distinct from it; the cases being different just in this, that the sun is a body, and circumscribed to its own portion of space, and therefore is not present everywhere where its light is present, any more than a flame is. For a flame is also, in a local sense, bound, to burning logs or to a wick, as the case may be, but the soul is incorporeal, and not circumscribed to a particular portion of space, but spreading entire throughout; like a sun that spread wherever its light reached, as well as throughout the body of the sun,[4] not being just a part of the whole that it illuminates, as would be the case if it were not omnipresent in it. For it is not the body that masters the soul, but it is the soul that masters the body. Nor is the soul contained in the body, as if in a vessel, or bag. It might rather be said that the body is in the soul.[5] For we must not think of intelligibles as liable to meet resistance from bodies. We should think of them as extending through the whole body, as though they ranged over them, or pervaded them. They must not, on the other hand, be supposed confined to some portion of space. For, since they are intelligibles, they have relativity only to intelligibles; that is, they must either be self-subsistent, or have their being within an intelligible of higher order. For example, the soul is, when engaged upon discursive thinking, an independent subject, but when

combination. In like manner Nemesius next compares the union of soul and body with a mixture without combination, such as that of water and wine. Then he moves to a new comparison, that of the union of soul and body with the intermingling of light and air in daytime. Here the soul is compared with light. But that introduces a difficulty. Ubiquitous as is the daylight, it is not everywhere producing itself, as it should, to provide a true analogy for the soul. Domanski (*op. cit.*, p. 61, Note 1) calls attention to a passage in Plotinus that could have inspired this passage on the union of light and air.

[4] This rendering accepts Matthaei's text and takes as subject the soul under the figure of the sun.

[5] Domanski, *l.c.* Note 3 gives a parallel in Plotinus to this notion of "the body in the soul." Plato (*Timaeus*, 35) describes the world-soul as "spread all through the body of the universe, and even stretching beyond, so as to wrap body about from without."

engaged in the activity of intuitive apprehension it is, as it were, a part of universal mind.[6] Therefore, if the soul is said to be in a body, it is not so said in the sense of being located in a body, but rather as being in habitual relation of presence there, even as God is said to be in us. For we may say that the soul is bound by habit to the body, or by an inclination or disposition towards it, just as we say that a lover is bound to his beloved, not meaning physically, or spatially, but habitually. For the soul is a thing that has neither size, bulk, or parts, transcending particular and local circumscription.[7] For how can something indivisible be said to be locally circumscribed? Since place and bulk go together, place being the bounds of the enclosing thing, wherewithin it encloses whatever is enclosed.

Suppose someone were to say, Well, then, my soul is in Alexandria and Rome and everywhere. He would be overlooking the fact that his form of speech itself implies locality, still. For the fact of being in Alexandria, or simply of being anywhere, implies place. Now, "in a place" the soul is certainly not, except by habit. For it has been shown that the soul is incapable of being circumscribed to a place. Therefore, when an intelligible is in the relation of habit to a certain place, or to a certain thing conditioned by space, it is a catachrestic use of words, to say that it is "there," because its activity is there, and we are accepting the notion of locality in lieu of that of habit, or activity.[8] For, when we say, "Soul is there," we ought to say, "Its activity is there."[9]

COMMENTARY

21. *An enquiry into the manner in which the union of soul and body is maintained.* Nemesius would have been ahead of his age if he had discriminated between consciousness and the soul which is the subject of consciousness. Consequently he is in severe diffi-

[6] Discursive thinking (*logizesthai*) proceeds from the initiative and energy of the individual thinker, and emphasizes the self-subsistence of the soul. Intuitive apprehension (*noein*) is like an action of universal mind through the individual. The distinction is Plotinian.
[7] See passages cited by Domanski from Porphyry. (*op. cit.*, p. 66, Notes 1 and 2).
[8] The imaginary disputant argues that Nemesius has made the soul ubiquitous. He retorts that he has made it non-spatial. We may compare Nemesius' notion of the soul's indwelling in the body by habit of predilection with that of Theodore of Mopsuestia that God indwells in the righteous, not by omnipresence, but by his favour (*eudokia*).
[9] Domanski (*op. cit.*, pp. 67, 68) supposes that the opinion of Ammonius Saccas, invoked in Section 20 (or its development by a Neo-Platonist author), is in fact being followed to the end of this section.

culties to express the relation of the soul to locality. It is, of course, consciousness that is subject to location, in being so related to the body and its organs as to share in its subjection to the conditions of place and time. But as Nemesius could not distinguish consciousness of which the soul is the subject from the being of the soul itself, he was driven to attributing to the soul a natural predilection binding it to its body, as the only way to avoid attributing spatiality to the soul.

TEXT

[M. 137.4–144.10.]

22. The above arguments would apply even more exactly to the union of the divine Word with his manhood. For he continued thus in union, without confusion, and without being circumscribed, in a different manner from the soul. For the soul, being one of the things in process of completion, and because of its propriety to body, seems even in some way to suffer with it, sometimes mastering it, and sometimes being mastered by it.[1] But the divine Word suffers no alteration from the fellow-

---

[1] Christian doctrinal writers commonly reversed the argument comparing the union of soul and body in man with that of God and man in the incarnation, so as to use the former to persuade of the latter. Not till a century after Nemesius was it generally recognized that the argument in this form favoured a Monophysite conclusion, by suggesting that Christ's manhood was by nature akin with the uncreated Logos. Nemesius takes the argument the other way round, and starts with the Logos who, being by nature immutable, must be held to be unaffected in himself by taking manhood. At the end of Section 17, Nemesius is seen to incline to the belief that a soul, once for all in the beginning created by the Logos, comes into actuality when God grants conception of its predestined body. We must therefore suppose that, in the incarnation, the Logos united with himself the soul for which was predestined the body born of Mary. Because of this union, Jesus "increased in wisdom and stature, and in favour with God and man." But the Logos did not increase. When the body was slain, its union with the Logos delivered it from corruption and raised it to glory. Jesus learned obedience by the things which he suffered, his soul having the true nature of soul, and being affected by what he experienced in the body. The Logos did not suffer or learn, but only sustained and revealed. Such is the Christology of Nemesius. When he says that the Word *continued* in union with manhood *unconfusedly*, he anticipates two of the famous four adverbs by which the Symbol of Chalcedon, A.D. 451, defined the nature of the union. This is remarkable from a writer of fifty years earlier. Some scholars have thought it too remarkable for credit, and have preferred to date the work of Nemesius in the second half of the fifth century. On a balance of arguments, it is safer to conclude the adjectives "indivisibly, unconfusedly" to be what might be expected from an Antiochene.

ship which he has with the body and the soul. In sharing with
them his own Godhead, he does not partake their infirmity. He
is one with them, and yet he continues in that state in which he
was, before his entry into that union. This manner of mingling
or union is something quite new. The Word mingles with body
and soul, and yet remains throughout unmixed, unconfused,
uncorrupted, untransformed, not sharing their passivity but
only their activity, not perishing with them, nor changing as
they change; but, on the one hand, contributing to their
growth, and, on the other, nowise degraded by contact with
them, so that he continues immutable and unconfused, seeing
that he is altogether without share in any kind of alteration.
Here Porphyry, who often spoke against Christ, shall be a witness on our side. The witness that our enemies bear on our behalf is cogent and uncontradictable. This Porphyry, then, in
the second book of his *Miscellaneous Questions*, writes, word for
word, as follows: "So, then, it may not be denied that any being
is liable to be assumed as complement to another being. It can
be part of a being, while preserving its own proper nature after
it has afforded completion to the other being, both becoming
one with the other, and continuing one in itself; and, what is
more, without suffering any change itself, it may, by its presence, transform those things in which it is, into the means of its
own activity."[2] Porphyry uses these words in discussing the
union of soul and body. If the incorporeity of the soul, then,
justifies this argument, much more does it apply in the case of
the divine Word, who is incomparably and truly incorporeal.
Porphyry's words clearly close the mouths of those who would
argue against the possibility of the union of God with man.
Average Greeks, however, scoff at it, saying that it is impossible,
incredible, and improper, that the divine should be joined to
mortal nature by way of mingling and union. To rebut their
charge, we appeal, then, to their own most approved witnesses.

Now there are some, and particularly among the Eunomians,[3] who say that the divine Word was united to the body, not

2 The work here cited is not otherwise extant. By "the thing assumed,"
Porphyry means the soul, which, by its activities, affects the body, of
which it is the complement.
3 The information here given about the Christology of Eunomius is unique
to this passage. Eunomius held the Logos to be a creature. But, to judge
from what Nemesius here says, he did not, like the earlier Arians, suppose the Logos to take the place of the soul in the body of Christ. Neither,
apparently, did he speak explicitly of the soul of Jesus, but only of the
faculties and senses belonging to the body taken by the Logos. Nemesius

by union of being, but by the uniting of the powers of either nature, and that it is not the being of the Word and of body that are united, or combined, but the powers of the body were infused with divine powers; and, by the powers of the body, regarded altogether as an organism, they mean the senses, just as Aristotle does.[4] According to them, therefore, the divine powers mingled themselves with the senses, and thus completed a union of Word and senses. I do not think that anyone would concur in their opinion, which represents the senses as identical with the faculties of the body. For it has been clearly defined above,[5] how that some things are proper to the body, some to the soul, and some are the property of both in common. Among the things common to both, and although they operate through organs, we placed the senses, while we said that the organs themselves belong to the body. It were better, then, to repeat what we said before, that, having regard to the nature proper to the incorporeal, the union of soul and body involves no confusion of one with the other; so that the more spiritual being is not impaired by the inferior being, but the latter only is profited by the more spiritual, seeing that the purely incorporeal nature

accuses Eunomius of confusing together the senses and faculties. He makes this out to be a too faithful following of Aristotle. But that is more ingenious than ingenuous, because Eunomius' reliance on dialectic was a well-known target for orthodox polemics, and the present passage offered another opportunity to insinuate that Eunomians were Aristotelians rather than Christians. The charge of confusing the faculties and senses is made the opportunity for Nemesius to draw a distinction between them. The senses are passive, while the faculties are active. Therefore, Nemesius held, in the union of the divine Word with manhood, all sense-experience and suffering of Christ reached no farther than the soul of Jesus, and did not touch the impassible Logos. On the other hand, the Logos could, and did, supply superhuman power to the faculties of his body of incarnation. We gather that Eunomius, whose Logos was not immutable and impassible in his proper nature, but only by grace of the Father, conceived that the Logos, to fulfil the Father's will, was reached by the things suffered through the senses, so as to endure while imparting endurance to the body. The fault of Eunomius is clearly in trying to unite senses and faculties into one system with no soul to hold them together. The rationalism of Eunomius, regardless of doctrinal tradition within the Church, did not incline him to reticence with regard to his own doctrine, and so freed Nemesius from reticence in refuting him. The phrase translated "by union of being" became a standard phrase of orthodox Christology in the fifth century, so that Eunomius' avoidance of it is a count against him.

[4] This is no more just to Aristotle than the former charge of explaining away, by the concept of entelechy, the substantiality of the soul.

[5] Nemesius may have in mind the opening of Section 7.

both spreads without obstruction through every part, and suffers no invasion, itself. And so union takes place, on the one hand, by the soul's power of pervading the body throughout, and, on the other, by the soul's immunity from invasion, whereby it continues unmixed and unconfused.

The manner of union is, therefore, not by divine favour,[6] as is the opinion of certain men of note, but is grounded in nature. For one might, very properly, say that the taking of a body was an act of divine favour, but that the unconfused union is a proper work of the divine nature, and not of divine favour, alone. For the doctrine of the different orders of souls, with their ascending and descending, which Origen introduced,[7] has

[6] Theodore, bishop of Mopsuestia, 392–428, would appear to have written his book, *On the incarnation* (sarcastically referred to by Leontius of Byzantium as *Against the incarnation*), while still a presbyter at Antioch. In this work he followed a long tradition of Antiochene theology in abhorring the use of expressions attributing circumscription to God, in incarnation. Theodore argued that, while the evil cannot escape from divine omnipresence, it is only the holy who enjoy communion with him. On this analogy, Theodore attempted to explain the incarnation as a communion of Jesus with the Word. This communion he held to have been unique, by the unique degree of divine favour, as it were, "concentrated" upon Jesus, such as to overcome all otherness of Jesus, in relation to the Word. Such communion, Theodore held, constituted union. But Nemesius sees that Theodore's argument is based upon a negation, namely, that God is such as could not unite himself with man. Nemesius retorts that it is because of what God is, that is, because of God's nature, that the paradox of incarnation is credible. The recently-discovered later works of Theodore show him following a line much closer to that of Nemesius than he followed in his notorious work of youth.

[7] The leap, which Nemesius here makes, to attacking Origen, might appear, though deceptively, to break connection with what he had been saying about the opinion of Theodore (his use of an anonymous plural need not make us suppose that he has anyone else in view but Theodore). That he should desire to refute Origen is the more natural, since Origen became the object of formal condemnation at Alexandria in A.D. 399, and at Rome in the following year. In fact, his obvious interest in refuting Origen, when it appears that he made great use of Origen's lost Commentary on Genesis, may indicate that he did not write *earlier* than A.D. 400. The particular subject of condemnation was Origen's doctrine of the pre-existence of souls. Part of this doctrine was the teaching that the soul of Christ alone had been in unfailing obedience to God from the very moment of creation of the intelligible world, and was therefore made the "own" of the Word, and predestined to be the means of his incarnation. Nemesius here implies that the doctrine of Theodore really involves the same notion of Jesus as had been propounded by Origen, and so was in danger of sharing the Origenist taint. Part of the score against Origen may have been the interest aroused by his speculations outside the Church.

nothing to warrant it in the Holy Scriptures, nor does it fit harmoniously with the rest of Christian dogma, and so is unacceptable.

COMMENTARY

22. *The union of soul and body illustrated from Christology*. In this section, Nemesius uses the exposition of an orthodox Antiochene Christology, and a refutation of Eunomian Christology, to illustrate and confirm what he has said about the union of soul and body. Seeing that in this very chapter he had alluded to the possibility that some of his readers may not acknowledge the authority of Scripture, it might be thought remarkable that Nemesius should show so little reticence on the subject of Christian doctrine as he does in this Section. It must be recognized, however, that a great change had taken place in regard to such matters, since the first half of the fourth century, especially in regard to the dogma of the incarnation. The doctrinal controversies concerning the nature and Person of Christ had removed the possibility of keeping all knowledge of such subjects from the non-Christian public, especially in a country like Syria, where the two elements in society had now for long mingled on easier terms than in the west. Moreover these controversies had taken a form so public and political as even to lead to open breaches of the peace, so that it was out of the question but that those outside the Church must have an idea of the issues on which Christians disagreed. Nemesius accordingly supposes that unbaptized readers will have some idea what he means when he speaks of the union of the divine Word with his manhood. The argument runs; "If the *Logos*, being God, could unite manhood to himself without yielding anything of his Godhead, there is no reason to doubt that soul can be in unconfused union with body." Logically, this argument should be without force for anyone who rejected Christianity. But the attitude of the public for which Nemesius wrote was not one of convinced rejection of Christianity. And this limited expedition into Christology conveys the suggestion that Christians have a consistent system of thought in which the problems of the nature of man find their true solution. This is good apologetic, especially when reinforced by the appeal to Porphyry, the representative of Neo-Platonism, the non-Christian system of thought that was intellectually the most respectable. Incidentally, Nemesius' handling of Christology, slight as it is, is acute and independent enough to be of some importance for the history of Christian doctrine.

[M. 145.1–150.4.]

IV. *Of the Body*

TEXT

23. Every body is a mingling together of the four elements, and was evolved from them. Immediately, however, the bodies of living creatures which have blood consist of the four humours, blood, phlegm, choler, and black bile.[1] Bloodless animals have the other three humours and what in them corresponds with blood. We say "immediately" when the thing is made of those constituents directly, in the way that the four humours are a mingling of the four elements, and that the different kinds of tissue which form the different members of the body are a mingling of the humours. So the humours can be compared, black bile with earth, phlegm with water, blood with air, and choler with fire. Every mingling of the elements is either solid, liquid, or gaseous. Aristotle would have the bodies of living creatures to be made directly of blood alone, since it is immediately by blood that all the members of an animal body are nourished and made to grow. Certainly semen is derived from blood. But, as it did not seem likely that the hardest bones, and tenderest flesh, and fat, all derived from one and the same thing, Hippocrates first preferred[2] the view that animal bodies are compounded immediately from the four humours, so that the more rigid parts are formed of the more earthy and coarse of them, and the soft parts of the more refined. Often, all four humours are found in the blood, as may be seen during phlebotomy. Sometimes serous phlegm is predominant, and, at others, black bile or choler. From this it appears how far men are uniform in constitution.[3] Some parts of living creatures are

---

[1] See Section 15. Note 3.

[2] i.e., in the controversy here canvassed, Hippocrates (fifth century) was the first to deal with the question, Aristotle resuming it in the fourth century B.C. Skard shows (*l.c.*) that this argument to reconcile Aristotle and Hippocrates, is Galenic. He will not credit Nemesius with resuming it from his own wide reading in Galen, and in Aristotle's *History of Animals*, but prefers the alternative of a lost work of Galen which Nemesius has followed slavishly. This estimate of Nemesius is too unfavourable to escape suspicion of prejudice.

[3] Nemesius has, no doubt, here reproduced an observation of Galen, whose notes of the results of many phlebotomies supported the conclusion, made by him in a medical interest, of the great uniformity of the physical constitution of man. Nemesius notes it, presumably, because it helps to universalize ethics.

20—C.J.

of one kind of tissue throughout, and some are of different kinds. Of the first kind are brain, membrane, sinew, marrow, bone, tooth, cartilage, glands, ligaments, films, fibres, hair, nails, flesh, veins, arteries, ducts, fat, or skin. And what might be called the immediate constituents of these are blood (in its pure state), phlegm, black bile, and choler. For muscle is composite of ligaments and fibrous sinews. And the parts composite of various tissues are the head, chest, hands, feet, and man's other members. For, when a head is divided up, the divisions are not heads, in the way that a sinew divided up gives portions of sinew, and so with vein or flesh. Every part composite of different tissues has components each of one kind of tissue; for example, the head is made up of sinew, flesh, bone, and so on. These composite parts are also termed organic.[4] The definition of homogenous parts is as follows: parts, of which, if they are subdivided, each subdivision is like the whole, and like the others: like, in this definition, is to be taken in the sense of identical.

Not every kind of living creature possesses every kind of corporeal member, but some such members may be absent. There are things with no feet, such as fishes or snakes, and some with no heads, like crabs and lobsters, or certain floating creatures. For these creatures, as they have no heads, keep their organs of perception in their breasts. Creatures that do not breathe air, have no lung. Some creatures have no bladder, as birds and all creatures that do not urinate. Things with thick shells lack most members, for in few of them is there the reality of a living creature. Some creatures appear to lack something that, in fact, they possess, like stags, which appear to have no choler, though they do possess choler, but dispersed through the entrails, and consequently not observable.

But man not only has all the members, but has them perfect, and such that they could not be changed for the better.

So, too, there is great variety among living creatures as to the positions of the different parts. Some animals have their teats on their breasts, other on their bellies, and others under their thighs. Some have two, some four, and some more. For Nature

---

[4] The English use is to distinguish as organs those members of the body that appear devoted to a specific function. A member which is recognizable as a unity serving certain purposes, such as head or foot, is not called by us an organ. But in Greek it was so called. Therefore each composite structure recognized as possessing this kind of functional unity was classed as organic.

generally makes the number of teats correspond with the number of young produced at a birth. Should the reader wish to pursue this subject in detail, let him read Aristotle's *History of Animals*.[5] It is no part of the purpose of this present book to go into such detail, but only to put before the reader outlines or sketches,[6] as one may call them. So let us pass on to discuss the elements, which is the matter next due for our examination.

COMMENTARY

23. *Man's body, in the light of comparative anatomy and physiology.* The point of this section, for Nemesius, is the emphasis which it lays upon the pre-eminence of the human body, as an instrument for the living of a creaturely life. For his use of Galen in this section, see Skard (*Nemesiosstudien* III, *Symbolae Osloenses*, Fasc. XVIII, pp. 31–39).

[M. 150.5–160.6.]

V. *Of the elements*

TEXT

24. The basic matter[1] of the universe plays the least direct[2]

---

[5] History is here used in the sense which we now particularize as natural history, which consists, in fact, of description and classification, rather than narrative.

[6] It has militated against the reputation of Nemesius for originality as a thinker that his so-called "outlines" on scientific and philosophical matters are so plainly reached by skimming books. His originality is, of course, not as a scientist or philosopher, but as a Christian, possessing some training in medicine and philosophy, in trying to integrate faith with the outlook of an educated man, in the secular sense.

[1] The ancients postulated a single first-principle of materiality, undifferentiated, and unexperienced by the senses. Known to the senses are the elements and the bodies which they go to form. The relation of these to the primal matter was the subject of a special theory which Nemesius passes by. Jaeger suggests that at this point Nemesius is drawing upon the work of Galen entitled *On the elements according to Hippocrates*. Skard (*l.c.*) likewise attributes to the influence of this work the sequence of ch. v upon ch. IV.

[2] Literally "the least" or "the last." Whereas bodies are seen to be composed of bones, flesh, fat, and the like, these in turn derive from the four humours by which they are built up in the process of growth and nourishment. The humours in turn consist of the four elements, which are the forms under which the basic matter of the universe is manifest. This basic matter thus lies at the end of a progressive analysis of the composition of the body, and so the opening sentence of this section is carrying on the

part in the composition of bodies. There are four material elements, earth, water, air, and fire,[3] to mention them in ascending order of activity, and by comparison with other bodies they are corporeal in a primary and simple sense. For every element is homogenous in all portions of itself. And while the basic matter is not thus homogenous with the elements deriving from it, each element is homogenous throughout itself. Now it is clear that earth, water, air, and fire are the elements, because in them appear the root-qualities,[4] both potentially and actively. Yet we never meet with any perceptible portion of any of these elements pure and without any other element mixed with it. For they have all to some slight extent suffered adulteration, and are mixed with each other in greater or less degree. But even in such a mixture the nature of each element declares itself. Each of the elements has two linked qualities which determine its characteristic form. For earth is dry and cold, water cold and wet, air (as concerns its proper nature)[5], moist and warm, and fire hot and dry. Now these qualities cannot possibly be themselves elements. For it is out of the question to constitute bodies out of incorporeal qualities, and it is likewise impossible for any other bodies but the four elements also to be elements, since they have not the corresponding quality in its radical form and active state. For otherwise there would be an indefinite number of elements, since any of the root-qualities is possessed in greater or less degree by everything that exists, so as to afford no criterion of what is relatively an element. It follows of necessity that that is an element which is corporeal and simple in its corporeity, possessing actively in addition the root-qualities, to

thought of the previous chapter. Jaeger (*op. cit.*, p. 71) must surely be wrong when he takes "the least part in the composition of bodies" to be a definition of the basic matter.

[3] The four elements first appear in a poem, *Nature*, by the Sicilian aristocrat Empedocles, of the mid-fifth century, B.C. From this start, the four-element theory underwent progressive elaboration down to the age of the Neo-Platonists.

[4] The theory of four root-qualities, hot, cold, moist, and dry, seems to be prior to the four-element theory, for the qualities, hot, wet, and dry seem to pick out fire, water, and earth respectively as corresponding elements. To these three, air is an obvious fourth.

[5] Air fitted with difficulty into the scheme, since it possesses its qualities, moist and warm, in no absolute degree. Its yieldingness offered an explanation of this, however, and the connection of air, warmth, and moisture with life might invest air with a distinction suited to an element. But the ancients were content that no other substances or qualities could compete with the accepted groups of four.

wit, hot, cold, moist, and dry. For these are the only qualities
that permeate things and change them radically. None of the
other qualities does so. For take the colour white. If you apply
it to a body, it does not transfuse it with whiteness, in the way
that heat makes it hot and cold chills it. And the like is true of
any of the other qualities.

The elements are mutually opposed, in the sense that one has
a pair of root-qualities while another has the opposite pair. For
example, water is opposed to fire, as a thing that is cold and wet
opposed to another that is hot and dry; or earth which is opposed to air as the cold and dry to the hot and moist. And as
these opposites could not be in union if no intermediary had
been ordained as a bond to bind them together, the Creator
ordained water as a mean between earth and air, which are
opposites, and gave it two qualities, namely cold and wet,
wherewith it might take part with the opposed extremes and
bind them together. For, as being cold, it is adapted to earth,
and in being moist it is at one with air. Again, as a mean
between water and fire, these also being opposites, God ordained
air, adapted to water, as being moist, and to fire by being warm.
And in such wise he united the opposed elements one to other
by means of appropriate intermediaries, which unite the opposites by binding together both themselves and the elements
they are connecting. For there is no better kind of bond than
that.[6]

So, then, God united each element to the element beneath it,
in respect to one of its root-qualities, and to the element above
it in respect to the other. For example, water is cold and wet,
but its coldness unites it to earth which is below it in the scale,
while its wetness unites it with air which is above it. In like
manner air is united with water below it by moistness, and with
fire above it by heat. And while fire is united with air below it
by heat, if we break off and turn back to the bottom of the scale,
then, by dryness, it is united with earth: and so earth also is
united by coldness with water, but, by retorsion of the scale,[7] it

6 We may conclude that it was an accepted philosophical dogma that there
can be no improving upon Nature. There seems, however, to be an allusion, here, to the closing sentence of a citation from the *Timaeus* in the
next section.

7 Nemesius imagines a vertical rectilinear scale, measuring subtlety,
mobility, and activity, with earth at the bottom and fire at the top. To
get direct relations between these two extremes, he converts his scale
from rectilinear into cyclic by the image of bending round a straight line
until it forms a circle.

is united with fire by dryness. For, in a manner of speaking, God bent back and turned round the ends of the scale (I mean fire and earth) to meet in full circle, so that the elements should be related not merely to the one above and the one below in a scale of higher and lower, but in a circular relation.[8] For when fire loses its heat but not its dryness it becomes earth. This is to be seen from thunderbolts, because, in a thunderbolt the fire, as it comes down to earth, is cooled off from excessive heat and solidifies into stone. Therefore every thunderbolt ends up as something between stone and brimstone. Brimstone is in fact a sort of frozen fire. It is not any longer actively hot, although it is potentially so, while, in fact as well as in potentiality, it is dry. Only the elements have the root-qualities in active form, while everything other than the elements has them only potentially,[9] unless it be but little removed from consisting of a single element. For the Creator in his wisdom devised that, lest the elements or the bodies made up of elements should ever by any means fail, the elements should be convertible both into one another and into composite bodies, and that composite bodies should be resolvable into elements again. And so, by process of perpetual transformations, they are kept continually in being. For earth, churned into mud, turns to water, and conversely water, thickening to mud, turns to earth, while when heated it vaporizes into air, and air, condensed and congealed, returns to water. When air, on the other hand, is parched dry, it turns to fire, while fire has but to be quenched and lose its dryness to vaporize. For air is both quenched fire and warmed and vaporized water. So, then, it is clear from these two facts that air is begotten of heat. For when water is warmed and when fire is quenched the common product is air. Thus according to its own proper nature air is hot, but cools in proximity to water and earth. So the lower atmosphere adjoining the earth is cold, while the upper air, which is nearest to the celestial fire, is hot. Now this variation is due to the softness and yieldingness of air, whereby it easily deviates from its natural state and is transformed. Aristotle says that there are two kinds of air, one vaporous and generated from the evaporation of water, and the

---

[8] Soot would count as earth. But more spectacular is the instance of the "thunderbolt" (meteorite), beloved of the meteorologists, including Posidonius.

[9] Wood, or sulphur, in being inflammable, has the potentiality of heat, but only reaches the actuality when transformed into fire by burning. Seawater would exemplify a near-element, being not pure water, but actively wet.

other fumy and produced by extinguishing fire. It is the latter
kind, he says, that is hot, while the vaporous air is also warm
when it is generated, but soon it cools, bit by bit, and progressively turns back into water. He was driven to the hypothesis
that there are two kinds of air[10] by the fact that things very high
up and far removed from the earth's surface appear to be colder,
as well as by the need to escape from certain other absurdities.[11]

All bodies, whether of plants or animals, originate from the
coming together of the four elements, and for the making of
these bodies Nature assembles the elements in their purest
form. Aristotle calls these bodies physical bodies[12] because they
are not made by conglomeration of matter but by all the elements being mingled throughout into the closest unity, so as to
make the body one particular thing in itself and different from
its constituent elements. This union of elements is such that
there is afterwards no way of distinguishing them apart, since
earth does not appear as such, nor water, nor air, nor fire,
because, by the coming together of the four, there has been
formed a particular unity differing from any one of the components and comparable with the fourfold prescription.[13] For,
in the case of the fourfold prescription, the medicament itself is
something quite different from any of the ingredients.

However, the cases are not quite the same. For the elements
are not mingled in bodies in the same way as the ingredients are
mingled in the medicament, by the juxtaposition everywhere of
very tiny particles of each ingredient. They are united by a
process of transformation. And bodies in corruption are resolved
again into their elements. And in this wise the universe endures
perpetually, and exactly suffices to bring to birth all existing
things, with nothing to spare and nothing to seek. Hence the
saying, "One thing is born, another dies; one thing dies,

10 *On generation and corruption*, Bk. II, ch. IV, Section 9. The reasons to which
Nemesius alludes are not in the text of Aristotle, but were those accumulated in the commentaries.
11 Aristotle's theory explained snow on mountain tops as due to water-
produced air, though the fire-produced upper air might be hot.
12 In contrast with bodies made by art or accident, plant and animal bodies
are constituted as such by the operation of nature. Aristotle's general
definition of a body as such is "something that extends in each dimension,
and is indefinitely divisible." It is in contrast with this that Aristotle is
said to have a separate definition of a physical, i.e., an organic body.
13 The concoction called *par excellence* "the prescription" was a mixture of
wax, tallow, pitch and resin. K. Reinhardt (*Kosmos und Sympathie*,
pp. 10–20, Munich, 1926) says that the prescription was often invoked
by Stoic writers in illustration of the union of constituents in a body.

another is born," applicable not only to the soul, as it was said above,[14] but to the body as well.

COMMENTARY

24. *Every body is constituted from an indestructible cycle of four elements.* Nemesius begins this section by summarizing the received four-element theory of the material universe. The reader must naturally wonder why, in a work on the nature of man, it should be necessary to digress so far. But, as has been said, we must seek the answer in a little tract of Hippocrates, *On the nature of man,* which can be almost reconstructed with the help of a commentary which Galen composed upon it (Berlin *Corpus Medicorum Graecorum,* Vol. v, 9.1), and an elaboration of it which he wrote, under the title of *On the elements, according to Hippocrates.* (Edition by G. Helmreich, Erlangen, 1878.) In this tract Hippocrates argues that the art of the physician is based upon the fact that man's body consists of permanently differing constituents, the maladjustments of which express themselves in suffering, for which there would be no occasion in a body that was everywhere formed of one single element. In Section 26, towards the close of the present chapter, Nemesius cites two sentences in which Hippocrates summarizes his refutation of the theory that all material existence is based on one ultimate form of matter. We can attribute to this Hippocratic theme the greatest influence on Nemesius. It gave him his cue for relating man's sufferings, and indeed all his sensible experience, to the constitution of his body. And this thought is so central to his treatment of the nature of man that he adopted, for his work, the same title as that of the tract of Hippocrates; and his aim is continually to interpret the conscious life of the soul in the light of what can be known of the human body. This whole chapter is the subject of a chapter in Jaeger (*op. cit.,* pp. 68–96, of which 68–77 cover the present section) entitled "the cycle of the elements," in which he shows how Nemesius reproduces the

14 The allusion is to the later part of Section 18, where the various beliefs were reviewed concerning the transmigration of souls. They all assume that, as a soul leaves one body by death, it passes into another body that is in the act of being conceived. And the Neo-Platonists drew the conclusion that soul is indestructible. It is unlikely that Nemesius believed in transmigration of souls in any form, but, on the other hand, he believed in the indestructibility of the soul. As an apologist, he accepts the support of the Neo-Platonists in this matter, without reference to the grounds on which they based it. And now he recalls it, as affording a parallel to the doctrine of the indestructibility of matter, which he has just enunciated.

world-view of Posidonius. The relation to Galen of this and the next two sections is discussed by Skard (*l.c.* pp. 39–41). The apologetic value of this discourse on the elements lies in Nemesius' Christian sense of the goodness and wisdom of God underlying the intricate pattern of material existence. And this value resides rather in the faith of the apologist than in the finality of the human science to which he makes appeal. He can leave it an open question whether there are two kinds of air, as Aristotle says, or only one, provided that, as far as human knowledge goes, it conforms with the good purposes of God towards us.

TEXT

[M. 160.6–166.4.]

25. The opinion of Plato is that three of the elements are transformable one into other, but that earth remains untransformable. For he likens each element to a rectilinear solid figure, comparing earth to the cube, as being the hardest of them to overturn, while he compares water to the icosahedron as being the steadiest of the remaining three. He likens fire to a pyramid,[1] as being the easiest to overturn, and air to the octahedron, because air is more mobile than water but less so than fire. From consideration of these shapes he deduces his proof that the three other elements are mutually transformable, one into other, but that earth resists transformation. He says that the three shapes, pyramid, octahedron, and icosahedron are constructed from scalene triangles, but the cube from isosceles triangles.[2] He asserts, therefore, that these shapes which are constructed from scalene triangles can be broken down and reconstructed as one of the others, but that, if a cube is broken

---

[1] There seems to be a pun in likening fire (*pyr*) to a pyramid, and some of the ancients derived pyramid from *pyr*. It is now thought that pyramid is derived from an Egyptian word. But it is possible that Plato saw some mystic fitness in the pyramidal shape, to be the symbol of fire. He certainly connected the shape with the sharpness of fire, saying, in *Timaeus*, xxi, "that which has the fewest bases must be the most cutting and keen," and, in the following chapter, speaking of earth as dissolved by the keenness of fire.

[2] Any triangle is reducible to two rectangular triangles by dropping a perpendicular from the apex to the base. If the triangle is equilateral, the rectangular triangles will be isosceles, and if otherwise they will be scalene. The triangles involved in a cube are rectangular isosceles triangles. For Plato's other figures the corresponding triangles would be scalene. This difference enabled Plato, through his ingenious, if fanciful, speculation on the solid regular shapes, to give a reason for the different behaviour of solids from that of water, fire, or air.

down, the parts cannot be put together again so as to make one of the other three figures, since it is constructed from isosceles triangles, from which it is impossible to build up any of the other three shapes. Conversely, none of the three, when broken down, can be built up into a cube. Of necessity, therefore, the bodies whose form corresponds with these shapes are related to one another in the same way that the shapes are related.[3] Meanwhile earth was not supposed by Plato to remain impervious, but to be penetrated by bodies of finer texture and thus regenerated,[4] though by no means transformed into the thing by which it is pervaded. For it is presently restored to its proper state, as appears when we put it into water. For if one throws a little earth into water and stirs it up, the earth dissolves into the water. But when stirring ceases and the water becomes still, the earth is precipitated. And that shows us how to think of earth in general.[5] Here there is no transformation, but mingling, which in due course separates out again. Plato also says that earth is broken up by the sharpness of fire, and when so dissipated is carried up in flame, or in a gust of air (that is, if it chances that air dissipates it) or in water (when it has been dissolved in water).

Another way to distinguish between the elements, Plato says, is that each element has three qualities. Fire has sharpness, fineness, and mobility. Earth, the other extreme among the elements, has the opposite qualities to those of fire, namely dullness, close texture, and immobility, so that, in respect of their qualities, fire and earth are opposites; a result that we did not get from the pairs of qualities under the other scheme.[6] Plato says that by taking qualities from these two extremes we get the middle elements. For, take two qualities of fire, fineness and mobility, and one quality of earth, dullness, and air is constituted, which receives its form by having the three qualities of

---

[3] Plato supposed the elements to consist of corpuscles so tiny as to be invisible, but that these corpuscles accumulated in such numbers as to form sensible quantities of the corresponding element. Each corpuscle he supposed to have the shape of the solid body to which the element is compared. And he explained the behaviour of the elements in bulk as due to the shapes of the corpuscles.

[4] The idea, here, is probably that soil is made fertile, when soaked with water, that iron is tempered by being heated, that the body is dependent on breathing air, and so on.

[5] Note the difference of this theory and that of the liquefaction of earth in Section 24.

[6] In Section 24 it is water and fire that are opposed.

dullness, fineness and mobility. Again, take two qualities of earth, dullness and close texture, and from fire the single quality of mobility, and there you have water, which receives its form by having dullness, close texture and mobility.

As sharpness is to dullness, so is fire to air, and as fineness is to close texture, so is air to water, and as motion is to stillness, so is water to earth. So, to be sure, air is to water as fire is to air, and water is to earth as air is to water. For it is the way of plain figures to be related by a single dimension, that is to say, by simple proportion, while, for comparison of solid figures, two dimensions are needed.

Another way of describing the qualities of elements is to say that earth and water are heavy, so as naturally to fall, and air and fire are light, so as naturally to rise. The Stoic phrase is that some elements are active and others passive. Aristotle, however, introduces a fifth corporeal element which is ethereal and rotatory, because he will not have heaven to consist of the four mundane elements.[7] He calls his fifth element rotatory because it moves in a circle round the earth. But Plato asserts explicitly that the heaven is made of fire and earth. For Plato says[8] thus: "Anything that has come into being must be corporeal, visible, and tangible. Nothing is visible unless fire is present. Nothing is tangible without solidity. Nothing is solid but there is earth in it. Therefore in setting out to make the body of the universe, God formed it of earth and fire. But two things cannot be well combined without a third thing to bind them together, for, if they are both to be joined, there must be a bond. Now the best of bonds is one that makes itself and the things it unites as complete a unity as possible. Proportion[9] is the thing best fitted to accomplish this."

So Plato designates as bond the two elements selected as middle terms in the above-mentioned scale.

COMMENTARY

25. *The Platonic theory of the elements.* Section 24 having outlined the Empedoclean theory of the elements as developed by Aristotle, Nemesius now gives an outline of the Platonic theory, from chs. xx–xxii of the *Timaeus*, and ends the section with a considerable citation from the opening of ch. vii. Jaeger (*op. cit.*,

7 Aristotle, *On the world*, ch. ii, adopting the theory of Anaxagoras.
8 The citation is from the opening of *Timaeus*, vii.
9 i.e., a mean must have obvious relation to the terms it connects.

pp. 77–96) argues that Nemesius' direct source is the lost Commentary of Posidonius on the *Timaeus*, and not, as Krause thought, Porphyry's Commentary. The point is not important for the understanding of Nemesius.

Nemesius seems, on the whole, to side with Plato against Aristotle, particularly on the matter of the fifth element. But his interest in scientific theories and their differences is clearly subsidiary to his apologetic interest in putting science to the task of illuminating human values. On this the controversy over Aristotle and Plato has little bearing. Two things may seem to move Nemesius to prefer Plato's theory. It enhances the wonder of creation, and, in teaching that earth remains itself through all its relations with the other elements, it offers a parallel to the doctrine that the soul preserves its own nature through all its union with the body.

TEXT

[M. 166.4–171.6.]

26. Those who favour the doctrines of the Jews[1] take a different line concerning the heaven and the earth from those we have been considering. For almost all others[2] . . . The first-mentioned persons, on the other hand, say that the heaven and the earth were not made from any pre-existing matter, since Moses says, "In the beginning, God made the heaven and the earth."[3] Apollinarius, however, will have it that it was out of the deep that God made the heaven and the earth, seeing that in his account of the world's creation Moses made no mention of the coming into being of the deep. Nevertheless in Job[4] we have, "Who made the deep." So Apollinarius will have it that it was from the deep as pre-existing matter that all the other things were made. He does not say, certainly, that the deep is uncreated, but that it is something that came into being as a

---

[1] This formula probably points to Origen's Commentary on Genesis, which, no doubt, discussed and defended the doctrine of creation *ex nihilo*.

[2] Although the manuscripts show no lacuna and the text is translatable, the sense indicates that something is missing. The "almost all others" are in contrast with the biblical and ecclesiastical writers, whose views nevertheless follow. What has dropped out, whether in MS transmission, or in (unrevised) draft, is that the "others" taught the eternity of matter.

[3] Gen. 1:1.

[4] This must be meant for a citation of Job 34:13, where the LXX has, not "the deep," but "what is under heaven" (presumably, "the earth"). There is no evidence of textual variation, and we must suppose that Apollinarius took it arbitrarily to mean "the deep."

first foundation laid down by the Creator before all corporeal creatures, to be the basis of all the rest. Further he says that the very name "the deep" points to the unknowableness of the primal matter.[5] But whether this is so or not, it makes no difference. For even if it be granted that the God of all things followed this order, he is shown to be God and Creator, and to have brought all things into being out of nothing. To those again who contend that there is a single ultimate element, whether it be fire, air, or water, the words of Hippocrates are sufficient answer, when he says, "If man were made of just one single thing he would never feel pain, for there would be nothing to give rise to pain if he were made of one thing only; while supposing that he were to feel pain, that one thing would cure it."[6] For there to be pain there must be perceptible change. But if there was only one basic stuff of the body, there would be nothing different into which it could change. And even if this

[5] This reference, unlike the earlier ones to opinions of Apollinarius, must be to some lost and unnamed work by the heresiarch or under his name. It might be by one of his more extreme followers. But the way in which it is here introduced suggests that Apollinarius had a great reputation in Syria as an exegete. We know from Jerome that Apollinarius was author of a vast number of Scripture commentaries. Accordingly we may suppose, with probability, that the reference in this passage is to his (lost) Commentary on Genesis. Dräseke (op. cit., p. 33) cites a passage from pseudo-Justin, Exhortation to the Greeks (which he vindicated as an apologetic work by Apollinarius), the sense of which comes very near to that which Nemesius attributes to Apollinarius. Neither passage amounts to a denial of creation ex nihilo.

[6] The citation is from an early part of the small work of Hippocrates entitled, On the nature of man, known to us through the fact that Galen appreciated it so highly as to write both a Commentary upon it and his work, On the elements according to Hippocrates, which, in the work, On the agreement of Hippocrates with Plato, Bk. vii, he describes as exegesis of Hippocrates, On the nature of man. This last work was a popular tract in defence of Hippocratean medical practice, with its developed pharmacology. Hippocrates had to overcome the view that blood, or some other one thing, underlay all health, so that, if anything went wrong with a man, it went wrong with all of him at once. Against this Hippocrates set forth his doctrine of the four humours, and their right balance in the constitution, with the practical aim of defending the use of a variety of remedies to correct disorder, according to its source. The bearing of his argument upon the theory of the elements is the concern, rather, of his commentators, first Galen, and then Nemesius. Nemesius is not citing from the Commentary, but from the other work (ch. iii, p. 15, Helmreich) which refers to the element theories of Thales, Anaximines, and Heraclitus in a passage (op. cit., p. 23) which Nemesius expands. The argument which follows the citation is summarized from Galen, who underlines the fact that pain always points to deficiency, excess, or bad tempering.

stuff were sensitive, nevertheless it would not feel pain if it never changed but always continued what it is. What suffers must of necessity have something that is causing it to suffer. But if man's constitution consisted of only one element, it would contain no quality at variance with the qualities of that one element. What would there be, then, to occasion suffering in such a living creature? And if it could neither undergo change or be affected by any suffering, how could it feel pain? So Hippocrates, when he had proved the impossibility that it should feel pain, made this concession, "supposing that he were to feel pain, that one thing would also cure it."[7] Now there is no one universal remedy for pain, but many remedies. Surely, therefore, man is not made of just one single thing.

Furthermore, with regard to the advocates of one basic element, the arguments with which each tries to establish his own opinion go rather to demonstrate that there are four elements. For Thales says that water is the sole element, and tries to prove that from it derive the other three elements, saying that earth is its sediment and air its vapour, while fire is a rarefaction of air. Then Anaximines says that air is the sole element. He too tries to show, from the same arguments, that the other elements are produced from air. Heraclitus and Hippasus the Metapontine,[8] in making fire the sole element, used exactly the same arguments to prove, as they also claim, that the other elements are begotten of fire. What they, and the advocates of water and air

[7] Galen, in the commentary, paraphrases thus: "If it be conceded that anything could suffer from itself, its cure would then be simple." i.e., that it should leave off making itself suffer.

[8] The MSS read Hipparchus. Jaeger (op. cit., pp. 94–6) shows that this misnaming of Hippasus in relation to this theme is so widespread that its origin must be long before Nemesius. He is thus encouraged to think of Posidonius, Commentary on the Timaeus, as at once the direct source for Nemesius and as the work in which the error first arose. For Thales and Heraclitus, see notes to Section 11.

Anaximines of Miletus, in the late sixth century B.C. taught that air is the primary element, and that all material substances are forms of it in varying degrees of condensation. We may see in such monist theories the keen desire of the primitive Greek thinkers to find a basic unity underlying the sensible universe.

Hippasus, of Metapontum in the "instep" of Italy, belongs to the same age, and was a member of the original Pythagorean discipleship. He moved, however, from Pythagorean orthodoxy in the direction of Heraclitus, with whom he is accordingly bracketed. He conceived of the soul as being corporeal and of an igneous nature, because the body is warm when alive, and becomes cold when the soul departs. Hipparchus, an astronomer of the second century B.C., is quite inappropriate for citation in this context.

respectively, do succeed thus in proving is that all the elements are transformable one into other. Now if they all turn one into other, it follows of necessity that they are all equally elements, since whichever of the four you take, it will be found that it, too, is derivable from one of the others. Now the body, as being the soul's instrument, has its various parts allotted to different faculties of the soul. For the body is well and aptly furnished to serve these faculties, lest any faculty of the soul should find the body a hindrance. For to each faculty of the soul there has been allotted its own portion of the body to be its means of action, as this book will show, as it proceeds. We may say that the soul has been given rank as craftsman while the body ranks as tool. The subject of craftsmanship is stuff, but the result is as the crafts-man makes it. (Suppose we liken the stuff to be worked upon to a woman; then what is done to it can be likened to adultery, or fornication, or honourable wedlock.)[9]

Now the faculties of the soul can be distinguished as imagina-tion, intellect, and memory, respectively.[10]

COMMENTARY

26. *The theory of elements concerns man in his body.* This section has all the appearance of an unrevised draft, containing great

[9] The argument of the last few sentences of the section is important and logically coherent. Stylistically it is grotesque. The most plausible solution is that we have here mere notes of the transition from the theory of the elements to discussion of the faculties of the soul, to which the saying of Hippocrates had pointed the way, and that an intended redraft never followed. The sentence before the bracket has troubled all translators. *Hyle* (here translated "stuff") is anarthrous, and in antithesis with "result." From the context, *praxis* must mean craftsman's work. The comment in brackets might be a gloss transferred to the text, and Matthaei, who calls it inept, would seem to take it so. But if we are right in taking the end of this section as a series of notes, we may conclude that it is a note for an argument, and by no means inept. The simile of the soul as a craftsman calls for qualification. The soul's work upon the "stuff" of corporeal life is not merely aesthetic. It is moral. The soul can be irresponsible and sinful in the use it makes of its instrument, and in its relations with it as body. The comment in the brackets is certainly to the point. But the manner of this conclusion to the section is certainly a possible indication that Nemesius died with his task unfinished.

[10] It transpires as we go along that Galen had localized these three faculties in the front, central and rear parts of the brain respectively. But he also saw that the ends of the sensory nerves joined the front of the brain. Nemesius' plan is therefore now first to deal with imagination, and show its close dependence upon the sense-organs, devoting a chapter to each of the five senses before completing this part of the investigation of the relations of soul and body by chapters on intellect and memory.

changes of idea without any attempt to smooth the transitions. First the ecclesiastic doctrine of creation *ex nihilo* is set out, in contrast with Greek philosophic ideas of a material substrate, formless and eternal, upon which God imprinted form. Next follows a very interesting note on Apollinarian exegesis, which indicates a road along which Apollinarius was able to approach so close to Gnostic dualism, and yet maintain a theoretical independence. This passage would be digression, were it not that it introduces the theme of a single substrate underlying the four elements as being one which is open to discussion, even on Christian presuppositions. This gives the cue for the really significant citation of the passage from Hippocrates, *On the nature of man.* Thence, by way of Galen's exegesis of this passage, Nemesius gains the conclusion that psychology and the elements are subjects in mutual relation. And the section ends with a scrappy indication of the way in which this mutual relation is to be developed. This will take place first under the heading of what Nemesius calls the three faculties of the soul, imagination, intellect, and memory. But it proves to be the case that, through the material structure of the brain and sense organs, these faculties all involve differences or changes in matter. So, the theory of the elements established, Nemesius turns next to the localization of faculties in bodily structures.

[M. 171.7–178.2.]

VI. *Of the faculty of imagination*

TEXT

27. Imagination,[1] to take the first of the three, is a faculty of the irrational[2] soul and acts by means of the sense-organs. A subject for imagination[3] is related to imagining in the same way that a sensible object is to perceiving. Imagining[4] is an affection of the irrational soul caused by some subject for imagination. An illusion[5] is an idle stirring of the irrational parts of the soul, in the absence of any subject for imagination.

[1] *To phantastikon*, imagination as a faculty.
[2] Nemesius will be found later to think of the irrational part of the soul as divisible into that which can be brought under rational control, and that which cannot. The seat of healthy imagination belongs to the former.   [3] *Phantaston.*
[4] *Phantasia*, a word in non-technical use. Stephanus gives meanings *visum, visio, impressio animi.* Nemesius' use, however, is clearly technical, for the process of making and relating mental images.
[5] *Phantasma*, phantom.

The Stoics use these four expressions, imagining, subject for imagination, imagination, and illusion, but they define imagining as that affection of the soul which both displays itself and points to the subject for imagination by which it is occasioned. For, suppose we see something white. The soul is affected in a particular way by receiving the impression of whiteness. And in just the same way that this sensation is aroused in the sense-organs when whiteness is perceived, the soul is affected when it thinks of whiteness; that is, by receiving within itself an image of what it thinks of. And they define a subject for imagination as something whereby the process of imagining is rendered perceptible. For example, something white, or anything else with a particular effect on the soul is subject for imagination. On the other hand they define imagination[6] as an idle mustering of images divorced from any subject for imagination. And they then define illusion as something that precipitates us into the idle mustering of images[7] in our imagination, but in the way that happens to people that have taken leave of their senses, or are suffering from an excess of black bile. Our difference from the Stoics is only that we make an interchange in the same set of terms.[8] Now, as organs, the faculty of imagination has, first, the front lobes of the brain and the psychic spirit[9] contained in them, then the nerves impregnated with psychic spirit that proceed from them, and, finally, the whole construction of the sense-organs. These organs of sense are five in number, but perception is one, and is an attribute of the soul.[10] By means of the sense-organs, and their power of feeling, the soul takes knowledge of what goes on in them. The soul perceives anything earthy by means of its most earthy and altogether bodily

6 *Phantastikon*, used adjectivally, and not as a noun, as above. The Stoics used it not very differently from the English "fantastic."
7 "Mustering of images," *helkusmos*; literally, a being carried away. It clearly concerns mental imagery, but such as is undeliberate, though not necessarily involuntary.
8 The interchange is in the Stoics making *phantastikon* mean what Nemesius means by *phantasma*. *Phantasma*, for the Stoics, becomes a pathological term.
9 With this sentence Nemesius returns to Galen from pseudo-Plutarch. Galen does not wholly free himself from the Stoic concept of corporeal soul pervading the body. He transforms it into this notion of psychic or intelligent "spirit" manifesting itself in parts of the organism, while being generated within the brain.
10 See Domanski, *op. cit.*, p. 95, Note 2. The probability seems to lie on the side of Siebeck, that the emphasis is the Neo-Platonist emphasis on the unity of the soul as the subject of perceptions.

sense-organ, that of touch. It perceives anything bright by means of its most brilliant sense, that of sight. Likewise it perceives the vibrations of the air with its airy sense-organ.[11] For air, or the vibration of air, is the basis of sound. Moreover, the soul apprehends flavours with its spongey and watery sense-organ, that of taste. For each object of perception is discerned by means of the sense-organ accommodated to it. If we follow this line of reasoning, therefore, seeing that there are four elements, there must be four kinds of perceiving, answering to the four elements.[12] But vapour, and the whole range of scents, has its nature intermediate between air and water, being grosser than air but more subtle than water (that this, or something like it, is the case is proved by the ailment known as a head-cold; for people with such colds inhale air in breathing but do not smell such scents as it bears, since, owing to the obstruction, the grosser portion of what they inhale never reaches perception). Therefore a fifth sense-organ, that of smell, has been invented by Nature for this reason, that nothing capable of being known should evade our perception.

Perceiving is not undergoing any change, but is the discerning of some change that is taking place.[13] For it is the organs of sense that experience the change, while perception merely discerns what is happening.

Nevertheless, the sense-organs are very often called by the name of the corresponding sense. Now sense-perception is the apprehension of sensible things. And yet this definition does not seem to define perception itself, so much as what it effects. And this is the reason that people have defined perception itself as an intelligent spirit reaching out from the soul's centre of authority to the sense-organs.[14] It has been defined, again, as the soul's power of apprehending sensible things, while a sense-organ is defined as an instrument for apprehending sensible things.

Plato calls sense-perception a co-operating of soul and body,[15] directed towards the external world. The faculty belongs to the

---

[11] i.e., the ear, in which the end of the sensory nerve is reached by the air, through the ear-passage.
[12] Since sight corresponds to fire, hearing to air, taste to water, and touch to earth. For this theory of the five senses, see *On the agreement of Hippocrates with Plato.*
[13] *Agreement*, VII. 6.
[14] In this sentence Nemesius, or Galen, comes as near as any ancient writer to recognizing consciousness as a fact distinct from the subjects of consciousness.
[15] *On the opinions of the philosophers*, IV. 8.

soul while a part of the body is the instrument. By means of imagining,[16] the two co-operate to apprehend external things. Now of the soul's faculties, some are like servants and attendants, while some resemble rulers and governors.[17] The faculties of thought and knowledge are of the ruler type, while those of perception, impulse and imagination[18] are of the servant type. For, with the greatest promptitude, and almost instantaneously, when movement is caused,[19] it takes place in obedience to the intentions of the mind. For we both will and move simultaneously and in the self-same moment, requiring no interval between intention and movement,[20] as anyone may see by moving his fingers. And some of the natural faculties are in subordination to the faculty of thought, and, in particular, those which we call the passions.

COMMENTARY

27. *How imagination starts at the soul and reaches to the four elements.* For the movement from ch. v to ch. vi see Skard, *Nemesiosstudien* III (*Symbolae Osloenses*, Fasc. XIX, pp. 46–7).

For this section, see Jaeger, *op. cit.* (Pt. I, ch. i, pp. 4–26), and Domanski, *op. cit.*, pp. 92–99 (ch. viii). Nemesius defines four terms relating to imagination. This is clearly in the Posidonian tradition, because it thinks of imagination as a faculty of the soul aiding and explaining human behaviour; and is likely, for this reason, to derive from a Neo-Platonic source. There follows a paragraph showing that the Stoics employ the same four words in a slightly different way from the Neo-Platonists. Domanski shows this fact to have been gathered by Nemesius from a passage in Bk. IV, ch. 12 of the work *On the opinions of the philosophers* commonly bearing the name of Plutarch. The great

---

16 The sense seems to be that soul translates sense-impression into mental images, and subjects these to the operations of mind, the apprehending of external things involving more than automatic reaction to sensation.

17 This image has a long history in Greek psychological tradition, and is represented most notably in the *Timaeus* of Plato.

18/19 At these two points the reading of Matthaei's best MS is preferred to the text which he prints, for reasons given by Domanski, *op. cit.*, p. 78, Note 2.

20 See Jaeger, *op. cit.*, p. 26. Nemesius is here reproducing, but in a changed sense, phrases from an argument of Galen against the Stoics, who thought that voice must have its impulses from the heart, since that organ is near. Galen replies that the nerves carry impulses instantaneously to any distance, so that nearness is not significant. Nemesius turns this immediacy of stimulus into an argument for the ascendency of the higher faculties over the lower.

difference between the Stoic use and that of Nemesius is that the Stoics contrasted imagination, as subjective, with sense-perception, as objective, while Nemesius thinks of imagination as having an indispensable function in the life of the rational living creature, man. The Stoic group can be attributed to Aetius. The Neo-Platonic source cannot be named.

From definition, Nemesius goes straight to the physiology of the faculty, which, he says, enjoys use of the brain and sense-organs. Here, his guide is certainly Galen, and Jaeger, *op. cit.* pp. 13, 14, gives parallels to most that is significant in Nemesius from Galen's work, *On the agreement of Hippocrates with Plato.* The rest he thinks to derive from the fundamental logical work of Galen, his fifteen books *On demonstration.* It contained much illustration from the medical field, and we have already seen that it was known to Nemesius.

In this section Nemesius makes three points, (i) that the material of imagination is derived from sense-impression, (ii) that the process of imagining, while answering to rational controls, is effected by the irrational part of the soul, (iii) that it is possible for it to be devoid of rational significance. In the course of the discussion, starting from the soul as possessor of the faculty, we are led by a continuous path to the four elements as determining the circumstances under which the work of imagination is done.

[M. 178.3–182.3.]

VII. *Of sight*

TEXT

28. The word sight is used in two senses, both for the mechanism of sight and the faculty of perception. Hipparchus[1] says that rays that extend from the eyes lay hold with their ends upon external bodies, as though grasping them with hands, and render them perceptible by the sense of sight. Mathematicians,[2] on the other hand, describe certain cones formed by the intersection of rays proceeding from the eyes. For the right eye sends

[1] The sentence is word for word from *On the opinions of the philosophers,* IV, 13. Hipparchus of Nicaea, *floruit,* 146–126 B.C., was an astronomer and is credited with the invention of trigonometry.

[2] It is not evident where Nemesius got this mathematical theory of vision, but it is much to the credit of his objectivity of approach to his subject that he includes this observation of the way in which the soul appears to be at the mercy of a mechanical circumstance of vision.

rays to the left, and the left eye sends rays to the right, and these, as they intersect, form a cone. It follows that, whereas sight can cover a large number of objects at the same time, it has precise vision only of what lies within the intersecting of the rays. So it often happens that, gazing at the ground, we fail to see the coin lying there that we are straining our eyes to the full to see, until rays from both eyes light upon that portion of ground where the coin is lying. Then we suddenly see it, as though at that moment we had just begun to take notice.

The Epicureans[3] say that images of things that we see impinge upon the eyes. But Aristotle[4] says that it is not a corporeal image, but something due to changes that take place in the surrounding air, starting from the things seen and ending with our sight. Plato explains sight by concurrence of rays,[5] the light from the eyes, on the one hand, flowing forth a certain distance into the air which is by nature akin to light, while on the other hand light is coming back from the visible objects, and extending through the intervening air, which is easily passed through and unresistant, to engage the fiery beams of sight. Galen, in his seventh book *On the agreement of Hippocrates with Plato*, also agrees with Plato in treating of sight, and makes the following observations gathered here and there from that work.[6]

"For if some portion or power or image or quality from the bodies that we are beholding entered in at our eyes, we should not know thereby the size of the object seen, even if it were, say, the hugest of mountains. For it is altogether against reason that the actual image of such an object should enter in at our eyes.[7] We must consider, surely, that the spirit of vision is not such that we can accord it the extraordinary strength to encompass everything that it beholds. It remains, therefore, that so long as we are using our eyes, the surrounding air constitutes an instrument of our vision, equally with the optic nerve in our own body. For the atmosphere is wont to serve any such purpose, since, whenever a sunbeam but kisses the uppermost air, it communicates the sun's power to the whole atmosphere. Yes, and the eye-gleam borne along the optic nerve, containing as it

3 The Epicurean theory is that objects keep emitting very thin films which correspond in shape and colour with the objects themselves and that perception follows from the impact of these on the organs of sight.
4 Cited from *Agreement*, VII, 7.
5 Cited from *On the opinions of the philosophers*, IV, 13.
6 For the way in which this passage is derived from Galen, see Domanski, *op. cit.*, pp. 101–2, Notes.
7 Thus Galen disposes of the Epicurean theory.

does the substance of the spirit of vision,[8] as it assails the surrounding air, works at the first onset a change, imparting itself to the full, and yet conserving itself till it strikes some answering body.[9] For the air, no less than the nerve from the brain, becomes the eye's instrument, to enable it to understand thoroughly the things it sees. Thus, as the brain is to the nerve, so is the eye to the air invigorated by sunlight. Inasmuch as the air is wont to assimilate itself to the bodies which it surrounds, it is plain that, given light, the air undergoes a change, in accordance with the quality passing through it,[10] according as the thing it comes from is red, blue, or glittering silver."

COMMENTARY

28. *The mechanics of sight.* In ch. vii, sight is taken, as the first of the five senses to which we have been introduced by considering the soul's faculty of imagination. It is put first, perhaps as being the most vivid sense, or because it offers the best evidence of the soul's vitality reaching out to the surrounding world through a sense. The chapter is in two sections. For Section 28, see Jaeger, *op. cit.*, pp. 27–30 and Domanski, *op. cit.*, pp. 99–102. The section is doxographic with the aim of showing the superiority of Galen's theory of vision to those of his precursors. It ends with a citation from Galen that trails off into a loose summary extracted out of three chapters. Galen recognizes an energy of the soul in looking, and conceives of a "spirit of vision" projected like a sunbeam into the air till it reaches its object of sight. No doubt the ancients, who credited the eye with so much power (as see their belief in "the evil eye"), were moved by the sensations of encountering gaze, directing the attention, and focusing upon an object, to feel that any purely mathematical theory of optics was insufficient.

---

[8] Since the "spirit of vision" is supposed to dart from the eye like a ray, it is comparable with a ray of sunlight. So the air is the connecting medium between sunlight, "eye-light," and the colour or gleam of objects, and somehow the soul is enabled to interpret visual impressions in terms of knowledge of surrounding things.

[9] This seems to express the sensation of focussing upon an object at moderate distance. It was taken to be a restraining of the ray of sight, as in the line of Herbert's hymn, "A man who looks on glass, on it may stay his eye."

[10] The puzzle was that colour seemed to be located in the coloured object. How could it get to the eye at a distance? Galen's answer is seen to be but a modified form of the Epicurean answer, in this respect.

TEXT

[M. 182.4–189.2.]

29. Porphyry, in his work *On sense-perception*,[1] says that neither a cone of vision, nor an image, nor anything else, is the cause of seeing, but the soul itself, which encounters the objects of sight and recognizes that it *is* what it sees, by virtue of the soul embracing all things that exist, and of all different kinds of bodies being simply all-embracing soul. For, as he will have it that there is one universal rational soul, he asserts accordingly that this soul recognizes itself in everything that exists.[2]

Vision operates along straight lines, and, in the first place, perceives colours. Along with the colour, it recognizes[3] the body so coloured, its size, its shape, relative position and distance away, together with the number of its parts, whether it

[1] No such separate work of Porphyry is otherwise known. It is probable that we have here the sub-title of one book of the five *On the soul, in answer to Boethius*, of which we read in Eusebius, Theodoret, and Suidas. Nothing of this work survives.

[2] This passage shows us that Porphyry had, in this work, developed a critique of the series of views resumed in Section 28, in that they all leave unanswered the question, How does the soul interpret what it receives through the senses? Domanski (p. 103, Note 1) cites Porphyry as saying that the soul "knows the principles of all things," so as to gather the significance of sense-impressions. But as Nemesius, from this passage on, withdraws from extreme Neo-Platonism, it is clear that the appeal to Porphyry here ends.

[3] We have here the first reference to *syndiaginōskein*, "knowing by co-ordination of perceptions." Jaeger develops the significance of this reference somewhat as follows: The dogma of Epicurus, that the senses are the sole avenue to truth, while error enters by way of opinion, challenged a closer consideration of those experiences in which the senses appear to tell us what is untrue. Among the Epicureans themselves there was already attention to such phenomena as the bent appearance of an oar in the water, or the round appearance of a distant square tower. Posidonius represents the early stage of the return to Plato, carrying with it an acceptance, again, of the fallibility of the senses. Posidonius also sought to reconcile the teaching of Aristotle with that of Plato. So the Aristotelian doctrine of a single perception operating through the several senses was now replaced by the doctrine that the soul co-ordinates and interprets the testimonies of the several senses. This is well represented in Galen's seventh book, *On the agreement of Hippocrates with Plato*, but not as fully as the theme is treated in Nemesius. In this book Galen refers to the fact that he has dealt more fully with these subjects in his work, *On demonstration*, and in its fifth book. This work was not primarily physiological, but concerned itself with the problem of knowledge. Jaeger concludes that this book is the source of the remainder of Section 29, after the Porphyry-citation.

is in motion or still, whether it is rough or smooth, even or uneven, sharp or blunt; as well as its constitution, whether, say,
it is watery or earthy, moist or dry. According to this view, the
special sense-object proper to sight is colour, since it is by sight
only that we apprehend colours.[4] But hard upon colour follows
perception of the body possessing the colour, the position in
which the thing seen may chance to be, and the space or distance between the person seeing and the object seen. For however many senses share in taking cognizance of a body, the first
thing they combine to recognize is its position; for example,
touch and taste,[5] though, except under circumstances to be
specified later,[6] these can only operate when the body they perceive is within reach. Sight, on the other hand, can operate also
from a distance. And since it receives its characteristic impression across an intervening space, it necessarily follows that
sight by itself can recognize the distance of its object, and, likewise, the size of its object, provided that the object can be
apprehended in a single glance. In those cases in which the
object is greater than can be apprehended in a single glance,
sight has to call upon the aid of memory and thought. For in
beholding the object piecemeal, and not as one whole, sight
must, of necessity, travel from one part to another, and the
object of perception, as the gaze travels, is always limited to
the part upon which the gaze is falling. But memory keeps
account of all that has been seen previously. Thought joins together the two elements, what is being perceived, and what was
previously perceived and is now retained in memory. Thus there
are two ways in which sight apprehends size, at one time unaided, and at another, with the co-operation of memory and
thought. As for a number of objects seen, when it exceeds
three or four, it is not taken in at a single glance, and as for
movements and the shapes of many-sided things, sight never

[4] The doctrine that colour is the peculiar subject of vision began with
Aristotle. Nemesius (or Galen) takes it as the basis for underlining the
partial character of this sense. It will be noticed that Nemesius is, in this
sentence, beginning to repeat what he has already said in the previous
two sentences, either as his own paraphrase of Galen, or as adding a
summing up to an introduction, both derived from Galen. The former is
perhaps the more probable, as intended to drive home the point that
each sense has its own limited *proprium* within which alone it is inerrant.
[5] The inclusion of taste here seems out of place, and the most probable
explanation is that Nemesius had before him a passage in which taste
was included with touch, but not in the context in which he has put them
together.
[6] i.e., where the range of touch is extended by using a staff.

apprehends these unaided, but always with the help of memory and thought. For one cannot count five, six, seven, or more objects, without calling in memory to help. Similarly, the eye cannot, by itself, recognize a hexagon, octagon, or polygon of a higher number of sides. Again when there is movement from place to place, the eye can take in start and finish. But if, to a first and second position, you add a third, only memory can keep count of it. Above and below, undulant or plane, as, likewise, rough or smooth, and sharp or blunt, are qualities open to perception equally by touch and sight, since these are the only senses which recognize situation.[7] But they employ thought as well.[8] For only an object that strikes a sense in one single impact is matter for unaided sense-perception. But things that make a multiple impact call, not for unaided sense-perception, but for the co-operation of memory and thought, as has been demonstrated above.

Sight is capable of penetrating transparent things to their very depth; first and principally the air, for that it penetrates without limit; and secondly water, when it is still and clear. For we actually see the fishes swimming in it. In lesser degree, it sees through glass, and other similar substances. Clearly this all requires light to be shining through the media. And that is the scope peculiar to sight.

But let no one be deceived into thinking that sight can perceive temperature,[9] because when we see fire, we know at once that it is hot. For if you were to carry your mind back to that point, you would discover that, then, when your eyes first beheld fire, they apprehended only the colour and shape of fire. But when touch joined in, we learned that it is hot, as well; a fact, gathered from the sense of touch, which memory retained. It follows that whenever we see fire now, we see only the shape and colour of fire. But by the action of memory thought adds the apprehension of heat to what we see.

The same thing takes place in seeing an apple. For if an apple makes itself known to us, not only by shape and colour but by scent and flavour, as well, sight surely has no apprehension of these latter qualities, to know that the object is an

7 This shows that the inclusion of taste above (see Note 5) was not deliberate. The statement fails to recognize the power of hearing and smell to locate an object of sense. In its bearing upon the inclusion of taste, above, it provides another sign of the unrevised state of the draft.

8 Thought directs these senses how to investigate their object.

9 Jaeger regards this passage as bearing the hall-mark of Galen's treatise of logic and philosophy, the work *On demonstration*.

apple. The soul, however, retains a memory, alike of the smell and the taste, and in the very act of seeing the apple, it associates these qualities with the shape and the colour. When, then, we suppose a wax apple to be a real apple, it is not sight that errs, but thought. For sight was not at fault, as regards its own sense-powers, since it registered shape and colour. There are then three senses, sight, hearing, and smell, that, with the air as intermediary, apprehend external objects out of actual contact. Taste does not operate except it can engage its object. Touch works by both methods, either in direct contact with bodies, or indirectly, for example, by means of a rod.

Sight, then, sometimes needs the confirmation afforded by other senses, for instance, when the object has been deliberately devised to deceive sight, as is the case with a picture. For the aim of painting is to deceive sight, it may be by reliefs and hollows that have no real existence, if the subject lends itself to perspective. Therefore, to detect a planned illusion, there is need of touch, in the first place, and, in some cases, also of taste and smell, as in that of the wax apple. At other times sight, acting by itself, represents its objects clearly so long as they are not far distant, and then sees as round, if seen a long way off,[10] what is actually a square tower. Sight errs again when we look through mist or smoke[11] or things of that sort that obscure vision. Looking through troubled water is similar. When one looks at an oar in the sea it appears broken. Similar things happen on looking through some transparent substance, as looking into mirrors,[12] or glass,[13] or anything else of that description, or at an object violently agitated.[14] For swift motion throws vision out, so as to see as round, things that are not round, and as still, things that are rotating.[15] Vision is thrown out, also, when the mind is preoccupied, as when someone sets out to meet a friend, meets him, and walks right past him, because his thoughts are on other matters. But this is not really a failure of sight so much as of mind. For sight saw and gave notice, but mind would not attend to the notice given.

---

[10] This was a classical example of aberration on the part of sight, arising without the intervention of external causes.

[11] The mention of smoke is perhaps prompted by the distortion of visual shapes caused by hot air rising from a fire.

[12] i.e., in a mirror, left and right are reversed.

[13] In glass and crystal, refraction takes place.

[14] A defined shape, when in such motion, is extended into the appearance of a blurred surface.

[15] The reference would appear to be to a spinning top.

Sight needs four chief conditions for clear discernment, unimpaired organs, measured motion, moderate distance, and the
air clear and light.[16]

<h3>COMMENTARY</h3>

29. *The soul co-ordinates and interprets perception.* (For this section, see Jaeger, *op. cit.*, pp. 30–53; Domanski, *op. cit.*, pp.
103–107.) Nemesius has now reviewed the physics of sight, its
physiology, mechanics, and geometry, and turns, in this section,
to the psychology of the senses, as illustrated by this sense. He
goes straight to the problem of the relationship between the
personal subject and external objects maintained through the
senses, and its solution according to Neo-Platonist idealism as
represented by Porphyry and his master Plotinus. But having
cited Porphyry, he draws back to the intermediate standpoint
of Galen, which acknowledges the responsibility of the soul for
making the best use it can of a team of servants (the five senses)
of whom none is infallible or all-competent. The discussion of
the subject at this level was, Jaeger thinks, to be sought in
Galen's lost work, *On demonstration*, which Galen himself
regarded as his most fundamental work. And Jaeger gives to this
section an added importance as being the best surviving evidence
of the character of Galen's lost masterpiece.

[M. 189.3–195.7.]

<h2>VIII. *Of feeling, or the sense of touch*</h2>

<h3>TEXT</h3>

30. The Creator devised each of the other sense-organs to be
dual, and located each of them in a certain place and portion
of the body; for he gave us a pair of eyes, a pair of ears, and
two nostrils for smelling. Also, in every living creature he
implanted two tongues.[1] In some creatures, for example,

---

[16] Thus, in the sense of sight, the soul has a servant liable to accidental
frustration. The soul cannot therefore trust itself to sense unreservedly,
as the Epicureans advocated.

[1] This dictum shows a surprisingly advanced knowledge of comparative
anatomy, outstripping Galen. There is unmistakable dependence upon
Galen in the opening sentences of this chapter. The dual character of the
sense-organs, and its relation to the nerves running from the two forward
lobes of the brain is treated by Galen in Bk. 8, ch. 10, *On the use of the
parts of the body.* In Bk. 9, ch. 8, the tongue, as organ of taste, equally with
the eyes, ears, and nostrils, is noted as being served by dual sensory

snakes, the two tongues separate, and in others, as is the case
with men, the two are joined up and made one. For this reason
he made there to be two ventricles in the front, only, of the
brain, so that the sensory nerves running from each ventricle
should constitute the sense-organs in pairs. It was of his abundant care[2] that he made them in pairs, so that if either were
affected, the other would be there to preserve that particular
sense. Yes, and even if a living creature lose most of the sense-
organs, it is no fatal detriment to life itself. But when feeling
goes, the living creature also perishes. Feeling, moreover, is
the only sense shared by all kinds of living creatures.[3] For every

nerves. Galen describes a dissection of the tongue, leading to a view of
the tongue as a dual organ, in his work, *On anatomical manipulations*, ch. 10.
In Bk. 10, ch. 10 of *On the use of the parts*, Galen says, "The tongues of
certain creatures, as, for example, snakes, are split in two, but in men
(since it would be of no advantage to man to have the tongue split,
either for eating or for speech) for good reason its parts are united, and
come together into the same organ." Galen, no doubt, supposed that
snakes got some advantage from their split tongue. He may have followed
Aristotle, *On the parts of animals*, Bk. 2, ch. 17, and supposed the snake to
have the advantage of a doubled enjoyment of taste. Actually, however,
the tongue of a snake is an organ of smell, rather than of taste. The ends
of the flickering tongue, questing in the air, pick up scent molecules, and
are then thrust into cavities in the roof of the mouth. The sensory nerves
running from these cavities to the brain carry the report of what the
tongue found in the air.

The independence of Nemesius relatively to Galen may be seen as
follows. Galen reaches the dual character of the human tongue by dissection, and thinks of the snake's tongue as split. His view of either is
teleological. Nemesius accepts what Galen gives, but has a view that is
genetic. There are two tongues, until and in so far as they are joined into
one. The magnificent generalization that thus appears in Nemesius must
have been reached by embryological studies. Galen was weak on embryology. Nemesius must therefore join to his knowledge derived from
Galen other knowledge derived from a source otherwise unknown to us.
And we must conclude that, on medical questions, Nemesius carries in
his own head information beyond what he found in the pages of his
favourite author. His debt, here, may be to the advanced anatomical
knowledge of the Alexandrine school of surgery. It is accordingly a false
estimate of our author that makes him just a stringer-together of copied
pieces.

2 The care of Nature for living creatures is a constant theme with Galen,
who sees in it a proof of the Creator's wisdom. Nemesius gives the thought
a Christian tone by attributing care to the Creator himself. Chrysostom
frequently finds proof of God's care in the order of Nature. We may
wonder how much Nemesius was responsible for establishing this theme
in the thought of Christian Syria.

3 This is an Aristotelian maxim. It may, nevertheless, have reached Nemesius by way of the pages of Galen.

living creature has feeling but, of the other senses, all creatures have not the full number. Some creatures have only some of them. The more developed creatures have them all. Since, therefore, a living creature would be in jeopardy, whether it should be or not be a living creature, in this matter of feeling, the Creator did not allot sensitiveness to one restricted part of the body, but spread the power of feeling over almost all the living creature's body. For, if we except bones, horns, nails, gristle, hair, and some other things of the same kind, every part of the body shares in feeling. It is the way with the sense-organs, therefore, to exercise two kinds of perception, one kind that is peculiar to itself, and the other in feeling. We may see this in regard to the eye. For it discerns colours, but also shares in feeling heat and cold. This last it does simply as part of the sensitive body, while it discerns colours as the organ of sight. The case is similar with regard to taste, smell, and hearing. But if we say that perceptions are mediated by the front ventricles of the brain, how, it must then be asked, is feeling maintained all over the body? It should be clear that consciousness of feeling is due to nerves proceeding from the brain, and spreading into every part of the body. And seeing that it often happens that, if a thorn pricks one's foot, the hairs of one's head immediately stand on end, some have deduced that the pain, or feeling of pain, is carried up to the brain, and so perceived. But if that argument were correct, it would not be the part pierced that smarted, but the brain. We should do better to say that the sensory nerve *is* brain. For, in a sense, it clearly forms part of the brain, as it has the vital spirit throughout itself, much after the manner that red-hot iron has fire throughout itself.[4] Therefore, wherever a sensory nerve may lie, that part of the body derives feeling from it, and is rendered sensitive. And there would be no impropriety in saying that what goes up to the head of the sensory nerve, and so to the brain, is not the sensation itself, but a certain consciousness and report of the sensation.

Objects of perception proper to feeling are such as are hot, cold, soft, hard, slippery, rough, heavy, and light; these things are recognized by feeling only. Feeling and sight have some common objects; as things sharp and blunt, rough and smooth,

---

4 Galen thought of the "vital spirit" as "distilled" in the front lobes of the brain. His largely Stoic background is responsible for this simile, meant to explain how the powers of the soul are exercised throughout the body, through "vital spirit" being "conducted" along the nerves.

dry and wet, thick and thin, above and below. For position
also can be the object of feeling; and size, if it is such as can be
comprehended by one application of touch; so can closeness
and looseness of texture, roundness (provided the object be
small) and various other shapes. In like manner, also, feeling,
with the aid of memory and thought, can perceive a body
moving in contact with it. It can perceive, also, number, but
only up to two or three objects, and then conditionally upon
their being small and easily taken hold of. But sight is more
effective than touch, for these objects, as is the case with things
level and undulant, for that is a variation of smooth and rough.
Undulant combined with hardness makes roughness, while
evenness and close texture makes smoothness. It is clear, then,
from what we have said, that the senses work in with one another
a great deal. For one sense shows up the errors of another; for
example, in a picture the eye sees certain things as though they
projected; let us say, a nose, or other things of that description.
But when touch is brought to bear on these things, it convicts
sight of error.

Again, as sight always operates with the air as its medium,
so likewise touch can use an intermediary, to wit, a staff, to
discriminate between hard, soft, and liquid; though this is
an excogitated discernment, involving thought. For this
kind of perception belongs in the highest degree to man, who,
indeed, has feeling and taste in higher degree than any other
living creature. He is, however, behind them in the other three
senses. For one animal excels man as regards one of these three
senses, and another animal in another, but a dog excels him
in all three at once. For a dog hears, sees, and smells more
keenly than a man, as can be seen when hounds are on a
scent.

Now the whole body, as we said before, is a single sense-
organ for feeling, but this applies in special degree to the inner
surfaces of the hands, and even more to the finger-tips. In
finger-tips we have, as one might say, exact arbiters of feeling.
For the Creator devised hands, not only as instruments for
taking hold of things, but also as the organ of touch. Therefore
human hands have the tenderest skin, while all over them,
muscle spreads under the skin. And so that they may be the
more sensitive to touch, they have no hair on them. Again,
the reason that no hair grows on them is the muscle that
spreads underneath. The harder the hand, the stronger its
grip. The softer the hand, the more delicate its feeling. So, too,

hard sinews⁵ are the better suited for imparting motion, while
soft nerve is the more sensitive. For nerves constitute the organ
of the sense of touch, since it is through them that sensitivity
of feeling is exercised.

COMMENTARY

30. *The sense of touch, and sensations of temperature and pain.*
In enumerating the five senses, it is usual to name the last as the
sense of touch. The heading of this chapter might, accordingly,
be rendered *On Touch*, were it not that the content of the chapter
shows that Nemesius regarded pain, and sensitiveness to
temperature, as within the scope of what he thinks of as the
distributed sense, by contrast with the senses located in circumscribed sense-organs. In this, as in the theme which runs
through chs. VI–XIII, that the body is the instrument of powers
exercised by the soul, Nemesius is, no doubt, reproducing the
thought of Galen. For this section, see Domanski, *op. cit.*,
107–110. In the interests of apologetic, Nemesius opens the
section with a reference to divine providence, which the reader
is left to keep in mind, and apply for himself, through chs.
VIII–XI.

[M. 195. 8–200. 3.]

IX. *Of Taste*

TEXT

31. We say that sight operates along straight lines leading from
visible objects. In smell and hearing, perception is not limited
to a straight line, but is from all directions. Touch and taste
discover their objects neither along a straight line, nor from
anywhere, but only when their own appropriate objects of
perception make contact with them, except in the cases already
noted.¹ Taste apprehends from juices. Its organ is the tongue,
and particularly its tip; but reinforced by the palate, through
which spread nerves from the brain, carrying to the consciousness of the subject that apprehension of taste that is taking

⁵ The same word, neuron, means a sinew and a nerve. Physicians distinguished them as hard *neura* (sinews) and soft *neura* (nerves). Nemesius
means that sinew is to nerve as a labourer's brawny fist is to a craftsman's
delicate hand. He concludes that the sense-organ of feeling is the whole
nervous system; a conclusion derived from Galen.
¹ The only case mentioned seems to be that of extending touch by use of
a staff.

place. Now, of juices, the different tastes, as we call them, are sweet, sharp, tart, astringent, sour, bitter, salt, and oily. These are the things which taste discriminates. By comparison with these qualities, water is said to be tasteless, in that it makes none of these impressions upon the sense of taste. By comparison with qualities of another kind, however, such as being cold and wet, water has its own proper quality.[2] Astringent differs from sour in drawing up the mouth more sharply. Those that have been named are practically all the simple tastes, but they are blended in a thousand different flavours. Every kind of animal and herb has its own particular flavour. There is one taste of pork, for example, and another of goats-flesh, so that we can recognize, by the flavour, the kind of meat that we are offered, without being told. Such a thing would not be possible, if everything that we taste had not a particular flavour of its own. No one, therefore, could name all these several flavours, since they are numberless, and yet quite different from each other. Even in those flavours in which one of the elemental tastes predominates, the difference of individuality of the flavours can be discerned. In dried figs, raisins, and dates, the one predominant quality of taste is sweetness. Nevertheless, the palate can distinguish their several flavours.

X. *Of Hearing*

Text

The sense of hearing perceives sounds and noises, and distinguishes high notes from low, and soft from discordant and loud. The organ of hearing consists of the soft[3] aural nerves from the brain, and the structure of the ears, especially the gristly portion, since gristle is particularly suitable, in connection with noises and sounds.[4]

---

2 This expression seems to attempt to say that though water has not a specific taste, it has a refreshing character that is its own.

3 Anatomists still speak of "hard" and "soft" nerves, and the aural nerve is distinguished as soft, in contrast with the nerve serving the facial muscles which is hard. Thus the nomenclature by which the ancients distinguished nerves from sinews has transferred itself into the vocabulary of the neurologists.

4 This observation was no doubt suggested by the resemblance of sinews to the strings of a harp or lyre. Investigation of the structure of the middle and inner ear was so far advanced as to show that there was something resembling a minute musical instrument constructed of bones and cartilaginous membrane adjoining the end of the aural nerve.

Men and monkeys are the only creatures that do not move
their ears, while all other animals that have ears move them.[5]

XI. *Of Smell*

TEXT

Smelling is through the nostrils, but reaches the surface of
the front ventricles of the brain. These surfaces are naturally
most akin to vapours, and so readily apprehend vapours. For,
as we said before, each of the sense-organs apprehends its own
objects of perception through a certain kinship and aptness for
them. The brain does not send down a sensory nerve,[6] in the
case of the sense of smell, just as it does with the other senses.
For the surface of the brain itself fulfils the office of the sensory
nerves, and receives the giving forth of vapours. Now the most
general distinction of vapours is into fragrant and foul, with,
in between, what is neither fragrant nor foul. There is fragrance
from bodies in which the humours are concocted in exactly
the right way, an indifferent odour where the constitution is
average, and where it is inferior, or quite unsatisfactory,[7] there
is an offensive odour.

COMMENTARY

31. *The remaining three senses.* This section, which the MSS
break up into the three chs. IX, X, and XI, constitutes a somewhat perfunctory completion of the survey, begun in Section
28, of the senses, their organs, and their manner of working.
Nemesius is, for the most part, composing loose summaries of
information derived from Galen. Domanski, whose interest is
particularly in the relation of Nemesius to Aristotle, notes that
it is Aristotle's list of tastes that Nemesius reproduces (*op. cit.*,
p. 111, Note 3). He concludes his discussion of the contents of
this section (*op. cit.*, pp. 111–114) with the suggestion that

5 This observation is unmistakably from Galen, who appreciated the
physical nearness of monkeys to mankind. Aristotle noticed that men
are singular in not moving their ears, but made no mention of monkeys
in this connection.
6 Actually there is a system of olfactory nerves, but quite different from
any other part of the nervous system. The "threshold" where the sensory
nerve-end joins the brain has a separate character for each sense, and
the ancients were right in thinking the sense-organs severally adapted
to their field of sensation. Skard, *loc. cit.*, notes that Galen's work, *On the
organ of smell*, is Nemesius's source here.
7 Nemesius here reproduces an unusual telescoped word, *mēdolōs*, meaning
"not at all," which is a particular favourite of Galen.

Nemesius is weaving together the ideas of some commentary on Aristotle, *On the soul,* with those of Galen's *Agreement of Hippocrates with Plato,* as part of his general tendency to keep on the Aristotelian side of the Neo-Platonists. Skard, however (*Nemesiosstudien* IV, pp. 47–8), argues that the intermediary, wherever Nemesius draws upon Aristotelian matter, is some work of Galen. From the point of view of apologetic, in an age when the ascetic interest dominated Christianity, it is remarkable how completely Nemesius eschews the suggestion that the senses are dangerous to the soul. The reader might rather gather that they were created to minister to man's enjoyment as well as to guard his safety.

[M. 200. 4–207. 14.]

XII. *Of the faculty of intellect*

TEXT

32. As regards the faculty of imagination, its possibilities and organs, its subdivisions and what they have in common and wherein they differ, has been sufficiently, if summarily, treated,[1] to the best of my power. As regards the faculty of intellect, on the other hand, its subdivisions are judging, approving, refuting, and essaying, while it expresses itself in recognition of objects, in virtues, in various kinds of knowledge and the principles of the several arts, as well as in deliberation and choice.[2] It is this faculty, also, which divines the future for us through dreams, a form of prognostication which the Pythagoreans say is the only true form, following the Jews in this.[3] The organ of the faculty of intellect is the middle part of the brain and the vital spirit there contained.

1 In ch. VI above.
2 The method of analysis, here, closely parallel as it is to that in ch. VI, points us to Galen, *On demonstration.* That Nemesius should be so brief in his extract suggests that he did not find Galen altogether satisfying as to the range of the faculty of intellect. He turns at once to another source, for authority to say that there is knowledge that finds no place in Galen's diagram.
3 This sentence presents us with difficult problems. The assertion that the Pythagoreans recognized no prognostication otherwise than such as comes from dreams receives no support from elsewhere in doxography. But in Origen, *Against Celsus,* i. 15, we have the statement that "Numenius the Pythagorean" said that Hermippus credited Pythagoras with deriving his philosophy from the Jews. In the same work, iv. 51, Origen says that Numenius allegorized the Old Testament after the manner of Philo, an assertion which is confirmed by Porphyry (*Cave of the nymphs,*

XIII. *Of the faculty of memory*

TEXT

The faculty of memory is at once cause and storehouse of remembering and recollection. Memory, says Origen,[4] is an image left on the mind from perceiving something actually taking place. Plato calls memory the preserving of both impressions and notions.[5] For the soul apprehends sensible objects

ch. 10), when he refers to a philosophic allegory of Numenius based on the second half of the second verse in Genesis. And, as, early in the next chapter, Origen is cited by name, we have good reason for suspecting that Origen is the source from which this passage of Nemesius is drawn. We shall naturally think of the *Commentary on Genesis*, and particularly of the prophetic dream of Abraham in Gen. 15. The Church recognized dreams and prophetic inspiration as the only legitimate forms of prognostication, and so Origen might well be glad to claim the concurrence of "the Jews" (by which formula he commonly means Philo) and "the Pythagoreans" (having, quite probably, no ground for what he says beyond what he inferred from his reading in Numenius). Philo has a great deal to say about dreams. He recognizes that many dreams are not significant of anything but the waking preoccupations of the subject. But he holds that the soul, when freed by sleep from the harness of the body, found in dreams an outlet for its inherent power of prevision. Most dreams, however, consist of enigmatic symbolism which calls for inspired interpretation. No doubt Numenius took over what he learned from Philo; for, as cited by Eusebius, *Preparation for the Gospel*, xiv. 8. 2, Numenius refers to a saying of Carneades that significant dreams are as like to dreams without significance as real eggs are to wax eggs. It will be seen, however, that Nemesius fits Philo's idea of the power of prevision inherent in the soul into his whole theory of intellect, and makes prophetic dreaming a normal exercise of the faculty of intellect. Remembered dreams (like yawning) are an accompaniment of waking, when the soul is putting on its fleshly harness again. They consist of trains of images constructed by the same brain-processes that serve discursive thought. If one can interpret these images, Nemesius seems to think, they contain knowledge which the soul has had in the timeless and intelligible world that is its true home. Thus, in dreams, it is the faculty of intellect, according to Nemesius, that ministers a knowledge of the future; a thesis that takes on a strangely modern air if we turn to Mr. J. W. Dunne's *Experiment with time*, and his claim to have found that "the faculty of precognition is a normal characteristic of man's general relation to time" (p. 91, 6th edn.).

[4] Jaeger argues that this is not the Alexandrine Father but another Origen, a Neo-Platonist philosopher of the same period of whom we have some scanty information. But see Note 5.

[5] Ch. xiii falls into two halves, the second being clearly drawn from Galen, and this first half being a psychological discussion that has, as Jaeger says, a Neo-Platonist ring. He credits Porphyry with being the source of this argument, and yet finds himself speaking of the "Origenism" of

by means of the sense-organs, so as to form an opinion about
them. But intelligible things the soul grasps directly with the
mind, and thereby forms a notion. When, therefore, the soul
preserves an imprint of things either felt or thought, it is said
to remember. When Plato speaks of a notion in this connection
he probably means not a notion in the strict sense[6] but something thought out. For things of sense are the direct subject of
memory, but intelligible things contingently so, since a memory
of thoughts is brought about by the images which are their
prerequisite.[7] Of notions in the strict sense we can only have
memory if they have come to us by our learning them or hearing
of them. They are not matter for memory in themselves. For
the apprehension of intelligibles does not come from any prior
process of imagining, but either from learning or by intuitive
understanding.[8]

Again, when we are said to call to mind something we formerly saw, heard, or otherwise came to know (the word
"formerly" having reference to time past), it is clear that what
was recalled was something that came and went at a certain
point of time. Memory, then, is of things no longer present,
and it is certainly not caused by those past events them-

Nemesius. We know, from Origen's *Commentary on St. John's Gospel*
(Bk. xx, ch. 7) that he believed that souls bring into their embodied life
learning which they have received in their previous existence in the
intelligible world. He is thus sufficiently "Neo-Platonist" to have supplied
that tint to the passage of Nemesius that we have before us. The *Commentary on Genesis* must have drawn Origen so far on to the ground trodden
by Philo that a discussion of recollection of pre-natal knowledge may well
have found a place there. In our passage of Nemesius, however, there is
visible also the influence of Aristotelian dialectic, and there is a reference
to the Epicurean emphasis on "opinion" as the fruit of sense-impression.
And these things would suggest the influence on our author of Galen,
On demonstration. It is, in fact, the synthesis of different traditions which
Nemesius achieves in this passage which exhibits most favourably a
quality of his thinking.
6 The distinction which Nemesius here draws between *dianoēsis* (discursive
thinking) and *Hē kyriōs noēsis* (the instantaneous knowing of truth,
without discursive thinking, or "notion in the strict sense") is not found
in those terms elsewhere.
7 Thus, one does not remember beauty. What one does is to recall images
that are beautiful, together with, it may be, discursive thought expended
on analysis of these images, in quest of a concept of beauty.
8 We seem to have here a critique of Plato's *Philebo* with a view to making
Plato's use of *anamnēsis* (recollection) in connection with the ideas a
catachrestic use of the word, and to show that the way in which intuitive
understanding establishes itself as conscious knowledge is distinct from
recollection.

selves.[9] When memory has been interrupted by forgetting, and the faded memory is recreated, we name it recollection. Forgetting is a casting-off of memory, sometimes for ever, and sometimes for a certain time, after which comes recollection. There is, however, a different kind of recollection, where the forgetting is not of anything felt or thought, but a recollection is made proceeding from intuitive understanding; and by that we mean notions that are present in every man without having been learned, like the notion that there is a God. Plato says that we have such a recollection of the ideas. (What an idea is we shall say later on.)[10]

So, then, the faculty of imagination hands on to the faculty of intellect things that the senses have perceived, while the faculty of intellect (or discursive reason) receives them, passes judgement on them, and hands them on to the faculty of memory.

The organ of this faculty is the hinder part of the brain (called also cerebellum and hinder-brain)[11] and the vital spirit there contained. Now, if we make this assertion, that the senses have their sources and roots in the front ventricles of the brain, that those of the faculty of intellect are in the middle part of the brain, and that those of the faculty of memory are in the hinder brain, we are bound to offer demonstration that this is how these things work, lest we should appear to credit such an assertion without rational grounds. The most convincing proof is that derived from studying the activities of the various parts of the brain. If the front ventricles have suffered any kind

9 Objects of sense are the immediate cause of images in the mind. But this causality ends with the moments of sense-impression, and when memory revives such images, it owes nothing to fresh causality proceeding from the objects.

10 This promise is never fulfilled. It is no way obvious how it could fit in with the purpose of the work to return to this theme. The sentence in brackets may really belong to Galen, *On demonstration*. But the sentence is, in any case, another indication of the unrevised state of the draft.

11 With this sentence we return to Galen, in his character of medical writer, and to his work, *On the use of parts of the body* (see Section 30, Note 1). The word for hinder-brain (*pericranis*) is not found elsewhere in literature, and may be a term orally current among the physicians of Nemesius' time and country. It is an indication that Nemesius does not hang entirely upon Galen's books, but that, rather, his deep interest in the subject of the human body had made him so earnest a reader of Galen. Modern studies have shown that, while accident to the cerebellum has the effect that Galen says it has, his conclusion that memory can be so strictly localized is unjustified. Memory depends upon the concerted action of different parts of the brain.

of lesion,[12] the senses are impaired but the faculty of intellect continues as before. It is when the middle of the brain is affected that the mind is deranged, but then the senses are left in possession of their natural functions. If the front ventricles and the middle of the brain are affected together, both thought and sensation break down. If it is the cerebellum that is damaged, only loss of memory follows, while sensation and thought take no harm. But if the middle of the brain and the cerebellum share in the damage, in addition to the front ventricles, sensation, thought, and memory all founder together, with the result that the living subject is in danger of death. Apart from lesions, these facts are in evidence in several other maladies and accidents, particularly inflammation of the brain. For we meet with patients suffering from that disease whose senses all work, and only their mind is deranged. Galen describes such a case,[13] of a man suffering from inflammation of the brain who was in a room, with a weaver working there. This man started up and took hold of some glass vessels, and running to a window he demanded of the passers-by whether they would like him to throw down such and such a glass vessel, naming each correctly. When some stopped and said that they would, he first threw the vessels down, one by one, and then asked those who were there whether they would like the weaver thrown down. Some of them, taking the whole thing for a joke, said, Yes. The man thereupon took and pushed the weaver out, and down he went!

Now this man's actual senses were in perfect order, for he could distinguish the glass vessels, on the one hand, and the weaver, on the other. What was deranged was his mind.

There are other cases where people fancy things that are not there, and think that they see things that in fact they do not, while being otherwise quite rational. These are people with lesions of the front ventricles only, while the middle part of their brains remain unaffected.

The working of any and every part of the organism is impaired by whatever ills affect it. For the living subject is the worse as regards the activity for which the affected part

---

[12] These observations on lesion seem to bespeak an extensive experience of head-wounds. Gladatorial fighting may have given Galen his opportunities, during his residence in Rome, from which he also gathered the non-traumatic "case" that follows.

[13] Domanski, *op. cit.*, Note 3 to p. 90, gives the passage from Galen, *On parts affected*, iv. i.

was naturally fitted; anyone with a bad foot, for example, can only limp, since walking is the foot's work.[14]

32. *The mechanism of mind and its supernatural aspects.* The two chapters forming this section are intimately bound together in subject-matter, as they are with ch. VI, and complete the programme announced at the end of ch. v. For the contents of the section we have studies by Jaeger, *op. cit.*, pp. 54–67 (Pt. I, ch. iii) and Domanski, *op. cit.*, pp. 80–92 (reviews of the two chapters).

While these two chapters are hardly more than very condensed notes strung together, the argument is both important and profound. The key to the argument is the fact that Nemesius, who no doubt accepts the condemnation of Origen, is so far Origenist as to believe in a modified pre-existence of souls, and to attach to that belief a modified form of the Platonic doctrine that souls possess a recollection of things they learned in the intelligible world before they were united to bodies. He does not reject the Platonic doctrine of ideas, though he shows no special interest in it. What he is interested in, and thinks the soul has brought with it into this world, is the intuitive understanding of a number of fundamental notions, which he calls "notions strictly so called," and instances the notion of there being a God.

In contradistinction to these notions is the body of knowledge and thoughts built up by discursive thinking (*dianoia*). The faculty of intellect is concerned with both the one and the other. The notions become the conscious possession of the living subject by the action of this faculty, the subject sometimes reaching this consciousness unaided, but often helped to do so by communications received from others; though the authority of such notions does not lie in the fact that all men agree in them. It is a supernatural authority, due to their being implanted in the soul itself. The faculty of intellect is simply the channel through which they come to embody themselves as conscious elements of thought (*noēseis*).

The more general activity of the faculty of intellect is to use the threefold instrument of the brain to carry on the process of

14 To Nemesius' chapter this is a lame ending. But on Galen's page it figured as a determined insistence that students shall view mental malady in strict analogy to the affections that impair the use of other parts of the body.

discursive thinking. Thereby the soul becomes possessed of
growing empirical knowledge through contact with the external world and with society. All activities of the faculty of
intellect unite for the one end of furnishing the soul with the
knowledge which it needs for the fulfilling of its destiny.

[M. 208.1–210.7.]

XIV. *Of thought and expression*

TEXT

33. The above, then, is one way of analysing our psychology,
namely, in respect to its correspondence with certain parts of
the body. With regard to the rational part of the soul, another
and different analysis may be applied, dividing it into what we
may term pure thought, and expression. Pure thought is a
motion of the soul that takes place in the rational mind, without
any kind of utterance, whereby it often happens that, in complete silence, we deal exhaustively with a whole subject in our
minds. In dreams, also, we discourse.[1] It is particularly in respect of this inward motion of the soul that we are all rational
creatures. It is more so, in this, than in our powers of expression.
For people who were born dumb, or those who have been
rendered voiceless by accident or disease, are, none the less for
that, rational. The activity of rational expression is by means of
the voice, and of some form of language. The organs of voice
itself are complex. There are first the intercostal muscles and
the whole chest. Then there are the lungs, the windpipe, and
the larynx, and of these particularly the cartilaginous part. The
vocal cords,[2] the glottis, and all the muscles that move these
parts, are the organs of vociferation. On the other hand, the
mouth is the organ of articulation, since, by the mouth,
language is (metaphorically speaking) moulded, fashioned, and
shaped. Comparing speech with a harp, tongue and uvula play
the part of the plectrum, and the roof of the mouth that of

---

1 Again we have expression of Nemesius' remarkable conviction that we,
and not some external agent, are the makers of our dreams.
2 Literally, "the sinews that run back." With the construction of a laryngo-
scope, the vocal cords could be observed closing together in vocalization,
and retracting when vocalization ceased. "Retracting sinews" is a more
accurate and scientific description than "vocal cords." As the end of this
chapter indicates, early thought about vocalization was dominated by
comparison with a stringed instrument. Skard, *Nemesiosstudien* IV, p. 49,
notes that Galen claims to have coined the term "retracting sinews."

sounding-board, while the teeth, and the extent to which the mouth is opened, fulfil the part played by the strings. To some extent, the nose contributes to pleasant or disagreeable utterance, as is evident with those that sing.

COMMENTARY

33. *How rational mind finds expression.* In the foregoing chapters, Nemesius has expounded how the brain works. He was here following Galen, expressing the results of Greek medical science at its most advanced. In ch. xiv, he turns back to something much more ancient, the Stoic psychology of introspection. The foundation of this was the recognition that what sense a man talks depends on what sense he has in his head. So a distinction was drawn between the faculty of rational thought, as it resides within the rational creature, containing indefinite potentiality, and the art of giving ordered and purposeful expression to what is in the mind. The chief part of the art of expression is language. And at this point the medical interests of Nemesius gain the upper hand again. There is the practitioner's observation that where speech has ceased to be possible, or even where it has never been possible, evidence can be seen of the presence of rational mind, on a par with that of the more fortunate. Finally, there is the anatomist's interest in the mechanics of speech.

[M. 211.1–213.9.]

XV. *A further way of dividing the soul*

TEXT

34. Some divide the soul in another way, into its faculties, forms, or parts, namely into the vegetative (also called self-nourishing and sensitive), perceptive, and rational. What are the organs of each of these parts is either already told,[1] or will be described later on. Zeno the Stoic[2] says that the soul has

1 The organs that have been dealt with are those of sense, thought, and expression. In chs. xxv–xxviii will be treated the organs of the bodily vital processes.
2 Zeno, a native of Cyprus, born 336 B.C., founded the school of philosophy at Athens which took its name from the *Stoa*, or Pictured Porch, where he lectured. He combined principles derived from Heraclitus with the Socratic tradition prevailing at Athens. The soul, according to the Stoics, extends spatially through the whole body. Seated in the sense-organs, it exercises its five faculties of sense, while it has a "directing part" generally thought of as seated in the heart. For this doxography, see *On the opinions of the philosophers*, IV. 4.

eight parts, and divides it into the directing mind, the five senses, the faculty of speech, and the generative powers. The philosopher Panaetius,[3] on the other hand, would say that the power of speech belongs to impulse, a most clear-sighted distinction,[4] and that the generative powers are not part of the soul at all, but are Nature working in us.[5] Aristotle asserts,[6] in his *Physics*,[7] that the soul has five parts, vegetative, perceptive, locomotor, appetitive, and intellectual. He says that the vegetative part is responsible for nutrition, growth, and procreation, and for the fashioning of our bodies. He calls the vegetative faculty also the nutritive, as naming the whole faculty from its most important function, that is, nutrition, on which the other functions of the vegetative faculty all depend. That, I say, is

[3] Panaetius, 180–108 B.C., Stoic philosopher from Rhodes, was the first to introduce Stoic philosophy to the west, when he went to Rome in company with Scipio. He was later head of the Stoic school at Athens, while his pupil Posidonius continued to influence the west, especially through Cicero and Seneca.

[4] The reason that Nemesius approves of the advance of Panaetius on the opinion of Zeno on the faculty of speech is that he regards impulse, like imagination, as something that belongs to the soul at both the rational and the irrational level. Speech is not automatic but voluntary, and so is a particular, highly rational, application of impulse.

[5] This opinion commends itself to Nemesius because he is, in regard to the nature of the soul, a creationist and not a traducianist. If the generative function is no part of the soul, the traducianist has not a leg to stand on.

[6] Domanski, *op. cit.*, p. 74, tabulates the psychology of Nemesius thus:

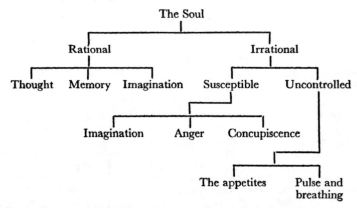

Domanski argues that it is predominantly an Aristotelian scheme.

[7] Nemesius does not mean the work usually so entitled, which does not deal with psychology, but the work *On the soul*, where the division here mentioned is in Bk. II, ch. iii.

what he says in his *Physics*. But in his *Ethics*[8] he divides the soul into two primary and general categories, rational and irrational. The irrational he sub-divides again into that which obeys reason and that which is not answerable to reason. Enough has been said in our foregoing chapters about the rational part of the soul.[9] We will next discuss the irrational part.

COMMENTARY

34. *A survey of psychotomies completed.* Nemesius is here rounding off what he has to say about the faculties of the conscious rational soul, before passing to the involuntary or unconscious aspects of our life.

[M. 213.10–218.8.]

XVI. *Of the irrational part of the soul, also called the passions*

TEXT

35. Some say that the irrational in us is a thing by itself, so that an irrational soul exists which is not part of the rational soul; in the first place because, in the irrational beasts, it is found by itself, whence it is clear that it is a complete entity by itself and not part of something else; and secondly because it would be most paradoxical that the irrational should form part of our rational soul.[1] Aristotle, on the other hand, affirms that the irrational not only belongs to but is a faculty of the soul.

8 *Nicomachean Ethics*, I. 13.
9 In Section 27, Nemesius has mentioned imagination as a faculty of the irrational soul. This is justified by the fact that there can be involuntary and pathological imagination. At the same time, there is imagination bidden and guided by the rational mind. Accordingly, Nemesius is able to say that in dealing with imagination, intellect, and memory he has been talking about the rational part of the soul.
  Margarites Evangelides, *Zwei Kapitel aus einer Monographie über Nemesius und seine Quellen* (Ph.D. dissertation, Berlin, 1882) begins his discussion at this point. He argues that the reference back, here, is to the last paragraph of the first half of ch. xiii, and that there is no reconciliation with the assignment of imagination to the irrational soul, made in Section 27. The inconsistency, Evangelides thinks, has arisen inevitably in the attempt to unite an Aristotelian psychology, based on the heart, with that of Galen, based on the brain. He admits that reconciliation is easy, if we regard imagination as a connecting link between the rational and irrational parts of the soul.
1 These two arguments are those of Numenius, who differentiated an animal soul, that perishes with the body, from an immortal rational soul. Nemesius does not refute them, but restates the Aristotelian psychology of the third book of the *Nicomachean Ethics*.

Further, as we said, he divides it into two, but couples both under one common title, appetite.[2] From appetite proceeds the movement of impulse. For yearning starts movement; that is, when living creatures are impelled by yearning, they proceed at once to a movement of impulse.

The irrational in us is partly not susceptible to reason, and partly obedient to reason. Furthermore, the part that obeys reason divides in two, that is, into the passions of concupiscence and anger.[3] Concupiscence, which is roused by things that we perceive, has the liver as its organ, while the organ of anger is the heart, a tough member, apt for strenuous movement, ordered for hard service and sudden onsets. In like manner the liver, a soft entrail, is fitting organ for soft[4] concupiscence. These two passions are called obedient to reason because, in men who live in harmony with nature, it is in the nature of these passions to obey reason, submitting or rousing themselves just as reason commands. Moreover, these passions are necessary components of a living creature, for life could not endure without them. But since the word "passion" is ambiguous, we must next resolve the ambiguity. Passion is used to mean bodily suffering,[5] such as comes from sickness or wounds. Equally it is used for passions of the soul, as in our present discussion where it is applied to concupiscence and anger. In a broad and general sense, however, passion, in a living creature, is whatever causes it either pleasure or grief. For, say that passion causes grief; nevertheless, the passion is not itself grief. If it were, whatever suffers anything must also feel grief. Now things without perception suffer (blows, it may be), but do not feel grief. So, clearly, the feeling of grief is not identical with suffering, but lies in perceiving what is suffered, and must be marked enough to call attention to itself. This, then, is a definition of passions

---

[2] *Orektikon.* See the second half of Domanski's first note to p. 74, *op. cit.*, where he argues against this being an opinion of Aristotle. The preferable reading would make this the opinion of Nemesius, and we should substitute "they are coupled" for "he couples." Appetite, for Nemesius, operates at two levels, as instinctive wishing or not wishing, or as the deliberate seeking of a satisfaction.

[3] *Thumikon,* which no one English word will render. The emphasis is more on courage and combativeness, than on the unpleasantness of anger which predominates in the English word.

[4] Soft in the sense of tender, easily hurt. While courage holds mischances at bay, concupiscence is exposed to them.

[5] *Pathos,* the Greek word for passion, need mean no more than an object "suffering" some fortuity, and does not necessarily imply feeling, as the English word does.

of the soul: passion is a movement of the faculty of appetite upon perceiving an image of something good or bad. Another definition is: passion is an irrational movement of the soul due to apprehending something good or bad. But, in a wider sense of the word, the definition is: passion is any change induced in one thing by another.[6] Activity, on the other hand, is energetic natural movement. Anything called energetic is self-moving. Thus, then, anger is, on the one hand, activity on the part of our warlike spirit, and, on the other, is something suffered by both parts of the soul, as well as by our whole body when anger drives it forcibly to corresponding acts. In this event, we have change in one thing caused by another, which accords with our general definition of passion.

There is another way of speaking,[7] according to which activity is called passion if it goes contrary to Nature, for, in this sense, activity means movement that accords with Nature, while passion is movement that is contrary to Nature. According to this way of speaking, activity that does not accord with Nature is called passion, whether self-originated or provoked, so that normal heart-beat is activity, but palpitations are passion.[8] It is no wonder, therefore, if the same happening should be described both as activity and as passion. For in as far as movements spring from the part of the soul where passion resides, they are in that sense activities, but in as far as they are inordinate and unnatural they are not so much activities as passions. So, then, according to either meaning of the word, passion is a movement of the irrational soul. Not every movement of the part of the soul where passion resides is called a passion, but only the more marked and those which attract attention. A slight and unperceived movement is not called passion, since, to be a passion it must be of noticeable magnitude. Therefore we must add to the definition of a passion that the movement is perceptible. For slight movements, escaping notice, do not, as we said, constitute passion.[9]

---

[6] The argument, from here on, is taken almost word for word from Galen, *Agreement* VI. i. (See Domanski, *op. cit.*, p. 116, Note 1.)

[7] This is the Stoic approach, where correspondence with Nature is the ethical aim. In as far as passions are irrational, in the sense of transgressing reason, they are contrary to this aim.

[8] The Stoics might call courage in battle an activity, but bad temper at home a passion. That Nemesius, instead, takes an illustration from physical health comes from following Galen.

[9] The quantitive clause comes again from Stoic ethics, which aimed at a rational apathy, attainable only in a broad way.

COMMENTARY

35. *The concept of passion.* The subject of the human passions, introduced in this chapter and section, opens a new stage in the argument of Nemesius. For, consideration of passion introduces that also of pain and pleasure, and so brings us to what had been a subject of age-long controversy among the philosophers, and one towards which Nemesius, as a Christian, is bound to take his own stand. From Aristippus of Cyrene, disciple of Socrates, and leader of a school from the beginning of the fourth century B.C., until Epicurus at its end, a succession of philosophers tried to identify, in some way, the good with pleasure. Against them other and greater thinkers asserted that pleasure is not an unqualified good, and is in fact often inseparable from evil. Plato tended to regard pleasure of the mind in things aesthetically or intellectually admirable as the only pleasure that is an unqualified good. Aristotle, in the *Nicomachean Ethics* demonstrated that pleasure serves the purpose of a stimulus to progress in virtue, and so claimed that the good, in pleasure, is to be estimated in relation to the ends which it promotes. Epicurus equated good pleasure with ataraxy or peace of soul, and expected a life of virtue to be the indispensable condition thereto. Such, in brief, is the controversial field, known to his readers, upon which Nemesius is now entering, and on the side of the moralistic philosophers. And accordingly he lays down as basis for his moral theory, what is, once more, an amalgam of the psychology of Aristotle with that of Galen.

[M. 218.9–220.7.]

XVII. *Of concupiscence*

TEXT

36. We said, then, that that irrational part of the soul which is susceptible to reason is divisible into the two passions of concupiscence and anger. Again, concupiscence divides into two, that is, into its pleasures and griefs. When fortune favours our desire, it ministers pleasure, but when it frowns, it causes grief.

There is again another division of desire, to make four different forms, inclusive of desire itself.[1] For seeing that all existing

---

[1] That is to say, one of the four divisions has no other name than desire. As appears presently, the four forms are desire, pleasure, fear, and grief. Hence the subject headings of chs. XVII, XVIII, XIX and XX. From the "some folk" who advocate this fourfold division—and they may well be

things are either good or bad, and some of them are ready at hand, and others are yet to come, we may, by following this clue, multiply two by two, and distinguish four forms of desire. There are good and bad, and each is either present or to come. For expecting good is desire, pure and simple. Good, when present, is pleasure. The expectation of evil is fear, and its presence, grief. So pleasure and desire are centred on what is good, and fear and grief on what is evil. And this is why some folk divide this passion[2] into these four forms, desire, pleasure, fear, and grief. And when we use the words "good" and "bad," it is either because the things are really so, or because we think them so. The evil passions[3] arise in the soul in these three ways; from a bad upbringing, from perversity, or through a poor constitution. For unless we are brought up well from childhood, and taught to govern our passions, we end by indulging them without restraint. From our perversity, again, false judgements get rooted in the soul's reasoning faculty, so that bad things are taken to be good, and good for bad. Certain consequences follow, also, from a poor bodily constitution. For splenetic people are testy, and those of a hot moist temperament are lecherous. But an evil tendency must be cured by acquiring good ways. Perversity must be cured by schooling and knowledge. But a poor physical constitution is matter for the doctor, who must win it over, as far as is possible, to normal temperament, by suitable diet, by exercise, and, should these be necessary, by the use of drugs.

COMMENTARY

36. *The cure of temptations arising from the passions.* The chapter does not really answer to the chapter-heading. Nemesius does not, like an Augustine, see in concupiscence a prime conse-

the Epicureans—Nemesius derives nothing but a way of breaking up his subject. He could not accept their identification of evil with fear and grief.

2 The Stoics said "the passions" (see Domanski, *op. cit.*, p. 119, Note 2). The limitation to concupiscence may well not be original with Nemesius.

3 These "evil passions" are clearly not fear and grief, as we might have supposed from what has immediately gone before. They are inordinate passion; plural because gathered under the two heads of concupiscence and anger, and evil when destructive of the good life as judged by Christian standards. Nemesius makes a fresh start, at this point, and begins to express his own convictions as to the principles which should guide the cure of souls. The pastor must value education and hygiene, as well as direct moral discipline. This wise and liberal ethic, at home in fourth-century Syria, was hardly so elsewhere.

quence of the Fall, but rather, like the Stoics, as evil only when
a disturber of the good life.

[M. 220.8—223.15.]

XVIII. *Of pleasures*

TEXT

37. Some pleasures are of the soul and some of the body, of
which the former, such as the pleasure of acquiring knowledge
and that derived from contemplation, affect the soul in itself.
For these pleasures, and their like, belong to the soul alone.
Bodily pleasures are those shared between soul and body. The
reason why they are called bodily is that they turn on things to
eat and drink and on sex relations. There are, however, no
pleasures, but only things endured, such as cuts, discharges, and
faults of temperament, that are restricted to the body alone.
For all pleasure is conscious, and we have shown that perception belongs to soul. It is plain, moreover, that pleasure is a
word that is used in many different senses. Pleasures are of
opposite kinds. Some are noble and some are base, some false
and some true. The pleasures of knowledge belong to the mind
alone, while pleasures of sense involve the body as well. Of
these last, some are natural and other unnatural. And whereas
the suffering of thirst is balanced against the pleasure derived
from drinking, there is no counterpoise to the pleasure of contemplation. So these considerations all show that pleasure is an
equivocal term.

Of the pleasures called bodily, some are both necessary and
natural, and without them life would not be possible; for example, the pleasures of the table, which bring satisfaction to our
need, and the pleasure from clothes which we have to have. On
the other hand, there are pleasures that are natural but not
necessary, such as normal and legitimate marital intercourse.
For this accomplishes the preservation of the race as a whole,
and yet it is quite possible to live in celibacy without it. Again
there are pleasures that are neither necessary nor natural, such
as drunkenness, lasciviousness, sordid love of money, and gross
over-eating, for they afford us nothing towards the survival of
the race, as does lawful marriage, nor towards the maintenance
of our own individual life, but even do positive harm. Therefore
a true man of God must pursue only the pleasures that are both
necessary and natural, while, at his rear, the man in virtue's

second rank[1] may indulge other pleasures besides, which, while natural, are not necessary, provided always that they are fitting, moderate, mannerly, seasonable, and in their right place. All other pleasures, in whatever guise, must be avoided. In short, those are to be accounted good pleasures that carry no grief bound up in them, involve no repenting afterwards, give rise to no countervailing harm, keep within bounds, and do not distract us from our worthier occupations too much or too tyrannously. Those are genuine pleasures which are in any way conducive to, or linked with, divine learning, the sciences, and the virtues. These are to be placed among the prime objects of pursuit, because they serve not merely our existence, or the survival of the race, but the good life, making us into noble and godly men, and leading us on to the very perfection of manhood, in soul and understanding. These pleasures are no mere remedies for such and such things that happen to us, as it might be the replenishing of bodily wastage. Nor is there any grief inevitably preceding, following, or counterbalancing them. But they are pure, and unmixed with any material strain, being exclusively pleasures of the soul.

For, as Plato puts it, some pleasures are false pleasures, and some are genuine.[2] False pleasures are all that spring from sense and a deceived judgement; and these have griefs wrapped up in them. True pleasures are all that belong only to the soul in itself, and spring from knowledge, mind, and thought. Such pleasures are pure and unmixed with grief, carrying no kind of repentance in their train at any stage. The pleasures that flow from contemplation, and the pleasure that follows from doing good, are not called passions but susceptibilities.[3]

---

[1] We have here the double ethical standard within the Christian Church, first occasioned by the Alexandrine conception of "true Gnostics" forming an *élite* within the community of believers and pledged to more stringent ethical standards than the clergy demanded of their congregations. The spread of organized monastic life from Egypt to Syria fixed the form in which the double standard was acknowledged there in the time of Nemesius, who accordingly thinks of the Church as an army drawn up in line of battle, with those who "truly live a life according to God" as the front-rank men, while ordinary members of the congregations are the rear-rank soldiers. Evangelides feels the irony of basing this distinction on Epicurus. But restriction to pleasures that are natural and necessary is an apt description of Christian asceticism in its negative aspect.

[2] Socrates makes this point early in his dialogue with Philebus, and argues for the same general conclusion which Nemesius is here invoking.

[3] A Stoic distinction.

23—C.J.

COMMENTARY

37. *The different kinds of pleasure.* The opening of this section is reminiscent of the first five chapters of Bk. x of the *Nicomachean Ethics*. Throughout the chapter, Nemesius clearly has before his mind, if not actually the argument about pleasure in the *Philebus* of Plato, at least that argument as rehandled by commentators, or as recast and conflated with the arguments of Aristotle, in ethical literature then recent, of which the *Philebus* was prime inspiration. Having said that perception belongs only to soul, while the body's only *proprium* is passivity to harm, and that most pleasures are enjoyed by means of a co-operating of body and soul, Nemesius proceeds to follow Epicurus in his division of these shared pleasures into three classes. Thence he proposes as ideal the ascetic life conceived after the Christian pattern, the proposition being based on (i) Epicurus' classification of pleasures, (ii) Plato's notion of pleasures which carry no grief involved in them, and (iii) Aristotle's doctrine of pleasures that urge us towards an end in virtue. The use of this combination would be proof of striking originality, if we had not reason to suppose that the arguments had been prepared by the Neo-Platonists in the interests of contemplative philosophy. But this fact will only have made the Christian form of the argument the better for apologetic ends.

[M. 223.15–225.14.]

TEXT

38. Some there are who hold that pleasure of that sort is properly called joy,[1] while they define pleasure as a becoming sensual. But this definition seems only to cover bodily pleasure. For that is, if you will, the satisfying and curing of the body's sense of need, and of the distress which need entails. For, supposing one is cold or thirsty, and assuages the distress that arises from cold or thirst, one enjoys the being warm or the drinking. These benefits, then, are accidental. They are not benefits intrinsically, or by nature. For just as being restored to health is a good thing, but dependent on circumstances, while being well is good naturally and by itself, so, likewise, those bodily pleasures are good according to the circumstances and because they remedy something, while the pleasures of contemplation are

[1] The distinction between *chara* (joy) as the sensation of the mind and *hēdonē* (pleasure) as the sensation of the body is of Epicurean origin.

good in themselves and by their very nature. They do not spring from any sense of need. Hence it is clear, therefore, that not all pleasure arises as the satisfaction of a sense of need. That being so, the definition is unsound which says that pleasure is a becoming sensual. For it does not include every kind of pleasure, but leaves out the pleasure that flows from contemplation.

Now Epicurus,[2] when he defines pleasure as the gradual taking away of what grieves, agrees with those who define it as becoming sensual. For he says that pleasure is being delivered from anything grievous. But since becoming anything is never identical, or even akin, with the corresponding completion, the birth of pleasure ought not to be identified with pleasure in itself. It is something quite distinct from actual pleasure. For birth is a state of becoming. And nothing in a state of becoming is both becoming and complete at the same time. A thing in a state of becoming is incomplete. But anything that gives pleasure does so instantaneously. Surely, then, pleasure is not a becoming. Again, becoming always implies that the condition did not exist previously. But pleasure belongs to the category of established actualities, so it clearly cannot be a becoming. Or, once more, becoming may be fast or slow, alternatives inapplicable to pleasure.

COMMENTARY

38. *A Neo-Platonist distinction of pleasures refuted.* With this section, we see at once that Nemesius has not before his mind

[2] Epicurus, 341–270 B.C., was born in Samos, and began to teach at the age of 32, as one who sought knowledge not for its own sake, like the earlier Greek philosophers, but for the sake of the happiness to which knowledge is the means. From 306, at Athens, he became the adored leader of a cult of happiness, supported by an outpouring of philosophic writing, in which the emphasis is on values belonging to the present life, and on the element of chance and the inexplicable in the universe. Epicurus' thought seems to have been conditioned by a great deal of physical pain, which goes to explain his negative approach to the concept of pleasure. On the other hand, Epicureanism came to be known as the "godless" philosophy. It was therefore particularly abhorrent to the Neo-Platonists, and it is undoubtedly a gibe, on Nemesius' part, when he drags Epicurus into his argument, to make him one of the supports of the Neo-Platonic error which he is attacking. In fact, Epicurus, who held that all mental pleasure is derived from the pleasures of sense, had really nothing in common with the Neo-Platonists, as regards the concept of pleasure. The Aristotelian argument that made pleasure an activity (*energeia*), and not a becoming, served Nemesius to knock out his opponents on the left (Epicureans) and on the right (Neo-Platonists) at the same time.

the text of the *Philebus*, but something mediated by Neo-Platonic hands. The famous proposition that pleasure is genesis, which was to provoke so much grave debate, begins with a jocular passage in the *Philebus* where Socrates cites the cynical saying of "certain wits" (the allusion is to Aristippus), that pleasure is always a genesis, and never by any chance an accomplished reality (*ousia*). His interlocutors yield to the truth in this saying, and Socrates draws the conclusion that pleasure cannot be identified with the Good. The saying clearly means that pleasure is delusive, a promise that is never fulfilled, a birth that is always an abortion. Aristotle, in the seventh book of his *Nicomachean Ethics* (ch. 12) attacked the phrase, "Pleasure is genesis" as a philosophic false principle. His arguments are largely reproduced by Nemesius in this section. But the proposition which Nemesius states and refutes is not the simple Platonic argument, but one developed in a Neo-Platonic sense. The "some" who are refuted begin by distinguishing between joy and pleasure but not exactly in the Epicurean sense. Joy, they say, the fruit of contemplation, is substantial. Pleasure, in belonging to the world of sense, is not. When the soul experiences pleasure, it is entering into the world of sense. So their definition of pleasure is that it is a birth into sensuality, a becoming sensual. The Platonic disparagement of pleasure has here taken a step nearer to dualism. It is not actual dualism. Plotinus was in reaction from the Gnostic dogmas, and regarded the things of sense as not actually bad, but only relatively so, as being but the faint and blurred reflection of the things that are really good, which the soul knows only by contemplation, since they belong to the suprasensual. This is, however, too close to dualism for Nemesius, who claims that pleasure is one thing, whether it be of the soul alone, or of soul and body together. He therefore brings the Aristotelian battery to bear upon the Neo-Platonist distinction, giving us a further instance of an eclecticism diverging from Neo-Platonism on the Aristotelian side.

[M. 225.14–229.6.]

TEXT

39. Once more, anything good must be either a state, an action, or a means. Being virtuous is a state, and doing a good deed is an action. Or again, being endowed with sight is a state, seeing is an action, and making use of one's eyes, legs, and so

on, is the means of seeing something etc. All the faculties of the
soul that are cognizant of good and bad are exercised in such
and such states. Whether, therefore, pleasure is a good thing or
a bad, depends simply upon these states, pleasure being in no
wise itself a state.[1] For it is not like virtue, or else it would not
so easily be changed into its opposite, grief. Nor is it a state as
being the opposite of its own negation. For a state and its
negation cannot co-exist. But people can have pleasure and
grief simultaneously; for example, those who scratch an itch. It
follows that pleasure is not a state. Neither is it a means, for
means do not exist *in vacuo*, but for the sake of other things.
Pleasure, however, justifies its own existence, without any other
end to serve. So it clearly cannot be a means. It remains, therefore, that pleasure is activity, wherefore Aristotle defines it as
activity that does not disturb our natural state. For anything
that hampers natural activity is a grief. Now prosperity is
activity that does not disturb our natural state. It follows that,
according to this definition, prosperity and pleasure are identical, and so the definition as such breaks down. So Aristotle
corrected it and said that pleasure is the objective of the unimpeded natural activities of a living creature: so as to connect
up pleasure and prosperity, and make them exist together,
without actually identifying them.

Not all activity is movement, but there is a kind of activity
that goes on in stillness, as with the divine activity as First
Cause. For the First Mover is unmoved. Now the activity of
contemplation, on man's part, is activity of such a sort, because
it takes place in stillness, because the object of contemplation
is unchanging, and the contemplating mind is at rest, seeing
that it is turned ever upon one and the same object. Now if the
pleasure of contemplation, being, as it is, the greatest, most
authentic, and truest of pleasures, happens in stillness, it is clear
that pleasures are better and greater in inverse proportion to
the disturbance they involve.

Pleasures differ in correspondence with the activities concerned. There are as many kinds of pleasure as there are of
activity, good pleasures corresponding with good activities, and

[1] Vice is a state. If a person is vicious, all the faculties of his soul, and with
them his judgements, are vitiated. The faculties of a virtuous man work
truly and his judgements are right. Both sorts of men have pleasures, but
with one they are wholesome and a good thing, and with the other a bad
thing; e.g., a good man has pleasure in his happy marriage and a bad
man in loose connections which do harm.

bad with bad.[2] It is plain, moreover, that different forms of pleasure correspond with the several senses. There are pleasures characteristic of touch, and pleasures characteristic of taste; there are pleasures of the eye, and ear, and nose. Those senses that are not in actual contact with their pleasurable objects, such as sight, hearing, and smell, are the purest in the pleasure they give.

There are two types of mind, one inclining to action and the other contemplative. Clearly, therefore, there must be two forms of pleasure consequent upon these two activities. Of the two, contemplation[3] is the purer. The characteristically human pleasures are those of the mind. For sensual pleasures are shared by man, as a living creature, with the other living creatures. Now since some folk prefer certain of the pleasures of sense, and others prefer others, the pleasures that are good in themselves are not those that seem so to worthless fellows, but are those that seem so to men of fine character. For a competent judge, in any matter, is not Tom, Dick, or Harry, but the man who possesses both knowledge and a balanced character.

COMMENTARY

39. *A true definition and criterion of pleasures.* Having disposed of the Neo-Platonic error that the nature of bodily pleasure is genesis or passive change, Nemesius now follows Aristotle's *Ethics*, Bk. VII, ch. 12 in establishing that pleasure is an activity, and accepts an Aristotelian definition based on the natural

---

[2] In general, activities are good or bad according to the state of the subject. But contemplation is an activity which is either good or non-existent. Some pleasures of sense are less ready to be vicious than others. What is meant is that good pleasures correspond with higher activities and bad pleasures with lower, though the pleasures corresponding with the lower activities need not be bad.

[3] Nemesius is taking the word *theōria*, contemplation, from Aristotle, with whom it means letting the mind study an object of knowledge, for no end other than the knowledge. But during the fourth century of our era the word had been taking on new and specifically religious associations, alike with Neo-Platonists and Christians. Christian writers of the fourth to fifth centuries use *theōria* of exegesis; Alexandrines for finding an allegorical sense in a historical narrative, and Antiochenes for discerning, through the plain literal sense, an underlying spiritual truth. *Theōria* also meant the characteristic occupation of monks, for which another name was mental prayer, in which heart and mind are given up to the quest for God and the knowledge of his will. It serves Nemesius' apologetic purpose to make none of these Christian associations of the word explicit. Neo-Platonist *theōria* was admired, and that opened an approach, on the part of the apologist, to the sympathetic attention of his readers.

activities of a living creature. What this definition means for Nemesius, therefore, can only be sought at the end of his enquiry into the nature of man. Pleasure being thus provisionally defined, the rest of the section is devoted to seeking a criterion of excellence for pleasures.

The first, preferring the calm and cool to the hot and agitated, is weighted against the ideal of an active life, and, in this, reflects the temper of the late fourth-century Church. The second, invalidating common opinion, finds the sound judge of pleasure only in such as have gone beyond untested opinion to soundly-based knowledge, and in whose natural disposition there is no disorder. The achievement, in finding a criterion, is not remarkable, but the firmness with which Nemesius clings to "what is natural" as an essential part of the criterion, is remarkable. It reflects his belief that "the nature of man" is not only a subject of question, but involves an ideal to be actualized.

[M. 229.7–235.6.]

XIX. *Of grief*

TEXT

40. The forms of grief are four;[1] pain, trouble, envy, and commiseration. Pain is a form of grief that makes us catch our breath. Trouble is grief that depresses us. Envy is grief provoked by other folk's prosperity. Commiseration is grief called out by evils that other people suffer. Every form of grief, by its essential nature, is an evil. For even though it may chance to be the grief of a worthy man at the destruction of good men, or at the deaths of children, or at the ruin of a city, yet he does not grieve for the sake of grieving, nor of deliberate choice, but as driven thereto by circumstances. But when such things occur, an actual contemplative will be completely unmoved, seeing that he has severed himself from present things, and cleaves to God; while any worthy man is schooled to be affected by such griefs only in due measure, not excessively, nor so as to behave as their captive, but rather as battling for the mastery of them.[2] Grief is the antithesis of temperate pleasure, as bad is opposite to

[1] Domanski shows that the definitions in this section are all Stoic definitions.

[2] Nemesius, who, in many ways, reproduces the liberal humanist outlook of Clement of Alexandria, is particularly reminiscent of him in this comparison of the contemplative (*theoreticos*) who has attained apathy (the state of independence of natural emotions, reached by a long ascetic training), and the "worthy man" (*spoudaios*) who has not yet come to so

good, while it compares with inordinate pleasure as one bad thing with another. Inordinate pleasures are bodily pleasures, and none other. For the pleasures of contemplation, though partaken in the highest degree and even to perfection, do not entail any element of excess. There is no grief, that is, opposed to such pleasures, nor are they the mere cure of previous grief.

XX. Of fear

TEXT

There are six different manifestations of fear; diffidence, shyness, shame, consternation, terror, and anguish. Diffidence is fear of taking action. Consternation is fear generated by some strong apprehension. Terror is fear caused by some impression without precedent. Anguish is panic fear, which is to say, helpless fear. We are in anguish when we are afraid that there is nothing whatever that we can do. Shyness is the fear of incurring adverse judgement, and is the least ignoble form of this passion. Shame is the fear that springs from having done some disgraceful deed; but shame is not unmixed with hope of deliverance. Shyness differs from shame in this, that an ashamed person is plunged in shame by what he has done, but the shy person only fears lest he should incur some bad opinion of himself. Ancient writers, however, often call modesty shame, and shame modesty (or shyness),[3] using the words indifferently (or improperly).

Fear starts with a chilling of the extremities, all the hot blood running to the heart, as to the centre of control, just as the mob, when frightened, rushes to the rulers of the city.[4] The organ of such grief is the pit of the stomach, for this it is that, at onsets of fear, feels a gnawing sensation. So Galen, in his work, *On demonstration*, Book III, says something to this effect: "People attacked by fear experience no slight inflow of yellow bile into the stomach, which makes them feel a gnawing sensation, and

high a state, but has attained metriopathy, or a habit of reaction strictly proportioned to the deserts of the causes of reaction, never being inordinately exalted or depressed by events. Domanski suggests that this particular distinction came to Nemesius directly from Porphyry.

[3] One Greek word represents modesty and shyness. Nemesius has an accurate estimate of shyness, but the older writers cover a wider range of meaning with the one word, so that modesty is at the other end of this range from the shame of disgrace. Nemesius is critical of these ancients, as showing in this matter a lack of discernment.

[4] This simile begins an allusion to the *Timaeus*, ch. 31 (end).

they do not cease feeling both distress of mind and the gnawing until they have vomited up the bile." For this gnawing sensation is felt just below the cartilage in the midst of the chest, known as the sword-shaped cartilage. The heart lies considerably higher, for, while the stomach is lower down than the diaphragm, the heart is above it. Ancient writers were used to say "the heart" when they meant the pit of the stomach. Thus Hippocrates and Thucydides, in describing the plague, speak thus: "And as soon as the disease fastened on the heart, it turned it over, and there ensued every kind of bile-discharge distinguished by physicians."[5] For, of course, it was the pit of the stomach that was thus affected and forced to vomit, and not the internal organ rightly called the heart.

XXI. *Of anger*

TEXT

Anger is the heating of the blood round the heart, taking place as a result of exhalation rising from the bile, or from the bile becoming turbid. That is why anger is called choler, and bitterness. Sometimes anger is a desire for revenge. For, when we have suffered a wrong, or think we have, we get angry, and the passion that then takes us is mingled of desire and anger. There are three forms of anger; wrath (also called choler and bitterness), vindictiveness, and rancour. For anger, when, in its beginning, it blazes up, is called wrath, or choler, or bitterness. But vindictiveness is choler grown chronic, and gets its name[6] from continuing, and being preserved in memory. Rancour, again, is wrath that bides its time to execute vengeance, and it gets its name[7] from the word for lying in wait.

Anger is "reason turning out the guard."[8] For when thought

5 Cited from Thucydides, *History of the Peloponnesian War*, Bk. II, ch. 49, but, no doubt, taken directly by Nemesius from its use in Galen's *Commentary on Hippocratean prognosis*, III. 30. There is no strict citation of any passage of Galen, but the medical knowledge of this section is all to be found in him.

6 There is a fancied connection, here, between *mēnis*, the lasting displeasure of the gods (or vindictiveness of men), and *mēnein*, to last, or continue; or again *memnēmai*, to remember.

7 Another fanciful etymology, connecting *kotos*, rancour, with *keisthai*, to lie.

8 In the passage of *Timaeus*, 31, cited above, Plato (though the passage has certainly suffered retouches) likens the heart to the guard-house of a city, implying, what Nemesius makes explicit, a likening of anger to the rushing out of the guard, when something has happened, either inside the city or without, that constitutes a challenge. Nemesius improves upon Plato's suggested relationship between reason and anger.

concludes that what has taken place is displeasing, anger makes a sally against it; if so be that rational thought and anger observe their respective natural functions.[9]

COMMENTARY

40. *The unpleasant emotions.* The essay on pleasure in Section 39 is now followed by a review of the unpleasant emotions, grief, fear, and anger. Section 40 is covered by Domanski, *op. cit.*, pp. 121–129.

[M. 236.1–240.11.]

XXII. *Of the irrational part of the soul over which reason has no control*

TEXT

41. The irrational part of the soul that is answerable to reason has now been reviewed. The part that is not accountable to reason is the nutritive, the generative, and the pulsatory faculties. The nutritive and generative are called natural faculties, and the pulsatory, vital.

XXIII. *Of the nutritive faculty*

TEXT

The nutritive faculty has four natural processes,[1] appetitive, retentive, digestive, and secretory. For it is natural to each

---

[9] What is said about anger in this chapter must be combined with what has been said about "courageous anger" in the middle of Section 35. Nemesius differs from the Stoics in his estimate of the place of anger in the good life, needing to leave room for righteous anger.

[1] Nemesius takes from Galen, *On the natural faculties*, III. 8, the scheme of four natural processes, of taking in, holding, breaking down, and casting forth, which enter into physiological function in several ways. In all probability this scheme of four processes goes back to Panaetius, the master of Posidonius. Tertullian, *On the soul*, XIV says that Panaetius divided the soul into five or six parts, and Posidonius into fourteen (the text reads seventeen). He goes on to explain that, by parts, Posidonius means faculties. Faculty, it here appears, means the capacity for performing a particular natural function. Posidonius considered every such faculty a partial manifestation of divine power immanent in the universe, which everywhere worked by some or all of the above four processes. Thus, for example, Posidonius explained the lodestone by saying that it

member of a living creature to draw to itself its appropriate
nourishment, to retain what it has so acquired, transform what
it retains into its own substance, and finally pass off the residue.
It is these processes that administer the nourishing of the members of the body, whereby their growth in either dimension
takes place.

Unwanted matter is evacuated, by passing through the
stomach, by urination, by vomiting, in perspiration, by way of
the mouth, nostrils, ears and eyes, in the breath and through
invisible pores. Apart from these last, evacuations are visible.
That through the ears is what we call wax, being the filth from
the ears; that from the eyes consists of tears and rheum; that in
the breath is a kind of smoke made by the heart's heat. It is said
that the invisible pores form the general ventilation of the body,
whereby, thanks to the porousness of the skin, most vapours
coming from deep down, from the contracting of the arteries,
make their way out. The organs of nutrition are the mouth, the
gullet, the belly, the liver and all its veins, the intestines, the
two bile-generators,[2] and the kidneys. The mouth begins the
preparation of the food for the stomach by chopping it up into
small pieces, using teeth and tongue. For, in mastication, the
tongue is of the greatest use, in gathering up the food and pushing it under the teeth, just like women grinding corn, who push
the grain by hand under the millstones. For, in mastication, the
tongue acts as hand. And when the food has been reduced in
this way, it is sent on its journey through gullet and stomach to
the bowels. For the stomach is not only the part that feels the
need of food, but is also an organ of passage for foodstuffs. For,
in the act of swallowing, the gullet[3] stretches up and sucks down
the food, and so passes it on into the bowels. Once the belly has
received the food, it separates what is good and nourishing from
what is gritty, stringy, and useless for food. It changes the good

exhibited two, only, of the four processes, namely the appetitive and
retentive. A self-nourishing plant or animal, on the other hand, would
exhibit all four. It will be seen that, in ch. xxiii, not only is the whole
body shown as employing the four processes in self-nutriment, but the
different organs are likewise shown to employ them in regard to the
blood. The whole chapter is derived, as regards its physiology, from
Galen.
[2] i.e., the gall-bladder, and the spleen, which the ancients supposed to
secrete "black bile."
[3] The Greek word *stomachos* included the gullet as well as that first section
of the alimentary canal to which we apply the name stomach. *Stomachos*
must therefore be rendered gullet or stomach as the sense of the passage
seems to require.

food into humours, and passes them on to the liver through those veins that draw the juices from the digestive organs and distribute them through the liver. These veins may be likened to the liver's roots, since they draw the nourishment from the stomach in just the same way that the roots of plants draw it from the earth. For the belly is comparable with the earth which provides the nourishment of plants,[4] while the corresponding roots are the veins which carry the humour from the stomach and from the intestines through the mesentery to the orifices and the bottom of the liver. And we can compare the liver itself to the trunk, while the branches and twigs are the veins that branch off from the main vein issuing from the lobes of the liver. For when the liver has received the humour from the belly it digests and assimilates it, since the flesh of the liver is most similar to blood, and so is suited to transforming humour into blood.[5] The purifying of the blood takes place through the spleen, the gall-bladder, and the kidneys, the spleen drawing off the dregs of the blood to replenish itself, the gall-bladder drawing off the bitterness still present in the nutritive juices, and the kidneys taking the watery residue and any bitter juices that still remain, so that the blood is afterwards pure and good, and can be distributed as nutriment to all other parts of the body, through the veins dispersed among them.[6]

Thus each several member draws blood into itself, retains it, and transforms it into its own proper nature, sending on what it does not need to the adjoining members, to yield them nourishment appropriate to their needs. In this manner every member draws its nourishment from the blood, and grows and

---

[4] Similes likening the human body to a plant go back to Plato and Aristotle; but the anatomists discovered that the blood-vessels made a system that could be likened to a tree with a two-fold trunk, branches, and twigs. The "power" in this system seemed partly comparable to that of a magnet, in that it incessantly drew in, and cast out. Brain, nerves, and spinal chord were also like a tree whose "power" was to bring sensation wherever it reached, and to set the muscles in motion.

[5] The naive assumption, here, is that because liver is like clotted blood, it is the blood-maker, having the power to turn the chyle into blood. Owing to this assumption, Nemesius follows his predecessors into attributing to the liver the work of body-building actually due to the heart and lungs.

[6] Aristotle asserted that blood was the sole nutrient of the members of the body. Hippocrates had argued to the contrary effect, that such dissimilar things as bone and flesh could not be equally transformations of one and the same substance. Therefore, he said, the other three humours must take part in the building of the body. But as phlebotomy revealed the fact that other humours mingled in the blood, it was readily concluded that the body-building "power" worked everywhere through the blood.

maintains itself; while the liver is the general purveyor of blood.

This department of the irrational functioning of the body is said not to answer to reason in the sense that it accomplishes its proper work by the laws of Nature, and not by any intention or choice of ours that it should do so.

COMMENTARY

41. *The functions of the soul that go on independently of reason.* What is called ch. xxii is really nothing more than an extended heading to the group of chs. xxiii–xxv, covering the functions stemming from what is called, in Domanski's chart, the "uncontrollable" irrational part of the soul, in contradistinction to those functions that are in any degree susceptible to control by reason. For commentary on this group of chapters, see Evangelides, *op. cit.*, pp. 21–28, from whom the following note is largely drawn.

Nemesius believes it possible to reach an authentic psychology only by taking evidence over the whole range of the life-functions of man, and in this group of chapters seeks to disclose the relation of those life-functions to man's anatomy and physiology. The knowledge of the ancients on these subjects may be said to begin with Aristotle, and the teleological physiology of his work, *On the parts of animals.* Herophilus and Erasistratus, at Alexandria, developed the knowledge of anatomy, a study that no doubt was much advanced in Egypt by the custom of the Egyptians of embalming their dead. A succession of schools led up to Galen. Nemesius, while he depends chiefly on Galen, shows that he had knowledge, by some means, of the Alexandrine surgeons, and tries to correlate his sources. The reason that he found Galen so attractive is that Galen, starting from the Aristotelian teleology, and his maxim "Nature never does anything in vain," inferred the glory of the Creator from his anatomical and physiological observations. In his work *On the use of the parts of the body* (iii. 10 and xvii. 1) he acknowledges the heart of true religion to lie in recognition of the divine care exercised in nature. And while Nemesius is dissatisfied with the clarity of his testimony to the substantiality of the soul, he fully accepts from him the conviction that, as substance, the soul is truly united to the body, so as to be affected in the genesis and decay of the body, and indeed by all its vicissitudes.

[M. 240.12–248.13.]

XXIV. *Of the pulses*

TEXT

42. The beating of the pulses is also called the vital process. Its inception, however, is from the heart, or, more exactly, from the left ventricle, which they call the vital-spirit ventricle. That ventricle distributes the natural heat of life to every part of the body through the arteries, just as the liver distributes nourishment through the veins.[1] So long as the heart is hot, just so long is the whole living body heated, and as soon as the heart grows cold the whole body grows cold with it. For the vital spirit is

---

[1] The distinction of function as between arteries and veins presented severe difficulty to the early physicians. They were misled by the disclosures of *post-mortem* dissection, which found the arteries collapsed, and the left ventricle of the heart empty of blood, the last completed act of the morbid organism having been to drive forward its last load of red blood. The ancients concluded, therefore, that the arteries were not blood-vessels at all, but ducts for "vital spirits," conceived as a hot and stimulating "gas." Praxagoras, in the late fourth century B.C., was the first to recognize that veins and arteries were in some way different in function. Somewhile later, Erasistratus proposed the clean-cut distinction which made the arteries purely carriers of vital spirit, and the veins the sole carriers of blood, of which a perpetually new supply was supposed to be manufactured by the liver, for continuous replacement of the loss through vaporization into vital spirit of the thin blood sucked through the capillaries. Nemesius reproduces the Erasistratian theory. It made terms with the phenomena of arterial bleeding by saying that, when an artery is severed, first of all vital spirit escapes invisibly (and the patient consequently faints). Then the contraction of the artery, as Nemesius says, sucks blood from the capillaries and squirts it from the wound in violent jets. It was supposed that the capillaries formed a sieve through which only the refined part of the venous blood was drawn by arterial suction. The same explanation was offered for the traces of blood found in the collapsed arteries of the dead. They were attributed to the process of concoction of vital spirit from the vaporization of refined blood. Galen (*On the natural faculties*, III. 14) added another theory, that where arteries reached the surface of the flesh, they drew in air, which, being carried to the left ventricle of the heart, regenerates the vital spirits. He also wrote a tract entitled *Does blood, in the course of nature, flow in the arteries?* in which he answered his own question in the affirmative. He could not, however, discard the old theory entirely, but supposed that, in the arteries, the blood-flow left room for vital spirit. He even explained fever as the result of an excessive flow of arterial blood, excluding the flow of vital spirit. By seeing that blood flowed in the arteries, and that blood was rejuvenated by respiration, Galen was within striking distance of discovering the circulation of the blood. But conservative opinion, such as that of Nemesius, was unwilling to follow him.

sent out from the heart along the arteries into every part of the body. It is a fair generalization that these three, vein, artery, and nerve, branch off in company, each taking its start from one of the three organs that regulate the life of man.[2] That is to say that nerves run from the brain as from the starting-point of movement and perception. From the liver as source of blood and nutriment go the veins or blood-vessels. From the heart as fount of the vital spirits proceed the arteries, as vessels for the vital spirit. And in working thus together, veins, arteries, and nerves benefit each other. For vein brings replenishment to nerve and artery; artery trades back to vein natural warmth and vital spirit;[3] while nerve provides both vein and artery, as indeed the whole body, with sense perception. Therefore, wherever you find an artery, there is refined blood; wherever there is a vein, exhalation is going on; and wherever a nerve runs, there is sensitiveness.

An artery distends and contracts with force, and yet in a modulated and regular fashion, for the movement originates from the heart. On the other hand, each time it distends, the artery forcibly sucks refined blood out of the adjoining veins, and this refined blood vaporizes and replenishes the vital spirits. Then, in contracting, the artery voids such waste products as it contains right through the surrounding body and out of the invisible pores, in just the same way as the heart, in breathing out, expels its hot smoke through the mouth and nose.

2 There are thus three vital organs, heart, brain, liver, each with its "power" distributed by ramification through the body; from the heart, vital spirit through the arteries, from the brain, psychic or sentient spirit through the nerves, and from the liver, nutrient blood through the veins. Cf. Galen, *Agreement*, v. 7.

3 It will be noticed that there is no mention of any benefit conveyed from artery to nerve, in this clause, where it might have been expected. We have seen that Galen supposes psychic spirit to extend along the nerves from the brain. For this reason, probably, he did not suppose vital spirit to pass from the adjoining artery to the nerve. Vital spirit was, however, held to be carried from the heart to the brain by the arteries running up to the head. Here we must suppose that, through the direct action of the soul, vital spirit becomes psychic spirit. See Evangelides, *op. cit.*, p. 30, Note 6 (vital spirit becomes psychic spirit in the forelobes of the brain). We must thus understand Nemesius, when he speaks of the soul as incorporeal, to be using the word in much the same sense as that in which it could be applied to a geometrical point. Relatively to the phenomenal world it has position; even if this is not strictly spatial, but only "habitual." It is so far localized as to transform vital into psychic spirit in the brain, and in this way maintain perception and consciousness. Galen makes the brain the seat of the soul (*On parts affected*, III, 9).

XXV. *Of the generative faculty, or concerning semen*

TEXT

The generative faculty likewise belongs to that part of the bodily functions not answerable to reason. For it is quite involuntarily that we emit semen when dreaming.[4] And the urge to intercourse is in our nature, for we find ourselves impelled towards it against our deliberate will. But the sexual act itself is unquestionably within our control, and is an act of the soul. For while it is consummated by organs subject to impulse, it is within our power to abstain and to master the impulse.[5]

The organs of the seminal process are, in the first instance, the veins and arteries; for it is in these that the seminal fluid is first generated by a transmuting of the blood,[6] in the same way that milk is generated from the blood in female breasts.[7] Indeed, seminal fluid is food for the blood-vessels, because they originate from semen at first conception. So, then, while arteries and veins concoct the blood into seminal fluid for their own sustenance,[8] any excess over their needs for that purpose becomes

[4] Bishop Fell compares the canonical ruling of Timothy, bishop of Alexandria (381–5), in his eighteen *Responsa Canonica*, that having sexual desire in a dream is no ground for abstaining, as though defiled, from the Holy Mysteries.

[5] The close of this paragraph seems to contradict its opening. But though the generative faculty may lie outside the control of reason, as touching its primary activities, no sooner do its operations mingle with those of faculties that are under rational control than sexual impulses which could not be inhibited can be turned from attaining the ends towards which they tended, by reasoned exercise of will. To this extent, they are under rational control.

[6] Nemesius, who does not admit that blood flows in arteries, here leaves uncorrected what he has taken from Galen, who credits the arteries not only with vitalizing the seminal fluid, but also with a share in its concoction from blood.

[7] The theory that, at the end of pregnancy, blood, turned back from the womb, entered the breasts, and was there agitated by vital spirit till it took the form of milk, is set forth at length in Clement of Alexandria's *Pedagogue*, I. 6. Galen, *On the care of the health*, 7, accepts the view that breast-milk is transformed blood.

[8] Hippocrates having overthrown the theory that blood is sole builder of body, early embryologists, finding the formation of blood-vessels preceding the presence of blood in the embryo, concluded that the humour from which they were formed must be semen. If so, then all subsequent growth and replenishment of blood-vessels must be due to the same humour. Hence proceeds the present argument, that the concoction of seminal fluid from blood is aimed first at the maintenance of the blood-vessels, and that the supply of semen to the genital organs follows only after the satisfaction of the first need.

semen. The first stage is that this is carried by a long and tortuous route to the head. The next is that it is carried down again from the head by two veins and two arteries. That is why excision of the veins that run round the ears and alongside the carotid arteries renders the individual sterile.[9]

The two veins and arteries in question end in a spiral and varicose system enveloping the scrotum,[10] whence seminal fluid is distilled into each of the two testicles. In each of these at last the seminal fluid borne by one vein and one artery separates off into actual semen charged with vital spirit by means of the varicose that immediately adjoins the testicles. It is for the sake of this process that each vein is escorted by an artery. Further, that the seminal fluid is carried by a vein is proved by the result of lewd indulgence. For men who have incessant intercourse and exhaust their seminal and generative fluid, subsequently, after violent straining, emit pure blood.[11]

Women have all the same genitals as men, except that theirs are inside the body and not outside it. Besides that, Aristotle and Democritus assert that the woman contributes nothing of semen to the generation of children. For, according to them, that which women emit is a discharge of the womb rather than semen. But Galen scorns the view of Aristotle,[12] and says that women do produce semen, and that it is the mingling of the two kinds of semen that produces the embryo. That is why, he says, intercourse is called, in Greek, "mingling." He admits that female semen is far from being full-developed, like the male, but says that it is still unconcocted and at a more watery stage. Since female semen is of this character, he continues, it serves to feed male semen. Also some part of the after-birth,

9 This is pure superstition. It is burlesqued by Rabelais in his account of the birth of Gargantua (*Gargantuan Chronicle*, vi), whom he describes as passing from his mother's womb up the hollow vein, and entering the world by her left ear. Rabelais, who became professor of medicine at Montpellier in 1530, was steeped in Hippocrates and Galen. In him we see the scientific spirit of the renaissance detecting the nonsense in its heritage from the classical age.

10 Galen, *On semen*, I. 5.

11 Ps. Galen, *On semen*, III. 3.

12 Not until the early nineteenth century were mammalian ova detected. Until then, conception presented a problem without a clue. Aristotle had the insight to see that menstruation is a mere discharge. But most physicians, including Galen, lured by the general parallelism between the sexes, and the derivation of male semen from blood, tried to account for menstrual fluid as female semen. Nemesius reports Galen's arguments without conviction. Embryology was Galen's weakest subject.

24—C.J.

that lines the horn-shaped extremities of the womb is compounded from female semen, as is the so-called "sausage-skin"
which receives the excretions of the embryo. In every kind of
living creature the female mates with the male when she becomes capable of pregnancy. Therefore, those females that are
continuously capable of pregnancy mate at any time, such as
hens, doves, and humans. But while other female creatures,
when pregnant, avoid the male, women grant intercourse at
any time. For hens, too, which lay almost daily, are mounted
almost daily.

Women, however, exercise their free will in having intercourse after conception, as they do in other matters; whereas
irrational creatures are regulated, not by any choice of theirs,
but under the working of Nature, so that they accept alike the
due measure and the set season.[13]

COMMENTARY

42. *The vital and generative processes.* This section is the subject
of a study by F. S. Lammert in *Philologus*, xciv (1941), pp.
125–141, in which he shows that, on one subject in each chapter, Nemesius diverges from the view of Galen, in favour of a
view previously prevailing. The observation is important, as
proving that Nemesius is no mere copier of passages from
Galen, but a wide reader on medical subjects. On the other
hand, he does not show a critical and professional judgement
on such matters, but writes as might a layman and amateur.
We may further infer that the public to which he addressed
this work was also given to reading works on health and medicine. And again, we may infer that Galen's prestige, if it had
already reached its zenith so far as practitioners were concerned, had not caused his doctrines to displace old established
theories from the minds of the general reading public.

The achievement of the section is the soundness of the foundation which it lays for the building of an ethic.

[13] Comparisons with animal behaviour indicate that the indeterminate
element in human behaviour gives it ethical character. The observation
is the more valuable in following so careful a limitation of the indeterminism in human conduct.

[M. 249.1–253.11.]

XXVI. *Another way of dividing up the faculties that control the life of a living creature*

TEXT

43. Some people classify the faculties in a living creature in another way. Some they call faculties of the soul, and some vital faculties. Those which they call faculties of the soul (or conscious[1] faculties) depend upon the will. Those that they call physical and vital faculties go on involuntarily. Conscious faculties divide into two, one group being faculties of impulsion and the other faculties of perception. Of impulsion there are three forms; first, locomotion, and the power of individual movement in every part of the body, then of utterance, and finally, of respiration. It is in our power to do these things, or to refrain from doing them. Physical and vital faculties, on the other hand, are not at our discretion, but go on, whether we will it so or not. Being nourished, growing, and forming semen are examples of physical faculties; and pulse is an instance of a vital faculty. The organs of these and the other unconscious faculties have been described already. We will speak now, therefore, about voluntary motion.

XXVII. *Of impulsion depending upon the will, also called the appetitive faculty*

TEXT

The origination of willed movement or impulsion, then, is in the brain, and (what is in fact part of the brain) the spinal marrow. Its organs are the nerves[2] proceeding from the brain

1 The ancients knew perception, but no such abstraction as "consciousness." That noun and the corresponding adjective therefore cannot rightly be used in translating a Greek author. It is clear, however, that very often the meaning that underlies the use of the adjective *psychicos* is just what we should represent by "conscious."

2 Galen seems to be the first writer to use the word *neuron* otherwise than for a sinew. The nerve threads qualified for the description *neuron*, because they were among the sinews of which the body is woven. But Galen, who recognized the nerves for what they are, treated them as the *neura par excellence* and found alternative words to describe other fibres, ligaments, and so on. Thus, by the time of Nemesius, the use of the word *neuron* predominantly, if not exclusively, in the sense of "nerve" was becoming established.

and spine, with the ligaments and muscles. Muscles consist of flesh, of nerve-strings, and of tendons with which nerve-strings are inter-woven. Some have supposed that muscles possess sense-perception, for that reason, on account of the feeling that is in the nerves woven together with the muscles. A tendon[3] (to resume definition) is made up of a ligament and sensitive[4] nerves. Sinew differs from nerve, in that every nerve has feeling in it, is round, and softer than sinew, and has its starting point in the brain. A tendon (or sinew), on the other hand, is at once harder, rooted in bone, insensitive in itself, and frequently band-like.

Hands[5] are the organ for taking hold of things, and are completely adapted for the arts. For, if one were to remove his hands, or merely amputate his fingers, one would render a man practically useless for almost every art; wherefore the Creator gave hands to man only, in view of his being rational and capable of arts.[6] Feet constitute the organ of locomotion; for by them we make our way from one place to another. Man is the only creature that sits, without needing anything to lean against.[7] For man alone bends his legs through a right angle in two places, at the hip and at the knee, bending the legs up at the hip and down at the knee. Whatever movement takes place by the operation of nerves and muscles involves the intervention of the soul,[8] and is accomplished by an act of will. Acts of perceiving and of utterance we have shown to belong to this cate-

---

[3] While the opening of ch. xxvii is reminiscent of Aristotle, *History of Animals*, iii. 6, the second half tends to leave Aristotle for the later physicians. This definition of tendon is not an Aristotelian definition.

[4] Literally, "light." It was still necessary to use such an adjective with *neuron* to show that nerves and not sinews were meant.

[5] Nemesius is here dependent (through intermediaries, no doubt) on a passage of Posidonius dilating upon the purpose of the human hand. It is a special interest of Posidonius to relate the characteristics of an organ to its function in life. Cicero works up the Posidonian praise of the human hands. Aristotle had called the hand "instrument *par excellence*," in the sense that the use of all other instruments depends on the possession of hands.

[6] Anaxagoras had said "Man is clever because he has hands." The teleology of Galen reversed the order, so as to say "Because man is clever and can use fine implements, God gave him hands." Nemesius simply follows Galen.

[7] So Galen, *On the use of the parts of the body*, iii. 3.

[8] Nemesius is again following Galen in making muscular impulse proceed from the soul, but goes beyond Galen, and reaches his own characteristic interest, by inferring an act of the will connecting the soul and the movement.

gory. Such, then, is the logical distinction to be made between the conscious and the purely physical operations. Nevertheless, it is to be noted that the Creator, in his supreme forethought, has woven all that proceeds from the soul together with whatever springs from nature, and the latter with the former. For consider the example of the voiding of excrements, an operation of the secretory process, which is one of the purely physical processes; for all of which, lest we should involuntarily disgrace ourselves by voiding in unsuitable places, moments, or circumstances, certain muscles have been made, as it were, guardians of the gate, in the matter of evacuations. So something that is an operation of Nature has been brought within the domain of soul;[9] and, because of this, we have the power to restrain evacuations, and to do so repeatedly and for a long while.

The soft nerves of sensation descend from the middle part and from the front lobes of the brain, while the harder motor-nerves proceed from the posterior lobe and the marrow of the spine; of these the nerves that spring from the spinal marrow are the harder, and of these again the hardest are those that spring from the base of the spine. The further, in fact, the spine-marrow is from the brain, so much is it the harder, and likewise the nerves that grow out of it.[10]

As we have been given sense-organs in pairs, so we have nerves springing out in pairs. Each spinal vertebra sends out a pair of nerves, one of which runs to the right side of the body, and the other to the left. For almost the whole of our body is symmetrically in two, a right and a left; and so it is with feet and hands, and with each of the other right and left organs, as it is likewise with the organs of sense.[11]

9 Though the example is inelegant, the general observation—that psychic and physical are intimately connected—is among the most valuable contributions which Nemesius makes in his study of the nature of man.

10 Nemesius, says Evangelides, is following Galen into one of his errors when he makes the motor-nerves harder (and so, by implication stronger) the farther they lie from the brain. Galen may have been influenced by his alternative theory of the origination of muscular movement, that it was caused by an outflow of psychic spirit from the brain along the nerve. So hard nerve might make up for deficiency of psychic spirit and the supposed observation might suggest that both theories were simultaneously true.

11 Thus Aristotle, On the parts of animals, III. 3, admiring the aesthetic symmetry. But Nemesius improves upon him with fresh anatomical knowledge.

COMMENTARY

43. *Consciousness and will.* Ch. xxvi forms one of the main
transitions of the book, because it opens the way to the consideration of voluntary action, and so, in turn, to that of moral
free-will. The cue has been taken from the close of the preceding
chapter, which has pointed to a contrast between women and
female irrational creatures in respect to coition. Women have
to autexousion (power of self-determination). Hitherto Nemesius
has followed the Hellenic tradition as represented, for example,
in Aristotle, *Nicomachean Ethics*, Bk. iii, in considering the life of
living man from the point of view of reason asserting itself as
the governing principle therein, against irrational passions. The
emphasis was upon reason, and not, as in this section, on the
soul as self-determining. But the Posidonian doctrine of *dynameis*
("powers") enabling particular portions of the life-process to go
on, and the discoveries of the physicians, had produced a view
of impulse independent of the reason-passion framework, and so
called for a new approach to the subject of self-determination.
Nemesius was not wholly an innovator in the argument which
he now develops. He shows this by his opening, "Some people
classify." It is not obvious who these people were, but their
threefold division of faculties stands in obvious relation to the
Galenic system of three principal organs, in the order brain,
liver, heart, with their ramifications of nerves, veins, and
arteries. We now see that the relationship of these ramifications
in ch. xxiv has been incomplete. The brain-nerve system has
been credited with no "power" except that of imparting sensitiveness to surrounding tissues. It is now brought to light that
the brain-nerve system has also the "power" of setting muscles
in motion. Evangelides (*op. cit.*, p. 51, Note 29) points out that
Galen was undecided between two explanations. One was that
the "psychic spirit" ran along the nerves, just as "vital spirit"
was driven through the arteries. The other was that while soft
nerves carried sensation, hard nerves imparted motion, as if
they were muscles at the root of the muscles. At the end of
Section 30 (M. 195.4) and in Section 43 (M. 252.16) Nemesius
accepts the second alternative. This suggests that the "some
people" of ch. xxvi, with their stress upon impulse, are post-
Galenic physicians. But Evangelides sees a definite motive in
the choice of alternative, that of placing impulse lower in the
scale than perception, which in turn is lower than thought.
Thus the life of the soul is carried on at different levels, though

all are equally part of the soul's life. And the different levels are the means by which the life of the soul is integrated with the automatic processes of the living body.

[M. 253.12–259.3.]

XXVIII. *Of respiration*

TEXT

44. Respiration, even, is a process involving the soul. For it is the muscles[1] that distend the chest, and that is the principal organ of respiration. The panting and sobbing breath that accompanies moments of great grief shows that the soul is here the driving force. Moreover, it is in our power to modify our breathing as we have need. For any pain in the respiratory organs or in members that share in their movement, the diaphragm, for example, or the liver, the spleen, the belly, intestines, or colon, makes us breathe short quick breaths; short, so as not to press more than necessary upon the part that is giving the pain, but quick, so that the number of breaths shall make good the deficiency in the several inhalations.[2] For, to take a parallel, when a leg gives us pain, we walk with very short steps, and the very same reasoning applies to breathing. It follows that, just as walking is an energy of the soul, so is breathing. But whereas we can live for any length of time immobile and not walking, we cannot hold our breath for a tenth part of an hour, or anything like so long. For if the vital heat within us is suffocated, its own fumes extinguish it, and death follows forthwith; as when you cover a flame over with any kind of vessel that has no vent, it is bound to go out, stifled by its own smoke. In view of the necessity of respiration, therefore, the soul goes on, even while we sleep, keeping up this side of its activity, knowing that if it were to rest from it, for ever so short a time, dissolution would ensue.[3] So once more we see, from

1 Muscles are moved voluntarily, and so lie within the domain of the soul.
2 Nemesius is here seen to attribute the rationality of the response of the respiratory system to pain not to Nature but to the soul of the subject. What he does not say is that the action, if rational, is instinctive, and not the result of reasoning. So rationality, which is an attribute of the soul, spreads into our instinctive actions.
3 Nemesius now takes a further step, and from attributing to the soul intuitive right action, goes on to attribute to the soul necessary directive government of vital process, divorced from consciousness altogether. The soul is said to "know" that it is responsible for maintaining and safeguarding life. But it is a hidden and innate kind of "knowledge."

this, how the action of soul mingles with the activities of Nature. For the soul is the driving force of respiration, by dint of using an artery, which is a physical organ in perpetual motion, like the other arteries, never remitting its work.[4] A lot of people, not understanding the process, think, for that reason, that breathing is a natural function, pure and simple.

The three causes of respiration are that we need it, that we have the faculty for it, and that the appropriate organs are present. The need for breathing is twofold; we have to keep up our natural heat, and we have to replenish the psychic spirit.[5] The natural heat of the body is, however, maintained by dint of both inhalation and exhalation. While inhalation first cools and then gently fans up the vital heat,[6] exhalation pours forth the smoky fumes of the heart. The replenishing of the psychic spirits is derived from the simple fact of respiration. For a certain modicum of air is drawn into the heart by its dilation,[7] the soul supplying the power required for this. For it is the soul that sets the respiratory organs in motion by muscular action; in the first instance, the chest, which in turn sets in motion the lungs and the bronchial tubes[8] which form an adjunct of the

[4] That the soul is behind respiration was taught by Aristotle (*On spirit*, 4), followed by Galen. Nemesius agrees, and provides an argument in support. The soul is responsible for voluntary muscular action, and for voluntary modification of respiratory movement. It is absurd to suppose that the rest of this muscular movement, exactly similar to voluntary impulse, takes place apart from the soul. Whence, otherwise, proceeds the perpetual pulsation of the heart and arteries except under impulsion of the same power that causes voluntary movement of the limbs?

[5] Psychic spirit is evidently used in a different sense, here, from that in which Galen uses it of the spirit in the brain, and issuing along the nerves. Lammert (*op. cit.*, p. 131) suggests that Nemesius may, at this point be, drawing upon a physician named Chrysippus, and in any case upon a source other than Galen. Evangelides points to Galen, *Agreement*, I. 6, which says "Erasistratus says that the left ventricle of the heart is full of vital spirit and Chrysippus says of psychic spirit." We have here a variation of vocabulary which probably lies at the root of such confusion as appears in Nemesius' account of "spirit."

[6] The heart is thought of as a fire that burns the more brightly for being fanned. The early physiologists were, in this way, rather at the mercy of their own similes. So Aristotle, *On Spirit*, 6, and Plato, *Timaeus*, 70.

[7] We have had another account of the generation of vital spirits at the end of ch. xxiv, where it is said to be nourished by the vaporizing of the most refined blood. That was Galen. What we have here is Chrysippus, who presumably thought that soul was in some way akin to air.

[8] Literally, "the rough arteries." From the lower end of the windpipe branch the two bronchial tubes, one running to each lung, and they in turn branch and branch, each smaller tube in this process being still of

lungs. The gristly part of the windpipe is the organ of voice. The membranous wrappings of the windpipe are organs of respiration, while the windpipe itself, combining gristle and membrane, is the common organ of voice and respiration. To go back to the lungs, they are a complex combining four different organs, windpipe and bronchial tubes, artery, vein, and the frothy flesh of the lung itself, which, as padding, fills in the spaces between the other organs, bronchial tubes, artery, and vein, so as to serve as a seat for them to rest upon, and also as a binder to hold them together. This lung-flesh, by Nature's process, concocts the air that reaches it,[9] just as liver concocts the humour from the belly. For that reason, just as the liver with its top lobes enfolds the stomach which needs warmth, so likewise the lungs envelope in their midst the heart, which needs the cooling of its surface that respiration supplies.[10] On

gristle. The whole system is known as the "bronchial tree." The "twigs" of the "tree" are finally extended as soft tubes ending in tiny bladder-like organs which carry out the respiratory oxidization of the blood. In the dissection of dead bodies, the similarity of the "bronchial tree" to a branching arterial system was so marked (the arteries being empty of blood) that the "roughness" of the trachea and "bronchial tree" seemed the most striking difference. This latter system was, therefore, taken to be arterial, but conveying air alone, and not vital spirits.

Nemesius now turns to trace the system upwards, towards the mouth. The gristle that he now mentions is the upper laryngeal cartilage. What he says about the membranous wrappings of the windpipe is to be explained by the fundamental error of the ancients regarding the arteries. They were all credited with a self-contained power of contracting and dilating, for the purpose of driving the vital spirits about the body. The windpipe must have this power, accordingly. Mere observation of the respiratory motion would seem to confirm the supposition that the windpipe was originating a pulsatory movement, by contracting and dilating itself. The muscular surroundings of the windpipe (trachea) were accordingly interpreted as being the mechanism of pulsation, as in this passage; an erroneous interpretation. Nemesius is right in saying that the trachea serves in two different functions, that of breathing and that of vocalization. This dual service was admired by Aristotle, *On spirit*, 11, and *On the parts of animals*, III. 3.

9 A third account of the generating of vital spirits. This time it may well be Galen who is the source, seeing that in his work, *On the purpose of respiration*, he defines that purpose as "the cooling of the natural heat," as in what follows here. It was at least seen that, in the lungs, the "process of conversion" was at work.

10 Dependent on Galen, Nemesius knew nothing of gastric juices. Merely the breaking-down process took place upon the food, under the digestive "power," producing chyle, which passed through the mesentery into the liver, which concocted it into blood by its appropriate "power." So Aristotle, *On the parts of animals*, II. 3 and III. 3, for the protection of the heart and stomach by the lungs and liver respectively.

to the windpipe joins immediately the throat, composed of three large structures of gristle.[11] From the throat follows the pharynx, then mouth, then the nasal passages, through each of which we inhale the outside air. The air thus inhaled passes through a perforated bone having the qualities of a sieve or of a sponge. Thereby the brain takes no harm from the extremes of quality of the air, as it would if the breath came to it unchecked.[12] So once more the Creator is seen, in this way, to have made a double use of the nasal passages, at once for breathing and for smelling; just as he designed the tongue at once for speech, for tasting, and as helping mastication. Thus the most important members share with the faculties of the soul the responsibility for our very existence, and for the inescapable needs of life. And if any such member has been omitted in this survey, it can easily be fitted in with what has been said.

COMMENTARY

44. *Respiration not automatic and independent of the soul.* The chapter headed "Of respiration" is, in fact, in two sections, only the first of which is about respiration. The great importance of this section in the argument of Nemesius turns upon the second sentence. The effect of purely mental grief upon the physical process of breathing, on the one hand, and our inability to hold our breath for more than a very short time, on the other, exhibit in epitome the terms of partnership of soul and body. We can say, Here the soul is clearly involved, for there are perception and will, the *propria* of soul. We can never say, Here the soul is not involved. In different manners, the soul is involved in every part of our life. The relation of Nemesius to Galen is worked out in detail by Skard, *Nemesiosstudien* IV, pp. 50–53, with a characteristic depreciation of the intelligence of Nemesius.

[11] i.e., the laryngeal cartilages and the hyoid bone, which together make up the vocal organs.

[12] Examination of the bone surrounding the brain led the early physicians to think of the brain as acting somewhat in parallel with the heart, being cooled and invigorated by taking in a modicum of air, through the respiratory motion, and passing off the fumes generated by its own activity. Chrysostom, in his eleventh homily "On the Statues," sees, in the crenellations of the skull, a providential outlet for the fumes of the brain. For this porous bone above the nose, see Aristotle, *On the parts of animals*, II. 10.

[M. 259.3–263.8.]

TEXT

45. It has been said[1] that all existing things can be divided into those that exist for their own sake, those that exist partly for their own sake and partly for the sake of other things, those that exist only for the sake of other things, and those whose existence is solely contingent and casual.[2] An exactly similar classification is applicable to the members of a living being. Thus, all those organs exist for their own sake of which we said that they subserve the centres of government controlling the living organism. For the framing of those parts is antecedent, and begins the formation of the body. They are called the natural organs in a special sense, and accordingly, like the bones, they are what are formed in the womb directly from the semen.[3] By contrast, yellow bile is something that exists for its own sake and also for the sake of something else. For example, it plays a part in digestion, and stimulates excretion. In regard to these operations it may be reckoned simply as one of the members partaking in the process of nutrition. That, however, is not all, for (just like vital spirit)[4] it contributes a degree of warmth to the body. On these accounts, therefore, it may be held to exist for its own sake. As the purging of the blood, on the other hand, it may be reckoned as existing for the sake of something else.[5] The spleen, too, contributes in no small measure to digestion. For as it is by nature sour and astringent, and since it pours out its excess of black bile into the stomach,[6]

1 Section 8 above.
2 Such as showers, in Section 8, with their parallel in the growth of hair, as described at the end of the present section.
3 So Galen, *On the use of the parts of the body*, xv. 6.
4 Literally, "vital powers" (*dynameis*). Posidonius explained every process in Nature by postulating a corresponding *dynamis* to enable it to be carried on. It is a Posidonian phrase that we have here, and used in exactly the same sense as the phrase "vital spirit" is used by the physicians. It seems best, for the sake of making the meaning easy for the reader, to translate "vital spirit" here. But the difference of words points to the difference of sources.
5 As an initiator of processes, the bile belongs to the upper end of the hierarchy of members, but as a by-product of the changes of the blood it belongs to the lower end. It is therefore one of the things that exists partly for its own sake, and partly for the sake of other things.
6 The spleen, being a ductless gland, does not in fact discharge into the stomach. The ancients may have been led to believe that it did, by discovering in the stomach substances that are common to the black and the yellow bile.

the spleen contracts and braces the stomach, so as to be a thorough stimulant to digestion. Beyond that, the spleen is the purging of the liver, and so may be reckoned as existing to some extent for the sake of the blood. The kidneys are also purges of the blood. Moreover they are exciters of sexual desire. For the veins which empty into the testicles, as we said, pass directly through the kidneys,[7] deriving thence a certain pungency provocative of lust, after the same manner that some pungent juice under the skin causes an itch. And inasmuch as the flesh of the testicles is more delicate than skin, they are the more stung by this pungency and cause an unreasoning desire to emit semen. These members and their like exist to some extent, therefore, for their own sakes, and to some extent for the sake of other things. By contrast again, glands[8] and flesh exist only for the sake of other things; that is to say, glands form a stay and support for the blood-vessels, which would otherwise, if loose and unsupported, be ruptured by the violent movements of the blood. Flesh, again, serves as a covering for the other members, in summer (by passing off moisture from within) to keep one cool, and in winter to play the part of a woollen felt, wrapping the other members round. The skin, in turn, is a general covering for the soft flesh and for all the other members internal to the body. The nature of skin is that of flesh that has been made callous to its environment and to bodies that come in contact with it. The skeleton is a support to the whole body, particularly the backbone which is commonly called the spine of the living organism. The nails, in all those creatures that have such things, are used for one operation, namely scratching, and besides that have a particular use that varies from creature to creature. To many of the animals, for example, those with hooked talons, they were given as a means of defence, and might be called their organs of combat. In many creatures they

---

[7] This statement is incorrect, though there is a relation, on the left side, between the testicular vein and the kidney vein which may explain the mistake. The consequences that Nemesius draws are due to the kind of guess-work whereby early physicians sought to relate conscious experience with anatomical observation, and are not to be taken seriously. Nemesius is right, on the other hand, in seeing that sexual desire has physiological causes, so that the morals of chastity are like dealing with an enemy within the gate.

[8] The function of glands was not recognized until the sixteenth century. Their proximity to the blood-vessels is due to the fact that they secrete their fluid from blood. But the early physicians were unable to detect this, and so saw in them nothing but shields for the blood-vessels.

are both a means of defence and armour for their feet, as in the case of horses and all creatures that have an undivided hoof. In the case of men, nails serve us not only to scratch and disperse the irritation of the skin, but also to enable us to grip light objects, and, in fact, we can pick up the lightest of things with the help of our nails, which make fast their grip by being placed at the back of the finger-tips, and by meeting nail to nail.[9] Hair grows out anywhere at random. For the smokiest vapours that rise from the body (so to say) congeal and become hairs,[10] wherever it may chance. However, the Creator did not make even hair to be entirely without profitable uses, but provided that, in spite of its random growth, it should complete the

[9] So Galen, *On the use of the parts of the body,* i. 7.

[10] Nemesius did not get this from Galen (unless from *On temperaments,* v. 1), and it differs from the theory of the origin of hair expounded by Plato in the *Timaeus,* and carried on by Aristotle, that hair is of the substance of the skin of the scalp, which is driven out wherever the fire from the brain has punctured a tiny hole, in the form of a cylindrical thread. But Athanasius, in his letter to Amun the monk, expounds what seems to be the theory that Nemesius repeats. Athanasius is arguing that an emission of seed in sleep carries no defilement of the soul. To prove this, he treats such emission as just one of a number of excretory actions of the body whereby it gets rid of what is useless or in excess. This natural system of excrement is the work of God, and therefore cannot defile. Athanasius says that "the sons of the physicians" give a list of widely different forms of excrement. The list starts with the head, of which the excrements are "the hairs, the waste products of the head, and the watery excrements." It is possible, therefore, that this theory of the origin of hair arose in the Alexandrine school of medicine. The question why hair grows in one place and not in another was a puzzle, and can hardly be said to have ceased to be a puzzle still. The growth of hair could not be attached to any point of the recognized nutritional system. And so Nemesius says that hair grows at random, and supposes that it is wherever the smokiest waste from the vital processes can find an outlet. This agrees with the suggestion of Athanasius that the "fumes of the brain" are the cause of man's head of hair. It thus seemed to bear witness to man's superiority in thought. He drew no consequences from a woman's longer hair. From the point of view of Nemesius, however, hair is something that does not exist for its own sake or for the sake of anything else, but is contingent and casual, so that it testifies to divine Providence that so purely accidental a thing is made to serve a useful purpose, just as if it were a designed organ coming under one of the other categories. That we should have what seems to be an Alexandrine view of hair in a Posidonian context may lend some slight colour to the view that Origen is the medium through whom Nemesius obtained his Posidonian ideas. Galen carries the "providential" explanation of growth of hair so far, in *On the use of the parts of the body,* xi. 14, as to say that women have no beards because, (i) as their place is to stay indoors, they do not need mufflers, (ii) they have no dignity to support, as a man has.

covering and be an adornment of various living creatures. For
goats and sheep it is a covering, and for men an ornament,
while for some creatures, such as the lion, it is an ornament and
a covering at one and the same time.

COMMENTARY

45. *Man's body is a microcosm.* The discussion of respiration, in
the previous section, ended by finding some pre-eminent organs
to be in particularly close and admirable partnership with the
soul in maintaining the business of life. This observation discloses a hierarchy among the organs and parts of the body,
completely parallel with the hierarchy of orders of being in the
natural universe. The body is no mere machine, but is rather
to be likened to a team in which there are leaders and sub-
ordinates; and the leaders are initiators, almost as though they
were in competition with the soul. The object of this section, in
the development of the argument, is to underline finally the
need of the soul to make terms with the body, as having in the
body a partner, rather than a mere instrument. This gives the
right starting point, as the discussion next goes on to the claims
of the soul to freewill. The hierarchy of being in Nature was the
subject of Section 8, which we saw to be essentially Posidonian,
however the matter reached Nemesius. The same can be said
of this section, partly because of the studied parallels, and
partly because of the language. That the greater part of it came
through Galen is shown in detail by Skard, *Nemesiosstudien* IV,
pp. 53-56.

[M. 263.9-269.16.]

XXIX. *Of voluntary and involuntary acts*

TEXT

46. Seeing that we have referred many times already to acts as
voluntary or involuntary, we must needs now state distinctly
what this means, or we shall not reach an accurate understanding of the subject.[1] Anyone who would discourse of involuntary
and voluntary acts must first of all lay down some rules and
norms, whereby it may be judged whether anything was done

---

[1] Ch. XXIX follows closely the pattern of the opening of the third book of the
Nicomachean Ethics. Domanski (*op. cit.*, p. 132, Note 1) sets out the parallel
passages side by side.

voluntarily or not. While, then, everything voluntary is embodied in an act, so too nothing can be deemed involuntary unless embodied in an act. In a little while this shall be demonstrated. Some authorities require that, for there to be anything truly involuntary, it must be not merely something suffered, but must involve doing something. So, before anything else, we ought to define an act. An act is something done rationally.[2] Acts bring in their train praise or blame. Also the doing of some of them brings pleasure, and of others grief. Some again the doer chooses and others he shuns. Further, of those he chooses, some he would choose at any time, but others only on their proper occasions. Things to be shunned divide in the same way. Again, some acts excite pity and are held excusable, while others are loathed and punished. So, then, the norms for judging an act to be voluntary are: that it inevitably brings upon the doer either praise or blame, that it is done with pleasure, and that it is something that some people choose to do either at any time, or at that particular time. And the norms for judging an act involuntary are: that it is held excusable or deserving of pity, and that it is done reluctantly and not by choice. With these definitions to guide us, we will treat first of involuntary acts.

XXX. *Of involuntary acts*

TEXT

Involuntary acts are either those done under constraint or those done unknowingly. In the case of the former, the origination of the deed lies outside the doer. For the cause that constrains us to do such a deed is something alien to us, and is not ourselves. Therefore, what defines a constrained involuntary act, originating outside the doer, is that the person constrained contributed no impulse of his own towards it. The source of the impulse is therefore said to be the effective cause of the act. The question, then, is whether involuntary acts are such things as the jettisoning of cargo by sailors who run into a storm, or someone consenting to suffer some outrage, or even to do some shameful deed, for the sake of saving his friends or his country. We should reply that such things are voluntary rather than involuntary. For it is essential to the definition of an involuntary act that the person constrained to it contributed no impulse of

2 Therefore no automatic movements of the body are acts.

his own towards it. For in acts such as those mentioned above
the actors willingly set their own members in motion, and that
is how they cast the cargo into the sea. And in the same way
those do so voluntarily who suffer outrage, or endure some
terrible fate, for the sake of a greater good; like Zeno, who bit
out his tongue and spat it at the tyrant Dionysius rather than
divulge secret mysteries to him, or like the philosopher Anaxarchus, who chose to be pounded to death at the hands of the
tyrant Nicocreon rather than betray his friends. [3] In general,
then, a man does not suffer or do anything involuntarily when
he either embraces a lesser evil out of fear of greater ills, or
accepts it in the hope of a greater good which he cannot otherwise successfully attain. For what he does he does by his own
preference and choice. And when such deeds are done they are
deliberate, although not in themselves such as a man would
choose to do. Thus, in these acts, the involuntary and voluntary
are mingled. They are involuntary, as regards the deed in itself, but voluntary when the circumstances are taken into
account. For apart from those circumstances no one would
choose to do those deeds. Nevertheless the praise or blame
attending such acts demonstrates that they are voluntary. For
there will be no word of praise or blame when things are done
involuntarily.

It is not easy to decide which course is preferable to the other.
In most cases one ought to choose what is grievous rather than
what is shameful, as Susanna and Joseph did. [4] Not invariably,
however. For, to be sure, Origen, rather than submit to be

---

[3] We must not suppose Nemesius to have had any care for historical
accuracy in writing this passage. He was dealing with what, to his age,
figured as aretology rather than history. Zeno and Anaxarchus were commonplace types of philosophic coolness and courage, and appear together
as such in Tertullian's *Apology*, ch. 50, though the stories that he attaches
to them are not quite the same. Diogenes Laertius, whose *Lives of the
Sophists* was most probably written in the mid-third century of our era,
gives us Zeno and Anaxarchus in that order. The *Lives* must be regarded
as mingled of legend and history. This Zeno, says Diogenes, was caught in
a conspiracy against the tyrant of Lipari, either Nearchus or Diomedon,
and gives two versions of what followed, the second of which is the tongue-
spitting episode. Anaxarchus, friend of Alexander the Great, Diogenes
says, landed in Crete, where his foe Nicocreon was tyrant, who had him
pounded to death in a hollow of the rock. The dying philosopher cried out
"You can pound the carcass of Anaxarchus, but Anaxarchus you cannot
pound." Clement of Alexandria and Origen both repeat this story, which
had become a favourite, centuries before Diogenes Laertius.
[4] For these examples, see The History of Susanna 5:23, and Gen. 39:12
respectively.

abused at the hands of the Ethiopians, offered incense,[5] and so
suffered the loss of all; so far is it from being easy to reach the
right decision in such circumstances! And still more difficult
than deciding what is right is to have the courage of one's convictions. For dreadful things in prospect are not so staggering as
when they are coming upon us. Sometimes, indeed, after we
have made our decision, we abandon it when the dreaded
moment comes. This fate befell some who were confessors. At
the outset, that is, they were steadfast, but in the end they gave
in, proving, when they actually felt the agony, not to be hardy
enough.

Let no one suppose that because lascivious desire or anger
have an inciting source outside the subject, these transgressions
are involuntary. For sure, it may be said that the charms of the
courtesan were what made the man that looked upon her crazy
for indulgence, and that it was the man who gave the provoca-
tion that excited someone's anger. But even though these motions had a first cause external to the subject, the subjects
nevertheless did their deeds themselves with their own proper
members. These cases do not fall within the definition of involuntary acts, because the subjects provided themselves with
a cause for giving way, in that poor discipline made them easy

[5] Epiphanius, in his *Panarion* (Book of all the heresies), Bk. II, Heresy 64
(Origen) ch. 2, tells us that, in view of the steadfastness of Origen, and his
influence for the Christian cause, the persecutors thought of the diabolical
plan of giving him the choice of offering incense to an idol or being
handed over to an Ethiopian to be subjected to abuse. He could not bear
the thought of the latter fate, and agreed to offer incense. In making this
choice, he did not do so with any willingness, but the persecutors threw
incense on to his hand, and he shook it off on to the altar. So he both fell,
by the judgement of the confessors, from his status of confessor, and was
expelled from the communion of the Church. This took place in Alexandria, and Origen, unable to bear the shame, removed to Palestine. So
wrote Epiphanius, before 380. The earlier evidences bearing on the removal of Origen from Alexandria to Palestine are quite incompatible
with this story of Epiphanius, who indicates that it is malicious hearsay
when he says that many do not credit Origen with having been reluctant,
in making his choice. The slanderous explanation of Origen's removal to
Palestine is to be explained by the Origenistic controversy which was
brewing up in the later years of the fourth century. There were certainly
monastic circles that thought nothing too bad to say of Origen.
In spite of his turning the single Ethiopian into Ethiopians, there is no
reason to doubt that Nemesius depends upon Epiphanius for this passage.
He probably supposed that it was among the Ethiopians that Origen was
being persecuted. Was not Ethiopia neighbour to Egypt? What concerned
Nemesius was the casuistry which the story afforded. Ecclesiastical cen-
sure pointed significantly at the guilt of the choice which Origen made.

captives of their passions. To be sure, those who so act are
blamed, as submitting to an evil willingly. So it is evident that
it is a voluntary act. For the subjects find pleasure in what they
do. And we have shown that an involuntary act is grievous to
the doer.

So much for an act that is involuntary as being performed
under constraint. It remains to discuss acts that are involuntary
because the subject does not know what he is doing.

COMMENTARY

46. *What acts are truly involuntary.* An act is not involuntary
because done under some stress from without. The last sections
have dealt with the soul, in its self-determination, as limited by
the structure and mechanism of the physical organism. The
next step is to show how this modified self-determination extends beyond the body, into the relations of the subject with
the outside world. Here Nemesius discovers that there is really
no such thing as an involuntary act which the subject does because compelled to do it by some force outside himself. For in
all instances that appear to fulfil these conditions, it turns out
that the subject could only be induced to do the deed because
his own will was partly consenting. So when men excuse themselves on such grounds, it is a false excuse. The conclusion which
Nemesius has thus reached in this section is that "an involuntary
act performed under constraint" is a *contradictio in adjecto*. The
only involuntary acts fall under the next chapter.

[M. 270.1–274.7.]

XXXI. *Of the involuntary act that is due to ignorance*

TEXT

47. There are many things that we do in ignorance that we are
glad, afterwards, that we did; like a man who should kill a foe
without meaning to, and is glad to have him dead, none the
less. This sort of act one cannot call voluntary, and yet neither
can they be called involuntary. Then again, there are things
that we do in ignorance, and grieve at having done them. These
acts have been called involuntary, on the ground that they are
things the doing of which brings sorrow in its train. So, then,
things done in ignorance are of two sorts, one producing a
result that was merely not intended, and the other a result that

was definitely not desired. Our next step is to consider these acts whose results are wholly undesired. For the mere unintended lies nearer to the voluntary, as having an element of the voluntary in it, mingled with the other; since it begins as unintended, but ends as voluntary. For what began as involuntary was turned, by the result, into voluntary. That is why the involuntary is defined as follows: an involuntary act is one which, besides being unintentional, is grieved over, and a cause of regret.

Again, doing a thing through ignorance is one thing, and doing it without knowing is another. For if the reason of our not knowing is something within our control, it is true that we do not know what we are doing, but we do not do it through ignorance. For example, a man does some ill deed when drunk, or in a rage. In the one case, drunkenness, and in the other, anger, is responsible for what he did, and yet did voluntarily. For it lay in his power not to get drunk. So he was his own reason for not knowing what he did. Things of that sort are said to be done not in ignorance but in blindness; and those are not termed involuntary, but voluntary. For this reason, those who do such things are censured by good men. For if such a one had not got drunk, he would not have done what he did. Getting drunk was voluntary on his part, and so, clearly, those things that he did when drunk were voluntary.

But it is when we have not ourselves provided the cause of our not knowing, but it simply fell out so, that we act through ignorance; for example, a man is shooting on the recognized range, and his arrow kills his father who chanced to be crossing it. So these examples prove that a man who does not know what is fitting, or esteems bad things as good, cannot claim to be the victim of an involuntary act, since his ignorance springs from his own wickedness, and he is surely reprehensible. But blame attaches only to voluntary acts. Surely then, it is not involuntary ignorance if it is of universals or of general notions, or of things that lie within our own control.[1] Only ignorance of some par-

---

[1] Aristotle defines a universal as "whatever may naturally be predicated of many things." The word "naturally," in this definition, contains the great assumption that there is an order in the universe which makes it intelligible. Aristotle differed from Plato in the explanation which he gave of the fact that the mind of man is aware of these things that "may be predicated of many things." They agree as to the fact itself; also that this awareness, unlike immediate sense-perception, is exempt from accidental error. On universals, therefore, there can be no genuine ignorance, so that, if a person acts as if some universal were otherwise than all men are aware that it is, he is not the victim of ignorance, but is himself excluding

ticular fact is involuntary ignorance. Of this or that fact we may
be ignorant without wanting to be so, but when we ignore some
universal, that is voluntary on our part.

Now that these terms have been defined, the next thing that
must be said is what we include under "particular facts." They
are what the teachers of rhetoric[2] call "details of circumstantial
importance;" who a person is, whom his act affects, what the
act is, to what is it done, where, when, how, why; in other
words, the character of the doer, the nature of the act, the
means, the place, the time, the manner, the cause. The character can be important, of either the doer, or of the victim of the
act, for example, the latter being the father of the man who
shot him without knowing. The act means what actually was
done, for example, that someone was blinded, although the
intention was only to slap his face. The means is exemplified by
the case of the man who threw what he thought was a piece of
pummice, when in fact it was rock. The place comes in, for
example, as the bend in a narrow passage, where one collided
with another whom he did not know was coming. An example
of the time is night, when a man slew his friend supposing him
to be an enemy. An example of the manner is a light, and by no
means violent, blow, killing someone. For the ignorance lay in
not knowing that a light blow would kill him. An example of
the cause is where someone gives a person medicine to make
him well, and the patient dies, because that medicine proves to
be poison to that particular man. While not even a lunatic
could be ignorant of all these critical circumstances, anyone
could be ignorant of most of them, or of the more important,

a knowledge which he possesses (e.g., of what is true, good, or beautiful).
A general notion is something the awareness of which is present to a
man in the same intuitive way as his recognition of universals, and is
equally exempt from the accidents of experience. For example, everyone
knows without experiment that the shortest way across a field is not round
the sides. There is a volitional element about awareness itself. Men can
ignore the universal, as they can a general notion. Equally they can ignore
their own exercise of volition, which is, of necessity, something the
knowledge of which is intimate to the subject himself.
2 Hellenic culture, during the fourth century of our era, was marked by a
disproportionate prestige of rhetoric. The "details of circumstantial importance" of which Nemesius speaks, are those critical for artistic perfection and clarity in setting out a rhetorical theme. Nemesius sees that these
are exactly the details which are critical for action truly adapted to the
circumstances of life, and so are those "particulars" (as opposed to
universals) on which a person may be accidentally, and so guiltlessly,
ignorant.

and act in ignorance. By the most important critical circumstances we mean, for what purpose the act was done and what form it took; in other words, the cause and the effect.

COMMENTARY

47. *Culpable ignorance makes an act not involuntary.* Only truly involuntary ignorance is excusable, while much ignorance is voluntary and the consequent action is likewise voluntary, and therefore is recognized as reprehensible. Domanski (*op. cit.*, p. 135, Note 1) again exhibits, by setting passages side by side, the influence of the *Nicomachean Ethics*, Bk. III upon this section.

[M. 274.8–277.3.]

XXXII. *Of acts that are voluntary*

TEXT

48. We have seen that there are two sorts of involuntary act; those done through ignorance,[1] and those done under constraint. Voluntary acts are the exact opposite to each of these two groups. A voluntary act is done neither under constraint nor through ignorance. That, forsooth, is not constrained which originates within ourselves. And that is not done through ignorance, where there is no particular circumstance that directly or indirectly affects the act, of which we did not know. Taking these two qualifications together, we define a voluntary act as one which originates within the doer, who, for his part, is aware of every circumstance attending upon his act.

The next question is whether natural functions, such as digestion or growth, are voluntary acts. It is clear that they are neither voluntary nor involuntary; since the categories of voluntary and involuntary rest upon our having a power of choice. In such things as digestion or growth, we have no power of choice; so that, although we are by no means ignorant of the way in which these things work, yet inasmuch as these processes are not within our power of choice, they cannot be termed either voluntary or involuntary. We have shown that deeds

[1] The last chapter has removed from the field of the involuntary those acts wherein the doer is responsible for having blinded himself, or where the result, though unintended, was welcome, while ch. xxx cleared out of the way excuses based on the plea of having acted under constraint. So, in seeking the definition of a voluntary act by way of antithesis, its opposite is seen to be an act done under external pressure and conditioned by ignorance to which no culpability attached.

wrought in wrath or lust are to be accounted voluntary, on the ground that the corresponding right conduct is praised, while offending therein is blamed, or even abominated. Moreover, such deeds carry pleasure or grief in their train, and originate within the doer. For it was within the power of the subject to avoid falling an easy prey to his passions, seeing that such conduct can be corrected by good upbringing. If this were not the case; if, that is, such actions were to be judged involuntary, then no beast or child can ever be said to do anything voluntarily; which is absurd. For we see how readily beasts and children come to be fed, needing no compelling. They come under their own impulsion, and knowing what they are about. They know all about feeding, and so soon as they see food, they are pleased, and hasten, as those that come to something that is well understood; while they are grieved if they meet with disappointment.

The criteria of the voluntary are, therefore, pleasure in the attaining, and grief in being disappointed; whence it is clear that anyone acting in lust or anger acts voluntarily. For even anger carries its own pleasure. If it were otherwise; and if one might not call the deeds of wrath and lust voluntary, ethical virtues would have no meaning. For these consists in striking the just measure[2] with regard to the passions. If the passions are involuntary, so too is the corresponding virtuous conduct. For deeds of virtue are, in fact, done under emotion.[3]

[2] Aristotle (*Nicomachean Ethics*, II. 6–8) teaches that virtue consists in reasonable moderation, avoiding excess on the one hand and deficiency on the other. To be devoid of natural passion would therefore be a defect, and not a virtue, just as much as an excessive giving vent to such passion. This definition of virtue is welcome to Nemesius because it involves the recognition that it lies within a man's control how far he indulges his passion. The doctrine of the mean was so well known that Nemesius appeals to it without elaboration.

[3] "Done with emotion," literally, done according to passion. Nemesius is clinging to the Aristotelian ethic, according to which, any act of virtue involves some passion exercised in moderate degree. We might paraphrase this as "involving a balancing of passions." The Alexandrine Fathers, Clement and Origen, sought to progress beyond metriopathy, or reasoned moderation, to apathy, or the negation of passion. According to them, supernatural Christian virtue was the fruit of one sole passion, the desire for God. Their doctrine promoted the cause of Christian asceticism, but might easily come to be dominated by Platonic scorn for the body and its attributes, and was unsuited to apologetic, above all, in Syria. And while it is clear that Nemesius held Christian asceticism in reverence, he obviously took the right line as an apologist, in working from the ethic of Aristotle and his doctrine of the mean.

Now no one would call that involuntary which is done after consideration and by free choice, where the impulse and the aim are from within ourselves, and where we have full and detailed knowledge of the circumstances. It has been proved that, where acts originate from within ourselves, they are voluntary. But since we have made frequent mention of free choice, and of things as lying within our power, we must now go on to discuss the nature of free choice.

COMMENTARY

48. *For some deeds our responsibility is undeniable.* The aim of Nemesius is now directed towards the establishment of man's moral responsibility. Chs. xxix–xxxii are devoted to an empirical psychology of action which brings out the fact that fully deliberate acts are far from being the sole exemplars of the voluntary, in human life, and that casuistry is so complex because of the admixture of reaction to circumstance with what is purely voluntary in our conduct. As an apologist, he begins his ethical discussion at a secular level, and proceeds thence, step by step, to a Christian conclusion.

[M. 277.4–282.11.]

XXXIII. *Of an act of choice.*

TEXT

49. What, then, is an act of choice? Is it, or is it not, the same thing as a voluntary act? Seeing that everything that is done by choice is also voluntary. The answer is in the negative, for the two things are not convertible as would be the case if choosing and what is voluntary were but one and the same thing, whereas we find that the scope of the term "voluntary" is the wider. For every free choice is voluntary, but not everything that is voluntary is done by free choice. Children, for example, and animals do things voluntarily, but certainly without deliberately choosing to. Anything that we do when angry, provided it is without premeditation, we do voluntarily, but it is certainly not done by an act of choice. Or, to take another example, some dear friend suddenly makes his appearance. We are so willing to see him as even to be delighted, but not because his coming was by our act of choice. Or a man unexpectedly finding a treasure is ready enough to accept it as a godsend, but not as due to his act of choice. From all these examples it may be

gathered that to act voluntarily is not the same thing as an act of choice. Can it really be, then, that choosing is the same thing as desiring? Once more we answer in the negative. For we can distinguish three kinds of desiring, lust, anger, and simply wanting a thing. But it is clear that neither anger nor lust is an act of choice, as may be seen from the fact that while men share with irrational animals lust and anger, they do not share with them their faculty of choice. For if while we have anger and lust in common with them, we differ from them when it comes to the faculty of choice, it is clear that the faculty of choice is one thing, but anger and lust are quite another. An intemperate person, in being overcome by his craving and acting accordingly, yet not by an act of choice, points us the same moral. In fact, free choice is at war with lust, over such a man, whereas if free choice and lust were one and the same thing there could not be war between them. Again, when the disciplined man acts as he has deliberately chosen, he does not act according to lust.

Once more, wanting something is not the same as choosing it. This is clear from the fact that not all the things that one may want are properly objects of choice. For we say that we want to keep well, but no one would say that he chose to keep well; no more would one say that wanting to be rich was the same thing as choosing to be rich. Wanting is a right word to use even when what we want is impossible of attainment; choice is the right word only when the thing lies within our power to attain it. So we may rightly say, "I want to be immortal." What we do not say is, "I choose to be immortal." For wanting applies to the end desired, while choice concerns itself with the means towards the end, the relation being the same as that between what we want, and what we deliberate how to get. For, what we want is the final result, while what we deliberate about is the means for reaching that result. It remains, then, that we make our object of choice only those things that we think we may be able to bring about. We want things of a kind that do not fall within our powers, as, for example, victory for a particular general. It is thus conclusively shown that an act of choice differs at once from anger, from lust, and from merely wanting a thing. Now that it is not the same thing as an opinion, either, is plain, both for like reasons, and also for different ones. For opinion is concerned not only with things that we might possibly do, but may equally have regard to eternal verities. Further, while we call an opinion true or false, we do not apply the adjectives true or false to an act of choice. Again, while opinion may be with regard to universals, choice has only to do with particulars. For choice is of things to be done, and such things are specific.

Neither is deliberation synonymous with an act of choice, as though it were an actual plan. For deliberation is an enquiry as to things that one might do. But when choice has been made of a course, it has been decided upon by process of deliberation. It is plain, then, that deliberation is about things that are still the subject of enquiry, but choice follows only when decision has been reached.

So now that we have stated what an act of choice is not, let us go on to say what it is. It is, then, something that mingles plan, judgement, and desire. It is neither pure desire, nor judgement, nor even plan in isolation, but is a combination of all three. For just as we say that a living creature is composed of soul and body, and that the body by itself is not the living creature, nor the soul by itself, but soul and body together, so likewise do we define an act of choice; that is to say, it is a kind of plan, followed by deliberation, which ends in a decision. It is clear from etymology,[1] however, that an act of choice is not a mere willing of something in the abstract. For an act of choice is a preferring one thing to another. No one prefers a thing, unless after deliberating, or chooses it, except he has passed a judgement. But, as we do not purpose forthwith to translate into deed every possibility that we esteem as good, an act of choice, and the course of action chosen by prior decision of the will, only follow when desire has been roused. Of necessity, therefore, choice and plan concern themselves about the same matters. And from these considerations we may gather that an act of choice is either the desire for some end within our power of attainment, reached after deliberation, or a deliberating about that end, incited by desire. For, when we make our choice, then we desire whatever it is that will has preferred.

But since we said that choice and plan concern themselves about the same matters, we will next make clear what are the things with which planning is concerned, and upon which we deliberate.

COMMENTARY

49. *Towards defining an act of choice.* An act of free choice is a more specialized and complex thing than many think. So

1 Free choice, in Greek, is *proairesis*, literally, choosing one thing before another, as the following sentence says.

Nemesius demonstrates in this section, and again, the *Nico-machean Ethics*, Bk. III, provides the model. (See Domanski, *op. cit.*, p. 140, Note 1 and p. 144, Notes 1 and 2.)

We now see the importance of the hint given in the last section but one, in the mention of the rhetoricians. The present section is, in fact, a valuable study in psychology. But it is pursued as a study in lexicography. The rhetoricians make exact definitions of the meanings of Greek words. And in this way they organize and make available the unconscious insights of past Greek thought, which has resulted in imprinting on the words their refinements of meaning. Nemesius' description of the natural, limited, and responsible character of human free choice may well be original. But it is presented as something that anyone could deduce from the established use of language.

[M. 283.1–288.15.]

XXXIV. *What things are subject for deliberation*

TEXT

50. Before we try to say what things are subject for delibera-tion, our best course is to define the difference between de-liberation and enquiry. For deliberation is not the same thing as enquiry, even though anyone who deliberates is making en-quiry about something; for all of which the two things are widely different. For example, it is matter for enquiry whether the sun is greater than the earth. But no one would say, I am deliberating of the sun being greater than the earth. For enquiry is the category including deliberation, as being the more general term. Every deliberation is, in a sense, enquiry, but not every enquiry is deliberation, as we indicated.

Sometimes we talk of considering, rather than use the word deliberation, as when one says, I am considering whether it is time to put to sea,[1] while we talk of considering, in other con-nections, such as learning, as when one says, I am considering mathematical propositions, not I am deliberating about such propositions. We often get our thoughts confused if we do not give discerning heed to our use of such terms, but take for synonyms what, in fact, are not synonyms. But once we have clearly established the distinction of meaning between "con-

---

[1] One would deliberate whether to go by sea or overland. But if, then, one chose to go by sea, one would have to consider whether conditions were suitable for putting to sea.

sider" and "deliberate upon," we can then safely approach the question, what are subjects for deliberation.

We deliberate, then, about things that depend on our free-will and are within the compass of what we can accomplish; things, further, of which the outcome remains uncertain, that is to say, things that could happen in one way, but equally could happen in another way. We say, "dependent on our free-will," because deliberation only applies where there is something to be done, and deeds are what are dependent on our free-will. For we do not deliberate about points of what is called "theoretical philosophy;" no, nor about God, nor about things that are bound to happen (by which we mean things that are always happening in a particular way, as, for example, the seasonal passage of the year), nor of things that, while they happen always in the same way, happen only at intervals, such as the setting and rising of the sun; nor, again, of things that, though they do not by nature happen always in the same kind of way, yet do so for the most part, such as, that a sixty-year old man is generally grey, or that a youth of twenty has down on his chin; nor, again, of things that fall out now one way and now another, without any rule, like the occurrence of showers or droughts or hailstorms; nor, again, of things that happen by luck, as we say, on the ground that they are among the less obvious possibilities. It is with this manner of things in mind that we say that subjects for deliberation are either "dependent on our free-will" or within the compass of "our agency," seeing that we do not deliberate on behalf of every man, nor as to every kind of matter, but only concerning such as depend upon our free-will or lie within the compass of our agency. For example, we do not deliberate how our foes, or people living in distant lands, would best govern themselves; though that is proper matter for their deliberation. Neither, even, do we deliberate about all things that can be done by our agency or lying within the scope of our free-will. There must be the further condition that the outcome remains uncertain. For if the outcome is manifest and acknowledged, then the matter is no longer subject for deliberation. Nor is deliberation in place concerning works or practice of science or art, for these (excepting a few arts that are called skilled, such as the art of healing, or of gymnastics, or of navigation)[2] have their fixed rules. We do deliberate about the skilled arts, as well as about whatever else lies within our power,

2 Aristotle gives these examples of skilled arts in the *Nicomachean Ethics*, Bk. III, ch. 3, with the addition of the financier's art.

is done by our agency, has its outcome uncertain, and is capable of being done in this way or in that. Further, it has been shown that deliberation is not about the outcome, but about steps leading up to it. For we deliberate not whether to be rich but how and by what means we shall get rich. To put the matter in a nutshell, we deliberate only about such things as are indifferently possible. And it is essential to make this distinction lest we leave anything in the argument lacking in precision.

The powers[3] whereby we are able to achieve anything are called our faculties; for we have a faculty corresponding to everything that we can do. If we have not the appropriate faculty, neither do we accomplish the corresponding deeds. So, then, the deed depends on faculty, and faculty upon our being. For the deed issues from the faculty, and the faculty proceeds from the being, in which, also, it reposes. So, then, as we have said, there are these three things, each in turn derived from the one before, namely, the potential doer, the faculty, and the possible deed. The being is that of the potential doer, the faculty is that which enables us to do the thing, and the possible deed is such as has that nature. Of possible deeds, some are unavoidable, and others open to our choice. Unavoidable things are such as we cannot prevent, or things whose opposites would be impossible. An open possibility is one that can be prevented, or one of which the opposite is possible. For example, it is unavoidable for a living man to breathe, and the opposite to this, namely, to live without breathing, is impossible. On the other hand, an open possibility is that it will rain today, but the opposite is equally possible, that it will not rain today. Again, of open possibilities, some are called probable, some improbable, and some indifferent. That a man of sixty will prove to be grey exemplifies the probable, that one of that age will not be grey, the improbable, and that he will be walking about or will not be walking about, or in general that he will do a particular thing or leave it undone, exemplifies the even chance.

So, then, the only things whereupon we deliberate are the indifferent possibilities. It is an indifferent possibility if we could do either the thing or its opposite. For if we had not that double possibility within our power, to do either the thing or its opposite, we should not deliberate. For no one deliberates where the outcome is assured, or about something impossible. Now if we can take only one of two opposite courses, and the

[3] From here, Nemesius' source for the end of the section appears to be Plutarch, *On fate*, 6 (Domanski, p. 148, Note 1).

OF THE NATURE OF MAN

course that we can take is assured, and beyond question, the opposite is impossible.

COMMENTARY

50. *The scope of deliberation.* The limited scope of our moral freedom is here illuminated by investigating the process of deliberating upon an action to be taken in the future. The theme of this chapter is developed from the argument of the opening chapters of the third book of the *Nicomachean Ethics* of Aristotle. Nemesius mentions the sixth book of the *Ethics* in Section 65 below, and there in terms which suggest that he has before his eyes, not the text of Aristotle so much as a commentary. The development of the psychology of deliberation by reference to the use of language, in this present chapter, is typical of the fourth-century rhetorical interest. It may be derived by Nemesius, therefore, from a contemporary commentary on the *Ethics*, and not be the fruit of his original speculation. (Domanski, *op. cit.*, pp. 145–7, Notes.)

[M.289. 1–294. 3]

XXXV. *Concerning destiny*

TEXT

51. Those who find in the courses of the stars[1] the cause of everything that happens are not only in conflict with the accepted notions of mankind but are bound to denounce politics as vain. For laws are absurd, courts (in that those they punish are guiltless) are an extravagance, and blame and praise are alike irrational; yes, and prayers are profitless, if everything happens just as it is fated to do. Heaven's providence and man's religion are banished at one stroke; added to which, man is found to be nothing but a plaything of celestial motion, seeing that the moving stars not only move man's bodily members to various actions but the thoughts of his soul as well. In a word, those who assert such things destroy the concept of the possible, at the same moment that they do away with free-will. And,

---

1 The dogma that all terrestrial affairs were ruled by the conjunctions of the planets, and movements of the other celestial bodies, was of old standing in Syria. The popular astrological fatalism to which it gave rise treated moral responsibility as illusion. Nemesius shows, however, that such fatalism makes nonsense of all serious thought, while itself resting upon a fantastic and baseless assumption.

thereby, they do nothing less than bring to ruin the whole concept of the universe. Then, too, they make the stars themselves wicked, as now procuring adulteries, and now inciting murders. Or, rather than the stars, it is God their Creator that bears the blame in their place, seeing that he made them such as would pass on to us an impetus to evil deeds which we cannot resist. So the monstrous doctrine of these men not only has such bearing upon human politics, but also denounces God as the cause of the most abominable crimes. Withal, their hypothesis is incapable of proof, and there is no need for us to take any further notice of it, so manifest is its blasphemous and absurd character.

We turn, then, to those who say that things are, at the same time, both in our own power and fated. For, they say, fate contributes something to each thing that is in process; as, for example, in causing water to be cold, each several plant to bear its own appropriate fruit, stones to fall and flames to rise; and, accordingly, fate causes any living creature both to obey its dictates, and also to move of its own accord.[2] When nothing external and fated opposes such movement, then it is perfectly possible for us (they say) to go as we please; we shall accomplish all that we set out to do. The advocates of this doctrine belong to the Stoics, to wit, Chrysippus[3] and Philopator,[4] with many other distinguished members of their school. But the only thing they succeed in proving is that all things happen in accordance with destiny.

For, if they say that, side by side with the working of destiny, we are granted impulses of our own, which are sometimes thwarted by fate but sometimes not, it is clear that everything, including what seems to lie within our own power, falls out as

[2] The Stoics tended to identify destiny with Nature, the world-soul, and God. Such identification only gives rise to difficulty when man as a moral agent is under consideration. To this difficulty the Stoics blinded themselves by saying that the difference between a moral agent, and all other things in the universe, is, itself, dictated by Nature.
[3] Chrysippus is here selected from the founders of the School as the most determinist.
[4] Our only knowledge of Philopator outside this passage is from an autobiographical chapter (ch. 8) in Galen's work, *On the detection and cure of disorderly passions, which each may carry out for himself* (R. Chartier's Paris edition, 1679, Vol. vi, pp. 531-2). Galen says that, when he was turned 14, he started hearing lectures in philosophy, at Pergamum, chiefly those of a disciple of the Stoic Philopator. This should date Philopator as early second century, A.D. and make his book, *Concerning destiny*, one of the latest in the Stoic tradition.

it is destined. Against these teachers, therefore, we repeat our former arguments, and prove their opinion absurd. For, if the same causes persist, there is, as they argue, every necessity that the same things should go on happening, and not in such wise as to give now one result and now another; since it has been assigned to them from all eternity how they should happen. Needs is, then, that the impulse of a living creature circumstanced, in every instance and in all respects, by the same set of causes should be as destined. And if our impulse attends upon inevitable causes, where is there anything left that is in our power? What lies within our power we must be free to do or not to do. There would be such freedom if, the circumstances remaining the same, it were possible for us now to take the initiative, and now to abstain. But if the impulse itself attends upon inevitable causes, it is plain that all to do with impulse itself is fated, even though it be by our agency and in accordance with our own nature, impulse and judgement, that it takes place. For, if initiative were such a thing as might possibly not be fulfilled, then the premiss, as stated, is a false one, namely that, circumstanced by the same causes, the same results must, of necessity, follow.

When it is applied to irrational and inanimate creatures, the argument follows the same course. For if they assign initiative to the category of things that are within our own power, because it is a natural quality with us, why should it not be said that it is in the power of fire to burn or not, as it likes, seeing that it is natural in fire to burn? And that, in a way, is what seems to be implied by Philopator in his book, *Concerning Destiny*.[5] Surely, then, what we do under the working of fate,

5 To appreciate the force of this argument, one must know that the Stoics attributed the order in the world to a "seminal principle" (or, as we should say, "formula") operative throughout the whole process of the universe. This "formula," conceived as essentially rational, could be personalized as Zeus, or the world-soul, or could be treated as impersonal, as Nature or destiny. A separate seminal principle, or "formula," was also attributed to each rational being, as the explanation of the rational form of his behaviour. The irrational in human conduct was explained as being the work of the passions, which had, therefore, to be regarded as at once an evil, relatively to the individual, and a product of Nature, which, *quâ* universal, must be good. It could, therefore, make no difference whether the seminal principle of reason was victorious over the passions, or whether the passions, as a product of Nature, disordered the rational pattern of life in the individual. Either way, it was a victory of Nature over Nature, and never could it be the triumph of a moral agent over destiny.

By thus exposing the illogicality of the Stoic ethic, Nemesius argues

lies not within our free will. For the same argument might be applied to harp or pipes or any other instruments, and indeed to all irrational and inanimate things, when used by anyone; and that would be absurd.

COMMENTARY

51. *Determinism is to be avoided.* The transition from deliberation to determinism has been prepared for by Nemesius having in view the work of Plutarch *On fate.*

Nemesius, whose investigation of moral responsibility has very much whittled down the field of human freedom, now turns to oppose the doctrine that there is no such freedom. He is aware that, although the moral interest was so strong in Stoicism, recent Stoic thinkers had, in fact, acquiesced in that doctrine. It was the characteristic weakness of Stoicism that its science was determinist, while its ethic called for the recognition of moral responsibility. This inconsistency is the object of Nemesius' attack.

[M.294. 4–298. 9]

XXXVI. *Of the dependence of destiny upon the stars*

TEXT

52. Now let us answer the Egyptian sages who say that, while it is true that destiny depends upon the stars, it can be modified through prayers and sacrifices for the averting of evil. For, they say, there are certain kinds of cultus that work upon even these very stars, fully to propitiate them and certain other and higher powers which are able to render them favourable. For this reason, they say, were devised prayers and cultus offered to the gods, and the sacrifices for the averting of evil. We retort that

that, when determinism is allowed into a view of the universe, it ends in driving out every kind of indeterminism. Conversely, if there be found in the universe any indeterminate, such as a man whose actions can be covered by no formula which answers to the general pattern of Nature, no realm can be vindicated for determinism, and any appearance of an iron rule of fate will prove illusory.

It may be gathered, from the form of Nemesius' allusion to Philopator's book, that the later Stoics, faced by systems that made moral responsibility a matter of concern and anxiety, laid their emphasis upon *ataraxia*, the untroubled state of being oneself, without moral struggle and its emotional disturbance. It was from such a quietism that Nemesius most needed to dissociate himself, if his somewhat subtle Christian ethic was to be taken seriously.

they thus make destiny one of the contingent, and not one of the determined, things. What is contingent is indefinite, and what is indefinite remains an unknown quantity. That is a situation that both brings to naught every possibility of prediction, and in particular, the kind which is called the casting of horoscopes, which these Egyptian sages themselves advocate before all other kinds, as being an effective and genuine expedient.

Now if they say that the influence of the configurations of the stars upon human destiny is both manifest and can be deciphered by the experts, and that, when the horoscope fails of its proper fulfilment, it is because divinely hindered, we then retort that this assertion also is absurd. In the first place, they thus make prayer and the cultus of the gods, the one thing that lies in our power, when nothing whatsoever besides does lie in our power. In the second place, we will dispute their contention that, while the whole of human activity and choice otherwise is determined by the particular conjunction of the stars, recourse to prayer alone lies within our power. For it is impossible to bring forward any reason why this should be so, or any necessity for it. In the third place, if there is some art and method of averting evil by sacrifices, whereby destined events may be thwarted from fulfilment, either this method is accessible to all men, or it is accessible to some, but not to others. If, then, it is accessible to all, there is nothing to prevent the fulfilment of destiny being totally overthrown, once all men have learned this art of thwarting the influence of the stars. If, on the other hand, this art is accessible to some men but not to others, what manner of men are they, and who makes the discrimination? But if it was destiny itself that some men should be worshippers of the divine and others not, it will be found that we are back once more at all things being fated. For this has now become clear about prayer and divine cultus (the sole thing, as they assert, that is in our power), that it is not inferior to the power of destiny, but superior. If, then, it was not destiny but something else that was responsible for these things, this other cause will then appear more properly to hold the place of destiny. For the possibility or hopelessness of reaching a successful issue by prayer settles the whole question of the power of destiny. For, to those who reach such an issue, destiny is nothing, and to those who cannot reach any such issue, all is destined. Thus it will be found that, to some men, all things are destined, while, to others there is no such thing as being destined. It is plain that whoever so orders things is most rightly the bearer of the name of destiny, and thus we shall find, once more, that all is destined; while, moreover, that agency, whether a spirit or some less obvious form of destiny, that apportions to mankind these two conditions, is (we shall see) unjust. For it does not share out to men, according to their deserving, knowledge of the way to propitiate the gods. For, wherein is this man more worthy than that, when all are mere tools of fate, and no one does anything of his own free will, or even so much as wills anything? For if things happen in this manner, no man is either righteous or unrighteous. So, no one deserves favour, or is undeserving of it. And that rulership is unjust, that does not give impartially to those who are all on the same footing.

COMMENTARY

52. *The astrological doctrine of the Egyptian priests refuted.* The ancient Egyptian priesthoods were famous among the Greeks for their astronomic lore. It was, of course, more astrological than purely scientific. We have a first hand account of this lore from the hand of an Egyptian high priest named Abammon in a work called the *Book of mysteries*, appearing among the writings of Iamblichus (edited at Oxford in 1678 by T. Gale). Porphyry had addressed questions to an Egyptian priest, and it is probable that this work is no fiction by Iamblichus, but a genuine reply received from a high representative of the Egyptian priesthood, glad to make common cause with the Neo-Platonists against the advancing tide of Christianity. The reply may be dated about A.D. 300. Nemesius most probably had his knowledge of the "doctrine of the Egyptian sages" from Neo-Platonic sources. Abammon believes, with the Neo-Platonists, that some men have a higher soul or "spark of divinity," deriving from a world above the stars. In this letter, intended as a reply to Porphyry, Abammon naturally adopts the Neo-Platonic view of the higher soul as being *nous*, or pure mind. The natural or lower soul, according to Abammon, is put into the body at birth by the working of the stars, and is constituted in accordance with the horoscope. The subsequent life corresponds with this pre-determination—hence the interest in casting horoscopes, which was, no doubt, part of the craft of the Egyptian priesthood. But, Abammon continues, those who have the divine spark have also the power to approach the higher divinities as suppliants. These divinities, according to Abam-

mon, are the deities worshipped in the temples of Egypt, who may, of course, be identified with deities worshipped under other names by the Greeks. The elect, or favoured race of men endowed with higher soul, can, by approved ways of prayer or sacrifice, win from the higher gods some modification of their destiny determined by the stars (who are lower gods), such, for example, as the recovery from an illness that would have proved fatal. Abammon seems to present this modification of destiny in the light of a correction, or overruling for good, of the destiny dependent on the stars, thus constituting a higher destiny. Hence the force of the argument of Nemesius. Nemesius clearly knows that the doctrine which he is refuting makes a division of mankind into two classes, of spiritual, and psychic or merely natural. Abammon seems to think of the higher soul as coming and inserting itself into the lower soul, perhaps at adolescence. Nemesius' conclusion is that all men have equally a measure of free-will, and that this disposes of the arbitrary doctrine that the stars determine human destiny. When, in the next section, he speaks of the opinion of "the wisest of the Greeks", it is not to contrast the Greeks with the Egyptians, so much as to imply that the Neo-Platonists, who follow the Egyptians, are not the wisest of the Greeks.

[M.299. 1–303. 5]

XXXVII. *Of those who say that the choice of actions lies with us, but that the outcome of those actions is destined*

TEXT

53. Those who say that the choice of actions lies with us, but that the outcome of those actions is as it was destined—and they are the wisest of the Greeks—have so far got the matter right, and yet so far are astray. For in attributing to us the choice of what we do, but not altogether charging us with the outcome, they speak most correctly. But when they invest fate with the part of determining the outcome, they are wrong. For they will stand reproved, in the first place, for making destiny something that is not self-complete, as only determining the one thing but not the other; and in the second place, for making fate a by-product of our purpose. For, upon that purpose of ours they make the operations of fate dance attendance, with the consequence that destiny is found rather to be set in motion by us, than we by it. So, man is mightier than fate, in the sense

that he is shaping destiny by what he chooses to do. What we ought to say is that providence shapes the outcome of our actions, for this work belongs to providence rather than to destiny. For the role of providence is to allot to each what is most suited to each. Consequently, the outcome of our choices will sometimes prove advantageous and sometimes not. Now if fate is, as the Stoics define it, some unbroken chain of causes and effects, that is to say, some order and concatenation of events that cannot be changed, then it reaches a conclusion that is not determined by its being profitable, but by some motive and necessity characteristic of fate. But what must we say of persons that are so silly and stupid as not to be capable of purpose? Did they turn out like that because they were so destined, or did they not? For, if they were not so destined, then here are things that fall outside the realm of destiny. But if they were so destined, it follows inevitably that we have not free-will. For if a person being incapable of purpose is the work of destiny, then it follows inevitably that destiny decides who shall be capable of purpose. And so these folk are where they started, saying that all things happen as they are fated. And that being so, the strife between reason and lust is an inanity, whether the struggle ends in continence or the reverse. For if it was of necessity settled that one man does the thing, and another does not, what good purpose is served by that upheaval and contention in the man? Yes, and furthermore it is equally fated, not only that one should do the thing, but that one should do it thus. What else, then, are folk saying, who make this assertion, but that even purpose itself belongs to the class of fated things? Well, then, it is free-will that battles with lust, and is victorious in the continent, and beaten in the incontinent. Therefore the form of the Stoics' original hypothesis will not stand, since it leads them to the conclusion that we have no free-will.

COMMENTARY

53. *Exposure of the Stoic failure to establish moral freedom on a logical basis.* Not fate, but only providence, leaves room for human free-will. Nemesius apparently dignifies the Stoics here, with the name of the "wisest of the Greeks" because they see that human affairs are in some way over-ruled. Destiny was, in their eyes, good. Chrysippus said that, if he knew that he was destined to be ill, he would try to be. Arbitrary choice of action they connected with ignorance, or doubt as to what was best.

Epictetus declared that he would choose sickness or death, if he knew that, as a member of God's universe, such was his appropriate fate. It was a Stoic presupposition that when choice must be made, it must be made unswayed by passion. When the destined course is known, the knowledge chooses for us. "Fecklessness", which Nemesius ingeniously makes the fulcrum for his refutation, was unconsidered in the Stoic scheme. Nemesius contends that fate, as such, is amoral, and not good.

[M.303. 6–307. 6]

XXXVIII. *Of the teaching of Plato on destiny*

TEXT

54. Plato uses the word destiny in two senses, as meaning both the concept of destiny and the working out of destiny. He conceives of destiny as being the world-soul. Its working out, he says, in having an inescapable source, fulfils an invincible divine law. This law he calls the rule of divine retribution, and says that it was given by the first and highest God to the world-soul[1] for the regulating of all things, and so that all things that happen might do so in accordance with it. He calls this law, "destiny working itself out", and "the rule of providence". For destiny is, he says, contained within providence, since everything fated is providential also. But the converse does not hold, that everything providential is fated. The divine law itself, which he says is at once both providence and fate, is all-embracing, affecting some things directly, and others indirectly. For it embraces directly, as being, as it were, the start for all else, each and every first cause. Such direct objects of that law

1 Providence, in the *Timaeus*, elevated to the primacy of the gods, is pictured as being faced, at the beginning, with matter in a state of confused and disorderly motion, or chaos. This chaos the Creator turned into order, by bringing into it the world-soul, which is the final cause of all that goes on in the universe. The world-soul constantly seeks the best that may be. It is Nemesius or his source, rather than Plato, that equates the world-soul with destiny. The divine law which Plato saw as being worked out through the world-soul is nearer to what Nemesius thinks of as providence, than to fate. It is invincible only in the sense that life and reason are invincible. Necessity (*anagkē*) takes the place in Plato more nearly of what Nemesius means by fate. *Anagkē* stubbornly asserts itself, in disregard of moral considerations, and is negatively victorious against the divine law of goodness, order, and reason, at least to some extent. In contrast, "divine retribution," *adrasteia*, while inescapable, is in moral correspondence with what men do.

are our proper assents, judgements, and impulses.[2] Whatever necessarily results from these is its indirect object, whereas our own free choice of what to do is its direct object. When we have done our part, the part of destiny follows on from what we have done, as indirect consequence. For example, we choose to go to sea. Here the law operates directly, but when once we are at sea, contingencies follow thereon, it may be shipwreck or not. Therefore Plato calls "contingent" those things that result from, and follow upon, our proper designs, that is to say, from and upon the things we originate and do. So, then, first causes, and our part in events, are matter for providence, while the consequences that follow inevitably and are not our doing, are fated.[3] For Plato says that what is destined was not determined from all eternity, but is contingent on our initiatives.[4] This agrees with the proverb, "the fault lies with our choice, and God is blameless", or "virtue knows no master", and with the fact of prediction.[5] For the entire argument to be drawn therefrom is to the end that choices, and some of the actions that result from them, lie within our power, while after-results, and how it all ends, are the province of fate and of necessity. It has been proved by what we have said above, that while this

[2] The souls of men, corresponding with the world-soul, are the children and choice creatures of providence, whose timeless design comes to fruition by their moral initiative. They are these first causes which are the direct object of the divine law.

[3] The world-soul, according to Plato, prevails upon matter, to improve it, as much as is possible. What opposes the world-soul in this task is the amoral causality, the anomalous and incomprehensible element of brutal necessity which arises in the world from matter. Providence, in Plato's belief, is largely triumphant by intelligent handling of this refractoriness of the material basis of the world. The mechanical consequences of acts are contingently providential, i.e., contingent relatively to providence. But it remains that when reason and mind have exercised all their initiative, the chain of cause and effect remains estranged from moral values. Nemesius superimposes a divine law upon Plato's providence and fate, to bind them together. This is not true to Plato, who saw the good purposes of the Creator at times suffering defeat, by the resistance of necessity; and that is something in which Nemesius will not follow him.

[4] As Plato saw it, inevitability was the attribute of *anagkē* (necessity), and not of the fulfilment by men of "what is destined" (the final purposes of providence). It was, in particular, amoral necessity that made men wicked; since no man wishes to be wicked, but is so only by bad rearing, bad health, or pressure of some kind from the material world.

[5] The first "proverb" is actually a citation from Plato's *Republic*, near the end of Bk. x. Prediction rests on superhuman knowledge. In the *Republic*, Plato directs consultation of the oracle of Apollo at Delphi, saying that "there is no other authority equally trustworthy."

exposition of Plato, wherein he gives the disposition and will of God the name of fate, and then subjects fate to providence, is inept, it diverges but a little from Holy Writ, which teaches that providence alone rules over all. Yet there is a serious difference, when he says that it is from necessity that the final consequences follow upon what we choose to do. For our assertion is that the dispositions of providence do not follow mechanically, but within a range of possibilities.[6] If providence could only follow mechanically, a first result would be that the greater part of prayer would be laid waste. For Plato's argument leaves prayer to affect only the beginnings of our actions, so that we may make the best choice what to do. But when once that choice has been made, further prayer is vain, since what follows is by mere necessity. But, as *we* draw the distinction, the power of prayer relates specially to what shall follow upon our choice. For we say that it lies with providence whether or not folk at sea are wrecked, and that, whichever in fact it is, is not the work of mere necessity, but is God's choice within a range of possibilities.

COMMENTARY

54. *A criticism of Plato.* In spite of the chapter-heading, only the first half of ch. xxxviii is concerned with Plato. In this half, Plato's doctrine is not stated in terms taken at first hand from Plato. Nemesius' most probable source of information is some commentary on the *Timaeus.*

[M.307. 6–311. 6]

TEXT

55. For it is blasphemous to say that God is subject to necessity, or that his will is bound by it. For necessity itself is his creation.[1] For, in the first place, he imposed necessity upon the stars,[2]

6 The Christian concept of providence rejects the Platonic dualism of matter and mind, as each being sovereign powers. In the Christian concept, God grasps the whole chain of causality, including that which extends beyond the reach of our initiative. God can introduce new factors into these further chains. Therefore a Christian can pray, not only, as Plato would, for guidance whether to put to sea, but, in putting to sea, for salvation from shipwreck. But man's prayer is useless, where God cannot master necessity.

1 Nemesius thus passes from Plato, with the justest criticism that can be made from the Christian side. The Greek doctrine of *Anagkē* is irreconcilable with Christian faith and hope.

2 By this sentence Nemesius turns necessity into the principle of order, whereas, as used by Plato, it was the negation of order.

making them move in the same way for ever and ever. Then he
set also the bounds of the sea. And he further imposed upon
universal Nature, and on particular kinds, the limits they must
observe. If any like to call those limits the domain of fate,
because such things happen inevitably, altogether and in every
respect according to that rule (for example, that everything
that, in its turn, comes into being, inevitably also perishes), we
have nothing to say against it. For our dispute with them is not
about terms. What we say is that God not only stands outside
the power of all necessity; he is its Lord and Maker. For in that
he is authority, and the very source whence authority flows, he
himself does nothing through any necessity of nature, or at the
bidding of any inviolable law. On the contrary, all things are
possible to him, including those we call impossible. To prove
this, he established once for all the courses of the sun and moon,
which are borne on their way by inevitable laws, and for ever
and ever will be thus borne, and at the same time to prove that
nothing is to him inevitable, but that all things are possible
that he may choose, just once he made a special "day" that
Scripture sets forth as a "sign",[3] solely that he might the more
proclaim, and in nowise invalidate, that divine ordinance with
which, from the beginning, he fixed the undeviating orbits of
the stars. In like manner, he made unending the lives of certain
men, Elias and Enoch, to wit,[4] in spite of their being mortal
and liable to corruption, so that, by all these signs, we might
recognize his authority, and know that his purposes are
unconstrained.

The Stoics, on the other hand, assert[5] that when the planets
have wheeled about until they reach, once more, the same sign
of the Zodiac, and the same height and position in it, which
each of them had at the beginning, when the world was first
made, at the stated periods of time, a burning up and destruction of all things is brought about. Then the world is recon-
stituted exactly as it was before, and the stars likewise go
through their motions all over again. Each single thing, they
say, happens in the same undeviating order as in the previous

---

[3] Josh. 10:13, 14.
[4] II Kings 2:11. (Elias) Gen. 5:24 interpreted by Heb. 11:5 (Enoch).
[5] This hostile account of the Stoic doctrine of the conflagration (*ekpurosis*)
at the end of the world-age is so remarkably like that in Origen, *Against
Celsus*, IV, 67, 68, and V, 21, 22, that we must assume that either Nemesius
knew this work, or that the account in Origen came to be a commonplace of Christian polemics.

world-cycle, and takes its course without a single change. For they will even have it that Socrates and Plato, and with them every single man of their time, whether of their friends or of the Athenian citizens, will live again, hold each their same opinions, meet with the same situations, and undertake the same courses of action, while every city, village, and division of the countryside, will likewise be repeated. Moreover they say that this rebirth of the world will take place not once but many times, or, rather, endlessly, and the same things will be repeated again for ever and ever. The gods, they then aver, not being subject to this periodic destruction, saw one world-cycle through, and, for that reason, know everything that is going to happen in each succeeding world-cycle in turn. For nothing will happen out of course that has not happened before, but all things will be just the same and unaltered, down to the last detail. Now some folk are saying that Christians made up their doctrine of a resurrection out of this doctrine of cosmic rebirth, but they are wide of the mark. For the oracles of Christ presuppose that the resurrection events will be once for all, and not repeated at intervals.[6]

COMMENTARY

55. *The Christian grounds for rejecting determinism.* God is above destiny; and the Stoics are ridiculous in their doctrine of cosmic rebirths. Such are the arguments of the two halves of this Section. Nemesius begins by a round statement of the theological answer of Christianity to determinism of every kind, that

[6] Nemesius is apparently dealing with a slightly different anti-Christian line of attack from that which Origen met from Celsus. Celsus assumes that the Christian teaching of the coming end of the world is a mere perversion of the doctrine of the *ekpurosis,* wherein the Christians say that, when all the rest of creation is destroyed, they will survive. Origen takes no notice of the suggestion that Christians are plagiarists. He gives his whole attention to showing that the Christian hope of bodily resurrection is not the crudity which Celsus thus makes it. And he ignores the fact that the Stoic doctrine is of world-cycles that go on endlessly, where the Christian doctrine of the end of the world is of an ending once for all. It would seem, therefore, that Nemesius had to meet a more recent development of anti-Christian polemic, the sting of which lay in the charge of plagiarism. Nemesius admits that Christians believe that the world will, at the end of the age, be restored to its pristine and paradisiacal state. But the restored world will not run the same course again, but an eternal and quite different course. The Christian doctrine of the finite present world-age is so essentially original that it cannot, he argues, have been plagiarized from the Stoic doctrine.

it is essentially blasphemous in its refusal to let God be God. The classical Greek concept of *anagkē*, which prevailed even with Plato, implied a despair of the supremacy of good which constituted the most excusable form of such blasphemy. Christians choose the alternative of seeing, in *anagkē*, God's will transcending mutability and our comprehension, and they do so, Nemesius says, because they have had the benefit of truth revealed in Scripture; in short, because they believe in miracle. So Nemesius concludes his case against determinism, in the first half of the section, while the second half forms an appendix in which he rebuts the charge, which we know to have been current, that Christian notions of resurrection were derived from pagan sources.

[M.311. 7–316. 11]

XXXIX. *Of free-will, or the power of initiative*

TEXT

56. In debating free-will, or in other words our power to initiate, the first point to establish is that we possess any such power. For there are many that hold the contrary opinion. That settled, there is the second point, namely, what things they are that lie within our power, and what is the extent of our authority. A third thing is to seek earnestly the reason why God, in making us, endowed us with free-will. To begin with the first point, let us first assert that we have free-will, and then prove it from facts which even our opponents will concede. For they say that the cause of anything that happens is either God, or necessity, or fate, or Nature, or fortune, or accident.[1]

Now, whatever God does is creative and providential. What springs from necessity is a motion from cause to effect that follows ever the same course. The working out of destiny is such that all things inevitably reach their destined end (it is indeed identical with that of necessity). The things that Nature works are birth, growth, and decay, and plants and animals. The tricks of fortune are singular and unexpected happenings. For fortune is defined as the coincidence and concurrence of two actions each of which arises from some particular purpose, to

---

[1] Basil and Theodoret are with Nemesius in asserting that neither God, Nature, fortune, nor accident, are to be blamed for the things which men do. Accident (*to automaton*) differs from fortune in being devoid of human interest.

produce something quite different from what was intended by either,[2] as when a man digs a ditch and finds a buried treasure. For one man buried the treasure, but not that the other man might find it. Nor did the other man dig for the purpose of finding treasure. The first intended, in his own time, to dig the treasure up again, while the second intended to dig a ditch. What fell out was something different from what either had intended. Finally, the fruits of accident are such things as befall inanimate and irrational things, devoid of nature or of art.[3] To which of these, therefore, shall we attribute those things that happen by human agency? (if, that is, we are not to admit that man himself is the cause and origin of his deeds).

It would be rank blasphemy to ascribe any man's shameful and wicked deeds to God. We cannot ascribe man's deeds to necessity, since they do not follow an invariable pattern. We cannot ascribe them to fate, because fate admits no range of possibilities, but only permits of one inevitable destiny;[4] nor to Nature, artificer of plants and animals; nor to fortune, since the deeds of men are not all singular or unexpected; nor to accident, for accident is the sort of thing that befalls inanimate and irrational things. Surely, there only remains the possibility that man himself, who both does things and makes things, is the initiator of his own works, and possessor of free-will.

A further consideration is this; if a man is the initiator of none of his deeds, it is in vain that he deliberates. For what use is taking counsel, if one is master of no single deed? Moreover, it would be a most monstrous thing that the fairest and most honourable attribute of man should turn out to be of no avail. For taking of counsel is with a view to doing something, and the undertaking and doing of something is the occasion for all taking of counsel. And still a further point is this; whatever powers of action we may have, the corresponding particular actions that employ those powers are ours as well. As we possess capabilities needed for various virtues, so surely those virtues themselves are ours to attain. And that those capabilities that can attain to virtue are ours is shown in that excellent saying of

2 This definition of fortune is from Aristotle, *Physics*, II, 4, 5, 6.
3 A dislodged stone rolls under the force of gravity. An animal takes shelter from heat or cold without reasoning why. Human conduct, Nemesius means, cannot be brought wholly within such a range of explanation. Rational creatures, as well as inanimate things, are, as Aristotle said, liable to accident.
4 That open possibility combined with fate is an illusion has been proved in chs. xxxv–xxxvii.

Aristotle about the ethical virtues, that "What things we learn by doing them, we also do from having learned them".[5] For, by learning to master pleasures we become temperate, and being temperate, we are masters of our love of pleasure. Or we may put it in another way, and say that anyone will admit that we have the power to rehearse and practise anything. Now rehearsal makes a thing habitual, and habit is second nature. So, if rehearsal is formative of habit, and lies within our initiative, then the attaining of a habit also is within our reach. And if certain habits are within our power, then the corresponding actions, springing from those habits, are in our power also. For deeds proceed from habits. For, surely, it is the habitually upright man that does the righteous deeds, and the wicked man likewise that does the wicked deeds. And surely, too, it lies with us to be just men or wicked, as we will.[6]

Now all our giving of advice and exhortation likewise demonstrates that there are things that lie within our power. For no one on earth would advise a person not to be hungry or thirsty, or not to take wings and fly, since it is not within our power to profit by such advice. It is plain therefore, that things that we can be advised to do, are things that lie within our power. One further and final consideration; laws would be inane if nothing whatever lies within our power. And yet, taught purely by Nature, every race of men observes some laws, which it lays down as knowing itself capable of acting in accordance with them. And the majority of peoples name gods as their lawgivers. For example, Cretans ascribe their laws to Zeus,[7] and Spartans ascribe theirs to Apollo. Surely, then, a knowledge of what is within our power must be naturally distributed throughout mankind. And we must add that conclusions identical with the foregoing are to be drawn from the existence of blame and praise,[8] while all such arguments disprove the thesis that everything is ruled by fate.

---

[5] This is the doctrine of the *Nicomachean Ethics*, the saying being cited, loosely, from II. 1. Aristotle's exact phrase is that "things we have to learn to do, we learn to do in the doing of them."

[6] For the parallels in Aristotle on habit, see Domanski, *op. cit.*, footnotes to pp. 158–9, as also parallels in Origen.

[7] Minos, the son of Zeus, whom Ovid calls *legifer*, was said to have given the Cretans laws in his father's name. The Spartan lawgiver, Lycurgus, sought confirmation of his laws from the oracle of Apollo at Delphi.

[8] The argument for free-will based on the consideration of praise and blame prevailed especially in Christian circles, and appears there first in Origen, *On first principles*, I. 5. 2.

COMMENTARY

56. *Human free-will demonstrated.* In this and the next three chapters Nemesius is concerned with the doctrine of free-will. He begins this chapter by enumerating the three themes to be dealt with, of which the first, that human free-will is no illusion, occupies the rest of the chapter. His ultimate source is the ethics of Aristotle, as may be seen from Domanski's footnotes, *op. cit.*, pp. 151–4. Aristotle knew, however, nothing of the conditioned nature of human freedom. Nemesius, for his part, fails to discover the psychological conditions binding our exercise of freedom; prejudice, limitation of view, and so on. But he advances far enough upon Aristotle for this not to make any serious difference, except that it is difficult to clear him from a suspicion of Pelagianism. In this he stands close to Theodore of Mopsuestia. The word *autexousia* for free-will, which he uses, does not belong to the vocabulary of Aristotle. The probable source of Nemesius, at this point, is therefore not Aristotle himself, but some later commentary on Aristotle's ethics. Domanski thinks it could be the famous commentary by Alexander of Aphrodisias. H. A. Koch is, however, inclined to think that it was a commentary of Syrian and Christian origin. The overt Aristotelianism of the Neo-Arian leaders, Aetius and Eunomius, would suggest the Christian circulation of such literature.

[M.317. 1–323. 14]

XL. *Of the range of things concerning which we have free-will*

TEXT

57. It has been sufficiently demonstrated that there are certain things that lie within our power, and that we are the masters of at least some of our actions. Now let us state what the things are that lie within our power. We say then, in general, that anything we do willingly is a thing that lies within our power. For no deed that does not lie within human power would be said to be done willingly.[1] The things in our power are, in a word, those that bring us blame or praise, or are the subject of advice, or the object of legislation; for so much has been proved already. In a special degree, everything that has to do with the soul lies within our power, together with things concerning

[1] If I say "I would willingly make myself invisible" I imply that, as things are, the word "willingly" is not applicable to making myself invisible.

which we take counsel. We take counsel about some proposed
deed, as having in our power the doing or not doing of it. And
further it has been shown (earlier in this work) how counsel is
taken in respect of things of even possibility, a possibility being
even when we can do either a certain thing or its diametric
opposite.[2] Our mind makes the choice which it is to be, and
this choice initiates action. These even possibilities are the
things that lie in our power, such as, whether to move or stay
still, whether to hasten or not, whether or not to grasp at things
not indispensable, whether to lie or tell the truth, give or with-
hold, rejoice over some good that comes to us or take it for
granted, or as many such things as there are, where vice or
virtue may enter. For, in respect of these things, we have free-
will.

Among actions of even possibility are the arts.[3] For every art
is concerned with creating something that can either be or not
be, of which the initiation lies with the artist, but not with the
thing that may be made. For nothing that is without beginning,
or that must exist, or that is bound to happen is attributed to
an art; neither is anything attributed to art, though having the
possibility of being otherwise than it is, if it contains within
itself the cause of its own being, as is the case with animals and
plants. For they are the work of Nature and not of art. If, then,
things attributable to art have their efficient cause external to
themselves, who is the cause of a work of art but the artist
himself, who makes it? For since the making of the work of art
lies with the artist, he is surely the origin and cause of what is
made. To be sure, therefore, there lie in our power both the
making of works of art, the virtues, and all activities of soul and
mind. And what the faculties of the soul are has been shown
already.[4]

[2] The subject of "even possibilities" is treated in the second book of the
commentary on Aristotle, *On interpretation*, composed by Ammonius, the
son of Hermeas, a late member of the Neo-Platonic succession at Alexandria, who died in A.D. 484. In this book he discusses providence, divine
foreknowledge, and free-will, and opposes the attribution of power to
fate. We may suppose him to be reproducing lines that the earlier Neo-
Platonists had pioneered, and may conjecture that Nemesius, in this
section, was much influenced by a Neo-Platonist commentary on some
work of Aristotle.
[3] In Section 50 it was said that most arts are not subjects for deliberation.
But that kind of deliberation concerned the "how." In this passage it
only concerns the "whether."
[4] The faculties of the soul have been the subject of investigation from ch. vi
on, and have been shown to work at different levels, rational and ir-

The man in the street supposes that the doctrine of human
free-will means that everything a man does, together with his
gifts and attainments, and even the fortune he enjoys is the
fruit of his own choice, and naturally rejects such a notion. But
men of sharper wit actually refute us by adducing a citation
from Scripture that, "A man's ways are not in his own power".[5]
"Good people", they say, "how can man have free-will, seeing
that his way is not in his own hands"? They cite again, "The
thoughts of men's hearts are vain",[6] so that we cannot bring to
fruition the thoughts that we conceive. Many such things they
say, not knowing what really is meant by free-will. For, of
course, we have not the choice whether to be either rich or poor,
or to be always well, or to enjoy rude health, or to command
either what men call a competency, or a fortune, or aught else
that is ruled by providence. But we have the power to do,
determine or promote either good or evil, in all those cases
where there is before us an even balance of possibilities; seeing
that an act of choice leads the way to every deed, and that not
the deed only but the choice itself is subject to judgement. This
is proved by what it says in the Gospel, "Everyone that looketh
on a woman to lust after her hath committed adultery with her
already in his heart".[7] Also Job sacrificed to God for the trespasses which his children committed in thought.[8] For the
beginning of sin and of good works alike is in an act of choice.
As for the actual deed, providence sometimes permits it, and
sometimes prevents it. So there is the part that we can play, and
the part of providence. What happens must necessarily depend
on both together. For if anything were the work of one only,
that excludes the other. The way things happen, then, is by an
intermingling of agency; now it will be by our initiation, and

rational. But we can hardly suppose that the "activities" (*praxeis*) of the
soul, here mentioned for the first time can be anything other than the
conscious rational thoughts and impulses.
[5] The citation is of Jer. 10:23, but is tendentiously inexact. The words of
Jeremiah are, "O Lord, I know that the way of man is not in himself; it
is not in man that walketh to direct his steps. O Lord correct me, but
with judgement . . ." The prophet admits the frailty of man, but certainly
not his moral irresponsibility.
[6] "The Lord knoweth the thoughts of men that they are but vain." Ps. 93
(94):11. It appears, from this "refutation," that there was, in Syria, a
non-Christian public acquainted at least with the Septuagint, but un-
reconciled to the Christian view of sin. The Syrian "man in the street"
would appear to have been frankly fatalistic.
[7] Matt. 5:28.
[8] Job. 1:5.

now by decree of providence, and now, again, it will accord with both at once.

Now providence is in some sense universal, and in some sense is concerned with particular things and persons. It follows of necessity that the particular providence must accord with universal providence. Thus, if the atmosphere is dry, everybody is also dry, although all may not be equally so.[9] And when the mother does not eat suitably, but gives herself up to gluttony, the consequence is that her children are born with their physical temperament disordered and their inclinations perverse. It is plain, then, from these considerations, that it may fall to the lot of some persons to have a difficult temperament, either through sharing the general circumstances of their parents,[10] or from the way their parents chose to feed, or because they themselves have ruined their bodies by gluttony, so that their physical temperaments turned out to be bad, ultimately because of human voluntary action; and providence is not wholly accountable for such situations.

When soul, therefore, yields to physical temperament, and

[9] This example gains force and clarity if we take it of the drought in the days of Ahab (I Kings 17, 18). This is represented in Scripture as a work of providence, for the correction of Israel. The general conditions affect the righteous Obadiah no less than the guilty Ahab, though it may be not so grievously, while a special providence is seen to preserve Elijah, who is also an example of free-will. "Elijah was a man of like passions with us, and he prayed fervently that it might not rain; and it rained not on the earth for three years and six months. And he prayed again, and the heaven gave rain" (James 5:17, 18). In this passage, providence almost seems to wait upon a human initiative. The single sentence of Nemesius under comment is, by itself, so obscure that it is probable that he is summarizing an argument known in some other way. It might only mean "the physique of the nomad Arabs is different from ours, but not in every individual."

[10] This is perhaps the sense, but there is strong probability that the text is corrupt at this point.

"Visiting the sins of the fathers upon the children" (Ex. 20:5) may well be cited as an exemplary work of providence. But the example taken by Nemesius bases the operation of this law rather on necessity than on providence, excusing providence because it is the hand of nemesis that is seen in the unhappy plight of the disordered. We have here, from Nemesius' own pen, the Platonic dualism of providence and necessity. This seems to show how hard it was for Greek men of learning to get free from the influence of Platonic notions, even when they wanted to. It also strengthens the probability that, at this stage in his argument, Nemesius was using a Neo-Platonic source, in some way. He gets back on to safe ground in saying that anyone has, within his capacities, different ways in which he can behave.

gives way to lust or anger, and is weighed down by poverty or puffed up by wealth, according as fortune apportions them, the evil so constituted is voluntary. For a soul that does not yield to faulty temperament, but corrects and overcomes it, changing it rather than being changed by it, succeeds in establishing for itself wholesome dispositions, by gentle training and a helpful diet. So, from considering those that go about things in the right way, it can be seen that those who do not, sin voluntarily. For it lies with us whether we concur with our faults of temperament, or work against them and master them. And when the man in the street puts up the excuse that his faulty temperament is the cause of his passions, he does not attribute vice to man's choice but to necessity, and caps that by alleging that the acquisition of the virtues does not lie with us either; an assertion which is monstrous!

COMMENTARY

57. *The inter-relation of human free-will and divine providence.* This section opens by summarizing the results that have been reached regarding the nature and extent of human initiative. The analysis of the nature of an art, which then follows, is likely to be derived from a rhetorical or philosophical commentary. It is to Nemesius' purpose, in providing, in the artist, a prime example of human initiative. Finally it is shown that the real problem of free-will is how to relate it to the working of divine providence.

[M.324. 1-328. 1]

XLI. *Why we were given free-will*

TEXT

58. It remains to say why we were given free-will. Straightway, then, we assert that free-will came to us as the necessary concomitant of the faculty of reason.[1] Next we say that transformation and change belong to creaturehood, and especially to creatures made with a substrate of matter. For the start of being is change, while becoming involves change in the material substrate. The truth of this statement can be seen by looking

---

1 Domanski, *op. cit.*, p. 161, Note 1, gives parallels from Alexander of Aphrodisias and from Origen; in this insistence upon the crowning glory of man, the double gift of reason and free-will, we see the Aristotelian psychology being influenced by a Neo-Platonic moment.

27—C.J.

at any plant, or at animals, whether they tread the earth, or fly, or swim. For change is incessant in them all. Furthermore, that free-will comes to us in company with the faculty of reason is quite clear to any that give good heed, from what has been said concerning the fact that there are things that are in our power. Nevertheless, it will not be out of place to recall these points at this stage, seeing that the argument which follows calls for it.

Of the rational faculty, part is devoted to contemplation and part to action. Contemplation is perceiving things, and how they consist. Reason on the active side is deliberative, and determines the right way to do things. The contemplative exercise of the faculty is commonly referred to as mind, while the active exercise is called reasoning; or the first is called wisdom and the second prudence. Everyone who deliberates does so on the supposition that the choice of things to be done lies with him, and that he will choose the preferable course as the result of his taking of counsel; further, that when he has so chosen, he will act upon his choice. There is every necessity, therefore, for one who has the capacity for deliberation also to be master of his own actions, for, if it were otherwise, it would be to no profit that he possessed the faculty of deliberation. And if things stand so, then free-will is bound to accompany the faculty of reason. For either a creature will not be endowed with reason, or, if it is endowed with reason, then it will also be master of what it does. And if a creature is master of what it does, without doubt it must possess free-will.

Now it has been shown that creatures made with a substrate of matter are mutable. Put together our last two arguments, and we get of necessity the result that man has free-will and is mutable. He is mutable because he is a creature.[2] He has free-

---

[2] As at the end of ch. 1, Nemesius here connects moral instability and physical instability as it exists in creatures living by means of material bodies. He goes on to attribute moral mutability even to incorporeal creatures. It appears, therefore, that it is inseparable in thought from creaturehood, as such, and not first and foremost to the instability of the body. A being morally immutable by nature would not be a creature, but a second God. To rational creaturehood, God adds the gift of ability to contemplate himself, and in varying degrees in different kinds of rational creature. But in them all, such contemplation generates moral immutability. The faculty of reason contains the possibility of the contemplation of God, but also that of preoccupation with and preference of creatures. Moral mutability is not identical with free-will, but free-will is the condition without which moral mutability, or, for that matter, moral immutability, would be inconceivable. The mingling of the two kinds of mutability in

will because he is endowed with reason. Anyone, therefore, that finds fault with God for not making man incapable of evil, while at the same time being endowed with free-will, is, though he may not know it, blaming God for making man rational, and not irrational. It has to be in one way or the other. Either man must be irrational, or, if he is rational, then liable to act now in one way and now in another, and so he must have free-will. Inevitably, therefore, every nature endowed with reason must also have free-will, and, as part of that same nature, be mutable. But creatures made with a substrate of matter are mutable on two accounts, first from being material, and then as being creatures. Such creatures as are not made with a substrate of matter are mutable on the one single account of creaturehood. And again, all such incorporeal natures as are concerned in mundane affairs, and descend to taking a share with men in their deeds, are mutable above all other beings of their kind. On the other hand, those whose incorporeal nature is so high as to be relatively near to God, enjoy blessedness in contemplating him. They are concerned only with their personal relation to God, and have weaned themselves completely from everything to do with passing activity and with matter. So they have become more and more habituated to contemplation and to God, and rest immutable. While, because they are rational, they have free-will, they are, for the reason given, in no wise mutable. Nor need we marvel. For those from among men who have given themselves to contemplation, and have severed themselves from affairs, have continued unchanging.[3]

I think, now, that in what has gone before it has been fully demonstrated that all creatures rational by nature were, from the first, most excellently made, and had they remained thus in accordance with their first creation, they would have been removed from all evil. Evil came to them by their own choosing.

man makes his preference of creatures before God more tentative than it would be in an incorporeal being, so that it is a subject for repentance and forgiveness (so Section 7).

[3] Cf. Athanasius, *Life of St. Antony*, 14, where the saint, after twenty years in the mountain, "had himself completely under control—a man guided by reason, who had attained stability." The rationale of this hermit life is before us in Nemesius. Reason sees that, of its two capacities, the practical confines to the sensible world, while the contemplative is free of the noetic world as well, and so is the higher. Contemplation of God fascinates the creature that attains to it, and stills him into an immutability of goodness that mirrors the immutability of God. This deliverance from mutability is the creature's salvation. Such was the gospel of the Desert Fathers.

Accordingly, those that have remained as they were made at the first enjoy blessedness.

Of the incorporeal beings, only angels fell away, and not all of them, but some only, that inclined to things below, and set their desire on things of earth, withdrawing themselves from their relations with things above, yea and with God.[4]

COMMENTARY

58. *The mutability of creatures.* The promise of the title of the chapter remains unfulfilled otherwise than in the first sentence. No doubt, the implication of this first section is that the use of free-will, for which it was bestowed by God, was that rational creatures, despite their creaturehood, should come, through continual exercise of right choice, and contemplation of God himself, to share the divine immutability. This conclusion is never made explicit. The explicit subject of this section is mutability as an attribute of creatures.

[M.328. 11–331. 2]

TEXT

59. It is clear, then, from what we have shown, that as we are mutable on account of our nature, we have faculties of choice[1]

---

[4] In this passage, Nemesius seems to identify angels with the "sons of God" in Gen. 6:2–4. His word "only" seems to exclude archangels from the fall of these angels. Such a view would go with the supposition that the serpent of Gen. 3:1 was an animal, and not a fallen archangel appearing as a serpent. Nemesius seems to have somewhat different speculations in view in the two passages, in Sections 7 and 58 respectively.

[1] "Faculty" throughout this section translates *dynamis* (power). But to substitute the word power in translation would be to obscure the fact that the reference is still to the Posidonian notion that for every activity that belongs to the life of man the Creator has given him the appropriate *dynamis*, or faculty wherewith he can fulfil that aspect of his being. Nemesius has been at pains to show how choices are made. But the assumption has been tacitly made that there is a *dynamis proairetikē* or will-power present, to implement the choice. This faculty has been called mutable because there is nothing in it *quâ* faculty that determines that it shall be used for good and not for evil. Nemesius will not allow, however, that, *quâ* faculty, it is evil or the cause of evil, any more than are any of the natural *dynameis* or faculties.

The mutability shows itself in the exercise of will, but it originates in the spiritual nature of man as a rational creature. Augustine would presumably have agreed with Nemesius that in itself the power to will is the gift of God in nature, and good; but he would have denied that bad upbringing or the acquisition of bad habit were sufficient explanation of the trend

that are mutable. But no one should blame God because we, having mutable faculties, are evil. For the badness is not in the faculties, but in our habits, and our habits are as we choose; and surely it is by our choice that we become evil. We are not so by nature. My meaning may be more exactly stated as follows. We said, above, that a faculty is that whereby we are able to do each several thing that we do. Every faculty that is concerned with the exercise of free choice serves for whichever alternative is chosen. For the same faculty enables us to lie or to tell the truth, just as one and the same faculty serves us to exercise moderation or to be wanton. But it is not one habit that enables us to follow opposite courses, such as wantonness and moderation, or lying and telling the truth. On the contrary, opposite habits lead to contrasted courses of action. For moderation springs from virtuous habit, and wantonness from vicious habit. Certain it is that evils do not come from the faculties, but arise from habits and from free-will. For it is not the faculty in question that prepares us to play the wanton, or to lie, but our free choice. For it lay in our power to tell the truth and not lie. Seeing then that vice is not faculty but habit, it is not he who bestowed upon us the faculty that is answerable for our evil deeds, but our habit that we have acquired, working through us, and at our bidding. For it was open to us to acquire, by exercise, the opposite habit, and not the bad one. And faculty differs from habit, in the fact that all faculties are natural, while all habits are acquired; as in the fact that faculties play their part untaught, while habits are acquired by learning, and by use. If, then, a faculty has the qualities of being natural and untaught, and a habit those of being acquired and learned, it follows that not nature but our bad upbringing, whence we acquired bad habit, is to blame for evils.[2] For all habit has been shown to be acquired. And that

towards evil that manifests itself in even the best nurtured and most innocent of mankind. Nemesius has not followed the matter so far back, but there is nothing to suggest that, if he had, he would have opposed Augustine. His object is clearly the justifying of God and not of man.

[2] Bishop Fell's seventeen illustrations of the agreement of the language of other Fathers with that of Nemesius are reprinted by Matthaei (pp. 399–400). Domanski (*op. cit.*, p. 161, Note 1), after saying that the argument of Nemesius lies entirely within the frame of nature, and is in collision with no doctrine either of supernatural grace or of divine wrath, points out the piquant truth that Bellarmine, while attacking Nemesius for Pelagianism, defends Gregory of Nyssa from a like charge, whereas the work, *On the soul*, printed currently among the works of Nyssen was nothing else than the first three chapters of Nemesius. And the words,

the faculties are, on the other hand, implanted by nature, is clear from the fact that all, excepting those suffering from some disability, have the same faculties. And that habits are not the work of nature is evident from our not all having the same habits, but some having one and some another; whereas natural attributes are the same in every individual.[3]

COMMENTARY

59. *We, and nothing of God's doing, are to blame for the ill we do.* The purpose of this section is to close the survey of man's free-will with a firm denial that the evil in man's life is due to any imperfection in God's gifts to man in his nature. So, having vindicated the goodness of God in nature, Nemesius is about to pass on to vindicate him in the matter of his providence. It is in this section, however, that Nemesius gives most handle to those who would suspect him of Pelagianism. It does not suffice to convict him. The Augustinian doctrine of an inherited pre-disposition to evil was not one that would come readily from the pen of any fourth century Greek churchman, because it was too reminiscent of the Gnostic doctrine that the body is the source of evil. Alternatively, if the entry of evil into human life was not due to the body, the fact of such evil must prove some pre-natal fall of the soul to have taken place, thus opening the door to Origenism. It is notorious that Augustine was never able to reach an assured view of the origin of the soul that would escape this dilemma. Nemesius, writing a decade before the Augustinian-Pelagian question had become a public issue, even in the west, was unconscious that there was any danger to avoid. He was chiefly anxious to claim that no blame attaches to God for our evil lives, but that we ourselves introduce evil,

"the free actions of men are not the work of providence, but proceed from the reasoning and counsels of men," with which Bellarmine epitomizes the justifiable teaching of Gregory, would apply admirably to what Nemesius has been saying in these last sections.

[3] Nemesius insists, as Pelagius did, upon the impartiality of God's gifts in nature. But Pelagius held it derogatory that God should be thought to require to assist man's will in a mysterious manner before man could be pleasing to him, and fit for eternal life. Nemesius, on the other hand, so emphasizes the differences of human attainment that some theological explanation is called for, over and above the attribution of evil to man's choice. Nemesius undertakes no such explanation. But as the Christian doctrines of election and grace are comprehensible only in the light of Christian faith and experience, we could not expect them to be discussed or disclosed in Nemesius' work of apologetic.

in the making of our free choices. The other side of the question, whether being such as we are, we could choose right, is not within his purview. He is writing as an apologist. His non-Christian reader, used to aretologies, would suppose man to be theoretically capable of virtue. And that would be the best thing for him to think, for only so would there be the opening to win him over to a serious acceptance of his own moral responsibility. In short, the issue upon which Pelagianism turns is something that lies outside the frame of Nemesius' argument.

[M.331. 3–336. 8]

XLII. *Of providence*

TEXT

60. Sufficient has been said already to show that man has free-will, to indicate in what respects his will is free, and to say why he was given free-will. But since not everyone who has it in mind to murder someone actually does so (in some cases it happens, but in others not, because the intention is thwarted and never attains its goal) we declared that providence (not fate) is in some sense answerable for what actually happens. A discussion of providence is the natural sequel to what has been said about human free-will. The argument may be taken in three stages. First let us treat of the reality of providence, then its method, and thirdly its scope. Now no Jew, even though he were beside himself, could fail to recognize providence,[1] knowing the wonders that took place in Egypt, and having heard, moreover, of the things that happened in the wilderness, events wherein providence was more clearly manifest to men

---

1 The difficulty of translating this sentence arises from the participle *mainomenos*, "raving," in apposition to the subject "a Jew." If it were not there, the sentence would clearly mean, "Yes, and a Jew would recognize providence." Some condition is required to balance the optative, and it is expressed in the participle. Ellebodius, followed by Orth, took the participle to mean "insane," so as to translate "a Jew would recognize providence—if he were off his head!" or, as it might be turned, "no sane Jew would recognize providence." But there is no reason why insanity should confer faith in providence, and the sense thus attained is unsatisfactory. If, however, *mainomenos* is taken to mean "deranged, not in full command of his faculties," we may render the sentence, "a Jew would recognize providence, even though he could recognize nothing else." The translation here given takes *mainomenos* as "even though mad," and does not follow Ellebodius.

than if they had seen it with their very eyes; having clearly perceived, besides, many such works of providence as admit no
possibility of doubt, in the prophets and during the Babylonian
captivity.[2] Christians, for their part, have all those things to
teach them the truth of providence,but, supremely, the divinest,
and, in its exceeding philanthropy, the most incredible of all
the works of providence, God's incarnation on our behalf.

It is not only, however, to Jews and Christians,[3] but to
pagans also, that we must make good our contention. Come,
then, and let us prove that there is a providence, arguing only
from such things as Greeks themselves believe. One might then
demonstrate the existence of providence by the same arguments
that we have employed to prove that there is a God. For the
continued existence of all things, especially where they are
subject to genesis and decay, the place and order of whatever
has being, maintained always according to the same pattern,
the utterly undeviating courses of the stars, the circle of the year
and the returning seasons, the equality of day-time and night-
time, when taken over the year, and the measured and utterly
regular lengthening and shortening of either—how could anything continue to be managed like that, if there was no one
thinking it out beforehand?[4]

Not only so, but the retribution that overtakes trespasses, and
even more, the circumstantial disclosure of the trespasses themselves in situations where there was no one able to bring home
a charge, proves the existence of providence. Both Hebrew
scriptures and Greek letters are full of stories to such effect. For
such is the story set forth in Scripture of the trials of Susanna,[5]
or in profane literature, of the poet Ibycus. For Ibycus was

---

[2] They could see providence in God's overruling of history so as to discipline
his people; predicted by the pre-exilic prophets, fulfilled in the captivity,
and crowned in the return of the pious remnant.

[3] The Greek *toutous* might here refer back to Jews and Christians, or to
Christians only. The present translation demands the former alternative,
while that of Ellebodius demands the latter. This is quite possible. The
difficulty in the way of Ellebodius is the absence of any word implying
"although" in qualification of Jewish knowledge of the revealed works of
providence.

[4] This recapitulates what is contained in the Stoic notion of general
providence, and adds the notion of One thinking it out beforehand, a
notion which was really derived from Scripture.

[5] In the *History of Susanna*, providence intervenes by raising up Daniel, and
giving him the insight to expose the false evidence of the elders. The
passage is the more appropriate to Nemesius' purpose because Susanna
(vv. 42, 43) has declared her faith in God's omniscience.

murdered by certain persons while no one was there to take his part or bear witness for him of these men's conspiracy. Nevertheless, as he was being done to death, he beheld some cranes, and cried out to them, "O ye cranes, avenge my murder." The city authorities tried to trace the murderers, but without success. Howbeit, some cranes flew over the audience seated at a performance in the theatre. But when the murderers saw the cranes, they laughed and said, "Lo, the avengers of Ibycus!" They were overheard by someone sitting near them, who informed the magistrates. The men were arrested and confessed to the murder.[6]

There are numbers more of such tales to be found in old-time writings. If anyone cared to collect them, he could extend this line of argument indefinitely. But though all evil-doers are not convicted in this way, while some seem even to escape scot free, let no one on that account deny that there is providence. For providence follows out its care for men not in one way only but in many and various ways.

Not the least cogent proof of the existence of providence is the structure and proportion of our bodies, which, though those bodies are subject to birth and decay, is yet preserved always constant. The forethought of providence is to be discerned in every member of the body, as the studious can gather, out of various treatises, for themselves.[7] Moreover, the variegated colouring to be observed in different animals, the beauty of which is maintained in every specimen, proclaims aloud the existence of providence.

6 Ibycus, of Rhegium (Reggio) in Calabria, flourished in the sixth century B.C. He was an erotic poet, and is credited with seven books of Dorian lyric poetry. He is also said to have invented the triangular cithern. His murder took place near Corinth. Plutarch tells the story in his work, *On garrulity*, 14, but knows nothing of any hue and cry. Ibycus was merely missing when the incident in the theatre took place. The moral which Plutarch draws is the advisability of keeping one's mouth shut. That, however, is no argument that the story was not commonly told with the moral "murder will out." Suidas (*s.v.* Ibycus) says that "the cranes of Ibycus" had become a proverb for the circumstantial revealing of crime.

7 Greek interest in the parts and bodies of men and animals took literary form in Aristotle, *On the parts of animals*. Nemesius no doubt had specially in mind Galen, *On the uses of the parts of the body*, with its observations on the way in which members are adapted by their structure to fulfil their natural functions. Nemesius now adds the telling point about the stability of the characteristics of the species in spite of the incessant change and decay in the individuals in which those characteristics are exemplified; in which Nemesius reads a divine purpose incessantly reaffirmed.

Commentary

60. *Approaches to belief in providence.* Chs. XLII–XLIV are no expected part of a work on the nature of man, and may be regarded as an appendix arising from the foregoing discussion of man's free-will. For, whereas Augustine sought to solve the problems of free-will by the mysterious action of God within individuals, Nemesius is evidently setting out to solve the same problems solely in terms of divine action surrounding the individual in the workings of providence. But, with that difference, Nemesius is as much minded as Augustine to "let God be God." So independent did these last chapters appear, to some of the ancients, of what had gone before, that they were treated as forming a separate opuscule, *On providence.* It is thus that Anastasius Sinaita (*Question* xviii) cites from the end of ch. XLIV as from a work of Nemesius with that title. Ch. XLII appears in a Munich MS under the same title.

In this section, Nemesius indicates that Scripture contains much to convince men of the reality of providence. Fourth-century pagan thought was ready to welcome tales of theurgy, and pagan literature and legend contained themes that might serve as a bridge to Scripture. Then there was the Stoic doctrine of a general providence, a kind of rationality of cause and effect, as though the world-soul had a goal towards which these things tended. Vague as it was, this notion provided Nemesius with a starting point, as he produces arguments for thought and purpose in the ordering of nature.

[M. 336.8–339. 16]

Text

61. Another thing that shows the existence of providence is the agreement among all men to acknowledge the need to pray and to perform divine service by means of sacred offerings and holy places. For how, or to whom, should anyone pray, if there were no mind guiding the world? Again that zeal to do good, which is naturally and keenly felt by those of unperverted character, points us to providence; for it is as looking for a recompense from providence that we choose to confer benefits even upon those who cannot requite us.

Take away providence, and forthwith wickedness is conceded to those who have the power to work it. Mercy and the fear of God are taken away, and at the same time virtue and godliness.

For unless God foresees, he neither punishes, nor distributes en-
couragement to those that do well, nor does he ward off their
hurts from those that are wronged. Who then would any longer
worship God, if he is nowise of the least service to us? Take
away providence, and prophecy and all foreknowledge is taken
away also. But any such supposition is out of accord with events
that are taking place almost every day. For many are the manifestations of divine aid to men in need. Many, too, are the
alleviations vouchsafed to sick folk through dreams, and many
have been the predictions, in every generation, that have seen
their fulfilment. Many are they whose hands are stained with
blood, or that have done some dreadful deed of ill, who pass
day and night in utter terror.

But the supposition that there is no providence is wrong.[1]
God is good. Being good, he is given to doing good, and to
do good, he must be provident. What need is there to recount
the works of the creation, their proportion and harmony,
their stability and order, and the service which each creature
renders to the whole? What need to point out that nothing
would be right if it were otherwise than as it is, that nothing
leaves room for improvement, and that nothing could spare
any attribute that it possesses? Nay, everything is made
perfect and good, everything was wisely and providently
created.

Let us, however, reserve this point for examination when we
come to discuss creation,[2] lest there happen to us what has befallen many writers on providence; for they extol creation when

1 This renders *allōs te*, on the supposition that Nemesius is using it in the
sense that makes what follows contrast with what has gone before. He has
been considering what would follow if there be no providence. He now
dismisses this assumption to assert God's goodness as creator. And this
introduces the distinction between the two forms of divine goodness,
revealed in creation and in providence respectively.

2 Matthaei argues that Nemesius has already spoken of creation at the
beginning of the book, and so proposes to read the indicative, here,
instead of the subjunctive. But the theme of the absolute perfection of
creation outlined in the last paragraph goes beyond what has been said
of creation, or rather, of the universe, in the first chapter. It would seem,
therefore, that Nemesius intended to follow the theme of providence,
which occupies the remainder of the existing work, with a chapter on the
perfection of creation, using the last word in its strict sense. For this, he
needs to prepare the way, by disengaging the notion of creation from that
of providence and the present universe. The fact that there is no chapter
on creation, together with instances that have been noticed, of lack of
revision in the work as we have it, would, once more, suggest that death
overtook Nemesius before his task was completed.

they should have been extolling providence.[3] The theme of creation leads us, it is true, to discourse of providence, but the two things are quite separate, since providence and creation are not one and the same. For the glory of creation is that all created things have been made well, but the glory of providence is to take good care of what exists. Now these two activities do not invariably go together, as can be seen from men of this or that craft or calling. For some of them set themselves the task of making something well, and have no care beyond the making; one might name, for example, carpenters, copyists, or modellers. Then there are others whose whole work is to take care of things, and to make provision for them, such as herdsmen or shepherds. While, therefore, we should so construct our chapter on creation as to show in suitable ways, that the things that have come into existence have been made well, our present argument on providence should show that the needed care has been bestowed on creatures since creation. How, then, is it that man invariably begets man, and ox always genders ox, while each kind of plant grows from its own particular seed, and from no other, in the absence of any providence? For if anyone contends that it is out of accordance with its original genesis that a thing progresses through a succession of stages, this is no different from saying that providence and creation go together hand in hand. For, if what was created makes progress through its own successive stages, it is clear that providence, also, originated at the creation, to continue its work. For the way things develop, once they are made, is the work of providence. The inference to be drawn is simply this, that the Maker of all things is, at the same time, their providence.

[3] Heinrich A. Koch, in his *Quellenuntersuchungen zu Nemesius von Emesa*, (Berlin, 1921) points out that Theodoret, the younger contemporary and compatriot of Nemesius, has ten homilies, *Of providence*, and devotes Chapter VI of his *Cure of pagan sickness* to that subject. Theodoret falls into the confusion of which Nemesius speaks. And Nemesius would not have made the distinction between providence and creation, had he not had in mind some doctrine of the perfection of the work of creation. The basis of this Optimistic doctrine of creation may be the scriptural phrase that "God saw" each detail of his creation "and it was good." Nemesius' most probable source is Origen's great *Commentary on Genesis*, which we know to have reproduced much of the optimistic philosophy of Posidonius. It is clear from Origen's *First principles*, III. 5, that Origen thought of an all-embracing providence of God in which the creation of this world was but one incident. It may thus be from Origen that Nemesius derived his distinction of creation from providence.

COMMENTARY

61. *Providence continues the work begun in creation.* The first part of the section continues the proof of the existence of providence by pointing to those human instincts which desiderate the existence of providence. The second part disengages providence from creation as its complement in revealing the nature of God.

[M. 339.16–343.5.]

TEXT

62. Anyone who gives consideration to human personal appearance, and sees how everyone in so many thousands is different, so that you never find two persons completely alike, cannot but marvel at such a work. And if he ponders the reason for it, must he not find that this individuality of shape, differentiated in respect of each individual feature, is due to providence? For, look! If all men faithfully reproduced the same stamp of countenance, what utter confusion would reign in our affairs? In what ignorance and darkness a man would be enveloped if he could not distinguish one of his own familiars, or discriminate a stranger, an enemy, or a scoundrel, from a dear and kind friend. In the famous phrase of Anaxagoras, "All were then undifferentiated," with a vengeance![1] If that were so, there would be nothing to stop one from having intercourse

---

1 This dictum of Anaxagoras is recorded by Diogenes Laertius, in his *Lives of the Sophists*, Bk. II. sect. 6.

Anaxagoras was born at Clazomenae in Asia Minor about 500 B.C. He migrated to Athens in the generation before that of Socrates. He is to be credited with bringing to Athens the spirit of scientific enquiry. A primitive physicist, his account of the universe began with the words, "All was undifferentiated; then came mind and put things into seemly order." Or, again, "Things began in homogeneity, and the whole world was compounded of small homogeneous particles." With Anaxagoras, mind enters the universe as a *Deus ex machina*. But when he speculated that the sun consisted of molten matter and was as big as the Peloponnese, Athenian opinion was shocked, and Anaxagoras, like a precursor to Socrates, was indicted for subverting the established beliefs. Pericles with difficulty obtained his acquittal, and he left Athens about 450 B.C., dying at Lampsacus some twenty years later. He seems to be the initiator of the theory that nature is the work of design, and Aristotle may be held to have been indebted to him for the conception of reason at work in the world-order. Our author has, therefore, chosen his citation particularly well to support the argument that differentiation is the supreme work of providence.

with one's mother or sister. There would be nothing to prevent robbery, or any other wicked deed, from being perpetrated openly, given the possibility of instant escape; for the criminal might be seen afterwards without fear of recognition. No law could be enforced, nor polity maintained. Fathers would not know their children, nor children their fathers; nor could any other human relationship be kept up, since every man, in dealing with others, would be as good as blind, being but little served in having sight, seeing that it would not serve him to distinguish anything except age and stature.[2]

Providence has been the donor to us of so great blessings, by differentiating the forms of men totally and universally, and never, at any time, omitting to do so. That is the strongest testimony to the existence of providence, namely, individuality, extending, as it does, to each single person being recognizable by exact detail of shape, feature and voice. And if, perchance every such detail is not exactly remembered, memory of the face suffices. For, as an overplus, providence gave us this, as well, our differences of complexion; so that the infirmity of human nature might have many kinds of aid. And I imagine that the host of different animals, that have a generally uniform appearance, as is the case, say, with daws and crows, have also certain differences of aspect whereby they recognize each other in mating.[3] Of course daws and crows flock together often, and in large numbers, but they separate to mate, each hen and cock knowing its own mate. Now how could they recognize one another unless each had some mark of individuality, which, though not easy to be discerned by us, is by nature easily seen by other birds of that feather?

Finally (since our argument is addressed to Greeks), tokens, oracles, omens and celestial portents, according to the ideas of their nation (as they themselves profess) assuring us that the events which they indicated will follow, have their power of signification always and entirely by reason of providence; and

---

2 Shakespeare's *Comedy of errors* embodies the theme that the existence of just two people who are virtually without difference of form could introduce endless confusion and absurdity into human affairs. This may measure the boldness of the fancy that here endeavours to picture the consequences of all human beings having exactly the same shape.

3 Daws, *corones*, and crows, *corakes*, are both mentioned in the Septuagint Old Testament, but not in the same passages. The probability is that this passage, whoever may have been its original author, arose from first-hand observation and reflection, and not from any literary source.

on the same account the events prove true to what was signified.[4]

COMMENTARY

62. *The recognizable identity of everyman a signal work of providence.* The maintenance of all individualities is the most remarkable work of providence and the most convincing proof that providence exists. In this section we seem to have something that is not in evidence as a commonplace. That is not to say that the theme was original with Nemesius. A man with a penchant for independent speculation would hardly compose his arguments in the form of a mosaic of other men's thoughts, as Nemesius is seen to do. The question of the authorship of the argument may be left open, in spite of the occurrence of the first person in it.

[M. 343.6–344.13.]

XLIII. *What is providence?*

TEXT

63. That providence exists is clear, both from what we have just been saying, and from what we shall be saying next. Let us now declare what providence is. Providence (for so we phrase it) is the care that God takes over things that exist. Another accepted definition runs thus: providence is that purpose of God whereby all existing things receive their most favourable outcome.[1] But, if providence is divine purpose, there is no possible

---

[4] Nemesius believed that true and inspired prediction takes place. As an *argumentum ad hominem*, in addressing himself to a Greek pagan, he will allow that their oracles and omens may sometimes not be delusions. But this is to establish the principle that, if there is anywhere true prediction, it depends on human contact with a mind which knows the future. To believe in prediction is therefore to believe that such a mind exists. It were then absurd to question the existence of providence.

[1] These two definitions of providence came to be well known, and stand at the head of Suicer's article on *providence* in his *Thesaurus Ecclesiasticus* or Lexicon of ecclesiastical Greek. The reason for this is not that the work of Nemesius was ever well known, but that these definitions, along with a number of passages from Nemesius, were included by the eighth-century Father, John of Damascus, in the second book of his *Exposition of the orthodox faith*. John received the posthumous approval of the seventh ecumenical synod, in A.D. 787, as the encyclopaedic theologian of orthodoxy, and his *Exposition* was accepted as a theological standard for the eastern Church. It is the more remarkable, therefore, that he should have not only adopted a large number of passages from Nemesius, in that part

doubt that everything that takes place does so in what, quite literally, is both the most excellent manner, and that most worthy of God's majesty; in fact they happen in the only way consistent with good, so that no better disposition could be looked for. Moreover, the Creator of existent things, and their providence, must be one and the same God. For it would be inconsistent and unseemly for one to create and another to care for what was created. For such a division clearly betrays limited powers.

What we are saying is amply reflected in the lives of living creatures, since everything that genders also takes care to feed its young, while man goes further and provides for his children everything else that their life requires, of whatever kind and in whatever quantity.[2] There are, it is true, creatures that make no provision for their young, but it is to be accounted mere infirmity on their part that they do not. It has been proved, therefore, that God is the God of providence, and that providence is his purpose being worked out.

COMMENTARY

63. *Definitions of providence.* Providence is God's care for the continued good of what he has created, the working out in detail of his beneficent purpose for every creature.

[M. 344.14–348.5.]

XLIV. *Enquiry into the scope of providence*

TEXT

64. We have established the fact of providence and its nature. It remains now to say whether it is general or particular, or whether it is both at once. Plato will have it that providence has sway both over the general conduct of the universe, and over particular events as well. He distinguishes three grades of providence. For, says he, there is a primary providence, that of the supreme God, which extends primarily to the ideas, but

of the work that deals with the Christian doctrine of the world and man, but have let the order and choice of divisions in Nemesius influence those of his own book. These facts throw a strong light upon the substantial contribution which Nemesius made to Christian thought, within the range of those subjects with which he concerned himself.

2 This passage is a development of the theme that is present in germ in Luke 11:13; divine providence inferred *a fortiori* from man's behaviour.

after that it extends generally over the whole of the universe; that is to say, it is a providence over heaven and the stars, and over all universals, namely over the kinds of things, their substance, quantity and quality, with other such-like general attributes, and their subordinate forms.

But there is a secondary providence, ruling the generation of ordinary animals and plants, and indeed everything that participates in birth and decay. And this providence is exercised by the under-gods that patrol the heavens[1] (now Aristotle also refers the generation of such creatures to the sun and to the Zodiac). The tertiary providence in the Platonic scheme is that which manages and directs actions which regulate the course of life, and orders those good things which we name natural, material or instrumental, together with their contraries. Of this providence, certain spiritual creatures, ranged about the earth, have been put in charge, to be guardians over human affairs.[2] The secondary and tertiary providence derive from the

[1] This means the sun, moon and seven planets. When astronomy recognized the relation of the paths of these heavenly bodies across the sky to the positions in the sky of the constellations of fixed stars, it had discovered the means of using these bodies as an accurate clock to mark the passing of the climatic and seasonal year. This was, of course, a great help to agriculture, since it was now known when to prune, sow, and the like. But the connection thus made between seasonal occurrences in animal and vegetable life and the motion and behaviour of the celestial bodies whose positions in the sky marked the advances of the year, came to be taken as a causal connection. If sowing at a particular time in the year brought the best harvest, it was supposed to be through the mysterious influence of the celestial bodies, personified as under-gods, who had announced the season. The Greeks called the zone of the sky which contained the paths of the sun, moon and planets, the zodiacal circle (literally "zone of the little living creatures") or Zodiac. In short, the Zodiac, wherein the sun, moon and planets moved against a background of constellations, was a true clock to tell nature's time for birth and decay, but superstition transformed it into the cause of birth and decay: and Plato and Aristotle accepted this inversion of the facts.

[2] The Platonic conception of tertiary providence rests on animistic foundations. Each man's tutelary *daimon* concerns himself with the man's activities, and minor deities preside over the stages of physical life, the house, and other circumstances which are individual to each person. These *daimonia* and minor deities are the agents of Plato's tertiary providence. They are thought to be in proximity to those for or against whom they work. *Daimonia* ought not to be rendered into English as "demons." In Christian thought, the word "demon" has gone steadily downhill, through having "angel" as its correlative. But in Greek paganism, *daimōn* and *daimonion* had rather beneficent than malevolent associations. Note that Nemesius says nothing against this tertiary providence in the Platonic scheme. The early Christian Fathers were very

28—C.J.

primary, so that the supreme God rules all things by his might, as ordering alike the secondary and tertiary agents of providence. It is praiseworthy in Plato thus to refer all things to God, and to describe all providence as dependent on his will.[3] He is at fault, on the other hand, in calling that a secondary providence, which the motions of the heavenly bodies effect, for what depends on them is not providence but fate and necessity.[4] For whatever be the conjunctions of the heavenly bodies, they are so of necessity, and there is no alternative.[5] And we proved, some time ago, that nothing to do with providence happens of necessity.[6] The Stoic philosophers, advocating belief at once in fate and in our own free-will, leave no possible room for providence.[7] But, in fact, they bring human free-will to nought, as

ready to accept the notion of a delegation, by God, to spiritual creatures, of portions and phases of the world process, without attributing to such creatures either spiritual perfection or the character of devils. This notion ceased to be in favour after the condemnation of the memory of Origen, who upheld the doctrine that each race of living creatives had its guardian angel. So Jerome, in his Commentary on Habacuc (i. 14) flatly denies that the maintenance of kinds of irrational creatures rests on any such basis, but places it under the *general* providence of God. It is a sign that the outlook of Nemesius is not that of a writer of days after the condemnation of Origen, that he should be so ready to christen Platonic doctrines of providence.

[3] Nemesius may not have been himself the constructor of this systematic view of Platonic providence. The signs are that he read commentaries on certain works of Plato, some of which may have been of Christian origin. Not only in this section, but elsewhere in the chapter, there are phrases that ring of the tenth book of Plato's *Laws*. The scheme omits mention of the world-soul, in regard to providence over universals, and it is difficult to give any meaning to providence over the Ideas. This suggests that either Nemesius or his hypothetical Christian source principally wished to claim Plato as a witness to providence as the work of the supreme God.

[4] The Syrian readers of Nemesius would not think of celestial beings (sun, moon and planets) as exercising their influence upon birth and decay by a use of free-will, as Plato did. For them, the heavenly bodies moved under mechanical forces, and the influence exerted by their conjunctions and oppositions were therefore thought to be no less predetermined than the positions of the several bodies in the sky at any moment. With this in view, Nemesius cannot endorse the Platonic doctrine without this amendment, that the part played by the heavenly bodies is mechanical.

[5] Nemesius is not here admitting that the celestial bodies have any influence upon sublunary affairs, but by insisting on the mechanical character of the movements of those bodies, seeks to exclude them from any part in providence, even allowing that they had such influence.

[6] Section 53.

[7] In spite of the Stoic use of the term providence (Chrysippus wrote a book, *On providence*), and the similarity of much Stoic terminology to that of the Church, Nemesius sees that the Stoics are speaking a different

we proved above.[8] Democritus, Heraclitus, and Epicurus[9] will admit neither general nor particular providence. Epicurus, in fact, says that what is blessed and incorrupt is neither involved in pains of its own nor is the cause of trouble to any other, because it is immune alike from wrath and favour. All such passions, Epicurus says, belong to imperfection. Wrath is alien to the nature of gods, says he, because it comes of being crossed, and divinity is never crossed. So these thinkers follow out their own principles. For as they hold that the universe just came together of itself, it is no wonder that they declare that there is no providence to take care of that which has no Creator? It is self-evident that what came into being of itself, must perforce continue of itself. Therefore our stand against them must be taken over their first opinion, namely that concerning creation. For once that is refuted, what has been said already will serve to prove the existence of a providence, and so we must reserve this refutation until its appropriate occasion.[10]

COMMENTARY

64. *Plato the best philosopher on providence.* In this chapter, Nemesius sets out to show that providence regards and touches the lives of individuals. Accordingly in this section, he selects Plato for preference over the later philosophers on this subject.

[M. 348.5–351.7.]

TEXT

65. Let us now consider the opinion of Aristotle and others who assert that providence does not extend over particulars;

language from Christians, and, as regards our faith in divine providence, are not allies but foes.

8 Section 53.

9 Nemesius apparently selects these three names as representing the mechanistic Atomists. See the notes to Section 11. It is surprising that Heraclitus should be thus inserted between Democritus and Epicurus. Presumably Nemesius associated Heraclitus with Democritus in some way, perhaps because of the fashion for calling Democritus the "laughing" and Heraclitus the "weeping" philosopher.

10 Nemesius sets out the Epicurean argument in the most favourable form, admitting that the conclusion follows from the premiss. This is because he had the intention of destroying the Epicurean theory of the self-origination of the universe, in the chapter on the nature of the work of creation which he never completed.

seeing that Aristotle, to judge by a hint in the sixth book of his *Nicomachean Ethics*, will have it that it is Nature that manages the details of our lives.[1] Nature, he says, is divine and inherent in all creatures, and suggests to each individual instinctively how to choose what is profitable and avoid what may do hurt. For, as he says, every living creature chooses out the nourishment suited to itself, pursues whatever is good for it, and knows by instinct what will cure its ailments. Euripides and Menander[2]

[1] The charge which Nemesius brings against Aristotle is just. Aristotle had a clear sense of design in Nature. All things strive for the good attainable by them, within their limitations. But Aristotle was agnostic regarding the relations of God with Nature, and of any moral government of the world that could be called divine providence. As for the Olympians, he says (*Nicomachean Ethics*, x. 8), "If there be any care of human affairs by them, as men think there is," philosophers should be the favoured of heaven.

The question is why Nemesius should refer to the sixth book of the *Ethics*, in this connection. It does not deal with the general theme of Nature seeking its own ends, but with deliberation, prudence, and mental ability. It is upon this book that Nemesius has drawn so heavily in his own ch. xxxiv. Perhaps Nemesius paid attention to the argument, towards the end of the book, that since intuitive reason, and judgment, are faculties that have their marked periods in a man's life, they must be gifts of Nature, and drew the conclusion that therefore the success of prudence in ensuring a man's interests is that upon which trust should be placed, rather than in any over-ruling of circumstances. He might therefore reach the view that Aristotle was "hinting" that Nature manages the details of our lives. It is possible, however, that this conclusion was not drawn by Nemesius from the text of Aristotle, but was derived from a Christian commentary on the Ethics, in which was criticised the self-sufficiency of the "prudent man" of Aristotle.

[2] The dramatist Euripides, 406–480 B.C. was the younger contemporary of the Athenian tragedians Aeschylus and Sophocles, and broke off from their technique, to mould tragedy to the changed outlook and mood of the Athenian public. It might seem strange that Nemesius should pick upon him as a denier of providence, because, as Tyrrell says in his edition of the *Bacchae*, Euripides sought to interpret the popular myths of the gods in a manner consistent with belief in a benevolent providence. His invention of the dramatic form, the *deus ex machina*, is for this purpose, and the dénouement is followed, in the *Bacchae* and the *Alcestis*, by a final chorus declaring that "manifold things unhoped for, the gods to accomplishment bring." The theme of *Ion* is that "the good at last shall overcome, at last attain their right" despite "the blind haste of mortals, and their little faith." Menander, 342–291 B.C., admirer and imitator of Euripides, and chief figure of the new comedy, is notable for his moral epigrams, and, on the whole, tended to show the gods as playing the part of providence. Nemesius might have in view such a character as Onesimus, in the *Epitrepontes*, who holds that the indifference of the gods throws moral responsibility on men, and concludes that "to each of us the gods have given a character that fits him to be master of his fate."

in certain passages, deny that any of the gods exercise providence, but declare that the mind in each individual is his
private providence. But mind knows only such things as lie
within our power, whether things to do, or arts to plan, or
objects for contemplation; while providence is concerned with
things that do not lie within our power, such as whether we
should be rich or poor, well or sick—things which mind cannot
in the least effect. But then (to return to Aristotle's opinion),
neither can Nature. For what Nature's works are is easily seen.
Then what have mind or Nature to do with the fact that
sometimes a murderer is punished and sometimes he gets off
scot free? Unless one says that the part played by mind and
Nature is providence, but that what determines the second type
of issue is fate. But if the part played by mind and Nature is
providence and the rest of what happens is fate, there remains
no place for free-will. That, however, is wrong, for we have
shown that what the mind does, whether for action or contemplation, is an exercise of free-will.[3] On the other hand, not all
that is providential is the work of Nature, although the work of
Nature be providential. Many things that happen under providence are not works of Nature, as has been shown in connection
with the discovery of murder.[4] Nature is a department of
providence, and not the whole. So much, then, for those who
ascribe particular providence to mind and Nature.

There are others[5] who allow that God cares for the perman-

[3] The allusion appears to be to ch. XLI.
[4] The case of Ibycus in ch. XLII.
[5] We shall hardly identify these "others" with any known philosophic
position. Rather, the expressions which Nemesius places upon their lips
are those of vulgar cynicism. The Greek philosopher was not "cynical"
in that sense. He had come face to face with the problem of the accidental
or fortuitous from early days, and found it particularly difficult to bring
to a clean solution. *Tyche* (chance, fortune, accident) had to be given a
place in the complex god-*daimōn*-providence-fate-necessity-nature. In
Bk. iv of the *Laws* of Plato the Athenian stranger observes how legislation
succeeds in bringing together the ideal and the accidental, which are
therefore capable of reconciliation. Plato concludes that, in some way,
God rules, while chance co-operates in his rule. This is to divinize *Tyche*.
And because politics combine principles and opportunism, cities worshipped *Tyche* or a *Tyche* of their own, as a goddess. This meant that *tyche*
must be justified at the bar of moral conscience. Philosophers accordingly
tended to argue that the accidental, could we but know it, is both intelligible and right. We may see how this was attempted in a passage that
lies very near to Nemesius at this point. This is ch. IX of Sallustius, *Concerning the gods and the universe* (Edn. by A. D. Nock, Cambridge, 1926).
Sallustius appears to have been one of those who surrounded the emperor

ence of the world-order, so that nothing whatever lapses from being, but that this is his only providence. They attribute the outcome of particular events to chance. That is why, they say, so many injustices, so many murders take place, and, to cut a long story short, why every kind of evil is rife among men. It is by chance, they say in explanation of these evils, that some men escape retribution, while others are punished, in a world where nothing ever falls out in accordance with strict reason or any law. And there, where neither law nor reason reigns, how can anyone assert, they ask, that God is taking care of things? Seeing that good men turn out most often to suffer injustice, to be kept under, and to live surrounded with a thousand ills, while wicked and violent men increase in power, wealth, position, and all the other desirable things of this present life.

COMMENTARY

65. *Where Plato is right, other Greeks err, regarding providence.* The section is an answer to those who refuse to acknowledge a divine providence extending to particular events and circumstances. These are of three sorts, (i) those who put the working of Nature in the place of providence, (ii) those who acknowledge no providence but that which proceeds from human minds, (iii) those who add to the last view the positive exclusion of any other rational factor, so that, apart from what man can do, all else is blind chance.

Julian in his revival of pagan religion. He was therefore, at most, only a couple of decades the senior of Nemesius.

Sallustius, in ch. VII of this work, declares that God cares for the permanence of the world-order. He does not mean, of course, that God intervenes in the world process to prevent something in it from perishing. Neither do the "others" in the passage of Nemesius. What Sallustius means is that the overthrow of the world-order is unthinkable because no other could be worthy of God. He defends providence with argument closely similar to that of Nemesius, and goes on to call *tyche* (ch. IX) a *dynamis* of the gods. This power works in ways that we call inexplicable or inequitable, but their total effect amounts to rough justice. Everyone gets what he really values, the bad the perishing goods of the body, and the good, the things that promote their immortal being. So *tyche* is not the antithesis of providence. Thus Nemesius is following Sallustius (or the moralistic tradition to which he belonged) and hoping to succeed where he failed, helped by the Christian dogma of the life eternal, in convincing the common man.

[M. 351.7–354.9.]

66. Now it seems to me that people who talk like this are ignoring many quite other principles[1] that bear on the working of providence, and, in particular, they are ignoring the immortality of the soul. For, by unthinkingly assuming that the soul is mortal they round off all human affairs within the span of this life, whence it follows that they have distorted views on what things are good. For they think just those people to be fortunate and happy who are rolling in wealth, who can plume themselves on their public honours, or can find complacency in the possession of any other blessings of this present life. But in proportion as they grossly exaggerate the importance of bodily and external well-being, they take too little account of the good of the soul. For those good things are the best that apply to the best in us. By so much the more, therefore, do virtues excel wealth, health, and all the rest, in proportion as the soul takes precedence of the body. Consequently a man is truly happy who has virtues, whether or not he has any other blessings besides. If he had virtues and the other blessings too, his is happiness in a broad and general sense.[2] But if he has virtues alone and for their own sakes, his is the clear-cut form of happiness. For some things are thought of in a clearly defined way, as when we say two ells of stuff, while others are thought of in a vague and general way, as when we say, "a heap." For you can take away two measures from a heap, and what remains will still be a heap.

Now if you subtract all bodily and external blessings from the condition of broad and general happiness, and leave nothing whatever but the virtues, it is, even so, a state of happiness. For virtue, even by itself, suffices for that state. Every good man, therefore, is happy, and every bad man wretched, even though the bad man have all the good things of fortune[3] (as they call

---

[1] These "other principles" prove to be (i) that spiritual good is imperishable and carnal goods transitory, (ii) that the state of happiness is qualitative rather than quantitative, (iii) that valuation based on knowledge of the present only is bound to be false, and (iv) that conduct based on such presumptions is impiety.

[2] The state of happiness that springs of being virtuous is something of precise and constant meaning. The vaguer presumption of happiness based on various grounds is apt to prove, on investigation, to be largely illusion. We may suspect that Nemesius has here overshortened his borrowed argument. [3] tyche.

them) heaped one upon another. But this truth is commonly
ignored, and folk suppose the well-fed and wealthy to be the
only happy men; wherefore they blame providence which
directs the affairs of men in ways that correspond not only with
what is under the eyes, but also with a divine foreknowledge
that we do not share. For since God knows that poverty is best
for a man who is kind and good while poor, but who, if wealth
were added to him would let it corrupt his judgement, he keeps
him poor; and for his good. Often, on the other hand, God
knows that a rich man would give more trouble if he lacked
possessions (for he would then engage in robberies and blood-
shed, or in some other and even greater crimes), and so he
suffers him to reap the profit of wealth. So it is often an advantage to us to be poor, to be bereft of our children, or have
our slaves decamp, when, through our children turning out
badly, or our slaves robbing us, the keeping of them would have
proved more bitter than their loss. For we, who do not know at
all what the future has in store, and see merely our present
circumstances, misjudge what will profit us. God, on the other
hand, sees what is to come as if it were present. These things are
addressed, however, to those who make themselves God's
judges. To them may also fittingly be cited those words of
Scripture, "Shall the clay say to the potter"[4] and so forth.

How shall we not shun a man who legislates in opposition to
the laws of God,[5] and issues decrees in opposition to the works
of providence, whereas he dares not breath a word against the
laws of men? Wherefore, leaving such extravagances, or, to
speak more truly, blasphemies, on one side, let us demonstrate
the error of denying particular providence while acknowledging
universal and general providence.

COMMENTARY

66. *The danger of adopting a cynical attitude.* The argument of
the grumblers errs by not considering the good of the soul, and
is, in fact, blasphemous.

[4] Isa. 45:9.
[5] This can hardly be other than an allusion to the *Laws* passage already
mentioned. The Athenian stranger proposed to legislate by bringing together realism and the recognized ideals of the moral law. But the man
who thinks *tyche* to be the heartless mocker of men conforms his conduct
to this amoral standard. Nemesius thinks of divine law as revealed in
Scripture, and points to the peculiar danger to a man's soul involved in
cynicism about the "tricks of fortune."

This section is a digression from the main argument, and arises from the mention of the "others," in the last part of Section 65, who grumble at their luck, and gird against the Ruler of the universe for permitting life to be so full of injustice. To this popular opposition to the Christian doctrine of providence, Nemesius replies with what might as well be a cynic diatribe against popular error as a piece of Christian apologetic. The presumption is that he had the diatribe ready to his hand, in some way.

The superiority of the happiness that comes from the attainment of virtues over that derived from any other source is a characteristic dogma of the philosophers of the Socratic tradition. But this dogma was not based upon belief in rewards and punishments in a life to come. It is the Christian in Nemesius that drags in the reference to the immortality of the soul, the point of which is that no judgement can be passed upon the fortunes of this life until the consequences of men's conduct for their destiny beyond the grave have been cast into the scales. But Nemesius completes the section without making this thought explicit; which is hardly credible had he been thinking the argument out himself, rather than rehandling an argument put together by someone else. The point of choosing the latter alternative, as a piece of apologetic tactics, is that the diatribe would carry some weight with thoughtful non-Christian readers, and so win them unconsciously on to the side of the apologist. In the same way, the earlier Christian apologists repeated the attacks upon immoral pagan mythology which had long been accepted as just by most people of culture, because it enlisted on their side those readers who might be at all accessible to their message.

Nemesius gives the diatribe a Christian turn again at the conclusion, where the murmurer is convicted of being not merely foolish but sacrilegious. And its conversion into a sermonette is completed by giving it a text (somewhat perfunctorily) in Isa. 45:9 (Septuagint text). Reasoned argument for belief in providence extending to particulars is resumed in the following section.

[M. 354.9–357.16.]

TEXT

67. For there are only three reasons that anyone can urge against there being a providence over particulars. These are,

that God does not know how fair a deed it would be to extend
his providence to taking care for particulars, that God is unwilling to do so, or that he cannot do so. But ignorance and
denseness are qualities altogether, and in the extreme, alien to
God's blessed nature. For he is knowledge, wisdom, and intelligence in very essence. And how could that be hid from God
which no right-minded man could fail to see, namely that if
every particular should perish, then the universe itself will
perish too? For the universe is the sum-total of all particulars.
God makes the universal form identical in every particular
thing of its kind.[1] God changes an existing form into something
different. If the form is destroyed, the corresponding particulars
disappear with it. While the form is maintained, so are the
particulars, and *vice versa*. And there is nothing to prevent from
perishing every particle that goes to make the world, if so be
that no care is being taken for them from above.[2] Then when
the particles perish, the universe will perish too. Should they
answer that God has a providence to this end only, that by
keeping all particulars from perishing, he may preserve the
universal forms, they are caught admitting that some kind of
providence over particulars exists. For it is by such providence
over particulars that God, on their own showing, preserves the
forms and the kinds of things.

Again there are others who say that God knows providence
over particulars to be good, but is not willing himself to exercise
it.[3] Now there are two reasons for which one may be unwilling
to do something. One is one's own indolence, and the other is
that the thing itself is beneath one. Who, then, would be so mad
as to charge God with indolence? especially considering that
the two parents of indolence are love of pleasure, and fear! For

---

[1] This argument is upon an Aristotelian basis. The forms have not an
existence on the same footing as and over against, the existence of particulars, but exist in the particulars of which they are the forms. Neo-
platonism had, in reconciling Plato and Aristotle, moved away from the
interpretation of Plato that gave the ideas a superior reality, independent
of other orders of existence; so that Nemesius could count that the force
of this argument would be acknowledged by those to whom it was
addressed.

[2] This doctrine of the momently sustaining of the material universe by God
is the counterpart of the doctrine of creation *ex nihilo*, and is Christian.
But it comes in very easily as a sequel to the argument that particulars
are dependent upon providence.

[3] At this point Nemesius meets those who say that particular providence is
left to spiritual creatures (e.g., *daimones*) or (with Sallustius) to a *dynamis*
of the gods other than direct divine action.

we are negligent of a duty when drawn aside by some pleasure, or brought to a halt by some fear. It is blasphemy even to think of either of these two alternatives as applying to God. But suppose that these objectors disclaim any imputation of negligence to God, but say that providence over particulars does not beseem him. Suppose that they say that it is incongruous that such blessedness should condescend to mean and trivial details, and be involved to some extent in profanation by the absurdities that spring from material circumstances and human caprice, and that, for that reason, God does not choose to exercise providence over particulars. In making such assertions, they do not see that they are investing God with two of the basest inclinations, an inclination to be scornful, and a propensity for being easily defiled! That is to say, either the Creator disdains ruling and managing particulars because he scorns them (a thing most monstrous to affirm), or else he must, as these folk suggest, be shunning defilement. Now the rays of the sun naturally draw up moisture of every kind, yet no one says that the sun (or even his rays) is sullied by shining on dunghills.[4] Everyone acknowledges that both sun and rays remain uncontaminated and pure. How, then, do they imagine that God can suffer profanation from the things that are being done down here?

These are not the doctrines of men who know what Godhead means. For the divine nature remains intact, incorruptible, uncontaminated, and above all mutability. For defilement, and everything of that nature, comes about through mutability.

Would it not be utterly absurd if an adept at any art, and particularly a physician,[5] should take thought for the broad

---

4 The thought of the sun's rays undefiled by what they fall upon was a commonplace. Mr. H. Chadwick has noted, in his *Origen, Against Celsus*, that Diogenes Laertius attributes it, as a primary observation, to Diogenes the cynic. Beginning with Origen it was used continually by Christian writers to prove the propriety of the incarnation. The reference which lies nearest to our passage, however, is in the *Hymn to King Sun* of the emperor Julian, who was the elder contemporary of Nemesius. Julian's involved argument is that as the material sun takes no defilement from that on which its light falls, the intelligible sun, symbolizing divine beneficence, can, without loss of purity, condescend, through agency of the lower gods, to human affairs. Julian belongs to the later Neo-platonism that follows Iamblichus. Nemesius may thus be answering the Neo-Platonists from their own armoury.

5 God as a physician is another philosophic commonplace. Plutarch uses it to explain delays in divine retribution, as like the doctor waiting for the right time to use a remedy.

exercise of his art, but take no notice of details, or if he should leave even the slightest point outside the scope of his art and his concern. Such a one would know that the part contributes to the whole. And is, then, God the Creator to be made out to have less sense than any craftsman?

COMMENTARY

67. *Providence over particulars beseems God.* It does not derogate from God's transcendence that he should exercise providence over particulars.

In this section, Nemesius leaves the method of answering specific opponents for that of exhausting the possible grounds for argument against providence over particulars. But it is easy to see that the argument with which he is really concerned is that it is not congruent with divine transcendence. And here it is probable that the Neo-Platonists are the unnamed opponents. The Neo-Platonist principle is that of the upward aspiration of the soul, not that of the condescension of the higher to the lower. To Plotinus, for example, the sensible world is substantially good, but with, and in spite of, its imperfections it remains a ladder by whose rungs the soul may climb to the realities of the spiritual world. Accordingly Plotinus disapproved of prayer for deliverance from calamities, since these should be becoming indifferent to the soul that is attaining communion with the world of intelligibles.

[M. 357.17–361.7.]

TEXT

68. Well, then, let us say that it is not because God is unwilling, but because of its impossibility, that God abstains from providence over particulars. But is it not plainly monstrous to speak as if God lacked some power and so could not do what were right to be done? It would be all the more so if one went on to assert that the impossibility is double, and that neither can God exercise providence in trifles, nor are such particulars, for their part, amenable to providence. We retort that it is God's nature to provide; and that they admit it when they concede him general providence, especially when we observe that, while trifles must not, of course, take precedence of the broad issues, the power that works in the greater matters may seep down for the preservation of the tiniest, and even of things that

to us are imperceptible.[1] For all things hang upon the will of God and derive their permanence and safety therefrom. Now, that tiny and multitudinous particulars form a subject upon which providence may be exercised can be seen from those many kinds of living creature which are under government and leadership. For bees and ants and most of the things that swarm take their orders from certain leaders[2] whom they follow obediently. But the best way to recognize the suitability of particulars to be the subject of providence is to contemplate human society, since the administration and care of law-givers and magistrates is there plain to see. Now, how can something that thus lends itself to being ruled by magistrates fail to lend itself to the providence of its Creator?

Now it is no small token that providence should rule even over particulars, that the recognition of such a providence is so widely distributed throughout our race as to be accounted a gift of nature.[3] For no sooner do we feel the pinch of necessity than we fly promptly to thoughts of heaven and take refuge in prayers, as though nature led us instinctively to seek succour from God. Now nature would not lead us by instinct, like this, to anything unreal by comparison with herself. For, at a sudden onset of troubles and fears, involuntarily and without stopping to think, we cry out to God: and wherever, in nature, something always follows upon another something, it points firmly

---

[1] The hierarchy of being, set out in ch. I, is the background to this argument. There it is shown that the lower exists for the sake of the higher, and that, for the sake of the higher, the lower is the object of God's care. Thus God's purpose for the higher may be said to "seep down" and embrace the lower.

[2] The exemplary character of the republics of bees and ants was a commonplace with both Christian and pagan writers. The latter see no theological bearing of the subject, but only a model of order. But Prov. 6:6 ensured that Christian writers would see a divine lesson for man in the insect republics. Theodoret, in his fifth sermon on providence, makes the divine purpose in them the more obvious by insisting that the insects are devoid of reason. Their order is therefore the direct work of God revealing what is his will for human society and the individuals of which it is composed. This view would not be readily accepted by any non-Christian, for whom the bees or ants would seem to be the producers of their own order. It fits the apologetic purpose of Nemesius to assume the latter estimate of the insect republics, and to use them and human society in parallel to prove that particulars are adapted to being governed.

[3] Nemesius can count on the assent of his readers to the doctrine that the natural order is rational. It carried the logical consequence that everything that can be established as being part of nature must be right and true. . .

to a conclusion that cannot be gainsaid.[4] What is it, then, that impelled those whose opinion we have been refuting to take up such a line as they do? The first reason, certainly, is that they assume the destruction of the soul in company with the dissolution of the body. The second reason is their inability to evolve a doctrine of providence over particulars. But that the soul is not thus mortal and that man's destiny is not bounded by this present life, is shown by the fact that the wisest of the Greeks believe in transmigration of souls,[5] and that souls attain different grades, according to the life they have lived, and have their different punishments: that is to say, these Greek doctrines, though perhaps quite wrong in this or that other particular, square with the truth, nevertheless, when they confess that the soul, after this present life is over, still exists, and renders account for its transgressions.

If the doctrine of a providence over particulars exceeds our comprehension—and surely it does that, as it is written, "How unsearchable are thy judgements, and thy ways past finding out"[6]—still we ought not, on that account, to deny that such providence exists. For we cannot measure the waters of the sea, or count the grains of sand. But, for all that, no one would assert that the sea does not exist, or that the sand does not exist. So, too, no one would deny the existence of man or any other animal because we cannot tell how many men or other animals there are. Go on to the number of particles of matter in the world, and we cannot conceive how many they are. And what is endless is incomprehensible. For while universals are often comprehensible to reason, particulars are beyond the mind's mastery. Now the individuality of any particular man is twofold. It consists first in his difference from any other man, and then in his difference from what he was in the past or will be in the future. For any man undergoes great change and alteration in himself as day succeeds to day, in his state of life and occupation, in his wants and desires, and in every other thing that follows from these things. For man is a living creature always in the act of becoming something fresh, and very rapidly transformed to meet a need or to adapt himself to an

---

[4] Whenever a man is *in extremis* he thinks of God. If there is no particular providence to answer him, the rationality of nature is overthrown.

[5] Chiefly associated with the Pythagoreans, this doctrine was accepted by Plato (see *Phaedo*, 15), to whom the phrase "the wisest of the Greeks" probably refers. In getting so near to the truth, Plato corroborates it, according to Nemesius.

[6] Rom. 11:33, but with the person changed from third to second.

occasion. It follows[7] of necessity that a providence that will fit itself to each particular must extend to embrace every difference, intricacy, divergence, and convergence, in all the teeming details that exceed the comprehension of man's mind.

COMMENTARY

68. *Particular providence is the response of infinite Mind to the needs of creatures.* In this section, Nemesius produces converging arguments based upon his extreme terms, God and particulars. Starting from the moral attributes of God, he argues that God is minded to provide for particulars. Observing particulars, he finds that their number and complexity is such as man's mind cannot grapple with, but that they seem adapted to government from above, and to look for such government. The two arguments meet in the wonder of divine Mind, omniscient and omnipotent, which can follow out, every instant, every ramification of particular being.

[M. 361.7–364.11.]

TEXT

69. It must be thus, if providence is to be suited to each individual and to each thing that he does; if, in short, the work of providence is to prove wholly appropriate. The differences between particulars are endless, and so, for sure, must be the resources of that providence that shall attend upon them all. Now if those resources are infinite, providence is beyond our comprehending. For that reason, our natural incapacity to comprehend it must not lead us to put out of court divine care for every creature. For, suppose that there is some situation that seems to you not to be well ordered. The Creator knows that it happens in that way for a very good reason. You, on the other hand, know nothing of that reason, and declare that there is no reason about it. For we experience in regard to the works of providence exactly what we experience in regard to other things that pass our comprehension. By a kind of guesswork, and that of a very vague order, we form an idea of the works of providence. From things that are happening, we gain a kind of conjectural picture of providence, and glimpses of its working.

---

7 The infinite demands of particular providence upon the power and wisdom of its Author prove it to be worthy of God.

At any rate, we speak of some things happening by divine permission. Now there are various forms of permission. And oftentimes God gives permission for a man, though righteous, to fall
into misfortunes, just so that he may reveal to others, as in the
case of Job,[1] what virtue is latent in that man. Another example
of divine permission is when God allows some monstrous crime
to be committed, so that, through the perpetration of an evident
outrage, some great and admirable vindication of the right may
be achieved, as when, by means of the cross, man's salvation
was attained.[2]

Divine permission appears in a different form where God, as
he did in the case of Paul, allows a godly man to suffer grievously, only lest his clear conscience and the might that has been
granted him should cause him to fall into spiritual pride.[3] One
man is forsaken of God for a season so that another man may be
corrected, and that others again, in witnessing that man's correction, may be warned by it. It was thus in the case of Lazarus
and Dives.[4] For it is natural that we should be restrained by the
sight of what happens to others, according to that admirable
line from Menander,[5] "The dread of heaven is fallen on us as
we behold what has befallen thee."

Again, one man is forsaken of God so as to promote the glory
of another, as in the case of the man who was born blind not

[1] Job 1:12 shows that Job's trials were by God's permission. Job 42:7–10
shows that, in the upshot, Job's virtues were made manifest to others. The
theme of the book of Job, that the tragedy of Job is resolved when we "see
behind the scenes," is no doubt the main inspiration of Nemesius in his
argument.

[2] This sentence diverges so far from the style of apologetic to those outside
the Church, as to suggest that Nemesius may have gathered this set of
scriptural "intimations" of the beneficent working of providence for a
sermon, on trust in providence, to be preached to the faithful. If this is so,
the fact that there has not been adequate rewording of the passage may
be regarded as another sign that the work never received final revision.

[3] II Cor. 12:7–10. Only those with a clear and Christian knowledge of the
passage could be expected to appreciate the force of this example.

[4] The reference is to the parable of Dives and Lazarus, Luke 16:19–31.
The first reason, Nemesius argues, for which Lazarus was allowed to
suffer as he did, was that Dives might be roused to works of charity. The
second reason is that, Dives dying uncorrected, the whole story should be
revealed by Christ in his preaching, and that, by this means, innumerable
hearers of the Gospel might receive warning.

[5] Grotius prints this sentence in his edition of the fragments of Menander
without naming his source, but it is almost certain that his source was this
passage of Nemesius, and that the play to which the sentence belonged
has otherwise perished. The fragment would appear to be part of the
words of the chorus to one of the *dramatis personae* in a tragedy.

through any fault of his or of his parents, but for the glory of the Son of man.[6]

Once more, one man is permitted to suffer that so he may arouse the zeal of another; that is to say that as the glory of the sufferer shines forth the brighter by his suffering, the rest come to think less of suffering as deterrent, in view of the hope of future glory, and their longing for those benefits that they expect. This is the case with the Christian martyrs,[7] as with those who have sacrificed themselves for their country, their people, their liege-lords, their children, or their faith.

Now if anyone should think it out of all reason that a godly man should suffer grievously so that someone else should be put right, let him reflect that this life is a contest[8] and a striving-ground for virtue. The victors' chaplets are splendid in exact proportion, therefore, to the pains with which they are won. That is why Paul was allowed to fall into countless afflictions; to the end, that is, that the crown of victory which he should bear off might be the greater, or rather, that it might be unsurpassable.

Well then, we conclude that the works of providence are well and fittingly done.

6 The incident of the man born blind is related in John 9:1-38. The purpose of providence in permitting the man's congenital blindness is discussed in verses 3 and 4.

7 So highly was martyrdom esteemed in the Church that in ecclesiastical literature it is assumed as self-evident that it is a supreme act of divine grace to call a disciple to lay down his life in fidelity to Christ. The "passions" or "acts" of the martyrs, in their character of the most popular form of Christian literature, from the fourth century on, show that this question of the suffering of martyrs severs the Christian outlook from that of outside society most acutely. No one inside the Church thought that there was need to explain why God permitted the persecutors to inflict suffering on the martyrs. Outside the Church, it appeared equally obvious that people who suffered as the martyrs did, must have fallen under the vengeance of heaven. Therefore Origen, in *Against Celsus*, VIII. 4, answers his pagan opponent by saying that the demons instigate persecution out of hatred towards God, and that God permits their success, only to make it work their undoing. That Nemesius should likewise treat the sufferings of the Christian martyrs as something that needed explaining, and that he should compare them with sacrificial patriotism, parenthood, and the like, show that he has now remembered the needs of apologetic.

8 For Paul's many sufferings and trials, see II Cor. 11:23-30. For his attainment of the crown, II Tim. 4:7-8. The combination of these two passages gives Nemesius a revelation of the working of providence in the life of an individual, upon which he can ground his conclusion.

COMMENTARY

69. *Intimations of the working of particular providence.* Section 68 has shown that if there is providence over particulars, its working must be so intricate that human minds cannot possibly overtake it. That being so, Nemesius now urges the impropriety of any human judgement passed upon incidents and situations in life regarded as resulting from the work (or negligence) of providence. That, however, is not to say that man's mind should be paralysed by the knowledge that the workings of providence surpass comprehension. Intimations of the goodness and wisdom of dispositions that at first appear cruel and senseless may sometimes come to us, and this should encourage us to think that goodness and wisdom run through every disposition of events, in all the world. This course is made easier if we regard what troubles us as permitted by God, rather than initiated by him. The later part of the section shows that while, for apologetic reasons, Nemesius suggests that intimations of the working of providence might be the fruit of any man's natural cogitations, his examples are all taken from Scripture, or inspired by Christian experience. These intimations, therefore, are really partial revelations. It would only, therefore, be as his reader began to regard Scripture as divine revelation that he would be willing or able to accept Nemesius' huge final generalization, drawn from a handful of particular cases, and would put his trust in providence.

[M. 364.11–368.10.]

TEXT

70. Now, that God arranges all things well and fittingly and in the sole way admissible, would be seen most surely by anyone who will view the matter in relation to two universally acknowledged facts.[1] God is good, and God alone is wise. Then, since he is good, he is of course a God of providence. Likewise, in view of the fact that he is wise, his care for every creature is of the wisest and best. For if he neglected providence he would not be good, while if he exercised it, but not well, he would not be wise. Anyone, therefore, who views providence in relation to

---

1 The Greek of this sentence suggests comparison of the theological truths of God's goodness and wisdom to two distant landmarks which help an observer to watch, without being confused, the movement of events in the foreground.

these two points will surely not pass adverse judgement on the works of providence, nor will he, for lack of due examination of the question, blaspheme against them. He will, on the contrary, accept all of them in good part, admire them all, and be convinced that they are all done well and fittingly, in spite of the fact that the man in the street supposes them inequitable.[2] So, do not let us bring down upon our heads the reproach of being personally and grossly foolish, in addition to the guilt of blasphemy.

Any statement of ours that all things fall out well must not— and this we must claim to be obvious—be supposed to cover human perversities, or anything that lies within our capacities and that we do. It refers only to the works of providence which are not within the scope of our action.

Well, then, how is it that men of God have died in bitter pains and been slaughtered when innocent of all offence? If, that is to say, we can presume that they were the victims of injustice, why did not just providence prevent their murder? For if their sufferings were well-merited, the men that slew them are surely guiltless. To such an argument, our reply is that the murderer always commits a wrong by his murder. A man who is murdered may deserve his fate or it may, for other reasons, be expedient for him to die. If he had committed crimes, monstrous, but all unknown to us, then he would have deserved his fate. It would, on the other hand, be a case where his death was expedient, if providence knew beforehand of some evil deed that he would commit, and that it would be best that his life should come to an end before the fatal situation arrived. (This may have been the case with Socrates, or with God's holy ones.)[3] But the man who did the deed committed the crime of murder. For he was not aware of this expediency,

2 This sentence compares strikingly with a short letter written by Gregory Nazianzen in his last days, in which he says that he can bear his sufferings cheerfully because he is persuaded "that nothing that happens to us from the divine Reason is without good reason, even though it appears otherwise to us." "Reason," here, is *Logos*, the "Word" of John 1:1, who is in the world as providence and was its Creator. If our Nemesius is the same as Gregory's friend, both men ended their lives with the same mind about providence.

3 We have here the notion that God might foresee that a good man, if allowed to live on, would meet a situation in which his perseverance would break down, and therefore permit the man to be slain by human agency before that situation was reached, while nevertheless bringing the agents of death to judgement. This notion is not Hellenic, and hardly is Christian. It appears in, and probably was inspired by, Wisdom 4:10, 11,

nor had he licence to do the deed, but he acted deliberately for the sake of gain and because he was a robber.

For what we do is our responsibility, but what happens to us is not, as, for example, if we were to be murdered. Death is in no sense an evil, were it not for sin, as may be plainly seen in the deaths of godly men. The sinner, on the other hand, finds death an evil, even though death comes to him in his bed, even though it be quick and painless, because the shroud of sin, which he procures, is evil. But to return to the point that the murderer commits a wrong by his murder. It is true that where his victim was deserving of death, a murderer is a self-appointed executioner. But where it was expedient for the victim that he should die, the murderer chooses the part of an assassin and an outlaw. The same arguments apply to those who, in war, butcher their opponents or load them with chains, or, when they have made them prisoners, use them with all harshness. They apply equally to those who covet and seize other men's goods. For it may very well be that, so far as concerns the people deprived of their possessions, they may be all the better for being relieved of them. Nevertheless, the people who coveted their possessions thereby committed a wrong. For when they committed the theft, they did so out of covetousness, and not with any thought of what might be expedient for their victims.

COMMENTARY

70. *The working of providence does not remove man's moral responsibility.* The actions of providence and the actions of men so fit together that the good will of God is done, but men bear the

which Cyprian understands in the sense that God's conditional foreknowledge is the reason that he permits his holy ones to suffer death prematurely. It is a notion at home in Pharisaism, where law-keeping and law-breaking are issues of life and death. "God's holy ones," in our passage, is a probable reference to the passage in Wisdom. More surprising is the application of the notion to Socrates. This might have suggested itself to the mind of a Hellenized Jew. Or Nemesius might have arrived at the idea himself. Theodoret, a generation later and against the same social background, in his *Cure of pagan sickness*, VIII, argues that Socrates has no right to be ranked with the Christian martyrs. Clearly there was a tendency for liberal fifth-century opinion so to rank him. And that tendency seems here to sway Nemesius himself, unless we suppose him to be making conscious concession to outside opinion. Perhaps this bracketing of Socrates with "God's holy ones" is indication that Nemesius, as a convert late in life, did not react automatically, like Theodoret, in accordance with ecclesiastical sentiment.

guilt of the sinful will with which they act. In this section, Nemesius begins a new movement in his argument, which is left incomplete when the book comes to an end with the end of the section. He has dealt hitherto with scepticism regarding the fact of providence, based on the infinite multiplicity of particulars. But a greater source of complication still is the varied moral initiative of the free rational creatures. The aim of this section is to extend the former argument, and show that, on the basis of a true theology, belief in providence should not cloud our recognition of man's moral responsibility. This is argued by consideration of evils which men are permitted to inflict on one another, and their effect upon the true welfare of the sufferer.

BIBLIOGRAPHY

CYRIL OF JERUSALEM

TEXT. The Munich edition of 1848–1860 in two volumes, the first edited by W. C. Reischl, and the second by J. Rupp.
The edition of Dom Touttée, 1720, is reprinted in Migne, *Patrologia Graeca*, tom. XXXIII. 331–1180.

FOR CYRIL'S LIFE, the article Cyrillus (2) by Venables, in the *Dictionary of Christian Biography* (W. Smith and H. Wace, 1877) gives the sources. There is but one monograph, J. Mader, *Der heilig Cyrillus, Bischof von Jerusalem, in seinem Leben und seinen Schriften*, Einsiedeln, 1891.

ENGLISH TRANSLATIONS. (Prebaptismal Lectures, and the five Mystagogic Lectures doubtfully Cyril's.)
Vol. II of the *Library of the Fathers*, Oxford, 1838. (Translation by R. W. Church.)
Vol. VII of *Nicene and Post Nicene Christian Fathers*, 1893 (revision by E. H. Gifford).
With the Greek text, by H. de Romestin, London, 1887.

FOR JERUSALEM, ITS TOPOGRAPHY AND BUILDINGS, the best work is P. Vincent and F. M. Abel, *Jérusalem*.

FOR PILGRIMAGES, the collection *Itinera Hierosolymitana* (Saeculi iv–viii), edited by P. Geyer in the *Corpus Scriptorum Ecclesiasticorum Latinorum* (tom. XXXIX. Vienna, 1898). The translation into English of the second of these *Itinera* by M. L. McClure and C. L. Feltoe is published in the *Translations of Christian Literature* (Series iii, Liturgical Texts) by the Society for Promoting Christian Knowledge, under the title *The Pilgrimage of Etheria* (London, 1919), and has useful introduction and notes.

FOR THE GENERAL BACKGROUND, H. M. Gwatkin, *Studies of Arianism*, Cambridge, 1882, remains more useful for this purpose than any other work in English.

454

NEMESIUS OF EMESA

TEXT. The Halle edition of 1802, edited by C. F. Matthaei and published by J. J. Gebauer is reprinted in Migne *Patrologia Graeca*, tom. LX. 503–818.

The Oxford edition of 1671, edited by John Fell and published by the University Press is reprinted in Gallandi, *Bibliotheca Patrum* (1765–81), tom. VII. 351–426.

FOR THE GENERAL BACKGROUND may be recommended:
Culture, W. W. Jaeger, *Paideia* (3 vols.), Oxford, 1945.
Philosophy, Article "Poseidonios von Apameia" by K. Reinhardt in Pauly-Wissowa, tom. XXII (i).
Doctrine, Article "Antiochene Theology" by J. H. Srawley in Hastings' *Encyclopaedia of Religion and Ethics*, tom. I.
Medicine. *s.v.* Galen, *Encyclopaedia Britannica.*

STUDIES. Those cited in the Introduction and notes, together with:
K. Burkhard, "Johannes von Damaskus Auszüge aus Nemesios" in *Wiener Eranos zur 50. Versammlung deutscher Philologen u. Schulmänner in Graz*, 1909. A Holder, Vienna, 1909.
A. Ferro, "La dottrina dell' anima di Nemesio di Emesa," in *Richerche religiose*, Rome, 1925, tom. I. 227–238. K. Gronau, *Poseidonius u.d. jüdisch-christliche Genesis-exegese*, Berlin, 1914.
F. Lammert, "Zur Lehre von den Grundeigenschaften bei Nemesios" in *Hermes*, Wiesbaden, 1953, tom. LXXXI. 488–491.

Indexes

GENERAL INDEX

Readers are referred to the respective Introductions for information on Cyril, bishop of Jerusalem (349–386), and Nemesius, bishop of Emesa (*c.* 400), not included by name in the index.
Page numbers in italics refer to footnotes only. The others are inclusive of text and footnotes.

BIBLICAL REFERENCES

Printed in the United States
51337LVS00003B/67-96

9 780664 230821